D0938808

For Bonnie —
Enjoy reading this book —
חזקי ואמץ גודל
In friendship! *Sandra Rapoport*

BIBLICAL
SEDUCTIONS

Books by Sandra E. Rapoport

Moses's Women
(coauthored with Shera Aranoff Tuchman)

The Passions of the Matriarchs
(coauthored with Shera Aranoff Tuchman)

BIBLICAL SEDUCTIONS

SIX STORIES RETOLD
BASED ON TALMUD AND MIDRASH

SANDRA E. RAPOPORT

KTAV PUBLISHING HOUSE, INC.

Library of Congress Cataloging-in-Publication Data

Rapoport, Sandra E.
  Biblical seductions / Sandra E. Rapoport.
      p. cm.
  Includes bibliographical references and index.
  ISBN 978-1-60280-154-7 (Hardcover)
  ISBN 978-1-60280-170-7 (Paperback)
  1. Sex in the Bible. 2. Rape in the Bible. 3. Women in the Bible.
  4. Bible. O.T. — Criticism, interpretation, etc. 5. Midrash. I.
  Title.
  BS1199.S45R37 2011
  225.8'3067082 — dc22

                                                          2010012729

Published by
KTAV Publishing House, Inc.
888 Newark Avenue, Suite 119
Jersey City, NJ 07306
Email: orders@ktav.com
http://www.ktav.com

(201) 963–9524

To my family with love and gratitude.

✠ S.E.R. ✠

It is only after you have come to know the surface of things, Mr. Palomar thinks, that you can venture to seek what is underneath. But the surface of things is inexhaustible.

—Italo Calvino, *Mr. Palomar*

TABLE of CONTENTS

✠✠✠✠✠✠✠

FOUR   David & Batsheva   241

ACKNOWLEDGMENTS

❊❊❊❊❊❊❊

In writing a book of this scope I enlisted much help.

Wendy Amsellem, beloved and brilliant Torah faculty member at the Drisha Institute in New York City, read the entire manuscript and checked my footnotes. Her suggestions frequently led to exciting discussions in Drisha's study hall as we searched for the most perfect understanding of text or *midrash*. The resulting revisions made the manuscript tighter, and my labor even more fun.

My friends and family came forward one-at-a-time when I told them about this new book venture, and offered themselves as test audiences. I shamelessly called on these wonderful women for individual reading sessions over the course of the two years it took to research and write this volume. To some I read entire chapters, to others only excerpts. I humbly name these women with love and gratitude, for their steady comradeship and encouragement, their wisdom and their insights: Judy Abramowitz, Rebecca Herschkopf, Danièle Gorlin Lassner, Lauren Merkin, Dinah Mendes, Linda F. Ossad, Sarah Kate Rapoport, Faanya Rose, and Shera Aranoff Tuchman.

In studying the books of Samuel I found I had numerous questions about soldiering and warfare, in particular about the physical and mental states of officers and fighting men both on and off the battlefield. I am fortunate that I was able to call upon Julius L. Lassner, Captain USMCR (Ret.), to be my military consultant. Captain Lassner answered my naive questions with patient wisdom born of his life experience.

I extend a special thank-you to Mia Diamond Padwa, who trusted me with her fascinating Harvard honors thesis on David and Batsheva. Another thank-you goes to David Ellenberg, who cyber-forwarded relevant articles to me. I offer still another thank-you to Dr. Diane M. Sharon for listening as I read my book proposal aloud to her in a West Side coffee shop in July of 2008, and for opening her personal library to me.

As he did with two prior books, Steve Siebert, computer expert, typesetter, troubleshooter and friend, formatted my manuscript with skill and meticulous care. This book's type face, "Book Antiqua," was Steve's suggestion. We particularly liked the way the "&" symbol used in each of the six chapter titles forms an intricate and beautiful knot; it is a metaphor for the complex relationships analyzed here.

Bernie Scharfstein and Adam Bengal of KTAV Publishing House have been that rare combination of excited yet patient advisers throughout the two years it has taken me to write this book. I have come to rely on their good judgement, their good humor and their friendship.

Chief Rabbi Lord Jonathan Sacks, Professor Phyllis Trible and Dr. Avivah Gottlieb Zornberg each read all or substantial portions of this book in manuscript form. I am indebted to them for the gift of their time, for their generosity of spirit, and for the boon of their enthusiastic responses.

Dorothy A. Austin and Diana L. Eck, Masters of Lowell House at Harvard University, graciously offered me a Resident Scholar position for the fall, 2010, semester, which meant I did the final edits and compiled this book's indexes while I was in Cambridge. But more fundamentally, it was an intellectual pleasure and a bracing challenge to teach undergraduates and also to deliver public lectures on the women of the Bible to audiences comprised not only of students, but also of professors, priests, and passionate lay people. Their questions and insights humbled and fueled me. Thank you, Dorothy and Diana.

My husband, Sam Rapoport, and my children, Ben and Sarah, have been my indispensable *aides-de-camp*, my "team" and my sounding-board. I entertained my husband literally for hours during long car rides as I read him every word of the manuscript. His spontaneous reactions were priceless; equally valuable were his thoughtful comments that surfaced hours or even days after the readings. Thank you for taking such pride in my work; half of it belongs to you.

Ben and Sarah have each been pressed to serve as my computer consultants, either in-person or, more challengingly, long-distance. Also, they both have listened as I talked through or read them portions of the manuscript, and each has at some point suggested — sometimes with an unaffected, brilliant non-chalance — an idea that sent me off on a research detour that invariably made the book better. Ben was my invaluable library genie, cheerfully and calmly fielding my middle-of-the-night e-mailed requests and finding and ferrying otherwise unavailable books and articles. Finally, Ben has produced this book's wonderful dust jacket. This book would not be what it is without your help.

Thank you, always, to my teachers, Rabbi Haskel Lookstein and Rabbi David Silber, for more than twenty years of Torah study and mentorship.

INTRODUCTION

✖✖✖✖✖✖✖

This book analyzes six stories in the Hebrew Bible in which the female characters' sexuality is used or abused. Certainly there are other stories that could have been included, but I have selected three stories from the Pentateuch, two from the Prophets, and one from the Sacred Writings. In three of these stories the women seduce the men; in two of the stories the innocent women are violently raped; and in one story not only is the woman forcibly taken, but that act is compounded by a murder.

There is a fascinating commonality in the three episodes in which the women initiate the seduction, and in the case that devolves into a murder and cover-up. In those stories, what I term the women's "sexual audacity" is explicitly rewarded by God with generational immortality. That is, the women ultimately bear sons who are ancestors of prophets, Davidic kings, even, potentially, the Messiah.

In the other two stories of violent rape it is the *midrash aggadah*—the legend literature—which connects the unmarried rape victims to the continuity of the Children of Israel absent an express biblical link.

Altogether, five women in these episodes of the Hebrew Bible are involved in audacious sexual behavior, but are *not* condemned in the Bible text. Using text, Talmud and *midrash*, I examine why these women give birth to sons who are uniquely linked to the Davidic dynasty and holiness. I also analyze the place their biblical sisters—two of the women who are violently raped—have in the Israelite and Davidic saga. What are these women's common characteristics, and how do they survive?

xxi

✠ ✠ ✠

I am fascinated by the stories of the biblical women who dared step *outside* the "tent," or whose fates found them when they took outrageous risks, chancing to venture beyond the real or meta-phorical four walls of their homes. What befell the curious, the innocent, the desperate and the inspired biblical women? How does the Bible present and portray their lives, thoughts and desti-nies?

Margaret Bruzelius, who teaches Comparative Literature at Smith, has analyzed adventure literature, in particular contrasting how that genre treats male and female heroes. She analyzes various fictional women heroes who "go out," or who have "experiences" (she says literature never calls them "adventures" if the heroes are girls), explaining why certain fictional females are never permitted to "win." According to Bruzelius, "the women who win are . . . 'stainfree.'"[1] Because I am a fan of adventure fiction (and of Professor Bruzelius) as well as a lifelong student of the Bible, I was struck by the fact that in the Bible this theory does not always hold. In the Bible, *not all* the women who step outside the tent are doomed to "lose;" nor do those who are stain-free necessarily "win."

This book examines six stories about women who stepped outside their expected roles. All of these women have unexpected experiences — perhaps their stories fall under Bruzelius's rubric of "adventures" — some tragic, some fortuitous. And, like all good and enduring stories, these stories have a twist. They are, cumulatively and severally, stories of seduction, desperation, survival, calculation, abduction, violence and, in one lone incident, a story of kindness. And importantly, five of the women who survive and are rewarded are, in counterpoint to Bruzelius's women of fiction, most decidedly *not* "stain-free." In fact, it is the two innocents, the stain-free girls, who are *un*rewarded in the Bible text.

I examine the story of Lot's daughters, who seduce their father in a mountain cave and bear his sons. The tale of Dinah, virginal only-daughter of Leah and Jacob, who sets foot outside her family tent and is abducted and raped by Shechem, the local prince. The drama of Judah's daughter-in-law, Tamar, who disguises herself as a harlot, seduces Judah, bears him twin sons, and is called "righteous." The story of King David's lust for Batsheva, wife of Uriah, his prized officer, and the king's plot to have Uriah killed in battle so that he can wed her. The tragic account of Princess Tamar, daughter of King David, who is lured, trapped, and raped by her half-brother, Amnon, sparking vengeful fratricide and a civil war. And finally, I examine the story of the young Moabite widow Ruth, who seduces Boaz, a tribal leader, and becomes great-grandmother of King David and forebear of the Messiah.

These biblical stories are at once disturbing and compelling. Some of them involve subtle seductions, others are outright abductions. Sometimes the seducer is a woman, sometimes a man; sometimes the seduced is willing, other times the victim is forced. Sometimes the act is condemned outright, other times it is condoned or praised. Often there is heated dispute among Bible commentaries and Torah scholars — ancient, medieval and modern, male and female — about the facts and the implications of these sexually charged dramas.

Because of their subject matter these chapters in the Bible are usually skipped over entirely when the Bible is taught to school children. At other times the stories are censored, or read uncritically, or, worse, misread. At the other extreme, they are the topics of fascinating doctoral theses not accessible to the ordinary Bible reader.

But these stories are important to analyze and understand; they are integral to the immortal Bible narrative. Often they are vignettes that function as the "glue" holding together sections of a larger story, or they provide the foils for the main actors, or they highlight societal injustices that cried out to be rectified. These stories are fascinating and disturbing for the very reason that every one of them describes biblical actors engaging in sexual behavior that is way beyond the pale of accepted social norms, and the consequences that flow from their behaviors.

We are fascinated by what befalls these biblical women because on some level we identify with them. We are driven to ask, what made this woman so desperate, that woman so curious, this innocent so foolhardy, or this stranger so courageous that she took that risk? Why did she commit incest, risk abduction, seduce a tribal chief? And to what avail? Did she win the day, or was she ruined in the process? Was she simply a beautiful innocent, preyed upon by those more powerful, evil or lawless than she? Does she disappear from the Bible narrative completely? And what of the men in their lives — what becomes of them?

These fraught situations are presented in the Bible text, discussed by the Talmud and *midrash*, and analyzed here.

※ ※ ※

A word about my use of the term *midrash*. It derives from the Hebrew root-word meaning to search, seek, examine or investigate. Whenever there appear to be gaps or inconsistencies in the Torah's narratives or dialogues, we can be sure that rabbis and commentators — ancient, medieval and modern, mostly male, but recently female — have searched for the meaning of the Bible text, and have stepped in to explain and resolve its ambiguities. Their work was originally passed down orally, but over the centuries has been transcribed, and it assists readers as they, too, seek meaning in the Bible text. It is this vast body of interpretive and legend literature that I refer to here collectively and expansively as *midrash*. All translations of quoted Bible passages and rabbinic *midrash* are my own.

※ ※ ※

Weaving together textual analysis and *midrashic* commentary — ancient, medieval and modern — this book retells these morally ambiguous, often tragic, sometimes triumphant stories. I explore the biblical characters' behaviors, motivations, and emotions; I discuss the context and the immediate and rippling consequences of these stories.

In the process the reader will develop a new understanding of the Bible's heroines and heroes. Sometimes they rise to greatness, other times they sink to depravity. But always, the Bible presents these fabulous stories for us to ponder. Understanding the biblical women and men in their adorned and unadorned glory allows us to hold a mirror up to ourselves, and to chart our own courses as we lead our modern lives, make moral choices, and seek to draw closer to the divine.

In addition to being a lifelong student of the Bible, I spent twelve years as an attorney specializing in investigating and litigating sexual harassment cases. The stage may have been modern-day America instead of the ancient Near East, but the issues were not unfamiliar to me; often I had already encountered them in the Bible. In retelling these selected biblical tales I invite the reader to confront the issues of healthy love, abuse of power, and forbidden passion, as part of the universal struggle for morality and spirituality.

This book illuminates these six provocative episodes through the lens of text and commentary, retelling the stories for women and men of all beliefs. These stories reverberate with ancient idiom but are as modern and relevant as today's headlines. I invite you to explore them with me.

Sandra E. Rapoport
New York City

PART

ONE

Lot

&

His Daughters

ONE

Lot & His Daughters

GENESIS 19:30-38

And Lot went up from Zoar and settled in the mountain, and his two daughters were with him, because he was afraid to settle in Zoar, so he settled in the cave, he and his two daughters.

And the elder one told the younger one, "Our father is old; and there is no man in the land to come to us in the [natural] manner of all the land.

"Let us give our elderly father wine and we will lie with him; thus will we live on through our father's seed."

And they gave their father wine that night; and the elder [daughter] came and lay with her father, and he did not know that she lay [with him] and that she arose [from him].

And it happened on the morrow, the elder said to the younger, "Now have I lain last night with my father; let us give him wine again this night, and you will come and lie with him, and we will live on through our father's seed."

And they fed their father wine on that night also; and the younger arose and lay with him and he did not know that she lay [with him] and that she arose [from him].

And the two daughters of Lot became pregnant from their father. The elder gave birth to a son and she called his name Moav; he is the father of Moav to this day.

And the younger also gave birth, and she called his name Ben Ami; he is the father of the sons of Ammon to this day.

We encounter Lot's daughters here at the low point of their young lives. These girls—known in the Bible only as "the elder" and "the younger"—in the space of a matter of days or even hours, have gone from being the virginal daughters of Lot and his wife in the city of Sodom, to motherless refugees huddling in a cave. They have been irrevocably transformed, much as the landscape they inhabit has been scarred and altered, by the sudden and cataclysmic destruction of their world.

The Bible reader must ask, How did they come to be here? For the answer let us hark back to biblical events that took place years before the evening described in chapter 19 of the book of Genesis, where the great drama of the city of Sodom unfolds.

LOT PARTS WAYS WITH ABRAHAM

Lot had parted ways with his dynamic and pious uncle Abraham some years earlier, after violent quarrelling had broken out between the two men's shepherds.[1] Their substantial flocks had overlapped one another grazing the same pastures,[2] and in the time-worn way of the world, the land was not big enough for both to live together in peace. So Abraham had offered Lot independence, suggesting that Lot go either to the north or to the south, and that he, Abraham, would be content to wander elsewhere in order to keep the peace. Lot portentously turned his face eastward, and when he saw the verdant, well-watered Jordan Valley, he chose to settle there, in the city of Sodom. The Bible tells us that at that time, well before God thought to destroy the cities of Sodom and Gomorrah, the valley—reaching to the settlement of Zoar—had the lush appearance of the Garden of Eden and the land of Egypt.

The alert Bible reader should detect the text's hints of evil events to come: The Bible tells us that Lot chose to travel eastward, *mikedem*, the same direction — and using the same exact Hebrew word — that Adam and Eve were banished when God chased them from Eden.[3] In fact, the Almighty stationed the heavenly guards at the eastward-facing gate of Eden, wielding the flaming and revolving sword of God in order to prevent unworthy mankind from returning there. The Bible text has made it plain that flight in an eastward direction is a flight *away* from the sacred space, the space of harmony and unity. The fact that Lot chooses to settle in the east — *mikedem* — is an indicator that Lot's vision is flawed, and that — like Adam and Eve, his biblical progenitors — he is making a wrong choice that will inform his character and will reflect tragically upon him for the rest of his days.

Lest we miss the reference to *mikedem*, the Bible also tells us that *in Lot's eyes* the Jordan Valley resembles the land of Egypt. This is a reference to Abraham and Lot's ill-advised journey into that land, where Abram's[4] wife — and Lot's sister, Sarai[5] — had been abducted by the Pharaoh. It was in Egypt that the Pharaoh, after glimpsing Sarai's fabled beauty, had held her prisoner in his palace, and subjected her to the terrors of abduction and near-rape. It is telling that *in Lot's eyes* the verdant land to the east reminds him of this same land of Egypt, a land of verdant natural physical beauty, but also one where immorality and sexual depredation rule, and from which he and his uncle and sister had narrowly escaped with their lives. By juxtaposing the Jordan Valley and Sodom and Gomorrah with Egypt, the Bible issues a subtle and tacit admonishment to Lot for his myopia in choosing to settle in Sodom because of its resemblance to Egypt. The careful reader expects that Lot will pay a high price for his choice.

So Abraham remained in Canaan, and resumed his isolated, nomadic life, and Lot parted from his uncle, settling in Sodom, the most lush of the cities in the valley. Lot even sought to straddle the best of both worlds — pastoral and urban — by keeping his flocks nearby, right outside the city walls.[6] He could not quite abandon his nomadic roots even as he strove to become a city dweller. Perhaps Lot felt he could weather whatever this Egypt-like city had in store, and that in the meantime — as was the case when they left Egypt—he would amass great wealth. We will see that Lot's abandonment of the semi-nomadic life in favor of an urban existence will spell trouble for him. In fact, the Bible loses no time in telling us in the very next verse about the character of the inhabitants of Lot's new home.

WHO ARE THE SODOMITES?

And the men of Sodom were evil and sinned before God exceedingly. Gen. 13:13

This verse is packed thrice-over with expressions of the corruption of the Sodomites, Lot's adopted neighbors. First it tells us that the men of Sodom were evil. Then it says that they were sinners against God. And third, that their cruel acts placed them beyond the pale of acceptable behavior. It is the rabbis of the *midrash*[7] who elaborate. The word "sinner" refers to the fact that the Sodomites sinned in matters of money and property in their daily interactions.[8] They refused to give even a penny to the out-stretched hand of the alms-seeker,[9] and they outlawed the centuries-old custom of offering hospitality, food and drink to wayfarers.[10] The word "evil"—or *ra* in Hebrew—is thought to describe worse behavior even than one who sins in isolated transactions; it indicates a more degenerated character trait, a totality and pervasiveness of evil, or *ra*.[11]

The *midrash* amplifies still further, explaining that the Sodomites contravened all seven of the basic rules of moral social behavior expected of the peoples of the ancient world, known as the Noahide Laws.[12] These are:

1. The prohibition against idolatry and a belief in One God
2. The prohibition against incestuous and adulterous relations
3. The prohibition against murder
4. The prohibition against cursing the name of God
5. The prohibition against theft
6. The prohibition against eating the flesh of a living animal[13]
7. The obligation to establish courts of justice and a rational social order.

In order to help us to understand the Bible's brief verse outlining
Sodom's execrable behaviors (and thereby appreciate the life Lot
has chosen for himself, and his daughters' place in it), the
Talmud[14] explains that the city of Sodom was established in a land
that God had blessed exceedingly. We are told that bread came
forth from the earth as if by magic; its earthy rocks yielded
sapphires, and its very dust was gold. But the inhabitants of
Sodom were haughty, and they worshipped only the god of
mammon, and sought to keep all strangers, travelers and
wayfarers away from their city so as not to share even the smallest
bit of their wealth. They viewed every passer-by as a potential
thief with designs on their good fortune. Even merchants were
prohibited from entering Sodom to trade their wares. The
Sodomites considered themselves completely self-sustaining, and
looked upon merchants from other cities as having only one
intention: separating the Sodomites from their coins. In fact, if a
wealthy traveler chanced into the city, they conspired to seat him
against a weak retaining wall, then they intentionally toppled the
wall, killing the stranger and keeping his purse.

Eventually, the word spread near and far that one entered
Sodom at one's own risk.[15] To paraphrase the words of the
Talmud,[16] the Sodomites "caused the sound of the footfall of the
traveler to be forgotten from amongst them." Over time, only the
unknowing or the desperate chanced to enter the city's gates.

The Talmud[17] devotes several pages just to explicating this
one verse in the Lot saga (*And the men of Sodom were evil . . .*). It
relates one heartbreaking story that is known by its introductory
words: "There was a certain maiden . . ." If we were reading
about any other town, those words might signal the start of a fairy
tale, involving as it does a virtuous and courageous maiden with a
tender heart. But instead this is a tragic tale, told by the rabbis of
the Talmud to illustrate why none of the Sodomites will have a
portion in the world-to-come. And as it involves the Sodomite
men, a virginal maiden and physical retribution for acts of
kindness to strangers, it is a portent for the next segment in the
Lot story.

The Talmud tells us that there was a certain maiden in
Sodom whose heart was compassionate, and who secretly brought

bread to the poor by hiding it in her water pitcher. The *midrash* tells us that her name was either Pelotit or Paltith, and that she was Lot's eldest daughter.[18] She was seen carrying her water pitcher to and fro in the streets—a common enough sight, as it fell to the maidens to fetch and carry the water from the town well. She waited until she was alone or until no one was looking, and as the opportunity arose she would reach into her pitcher and give the secreted bread to a pauper. She was eventually found out by the Sodomites, who determined to make an example of her by punishing her horribly. They smeared her naked body with honey from head to toe, making a brutal mockery of the girl's sweet nature. They then bound her and stretched her out atop the city wall. The honey attracted swarms of bees who stung the maiden repeatedly, and bit her until she died. It is said that her unheeded, agonized cries—her *za'akah* in Hebrew—went on for hours and rose even to the Heavens. In the words of Nehama Leibowitz,[19] "it was this one deed, *this cry*, that weighted the scales against them," causing God to determine and seal the Sodomites' fate.

The *midrash* picks up on the Bible's use here of the Hebrew word *za'akah*—outcry. The word is used in Gen. 18:20 and 21 when God is contemplating annihilating Sodom and Gomorrah, and again in the Lot story in Gen. 19:13 when the angels are explaining to Lot the reason he must hurry and exit Sodom (*because the 'za'akah' of this place has become great before the presence of the Lord, and He has sent us to destroy it*). The reader should be alert to the Bible's use of this particular word, as it indicates a visceral cry of extraordinary anguish. Whenever this word *za'akah*—outcry—appears in the Bible text, it is virtually certain that God's appearance is not far behind.[20] It is said that this *za'akah* is so elemental and profound that it catches God's ear.[21] It is this special quality of anguished, hopeless crying out that the Talmud uses as a springboard for its eloquent story of the hapless Sodomite maiden.

The Talmud's gruesome tale evokes in the reader precisely the emotions intended: revulsion and anger at the Sodomites, and a disapproving wonderment that Lot, raised in Abraham's household, should not only prefer to live among such people, but also appear to flourish there.[22] This is especially so if, as the *midrash* suggests, the maiden in the tale was Lot's eldest daughter. Lot's seeming acquiescence to Sodom's evil and perverse nature early on only foreshadows his "sacrifice" of two of his other daughters later in the story. It also provides important background to the cave seduction by these selfsame daughters following the destruction of Sodom.

One might wonder how Lot was able to ingratiate himself into the Sodomite society given that he, too, came to them as a stranger. We will see as the story unfolds that he never does become fully integrated in the eyes of his Sodomite neighbors; they turn on him in an instant when it suits them. Lot was ever the stranger in their eyes.

The Talmud implicitly allows us to draw the sexual parallels in the tale: a compassionate, blameless maiden is treated to the Sodomites' violent perversion of her kind act of hospitality by being stripped, publicly shamed and abused, bound and "stung" to death. The reference to bee stings in the tale is a thin veil to the underlying sexual nature of the violation, one that will echo in the coming verses. The reader can entirely appreciate and applaud that God finally responds to this innocent's bootless cries. The Almighty has had enough!

LOT AND THE TWO ANGELS

Lot, apparently, has not. It is this city of Sodom that Lot inhabits for many years, except for the intervening, terrifying episode in Gen. 14 when he was taken prisoner in the battle with the Four Kings and eventually rescued by his valiant uncle Abraham.

We encounter Lot, a town judge,[23] sitting at the city gates as evening falls. He sees two angels dressed as men arriving at the entrance to Sodom. The two strangers are none other than two of the three angels who had visited Abraham in the heat of the day in the Bible's prior story (Gen. 18). The Talmud[24] is specific, naming Abraham's three angels and their tasks, as each angel is usually assigned but one mission at a time.[25] They were the angels Raphael, Michael, and Gabriel. Raphael came in order to heal the aged Abraham's wounds after his circumcision; Michael's task was to relay to Sarah the news that she would bear a son in a year's time; and it fell to the angel Gabriel to destroy the city of Sodom. But because of the twofold task ahead—the rescue of Lot and the destruction of Sodom and Gomorrah—the Bible tells us two of Abraham's three angels appeared that same evening at the gates of Sodom. The angel Raphael had completed his assigned task and returned to the heavenly host, and God pressed the angel Michael into service once more. The angels Michael and Gabriel[26] —referred to in most of this portion of the Lot story as "men"— will rescue Lot and destroy Sodom.

It is significant that the Bible uses the term "angels" in the first verse of the Lot story (Gen. 19). They were referred to as "men" in the Abraham story because their task was a uniquely mortal one: visiting the sick. But here in the Lot story they are introduced as "angels" because they will be calling upon supernatural forces to destroy Sodom and Gomorrah.[27]

They waited until late in the day before entering the city because they were, at their essence, angels of mercy, and had hoped that Abraham would be successful in his plea to the Almighty to spare the cities from annihilation.[28] Only when Abraham was unable to wring any more mercy from God than a promise to spare the cities if but ten righteous men could be found, did the angels move into position. We should remember that the angels were also sent by God to reconnoiter the evil city of Sodom. Was it truly past saving? And the corollary question if the answer to this first inquiry were "yes:" Was Lot alone worthy of being saved?

In our continuing hunt for textual details about Lot that will supply us with clues to his personality—and so that we can better understand his upcoming behaviors toward and with his daughters—the *midrash* offers assistance. The rabbis of the *midrash*[29] have compared the manner that Lot welcomes the two strangers here in chapter 19, to the manner that Abraham greeted the three men in chapter 18, mere verses before the Lot story. Has Lot's character retained the quality of graciousness and hospitality that he learned at Abraham's knee, or have the past fifteen-plus years of living among the Sodomites altered him? Is Lot worth saving?

First of all, the reader learns from the biblical narrator that the two angels arrive at the gates of Sodom in the evening. It was earlier *on that same day* that the angels had visited Abraham and Sarah's tent in the groves of Mamre.

In the Abraham story,[30] the Torah referred to the three desert visitors as "men," yet Abraham knew them to be angels.[31] There is much *midrashic* discussion that Abraham's high level of intuition enabled him to discern God's presence—the *schechina*—hovering over the strangers, even though the three angels appeared at his tent dressed as men.

Here in the Lot story we see, to the contrary, that at the outset the biblical narrator calls the two strangers "angels" in Gen. 19:1, but that thereafter Lot and the Sodomites refer to them as "men." The *midrash*, which expresses a growing cynicism about Lot, views this ability to perceive holiness as a litmus test of the man's spiritual evolution. Lot fails to perceive the two strangers as the angels we know them to be, because his degraded spirit[32] has blocked his ability to see clearly. This selective myopia, referred to when Lot parted from Abraham, is a thread we will follow in the Lot story.

On the other hand, some commentaries see the man/angel dichotomy as *inversely* related to the person perceiving them. One *midrash*[33] explains that Lot and the Sodomites perceived the angels *as angels* precisely because their spirit was too corrupted to allow them to perceive the humanity of the two wayfarers; a kind of magical mirror held up to reveal their own characters. But either way, we note that as the story progresses Lot is struggling with his waning ability to perceive what is right and good, especially after he allowed himself to be influenced by the conscienceless Sodomites.

HOSPITALITY TO STRANGERS

We should ask, Why was Lot still sitting at the gates of Sodom at eventide? Should he not have been at his home as darkness was falling? One view stresses Lot's role as a judge in Sodom.[34] Typically, judges sat at the gates of the city in order to be visibly available to all the townspeople, the better to handle the ongoing business of judging. It apparently fell to one of the judges to remain at the gate until the marketplace shut down for the day, in case there were any lingering disputes to be settled between merchants and buyers, or among any of the townspeople. As long as there were people about, a judge was expected to remain on duty. The text mentions only that Lot was present — so we can assume that he was the on-call judge who was left alone at the gate of Sodom that fateful evening.

There is also a view that Lot's character was still salvageable at the time he was visited by the two angels. One *midrash*[35] tells us that from time to time Lot returned to the city's gates in the evening, after all work had been completed for the day and when the area was deserted. He kept a lookout for wayfarers and when no one else was about, he was able secretly to bring any strangers to his house for the night, sending them on their way early the next morning, before the city's populace awoke, thus avoiding detection. According to Nehama Leibowitz,[36] "Lot tried to maintain Abraham's way of life even in the heart of Sodom, striving to preserve, at the risk to his life, the elementary obligations of hospitality to strangers, in a city where such behaviour was forbidden by law. Naturally his attempts were doomed to failure, resulting from his inability to choose between Abraham and *his* environment and Sodom and *its* environment." So the reader begins to appreciate that Lot is no Abraham. But that Lot took the considerable risk by harboring strangers is weighed to his credit.

Still another *midrashic* opinion[37] is that on the contrary, Lot had fallen out of the habit of issuing hospitality to strangers since he took up residence in Sodom, and that over the years he had turned his face away from wayfarers. Sodom had no hostels or inns to accommodate travelers like all other towns and cities of the day.[38] But because Lot had retained a spark of the generosity learned from his uncle Abraham, when he saw that these two strangers — men of unusual tall bearing[39] and apparent substance[40] — genuinely intended to spend the night in the streets, Lot grew embarrassed, feared for their safety, and offered them a place for the night.

IN ABRAHAM'S HOUSE

As regards Lot's uncle Abraham, we recall that he sat on the threshold of his tent at noon on the day after his circumcision, keeping a lookout for wayfarers. Let us examine Abraham's behavior as he greets his three strangers in the previous chapter.

When Abraham saw the three men approaching his tent earlier that day, he ran to greet them despite his advanced age of ninety-nine years[41] and his physical discomfort. He entreated them to tarry with him, saying "My sirs, if I find favor in your eyes, pray do not pass your servant by." He offered them some water to wash their dusty feet, and bade them to rest in the shade of the tree. He told them that he would fetch a piece of bread for their meal, and that after they ate and drank and rested they could go on their way. The men agreed to his simple offer of shade, bread and water. But Abraham was a master of understatement. He promised a meager snack but delivered a veritable feast.[42]

After settling the strangers under the tree he hurried into his tent, summoning his wife, Sarah: "Hurry, hurry! Guests are come! Quickly knead three measures of meal and fine four and bake bread and cakes!" Sarah understood the importance of guests in their household, and prepared the bread and the cakes herself, not relegating the work to a kitchen maid, despite her own advanced age of eighty-nine years. One can imagine that the unexpected delight of having three strangers to fuss over, to ply for news, to break the monotony of their solitary and nomadic existence, booted the aged couple into high gear.

We can envision that Abraham barely slowed his pace as he rushed through the tent and shouted instructions to Sarah. In fact, the text is not content with using the verb *to hurry* twice in verse 6: once when narrating Abraham's hurrying and again when Abraham instructs his wife. In verse 7 the narrative also tells us that *he ran* to the sheep-fold, selected a tender, goodly young lamb from among his flock, and only after assuring himself that the lamb was choice did he *hurry* to turn it over to his household lad (some say it was his eldest son, Yishmael[43]) to slaughter, marinate and cook it forthwith.

Abraham is presented as a blur of action, and the reader cannot but be struck by the instantaneous transformation of the sedentary, recuperating man who greets us in verse 1, into the spry, purposeful fellow in verses 6 through 8.

Three times the Torah text uses the verb *to hurry* when describing Abraham's reaction to his visitors. It leaves the reader in no doubt of Abraham's touching and obvious delight at having guests notwithstanding his painful recuperation, and importantly, of the fact that his wife, Sarah, is integral to the ingathering and the preparation. The Bible narrates that Abraham himself—again not a servant—brought butter and milk as well as the cooked lamb that he had ordered prepared, and set it all before his visitors. And he stood by[44] as they consumed the small feast, at-the-ready to see to their every need.

This is a well-oiled procedure we are witnessing in chapter 18. Abraham and Sarah are a team, and have repeated this routine hundreds of times throughout the years. This visit seems to come at a perfect time, interrupting the baking torpor of the desert noon, and lifting the old couple out of their physical and emotional doldrums. Abraham is suffering the painful after-effects of a self-circumcision, and Sarah is miserably resigned to her childlessness. Little do they know that during a prosaic meal eaten in the shade at the open tent flap the three strangers will impart news that will alter the couple's lives forever.

IN LOT'S HOUSE

With Abraham's model behavior as a basis for comparison, we now pay close attention to the Bible's narrative details regarding Lot. It is these differences between the two men's behavior that will provide clues to the inquiring reader about Lot's character.

We return to our reading of chapter 19, where the Bible shows us Lot in action. He sees the two angels approaching Sodom as evening falls. He perceives them as men—perhaps with a radiance surrounding them[45]—and rises from his seat at the gate. He approaches them, bows low to the ground in a show of courtesy, and addresses them: "Here, now, Sirs, turn from your path and come to the house of your servant, and stay the night. Wash your feet, then rise up early and go on your way."

Given what we already know about the "welcome" Sodomites offer to wayfarers, we can imagine that Lot has approached
the two strangers, extending his invitation in a whisper, in case
any chance passerby should overhear.[46] We note that Lot
approaches the strangers at a walk, and not at a run, as Abraham
did. But to give Lot his due, he appears to rise to the occasion,
demonstrating to the reader and to himself that he is, after all,
Abraham's nephew, and that offering hospitality to strangers had
been drilled into him over the many years he spent as a member
of Abraham's household. Perhaps the Sodomites might overlook
Lot's whispered approach to the strangers, thinking he was
enticing them into his home in order to fleece them. The Sodomites might even smirk in appreciation of his cleverness. That he
would house the strangers out of simple generosity is not an act
the Sodomites would expect from a fellow judge.

Another inference the reader can make from the suggestion
in the *midrash* that Lot had risen to the respectability of a magi-
strate in Sodom, is that he had internalized the Sodomite values to
the extent that the others felt confident he would enforce their
rules *against* offering hospitality. We will see the confirmation of
this when in coming verses the Sodomites expect Lot to turn the
strangers over to them.

But viewed as a Sodomite, Lot's offer is generous. He risks
censure at the very least for housing the strangers — likely even
more serious punishment if he is found out — so it is to Lot's credit
that he actively sought to keep them from harm. The *midrash*[47]
cites this as a reason Lot is worthy of being rescued from Sodom's
fated destruction. Unfortunately for Lot and for his family, his
offer of hospitality and a measure of protection to the two
strangers marks the high point of his courage. We will see that as
concerns his own family the man Lot behaves in a craven and
reprehensible way.

His offer to the men to sleep first and wash up later is a
calculated one. It would be more courteous and natural to offer a
dusty traveler to wash his feet *first*, and then to rest afterwards.
But Lot's offer is reversed. Lot expects that the Sodomites will
likely come knocking on his door to inquire about the strangers.
He cleverly figures that if the men rest right away, then at least by

the time any Sodomites come to check, the strangers' still-dusty, sandaled feet will lead the Sodomites to assume that the men had only just arrived moments before, and he would thereby avoid any unpleasant consequences.[48] Lot is covering his back, acting in a generous manner by Sodomite standards by even offering the strangers a place to sleep, but at the same time he is leery and almost expectant that they will be found out.

When viewed in light of Abraham's encounter with the angels in the prior chapter, Lot's offer appears paltry and grudgingly tendered. Notably absent here is any proffer of food or refreshment. It seems that such an offer would be a surefire way to tempt desert wayfarers to agree to tarry overnight. Instead, Lot's offer of hospitality is a bare one. And the strangers respond in kind, saying, "No, thank you. We will spend the night in the street." It is extraordinary that the strangers refuse his offer of a bed for the night! We can imagine that the perceived effrontery of their rejection surprises Lot. So he tries again, entreating them forcefully to stay with him, cautioning them that if they were to sleep on the street they would be easy prey for roving Sodomite thugs.[49]

We recall that with Abraham their response was positive and immediate. It is possible that the angels had no reason to expect that Lot — or any of the Sodomites for that matter — would offer them hospitality for the night, and so quite logically they came prepared to sleep out-of-doors.[50] It is also possible that because they were angels they bore no fear for the reputedly vicious Sodomites,[51] whom they could smite with a mere gesture. And after all, they only had to pass the night until it came time to fulfill their appointed missions early the next morning.

Because their preordained mission included rescuing Lot, one would think that the angels knew in advance that they would not be sleeping out in the street. They needed to quickly become reconciled to accepting his hospitality — however grudging — and face Lot with friendly countenances.[52] The angels' demurral might thus have been strictly *pro forma*, allowing Lot to rise to the moment and entreat them to stay with him. The angels were allowing Lot to accumulate "grace points," to justify their saving him from the doomed city.[53]

We see that Lot does, in fact, entreat the men exceedingly to stay at his house. He might have said, "Sirs, you must have a care *here*—for in Sodom you would not survive a night on the streets!" Perhaps he even tugged at their sleeves and gestured that they should enter his house through the side door,[54] to keep their coming a secret from the prying eyes of the Sodomites. And the strangers relent, following Lot to his house cloak-and-dagger style through a circuitous route of back streets, in an attempt to avoid detection.[55]

Lot prepares a meal with wine and unleavened *matzot*, perhaps indicating to the reader that this event occurs on the second night of the future holiday of Passover,[56] and the Bible tells us that the angels ate the meal. We incidentally learn from this verse the proper, courteous manner of behaving as a guest in another's home. For although the angels had no need of food or drink, they appeared to consume it in order to show respect to Lot, who had prepared it for them.[57]

Conspicuously absent from the Torah narrative is any mention of Lot's wife. This, too, is in marked contrast to the Abraham narrative. Lot's wife was apparently furious with her husband for bringing the strangers home and endangering the entire household. What's more, she refused to set out so much as a salt cellar for the guests, so opposed was she to offering them either a bed for the night or a meal to eat. One *midrash* teaches that it is an illustration of "measure-for-measure" that Lot's wife was later turned into a pillar of salt as she fled the burning city of Sodom. Because she had sinned through the medium of salt—an offer of the expensive commodity of salt on the table is a measure of one's hospitality—salt was part of her downfall.[58]

Nor is there any indication that Lot involved his two unmarried daughters in his preparation for the guests. This also is in contrast with Abraham, who involved at least one other member of his household in addition to his wife, Sarah, in his bustle to set out a meal for the three angels. In reading the Lot story the reader perceives no inkling that anyone other than Lot himself is out and about fussing and cooking or making ready for the guests. One must consider that if Pelotit, the Talmud's kind-hearted but doomed maiden, was in fact Lot's eldest daughter, perhaps Lot chose not to involve his other family members in this incident of hospitality in a cautionary reaction to her awful fate. Perhaps he felt that his standing in the community protected him from the Sodomite injunction against kindness to strangers. Whatever his reasoning, Lot chose to act solo. He alone set out the fixings for their prepared meal. He alone baked the *matzot* for them to eat. The whole atmosphere reminds us of a person readying his lonely dinner meal. There seems to be no joy in the preparation of it.

The Torah's word for the repast Lot set out for the strangers is *mishteh*, the Hebrew word for feast. This is curious, as the text indicates only that he set out *matzot* for them. What else did Lot serve the men that would allow the Torah to suggest that it was a feast? We note the Bible's word-clue embedded in the Hebrew word *mishteh*. The root-word is *shoteh*, meaning *to drink*. The Bible is telling us that Lot set out wine as well as the unleavened *matzot* for the two strangers. This is certainly a significant variation from the meal laid out by Abraham in the prior chapter. Milk or cream, plus water to rinse their feet, were the only liquids set before Abraham's angels, and the Torah conspicuously did not refer to Abraham's generous meal as a feast; it is described only as a "meal."

The *midrash* is quick to pick up on this textual clue to Lot's character.[59] We are told that Lot loved his wine, and needed nothing more than the invited strangers as an excuse to imbibe. This is a weakness in Lot that will echo in the biblical text later on in his saga, when we encounter Lot and his daughters huddled in a cave after the destruction of Sodom and Gomorrah. Lot's love of wine plays a central part in the seduction scene and frames our last glimpse of him in the book of Genesis.

THE SODOMITE SIEGE

But before they lay down, the men of the city, [all] the men of Sodom, surrounded the house, both old and young, all the people from every quarter.

And they called to Lot, and said to him, "Where are the men who came in to you this night? Bring them out to us so that we may know them!"

And Lot stepped out onto the doorstep and closed the door behind him.

And he said, "I pray you, my brothers, do not act so wickedly.

"Behold now, I have two daughters who have not known [any] man. Let me, I pray you, bring them out to you, and you may do to them as is good in your eyes. Only unto these men do nothing, for they came under the shadow of my roof."
Gen. 19:4–8

Lot's two visitors have eaten and drunk what he placed before them. But before they have the opportunity to retire for the night, the entire population of the city of Sodom—a noisy mob comprised of young and old alike—converges on Lot's house and surrounds it. We can imagine the scene that the Bible outlines for us in Gen. 19:4–14: Night has fallen, and a horde of townspeople are marching toward Lots' house, their feet sounding like a muted thunder. Some of the men carry torches to light the way. Their faces are a study in brutish determination, and some of them are wielding clubs. There is no doubt that they are bent on a lynching. The crowd advances on Lot's house from all points, precluding an escape. The angry din reverberates within the house and terrifies Lot's wife and two daughters, who have likely barricaded themselves in a back room and are listening and watching intently through a small window as the scene unfolds.

When the mob arrives at Lot's house, several thugs call out loudly, in voices laden with menace, "Hey, Lot! Lot! Where are the men who came into your house tonight? Bring them out to us, so that we will know them!" A raucous roar of laughter accompanies this last shouted demand. There is no doubt in anyone's mind what the Sodomite multitude intends: they are flexing their fists, pumped with adrenaline, and ready to brutalize, gang-rape, and kill the two strangers.[60]

A careful reader should be alert to the use of the Hebrew word *nedah*—meaning *we will know [them]*—in the text (at Gen.

19:5). Depending on the context, the root-word, *de'ah*, meaning *to know*, is a verbal flag that some sort of sexual event, or "carnal knowledge" is about to occur.[61] Being alert to the presence of the Hebrew verb *to know* in these stories is thus another tool the reader can use to understand the action. It will recur in the Lot story as well as throughout this book. At this moment in the Lot story the *midrash* understands that the unruly mob is intent on sexually assaulting the strangers. Many of the commentaries explicitly say that the assault was to be homosexual in nature.[62] But despite these overtones, the scene is more about brutality and domination than it is about sexuality.

Modern-day Bible scholar Tikva Frymer-Kensky adds an additional layer of meaning to the mob's phrase, *Let us know them!* She posits that "the proposed rape of the traveler is like the rape of a newcomer in jail. The purpose of such a rape is . . . the assertion of dominance and the dishonoring of the man forced to submit."[63] She considers the possibility that the men of Sodom might only want to know what the strangers are made of; that is, that they might have planned to assault and pummel them, to assert their dominance and show them who's boss, short of actually raping them. She emphasizes that whether or not the "knowledge" of the strangers was planned as carnal, its intent in any event was "to emasculate the traveler, strip him of his pride and his honor, and render him submissive and nonthreatening."[64] Even so, an assault short of an actual rape is still considered heinous and depraved.

The *midrash* expands on the Bible's phrase, *the men of Sodom surrounded the house, both young and old, all the people from every quarter.* Apparently the entire population of Sodom turned out for this nighttime mob scene. It was not merely the dregs of the Sodomite society, but also the city's "elite," including members of the city's ruling class, who marched on Lot's house.[65] Every Sodomite had a stake in making an example of Lot's invited guests, and, if it came to it, of Lot himself. Lot had violated a foundational tenet of Sodomite law and custom by sheltering the strangers, and the entire city was there to effect his humiliation.[66] While the young, hot-headed and hot-blooded men were the instigators, even the oldest of the old men cheered the young bucks on to do their worst.[67] The Bible wants the reader to appreciate the pervasive corruption of the *entire* Sodomite society. Hence the Bible's use of seemingly repetitive phrases *young and old alike, all the people* explaining who it was that converged on Lot's house.

> *And they said, "Stand back! This one fellow came in to sojourn [among us], and now he judges us! Now will we deal worse with you than with them!" And they pressed very hard against the man, against Lot, and they were about to break down the door.*
>
> *But the men put forth their hands and pulled Lot into the house with them, and they shut the door.*
>
> *And they struck the men that were at the door of the house with blindness, from the smallest to the greatest [of them], so that they struggled in vain to find the door.* Gen. 19:9–11

As if the prospect of raping Lot's guests were not sufficient to consign the Sodomites to the imminent hellish consequences of their behavior, the *midrash*[68] tells us that they also intended to make a public example of the two strangers by sexually abusing them *in front of their host*. We are reminded of the Talmud's tale discussed earlier in this chapter of the compassionate maiden who was tortured and murdered by the Sodomites for giving a crust of bread to a beggar. The Sodomites likewise view Lot's behavior here as a capital offense, and in their perverse world this means that they can capriciously and arbitrarily carry out the sentence on the *object* of the kindness if the mood suits them. The intention is to deter anyone in the future from even contemplating extending a hand to a stranger in need.[69] Let it be known that in Sodom they are prepared to make bloody examples of both the compassionate Sodomite and the unfortunate supplicants. No one is safe from their reach.

And yet, we are surprised to read that by some unwritten rule or a seeming vestige of decorum[70] the rabble remain *outside* Lot's house, at least initially. They do not enter his house by force to get to the two men. Evidently it is important to them that Lot surrender the strangers by his own hand. It would seem they require Lot to be complicit[71] in their intended brutality.

The Bible is implicitly asking the readers to measure themselves against the events unfolding before Lot's eyes. The aroused and wicked Sodomites are demanding that Lot turn over his guests to them for their sport. How should Lot have responded in the face of this mob? Perhaps we are meant to ask what Abraham, Lot's uncle, role model, guardian and literary doppelganger would have done?

The Mishnah[72] teaches us that if an extortionist were to demand of us, "Give me one of your women as a sacrifice, so that I may defile her and spare the rest of you," we are forbidden to forfeit the one woman, sacrificing her to save the others. So, too, we are forbidden to spill another's blood to save our own life, or to turn over an innocent to satisfy the blackmailer, even if this refusal would result in all of us dying at the extortionist's hand.

The Mishnah is teaching us that the proper way for Lot to respond to the Sodomites would have been to refuse their demands categorically. And as for learning from his uncle Abraham, unfortunately Lot had been standing with Abram and his wife, Sarai, at the gates of Egypt years ago when Abram sinned greatly[73] by exchanging her for a king's ransom in order to save his own life (Gen. 12:11). Lot learned first-hand that when faced with the direst of moral choices, one is "permitted" to place a female family member at risk in order to save one's own skin. Let us see how Lot implements and compounds this lesson.

Lot and the two strangers are standing just inside the door to his house. All three men have heard the mob's demands, and Lot realizes that he has but a few moments before the crowd storms his door. He is faced with a nightmarish choice: Either he must turn over the men whom he has invited into his home and to whom he has offered protection, or he must stand his ground in the face of the mob, bringing their ire and violence upon himself. His fear must be palpable and very great. All his years of building up his wealth and reputation in this city might actually be for naught if he mishandles this. What to do? What to say? He is not a brave man, or a particularly moral one; Nehama Leibowitz calls him "an average man, a study in mediocrity."[74] He is a weak man with a love of material wealth and comfort. That he now faces an evil that is to some degree of his own making — as he freely chose to live among these people — does not lessen the drama or danger of the moment.

LOT OFFERS HIS DAUGHTERS

So Lot steps outside and closes the door behind him. He is not a young man, and suspects, perhaps, that his best effort may not be good enough to save the day. Still, he draws himself up to his full height and takes a deep breath. Hands lifted in a mime of supplication, Lot raises his judicial voice to quiet the crowd so that he can be heard. "My brothers! Don't, I pray you, do this awful thing!" Perhaps the crowd murmurs impatiently at his plea, and pushes closer, jostling him. He can actually see the unquenchable lust in their eyes, smell their feral intent, and in a flash he realizes they are past reason. He must offer them something of what they want or all will be lost. In a rush he says, "Here now, I have two virgin daughters who have not known any man. If you will it, I will bring them out to you instead, and you may do to them as seems good in your eyes. But as for these men, do nothing to them, because they have come under the shadow of my roof and my protection."

Lot cannot hear — and would not even consider — his daughters' gasps of shock and fear as they listen at the window. They grip one another tightly, their mother perhaps stretches her arms about the two young women, and they all hold their breath, dreading what the mob will do next.

The spokesmen say, "Press closer! Closer still!" And they sneer and say, "Listen to this one! He is but a newcomer here, and he dares to judge us now, telling *us* what to do! Well, we will treat *you* even worse than we will treat *them*!" And the crowd presses even closer to Lot, and they prepare to break down the door.

The two angels reach their arms around the doorway and pull Lot toward them into the house, and close the door securely. And as for the mob who are still crushing up against Lot's door, the angels strike them, one-and-all, from the youngest ruffian to the oldest thug, with blindness, so that they scrabble in vain to find the door latch.

Let us closely examine Lot's offer of his virgin daughters to the marauding Sodomites. Immediately, there are many questions that trouble the inquiring reader. In verse 7 Lot begs the Sodomite mob *not to do this evil thing* when they demand that he turn over the two strangers for their sexual pleasure and abuse. Yet just moments later, in verse 8, he is offering his two daughters *who have not yet known a man* as a placatory substitute. Is Lot saying that sacrificing his virgin daughters to the crowd does *not* qualify as an "evil thing," while surrendering the strangers does?

The *midrashists* teach us that Lot had five daughters. The eldest was Pelotit, the Talmud's "certain maiden" whose compassionate heart led the Sodomites to torture and kill her. The next two were already married at the time of our story, living with their Sodomite husbands in a different part of the city.[75] Lot's two remaining daughters were betrothed,[76] living at home at the time of the incident of the two strangers.[77] This places Lot into an even deeper moral morass. For we are taught that as regards virgin girls who are betrothed in marriage, a man must allow himself to be killed rather than to despoil them.[78] Such women are positively forbidden to other men, having been promised and contracted to their future grooms, but still living in their father's house until they marry and move into their husband's domain. So even to save his own life Lot was forbidden to offer up his betrothed virgin daughters to the Sodomite mob.

Ramban, the great 13th-century Torah scholar, who unreservedly condemned Abraham for trading his wife's honor for his own life in Egypt,[79] is similarly outspoken in his denunciation of Lot for his comparable behavior here,[80] condemning Lot twice-over. First, Ramban condemns Lot for his cowardice. Even in that far-distant time and place he owed his daughters—and his wife, too, for that matter—the highest measure of protection. According to the commentary,[81] Lot should have fought to the death for his daughters' honor, and instead he offered to hand them over to the mob. And second, continues Ramban, Lot must be condemned for his depraved heart. He was evidently so much a Sodomite by this point that the notion of prostituting women—here his own virgin daughters!—was not abhorrent to him.

So we see that far from condoning Lot's behavior, the Bible provides us with sufficient detail to allow the reader to cringe and gasp at Lot's offer to throw his daughters to the ravening mob. We appreciate, for instance, that when the two angels' focused radiance smites the Sodomites with blindness and stops them in their tracks, this immediately highlights for the reader the parallel to Lot's *moral* blindness, which we already have witnessed throughout his story, and which we will observe as the story continues.

The thread of the theme of hospitality runs visibly through these early Genesis stories. We have seen that the Bible first presents Abraham (and Sarah) as prototype purveyors of desert hospitality, and that Lot's weak imitation of this prized quality of generosity to strangers is a window into his character. The hospitality comparison is a device that allowed the reader to see Lot's descent from moral indifference into moral bankruptcy. This latter state is graphically illustrated in this episode in which Lot offers his daughters to the Sodomite mob.

The universal reaction of Bible readers to Lot's offer of his two virgin daughters to placate the Sodomites is horror, disgust, and condemnation. Genesis 19:8 presents an almost Gordian scenario for us to unravel. On the one hand, Lot gamely steps out onto his front steps and faces down the mob of brutish Sodomite townspeople. He intends to protect his two house guests — complete strangers — from harm. This is praiseworthy behavior by any standard. On the other hand, the same verse has Lot substituting — and offering — almost immediately, his own two virgin daughters to the mob instead! By any standard of morality this is repugnant and reprehensible behavior. Ordinarily, such conflicting moral clues would allow the reader to feel a justified ambivalence about the character in question. But here, Lot's offer of his virgin daughters is so morally wrong that Lot has fallen completely from grace in the reader's eyes, as a father and as a man. It falls to us to examine how this difficult verse has been perceived by generations of Bible scholars. How is Lot's behavior understood or explained?

Ovadia Sforno,[82] the 16th-century Italian Torah commentator, condemns Lot's offer as morally wrong. He also suggests the slim possibility that Lot's offer could have been a pretext, tossed out at the spur-of-the-moment in attempt to stall for time and to create a diversion. *Sforno* says that perhaps Lot expected that before the mob would be able to lay a hand on the two young women, their intended husbands would arise against the mob and protest. In the ensuing melée and confusion, the strangers as well as the girls could be spirited to safety.

Another *midrash*[83] suggests that when Lot addressed the mob as "my brothers" in verse 7, he was not being merely rhetorical. He was personally acquainted with the men who had come to his door, and was in fact related to them by marriage, as they were his wife's brothers and cousins. This notion would support the possibility that Lot thought that his offer of his daughters would not be accepted. Because after all, the mob's main object was the two male strangers.[84] *They* had not demanded that Lot turn over the young women, so perhaps his in-laws among the crowd would recognize his offer as a reckless stalling tactic, and would not expect him actually to sacrifice his daughters. In considering this minority opinion, the remote possibility arises that Lot might have calculated all of this when he offered his daughters to the mob, never expecting that he would be forced to make good on his offer. There is the smallest possibility, according to this reasoning, that Lot intended his daughters no harm, and thus should not be damned in the readers' eyes.

But modern Bible scholars[85] view the scenario through a more prosaic lens. They have noted that the prevailing societal code of the ancient Near East granted the father an enormous authority over the governance of his family. Ancient Israelite law[86] allowed a father to punish his offspring with impunity, banish them from his household, sell them into indentured servitude, or even offer them as concubines to pay off a debt. Professor Leila Bronner says that this was especially so as regards the father's control over his daughter. Not only could he sell her, but he also could give her over in marriage, or annul her vows. The father possessed complete control over his daughter's "body, mind and destiny."[87]

It is not an overstatement that we appreciate for this analysis that male offspring were prized in biblical times. The sons—not the daughters[88] — inherited their father's property, and also could bear arms in times of war, so consequently the assets and strength of a tribe or family were measured by the number of its sons. Whereas a daughter was useful as unpaid domestic labor, and perhaps could be traded in marriage for the father's political purposes.

Another strong societal norm at that time was the ingrained Bedouin code of hospitality[89] requiring that strangers be offered food, water, and a bed for up to three days, even if such an offer presented economic hardship for the host. The Bible text at Gen. 19:8 (*only do nothing to these men for they have come under the shelter of my roof-beam*) suggests that Lot had this code in mind when he stepped out of his house to confront the Sodomite mob.

It is interesting briefly to note another powerful indicator of the mores of the time: the Code of Hammurabi.[90] Section 130 of that pre-biblical code states that "if a man violate the . . . betrothed of another man, **who has never known a man and still lives in her father's house**, . . . this man shall be put to death." The situation with Lot differs in that the Bible text only tells us that his daughters were virgins, and not that they were betrothed (this latter was inferred by the commentaries).[91] Also, the Bible text is clear that Lot offered the girls to others rather than violated them himself. But it is nevertheless striking that the language of the Bible text (*I have two daughters who have never known a man*) and of the Code are nearly identical. The norm is clear: In the ancient Near East a betrothed virgin was offered a high level of protection, so much so that violators of this dictum were executed.

This normative code of behavior should not have come as a surprise to the Sodomites. Avivah Gottlieb Zornberg[92] points out that the sin of the pre-Flood generation was primarily the sin of sexual immorality. Rashi adds that the additional sin of robbery sealed their verdict.[93] Zornberg emphasizes that indiscriminate punishment — where innocents are killed along with the guilty — such as that of the blanket destructiveness of the great Flood, comes to punish such sexual sin compounded by theft. For what is sexual rapaciousness — such as abduction and molestation of young girls — but a theft of their innocence, their lives and their futures? The Sodomites, as we have seen, have duplicated, to a

large extent, the antediluvian sin of sexual immorality compounded by theft. The Sodomites were on notice after the world
was destroyed by the Flood that the divine powers did not suffer
this sin lightly. And in fact, the Sodomites are fated to suffer a
similar punishment, in that their world also will come to an end
through the instrumentality of the destruction — through fire, this
time, and with the exception of Lot and his two daughters — of
every living being in Sodom, Gomorrah and the cities of the plain.

So we see that the societies of the ancient Near East were
cognizant of the proper way to treat betrothed virgins. There also
were other codes of behavior that were common and widespread.
We already have demonstrated that the Bible endorses extending
hospitality to strangers. The ideal is clearly to offer a measure of
succor to the stranger, both for its humanitarian purpose and also
possibly in order to promote commerce among far-flung communities. As we have seen, keeping to this ideal looms large in
the Lot story because it is pitted against his duty to protect his
own family, in particular, his innocent daughters.

Another way to understand Lot's offer of his daughters is to
bear in mind that he was a product of the ancient Near East
society where the rules of hospitality protected only the males.[94]
This would allow the reader to see Lot as upholding the only code
of hospitality he knows when he says to the mob, *Here, now, I have
two virgin daughters who have not known any man; I will bring them
out to you, and you can do to them whatever is good in your eyes;* **only
do nothing to these men, for they have come under the shelter of
my roof-beam.** (Gen. 19:8, emphasis added.) Professor Phyllis
Trible characterizes this exchange as an attempt by Lot "to
mediate between males. . . . Conflict among them could be solved
by the sacrifice of females. The male protector, indeed the father,
became procurer."[95]

This revolutionary notion is borne out not only in the scene
before us, but also in the clearly ironic and dramatic doings in the
cave scene at the end of Lot's story in Genesis 19 (the reader was
given a glimpse into the text at the first page of this chapter).
There, the Bible's final characterization of Lot is as the *object* of his
daughters' desperate sexual gambit. Our reaction there is a rueful
nod, as we see how circumstances have permitted a turnabout.

Lot, desperate to save himself and the two strangers from the abuse of the Sodomite mob, had earlier offered his powerless virgin daughters as a sop to the Sodomites' blood-lust. Later, after the destruction of Lot's world, these same virgin daughters, in an extreme act of desperation and survival, will themselves employ their untried sexuality to control Lot and seize a future.

The reader should bear in mind that while this chapter tries to make sense of Lot's behavior, and to understand the man who will be the object of the final cave seduction, neither this author, the Talmud, nor the biblical commentators in any way condone his actions. As was described earlier in this chapter, the Talmud disallows valuing one life over another. Further, *Sforno*[96] clearly and eloquently makes the case for the *midrashists*[97] that Lot's offer of his daughters transgressed not only moral decency, but also the code of behavior that required a father to protect his daughters' honor even if it meant his own death. *Midrash Tanchuma*[98] concurs, expressing disgust with Lots's behavior: "It is the way of the world that a man would fight to the death to protect his daughters and his wife. Yet 'this one' [*i.e.*, Lot] hands his daughters over for immoral purposes without demurral."

Indeed, in weighing the competing and compelling legal and moral obligations—hospitality versus sexual morality[99]—"critics and commentators conclude that Lot simply does not value his daughters highly enough to place their safety above his duties to the strangers who sheltered under his roof."[100] Lot, a weak man, a product of his time, of his preference, of his Sodomite society, made the horrifyingly wrong choice, honoring one important societal tenet—protecting one's house guests—over the deeply-rooted and morally compelling one: safeguarding his daughters' honor and lives.

THE ANGELS INTERVENE

The offer of his daughters has barely passed from Lot's lips when we see that the Sodomites do not appear even to consider tarrying with the proffered young women. In the Bible text they ignore his offer, and, still bent on man-handling the two strangers, they shout at Lot to "Stand back!" Then, pushing rhythmically against

Lot's door in an attempt to batter it down, they mock Lot, saying, "Listen to him! He is but a newcomer here, and he dares to judge us now, telling us what to do!" Addressing Lot, they taunt, "We will treat *you* even worse than we will treat *them*!" The scene has degenerated, and Lot realizes in that moment that his gambit has failed, and that his guests, as well as his household and all that he has built here in Sodom, are now forfeit.

Lot and his wife and daughters do not know it, but they are about to be saved by the miraculous intervention of the two strange men, whom we know to be messenger-angels from God. Almost as if the strangers are impatient with the dangerous human drama that has unfolded on Lot's doorstep, they stretch out their hands in the nick of time and grab Lot, pulling him back into the house, securely shutting the door on the mob. Clearly the time for talking is at an end. As for the unruly throng, they are instantaneously and miraculously struck, one and all—from the youngest to the most distinguished among them—with blindness. And amid the chaos that results, they grope in vain for Lot's door handle.

It is interesting to note that the action in these verses takes place on Lot's threshold. The mob comes up to the door but does not make it through into the house; the angels reach around the door and grab Lot back over the threshold, shutting out the mob; the mob is blinded and they grope about at the threshold to Lot's house. There is also a faint tinge of sexuality to the threshold. Lot was willing to pass his two virgin daughters over that threshold and give them to the mob, but was prevented by the angels' intervention. Also, if the mob manages to batter down his door and cross Lot's threshold, they will abuse and violate Lot's guests. The reader can practically see the moral and physical tug-of-war going on in that one spot.

The *midrash*[101] tells us that the Hebrew word for blindness used in Gen. 19:11, *sanverim*, is a compound word meaning "thorns of light." It is an unusual and apt word, and the reader can almost feel the piercing, supernaturally-bright light that must have emanated from the angels, in a flash blinding the Sodomites and foiling their planned attack. To the modern reader the *sanverim* might be akin to a blinding laser burst and its afterburn.

We can appreciate the irony of the scene: The Sodomites, emboldened by decades of rampant, unchecked evil and licentiousness, are unprepared to be thwarted by two solitary wayfarers. When the mob is miraculously struck with *physical* blindness, the reader understands that this is the perfect concomitant to their pervasive *moral* blindness. Lot, saved by a hair's-breadth from suffering at the Sodomites' hands, could easily have suffered their fate, as well. Certainly he has been wearing blinders for all the years he has lived amongst them ignoring their lawlessness and perversity, and profiting from it. That Lot is spared is primarily due to his uncle Abraham's intervention with the Almighty,[102] and not to his own merit.

ESCAPE FROM SODOM

Once he is safely within the house, Lot wails to the strangers, "Oh, why have you come here?!"[103] And the angels, still grasping Lot tightly, respond urgently, perhaps even shaking him to get his attention, "Who else lives here with you? Your sons and your daughters? A son-in-law? Everyone that you have in the city you must remove from this place, for we will be destroying it utterly, because their outcry is great and has reached God, and He has sent us to annihilate it!"

In a daze at the news he has just heard, Lot leaves his house through a little-used door, and hurries to the homes of his sons-in-law and prospective sons-in-law.[104] Breathless from his run as well as from his narrow escape from the terror of the mob scene, Lot exclaims to them, "Arise! You must leave this place, because God will be destroying this city! You must fear for your lives!"[105] He might even have grasped their arms, turning in a frenzy from one to the other, urging them out of their seats and tugging them toward the door. But to no avail. The young Sodomite men see only a wild-eyed, disheveled old man, who appears as if he has taken leave of his senses. Gone is the staid, judicious Lot they are familiar with. They think perhaps the old man is jesting with them for some purpose known only to him, and they placate him and tell him to go on back home; they will not evacuate Sodom.

"Don't be absurd," they say to Lot. "This city is as strong as ever, we have nothing to fear.[106] Go on home and leave us be."

Lot's frantic energy drains away, and he slowly makes his way back to his house. He does not even notice if the crowd has dispersed; he is in despair. As he climbs the stairs, he takes no notice of the black night sky that is blushing faintly on its eastern horizon with the faintest light of dawn. The *midrash* relates that at that precise moment the moon and the sun occupied the night sky simultaneously,[107] at the fleeting instant when the old day was dying and the new one breaking. The dawn light piercing the horizon is the harbinger of God's imminent final judgement of Sodom. Lot, poised between the old day and the new, has no inkling what this day will bring.

> *And when the morning arose, then the angels hastened Lot saying, "Arise, take your wife and your two daughters which are here, lest you be consumed in the iniquity of the city."*
> Gen. 19:15

As the night wanes, the two angels, seeing that Lot has returned alone from his fruitless mission, urge him to hurry. They press Lot saying, "Arise! Make haste! Take your wife and two daughters who are found here in your house. You must abandon your married daughters and their husbands if they refuse to leave Sodom.[108] There is no time to lose! Be quick, all of you, lest you be caught up in the city's iniquity and be swept away and obliterated along with it!" The angels know, if Lot does not, that the whirlwind of destruction will not discriminate between the damned and the deserving.[109] For Lot to be saved he must be gone from the doomed cities of the plain.

The Talmud[110] and *midrash*[111] inject a wonderful allusion to the coming cave scene into the angels' exhortation to Lot to hurry. The *midrash* focuses on the angels' reference to Lot's daughters *who are found* in his house, noting the slightly odd wording. Why did the text need to include the Hebrew word for "who are **found**" (*hanimtza'ot*), when the meaning would have been clear without it (*Take your wife and daughters who are **in** your house*)? The response is that the Bible text here in the Lot story is hinting to a later biblical reference to King David, where similar odd wording occurs.[112] Bryna Levy[113] points out that the *midrash* makes the extraordinary statement that "God **found** David **in Sodom**."[114] How could this be so? Our verse in the Lot story, noting Lot's **daughters** "who are **found**" in the house, hints to the reader that Lot's two daughters are destined to be the source of two special "finds" in the future. They will give birth to the progenitors of two nations, Moav and Ammon. From Moav will descend Ruth, great-grandmother of King David,[115] and from Ammon will descend Naama, wife of David's son, Solomon, and mother to Rechavam, also a future king of Israel. Later in this chapter we will discuss this double provenance of the Davidic dynasty, descending from both a Moabite and an Ammonite, traceable directly to Lot's two daughters.

Meanwhile, the angels are impatient to be on their way with Lot and his family. They know that a man could walk a distance of four miles in the time it takes the sun to go from barely dawn to showing itself over the horizon.[116] They are anxious that Lot be at least that distance from Sodom by the time the sun is fully up. They are charged by God with rescuing Lot and destroying Sodom on this very day, and they cannot begin their macabre task of destruction if Lot tarries.

So far in the Lot episode the Bible has narrated the action in rich detail, allowing — even encouraging — the reader to draw conclusions about Lot's character.[117] We have seen him as grudgingly hospitable, myopic, craven, rash, manipulative, and argumentative. Now, as his laboriously constructed world-within-a-world comes crashing down around him, we will see not only what Lot is made of, but also how his character and behavior influence his daughters' actions in the final cave scene.

> *And while he lingered, the men laid hold upon his hand, and upon the hand of his wife, and upon the hand of his two daughters, the Lord being merciful unto him. And they brought him forth, and set him outside the city.*
>
> *And it came to pass when they had brought them out that he said, "Escape for your life! Do not look behind you, nor may you stay in the plain. Escape to the mountain, lest you be consumed!"* Gen. 19:16–17

The Bible continues its story in verse 16, using a wonderful and rare Hebrew word to allow us to "see" Lot. Using the word *vayitmahmah*, the Bible tells us that Lot *delayed*.[118]

Lot turns in a circle, surveying his prosperous home and its possessions. The angels are at the door and the sun is coming up, Lot's city will soon be a smoldering pile of ash, and still Lot drags his feet. The *midrash*[119] tells us that Lot could be heard exclaiming, "How can I leave my life's treasure; my silver coins, my gold, my precious stones, my priceless pearls?!" He even tried to cram some of it into his pockets, and some more into an improvised bundle[120] to carry on his back.

There is no time to be lost, yet Lot is tragically dilatory here, so much so that the men/angels grasp Lot's hand, and the hands of his wife and two daughters, and forcibly drag them from his house, quickly and magically depositing them outside the city of Sodom.

This verse opens a window for the reader into the biblical narrator's feelings about Lot and his behavior, inserting the phrase *because of God's mercy on him*. Is this phrase an explanation for the angels' extraordinary rescue of Lot? The phrase suggests that the Bible text is wrestling with the same *sub silencio* question we are struggling with: Why is Lot being saved while the rest of Sodom will perish? Lot certainly does not seem worthy of all this trouble: two messenger angels sent to reconnoiter; an overnight stay that foments a mob scene; a miraculous intervention by the angels to prevent a lynching. In the face of God's helping hand Lot flouted the laws of moral behavior, offering to sacrifice his virgin daughters; and now, on the point of actual rescue, Lot is almost unbelievably ambivalent. In fact, the *midrash*[121] tells us that the appearance of the phrase *because of God's mercy* in the same verse with Lot's procrastination teaches us that God actually has judged Lot *un*worthy of rescue at this precise point, but that only His quality of mercy and Lot's relationship to Abraham save Lot from sharing the fate of the Sodomites.

The biblical reader understands that in the book of Genesis, morality, the journey toward knowledge of God, and the building of family are everything. Lot has been traveling in the wrong direction certainly from the moment he parted from Abraham and chose to settle in Sodom. Here at this precise moment we see that his persistent moral blindness should have rendered him beyond saving. The *midrash*[122] tells us that Lot's reluctance to leave the city, even in the face of the angels' revelation that the place is to be destroyed, proved he really was undeserving of rescue. In fact, the angel Gabriel, who represented God's attribute of justice and was partnering the angel Michael in this dual enterprise, gave up on Lot completely at that point. It was the angel Michael who alone persisted in his assigned task and proceeded to remove Lot from the doomed city. Lot may be the most righteous man in Sodom, but that sobriquet damns him with its faint praise.

Still, Lot, his wife and his two unmarried daughters are removed from the doomed city by the two men, and the angel Michael[123] instructs Lot as follows: "You must flee for your life! Leave your money, your flocks and your worldly goods.[124] Do not look back, and do not tarry or stop anywhere on the plain. Flee to the mountain lest you, too, be obliterated!"

> *And Lot said to them, "Oh, not so, my Lord.*
>
> *"Behold now, your servant has found grace in your sight, and you have magnified your mercy, which you have shown me in saving my life. And I cannot escape to the mountain, lest some evil overtake me and I die!*
>
> *"Behold now, this city is near to flee to, and it is a little one. Oh, let me escape there! (Is it not a little one?) and my soul shall live."* Gen. 19:18–20

But Lot, true to his character, rather than thanking the men and running with his family, lingers and opens a negotiation with them. Lot begs, "Please, no, my lord! See now, your servant has found favor in your eyes, and your kindness to me has been great, as you have surely saved my life. But I will not be able to flee to the far mountain as you have instructed, lest the evil of these cities and the plain catch up with me, and I will die along with them. Behold, please, this small city nearby. It is close enough for me to escape to it — is it not small? — if I could but flee *there*, my life will be spared."

Lot is seeking a shorter and easier escape route, and he shudders at the prospect of living in the wilds. The *midrash*[125] tells us that Lot whined to the angels, asking, "But where shall I run to?" And they replied, "Go to your uncle Abraham, who dwells on the mountainside." But Lot has no intention of following this directive. He is a city-dweller, and his days of living the nomadic life in desert and mountain foothills, living off the land with frequent pitching and un-pitching of his tent, ended when he parted with his uncle years before. He has no desire to be back under Abraham's watchful eye, his every move scrutinized and measured by his uncle's moral yardstick. Lot also is hoping that because the small, nearby city is not as long-standing or established a city as Sodom and Gomorrah, that its nature would not have ripened to such a level of evil that God will destroy it along with everything else on the plain.[126] His foolish hope is that he can ride out the destruction right there, in the nearby town of Zoar, and resume his urban life after all the dust has settled.

THE DESTRUCTION OF SODOM

The angel Gabriel[127] replied to Lot that his plea — albeit self-serving — on behalf of the small city of Zoar has softened God's heart, and for that reason the small city would be spared. "So make haste and flee to Zoar! For I cannot begin my task of destruction until you arrive safely there."

As the first fingers of light spread across the eastern horizon, the men of Sodom were just beginning to awaken.[128] They had fallen into exhausted sleep after their night of marauding culminated in their being struck blind by Lot's angels. Now, as they opened their eyes, they congratulated themselves that their blindness had been only a temporary inconvenience. Perhaps they even imagined it in their wrought-up state. They hardly had time to make their way back to their homes before, unbeknownst to them, the *shechinah*, God's presence, descended from the Heavens to wreak destruction and death upon them.

> *And God rained sulphur and fire onto Sodom and Gomorrah; the brimstone and fire emanated from God and from the Heavens. And He destroyed these cities and the entire plain,*

and all the inhabitants of the cities, and the vegetation of the soil. Gen. 19:24–25

At the exact moment that Lot and his wife and daughters set foot in the town of Zoar, there was a deafening crack of thunder. The dawn sky darkened to black and the air concussed with a supernatural boom. The pelting rain almost instantly turned — unbelievably! — to sheets of searing flame.[129] The stench of sulphur filled their nostrils and mingled with the horrific smell of burning flesh. They could hear the not-so-distant cries of the people of Sodom, and the bleating of the animals, even through the deafening sound of the thunder, which shook the earth like an avalanche of boulders, and rolled on and on.

The two girls had heard the two powerful strangers implore their father, Lot, to head for refuge in the craggy foothills that rimmed the plains cities. They had listened, too, as their father had demurred and bargained with the two strangers, the powerful and frightening men whom he called "masters,"[130] begging them to spare the tiny, outlying settlement of Zoar from destruction. It was toward Zoar that the four of them had run, only to find it a desolate and abandoned place, its streets empty as a graveyard. The people of Zoar had fallen victim to the abject fear that they would be engulfed in the inferno that was consuming the nearby cities of the plain, so they had picked up and run from their homes in terror.[131] Amazingly, the girls had had the presence of mind to grab some abandoned foodstuffs and skins of water and wine in their haste to escape the ghost-town of Zoar, and the four refugees ran, after all, to the shelter of the nearby mountains. The girls were the most fleet-of-foot, then came their mother, with Lot following last of all.

And in the split-second when they paused to catch their breath, the girls saw their own mother turn her head over her shoulder, squinting through the acrid smoke behind her husband.[132] Perhaps she had forgotten the strangers' admonition; perhaps she never heard it.[133] Perhaps in her confusion and fear she looked back, hoping to see her two older, married daughters escaping Sodom at the last moment.[134] She might also have been straining to see if her father's house had escaped the destruction.[135] According to the *Zohar*,[136] Lot's wife looked behind her, turning her face to Gabriel, the angel of destruction. The *Zohar* explains that once Gabriel saw her face, his power of destruction touched upon her, too, and she became a pillar of salt.

The *Netziv*[137] offers an amazing *midrashic* explanation for Lot's wife's demise. At the exact hour that God began the destruction of Sodom, the evil Satan was released as well. As was Satan's wont, he envied Lot's rescue. He dogged Lot's steps as he and his wife and two daughters fled the city, hoping for a chance to taint or prevent God's act of deliverance. Powerless to undo God's rescue of Lot, Satan seized his momentary opportunity to wreak misfortune upon Lot's wife. He jostled her as she was being ushered away from Sodom, causing her to turn her head and look behind her. So it was, that at that instant Lot's wife was turned to salt.

We see that the *midrash* appears loath to assign a purely negative motive to Lot's wife at the moment of her death. All three — Lot and the two girls — watched in horror as the woman remained rooted mid-stride, as — in the fraction of the instant it took to blink their eyes — she became covered in salt and ash. First her head, then her shoulders, and finally her toes were consumed by it, until no living flesh remained, and she literally became solid as a pillar.[138]

The girls heard their father gasp, "Edis! Edis, what have you done!"[139] He could not know that in looking behind her his wife had beheld the back of the Divine Presence, God's majesty, known as the *shechinah*, as the Almighty — cloaked, so-to-speak, in the divine attribute of justice — rained the plague of destruction and death onto Sodom.[140] Lot's wife could not witness such a fearful spectacle and live, and so instead of being burned to death by the raining sulphur, she became instantly encrusted with salt.

There was no time to mourn her. The horrified girls, registering that their mother was lost to them forever, continued running, tears streaming from their eyes. Amidst the searing heat and the falling ash, the two girls stumbled over strewn rocks, dragging their father along with them. The girls had thought that the small city of Zoar would be their refuge; but when they arrived there and saw that it was bereft of inhabitants, they deduced that the fire would soon engulf that small city as well. So they fled from Zoar to the foothills, the nearest location that, while it rimmed the doomed valley, did not appear to be touched by the flames.

The Bible tells us that Abraham could not sleep. He arose early that morning, stood in the half-light of dawn, and kept watch from the very same nearby mountain top where just the previous day he had pleaded with God to spare the righteous of Sodom. He thinks that if God had reacted mercifully to his pleas that one time, then perhaps God would again be merciful, and allow him to perceive that his nephew Lot had been spared.[141] Actually, Abraham is fated never to see Lot again, but he does not know this, and at this moment he is watching avidly from his vantage point.

What he sees as he gazes toward Sodom and Gomorrah and the plain of Jordan is—behold!—black smoke rising straight up from the earth like the smoke from the burning kilns of the lime pits. Abraham sees the billowing columns of black cumulus smoke, the immediate aftermath of the fiery rain that fell from the heavens. He sees thick black and gray ash rising in a cloud and hovering over the valley, so that even the birds over Sodom and Gomorrah fall from the sky. Particles of ash are borne on the air as thick as a desert dust storm, and he sees that not even a tree is left standing.[142] There is no daylight over the plain of the Jordan, only an artificial darkness and an acrid hell, and the unceasing din of earth tremors and the supernatural thunder.

God had destroyed the evil cities of the plain of the Jordan, but God spared Lot, Abraham's nephew, from the conflagration of the city he had inhabited. Ironically, Abraham was unaware that God had indeed saved Lot, or that Lot had fled from Zoar, along with his two daughters, seeking refuge in the low-lying mountains.

SEDUCTION IN THE CAVE

Lot dwelled in the mountain, he and his two daughters with him, because he feared to stay in Zoar; so he dwelled in a cave, he and his two daughters. Gen. 19:30

While there is dispute among Bible commentaries concerning interpretation of and responsibility for the coming incestuous seductions, there is virtual unanimity that the girls genuinely thought that the end of the world had come.[143] One *midrash* tells us that the girls thought they had witnessed a complete annihilation of both people and vegetation, akin to God's destruction of the world by flood[144] centuries before; only this time the "flood" was molten fire.[145] Another *midrash* explains that they thought that the small settlement of Zoar was the very last outpost of humanity, and that when their father abandoned even Zoar to flee to the mountain, he fled because he knew that Zoar, too, was but minutes away from a similar destruction.[146] The girls thought they were the last living persons on the face of the earth.

At this point in the story, poised as we are to analyze the seduction in the cave, it would be fitting if we could call Lot's daughters by name. As we already are aware, the Bible has not assigned them names. This despite the Bible's general practice of naming those people with significant roles to play in the stories' human and political dramas. In fact, as we will learn in coming chapters of this book, often the person's name reflects his or her true nature or fate, functioning as a valuable key to the reader. Also, as we already have seen, whenever there is an ambiguity or a gap in the Bible text, the *midrash* is sure to seek to explain or resolve it. One would think, therefore, that the *midrashim* would have assigned names to the two girls, considering the pivotal role they play in the coming scene. But only one obscure *midrash* does so,[147] calling the elder girl Pheiné, and the younger Thamma. It is entirely probable that the girls are referred to simply as "Lot's daughters" in the text because that epithet identifies them better than their names would. Their past and future behaviors are judged by their relationship to their father.

What is in store for these two officially unnamed girls who are running for their lives?

We read that Lot and his daughters headed into the hills because Lot was understandably terrified to linger in Zoar despite the angels' assurance that the small city would be spared. He saw that the conflagration of Sodom and Gomorrah and the cities of the plain began before he even reached the safety of the city's gate.

Who knew if the fiery destruction would spread to that outpost city, too, and engulf him there?[148] Better to abandon his initial preference for remaining in the small city in the Jordan plain, and head for the mountainside. Lot thought if he reverted to the angel's initial instruction the fires would not follow him.[149]

There is strong *midrashic* opinion[150] about the phrase *and Lot settled in the cave, he and his two daughters*, interpreting it to mean that Lot was on some level desirous of being alone with his two virgin daughters, and that for this improper reason he abandoned the city of Zoar after his wife's death and fled with them to the isolation of the cave. The Talmud[151] connects Lot's decision, years earlier, to part from Abraham and settle in Sodom, to the present cave incident. The phrase used in the Bible back at the time of the parting of the ways (see Gen. 13:10–12) is *Lot chose the Jordan valley . . . and Lot **dwelled** in the cities of the plain, pitching his tent near Sodom*. The Talmud sees, in Lot's choice of the fertile but immoral city of Sodom, the genesis of his descent into sexual depravity that culminates *here*, when he **dwells** in the cave with his daughters. The Hebrew root-word employed in both narratives is identical: *yashav*. The commentaries,[152] having tallied the uses of the portentous word *vayeshev* — meaning *and he dwelled* — in the Bible, conclude that in nearly all the places where the term is used in connection with settlement of a biblical actor, it is a harbinger of serious troubles to come.

By itself this word coincidence might not convince, but in biblical parlance Lot's choice of Sodom was a fatally incorrect one. His moral compromises in remaining in Sodom and rising to the top of its societal ladder doomed him; and his behavior in offering his virgin daughters to the Sodomite mob, and his lethargy about escaping the city, demonstrate his poor judgement, an opportunistic moral sense and his weakness of character.

There is one *midrash* which suggests that once the three refugees reached the mountain they intended to dwell there like civilized people and in a chaste manner. It is of course theoretically possible that although they lived in the cave alone together, they intended a chaste life, with Lot occupying the main area of the cave and his daughters separate quarters,[153] perhaps a second, smaller cave chamber adjacent to the main opening. Or perhaps they roped off a private area using a large swath of cloth. This attempt at civilized habitation is credited to the two girls, to whom the task fell to make a temporary dwelling as best they could, in light of their motherless state.

The suggestion of this lone *midrashic* voice is overshadowed, however, by the incontrovertible facts of the cave seductions in the coming verses. The implicit unanswerable question persists among the commentaries: If Lot had *not* chosen to live in extreme solitude in the cave — if they had proceeded, instead, to the society of his uncle Abraham's compound, as the angels intended — would the incestuous seductions we are about to encounter never have taken place?[154] The question is purely academic, as the Bible continues its narrative:

> *And the elder [daughter] said to the younger one: Our father is old; there is no man left in the land to come to us in the usual manner of the land. Let us give our elderly father wine and we will lie with him; thus we will live on through our father's seed.* Gen. 19:31–32

Lot's daughters are in an untenable situation. They believe that the world has been destroyed. The Bible does not tell us how much time has elapsed between the day that Sodom and Gomorrah were destroyed, and the present verses. But we can assume that Pheiné, the elder daughter, has spent much time peering out of the cave opening, watching the yellow-black pall of sulphurous smoke hovering low over what was once their lush valley and is now a desolated landscape. She sees no movement at all; there are no people about, no animals lowing, not a single bird flying overhead. Her nostrils are filled with the searing smell of burned flesh, bone and stone. As far as her eye can see there is not a tree standing, nor even a blade of grass. The air seems to ripple as she watches; it is so very hot that neither she nor her younger sister nor their father have ventured outside the cave for fear of being immolated.

Her thinking must have been along these lines: "My sister, when we were living in Sodom we were like princesses; papa was an important man, head of the court, and we wanted for nothing. Mama cared for us, men came to court us, and our future husbands were selected and approved by papa. But that world is lost to us. *Everyone* is lost to us! Mama is dead, our betrotheds have perished in Sodom along with our elder sisters and their families.

"And our father is useless to us now. He was so afraid when the mob surrounded our house on that last night in Sodom that he almost sent us out into the street to be set upon as if we were strangers! He has not come back to himself since our escape, when he watched mama turn to salt and ash. Just look at him! He lies there, huddled against the wall of this miserable cave, taking only the nourishment we are able to coax into him. And can you not see, now, how old he has become? He will not rouse himself to venture from this cave to seek out any surviving men who might even be suitable mates for us. Nay, he will not *ever* leave this place, I know it in my bones.

"Thamma, my sister, we must think! What is to become of *us*? We are still young! Must we suffer our father's fate and decay here in this cave? Surely we have been spared for a reason. Perhaps the Lord of our great-uncle Abraham sent his messengers to take us out of Sodom so that we would begin the new world! Could that be it, do you think? And if that *is* the reason, what are we to do? There are no men left alive who would take us as wives in the natural way of the world as we knew it."

Her younger sister, accustomed to being led and guided by her elder sister and her mother, thinks about what Pheiné has just said, and asks the logical question: "But if there are no men left alive, how can we have children and repopulate the world? We are lost!"

And in response the elder girl throws down the forbidden gauntlet and cold-bloodedly proposes the incestuous couplings described in Gen. 19:32–36 and quoted at the outset of this chapter.

"No, Thamma, there *is* a way: We will lay down with our father." When her sister gasps and cringes at the pronouncement, the elder girl presses on: "We have no choice — there is no one else left alive! We will ply him with wine so that he falls deeply asleep, and then we will lie with him in the manner of women. We will rupture our female membranes ourselves, before we lie down with him,[155] and the act will be swift. And with the Lord's help we will become pregnant. And thus we will continue our father's seed, and we will live on even after our deaths, through our children's seed. And the world will not perish this day."

The Bible commentaries are vociferously divided about the elder sister's proposal. Some label it incestuous and unredeemed; others see it for what it is but name it inspired, desperate, and even noble.

On the side of condemnation, Rashi[156] states outright that because the elder sister boldly initiated the incestuous relations, she is disgraced in the text in verse 33, which states *the elder [daughter] lay down with her father.* The commentary points out that this differs from the text concerning the younger daughter (in verse 35), which does not link the younger daughter explicitly with "her father." Verse 35 only states indirectly that *the younger [daughter] arose and lay with him*, thereby sparing the younger girl's dignity.

And some *midrashim* concur,[157] labeling the daughters' seduction of Lot as *z'nut* in Hebrew, defined as harlotry or fornication. They place the major burden for the illicit act on the shoulders of the elder daughter, who suggested, initiated and orchestrated the incest. Motivation and desperate circumstances do not appear to mitigate their analysis.

Still other *midrashim* disagree with Rashi and try to make sense of the incident in the cave while resisting labeling it harlotry. *Alschich*, for instance, states that the incest was justified because the girls believed all the physical evidence that surrounded them: She says, *there is no other man in the land . . .* The world for all intents and purposes had been destroyed utterly, sparing only the three refugees in their cave. The girl also analyzed the situation unemotionally and acted with intuition and cleverness, proposing to feed Lot wine in order to make him feel stronger and more virile for what they had in mind. The wine would also act as an anodyne, rendering their father inert for the duration.

Still other *midrashim*[158] blame Lot, stating that he had lusted after the girls in his heart, and in fact had selected the remote cave to dwell together with them in order to indulge his secret and forbidden desires. As proof, the rabbis cite a discussion in the

Talmud[159] on the subject of how the intentions behind a person's deeds impact their worth. The Talmud deduces Lot's intentions in this episode by his past and present actions. It quotes the verse from Proverbs (18:1) saying that "he who isolates himself seeks to satisfy his own desires," and points out that Lot isolated himself on two occasions: Once, years before, when he split off from Abraham and settled in Sodom,[160] and again now, when he flees even the small city of Zoar and isolates himself in a cave with his two daughters. His intentions and inclinations were, and continue to be, to pursue licentiousness.

On the side of reading the text as offering a justification for the girls' seductions, many *midrashim* reason, with *Alschich*, that the entire purpose of the daughters' incestuous act was a noble one: to maintain and repopulate the human race. There was to be no thought of physical gratification. In fact, *Alschich* explicitly states that the daughters derived *no* enjoyment from their acts of incest with Lot.[161] They had a job to do, and they did it, gritting their teeth all the way. The same *midrash* cites kabbalistic sources that credit Pheiné, the elder daughter, with fiercely maintaining the focused intention, throughout her sexual coupling, that her union with Lot would produce the ancestor to the Messiah. We will soon see that tradition holds that this indeed may turn out to be the case.

Bible readers should pay special attention as we read these latter *midrashim* (the ones that are sensitive to Lot's daughters' motivations). We must appreciate that while of course we cannot know what was on the daughters' minds when they staged and carried out these incestuous seductions, it is fascinating that many of the rabbis were loath to tar the two girls with the brush labeled "harlotry." So they infer a permissible inspiration from the Bible's wording of verse 32.

In suggesting that Pheiné was focused on saving Lot's line from extinction rather than on fleeting sexual pleasure, the *midrash* emphasizes the elder daughter's words: *thus we will live on through our father's seed*. The *midrash*[162] notes emphatically that the Bible text does *not* have the girl say "we will live on through our father's **child**." There is a world of difference between the two words, allowing the careful reader to perceive, along with the *midrashists*, the elder daughter's *motive*. It was continuity of their line, not the ticking of her biological clock or the need for sexual release, that drove her to breach this taboo. The girl foresaw that with their elderly father's death not too far in the future, she and her sister would decay and eventually likewise die without leaving a genealogical trace, unless they acted immediately. This fear of extinction was the girls' paramount motive, and, according to Samson Raphael Hirsch, it "was a moral one."[163]

Other *midrashim*[164] concur, with one *midrash*[165] offering a particularly sensitive reading of the elder girl's argument to her sister. It suggests that if the Almighty had passed judgement on Lot's two daughters solely on the basis of their *deeds*, the girls would have been deemed guilty of incest and deserving of the extreme punishment of public burning. But before condemning them in such a manner the Almighty also looked into the girls' innermost, uncensored *thoughts*, and saw that they genuinely believed the world had been destroyed by fire and that incest was the only alternative to extinction. Their intention was a moral one, and for this reason they did not die by fire as did the other Sodomites. Instead, their wombs were opened and they conceived and gave birth to two sons, progenitors of two great nations, kings in Israel, and the Messiah.

Sforno cites the Talmud[166] to support the commentaries' guarded acceptance of Lot's daughters' seductions of their father. The Talmud's precept is that in the process of honoring God, there may be rare instances where it is necessary to perform a transgression. In assessing the predicament in the cave after the annihilation of Sodom, the girls reasoned that to honor the Almighty and to continue to populate His earth, there was no alternative for them but to transgress the incest taboo.

Frymer-Kensky, discussing the biblical incest taboo,[167] points out that "the act of the daughters of Lot was a very special type of incest." Usually it is the father who initiates this forbidden sexual encounter, thus abusing his position of trust and power. Here, though, Lot did not pursue his daughters while he was either sober or inebriated. Whether he consciously participated in the act begs for closer analysis. Frymer-Kensky acknowledges the suspicion of modern Bible readers that Lot may not have been totally unconscious of what was going on. The commentaries suspected this as well, and the *midrashim* deal with just this question.

> *And they gave their father wine that night; and the elder [daughter] came and lay with her father, and he did not know that she lay [with him] and that she arose [from him].*
>
> *And it happened on the morrow, the elder said to the younger, ". . . let us give him wine again this night, and you will come and lie with him, and we will live on through our father's seed."*
>
> *And they fed their father wine on that night also; and the younger arose and lay with him and he did not know that she lay [with him] and that she arose [from him].* Gen. 19:33–35

One point of discussion among Torah commentaries is whether Lot had any awareness of the seductions. It already has been mentioned that Rashi's position is that Lot was fundamentally immoral and inclined toward sexual promiscuity. According to Rashi and the Talmud,[168] Lot's passive acquiescence to the seductions in the cave is the predictable end to a life lived cheek-by-jowl with the illicit in Sodom. The reappearance here of wine as a facilitator echoes Lot's inclusion of wine at his meal for the two messenger-angels. Lot enjoyed his liquor, and his daughters knew his weakness and used it. Notwithstanding the liquor-induced sleep, *Alschich* goes so far as to say that Lot was on some level aware of the incestuous couplings, and that he had even enjoyed them.[169]

According to the Talmud,[170] the Bible text is packed with indications that Lot was aware of what was happening to him, at least on the night of the *second* seduction. It is reasonable to assume that Lot accepted the offer of wine with alacrity because of his propensity for the drink. But it is also likely that this is the first time that he has been given any wine since his escape from Sodom. We can derive this from the Bible's unadorned statement that *they gave their father wine* **that night**. Whatever the quantity — and the Bible gives us no indication of the amount of wine Lot drank — it evidently was sufficient to render him insensate for the duration of the first seduction. Perhaps this is because he had not had much to eat, or that he was already tired out, or that he was in shock after witnessing his home and his wife wiped out before his eyes. The result was that on the first night his elder daughter was able to lie with her father without Lot's knowing when she lay down or when she arose.

The Talmud and numerous commentaries[171] advance the notion that Lot was, in fact, aware that some form of sexual activity had gone on in his bed after Pheiné arose from him. Siftei Chachamim states emphatically that notwithstanding the text's statement that *he did not know when she lay down and when she got up*, this is true only for the *first* night's act of laying down. Certainly afterwards, on the *second* night, when Lot was again plied with wine, he surely was reminded of what had occurred the prior night when he was gotten ready for bed in the same manner. He remembered, yet still he drank the wine and lay down for the night. The commentaries are certain that Lot was aware of what was in store for him on the second night.

The Talmud derives its certainty from the text's Hebrew word *bekomah*, meaning *when she arose*. In verse 33, the first time the word is used after the elder daughter has cohabited with Lot, the word is spelled with the letter *vav*. In verse 35, the second time the same Hebrew word is used to narrate *when she arose* concerning the younger daughter, the word is spelled *without* the *vav*. The rabbis are accustomed to reading the textual word-clues in the Torah text, and they deduce that the difference in the spelling of the identical word in an identical phrase was intended as a hint to a difference in Lot's *awareness* in nearly identical circumstances. Lot did not have any inkling of what was in store for him on the *first* night; but he had sobered up by the next morning,[172] and by the second night, says the Talmud, *he knew*.

> *And the two daughters of Lot became pregnant from their father.*
>
> *The elder gave birth to a son and she called his name Moav; he is the father of Moav to this day.*
>
> *And the younger also gave birth, and she called his name Ben Ami; he is the father of the sons of Ammon to this day.*
> Gen. 19:36–38

The reader learns from these verses that each daughter became pregnant from her **one** incident of intimacy with Lot.[173] This is considered highly unusual and should surprise us, because in the book of Genesis it is a rare thing for a woman to conceive almost immediately. In fact, possibly the prime themes of this first book of the Bible are the conjoined issues of fertility, family, and succession. As we read Genesis — known as the story of the *patriarchs* — we see that the book tells a heartfelt parallel story: that of their wives, the *matriarchs*, mothers of the future Israelite nation. Three of these four women spend years of their lives in a miserably barren state. In Sarah's case she does not conceive until she is nearly ninety! The plots of the Genesis stories actually revolve around the fertility issue in all its permutations: the desire for children; the shame and pain of childlessness; the ill-fated plots to conceive; the machinations to inherit the covenantal blessings; and the envy of the unloved over the favored ones. Generations of conflict are fueled by this single issue.

So the Torah commentaries are agog at verse 36 of chapter 19 of Genesis — our present story — where the Bible in short order announces the two pregnancies and the births of male offspring. This verse comes directly after the statements that each of the two daughters slept with their father *on that night*, underscoring the one-time nature of the event. It also signals the end of the Lot story. His unnamed daughters have succeeded in their desperate plan to continue their father's line, and although the girls are never named in all of chapter 19's thirty-eight verses, the story ends with the double-mention of each of *their sons'* names, almost as if to compensate for the omission. The text is clearly ambivalent about this episode, and the *midrashists* read these textual clues and label the daughters' goal as noble, but the means abhorrent. So the girls go unnamed except in the *midrash*; in compensation, the Bible gives the reader an assurance of their sons' immortality via the repetition of the phrases *he is the ancestor. . . to this day* for each of the named boys.

But this is not a pat ending. Some questions persist about the meaning, in biblical terms, of the immediacy of the girls' conceptions, and also about the illustrious ancestors who are destined to emerge from their line. The answers to these questions will invite the reader to assess whether or not the daughters' behaviors were justified, and will, hopefully, have shed new understanding onto a difficult and mostly unmentionable episode.

The Talmud and the commentaries discuss whether and how a woman can become pregnant from a first incident of intimacy, and what this signifies. The rabbis' focus is not on the gynecological possibilities, but on textual patterns in the larger biblical narrative. For if three out of the four matriarchs suffered extreme hardship becoming pregnant — and all four of those women were revered or well-loved in their time, and were chosen by God to partner the forefathers of the Hebrews — then what does it mean that these anonymous, perhaps forgettable, morally ambiguous daughters of Lot conceived nearly immediately and gave birth to future kings?

Concerning the speed of their conception, the *midrashim*[174] explain that the girls deliberately broke their own maidenheads beforehand so that the sex act would not be as difficult and drawn-out as it would ordinarily have been for a virgin. Because of this clever preparation, it was as if this had been their *second* sexual experience and not their first. And as was discussed earlier, this also supported the elder daughter's statement that they were engaging in this incestuous mating in order to repopulate the world, and not for their own prurient pleasure. According to one *midrash*[175] this was the reason the Almighty allowed them to conceive right away; He appreciated the desperation that propelled them, the revulsion they had to overcome, and their noble mission. The daughters became pregnant quickly, forestalling the need to repeat the repugnant acts.

The *Netziv*[176] raises the problem of the gender of any resulting offspring. The commentary posits that after the elder daughter endured her one night with Lot she was intent that her sister follow suit. He suggests their whispered conversation when the younger girl balked when it came her turn. The elder sister grasped the younger girl's shoulders, stared into her frightened face, and argued forcefully: "What good will all this do if only *I* were to become pregnant? Sister, you *must* go through with this and lie with our father this night. We must pray that one of us has a girl child and the other a boy, so that they will be able to mate and continue the line if no one has survived this devastation. You *must* do this!"

The commentary poses this gender problem in order to underline the cold-blooded nature of the girls' acts, so we see that while it was certainly incest, there was very little "sexuality" at work here. The girls undid their virgin state beforehand, and did their best to "anesthetize" their father. In modern terms, the cave might as well have been an *in vitro* clinic; Lot was a sperm donor, giving up his seed for purpose of procreation only. The *Netziv* is putting the best gloss on the girls' seduction of Lot.

An important remaining question is whether, in allowing Lot's daughters to become pregnant, God was rewarding them for their outrageously brave but immoral behavior? It would seem so. Frymer-Kensky[177] says the girls' goal outweighed their means of achieving it. Lot's "daughters' goal was *children* rather than sexual intimacy. . . . Genesis is interested in *seed*, not in sex. And the ancients believed that a woman *could* obtain seed from an unconscious . . . male." In this situation it is fitting that God would reward Lot's daughters with issue who would not merely survive them, but who would perpetuate the girls' characteristics. They were possessed of a bold initiative, courage, audacity, cleverness, ability to sway others, singlemindedness, clarity of vision, and yes, the legacy of engaging in questionable sexual liaisons.

We have outlined here the characteristics of progenitors of kings. Unfortunately, Moav and Ammon, the nations destined to descend from Lot's daughters' sons, were also labeled as a special class of future enemies of Israel. The Talmud[178] cites the book of Deuteronomy (2:9), where God commands Israel *not to oppress or to incite war against Moav or Ammon*. This is a strange injunction offering a measure of protection to Ammon, the people who wickedly refused the Israelites food and water once they knew that the Israelites were forbidden to initiate a conflict with them; and to Moav, the nation that later sent the prophet Bilaam to curse the Israelites. The Bible also forbids Israel from annexing the land of the nations of Ammon and Moav (Deut. 2:19),[179] because God had given it to *the children of Lot* for a possession.

It is difficult for the reader to appreciate this special status that the future nations of Moav and Ammon enjoy in the Bible. Are they enemies or are they protected? Apparently they are both. This ambivalence derives from their foremothers, Lot's daughters. The Talmud explains the duality that Moav and Ammon embody for the Jewish people. On the one hand, the nations of Moav and Ammon are, indeed, adversaries of Israel. On the other hand, Moav and Ammon also beget illustrious and righteous women who champion Israel. As we will discuss in depth in Part Six of this book, Ruth, the great-grandmother of King David, was herself a Moabite. And Naama, an Ammonite, was wife of King Solomon, and the mother of Rechavam, another future king of Israel.

This duality has its genesis in our story. The Talmud explains that the elder daughter named her son "Moav," which in Hebrew means "from father." This brazen statement of the boy's incestuous origins is frowned on by the commentators, who much prefer the younger daughter's naming of her son. She called her son "Ben Ami," meaning "the son of my people," avoiding a direct reference to his incestuous origin. The reward for the younger daughter's "cleaner, more refined speech" is the Israelites' prohibition against inciting or in any way oppressing the nation of Ammon. And as for the Moabite descendants of the elder daughter, while Israel could not incite war against them, they could levy taxes against them and defend themselves if attacked.[180]

Still, the Bible does assert (Deut. 23:4) that Moav and Ammon *are banned from the congregation of Israel.* According to the *midrash*[181] this is precisely because they acted ungenerously to the children of Abraham, ignoring the fact that as descendants of Lot and his daughters, the two brother nations owed their very existence to the generosity of their ancestor Abraham. It was Abraham who rescued Lot and his family twice: once in the war against the five kings, and once again when Abraham pleaded with God to spare the righteous of Sodom from annihilation. As such, Moav and Ammon should not have refused food and water to Lot's kin—their Israelite brethren—or sent Bilaam to curse them. The future refusal of food and water even echoes the absence of hospitality of the Sodomites, and the perversion of hospitality of Lot, their forebear.

Yet the Talmud[182] recognizes the praiseworthy audacity of Lot's elder daughter, and says that notwithstanding all the problems attendant to this cave seduction, she should be recognized for her forwardness. In the truest sense of the word, Pheiné bravely stepped forward and "went first" with Lot, and her reward was that her descendant produced the Davidic progenitors four generations *before* her sister: Ruth the Moabite gave birth to Obed, who was the father of Jesse, who in turn was father of David, who fathered Solomon. The younger sister's royal issue came a generation later, with Solomon's son, Rechavam, whose mother was Naama the Ammonite.

The *Zohar*[183] presents an extraordinary *midrash*. It sees God's hand, so-to-speak, directing the behavior of Lot's elder daughter. The commentary reminds us of the spelling difference we discussed earlier, but interprets it differently.[184] Regarding the **extra letter** *vav* in the Hebrew word for *when she rose up*, the *Zohar* reads it as signifying that **Heaven was an accomplice** to the **elder** girl's bold act! Says the commentary, God had a hand in her ostensibly illicit behavior, because the Almighty intended her daring act to bring about the birth of the Messiah. And as we will see, this indeed comes to pass, as Ruth, the Moabite great-grandmother of King David, is a direct descendant of Lot and his elder daughter, and is thought to be the progenitor of the Messiah, whose provenance is Davidic.[185] According to the Talmud,[186] this was the elder daughter's reward for her courageous and audacious act.

CONCLUSION

The Bible and the *midrashim* stop here in their narration of the story of Lot and his daughters. There is no further mention of the daughters or of Lot in the book of Genesis after the conclusion of this episode at verse 38 of chapter 19.[187] Once his daughters have lain with him and continued his seed, Lot is of no further consequence to them or to the Bible reader. This weak, avaricious, immoral man owes his biblical immortality to his daughters' acts; he literally disappears in their wake. We can speculate whether Lot ever emerges from his mountain cave, but it is of no consequence from the standpoint of the biblical narrative. My own thought is that he died in the cave and was buried there by his daughters, sometime after he contributed his seed to posterity and before the young women emerged to rejoin civilization.

And as for Pheiné and Thamma, Lot's two daughters, we know that they lived on, and that they survived rough pregnancies even by ancient Near East standards. My suspicion is that they midwifed each other and gave birth to their sons in their isolated cave home. Possibly the small family was fed and watered from a mountain stream, and they became adept at finding and surviving on edible mountain vegetation, augmenting their diet by trapping and killing small animals that found their way into their sheltered cave dwelling.

After their sons were born but before they had been weaned, Pheiné, the elder sister—ever the adventurous one—prodded Thamma to risk venturing with her from their cave and rejoining the emerging society they could view distantly from their mountain vantage point. After the fiery destruction of Sodom and Gomorrah and the cities of the plain, it is likely there were more than a few husbandless refugees wandering the countryside as it rejuvenated, so young women alone with suckling babies were probably not an uncommon sight. Perhaps Lot's daughters, and other young mothers, made their way to Zoar, the nearby city that had only been deserted and not destroyed, and they set up housekeeping there.

The two daughters of Lot may have revealed their identities, or perhaps they kept their past a secret. It is likely they married, as the young women were focused, resourceful, brave, and determined to survive and to provide for their young sons whom they expected were destined for greatness. They saw their sons grow to manhood and in turn marry and have families. The daughters of Lot lived to witness the success of their audacious plan.

This chapter has retold the story of Lot, whose sheltered, pampered daughters find their world destroyed, and who, in a mountain cave, commit incest with their father in order to perpetuate humanity. Some call it harlotry, but the biblical evidence reveals it to have been a desperate and heroic exploitation of their own femininity for the noble purpose of survival.

PART

T W O

Dinah

&

Shechem

TWO

Dinah & Shechem

GENESIS 34:1–4

*Dinah – daughter of Leah, whom she had borne to Jacob –
went out to look over the daughters of the land.*

*Shechem, son of Hamor the Hivite, prince of the land, saw
her; and he took her, lay with her, and violated her.*

*[Afterwards] his soul clung to Dinah, daughter of Jacob;
and he loved the maiden, and he spoke to the maiden's heart.*

*And Shechem said to his father, Hamor: "Take this girl for
me for a wife."*

The spare story of the rape of Dinah, the only daughter of Leah
and Jacob, is told in typically laconic biblical fashion in these four
verses. The rest of chapter 34 of Genesis — thirty-one verses in
all — describes the aftermath of the abduction and rape: Dinah's
father's silence; her brothers' anger; striking the deal for Dinah's
bride-price; the deceptions; the vengeance wreaked by Dinah's
brothers upon all the Shechemites; Jacob's chastisement of his two
sons; and finally, their stated reason for their behavior.

It is conspicuous that Dinah does not speak at all throughout
this entire incident. And nowhere in the biblical text is there any

indication of her feelings throughout this brutal chapter. But there are clues in the text, and the *midrash* and Talmud pick up on these clues, helping to unravel the "back story," in the process enabling us to reach a deeper understanding of this troubling chapter. We are able to answer questions such as: How old was Dinah at the time of her abduction? Why did she "go out?" Why was Dinah unattended? What is Jacob even doing in the city of Shechem? What motivated Shechem to abduct her; was it Dinah's beauty, or was it something else entirely? Was Dinah to blame for what happened to her? Is this the story of a rape or is it a love story? Why does Dinah's father remain silent? Are her brothers' actions justified? Does Dinah leave Shechem's palace willingly? What becomes of her after her rescue?

As with other complex and fraught stories in the Bible, we see that the story is not as straightforward as it seems at first blush. We will come to appreciate it as nuanced, multivalent, and fascinating.

JACOB ARRIVES IN SHECHEM

> *Jacob journeyed on to Sukkoth, and he built himself a house; and for his livestock he made shelters [sukkot]; therefore he named the place "Sukkoth."*
>
> *Jacob arrived safely at the city of Shechem in the land of Canaan, upon his arrival from Padan-Aram; and he camped before the city.*
>
> *And he purchased the portion of the field upon which he pitched his tent from the hand of the sons of Hamor, the father of Shechem, for one hundred kesitas.*
>
> *And he erected an altar there, and he cried out, "God, the God of Israel!"* Gen. 33:17–20

The story of Dinah is also, largely, the story of Jacob. It is the story of family, of generational conflict, of violence, of female helplessness, fear of strangers, and a study in context. In order to understand why Dinah "went out," and why Shechem kidnapped and raped her, we should take a small step backward in the Genesis narrative.

Jacob has come to the city of Shechem by way of a dot on the ancient Near Eastern map that he named "Sukkoth." He stayed in Sukkoth for eighteen months,[1] grazing his substantial flocks, lingering there perhaps even longer than he had initially intended. Still, this is understandable. Jacob's wealth is in his flocks and his livestock. He has spent the past twenty years being baked by the desert sun, buffeted by its winds, laboring nearly single-handedly to build a husbanded herd from a few grizzled sheep grudgingly given to him by his uncle Lavan. He has arrived in Sukkoth in need of a respite from labor, travel and flight. Knowing he was facing winter and the rainy season,[2] Jacob built himself a house fit to withstand the elements, and also erected shelters, *sukkot* in Hebrew, for his herds of livestock.

Jacob rested in his watertight home in Sukkoth, reflecting gratefully on his narrow escape. This is because for the first time in twenty years, after hiding out in Haran in the home of his uncle Lavan, Jacob was now no longer a fugitive. He recalled how he had set out for his father's home laden down with his four wives, eleven sons and one daughter, and his cumbersome caravan of oxen, donkeys, herds of sheep, camels, household goods, servants and tents.

Then, on the way, his worst nightmare had come true: His brother, Esav, who had sworn an oath twenty years earlier to hunt him down and kill him for tricking him out of his father's blessing, was on the march from the fields of Edom. It was only a matter of hours before their paths would intersect and Jacob would face Esav and his complement of four hundred soldiers. Jacob had known he had no chance against a brother intent on exacting revenge. After all, Esav had spent the twenty intervening years becoming a great and feared hunter. So Jacob had sent runners to Esav's camp, bearing gifts and herds of livestock and begging favor in his eyes. Jacob received no word of conciliation, and he became terrified. He reckoned desperately that his only possible defense was a passive one. He divided his family into two camps, thinking that if Esav were to attack the first camp, perhaps the second would survive destruction. Jacob also offered a heartfelt prayer to God, begging salvation from his brother's hand.

Jacob had spent a sleepless night, patrolling the river bank that bisected his two camps, every night-sound magnifying in his imagination, fueling his fear. He fully expected that the morning would bring a hopelessly one-sided massacre, and that he would be forced to watch as his family was slaughtered, and his herds laid waste or confiscated as booty. Jacob genuinely thought this was his last night on earth. The Bible tells us that in his emotionally distraught and anxious state, he wrestled throughout the night with an *ish*, an unidentified man or man/angel who, according to the *midrash*, had his brother's face.[3] As dawn broke, Jacob wrested a blessing from the man. He was given the promise of the additional name of "Yisrael," from the Hebrew root meaning "he prevailed" in his struggle with an angel of God. But Jacob did not walk away from his nocturnal battle unscathed; he suffered a dislocated hip,[4] so that afterwards he walked with an uneven gait.

With the sunrise came the meeting that Jacob had dreaded for the past two decades. But instead of a rout, Esav ran forward and embraced Jacob, kissed him, and the brothers wept in each other's arms. And Esav agreed, after all, to accept Jacob's gifts of tribute, and to put aside his long-nursed anger. The brothers agreed to part, and Esav returned to Seir, in Edom, while Jacob proceeded to Sukkoth.

So it is no wonder that Jacob built a house and lingered through the rainy season in Sukkoth. He was keenly aware that God had caused his brother to have a change-of-heart, sparing him from death at Esav's hand, and his family from death or servitude. Jacob needed to erect an altar and give thanks to God. He needed some time to get his bearings, rest his hip,[5] and put some time and distance between himself and his brother. Also, Jacob was no longer a young man. The *midrash* tells us that he was a rugged man of eighty-four years old when he wed Rachel,[6] and then spent the next twenty years in his father-in-law's house working for him and building up his own herds. So at 104 years of age, even if Jacob were still a vigorous man accustomed to a life out-of-doors, he perhaps relished some time spent in a comfortable house before decamping once again and journeying to Beit-El.

This is why the Torah text tells us at Gen. 33:18, *Jacob arrived intact at the city of Shechem.* The Hebrew word for whole or "intact" is *shalem*, and the Talmud[7] explains that Jacob was aware that a three-fold miracle had been performed on his behalf, saving him from harm at the hand of the brother he had wronged. Says the Talmud, he arrived at Shechem alive, *physically* intact after his nighttime encounter with the man/angel; whole, too, in his *material* wealth, as even the considerable gifts of herds of livestock he gave to Esav did not make much of a dent in Jacob's personal fortune; and also whole *spiritually*, in his awareness of God's providence. The word *shalem*, from the same root as *shalom*, can also mean that Jacob arrived in Canaan *in peace*,[8] which had been his fondest wish when he had fled his father's house a quarter-century earlier. It can also mean, in the context of having just survived the potentially deadly confrontation with Esav, that Jacob is relieved and content to leave conflict behind him, and that he comes *shalem* — "in peace" — to the city of Shechem.

To express his gratitude Jacob contributed to his new "home" city of Shechem in three ways: He struck and minted a new coin — called a *mu'ah*[9] — for the city, which was of significant commercial and political benefit since until that time the city of Shechem had no currency of its own; he built a new and enlarged communal marketplace; and he established public bathhouses.[10] Jacob set an important precedent by sharing his good fortune with the municipality in which he sought to dwell.

Of course, while no doubt he engendered goodwill among the commonfolk for his good works, it is certain that Jacob also raised his profile among other Shechemites, perhaps stimulating envy or anger at their having been overshadowed in the public eye by an *arriviste* — a wealthy newcomer, a nomad and a Hebrew. This notion is borne out later in the story of Dinah and Shechem.

The modern Torah commentator Avivah Gottlieb Zornberg has taught that this "wholeness" or "peace" that Jacob experiences in this verse is evanescent indeed. For it is but a momentary breath between his near-death experience with Esav and the brutal events yet to come in the city of Shechem.

JACOB PURCHASES LAND IN SHECHEM

Jacob was on the move. He arrived at the city of Shechem well-rested after his sojourn in Sukkoth, with his family and fortunes intact. It was no mean feat to have escaped the quicksand of his father-in-law's compound in Padan-Aram, but Jacob survived that break as well as his terrifying encounter with Esav and his armed escort.[11] Jacob may have limped, literally, into Sukkoth, but after eighteen months he walked out straight and tall, his body healed, his flocks and livestock fat and healthy, his family of several hundred persons overflowing his Sukkoth compound and ready for new horizons.

At the end of a week's trek[12] Jacob drove his caravan directly opposite one of the gates of the city of Shechem[13] and camped there. The *midrash* actually describes the layout of Jacob's encampment, saying that he positioned his sons' tents arrayed to his right and to his left, placing his own tent at the very the center of the compound.[14] He had scouted the landscape and found a good-sized tract of level land, relatively free of the ubiquitous rocks and boulders that are characteristic of the Canaanite terrain.[15] He chose to pitch his tents on this habitable parcel, and the Torah's words in Gen. 33:18 are that he camped at the very "face of the city."

He might even have given passing thought to setting up house inside Shechem proper, as he had done in Sukkoth, but because of the encroaching Sabbath it is said that Jacob had time only to pitch his tents and make camp outside the city. One *midrash*[16] does say that he set up his home *within* Shechem, while his sons and flocks remained camped outside but still nearby. Presumably such a comfortable city dwelling might have been in deference to Jacob's advanced age.

The *midrashic* literature has numerous references to this tract of land that Jacob purchases in Shechem.[17] Interestingly, the city or town of Shechem has a dual history in Bible lore; it embodies a level of ambiguity that is reflected in the stories that take place there. The Talmud even labels it as a place perhaps predestined for misfortune.[18] For instance, Shechem bears the distinction of being the place not only where Dinah will be kidnapped and raped and where the inhabitants are wiped out, but also where in coming biblical chapters Joseph is sent by his father to find his brothers.[19] And when they are not to be found in Shechem, Joseph seeks them out in Dotan, where they plot his murder and then sell him to a passing caravan. It is also the place where, in years to come, the united kingdom of the house of David will, tragically, be split into two, inciting civil war. This is the biblical city's violent and agonizing legacy, so much so that Abarbanel[20] calls Shechem "the city of blood."

Yet it is also considered a holy place, as it is one of the few portions of the land of Canaan that is acquired outright by Israel and paid for in cash (the others are the Cave of Machpela by Abraham and the threshing-floor of Arona the Jebusite by David). Also, various legends state that Jacob's parcel of Shechem is the site of the Garden of Eden; the spot where the Children of Israel receive the Torah; the site of the Holy Temple in Jerusalem; and the site where the children of Israel receive both the blessings and the curses from Moses at the end of his life. It is even said that this is the precise place to which Joseph's bones will be carried by the children of Israel forty years after their Exodus from Egypt, and where they bury his remains.

The rabbis of the *midrash*[21] must have sought to assign some level of poetic closure to Shechem, a place of such intense personal suffering. We are told that it is in Shechem that Joseph's bones are laid to rest — that his brothers' children's children keep a sacred promise and return Joseph to the very same spot that marked their grandfathers' betrayal of him several lifetimes ago.

The Torah tells us that Jacob camped *in the face of the city*, or colloquially, *in front of the city*. Yet it has already informed us that he arrived at the city of Shechem; one would think that is sufficient information requiring no embellishment. We learn from the *midrash*[22] that the extra phrase *in the face of the city* indicates that he made his camp where the "main faces" or honored men of Shechem congregated. We are expected to appreciate that there was a calculated reason for Jacob's encampment.

On the other hand, the *Netziv*[23] states that Jacob was a loner, and that he certainly did not set up his dwelling *within* the city of Shechem. Any business that Jacob conducted in Shechem remained distinct and separate from his family's living quarters outside its gates. But it is certainly possible that Jacob found temporary shelter or set up the equivalent of an office within the city proper precisely in order to be close to the local power center. If he intended to do business with the elders of the city he was sufficiently canny to appreciate that he would do well to position himself in their neighborhood. This is important information for our story, as we are about to be introduced to Prince Shechem and his father Hamor, the city's first family.

Jacob, himself the head of a wealthy and powerful nomadic clan, is adept at assessing the worth of a place and scoping out its power structure. He has a keen eye for men and for livestock, as his very survival depends on his ability to get along and trade with the peoples among whom he wanders. His reputation surely precedes him; he must be known far and wide as the nephew of the wily Lavan, as the man who enriched Lavan and who also became wealthy in his own right. Jacob's arrival at a city, especially if he has combined his arrival with an open hand for the commonweal as Jacob has done here, must have been an occasion for the town fathers to smile. For Jacob brought goods as well as custom to the town. He would be spreading his not-insignificant fortune among them for as long as he and his family tarried there.

He purchased the portion of the field upon which he pitched his tent from the hand of the sons of Hamor, the father of Shechem, for one hundred kesita. Gen. 33:19

The Torah text introduces the reader to Prince Shechem in Gen. 33:19, three verses *before* it names him as Dinah's abductor in Gen. 34:2. We first learn of him when Jacob purchases this choice tract of land directly from Shechem and his brothers, the sons of Hamor. The negotiation and consummation of the real estate transaction place Jacob and his family members squarely in the limelight and in the sights of Shechem, the most prominent person in the city.[24]

It is unknown whether Shechem drew his name from that of the city, or whether the city adopted his name.[25] The Hebrew term *Ir Shechem*, meaning "city of Shechem," could mean both a city *named* Shechem, or the city *of the man named* Shechem.[26] But either way the Torah text is deliberately assigning the man named Shechem the top billing in this new dwelling place. The message of the eponymous Prince Shechem's prominence is loud and clear, and this fact, too, will assume significance as our story unfolds.

When the Torah tells us that Jacob himself purchased the land from Shechem and his brothers, it intentionally gives Hamor second billing. The *midrash*[27] tells us that Hamor may in fact have been ineffectual or senile; that his very name—meaning donkey or jackass—is a window into his character. Hamor had long before designated his son Shechem as the custodian of the family interests, so that the person to be reckoned with not only in Hamor's family but also in the city of Shechem itself is not the father, but the son, who is known to be exceedingly clever and possessing a sharp mind. We can appreciate that the Bible pitted Jacob against a person equal to him in acuity in business matters.

The Bible states the purchase price for the plot which Jacob chose for his family compound: Jacob paid *one hundred kesita* to Shechem for the land. We have no definitive way of knowing whether Jacob paid value for the property or whether he paid top dollar, and to complicate the matter there is varying *midrashic* opinion as to the worth of a *kesita*. It is said that one hundred *kesita* equaled one hundred pieces of silver; alternatively, that the price of one hundred *kesita* was the equivalent of one hundred precious stones, one hundred head of sheep, *and* one hundred *sela*.[28] It is said, too, that a *kesita*, from the Hebrew root *keshet*, meaning ornament, is a precious stone or decoration that is set into earrings and bracelets.[29]

And finally, the Talmud[30] cites Rabbi Akivah as saying that in his travels to Africa he heard that the coin known as the *ma'ah* was also referred to as a *kesita*. We recall that the *ma'ah* was the name of the small coin that Jacob minted and introduced to the Shechemites, so it is fitting, according to the Talmud, that Jacob's payment for the tract of land should be translated into his coinage. It is also said that one *ma'ah*, or *kesita*, was worth twenty *shekels*,[31] which would make the purchase price of Jacob's plot of land 2,000 *shekels*, an exorbitant price.

These various *midrashic* definitions of a *kesita* strongly suggest that Jacob paid dearly for the tract of land he bought in the city of Shechem. This fact, too, will assume import in our story, as the Torah text is cluing us into the picture of the wealthy and determined noble clansman named Jacob who arouses the avaricious curiosity of Prince Shechem.

The only real estate transaction to which we can compare Jacob's purchase is Abraham's earlier purchase of a gravesite for his wife Sarah in Gen. 23:16. There, the Torah tells us that Abraham weighed out and paid to Ephron the Hittite his asking price of four hundred *shekels* of silver in universally negotiable silver coins for the Cave of Machpela and its surrounding fields. He paid Ephron in full view of the people of the land who had gathered to watch the transaction, so it became public knowledge that Abraham was the rightful owner of the land specified in the Bible text.

We can assume that Jacob followed in his grandfather's footsteps and purchased the desired plot of land in Shechem at the asking price both in order to quickly close the deal and also so as not to appear mean or a sharp operator in Shechem's eyes. Jacob's fortune was on-the-hoof, spread out and grazing over the city's outer acreage, so he could not very well plead poverty in any negotiation. Moreover, Jacob desired to establish himself quickly as equal with the town's nobility, and to settle in for awhile; after all, this is presumably the reason he sought to purchase the choice plot of land in the first place.

For all these reasons we can appreciate that Jacob, through his philanthropy as well as because of his purchase of this choice piece of property at the asking price, is now the talk of the town, and the members of his family are objects of curiosity and are considered desirable trading partners.

We should remember that Jacob has spent all of his married life to-date — twenty years — in the midst of a quasi-hostile nomadic family.[32] The Torah tells us, in Jacob's own words, that Jacob worked as shepherd of all his uncle Lavan's flocks; that he personally bore the expense of every single ewe or goat that was stolen or mangled; that he was on watch day and night, in heat and in frost; that during all the years spent in Lavan's house he never once slept soundly because he was in a state of constant vigilance over the flocks entrusted to him. The result of Jacob's meticulous care was that Lavan's flocks were the envy of his nomadic neighbors. Lavan's sheep were fat and plentiful, their wool clean, fluffy and choice. And we know that Jacob, too, grew wealthy in sheep and livestock.

As the years passed Jacob never forgot that Lavan had tricked him, giving him his eldest daughter Leah to wed instead of Rachel, Jacob's heart's desire. Jacob had served fourteen years of indentured servitude to earn the hands of Lavan's two daughters in marriage, and six additional years to earn his own flocks, with the wily Lavan changing his wages a hundred times in order to keep Jacob dependent and to prevent him from leaving Haran. But despite this ill-treatment over those twenty years, Jacob kept his peace and said nothing.

It was only when Jacob heard Lavan's sons murmuring bitterly and avariciously, saying, *Jacob has taken all that belonged to our father; he has amassed all his wealth from that which belonged to our father*, that Jacob knew it was past time to leave. He noticed that his father-in-law was now looking at him askance, as if he no longer trusted him. Jacob was forced to admit that even after toiling for two decades to make Lavan and his sons wealthy beyond their dreams they nevertheless mocked him, resented him, and harbored a growing suspicion of him.

So Jacob, heeding God's instruction to *return to the land of your fathers,* consulted with his two principal wives, Rachel and Leah, out in an open field, away from prying eyes and listening ears. There, with their agreement, he plotted his escape from their father's house.

This is the Jacob who has arrived at Shechem after resting in Sukkoth. He has managed to escape intact from both Lavan's avaricious clutches and the feared encounter with his brother Esav. He is an elderly, once-vigorous outdoorsman with a keen business sense. He is the head of a wealthy nomadic clan and is a personage to revere. Not only is he wealthy in herds and livestock and servants, but he also has fathered eleven strapping sons and a young daughter. The sons for the most part are grown, some possessing families and households of their own. They all live and travel together, comprising a nomadic clan of enormous wealth and power, confidence and might. It follows that their business success relies on their mutual trust and their concomitant wariness of outsiders.

DINAH AS A PRIZE

Dinah is named in the Bible as Jacob's only daughter. She is, in fact, Leah's last-born child after the birth of her six sons. We note that when the Bible announces the birth of each of Leah's sons, it says that it is Leah who names the boys, and the Bible also gives the explanation of the child's name. It is curious, though, that after Dinah's birth there is no textual explanation of *her* name. After the birth of Zevulun, Leah's sixth son, the Torah text simply states, *And afterwards she gave birth to a daughter, and she called her name Dinah.*[33]

Leah has amply fulfilled her mission as first wife of Jacob by easily producing, in relatively rapid succession (with a short hiatus after the first four sons are born), six healthy male heirs. Though the Bible tells us that she *is hated* (Gen. 29:31), and that she is aware every waking moment that Jacob prefers her exquisite sister Rachel to her, she wrings every drop of satisfaction she can from the fact that she is lushly fertile while her sister is unable to conceive. Leah is staggered by the extraordinary fortune that causes her term of gestation to last only seven months[34] instead of the normal nine, allowing her to bear more children in a shorter period of time. Leah also knows that this breeding success guarantees that Jacob will continue to seek out her tent. But Leah's happiness is marred by the fact that her husband nevertheless spends most nights with Rachel. We deduce Leah's tortured state-of-mind from the text's brief captions after she names each of her sons.[35] For instance, after her first son is born she names him *Reuben*, translated from the Hebrew to mean "see my son!" as she explains, "God has seen my humiliation at being the hated one, and has given me a son before my sister. Surely *now* my husband will love me."

Of course he never does, and this theme of naming her sons as a reflection of her misery, her hope and her increasing hopelessness as the unloved wife, continues five more times.

THE MEANING OF DINAH'S NAME

After the birth and naming of Dinah, the Talmud and *midrash* view the *absence* of the usual explanation of her name as a textual gap, and they step in to offer reasons for and explanations of Dinah's name.

Understanding Leah's abject misery at being unloved, and her deep disappointment that her fertility still does not convert Jacob's heart in her favor, the Talmud's explanation of Dinah's naming outlines an act of selflessness, and a *midrashic* marvel. Amidst a discussion on the power inherent in an individual's prayer for a miracle, the Talmud[36] relates a bizarre but eloquent tale that endears Leah to us. First it refers us to the verse (Gen. 30:21) that announces Dinah's birth. We note that the first word in the verse is *Afterwards* . . . The Talmud asks, to what does the word "afterwards" refer — after *what* is Dinah born? The great sage Rav tells us that this refers to *after Leah rendered a judgement* about herself; only then does she give birth to a daughter and name her Dinah, from the Hebrew word *din*, meaning "judgement."

Leah's self-pronounced judgement[37] occurred after she gave birth to her sixth son, Zevulun. The Talmud teaches us that Leah, Rachel and Jacob knew through divine intuition or prophecy that Jacob was fated to father twelve sons who would grow to be the twelve tribes and ultimately form the backbone of the future Jewish nation. Leah did some elementary calculations and realized that since six of the twelve had already emerged from her own womb, and each of the sisters' handmaidens had produced two sons apiece, that totaled ten, leaving only two covenantal sons yet unborn to Jacob. Leah prayed fervently to the Almighty that the pregnancy she had just realized she was nurturing should yield a *girl*-child, thus allowing her sister Rachel to bear the last two sons. In this way Rachel would be the equivalent, at least, of the two handmaidens, and—if she were blessed with conception—would be in line to produce her one-sixth share of the future children of Israel.

We are told that God heeded Leah's unselfish prayer, and immediately transformed the fetus within her from a male into a female. Thus, at the baby girl's birth, *after Leah had begged that a judgement be pronounced upon her changing her unborn son into a daughter*, Leah jubilantly named the girl Dinah, meaning "judgement." Dinah's birth was proof that Leah's prayer for judgement was assented to by the Almighty. Another Talmudic *midrash*[38] even suggests that Dinah was born with a twin sister; Leah's double gift for her selfless request, perhaps.

These Talmudic tales have a two-fold purpose. First, they enable us to understand Leah a bit better. Despite her misery at losing out to her younger sister Rachel in the quest for Jacob's love, she retains a measure of unsullied affection and loyalty for her sister. Leah shunts aside her own unhappiness and adds her own prayer to her sister's in order to spare Rachel from the humiliation of bearing fewer covenantal sons than the handmaidens. We are meant to be in awe of the power of such selflessness. See what it can do! Selfless prayer can and does arouse and marshal the Almighty's attentions. Leah's newborn is a girl in fulfillment of her prayer, and her sister very shortly— within months, we are told[39]—gives birth to her first child, a son whom she names Joseph.

The second purpose of the Talmud's tale about the switched genders is to highlight for the reader that this sole daughter of Leah and Jacob bears a heavy burden. She is, at her birth, the evidence that God judged Leah's prayer to be worthy. Further, as Dinah grows, and features so prominently in our present drama, she emerges as an emblem of judgement for virtually all of the story's actors. The very personal tragedy for this young and sheltered girl is that she is innocent of wrongdoing, and yet is snatched into a whirlwind of desire, anger, lust, outrage and revenge. We will try to understand—if not accept—the judgement that fate has pronounced on her as we unravel the story in chapter thirty-four of Genesis.

It is also possible that the reason the Bible fails to state a reason for Dinah's name is that she is a daughter and is therefore of lesser consequence than her brothers in the tribal scheme of things. Leila Leah Bronner has written that "biblical law clearly places daughters on a lower rung than it does sons."[40] It should therefore be sufficiently significant, if we consider the biblical context, that Dinah is singled out and named at all in the text heralding her birth, as female characters are mentioned "only when they play dramatic roles [or] as calamity befalls the family."[41] Unfortunately, we are about to witness the validity of this proposition.

DINAH, DAUGHTER OF LEAH, "GOES OUT"

So we must ask, Who is this girl named Dinah?

First and foremost, she is the sheltered only daughter of Leah and Jacob. Arriving with her parents and brothers at Shechem when she was only seven years old,[42] Dinah grew from childhood to girlhood on the outskirts of that city. Soon after their arrival, Jacob purchased the plot of land and settled in, living in relative peace for about five to seven years. Dinah's beloved brothers, Shimon and Levi, were themselves strapping lads when they first arrived at Shechem, and over the ensuing years they grew to young manhood.

Rashi tells us that the Bible first identifies Dinah as "daughter of Leah" because she shared an immodest or wanton characteristic with her mother.[43] He deduces this from the earlier incident of the *dudaim*, or mandrakes, when Leah—sick with longing for Jacob, who preferred spending his nights in Rachel's tent—bartered a night in Jacob's arms for a fertility talisman which she gave to her barren sister.[44] The text there says that *As Jacob returned from the field in the evening, Leah **went out** to greet him, saying, "Come to **my** [tent], because I have surely hired you with my son's 'dudaim.' "*

Rashi would characterize Leah's "going out" as a brazen or forward step; as behavior unbefitting a proper modest woman. Along these lines another *midrash*[45] says that Leah was adorned to entice Jacob when she "went out" to greet him, and posits that perhaps in our story Dinah's clothing, likewise, attracted and seduced Shechem into snatching her.

In order to understand these commentators we must forget, for argument's sake, that Leah legitimately "went out" to greet her lawfully wedded husband, or that such behavior should have been acceptable and even admirable even in biblical times. If we accept Rashi's implication we must also dismiss, again for argument's sake, the sound and legitimate notion that a young girl should never be held responsible for her own rape. To Rashi it is the "going out" behavior that Dinah is thought to have imitated in our story, and for this reason the text labels her "the daughter of Leah." "Like mother, like daughter," says the commentary.

But we should ask, even if this is the moral yardstick against which the *midrash* initially holds the young girl Dinah, what is so bad about that? After all, Leah, Dinah's mother, nurtured fully one-half of the children of Israel, and it is likely that she bore the burden of the practical business of mothering them *all* after Rachel died in childbirth. Also, it is Leah — and not Rachel or the handmaidens — who merits burial in the hallowed Cave of Machpela next to her beloved Jacob and alongside Abraham, Sarah, Isaac and Rebecca. These are not the hallmarks of a disgraced or censured woman. Thus, we can conclude that Leah's "going out" neither marked her nor branded Dinah.

In fact this latter notion — that Dinah is blameless in this story — is the opinion of most commentaries. The *Akeidat Yitzchak*, for instance, the 15th-century Spanish Torah scholar,[46] states unequivocally that by referring to Dinah as "the daughter of Leah" the Bible means only to compliment the girl, and that her "going out" was *not* a departure from traditional Hebrew conduct. The Abarbanel stresses that when Leah, Dinah's mother, "went out" onto her doorstep to greet her husband, this was a wholly legitimate act done with only the best of wifely intentions;[47] and that therefore, comparing the girl Dinah's "going out" to her mother's is also free of the stamp of wantonness.

Even *Ohr HaChayim*, the 17th-18th-century Moroccan Torah scholar who was concerned that perhaps Dinah had adorned herself in a manner that enticed Shechem, concurs that her "going out" was legitimate. Sounding quite modern in his analysis he says that as an only-daughter Dinah longed for female playmates of her own age. He posits that her "going out" was a guileless stepping outside her tent in search of girlhood company. Hirsch adds that Dinah was acting in a manner that was natural and normal for a curious young girl,[48] and the *Malbim* states plainly that Dinah cannot be faulted for her behavior in any way.[49]

Modern Bible analyst Leon Kass agrees, stating that Dinah, the victim in our story, must not bear the blame for what is done to her. She had innocent intentions and really was too young and too sheltered to understand and appreciate the dangers of stepping outside. Says Kass, "If blame is to be meted out, it should go instead *to Jacob.*"[50] In fact, Jacob's casualness about settling among hostile Canaanites will be discussed later in this story.

The picture we draw of the Dinah in our story, then, is of a girl between the ages of twelve and fourteen years of age.[51] She is referred to in verse 4 of this chapter as a *yaldah,* or "girl" in Hebrew, indicating that she was a minor, a female still deserving of her father Jacob's protection.[52] Another measure of Dinah's age at the time of our story is that she was only months older than her half-brother Joseph, the son who was born to Rachel through Leah's *midrashic* prayer discussed earlier. And Joseph, in upcoming chapters of the Bible and after the passage of some years, is sold to Ishmaelites at the age of seventeen.[53]

Even the Bible's reference to Dinah as a *na'arah* in verse 3 of the text means "a girl from infancy to adolescence: [a] damsel, [a] maiden."[54] She is a lovely and lively young girl who knows she is cherished by her mother and father for her singular uniqueness — she is, after all, the only daughter of the head of their clan—and is teased and protected by her eleven older brothers. Shimon and Levi, her whole brothers by Leah *and* Jacob, generally keep a special watch over her, cautioning her about the dangers of venturing from their encampment, as the family alternatively roams and settles amidst strange peoples.

There is always the possibility, of course, that the Bible first identifies Dinah as "daughter of Leah" to remind the reader that Dinah was Jacob's daughter from his *unloved* wife, and to suggest perhaps that Jacob's passive behavior in the upcoming incident at Shechem reflects his ambivalent feelings about the girl's mother, Leah. As the story develops we will see if that theory fits.

As far as Dinah's appearance is concerned, the Bible tells us when it is describing Joseph's appearance in upcoming chapters (at Gen. 39:6) that Joseph is *handsome of face and also of form*. If Joseph is the male embodiment of the female child that Dinah miraculously became (following the *midrash* discussed earlier), it is fair to assume that Dinah was likewise lovely of face and of figure. It is unlikely that the Almighty would have granted Leah's wish but substituted an ugly girl-child in place of a beautiful son. In fact, the Abarbanel reveals[55] that not only was Dinah lovely of face and form (mirroring her brother Joseph), but that quite simply she was *eshet chen*; meaning, in Hebrew, that she was a girl of charm and grace.

So at the time of our story Dinah is still in her girlhood. She is immature, wide-eyed, lovely, energetic, and — vitally important to this story — she is innocent.

SHECHEM SEES DINAH

While Jacob is preoccupied with selecting and acquiring his choice real estate parcel in the city of Shechem, Dinah and the women within his household and inside his bustling compound go about their daily tasks. There are sheep and livestock to be tended and fed; household clothing to be washed and mended; vast quantities of food to be gathered and prepared for the hundreds of mouths in the clan; countless numbers of water jugs to be dipped and carried from the town well or watering place. Shechem was larger than a town but was not quite a metropolis; it is virtually certain that every move the Hebrews made both within and without their compound was watched and commented on to the town fathers.

To be sure, if newcomers to the gigantic metropolis that was ancient Egypt are noted[56] and taken before the king, then doubtless every newcomer to Shechem is also noted, and their appearance, clothing and movements scrutinized and talked about. Doubtless Prince Shechem knew within hours of Jacob's family's encampment that he counted one untouched flower of a girl among his retinue.

Jacob and his sons are by now accustomed to arriving at a new place, setting up camp, and making themselves known as peaceful newcomers to the town fathers. Jacob's *modus operandi* was to flex his economic muscle with the powers that be, while simultaneously keeping his private life out of the public eye. This practice has stood Jacob in good stead until now, and might have continued to shield his female family members, except that this time Jacob has seen fit to purchase a landhold. This public real estate transaction put Jacob as well as his household into the limelight, and brought him to the attention of prince Shechem.

Prince Shechem has sat with Jacob and his sons in their tents, broken bread with them, haggled a bit, and taken their substantial coin as the price of the land deal. It is quite possible that, in the ways of nomadic clans, Jacob's daughter Dinah was one of the serving girls who brought refreshment to the men for a celebratory toast solidifying the purchase. Perhaps, as Abarbanel suggests,[57] that is how Shechem first glimpsed her. *Ohr HaChayim*[58] states unequivocally that unless Shechem had already seen the girl Dinah, daughter of the famed Jacob, as she moved about in her own tent and compound, he would not have committed the rape. So it is possible that Shechem leaned over to the man on his left and inquired, "Shimon, tell me, pray, who is this maiden who stands at the door and directs the serving girls?" We can envision Shimon, or his brother Levi, or even Jacob himself responding, "You will excuse us, milord Prince Shechem, but that is our baby sister; pray do not concern yourself with the likes of her."

We appreciate that Jacob and his sons are content enough to conduct business with the city fathers. But they have never in the past — and do not intend to start now — permitted locals to fraternize with their womenfolk. They are circumcised Hebrews, after all, and remain different or "other" and overwhelmingly aloof socially from the people with whom they do business.

The Bible text doubly identifies Dinah as *daughter of Leah* **and** *who had been borne to **Jacob** .*[59] The *midrash*[60] says that this seemingly unnecessary add-on (of course she was *borne to Jacob* if she was the daughter of Leah; why the need for the double reference?) is to teach the reader that Dinah's attraction for Shechem was precisely *because* she was *Jacob's* daughter! Dinah was the only daughter of Jacob, the wealthy Hebrew clan leader, and this made her close to irresistible to Shechem.

The *midrash* emphasizes that Dinah "the maiden was very beautiful,"[61] so perhaps Dinah's youthful beauty — and not solely her father's fortune — was enough to spark Shechem's interest. But the biblical text deliberately omits a physical description of Dinah. Earlier in Genesis we were told of the physical beauty of Sarah, Rebecca and Rachel, Dinah's forbears, and we saw that terrifying consequences can flow to women who are described as "beautiful." (The stories of those abductions and close calls appear in the next section.) Perhaps the Bible omits details of Dinah's appearance precisely to avoid what had occurred to earlier biblical beauties. Of course, the Bible's silence on Dinah's appearance does not preclude or forestall the events we will read about in this chapter. She still falls into Shechem's grasp.

Perhaps, too, the depth and richness of Jacob's pockets opened Shechem's eyes to the possibility of joining his family with this royal nomadic clan. It is likely that it was a combination of these circumstances that caused Dinah's untouched loveliness to act as catnip to this man who was the prime catch of the city of Shechem. But it was also likely that her family's protectiveness and socially aloof manner limiting social contact with him roused Shechem's vanity and resentment. He *had* to have her, and the fact that Jacob and his sons treated it as an impossibility merely made him more determined.

THE KIDNAP OF DINAH'S GRANDMOTHERS

Bible readers will recall that Jacob's father and grandfather each experienced an actual or potential abduction situation where their beautiful wives were seen, desired and taken, or nearly taken, by the ruler of the city-state that the patriarchs were visiting. The highwayman-like credo of "see-and-take"[62] apparently applied not only to material goods, but also to desirable human traffic, especially females. This was so prevalent that as Abraham and

Sarah approached the gates of Egypt during the desperate days of a severe famine, he proposed the famed wife/sister ruse to her.[63] Abraham said to his wife, "Behold, now I know that you are a beautiful and fair woman to look upon. Surely, when the Egyptians set eyes upon you they will kill me, your husband, in order that they may possess you. For this reason I beg of you, *please say you are my sister.* In this way things will go well for me for your sake, and I will be kept alive on your behalf."

This was the first time Abraham presented his wife, Sarah, as his sister. At the time he made this plea to his wife, Abraham was just a nomad with a vision; he had no fortune to speak of. He hoped that instead of having him killed and conveniently out of the way, the king of Egypt would woo him with gifts in order to possess "Abraham's sister" Sarah. This ruse worked fairly well, enriching Abraham with herds of sheep, oxen, camels, donkeys and numerous servants. While Abraham was being enriched, Sarah suffered the horrors of abduction and near-rape at the Pharaoh's hands; she was saved from being sexually violated by a God-sent plague that affected the Pharaoh's sexual organs, precluding intercourse. Sarah was returned to Abraham otherwise unharmed.

Some years later,[64] the nomadic couple approaches the Philistine city of Gerar with their retinue, and Abraham—again in fear for his life—employs the same wife/sister ruse, this time with the Gerarites. Sarah's fabled beauty has caught the eye of king Avimelech of Gerar, and he sends his soldiers to Abraham's camp and takes Sarah off to his palace against her will. Abraham remains unharmed while once again Sarah experiences the terrors of abduction. She narrowly escapes rape, the Torah tells us, because God Himself appears to the king in a dream, forbidding him even to come near to Sarah, as she is already wife of another.

When faced with the great genital plague years before, the Egyptian Pharaoh had deduced at once that Sarah was forbidden to him, and he said to Abraham, "Why did you not tell me that she was your wife and not your sister?! Thinking Sarah was your sister, I might have taken her as my wife! But as she is already your wife, take her and go!" The Egyptian king made no mention of the fact that he took her against her will; presumably that was a permissible way for royals to behave when they saw and desired a beautiful and eligible female. What stopped him cold and caused him to return Sarah unharmed — and with abundant gifts — was that Abraham and Sarah's God intervened, making it abundantly clear that even the king of all Egypt was forbidden to rape another man's wife.

King Avimelech's responses years later differ from the Pharaoh's in one important respect: Avimelech explicitly blamed Abraham for nearly causing him to commit "a great sin."[65] Mention of or even allusion to a "sin" was never made explicit by the Pharaoh; we only realize the Egyptian king's horror at his behavior as we witness his lightning-quick relinquishment of Sarah once he comprehended the reason for the genital plague. The great sin referred to by Avimelech was the same as the Pharaoh's: he had come dangerously close to transgressing the universal proscription against sexually molesting the wife of another.

The third episode of near-abduction that precedes the Dinah story occurs when Dinah's grandparents, Isaac and Rebecca, seek refuge from another great famine and settle in Gerar, the now-familiar home of the Philistine king Avimelech. When Isaac is accosted by the Gerarites about Rebecca, he, like his father before him, genuinely fears for his life. He is certain these lawless men will kill him without qualm if they learn she is his wife, as his death would leave the beautiful Rebecca fair game for them. So Isaac offers the wife/sister ruse, and remarkably, she is not taken from him.

Isaac and his "sister" live peaceably among the Philistines perhaps for years, until the king happens to see the "brother and sister" behaving toward one another as husband and wife. The *midrash*[66] tells us that perhaps Isaac let down his guard after being lulled by the passage of time and grew physically demonstrative toward Rebecca; or that the king, increasingly curious about the pair, actually spies upon them in their private living quarters. Either way, when the truth is known the king erupts in anger to Isaac saying, "For sure she is your wife! Why, then, did you tell me she was your sister? Do you see that you could have caused one of us to lie down with your wife, thus bringing shame and guilt upon our heads!"

So the king cautioned all the Philistines that any one of them who so much as touched Rebecca, wife of Isaac, would be put to death. And Isaac and Rebecca, who have incurred envy in the hearts of the Gerarites on account of their great wealth, soon depart from the city.

What do we learn about the mores of the ancient Near East from these three stories? Importantly, the third story never actually escalates to an abduction; Isaac manages to keep Rebecca safe by successfully proffering the wife/sister ruse. Or perhaps the Gerarites' memories of the similar scenario with Abraham and Sarah years earlier—and their narrow escape from divine retribution—kept them in check. But fundamentally, the three stories give us a glimpse into the social mores of the Egyptians and the Canaanites when faced with abducting a strange woman. And this in turn sheds light on the Dinah story.

Abraham *knew* that Egyptian moral practice was so degraded that the Pharaoh's soldiers were posted at each of the country's entry points with orders to summarily confiscate anything that they thought would strike the Pharaoh's eye. This included beautiful women. Apparently their custom frowned upon taking a beautiful *married* woman from her husband's side, so Abraham, a keen lifetime nomad with his ear to the ground, devised the wife/sister smokescreen in a desperate move to stay alive. If the woman was his sister, with no husband extant, then either she was a virgin or she was available to another man. We must assume that the woman's virginity was an important element in the abduction, as the age-old practice of saving the choicest of the maidens for the king's harem was a well-known ancient Near Eastern practice.[67]

Abraham was in a trap: If he had stayed in Canaan he would almost certainly have died in the great famine there. Migrating to Egypt was his desperate move to save his household from starvation, and he saw no alternative but to sacrifice Sarah "in order that it may go well with me for your sake." A Hobson's choice to be sure: Sarah's abduction in exchange for his life.

Abraham was *certain* that the Egyptians would not kill the *brother* of the exquisite Sarah.

And as we see from Pharaoh's quick release of Sarah when his genitals became enflamed, the king knew instantly that his plague was the result of his having taken the wife of another. Whether this marital detail alone would have stopped him cold and saved Sarah from rape is doubtful; God's intervention struck the Pharaoh with terror, and the king calculated that ravaging one woman, however desirable she happened to be, was not worth the risk. She was wife of another and not a virgin after all. So he sent her back to her husband and let them both go free.

Abraham is emboldened by his success with Pharaoh. The biblical text actually tells us, in Abraham's own voice, that since the incident in Egypt he presents Sarah as his "sister" everywhere they travel.[68] It is perhaps inevitable, then, that some time later we see history repeat itself, with Sarah's abduction by Avimelech, king of Gerar. But this time the Torah tells us that Abraham proffers the wife/sister ruse because he *knows* the Gerarites "have no fear of God," and will kill him to possess Sarah. Avimelech's outraged speech to Abraham focuses on the "great sin" and "offense" that he *would have unknowingly committed* if he or a countryman had taken Sarah—already the wife of another—to his bed. The king, like the Pharaoh before him, heaps gifts and even silver coins on the "wronged" couple.

Again we understand that the "seeing-and-taking," while it was no doubt a contravention of the rules of Abraham's God, was ordinary practice for the Canaanites. And while the virginity of the maiden was important to the king, apparently his "great sin" would have been lying with the wife of another. The king's guilty dream—in which God threatens to kill Avimelech and also wipe out his entire court if he so much as touches Sarah—saves him and his royal family from God's plague.

The king also knows that his abduction has shamed Sarah, and so in a highly unusual move he addresses her directly in the text[69] and, in a half-hearted apology, informs her that he "has given her brother one thousand pieces of silver as a covering of the eyes." This enormous sum of money is the price of her virginity that he never despoiled—not because he did not try, but because she was already the wife of another. Avimelech publicly pays the thousand pieces of silver as a proclamation that Sarah's reputation as a married woman remains unsullied. The huge sum also indicates to one and all that the king accords Sarah, the wife of Abraham, much honor.

And finally, in the third incident, when Isaac dwells in Gerar during a famine, the Bible tells us that the men of the place send out inquiries about the exquisite woman in his retinue, asking, "Is she a virgin?" The mores of the Canaanites have not changed a whit. Isaac's life is on the line as was his father's, and he offers the wife/sister ruse, this time successfully. In Avimelech II's speech to Isaac after he discovers Isaac and Rebecca are not siblings, we see proof that the rules of the game remain unchanged. Had he or anyone from Gerar lain with Rebecca it would have brought "guiltiness" upon them because she was already a married woman. Not a word is said about the rectitude of bringing pain or shame upon the potentially despoiled virgin.

We must conclude from these stories that ancient Near Eastern royalty took it as their right — a version of *droit de seigneur* — to see, to take and to despoil any non-royal virgin girl who struck their fancy. Or that perhaps, if the woman was presented as a "sister," it was the illusion or fiction of her consent that legitimized the taking. The "privilege" of being desired and sought by the king outweighed — in the minds of the royal abductors if not in the mind of the woman — the shame and pain of the taking.

The question for our purpose, then, might be whether royals were permitted to do this with impunity when the virgin girl belonged to the family of another highly-placed family or clan. Was seeing-and-taking the accepted *modus operandi* in such circumstances, or was the desirous male expected to open a negotiation with the girl's royal family first? As these prior incidents attest, the Bible text indicates that such takings were considered "a great sin" even among the Egyptians and Canaanites.

Shechem's kidnap and rape of Jacob's virgin daughter was a sin and an outlaw act. We will see that in the Dinah story Prince Shechem's desire for Jacob's daughter was likely complicated by his earlier, shunned rejection as a suitor by her father and brothers, or by some other perceived slight. The result is that what is at work here is not pure lust, as was the case with Pharaoh and the two Avimelechs. Shechem is out for revenge, at least initially, and the seeing-and-taking occurs between two socially equivalent and powerful clans. In Shechem's eyes the girl Dinah is merely the instrumentality of getting the better of her father Jacob.

QUESTIONS ABOUT JACOB'S ACTIONS

A word here about Jacob's lack of vigilance. Given the mores of the Canaanites, it is curious that Jacob was not more proactive in protecting Dinah. As Kass says, "shrewd and wise in the ways of the world, Jacob certainly should have taken precautions to instruct and protect his daughter."[70]

It was well known, certainly within the family, that Jacob's mother and grandmother each had experienced a traumatic forcible abduction or a near-abduction when the family came to a strange city. As such, certainly Jacob should have issued his family a stern, cautionary warning against the strangers in the city of Shechem. Exhorting them to "Remember to be vigilant! Keep a close watch on our wives and daughters!" would have been the very least he could have done. Or more forcibly and in character, he should have ordered a redoubling of the guard over his womenfolk. Yet we read only that *Dinah went out*, as if it were a commonplace event, and she had no fears of any untoward consequences. Perhaps that was the case.

While the text is silent, the *midrash* is outspoken in its chastisement of Jacob in this regard. We are told that certainly for all of Jacob's life, and even earlier, it was well-known that the kidnap and despoiling of virgins, certainly by royals, was a commonplace.[71] Abraham and Isaac had been aware of this danger to their womenfolk, and also that they, as the husbands, were themselves at the sword's point.[72] Fear for their lives caused them to prepare as best they could given their nomadic lifestyle and their need to rely on the prosperity — and to some extent the hospitality — of foreign cities in times of famine. The danger was real, it was great, it was prevalent, and Jacob should have warned his family against it when he arrived in Shechem.

Moreover, why did Jacob feel the need to camp right in the face of the city in the first place? Why court trouble? It would seem that the example set by Abraham and his nephew Lot all those years ago — where Lot's choice of the city life in Sodom over the nomadic life ended in disaster — would have warned Jacob against settling in Shechem. In our search for answers we must note that conspicuously absent from the verses narrating Jacob's settlement in Shechem is any word of a famine in the land necessitating Jacob's settlement there. Nor is there a mention in the Torah text of any war in the area or any physical threat that would have led Jacob to seek protection in the city. So we must ask, as does the Abarbanel,[73] whether Jacob unthinkingly put his family in harm's way and would have done better by camping farther afield. As the story plays out the answers will become glaringly clear.

There is also the unfinished business of Jacob's earlier pledge at Beit-El, the site of his dream of the ladder with ascending and descending angels and his stopping place while on the run from his brother Esav. It was in Beit-El that he had made a sacred pledge to God: *Then Jacob took a vow saying, If God will be with me, and guard me on this way that I am going, . . . and I will return in peace to my father's house, . . . then this stone shall become a house of God.*[74] As we have seen, Jacob did indeed emerge whole, intact — *shalem* — from twenty years of trials, dangers and a near-death experience. The Bible even hints to the reader — and perhaps to Jacob, as well — by use of the word *shalem* in Gen. 33:18, as he arrives at the city of Shechem, that ironically, this echoes the moment of Jacob's vow to return *b'shalom* (in peace) to his father's house and to Beit-El (which in translation means "house of God").

But as the Dinah story opens we see that Jacob does *not* return to his father's house, nor does he make his way back to Beit-El. Instead, he delays, settling outside the city of Shechem. And so begins a descent into tragic happenings.

The *midrashists* are vocal in their chastisement of Jacob for failing to live up to his vow. Zornberg explains that "The Rabbis, in general, breathe no word of disapproval for any of Jacob's apparently more dubious acts: his acquisition of the birthright, his 'taking' of the blessing, his financial negotiations with Laban. The harshest criticism — and the suggestion that he was terribly punished — is leveled against Jacob's delay in fulfilling the overt thrust of his vow at Beth El."[75] The *midrash*[76] advances the extraordinary claim that because Jacob delayed the fulfillment of his vow, he was punished through his daughter, Dinah's, sufferings at Shechem's hands!

According to other *midrashim*,[77] when Jacob and his family were traveling on the road from Lavan's house and the news reached them that Esav was on the march, Jacob took the unusual action of hiding his only daughter in a wooden chest. She was so very lovely that Jacob feared that if Esav were to see her he would desire her and take her from him. Jacob thought, *my brother is not worthy of her, I will hide her from his sight.* Jacob's great fear was that he would be unable to stop his brother from taking the girl if he chose to do so. After all, Esav was a warrior who had sworn to kill him twenty years earlier, and was now marching to meet him with four hundred armed men. So Dinah was shut away in a stout wooden box and cautioned to be silent for her own protection.

But however logical such protective, preemptive action might seem to the Bible reader, the *midrash* tells us that God was displeased. The Almighty considered that Jacob had sinned by withholding his only daughter from his brother, who was a circumcised Hebrew and ostensibly a worthy husband for Dinah. Jacob's punishment for this distinct lack of compassion, generosity and kindness towards his brother was that his prized daughter would in the future be "taken" by another man; this one *uncir*cumcised. Who knows, posits the *midrash*, but that the young girl, Dinah, would not have been a purifying, positive influence on Esav the hunter? But of course, we will never know, because Jacob withheld her from him.

The *midrashic* position is that Dinah's rape and the violent aftermath are a measure of comeuppance for Jacob, the uncharitable, arrogant man who has delayed fulfilling his vow to return to Beit-El; who has withheld his daughter from the eyes of

his brother;[78] who is so shortsighted that he thinks he is *shalem* —
complete — when he arrives at the city of Shechem. Little does
Jacob know, the *midrash* seems to be saying, that he is poised on a
cliff's edge when he thinks he is standing on safe ground.

Disturbing and unresolvable for the reader, if we follow this
reasoning, is the matter of vesting on the innocent Dinah the sins
of her father. We will see how the text and *midrash* deal with
Dinah. We will see, too, as the story unfolds, that Jacob will have
cause to regret his tarrying in Shechem.

SHECHEM LURES DINAH OUTSIDE

Prince Shechem was unaccustomed to feeling frustrated. He was
the canniest man in the city, deferred to by his father and brothers
as well as by the city elders. His land deal with the nomadic
chieftain, Jacob, had just been concluded and his, as well as his
fellow Shechemites', purses were fatter as a consequence. What's
more, he had never before been in the position of being rebuffed
when he expressed an interest in a girl. In the past all he had ever
had to do was crook his eyebrow at a maiden and her fathers or
brothers fell over their feet as they sought to please him. He was
tall, he was not bad to look at, and all things considered Shechem
knew he was a prime "catch."

Shechem could think of nothing but the wealthy clan leader's
daughter. Even in his own home, or as he went about his day, in
his mind's eye he saw the slip of a sloe-eyed girl with abundant
blue-black hair flowing like silk past her waist. He had admired
the girl when he had been a guest in Jacob's tents during the
recent land deal.[79] In truth, Shechem had watched the girl grow
over the past five years or so, almost from the moment Jacob first
came to settle in Shechem. The girl was only seven years old
then,[80] but she was exquisite and glowed with promise. Shechem
felt he had waited long enough.

Having had his interested queries about the girl rebuffed by
the powerful and secretive Jacob and his sons,[81] Shechem's blood
was on a slow boil. So he brooded.

*The nerve of them! What is she but the brat of a desert rat, a
glorified tent-dweller, a nomad without a real roof over his head*, he

thought.[82] *They should be grateful I would even cast my eye in her direction. The way they keep her under wraps in their women's compound is a guarantee that she is pure and untouched. What is she, a princess? It is unlikely that anyone better than myself—a prince in my own city—would come along for her, after all.*

Having never before felt the sting of rejection, the girl he could not possess took on enormous importance in his idle mind. So Shechem did what he did best; he hatched a plan.

The *midrash*[83] tells us that Dinah is identified in the Torah as daughter of *both* Leah *and* Jacob in order to highlight qualities of both parents that the girl might possess. We already know that when we were first introduced to Dinah's father back in Gen. 26:27, the Torah referred to Jacob as *a tent dweller*. Here, then, is a clue into both Dinah's character and Shechem's reason for luring the girl outside. The young girl Dinah, like her father before her, stayed close to home.[84] She surely occupied herself in the women's tents, following the example set by her mother Leah. She applied herself to learning all she could about the homely tasks that would fall to her as a woman of the clan of Jacob. She spent her time preparing food, combing wool, spinning it into thread, weaving the thread into cloth, dying the cloth, fashioning clothing for herself, her mother, and, as she became more adept at the task, weaving cloaks for her father and brothers. She was not a shepherd, as her aunt Rachel had been; that task now fell to her brothers. Proper females of her clan were expected to keep busy within their tents.

Dinah was content with this, as she knew she would someday take her place as the head wife of her own household, and she wanted to be ready. Moreover, she strove to be the best, like her mother Leah and her aunt Rachel. And if sometimes she peeked wistfully beyond her mother's compound on her way to and from the well, or as she assisted in the serving of food to her father's visitors, she was sufficiently disciplined in the age-old ways of her family to simply peek and sigh and imagine. And, as Abarbanel points out, the Torah text says that Dinah went out to see *the daughters* of the land. The *midrash*[85] explains that she was curious about their clothing, their jewelry, the way they dressed their hair. As the only girl in a household of boys and men, Dinah was naturally inquisitive about the ways of the maidens. She was an innocent, and her behavior was innocuous.

Truth be told, she was more than a bit leery of venturing out of the women's compound. From the gossip of the maids and the servant girls she heard that the men of the city of Shechem were hanging about, asking questions about the women of the family of Jacob who stayed within their own tents. The Shechemites were handsome to look at, though from what she could glimpse, not as handsome as her own grown brothers. Though she did notice that the girls of the city did not cover their heads, arms and legs. She had seen tanned limbs showing from between the skirt folds as the Shechemite girls walked to and fro near the well. And the fascination of dangling earrings, decorative toe rings, and the cheerful jangle of arms decorated with circles of silver bracelets; all these strange things interested Dinah, the daughter of Leah and Jacob.

She never forgot her brothers' severe admonition. Shimon and Levi had warned her privately that she must stay within the tent walls. *Take heed, our sister. It is not safe to venture outside so close to a city. A sheltered girl such as yourself, raised in desert tents, is no match for wild city boys. They are like a snake,*[86] *and will snatch you and bite you before you know they are even there. Stay inside like a good girl.* Dinah was not quite teen-aged, and so was not yet touched by nascent rebelliousness. She heeded her brother's warnings, and as their only sister she was accustomed — and entitled — to their protectiveness.

But Dinah's brothers failed to take into account market day. On that day each week the women from Jacob's compound ventured forth as a group and, with two burly male servants as their escorts, walked the stalls of the city's markets. Dinah had only once been selected by her mother to join the retinue, and it was on that single foray that Dinah's eyes had beheld the wonders of city life. Her nostrils sniffed the baking breads, her stomach turned at the odor of the charred and forbidden meats; her ears delighted in the squawking of crated fowl, the hawking of the fish mongers. And her young heart leapt to see other young girls — none of them held as closely as her mother guarded her single daughter — skipping by in the dusty pathways, chattering one to the other, casting curious and censuring glances at the strange, aloof Hebrews.

It was on market day that Shechem, standing by the market entrance with his brothers and some friends, spied the girl Dinah.[87] He recognized her at once from having watched her serving in her father's tent. This time, however, it was not an easy sighting. She was flanked by her mother and her aunt, and she — as were they — was swathed neck-to-toe in distinctively patterned homespun robes. As she was still but a girl her hair was loose and thick and glinted blackly in the sunlight. Her eyes never looked his way, but he could see they were large and fine. Her camouflaged willowy, sapling figure, so unlike the young women of his acquaintance, set off sparks within him. And though he jostled through the crowd to get a better look at her, all he was able to glimpse was her lithe arms[88] holding a basket of fruit.

Ah, the precious daughter of the mighty Jacob[89] *makes an appearance at last,* thought Shechem. He banked his twinges of lust, driven as he was by the need to pay Jacob back for the snub of rejection. He knew Dinah was still a girl[90] and thus under her father's protection. So he wracked his brain to find a way to snatch the girl from beneath her father's nose. *That would really teach the old man a lesson. I'm good enough to share a meal and a pipe and a land deal; he can give me his coin, but he won't even give me the time of day with his daughter. Well, we'll see about that. I'll soon show him and his he-man sons that Prince Shechem is not someone to be ignored.*

Shechem's resentment of Jacob pitted him against a fellow-nobleman, for Jacob and his sons were considered leaders of a great tribal family. For this reason Jacob's lone young daughter, Dinah, was considered a princess, as she was the full daughter of the clan's leader and his full-status wife.[91] She was thus at once both forbidden to Shechem as well as a prize to wrest from an interloper. He knew that Dinah would be well-guarded and also that she, herself, would not be looking for trouble.[92] He had thought to accost her the next time he saw her in public, and so Shechem watched and waited for Dinah for three weeks, over three successive market days. But she was not among the women who came from the tents of Jacob.

Shechem is experiencing a swirling maelstrom of disappointment, resentment and desire.

We can appreciate that Shechem resents the wealthy Jacob, a newly-arrived nomad who has come to the city that Shechem calls his own and has endeared himself to the denizens by his public philanthropy.

We can also appreciate that Shechem's ego might have taken a bruising when Jacob and his sons scoffed at and rejected his attempts to meet Dinah, their youngest sister and only daughter.

There is yet a third reason that might be motivating Shechem to bring Jacob down a peg or two by snatching his only daughter. Shechem is a smart and willful young man. He already has gotten Jacob to pay top dollar in the land deal. If he has now been rejected in his direct attempt to meet and perhaps negotiate for the girl Dinah, then he might very well have conceived of a way to best Jacob at the bargaining table once again. Perhaps this was his plan: Shechem knew that Dinah would command the highest possible bride-price as a nearly-royal and entirely choice and innocent maiden. Having already been rebuffed in his direct approach for the girl, Shechem decides to beat Jacob at his own game. Frymer-Kensky suggests[93] that instead of offering the clansman top dollar for the untouched girl, he resolves to take her by force and rape her, thereby shaming Jacob into lowering the exorbitant bride-price for a virgin to that for "used goods." Or perhaps he might no longer desire her after he was done despoiling her. It was quite likely that he would have no further use for the girl after spending his passion and stealing her innocence. It would serve Jacob right for snubbing him, and after all, the girl was only a girl, and she was expendable.

So Shechem, a man of action, resolves upon a plan. He would create a diversion to grab Dinah when she is alone.

A SILENT DINAH IS "TAKEN"

As we discussed earlier, Rashi is proponent of the notion that Dinah imitated her mother's behavior by "going out" of her tent, thus tempting Shechem into snatching her. This notion is unsatisfying. It is morally reprehensible to blame a twelve-year-old girl for inadvertently "tempting" a grown man into abduction and rape. Rashi's notion is supported only by the repetition of the "going out" phrase that appears in the Bible text both with Leah and with Dinah. We might even ask rhetorically, what of the same Hebrew phrase used to describe *Jacob's* "going out" from Beersheva in Gen. 28:10? Does *his* "going out" also invite sexual violation?

Other *midrashists* are not convinced by Rashi's reasoning, perhaps because an examination of the facts and circumstances presented in the Torah text suggests more convincingly that the girl was *not* the biblical actor to blame for her own kidnap and rape. *Pirkei d'Rabi Eliezer*, Yalkut Shimoni and *Sforno*, for instance, are emphatic that Dinah is mentioned *five times* in the Torah text as "Jacob's daughter" precisely to remind the reader that just as Jacob was a tent dweller (Gen. 26:27), so, too, was Dinah. They reason that Shechem was motivated by an intense desire to do harm to the mighty and respected Jacob, and thought both to slake his lust with the girl *and* to harm Jacob in one fell swoop.

We will see that the girl Dinah is completely silent in the biblical text. Incredibly, she does not utter a word — except in the *midrash* — before, during, or after the rape. But as is the case with many a biblical silence, it is a deliberate clue to understanding Dinah's place in the biblical narrative.[94] The reader must face the possibility that this entire tragic episode is not "about" Dinah, though she is its instrumentality, its victim, and its sacrifice. We must read the text and *midrash* with the understanding that this tale lays out a power play between two powerful ancient Near-Eastern clans; it illustrates a tug-of-war and a stand-off between the aged patriarch Jacob and his sons — princes in his own nomadic family. It is a story of the conflict between a desire to maintain the status quo, to purchase peace at any price, versus drawing a line in the sand and declaiming, "enough!" It is another dramatic illustration of the human consequences of individual acts of lawlessness.

It is precisely because Dinah is silent in the Bible text that the *midrashists* fill in the gaps. The function of the *midrash* here is to give Dinah a voice, to give flight to her thoughts and emotions. So the *midrash*[95] tells the story of the girl Dinah who kept to her mother's tent. Interweaving the details set out in the *midrash* with the spare biblical text, we can envision how the abduction could have taken place:

Even when the women of Jacob's house ventured outside the compound to draw water or to visit the city marketplace, Dinah held back. Shechem was aware of all this because he had set up surveillance over Dinah, and watched her daily movements. So he approached some of the local girls and asked them for a favor. "I want to play a little trick," he might have told them, "and I need your help. Midmorning tomorrow I want you and eight or ten of your friends to bring your jumping ropes, your drums and your whistles to the side of the Hebrews' compound. I will be waiting for you there. At my signal, you will play and laugh and beat your drums, sing your songs, and make an unholy ruckus." Only too glad to accommodate the local prince, the girls agreed to do as he bid them.

The next day, at the appointed time, a small crowd of town girls gathered outside the border marking the women's tents of Jacob's family compound. Shechem had chosen his moment well, as Jacob's sons and virtually all the men had gone out to the fields much earlier to tend to their livestock, and would not be back for hours. At Shechem's signal from behind a nearby gnarled tree the girls began to play and dance, thump the drums and blow their whistles, moving in a hypnotic circle to the beat of their own music. Dinah was momentarily alone in her mother's tent, as the women were out and about doing chores elsewhere within the compound. No one suspected that Dinah would come to any harm inside her own home.

Whatever can that noise be? Dinah must have thought, and she pulled back the tent flap to take a look. She stood in the doorway and beheld the local girls dancing before her[96] in a circle, moving with grace to their own beating instruments. Her smile bloomed on her face. *How lovely they are, and what a nice sound their drums and whistles are making.*

That was all the opportunity Shechem would have needed. He stepped out from behind the tree, clamped his hand over Dinah's mouth, grabbed and then easily carried the struggling girl to his waiting mount.[97] He threw a heavy blanket over her head and held her fast as he sped away to his palace. The kidnapping was over in the blink of an eye. The local girls, once they realized what had happened, perhaps thought what a strange game Prince Shechem had been playing. They would have shrugged their shoulders, picked up their toys and drums, and dispersed back to their homes. Quiet reigned once again in Jacob's compound.

Later that night, when the Shechemite girls recounted their adventure to their parents, they were told that Prince Shechem knew what he was about, and they were cautioned not to say a word about the incident to anyone. The *midrash*[98] tells us that the Shechemites were entirely dependent on Prince Shechem, and that they were accustomed to turning a blind eye to his escapades.

THE RAPE OF DINAH

Shechem, son of Hamor the Hivite, the prince of the land, saw her; **he took her, he lay with her, and he tortured her.** Gen. 34:2

The *Netziv* tells us that Shechem spirited the captive Dinah away to his private chambers. His rooms were situated in a secluded portion of the palace so that her cries for help, if they were even audible, would have been considered Shechem's private business, as the servants were schooled never to question the prince's comings and goings. It is even possible that Shechem had executed an abduction such as this one before,[99] as his actions were quick and practiced. Members of his household knew enough to play "deaf and dumb;" Prince Shechem was the law.

This is the reason that the *midrash*[100] roundly condemns not only Shechem, but also the people inhabiting the city of Shechem, for Dinah's abduction and rape. They were complicit in the prince's behavior because they not only knew exactly what had occurred, but they also affirmatively and implicitly kept silent in the face of the girl's abduction, and even, perhaps, her cries for help. Shechem's exalted position in the community was the reason no one came to her aid. As such, according to Maimonides and the *midrash*,[101] we begin to appreciate that under nomadic law they must *all* share in the coming retaliatory punishment for the rape.

The Bible reader is sick with dread at what the girl Dinah must be facing. In fact, the Bible presents the first in a series of triple verbs when it narrates, in spare, harrowing language, what was done to her. *He took her; and he lay with her; and he tortured her.* Each verb describes but a portion of the horrifying nightmare that she endured.

First, *he took her.* As we already have described with the help of the *midrash,* Shechem abducted Dinah from the doorway of her home. The *midrashists* use various synonyms to explain the Hebrew word *he took.* Mizrachi calls the taking "a theft." He sees Shechem's unlawful act as a kidnapping. One instant Dinah was a carefree, curious girl on the cusp of young womanhood. The next she was a kidnap victim subjected to the tearing, indescribable horrors of physical attack and sexual violation. The *Malbim* calls the taking "a robbery" by Shechem of Dinah's youth and innocence.

We can appreciate the Bible's eloquence in its verbal restraint. It simply tells us that Shechem *took her.* It is an unambiguous expression of a kidnapping, of an abduction, a taking against her will. Can we even allow our imaginations to open the window on what a sheltered Hebrew girl surely endured at the hands of an angry, sexually experienced, powerful and virile Canaanite man?

Second, *he lay with her.* The *midrash*[102] tells us that this phrase means that this was the first stage of the sexual attack that Shechem perpetrated on Dinah: he lay with her, first, in the natural manner that a man would take a woman. But the *Netziv* and other *midrashists*[103] say that we know from the verbal sequence in the Torah that this was no soft and easy coupling. To the contrary, it was forced and violent from the very first moment. It was a kidnap followed by a rape, says the commentator, an unambiguous physical violation of a young girl.

Third, *and he tortured her.* This third phrase is an elaboration on the first two. This was the third strike against an utterly innocent girl. The *midrash*[104] teaches us that this phrase means that Shechem sodomized Dinah, forcing himself upon her in the unnatural manner that a man would rape another man. Other commentators[105] say the rape became a compounded torture for

Dinah because Shechem forced her into *repeated* sexual acts; that Shechem's appetite for Dinah was insatiable once *he took her*. This is the reason the Bible adds the third phrase *he tortured her*, or *he made her suffer*. He used her repeatedly. And because the girl was innocent—practically a child herself—Shechem's cruel, repeated and excessive use of her sexually was pure torture for her.

The *Netziv*[106] elaborates, saying that the "torture" for Dinah only began with the physical. Another *midrash* says that Shechem is likened to a snake who struck out at the girl in stealth, took her, and also bit her.[107] So her physical suffering is more elaborate even than the reader might have imagined. The *Netziv* acknowledges that the primary torture was, of course, during the rape itself, but in the mind of a conscientious and sheltered girl her suffering extended to afterwards, as well. In the moments of the aftermath, Dinah's terrors focused on her predicament. It is likely that as she lay there alone weeping, in physical and mental shock, she thought, "What is to become of me?!"

Once she realized she was not to be killed, the commentator suggests that Dinah suffered the terror that she was doomed to be forever shamed, sullied, branded and—critical for a female in that time and place—unmarried. Her status and currency revolved around her virginity and marriageability. Now, she feared, even if she were fortunate enough to make it back home alive, she would be a *persona non grata* in her father's world, marked forever as the Hebrew girl who had been defiled by the uncircumcised Canaanite.[108] Thus we see that Shechem's "torture" of Dinah had serious psychological repercussions layered over her physical injuries.

This is perhaps why the Talmud[109] says that the Torah adds the third verb of *inuy*, or torture, *after* it says that Shechem *took her and lay with her*. It is to clarify how Dinah reacted to the violent sexual intercourse. Says the Talmud, Dinah obviously did not derive pleasure from the act, or else the Torah would not have used the term for torture or infliction of suffering immediately after the statement *he lay with her*. We are meant to understand that the girl was in great pain of both body and mind after Shechem forced himself on her.[110]

In yet another portion of the Talmud[111] the sages again inquire, What, specifically, was the "torture" or "affliction" referred to in this verse? The answer lies in an examination of the same word (*inuy*) when it was used a bit earlier in the Jacob saga (at Gen. 31:50). The same word for "torture" appears when Jacob's father-in-law Lavan chases after him, finally agreeing to withdraw his objections to his daughters and grandchildren accompanying Jacob back to his own father's house. But before Lavan takes his final leave of Jacob and his household, he metaphorically shakes his finger at his son-in-law, scolding and cautioning him never to "afflict" Lavan's daughters—Jacob's wives, Rachel and Leah. Lavan uses the same Hebrew word for "torture" or "suffering"—*inuy*—that is used by the Torah in our story to describe Shechem's abuse of Dinah. One interpretation of Lavan's use of the term is that it would constitute "torture" of Jacob's wives if he were to *withhold* sexual relations from them, and take additional rival wives into his bed.

The reader therefore asks, What is the proper definition of the Hebrew word *inuy*—torture? Does the word refer to *with-holding* of sexual relations, as in Lavan's warning to Jacob, or does it refer to forced and excessive physical abuse of a virgin, as in Shechem's rape of Dinah?

Interestingly, both verses in the two stories also include the Hebrew word for "taking"—either the taking of a rival wife, or, in our story, the taking/abduction of the girl Dinah from her father's house. The use of the words "torture" and "taking" of a female would indicate a link to sexual behavior when these words and phrases are used in tandem in the Bible text.

Still, the question about the word *inuy* persists. How can we reconcile two opposite usages of the same word?

The solution to any such verbal ambiguity must be sought in the contextual use of the words. In the earlier Jacob story, Lavan is concerned that in the ongoing familial battle for Jacob's affections and sexual favors Jacob might bring yet *another* woman to his bed. *This* behavior, in a father's eyes, would have consti-tuted "torture" for his two daughters, Jacob's main wives.

In the present story, in the context of this verse, where first Shechem *takes* Dinah, then *lays with* her, and then *tortures* or afflicts her, the meaning of the word *inuy* clearly refers to the forced infliction of sexual behavior upon a virgin. That the word for "torture" refers to sexual behavior is clear in both stories. *But depending upon the state of mind of the woman involved, the sex act could be either desired or abhorred.* For Jacob's rival wives, his conjugal intimacy in their beds was a prize; in our story, the forced and repeated sexual violation of the young girl Dinah was detestable and tragic.

Lest we think that perhaps our sympathy to Dinah's plight might skew our analysis of the gravity of Shechem's behavior, the *midrash*[112] tells us that even among the Canaanites the torture and kidnapping of virgins *was not done*.[113] Quite possibly there was a similar rule among the broader civilization of that part of the ancient Near East. Such a credo would make sense in societies which of necessity prided and traded upon virginity, and whose landed fortunes passed through primogeniture. A virgin girl was counted as a measure of family's wealth because she had a value that could be bartered, and, too, a person's provenance depended upon the certainty of his parentage.

For these reasons the Bible reader expects that Shechem must know to a reasonable certainty that his lawless behavior is inviting a serious backlash even beyond what was prescribed in the contemporary law codes.[114] In fact, Bronner states that in biblical times rape "was considered an outrage" against the family or clan.[115] And other sources[116] clearly state that even among the Canaanites it was forbidden to lay with a virgin without the benefit of a marriage contract. A cursory examination of the Bible's penalties directed against a rapist[117] of a betrothed virgin girl suggests that because such behavior was outlawed, it virtually invited violent retaliation, and the prescribed penalty, beyond payment in silver coin, included the rapist's death by stoning.[118] We will see how Shechem meets his fate later on in our story.

AFTER THE RAPE - SHECHEM'S REACTION

*[Afterwards] his soul **clung** to Dinah, daughter of Jacob; and he **loved** the maiden, and he **spoke** to the maiden's heart.*

And Shechem said to his father, Hamor: "Take this girl for me for a wife." Gen. 34:3–4

Here the Bible reader is faced with a dramatic turnaround. Our heads are reeling! In verse 2 Shechem kidnaps and violently rapes the innocent girl, Dinah; in verses 3 and 4 we learn that he now "loves" her and wants her for his wife. What are we to make of this? Does Shechem's apparent *volte-face* whitewash his lawless and unconscionable acts? If we follow our instincts and unequivocally condemn him, are we unfairly looking at the event through twenty-first century eyes? Is Shechem's offer of marriage reasonable given ancient Near East sensibility and practice? And what of Dinah? What does *she* want?

Examining the Bible verses, we are faced with a second triad of verbs describing Shechem's *behavior*. The first, of course, occurred before and during the rape. In verse 2, we read of Shechem's *actions*: he *took her*; *lay with her* and *tortured her*. Now, after the rape, in verse 3, we read of Shechem's *emotions*: he *becomes deeply attached to her*; *loves her*; and *speaks to her heart*. We must assume that the two verses' similar cadence and structure are meant to be read in light of each other; that we should examine whether the one triad informs the other.

Let us analyze Shechem's actions *after* the rape.

First we read that **his soul clung to Dinah**, *daughter of Jacob*. The Bible's narrative voice is telling us that Shechem *became deeply attached* to her. The Ishbitzer,[119] the great 19th-century Hassidic master, deduces that after experiencing sex with Dinah, Shechem lost all desire for the Canaanite girls of the land; that he had eyes only for her. As a result, another *midrash*[120] tells us, Shechem now seeks a permanent relationship with Dinah. Perhaps his attachment to the girl came as a surprise to him; after all, he had kidnapped and raped her without a thought to her sensibilities and to the devastation he was wreaking on the Hebrew girl's life. He had been slapping back angrily at Jacob, and managed to despoil the one vulnerable asset belonging to Jacob that he could get his hands on. We get the impression that neither he, nor Dinah, nor the Bible reader is expecting Shechem's own tender reaction to his savage behavior.

The reader should note that the Bible is clear: It is *to Dinah, daughter of Jacob*, whom Shechem has now apparently cleaved.[121] The text emphasizes her relationship *to her father* when it describes Shechem's softened feelings. We might compare this to the case of a kidnapper who abducts *the daughter of the Prime Minister*. It is not just the girl herself who has been taken, however much her captor is enamored of her at the time and even the morning-after; in fact, she is almost beside the point. Rather, it is the girl's value to her wealthy and honored father that makes the taking—and the subsequent attachment—meaningful to her captor. As we analyze Shechem's behavior the Torah text wants this relational detail to be front-and-center in the reader's mind, and that is the reason it repeats it here after first reminding us in verse 1 that Dinah was *born to Jacob*. *Sforno* supports this reading of the text by emphasizing that the Bible uses the phrase for yet a third time in verse 19 later in the story, saying that Shechem did not delay his own circumcision *for he wanted Jacob's daughter*.

The phrase *and his soul clung to Dinah, daughter of Jacob* has been interpreted as saying that Shechem was willing to live with Dinah in a legitimate, married fashion, according to *her* sights and sensibilities and accustomed manner of living as the daughter of Jacob.[122] Her innocent and aristocratic manner, her guileless beauty, her softspoken nature—all of the behaviors that befit a princess who has grown up in the house of the mighty and wealthy Jacob—these hallmarks of the young girl, Dinah, have drawn Shechem to cling to her. The *Malbim*[123] would agree, saying that Dinah was equal to Shechem in stature, as close as she could be to a princess. This appealed to Shechem, the prince. Her father's eminence as a tribal nobleman made Dinah a fit mate.

Still, the contrast between the verbs in verses 2 and 3 is striking; almost impossible to believe. It calls to mind a Jekyl and Hyde personality switch: First Shechem engages in kidnap, rape and abuse; mere hours later he feels attachment and love for the girl, and speaks to her in cajoling terms. Such a behavior switch fits the classic pattern of spousal abuse: Unprovoked anger and violence followed almost immediately by remorse, sincere promises of reform, placating words, even gifts. Unfortunately, such a cycle of abuse and remorse has been shown to recur absent outside intervention. It seems to me that a version of this pattern of abusive sexual dominance is occurring in verses 2 and 3, where we see Shechem at work during the rape and afterwards. Let us attend closely to the Bible's language and see if he is genuine; if his protestations of love and desire for marriage to his abused victim ring true.

In order to understand the apparent about-face presented in the Bible text, it behooves us to closely contrast verses 2 and 3. This analysis will inform our understanding of the next two verbs in the triad and of Shechem's post-rape behavior.

Let us engage in the useful exercise of matching the *emotional* verbs *after* the rape (verse 3) to the *action* verbs *before* the rape (verse 2).

In this way we connect the Bible's first emotional **post**-rape phrase — *his soul clung to Dinah, daughter of Jacob* — to the earlier action phrase *and he took her*. This correlation makes sense to us, as we already have suggested that Shechem's *taking* of Dinah is likely to have been motivated by his reaction to Jacob's wealth and possibly Jacob's rejection of Shechem as a potential suitor. Read together, then, we see that the fact that *she was Jacob's daughter* is also a likely reason for Shechem's feeling of attachment to Dinah afterwards. The combined sentence economically tells the story: *Shechem's soul clung to Dinah, daughter of Jacob, whom he had taken.*

The second *emotion* phrase in verse 3 is *and* **he loved the maiden**. On its face, it would seem that after Shechem raped Dinah he came to love her. Let us match this phrase to its earlier *action* counterpart in verse 2. The partner phrase there is *and he lay with her*. Read together, we see that *after he lay with her, he loved the maiden*. Shechem's "love" for Dinah is tied to having laid with her "in the natural manner," to use Rashi's expression. How are we to understand this?

Quite simply, this utterly innocent and beautiful young girl appealed to Shechem.[124] She was lovely when he snatched her from her doorstep; gazing at her even *after* he "took her" in rough violence, her youthful loveliness was still undimmed.[125] Her lips did not curl in curses of him and of his treatment of her; it is certain she did not even know how to curse him even if she had wished to do so. She was miserably wretched and weeping,[126] but was still objectively beautiful to behold. Quite possibly this was a unique experience for Shechem. Perhaps the women he had "taken" to his bed before this — either willingly or by force — appeared haggard or undesirable to him the morning-after. Or perhaps Dinah's hitherto untouched virginity was a unique sexual experience for Shechem and it is *this* aspect of Dinah that he professes he cannot live without. We deduce this from the Bible's repeated use of the term *na'arah*, meaning "maiden," emphasizing that this untouched aspect of Dinah is the reason for his "love" for her.

The third phrase used to describe Shechem's *emotional* behavior is ***and he spoke to the maiden's heart***. The *midrash*[127] explains that Shechem tried to entice Dinah with words that would "settle onto her heart." We imagine that he would try to convince, cajole, or placate her. But no. According to several commentaries,[128] Shechem's speech to Dinah is, "Please, Dinah, don't cry so bitterly. Marry me and you will have riches that far exceed your father's. Your father's wealth is sufficient to acquire only *fields*; and he paid dearly for those. But I will marry you and you will acquire fields, vineyards, a granary, *a city*. For I am prince over all the land that your eye can see."

Shechem's simulated speech tells the reader that the *midrash* suspects that this leopard has not changed his spots; Shechem attempts to entice the girl he has just raped with *mercenary* arguments focusing on himself. He speaks to her as if he is conducting a business deal, and this may in fact have been the case. We already suspect that his motivation in snatching Dinah was at least in part because of the lure of her father's fortune. Here we have the evidence in the *midrash's* version of Shechem's words. We must ask rhetorically, what understanding can Shechem have had of Dinah's fragile and bloodied state if he can try to sweet-talk her *in this manner*? Here, when he is supposedly at his most eloquent, trying to cajole the girl he has just abused, he speaks to her not of "flowers," but of lucre. The answer is that Shechem's *midrashic* words reveal his heart. They also reveal his utter failure to appreciate the inner worth of the gentle girl who is the object of his speech.

The Bible reader can infer from this third phrase (*and he spoke to the maiden's heart*) that the abduction, rape and suffering that Dinah experienced at Shechem's hand was in no way softened by the first two phrases (*i.e., his soul yearned for Dinah, the daughter of Jacob* and *he loved the maiden*).[129] On the contrary. Shechem, the man of action, was reduced to *speaking* in a cajoling manner precisely because his yearning and love had made no dent in Dinah's misery. Her fear and abhorrence of him did not abate even after he ceased his sexual predations. In fact, in order to gauge the depth of Dinah's misery the Torah sets up this unusual attempt by her rapist to try to calm her. The great effort expended by Shechem as he "appealed to the girl's heart" is in direct proportion to Dinah's deep feelings of terror, physical pain, and shame.

In light of this analysis, matching the third and final post-rape verb in verse 3 (*and he spoke to the maiden's heart*) to its partner in verse 2 (*and he tortured her* or *and he made her suffer* or *and he debased her*) yields still another textual synthesis that makes sense to the reader: *Shechem spoke to the maiden's heart because he had tortured her.*

Professor Phyllis Trible[130] interprets Shechem's third phrase (*and he spoke to the maiden's heart*) as his "pursuit of Dinah" after the abduction and rape, because in the Bible the term "to speak to another's heart" connotes reassurance, comfort, loyalty, and yes, love. Trible says a man will "speak to a woman's heart" when she is "the offended party," and he owes her some degree of comfort. This is certainly the case in the present story. So if we believe the biblical narrator speaks the truth, we must assume that Shechem is, in fact, strongly drawn to Dinah, daughter of Jacob; that he has discovered that he "loves" the maiden; and that he is — however backwards it may seem to the modern reader — courting or pursuing her now, *after* he has already abducted her and forced her sexually.

The Bible text is sympathetic to Shechem in the verses following his rape of Dinah, at the same time that it does not flinch from condemning his lawless predatory behavior towards her. Amazingly, one *midrash* attributes Shechem's "three languages of love" in verse 3 to God's love for the Children of Israel.[131] Shechem's "terms of endearment" — *his soul cleaved; he loved; and he spoke to her heart* — are recognized as poetic and affecting, notwithstanding their vile source. Other *midrashim*[132] even recognize two additional terms of endearment attributed to Shechem other than the ones presented in the Bible at verse 3; they are *longing* (verse 8) and *wanting* (verse 19). But they are expressly credited nevertheless to "that wicked barbarian, Shechem."[133]

The commentaries — as do we — have enormous difficulty reconciling the cunning, calculating businessman and rapist who appears in the text in verses up to and preceding the rape, with the tender lover in verses 3 and 4. His emotions post-rape seem admirable, but his behavior toward Dinah was unforgivable.

Avivah Gottlieb Zornberg lays to rest the question of whether Shechem really loved Dinah. In discussing the paradigmatic act of sexual sin, Zornberg identifies it as an arrogant act of "rapacious self-assertion." Such a sexual act — virtually identical to the seeing, taking and torturing that Shechem engaged in here — is the very *antithesis* of love, according to Zornberg. Instead of "I-thou," such an act can best be characterized as "either-me-or-you." "Essentially, this is a sexuality of cruelty, not of erotic relationship."[134]

Shechem cannot have it both ways; when he abducted and raped Dinah — the Torah unambiguously defines it as *inuy*, an act of sexual cruelty — he damned himself, even pronounced his own death sentence. The consequence of such a sexual sin, in biblical terms, is always a "mass destruction" (such as occurred to the generation of the Flood and to the cities of Sodom and Gomorrah) that "washes away all selves, innocent and guilty alike."[135] We will see that Shechem the man, as well as his entire city, will, indeed, be punished for his sin.

This discussion highlights that Shechem's character is complex. He is not easily characterized as unqualifiedly evil. It is this complexity that creates unbearable tension for the reader and raises the justifiably strong emotions of outrage, anger and possible compassion. All of these emotions are evinced as the story continues.

Shechem was acutely aware that his brutality toward Dinah has made her virtually unmarketable as a bride to another. The *midrash*[136] tells us that knowing this, and desiring her, he spoke to her in the aftermath of the violence reassuring her that he would take her as his bride, so she need not weep and worry at being covered in shame. The modern reader's perception of this offer of marriage as the height of arrogance might not be a fair assessment from the standpoint of the biblical actors. To a twenty-first-century woman, being bound in marriage to the very man who has brutalized, raped and sodomized her would constitute a nightmare and a life-sentence of abuse. But to a raped virgin in the ancient Near East this may be her last best chance at marriage; and in fact the Bible offers marriage to her rapist as a consolation to her for this very reason.[137] And as Shechem is wont to point out to Dinah, he is, after all, a prince, and thus is by all accounts a prize.

AFTER THE RAPE – DINAH'S REACTION

The pressing question for the Bible reader is whether Shechem's turnabout in verse 3 mitigates his violent behavior toward Dinah in verse 2; also, conversely, whether his lawless kidnap and rape of Dinah in verse 2 vitiates his profession of love in verse 3. We must also ask whether Dinah reciprocates Shechem's tender feelings toward her, or whether the rape has hardened her heart against him.

Dinah is utterly silent in the Bible throughout this entire incident and its aftermath. But, mindful of Zornberg's teaching that the *midrash* speaks in the voice of the woman,[138] we are reliant upon the *midrash* and Talmud, and of course on minute examination of the verses of Chapter 34 of Genesis, in order to decipher Dinah's reaction to her rape.

The *midrash*[139] explains that Shechem's tender but somewhat desperate attempt to calm and placate Dinah is necessary because the girl cowered from him after the rape. She could not abide his touch, was in a state of near-hysterics, and wept inconsolably.

Because Dinah does not speak at all in the Bible text, the reader must attempt to gauge her reaction by what the Bible *has* divulged: We are told that she went out to see the daughters of the land; we are told what Shechem did to her (verse 2), and then we are told how Shechem felt about her afterwards (verses 3 and 4). Very soon we will be told about Dinah's father's and brothers' disparate reactions to the news. But there is not a word in the text that indicates that Dinah reciprocates Shechem's newfound tenderness.

On the contrary, at this very moment we can only infer that Dinah is curled up on the bed, swathed in blankets, her arms covering her eyes as she keens in physical pain and psychic misery. She is distraught and cannot think past the moment. Her rapist is leaning over her, speaking in what seems to be a kind voice, professing his love for her. She thinks, *What kind of trick is this? What is he saying? What will he do to me now? Will I be killed?* Some of Shechem's words are penetrating the fog of her pain and distraction. In fact, he is at this very moment earnestly begging her forgiveness.[140]

An unusual verbal artifact in the Hebrew Bible text yields a clue as to Dinah's actual age and girlhood at the time of her rape, and thus can help the reader gauge her reaction afterwards. Verse 3, which tells us that Shechem loved the maiden and spoke to the maiden's heart, twice spells the word *na'arah*, or maiden, *without* the final letter *hay*. The word therefore reads *na'ar*, which means the *male* youth instead of the *female* maiden. It is only the context which supplies the female meaning, spelling, and vocalization to which we are accustomed. The *midrash*[141] explains that the reason the Bible spells the word *absent* the feminizing last letter is to hint to the reader that Dinah was still a trim girl—as slim as a tomboy—when Shechem raped her. She is in fact still but a girl— *yaldah*—one verse later when he professes his love for her and tries to calm her, appeal to her and endear himself to her. Elsewhere in the Bible, when the context refers to a grown woman who has reached adulthood with all the physical, feminine characteristics that that state implies, the word *na'arah* is spelled *with* the feminizing letter *hay*. But here the word is spelled without the letter *hay*, indicating that Dinah is not yet a woman.

So Dinah is still a girl, and she thinks and feels as a twelve- or fourteen-year-old will do. She has been hurt grievously, and she no doubt wants her mother and the familiar comforts of her home as would any young girl in her predicament. But she has been sexually violated by an uncircumcised man,[142] and she knows that thus shamed, she can never return to her mother's tent. Her life is upended, her future precarious. In fact, not only is Dinah silent throughout this nightmare, but so is her mother, Leah.[143] In past episodes the matriarchs have not hesitated to speak up about or on behalf of their sons (Sarah for Isaac; Rebecca for Jacob; Rachel when she begged Jacob for sons); yet here, Leah does not speak, and her daughter Dinah is existentially alone.

It has been posited that what Dinah endured at Shechem's hand was not rape, but a marriage by abduction.[144] That is, that her kidnap and forced sex was, in that time and place, an understood means of taking the girl in marriage. This notion is unsupported by the text, and is pernicious because it implies that Dinah had tacitly consented to her own rape, a fact that the Bible explicitly rules out when it states (in verse 2) that Shechem took her, lay with her *and tortured her.* **The text nowhere supports the idea that what took place between Dinah and Shechem was a consensual sexual encounter.**

In fact, to the contrary; in verse 3 we read that Shechem tries hard to speak to the maiden's heart of his newly-discovered "love." If kidnap and forced sex were an acceptable method of marriage, Shechem could have saved his breath; it would have been unnecessary for him to sweet-talk the girl if she already legally belonged to him.[145] Also, if the abduction and rape *were* an accepted means of marriage, why, then, does Shechem tell his father in verse 4 to go to Jacob in order to "go take this girl for me for a wife?" If there already had been a *de facto* marriage, the discussions between the two fathers or heads-of-family would have been unnecessary. And in verse 7 the biblical narrator twice decries the kidnap and rape in the strongest possible terms. It is called an "obscene abomination," and then we are told simply that "such a thing is not done."

Finally, in verse 31, Dinah's brothers will have the last word and laconically explain why they put all the men of the city to death and lay the city to ruin. They say, *Should he treat our sister like a prostitute* and we stand by and do nothing? So it is clear from the text that Shechem's taking of Jacob's daughter was a lawless act, and not an acceptable method of acquiring a wife.

As for the question of whether Dinah loved Shechem, the Bible text is absolutely silent. Despite, perhaps, a romanticist's need to project Dinah's emotion onto this silent canvas, **there is no textual evidence whatsoever that Dinah loved Shechem.**[146] The only word of love here is attributed to Shechem, where the Bible says after the rape that *he loved the maiden.*

Yet there is a hint in the *midrash*[147] that suggests that perhaps Dinah grew enamored of her captor; that when her brothers, Shimon and Levi, storm the prince's palace (in verse 26) in order to rescue her, she did not go with them willingly. This *midrash* says that her brothers "dragged her outside." The reason this *midrash* has persisted despite the vast body of rabbinic lore to the contrary is perhaps due to the simple and convincing word-play on which it hinges.

When Shechem kidnapped Dinah in verse 2 the Bible used the Hebrew word *vayikach*, meaning *and he took her*. When Dinah's brothers come to extract their sister from Shechem's palace in verse 26 the Bible uses the plural version of the same word: *vayik'chu*, meaning similarly *and they took her*. If the word implies a forced taking in verse 2, then the re-taking of Dinah in verse 26 may well have been against her will also.

What might have been at work, if we follow the view of this *midrash*, is a prescient case of "The Stockholm Syndrome." This syndrome is a psychological response by an abducted hostage who counterintuitively displays signs of loyalty to her abductor, regardless of the personal danger in which the hostage finds herself. This syndrome was described in 1974 when victims in a Swedish bank robbery, held hostage for six days, became emotionally attached to their abductors and even defended them after they were rescued. Psychiatrists and psychologists consider such behavior a prime example of "identification" by the victim with his captor in order to best insure that she survives the ordeal.[148]

Perhaps the girl Dinah automatically and unwittingly employed this defense mechanism after she was taken, raped and tortured. She was, at most, fourteen years old, and was terrified, injured, and deeply ashamed. A "rescue" and return to her family compound held no attraction for her because she knew enough after a simple calculus to appreciate that a female who had been shamed and defiled by an uncircumcised stranger would not be considered valued bride material among her people. Moreover, here was her captor speaking softly to her of love and marriage. "Better the devil she 'knew' " — this is Shechem — "than the devil she did not know" — this is the unleashed anger of her father and brothers — might have been Dinah's unvoiced, reluctant response when Shimon and Levi storm the palace and drag her outside to safety.

And the *midrash*,[149] aware of Dinah's fraught psychological state, presents us with her internal, agonized worry: "Oh, where will I hide my shame?!" she cries over and over to herself. Would her shame have been more effectively ameliorated had she married her rapist, as was the law of the Hebrews in the ancient Near East,[150] or if she were spirited away to live out her life hidden in her brother Shimon's house?[151]

Frymer-Kensky reads the language of verse 3 as indicating that Shechem's words "spoken to Dinah's heart" were success-ful;[152] that what began as a kidnap and rape was turned into a "poignant scene" between the rapist and the maiden, implying that perhaps Dinah did *not* wish to be rescued.

But even Frymer-Kensky acknowledges that the serious problem of the abduction and rape "will not be easily resolved," for the reason that "Shechem has 'done her wrong' [and] de-graded her and her family."[153] In fact, it is incontrovertible that Shechem is working very hard to appease and calm Dinah after he has raped her. The logical deduction is that Dinah does not recip-rocate Shechem's infatuation.[154]

But we cannot *know* what Dinah felt that awful and fateful day, as she is absolutely silent in the Torah text. The *midrashim*, the Talmudic as well as modern commentaries, and the analysis presented here, offer the reader Rashomon-like analyses of the possible scenarios, using the word-clues presented in the Bible. Was Dinah abducted and forced sexually by Shechem? According to the Bible text this is a certainty (*and he took her; lay with her; and tortured her*). Did Shechem have a change-of-heart afterwards?

According to the very next verse, this seems to be the case (*his heart cleaved to Dinah the daughter of Jacob; he loved the girl; and he spoke to her heart*).

But what is *unsaid* in the spare text of verses 2 and 3 gives the commentaries and Bible readers pause. We want to understand Shechem's behavior. Why did Shechem abduct Dinah in the first place? Was she targeted? Did the abduction stem from the real estate transaction? Was the abduction and rape a calculated acting-out of his resentment against Jacob? Was he also attracted to Dinah's beauty? Did he fall in love with her almost against his will after his night with her?

And of course we wish to understand what Dinah was thinking and feeling before, during and after her kidnap and rape. Why did she go out to see the daughters of the land? Did she somehow invite the rape? Did she despise her rapist afterwards? Was she shamed beyond words and did she desire her own death? Was she inconsolable, or was she comforted by Shechem's words? Did she wish to remain with him? Did she resist rescue by her brothers? What happened to her afterwards?

It has been suggested that Dinah's brothers' enraged response of dragging her from Shechem's palace precluded her from freely choosing a marriage to her rapist over an unmarried, shamed life among her own people.[155] Perhaps this is so. Perhaps Dinah was weary of being "pushed around" and "acted upon." After all, years before Jacob had shut her up tight in a wooden chest to hide her from Esav's lascivious eyes; now, Shechem has kidnapped her from her father's house and forced her sexually. Her rapist then orders his father to "**take** this girl for me for a wife." And finally we will see how her father and brothers preclude any choice on Dinah's part. Her brothers will drag her from Shechem's palace and spirit her to a "safe house" for her own good.

More likely, however, Dinah resisted her brothers' rescue because she could not bear to return to her family a shamed woman.[156] Perhaps she very literally could not bear to show her face in the light of day after enduring the acts of defilement that Shechem forced upon her. Dinah begins the day as a carefree girl; she ends it an abused rape victim. Is it any wonder that she wraps herself in a sheet and huddles on the floor in a corner of the locked room? The terrified girl expected that it would be Shechem who would walk through the door, and that she would again be subjected to unspeakable shame. Instead, it is Shimon who smashes the lock, and finds his sister stiff with fear, shame and pride. It is no wonder Dinah could not even speak to her brothers when they discovered her cowering in the room that had become her prison. She, who had thought she held no more tears within her, weeps silently onto Shimon's shoulder as he carries her out of the palace.

We note that things and events happen *to* Dinah rather than *with* her. *Otah*, meaning *to her*, is the word used in the text when Shechem abducts her in verse 2; its corollary, *et Dinah* — to Dinah — is used again when her brothers take her back in verse 26. The Hebrew words imply her lack of consent. A 21st-century reader might posit that perhaps Dinah would have preferred to have made her own choice — whether to consent to marry Shechem, or to return to her father's house — that is, to have had some say in her own destiny. Sadly for Dinah, as a daughter from a tribal family of the ancient Near East, freedom of choice was never to be her fate. And the Bible text nowhere reveals Dinah's preference, leaving it to the reader to infer. Later on in this chapter I will examine what became of Dinah after the family picked up stakes and left the city of Shechem.

Throughout these analyses, the tension that the Bible has set up between the kidnap and rape in verse 2 and the rapist's quick expression of love in verse 3 persists. Should verse 3 cancel out the horror and dishonor of verse 2? For this writer, and for the raped and abused Dinah, the answer must be that it cannot.

Let us now explore the aftermath of the rape from the point of view of the story's actors, and follow the plot as it thickens.

❈ ❈ ❈

GENESIS 34:5–19

Now Jacob heard that [Shechem] had defiled his daughter Dinah, while his sons were with his livestock out in the field; so Jacob kept silent until their return.

Hamor, Shechem's father, went out to Jacob to speak with him.

And Jacob's sons came from the field when they heard; the men were distressed and very angry, for he had committed a disgusting outrage in Israel by laying with the daughter of Jacob, as such a thing was not done.

Hamor spoke with them, saying, "My son, Shechem's, soul longs for your daughter; please give her to him as a wife. And intermarry with us; give your daughters to us, and take our daughters for yourselves. And you shall settle with us, and the land will be before you; settle and trade in it, and acquire a portion of it."

Then Shechem said to her father and to her brothers, "Allow me to gain favor in your eyes; whatever you tell me [to give] I will give. Inflate upon me greatly the marriage contract and gifts, and I will give whatever you tell me; and you will give me the maiden for a wife."

Jacob's sons answered Shechem and Hamor with trickery, and they spoke (because he had defiled Dinah, their sister), and they said to them, "We are unable to do this thing, to give our sister to an uncircumcised man, for that is a disgrace to us. Only on this condition will we acquiesce to you: if you will become like us, and circumcise every male among you. And then we will give our daughters to you, and we will take your daughters to ourselves; and we will settle with you and become a single people. But if you do not heed us and become circumcised, we will take our daughter and go."

And their words were satisfactory in the eyes of Hamor and in the eyes of Shechem the son of Hamor. And the youth did not delay doing the thing, because he wanted Jacob's daughter; and he was the most respected [member] of all his father's household.

THE AFTERMATH: JACOB'S SILENCE

The enormity of the personal tragedy that Shechem perpetrated on the girl Dinah takes up a mere four verses of chapter thirty-four of Genesis, while the aftermath is described in detail for the rest of the chapter's thirty-one verses. After agonizing about Dinah's experience and her reactions, the reader is anxious to read about Jacob's response, and about how Dinah's brothers will take the news of her kidnap and rape. Suspending our foreknowledge of the ending, it is worthwhile to describe and examine the post-rape drama so that we can better understand Dinah's brothers' depression, anger, shame and duty. The depth of their emotions informs their behavior toward Dinah, toward her rapist, toward his father, toward the men of Shechem and the rest of the city's inhabitants. It also sheds light on their responses to their own father's fear and the anger he vents on them. At all times, we must bear in mind that Dinah is the innocent victim in this tragic tale of resentments, lust, calculation, regret and revenge. This section will analyze the aftermath of the rape in this light.

First the Bible tells us, in verse 5, that *Jacob heard that he [Shechem] had defiled his daughter Dinah*, but because *his sons were with his livestock out in the field, **Jacob kept silent** until their return.*

Jacob's behavior evokes conflicting emotions in the reader. On the one hand, verse 5 seems completely logical. We can perhaps understand Jacob's reluctance to take on the prince of the city without backup from his sons. For we know that Jacob is not a young man. The *midrash* places his age at between 104 and 117 years.[157] Perhaps he first heard of his daughter's disappearance from her mother, Leah, who found Dinah missing when she returned from her own chores of supervising the meals for the enormous household. Leah must have been frantic, as the girl was not one to wander about. Perhaps Jacob at first dismissed the matter as one that would resolve itself in short order. Perhaps it became known through one servant whispering to another and to another, as the marketplace grapevine was speedy and brutally accurate. Regardless how it became known to him, the text tells us *Jacob heard* of the rape, and the *midrash* tells us he heard about it on the very day of her defilement.[158] The important point for Jacob is that the rape has become public knowledge. Dinah's personal tragedy has now become a public scandal.

We can envision this old man quaking with fear and indecision. The text invites us to imagine his thought process: "What should I do? I am alone and old, and even when my sons

come back from the fields we are a pitiful few and the Shechemites are many. This will surely mean a war. And such a war! The
Perizzites and the other Canaanites will surely side with the
Hivites against us![159] We will be outnumbered and will surely
perish! Did I survive Lavan's house and my brother Esav and his
soldiers just to die here?"

So it is possible to read these verses as they are written,
understanding that because of Jacob's not illogical fears, and in
order to buy time, he remains prudently silent until he can confer
with his sons.[160]

But on the other hand, the Bible reader has just left Dinah in
physical and psychological tatters in Shechem's palace. We ache
for her, and we feel intense disappointment at her father's silence.
We who have been raised on tales of derring-do would like
nothing better than for Jacob — quite the man of action in his
youth — at the very least to utter the words of outrage that will
condemn Dinah's captor. The *midrashists*, too, are troubled by
Jacob's silence. Their hero, Jacob, may be silent, but in their minds
his silence does not equal passivity. So they tell us in detail what
Jacob *did*.[161]

When Jacob hears that Dinah has been raped, he speaks not a
word. Fear and shock were the reasons at first, but almost
instantaneously his calculating mind tells him to "play dumb."
And so the frightened but thoughtful Jacob keeps silent, feigning
deafness.[162] The servant or messenger who relays the awful news
evinces no response from Jacob, and leaves the patriarch's tent
disappointed. The *midrash* details what happens next.[163] Jacob
immediately calls in two of his most trusted servants who are also
experienced men-at-arms. He instructs them to make haste to
Shechem's palace, to slip inside and bring Dinah out. Jacob is
hoping to effect a commando-like lightning-raid, take the enemy
by surprise, and thus retrieve his daughter.

Unfortunately, Shechem is ready for them, and with his own
armed men he easily repels the raid. But he does not harm Jacob's
men. He figures he can turn them to his own use. So Shechem
puts his arms about Dinah and kisses her in full view of Jacob's
servants, whom Shechem instructs to watch from afar. Shechem
calculates that they will report back to Jacob that his daughter is

alive, is being held in Shechem's palace, and that Shechem appears to treat her with some affection and care.

When Jacob's two servants relay all this to their master, he knows to a certainty that the news of Dinah's abduction is not mere rumor; his daughter Dinah has in fact been defiled by Shechem, a powerful and clever man. Jacob appreciates that he has been rendered powerless until his sons' return. So Jacob does the next-best thing: he dispatches two of his wife's most trusted and experienced handmaidens to Shechem's palace with orders to watch over Dinah, to see to her needs and to remain steadfastly by her side. Shechem does not refuse entry to the maidservants, and in this way Dinah is comforted.

Jacob's textual silence, then, while it arouses the reader's indignation, is perhaps understandable if we put ourselves in Jacob's place. He must be feeling the unbearable weight of his guilt for having settled in that city instead of traveling onward to Beit-El and after that, back to his father's house. Jacob must surely be thinking that when he paid *one hundred kesitas* years before for the plot of land outside Shechem he had no foreknowledge that the purchase price would include his daughter's precious virginal blood.[164]

HAMOR APPROACHES JACOB

Shechem sends word to his father, ordering him to *take this girl for me to be my wife!* To be sure that his father heeds his words, Shechem also dispatches three of his men to Hamor's house to underscore his serious intent,[165] emphasizing that time is of the essence. The implication is that Shechem is in charge; but he still needs his father Hamor to make the ceremonial overtures to Jacob. It is obvious that the prince would not brook any hesitation on the part of Hamor. The reader should note that his imperious command to his father to "take this girl" uses the same Hebrew word for "take" as was used in verse 2 when Shechem abducted Dinah. This emphatic and commanding language associated with Shechem is likely a deliberate move by the text to allow us to appreciate his power and willfulness over not only Jacob's daughter, but even over his father.

Dutifully, Hamor goes out to speak with Jacob, to set up a meeting between the father of the prince of the Hivites and the father of the young princess of the house of Israel.

The Bible tells us exactly what Hamor says to Jacob and his sons, Dinah's brothers. It is likely—given Shechem's manner and bearing, coupled with the importance of the matter to him personally—that Shechem scripted the precise words as well as the scope of what his father was to say. We assume this because Hamor's words are eloquent for what they do *not* say!

Hamor spoke with them, saying, "My son, Shechem's, soul longs for your daughter; please give her to him as a wife. Intermarry with us; give your daughters to us, and take our daughters for yourselves. And you shall settle with us, and the land will be before you; settle and trade in it, and acquire a portion of it." Gen. 34:8–10

Note that **Hamor breathes not a word to Jacob of the abduction and rape of Dinah**, and of her present captivity. Astonishingly, if the reader had not suffered along with Dinah through the prior verses, we would have no inkling from Hamor's speech to Jacob that anything was amiss. He speaks for all the world as if this were a fairytale romance, awaiting only a nod and a handshake from both fathers and an exchange of gifts, to effect the match between his son and Jacob's daughter and a mingling of the two clans.

There is no doubt that that is precisely the scenario Shechem seeks to present. **He and Hamor open the discussion with Jacob and his sons with a deception**: not a word is to be uttered about Dinah's kidnap and rape, nor is there an offer of apology. They are possibly calculating that because Jacob was silent on the matter (verse 5), perhaps the brothers are not yet aware of what has befallen their sister. We must ask, what does Shechem seek to gain by this deception, this omission of the most salient facts in the negotiation? We have presented one argument that perhaps he intends to drive Dinah's bride-price down under the theory that she is no longer a virgin (never mind that he deflowered her!). But here, it seems possible that he wishes to present himself in the very best light to Dinah's father and brothers. And perhaps, too, Shechem's arrogant willfulness insulates him from the moral gravity of what he had done to Dinah, so that he actually thinks that Jacob will be glad of the offer of marriage, and never mind the circumstances.

This is borne out by Shechem's willingness in later verses (11, 12 and 19) to offer Jacob anything he might see fit to require in a marriage contract, implying that no price will be too high, no gift too extravagant for him to present to her family. Shechem is eager to believe that Jacob will accede to having him as a husband for his only daughter, except for the pesky condition of the required circumcision. And we see that he is the first Shechemite to submit to the condition and put himself under the knife. While the Bible text states in detail Hamor's words as well as the brothers' condition, nowhere do either Hamor or Shechem mention Shechem's rape of Dinah. In Shechem's reckoning, the rape he committed does not factor into the calculus of his worth as a prospective member of Jacob's family or as a mate to her. He cannily leaves it out of the discussion completely, knowing it would likely to spoil the deal.

The fact of Hamor and Shechem's active omission of any reference to Shechem's abduction and rape of Dinah in their discussions with her father and brothers is an unqualified lie. So is the omission of any reference to the fact that Shechem was still holding her prisoner. Dr. Paul Ekman, noted expert on the subject of lie detection and truth-telling, defines lying as "a deliberate choice to mislead a target without giving any notification of the intent to do so."[166] Concealment and misdirection are just two ways to lie, says Ekman, and Shechem engages in both in his "negotiations" with Dinah's brothers. Understanding Shechem's deception behavior is important, as the brothers' imminent answer to them will be a response in kind.

Shechem and Hamor are adept at telling their audience only what they think the audience will tolerate. The *midrash*[167] says that when they present their request to their fellow Shechemites that they all submit to the condition of circumcision, they tell their countrymen that *they* will have first pick of the Israelite girls (verse 21) — not that the Israelites will have first chance to give and to select wives, as the offer states (verse 9). Further, that Jacob's livestock, his possessions and all their animals — camels and donkeys included — will become "ours"[168] (verse 23). Hamor and Shechem speak convincingly to their countrymen saying, "These people are exceedingly heavy with wealth. What's more, they are relatively few in number, while we are many and strong. In the end, everything that belongs to them will be ours. Whether we pay them for their houses and fields, or take them by theft and by force, in the end we will own it all."[169]

Hamor also knows that "the land" is precious to Jacob[170] and his family, and so, when speaking to Jacob and his sons, he inserts (at verse 10) the incentive that once their two clans are joined Jacob will be able to avail himself of all the land he sees. But the sly Hamor is careful to use a term that hints at "dwelling on a *temporary* basis" (the word is similar to *sukkot*, meaning temporary booths)[171] rather than permanently owning the land. Hamor and Shechem have no intention of allowing Jacob and the Israelites to fully integrate into their society. They intend to dominate, overrun and ultimately control all that Jacob calls his own.

So we see that Shechem readily agreed to whatever condition the brothers placed in his path, all the while planning to sell the idea of circumcision to his countrymen in the one way he knew would win the day: he would ensnare them with their own avarice for Jacob's wealth.

THE AFTERMATH: THE BROTHERS' REACTION

In the meantime, and taking a small step backward in this rapidly-moving story, the Torah tells us that *Jacob's sons came from the field when they heard;* **the men were distressed and very angry,** *for [Shechem] had committed a disgusting outrage in Israel by laying with the daughter of Jacob, as such a thing was not done.* (Gen. 34:7)

Somehow, the brothers hear about what has happened to their sister, and they drop what they are doing to hasten back to their father's tent.[172] The Torah presents two reactions: first, that when they hear about the rape they are saddened or depressed[173] at the news, and second, that they are hotly angry.

First, they are saddened at the shame, debasement, and physical violation that their sister was made to suffer. They, too, feel her humiliation, according to the *midrash*.[174] Their deep sadness is for the loss of their childhood playmate and sister. They are in real pain at having to renounce, or give up, "their pure, innocent Dinah . . . [whom] they had lost even if they would succeed in getting her back out of the hands of Shechem."[175]

Coupled with their feelings of loss and mourning, the brothers are shamed by Shechem's vile deed because the rape debases not only their sister specifically and terribly; it also brings disgrace upon Jacob's entire family. And, as we have seen, revenge of some sort *against Jacob* was part of Shechem's initial reason—if not a prime motivator—for the abduction and rape of Dinah: he sought to ravage *the daughter of Jacob*, to strike a blow against Jacob in particular.

As for the brothers' hot anger, this is, perhaps, the more predictable reaction. Shechem's violation of their sister filled Dinah's brothers with "fiery indignation."[176] The Torah explains the brothers' anger saying, it is *because he [Shechem] had done a disgusting deed to Israel to lie with a daughter of Jacob*. The "disgusting deed," the rape of Dinah, is, in the Torah's words, a *nevalah*. The root-word for *nevalah* means, in its various uses, ruin, rubbish, a withering, a death of moral forces, a previously healthy, strong being turning to ruin, and to treat something as if it were worthless. A *nevalah* is an act showing utter moral degeneration; a disgraceful act.[177] This is the word used by the biblical narrator to justify Dinah's brothers' depression and anger when they return from the field. It is not an everyday biblical occurrence to call an event a *nevalah*, so this is the reader's clear clue to how the brothers interpret the awful news. Shechem's act was unheard-of, and the brothers' emotional reactions are real and appropriate responses to the news of their only-sister's rape.

Another puzzle piece that rounds out the picture of the brothers' reactions is an appreciation of their ages. The *midrash*[178] tells us that Shimon and Levi, Dinah's full brothers from their mother Leah, were, respectively, about sixteen and fifteen years old. This is old enough to be a shepherd, old enough to have their emotions—shame and indignation and anger—run hot in their strong and virile young bodies, and also young enough to resent their father's silence and to choose to avenge their wronged sister themselves.

And the Torah text actually tells us the reason for the brothers' dual reaction: *Because he [Shechem] had committed a vile outrage in Israel to lay with the daughter of Jacob; for such a thing was not done.* It was widely known and accepted among the Canaanite nations[179] — it was not simply a quaint convention applying to the family of Jacob alone — that violating a virgin from such a respected family was simply not done. Or, alternatively, that even if the Canaanites *did* do such loathsome acts as abducting and despoiling virgins (the *midrash*[180] points to Jacob's grandmothers' harrowing experiences as an example), still they knew for certain that *for Israel or Jacob* this was a vile deed — a "predatory behavior"[181] — not to be tolerated, as Jacob was a man of stature, considered "a prince in Israel."[182]

THE AFTERMATH: SHECHEM'S PLEA

Even though Shechem dispatched his father, Hamor, to negotiate with Jacob — one father addressing another — we see from verse 11 that Shechem has injected himself into the negotiations.[183] *Both* Hamor and Shechem are now addressing Jacob and his sons. Shechem has jumped in either because his father was a poor negotiator or simple-minded[184] and Shechem feared he was not making a convincing case on his behalf, or because Shechem's impulsive and aggressive personality propelled him to speak his mind on a matter that concerned him so intimately.[185] Or perhaps Hamor told his son that in his own mind he saw no hope of success, because speaking as a father, Hamor knew that in Jacob's place no amount of compensation would be an acceptable exchange for his daughter's stolen honor.[186]

Shechem is eager to marry Dinah, to negotiate a bride-price for her that will be so generous in her father's eyes (and in the eyes of their world) that it will, effectively, erase the deep shame of his having taken and defiled her. We can envision the scene of the negotiation. A long table is set up in Jacob's luxurious tent.

At the head sits Jacob, the aged patriarch and clan leader, and ranged to his right along one side of the table and standing along the tent walls are Dinah's eleven brothers. To Jacob's left and seated opposite the brothers are Hamor and Shechem, the royal rulers of the city. Shechem seeks favor in the eyes of Jacob and the brothers, and tells them to name their price for Dinah and he will meet it; his goal is that they will give him "the maiden" for a wife.

If this is a negotiation, it is a strange one, indeed. Shechem, who surely drove a hard bargain when he negotiated a top-dollar price from Jacob in the earlier land deal, actually appears to hand Jacob the reigns in this transaction. This tactic would ordinarily assure that his adversaries would not doubt his sincerity now — when he offers to give them whatever bride-price they demand — as they already know him to be a formidable negotiator. But here we see that Shechem's open-handed offer is not the issue. For the brothers, the sole issue is the besmirched honor of the family and, integral to that, Dinah's extreme personal dishonor. This is their preoccupying interest, plus their desire to wrest her from Shechem's clutches. With these goals in mind they respond to Shechem.

THE BROTHERS RESPOND TO SHECHEM

An aspect of the negotiation that often is overlooked in the romantic rush to legitimize Shechem in light of his about-face — although Hamor and Shechem never raise the subject — is the brothers' keen awareness that *Dinah is still being held in the house of her abductor; she has not been freed.* This turns the "amicable" conversation between Hamor/Shechem and Jacob/the brothers into a sham. The fact that their sister is still *in extremis* colors the brothers' responses to Shechem's offer that he will pay whatever bride-price they will name. In the words of one commentary, "All this sounds very nice and fair, and would indeed be so had the gracious lord had the grace to first return the girl to her family, and then, when she was free, sue for her hand." [187]

But because Dinah is still being held prisoner, the negotiation is not a "free" one,[188] and the brothers' goodwill as well as the girl's agreement to marry her rapist cannot be expected or inferred.

Modern-day events that reveal negotiations between terrorists who kidnap innocent civilians and the law enforcement authorities who promise anything in order to secure the hostages' release, are a testament to this. What Hamor and Shechem are attempting to do is to put the gloss of legitimacy on "an act of bare-faced rape and violence."[189] The reader should understand that the brothers will dissemble, will appear to agree, while all the while plotting their sister's rescue and the defeat of her captor. The captor — their sister's rapist — is an outlaw beneath his princely trappings, and the brothers will use whatever means they have at their disposal to outwit him and free their sister.

This is precisely what the Bible tells us in verse 13: *Jacob's sons answered Shechem and Hamor **b'mirmah — with trickery** — . . . because he had defiled Dinah, their sister.* The various *midrashim* also translate the Bible's word *b'mirmah* as "with cleverness" or "with wisdom."[190] The absurdity — the impossibility — of any pretense at honest, arm's-length negotiation while Dinah is still being held captive is not lost on these commentators. The brothers' "cleverness" was to pretend to come to a plausible agreement when in reality their overarching intention was to overcome Shechem and his countrymen and rescue their sister. Shechem's defilement of Dinah cancelled out the rules of good-faith negotiations. In their minds Shechem had thrown down the gauntlet and they were taking up the challenge, fighting fire with fire, guile with guile, deception with deception. [191]

The text demonstrates this. The brothers state clearly at the outset in verse 14: *We are unable to do this thing, to give our sister to an uncircumcised man, for that is a disgrace to us.* This is their first response to Shechem's offer, and it is utterly true. They tell Shechem and his father that they cannot give their sister to him; that such an act is a humiliation to their clan. If Shechem had truly understood and believed the brothers, he would have ended the discussion then and there and the two sides may well have engaged in a pitched battle. But Shechem took their words to be their opening gambit in the negotiation. The brothers' next words — stating the condition that Shechem and all the males of the city undergo circumcision—was understood by Shechem to be the main hurdle to an agreement. Verse 17 sums up the circumcision ruse: *But if you do not heed us and become circumcised, we will take our daughter and go.*

The brothers' response was intended to allow Shechem to assume that if he and the entire male population of his city were to become circumcised, the marriage could go forward. And indeed, *their words were satisfactory in the eyes of Hamor and in the eyes of Shechem.* Shechem was so anxious to resume sexual relations with Dinah, *Jacob's daughter* (verse 19), that he was the first one to undergo circumcision. And because *he was the most respected of all his father's household* and the prince of the city, he expected his countrymen to follow suit.

✠ ✠ ✠

GENESIS 34:20–31

Hamor and his son Shechem came to the gate of their city; and they spoke to the people of their city and said,

"These people are peaceable toward us; they will settle on the land and trade within it, and the land, behold, is large [enough] for them. We will take for ourselves their daughters as wives, and we will give our daughters to them.

"But there is one condition; the people will only acquiesce to dwell with us and to become a single people if all our males become circumcised as their males are.

"Their livestock, their possessions, and all their animals — will they not be ours? We must only acquiesce to them and they will settle with us."

And all the people going out of the gates of his city heeded Hamor and his son Shechem; and all the males who went forth out of the gates of his city were circumcised.

And it happened that on the third day, when they were in pain, that two of Jacob's sons, Shimon and Levi, Dinah's brothers, each took his sword, and they came confidently to the city and they killed every male.

And Hamor and Shechem his son they killed at the point of the sword; and they took Dinah from Shechem's house and they left.

Jacob's sons came upon the slain, and they plundered the city that had defiled their sister.

Their flocks and their cattle and their donkeys and whatever was in the city and in the field they took. And all their wealth, and their children and wives they took captive, and they plundered, too, everything in the house.

And Jacob said to Shimon and Levi, "You have aggrieved me, and you have caused me to be hated among the inhabitants of the land, among the Canaanite and among the Perizzite; and I am few in number and if they should gather together and attack me I will be annihilated, I and my household."

And they said, "Should he treat our sister like a harlot?!"

CONVINCING THE SHECHEMITES

So Shechem and Hamor gathered the city's fathers at the gates of Shechem and, speaking to them and to as many of his fellow Shechemites as crowded around, Shechem and his father began to talk.[192] First and foremost, they told their neighbors that Jacob and his family had come in peace.[193] Furthermore, they convinced the elders that it would benefit them economically and socially to accede to the brothers' condition and become circumcised. The Shechemites would have the pick of the Hebrews' beautiful daughters to take as wives, and they would eventually acquire all the Hebrews' vast flocks and livestock. They had nothing to lose by absorbing Jacob's family into their society to live as one people, and much to gain. The single precondition of circumcision was but a fleeting physical inconvenience they must endure beforehand.

There is nothing in the Torah text that says the Shechemites demurred or objected to being circumcised. This may be because the mere act of circumcision was not unique to the family of Abraham; other ancient Near East societies also practiced it,[194] only not, of course, in the manner of the Hebrews, where it symbolized their Covenant with the One God. It is also possible that the Shechemites were eager for "new blood;" that is, a new society of women to choose from, and an infusion of new breeds of sheep and livestock, donkeys and camels to augment their own.

Frymer-Kensky agrees that economic considerations drove the Shechemites to accept the brothers' condition. They were eager to form some sort of union with Jacob, whose flocks were prime, abundant and legendary. The urban Shechemites would thereby gain a "pastoral partner, a market for their agricultural and urban products, and a steady supplier of meat, wool, [and] leather."[195] And not insignificantly, they would also enlarge their choice of marital partners.

But the *midrash*[196] reads the Bible text closely, and sees a dark shadow of compulsion in verse 24, which states: *And they heeded Hamor and his son Shechem, all those who came through the city's gates; and all the males who exited the city gates were circumcised.* The repetition of the phrase "city gates" in the context of Shechem's outlining to the Shechemites his "request" that they all fall in with his wishes leads the *midrash* to a different conclusion than a simple reading of the text would indicate.

Once Shechem put the word out and gathered the elders, the members of the court, and the upper-crust at the city's gates, the other curious Shechemites crowded around, as well. His clever plan was to attract everyone to *the city gates* and then to make his pitch, hoping for unanimous voluntary compliance. But in the event some of the males demurred — an understandable and predictable reaction — Shechem was ready. He had quickly and surreptitiously closed off the area surrounding the open square at the city gates, trapping the Shechemites inside.

Human nature being what it is, the proposal to absorb Jacob, his household, his wealth and his flocks is easy for the crowd to accept. But once Shechem explains the condition of mass circumcision, there is a movement among the men toward the exit. They have no intention of putting themselves under the knife; that was going *too* far. But the prince has closed them in. The Shechemites understand, then, that his proposal for "voluntary" compliance is a veiled demand. The forced, mass circumcision[197] occurred right there, in tents hastily erected *at the city's gates*, and was performed by Shechem's servants. The Shechemites understood that in this matter they were pawns in the hands of their prince. They were being forced to suffer the crude surgery because of Shechem's lust for the Hebrew girl he had stolen.

THE BROTHERS EXACT REVENGE
AND RESCUE DINAH

Still, the Shechemites do not protest, because after all is said and done they are eager to lay their hands on Jacob's wealth.[198]

Shimon and Levi bide their time. Perhaps they are waiting to see if their father will authorize a raid to extract Dinah from her captivity. It is possible that the brothers, sensitive to the fact that they — and their sister Dinah — are children of Leah, and not of Jacob's favored wife, fear that Jacob's silence and inaction mean that he will do nothing to rescue the girl![199] In which case, the brothers realized, Dinah's fate is in *their* hands.

So they wait until the third day following the circumcisions, when the Shechemites are in a state of great pain and discomfort. Some *midrashim* say that "the third day" specified in verse 25 actually coincided with the third day after Dinah's rape;[200] that *that* was the actual day of the circumcisions, the day the Shechemites were distracted with pain.

The Shechemites' discomfort was exacerbated by their acute feelings of regret for having allowed themselves to be convinced to be circumcised.[201] They feel nothing for Jacob's God, nothing but avarice for Jacob's wealth and holdings, and the future promise of intermarriage with the virginal Hebrew girls is a distant event that offers them no immediate surcease. They grumble and speak bitterly amongst themselves about what their prince's latest sexual escapade has wrought upon them. What's more, they realize, too late, that Hamor and Shechem have glorified the benefits and belittled the discomforts of the deal they struck with the girl's brothers. The Shechemites rue the day their prince abducted the virgin Jewess, and think that *this time* they are paying dearly for turning a blind eye to his lawlessness.

It is on this day that Shimon and Levi, Dinah's brothers, take up their swords and, in the guise of bearing healing elixirs, they enter the city and, while the men of the city are napping,[202] catch them unaware and slay them. Next, they enter the palace on the same ruse and seek out[203] Shechem's chambers. First, as they did in all the other houses they entered, they send any Shechemite women and children from the chamber, so that they are alone with the prince. Then quickly and silently the brothers run their swords through the rapist and his father.[204] Dinah's brothers — likely in their late teens at the time of their revenge[205] — cannot resist staring into Shechem's stunned eyes before killing him, willing their sister's defiler to go to his death knowing that Dinah's brothers had avenged her rape.

Their grisly duty done, they exit the chamber soundlessly and close and secure the door behind them, escaping undetected.[206]

When the Bible narrates the events of *the third day* (verse 25), it first identifies Shimon and Levi as *two of Jacob's sons*. It further identifies them as *brothers of Dinah*. A *midrashic* understanding of the first expression is that their avenging killings were done against the wishes of their father, Jacob, and that the two sons acted alone.[207] As for the phrase *brothers of Dinah*, this does not serve as a useful identifier for the actors in this segment, considering that Dinah had *eleven* brothers. But there really is no ambiguity for the Bible reader. The verse sandwiches the two brothers' names between the names of Jacob and Dinah, so the first ambiguity is laid to rest almost immediately. *And two of Jacob's sons, Shimon and Levi,* **brothers of Dinah***, took their swords . . .* We are meant to understand from the phrasing that the two sons of Jacob who did this deed *also* were the *only* two of Dinah's "brothers" to bear that sibling banner. The *midrash*[208] explains that because Shimon and Levi put their lives in jeopardy in order to save Dinah, *only they*, of all Jacob's sons, behaved toward her in the truest manner of "brothers," and so the Torah identifies them as such.

The brothers' revenge killings of Shechem and Hamor, while they might remind modern readers of frontier justice and vigilantism, are an understandable measure-for-measure act in the context of the ancient Near East. In the eyes of the brothers, of Jacob, of the Shechemites, and of the surrounding Canaanites, killing their sister's kidnapper/rapist (as well as Hamor, his enabler) was seen as necessary and possibly expected behavior.

Malcolm Gladwell, in his book *Outliers*[209], discusses the herdsmen's "culture of honor," a version of which we are witnessing here in these verses describing Shimon and Levi's behavior. Gladwell describes a culture where herdsmen in one family or clan will perceive an insult to one member of their clan as an insult against the entirety, and will carry out revenge accordingly. This culture took hold many centuries ago, and persists to this day among herdsmen of the Scottish Highlands, Sicily, Basque Spain, and even the mountains of Kentucky. The harsh life of the herdsman bred fearless families who populated inhospitable terrain, lived on remote farms, herded sheep, and were dominated by powerful patriarchs. The credo was quick and merciless retaliation for — at its most benign — overgrazing by another clan's sheep, for example, and swung to revenge killings for more serious assaults against family members. Clan members' memories were long, and the reach of clan justice stretched sometimes for over a century, leading oftentimes to thousands of deaths.

In light of Gladwell's description, we can appreciate Dinah's brothers' response to their sister's rape. They were responding consistently with the "herdsman's culture of honor" that persisted in the ancient Near East among powerful nomadic families. The brothers were avenging their virgin sister's honor as well as the honor of their clan. This was the clan's manner of effecting justice, and as I already have discussed, Shechem and Hamor had every reason to expect a retaliation would be targeted and forthcoming.[210] "Violence [in such 'culture-of-honor' situations] wasn't for economic gain, it was personal. You fought over your honor."[211]

Shimon and Levy's ringing last words support this statement: *Should our sister be treated like a harlot?!* Dinah's personal honor was identical to the family's honor in their eyes.

Remember, too, that Shechem and Hamor affirmatively did *not* bring up the fact of Dinah's abduction and rape when they were negotiating a marriage price, nor did Shechem set Dinah free. This cover-up behavior is evidence both of their guilty knowledge of Shechem's wrongdoing and of their attempt to avoid the predictable consequences and backlash flowing from it.

Despite Hamor and Shechem having deliberately ignored the act of rape, they were still made to pay with their lives for it. As we see from the Bible text, Dinah's brothers had "blood in their eyes" and they executed a premeditated commando-style raid to retaliate for Shechem's violation of their sister. Shechem had stolen Dinah's innocence, robbed her of her future, killed any hopes she had had to live her life as a proper Hebrew princess. As such, he paid the penalty with his own life.

By instructing any servants or onlookers to leave the two men alone in their rooms, the brothers "bought" time in which they were able to move swiftly and undetected from house to house, encountering no resistance.[212] Once the city — of anywhere from 500[213] to 5,000[214] inhabitants — was secure, and Shechem and Hamor were dead, Shimon and Levi moved through Shechem's palace, found Dinah — who had been secreted in a locked room — carried her outside, and brought her back alive to their father's camp and her mother's arms.

Earlier in this chapter I discussed whether or not Dinah went willingly with her rescuers. There is some *midrashic* indication that the brothers dragged Dinah from the palace.[215] While it may certainly mean that she wished to remain *with Shechem*, it is more likely that she did not wish to be subjected to the inevitable humiliation and censure that a girl raped by an uncircumcised Canaanite would face.[216] Dinah's shame was so great that she dreaded being brought out for her brothers to see; she feared being brought home to face her father's temper. That the brothers "took Dinah and left" may mean what it says: that they bundled her up, hid her face from any prying eyes, carried her out and brought her home. Later on in this chapter I will discuss Dinah's fate after her return.

The *midrash*[217] explains that it was permissible under the Hebrews' code of laws to rescue Dinah *alive* and return her to her home. It was *not* required that *she* be put to death — as was her rapist — in order to avenge the shame brought upon her and upon her father's house. Because Dinah *had been forced* to submit sexually to her abductor and was held prisoner in his locked palace against her will, law and lore hold her blameless. Her rescue and return to her father's house was proper from the point of view of the clan. Whether it was what Dinah preferred is, of course, never discussed in the Bible, but was explored earlier in this chapter.

Problems arise when we read that the brothers kill *all* the males in Shechem as they lay recuperating from their circumcisions. It is not clear to the *midrashists* whether it was Shimon and Levi acting alone—or whether the nine other brothers acted either on their own or in concert with the other two—to kill all the town's men. Did Dinah's brothers go too far? Or should this entire event be considered, in effect, a wartime situation, so that their plundering of the city and taking the women and children as captives was permissible?

In the words of one commentator, with the killing of all the men of Shechem begins the "blameworthy part" of the brothers' behavior.[218] Killing Shechem and Hamor was considered an acceptable, measure-for-measure execution of clan-style justice. But the fact that they went further and killed the city's ailing and unarmed men and looted their city, in effect made the town's inhabitants "pay for the crime of their lords."[219] This was perhaps unjustified.

While the brothers' killing of the town males is often condemned, there is *midrashic* argument cited by numerous and varied sources, including Maimonides,[220] that credibly mitigates the brothers' **revenge on the entire city**.

When Shechem abducted Dinah, took her against her will to his palace, and raped and abused her, this was not done without at least the tacit knowledge of the city's inhabitants. In fact, the commentaries are clear that **the entire city actually knew** about Dinah's kidnap and rape.[221] The dancing girls who lured Dinah knew; Prince Shechem's household servants and kitchen staff knew; his father and the town elders knew; and the knowledge of his deed passed quickly through the medium of gossip among the town's inhabitants so that by day's end the entire city knew that Shechem had "taken" Jacob's daughter. Ironically, only Jacob's sons, out in the fields, did not know.

Whether the Shechemites had witnessed this type of behavior by their prince on prior occasions, or whether this was a first, the townspeople knew precisely what Shechem had done to Dinah, *and that it was forbidden*. According to the Noahide Laws[222] that governed the post-Flood peoples, seducing and forcefully violating the daughter of one's fellow man was punishable with the death penalty.[223] The city's inhabitants, by turning a blind eye to Shechem's lawlessness and to an innocent girl's plight, were *all*, therefore, morally and legally culpable. They were obligated not only to stop Shechem, but — if they were powerless to interfere during the actual abduction and rape — they were still required to bring Shechem to justice afterwards. Instead, they did nothing. And for this reason they were *all* liable for the death penalty.[224]

The reader will recall that in Part One of this book, in the discussion of Lot and the city of Sodom, the Talmud specifically cites the Sodomites' deafness to the pleas of an innocent and blameless maiden as the final reason for the city's utter destruction. Perhaps the brothers' revenge on the men of the city of Shechem is a similar exacting of justice for a like crime.

Here, in verses 25 and 26, there is an odd sequence to the brothers' actions that suggests why they slay all the males in the city. The text says that they first killed every male, *and then* that they slew Hamor and Shechem. Why did they not go directly to the palace and slay their main foe straightaway? One *midrashist*[225] notes this and suggests that Shimon and Levi had come by stealth into the city, intending just that; to do away with Shechem and to free Dinah, then return swiftly to their camp. But all the city's inhabitants, anticipating some sort of reprisal by Jacob, had encircled the prince's palace, forming a human barrier, protecting their king and his son. With this act, the people of the city became accomplices after-the-fact to the kidnap and rape of an innocent girl. Shimon and Levi had no choice, then, but to slay them all if they were to achieve their objective and rescue their sister.

Perhaps the most compelling argument in favor of the brothers' actions is that this entire episode constituted an actual battle, a war, in effect, between Prince Shechem and his father and the city that bore his name on the one hand, and Jacob, his sons, his children and his possessions and way of life on the other.[226] Shechem drew first-blood when he abducted Jacob's only daughter, raped her, and held her incommunicado in his palace. That Jacob and his sons bided their time, strategized their retaliation, and simultaneously held "peace talks" with the enemy is wartime *modus operandi*. A lightning-quick, bold commando raid freed their hostage sister and won the day, and to ensure their future safety they killed the enemy males in addition to the rapist and his father.[227]

There is even a prior Biblical instance in Genesis of hostage-taking of a Hebrew by a Canaanite king, and of a swift, audacious rescue by a close relative. It takes place in chapter 14 of Genesis and is known as the battle of the Four Kings against the Five Kings. It is a story of luck; of a battle that is waged and won by dint of surprise and raw courage; of a successful rescue and homecoming. This is the story of Abraham's rescue of his nephew Lot, who had been taken captive when Sodom was attacked. When Abraham hears about Lot's situation, Abraham plans and executes a daring nighttime ambush. The battle was surely not a bloodless one, but the Bible tells us mostly about Lot's rescue by Abraham, and of the return of Lot's wealth, women and possessions.

There is no hint in that story that Abraham's military action constituted an overreaction; it is understood that Abraham and his servants are few in number; that to save Lot Abraham is justified in employing tactics of ambush, deception and bloodshed. It is likely that in the ancient Near East it was known that swift and ruthless reprisal was necessary in order to retrieve captives or hostages. This is understandable, as in a nomadic society war captives—if they are kept alive—are portable currency. They can be sold as slaves in a moment, and transported down an unfamiliar route, never to be seen again. Speedy and fierce ruthlessness is therefore the essential mode of rescue if liberator and hostage are to make it home alive.

Dinah's brothers' deception and incursion into the enemy's midst was brilliant, necessary, and fraught with danger. They literally took their lives in their hands when they walked into the palace with their swords unsheathed. Rather than heap censure on them for overreacting, perhaps the reader should transport him- or herself to the Shechemite city, or into the prince's locked bedroom, and ask what the correct course of action was in that time and that place, given the stakes.

[Afterwards,] Jacob's sons took booty from the city that had defiled their sister. Gen. 34:27

Some analysts look askance at the brothers' taking booty from the city. Was it necessary, after all? It has been said that what began as a noble effort to rescue their sister was tainted by the looting.[228] The argument is that taking spoils in effect turned the brothers into "takers," like the Shechemites.

In fact, in the Bible, the taking of spoils is problematic. The most dramatic example of misuse of spoils occurs many years in the future, when king Saul disobeys God's command and not only takes choice spoils from the Amalekites after a battle, but also spares their king from death.[229] It is for this act of disobedience, misplaced compassion, and failure to own up to his error, that God takes the kingship from Saul and gives it to David. Similarly, centuries later, in the Persian kingdom of Shushan, after Esther and Mordechai have foiled Haman's plan to annihilate the Jews, they wage a pitched battle against those bent on destroying them. *Megillat* Esther tells us that while the Jews slew 75,000 of their enemies, they *did not take any spoils* in that war.[230]

The *midrash*[231] understands verse 27 (*Jacob's sons **took booty** from **the city** that had defiled their sister*) to be the biblical narrator's *explanation* for the brothers' looting of Shechem. As was suggested earlier, the Bible says that "the city" — and not only Shechem, the rapist — had defiled Dinah by allowing her to be taken and ravished with their knowledge. Thus, taking spoils from the offending *city* and laying waste the city itself mirrors precisely what befell Dinah, and as such may be justifiable. It also might be a biblical hint that because Shechem the man and Shechem the city bear the same name they are indistinguishable for purposes of the brothers' revenge.

As spoils of war, Jacob's sons took the Shechemites' gold and pearls, their silver coins, their hoarded treasure, their sheep, cattle and donkeys.[232] They denuded Shechem's palace, leaving nothing but ruins in their wake.[233] They laid the city as well as its surrounding fields to waste so that it could sustain no life. As for the Shechemite women and children, they took them into their camp as part of the spoils of war. Jacob's sons intended that there would be no Shechemite family left intact[234] to spread the tale among the Canaanites that Shechem had despoiled their sister.

In a striking and ironic parallel, the very items of wealth that Shechem listed as an incentive in his argument to convince his townsmen to agree to circumcision ("Jacob's daughters, his women, his possessions, his sheep, cattle and donkeys—*will they not all be ours?*") are the same items of booty that Jacob's sons took as victor's spoils.[235] The Bible text (verse 23) is clear: The Shechemites had planned to take all of Jacob's wealth, women and livestock after they acceded to circumcision! What Jacob's sons did was turn the tables on them through stratagem and raw bravery. This equivalence is often overlooked in a rush to condemn Jacob's sons' behavior as an overreaction. But this measure-for-measure yardstick makes the brothers' actions more understandable, though the cruelty of war and death is never easy to bear.

JACOB BREAKS HIS SILENCE

For the first time in this entire sad and tragic episode, Jacob speaks up. He addresses Shimon and Levi saying,

> "*You have upset me, brought trouble to me by besmirching my reputation among the inhabitants of the land, among the Canaanites and the Perizzites. And I am few in number, and they will [now] gather themselves against me and attack me, and I will be destroyed, I and my house.*" Gen. 34:30

Jacob's anger centers on two arguments. His first concern is for his honor as a man-of-his-word; his second concerns his fear that the surrounding Canaanites will exact revenge by banding together and waging war against him.

As for Jacob's first admonition, he tells Shimon and Levi that by their act of killing all the males in the city they have clouded his honor among the surrounding peoples. Jacob is referring to his sons' having ignored the pact they struck of coexistence-for-circumcision; that they gave their word and then ignored the agreement and slew the men even after they had submitted to the condition. Jacob is a nomad, and his good name and the ability to travel, trade and be trusted is crucial to his existence. He feels dishonored by his sons' actions.

With Jacob's second reproach he admits to a fear of reprisal by the surrounding Canaanite nations. *And I am few in number* is his explanation. He worries that the surrounding nations, in a show of camaraderie with the Shechemites, will band together, outnumber and attack him, and annihilate him and the entire family he has worked for decades to create.

Both Jacob's arguments make perfect sense on their face. Honor and security — the moral and the practical reasons for his anger — are sullied and endangered by Shimon and Levi's audacious victory over Shechem. Not only will Jacob be hampered in his ability to trade if his honor is questionable, but if the surrounding peoples become his sworn enemies, he and his family are exposed and vulnerable to attack wherever they wander.

But on closer examination, Jacob's angry condemnation of Shimon and Levi raises some questions. This writer cannot help but contrast Jacob's speech here with his silence in reaction to his daughter's kidnap, rape and captivity. The common element of fear is present in both his reactions, but instead of experiencing sympathy for a wronged and terrified old man the reader is losing admiration for a father who cowers in silence when an innocent girl is ravished, but lashes out in anger when she is avenged. Where was his anger and outrage *then*?

And why lash out at the two sons who showed courage and risked their lives to free their captive sibling? In light of the pervasive sibling rivalry and hatred, the mistrust and blood-feuds that we have seen thus far in the book of Genesis, Shimon and Levi's courage and success at retrieving their sister Dinah are to be lauded. Yet not a word of praise issues from Jacob's mouth, or gratitude to them for saving his daughter. Perhaps Jacob just does not see the correctness and symmetry of Shimon and Levi's act of brothers-saving-sister. The Bible reader knows that still to come in the biblical narrative is Jacob's utter disregard for his sons' sensibilities when he shows blatant and inappropriate favoritism to his son Joseph.

We should reflect that so far in his own life Jacob has engaged in a pattern of filial behavior that is far from blameless. He has tricked his father and wronged his own brother, fomenting an escape into the desert and two decades of hatred and fear; he has wed two sisters, exacerbating and enabling the women's lifelong rivalry; he treated his wife Leah so badly that she spent years in misery knowing she was hated; and he exploded in anger at his beloved Rachel when she pleaded with him to intercede on her behalf to end her infertility. Obviously, Jacob is not adept at communicating effectively with those closest to him. Here, when he should be tenderly receiving his daughter back into the fold, he never interacts with her at all, instead issuing an angry harangue at his sons, her liberators.

Also, given Jacob's past deceptions and trickery, one could say that Shimon and Levi's deception and rout of the Shechemites is a "chip off the old block." If Jacob recognizes the mirror held up to himself, there is no inkling of this in the text. Perhaps, seeing too much of himself in his sons' actions, Jacob lashes out in anger; he does not wish them to be as he was.

Sadly, Jacob's anger does not diminish with time. Half a lifetime into the future, on his deathbed, Jacob will again express his disapproval of Shimon and Levi. There, in Gen. 49:5–7, Jacob harks back to their teen-aged killing spree in Shechem. Addressing Shimon and Levi as a dyad rather than individually, he says: *Shimon and Levi are brothers; [but] instruments of violence are their means of acquisition.* Interestingly, though, Jacob begins by acknowledging that these two—of all his sons—have earned the right to be called "brothers," caring, as they have done, for even the weakest member of the communal whole that is their family.[236] Perhaps, all those years later, Jacob is expressing an indication that their act of brotherhood was laudable.

Nevertheless, Jacob goes on to curse the two brothers' anger and cruelty,[237] — though he does not curse the brothers themselves — and he predicts that they will disperse among the other tribes rather than own portions of land within the community of Israel.

But there is a subtle indication in the Bible a mere five verses earlier in the same deathbed scene that Jacob has, in fact and over time, come to "affirm"[238] Simon and Levi's conquest of Shechem. Jacob says to Joseph, in referring to his future inheritance, that he will give him "the portion which **I** took out of the hand of the Amorite with **my** sword and with **my** bow." (Gen. 48:22, emphasis added.) It is fascinating and significant that Jacob, at the end of his life, has seemingly come to adopt the two brothers' audacious conquest *as his own.*

So we see that Jacob goes to his grave ambivalent about the brothers' actions. While he appears to soften somewhat toward Shimon and Levi for having acted "as brothers," and even refers to their conquest as his own, still he harbors anger at their youthful violence in Shechem.

As for Jacob's second argument — the practical concern of fear of reprisal — one can ask, where is Jacob's derring-do, the courage and spunk that he showed when facing down his brother's army? For that matter, he need only reflect that his eleven sons have just this day overcome a city of anywhere from five hundred to five thousand people. And now that the few have utterly destroyed the many — with no loss of life among Jacob's sons — it would seem that Jacob's fear would be unfounded. To the contrary, it would be more logical that when the surrounding peoples hear about what the sons of Jacob have wrought in Shechem, rather than rush to attack they will now run for cover when Jacob's clan is on the road. We will see that that is in fact the case.

SHIMON AND LEVI RESPOND

Shimon and Levi have the last word in this chapter and in Dinah's story. Their response is only four Hebrew words, but it is pitch-perfect; these two exhausted warrior-shepherds have just rescued their captive sister and slain more men in one day than professional soldiers might slay in a lifetime. Their laconic response is the distillation of their motivation. To Jacob's two-pronged verbal attack they respond: *Should he treat our sister like a harlot?!*

Let us imagine the scene. Shimon and Levi, two fit and agile young men barely finishing the second decade of their lives, are, in today's parlance, mountain men. They reside in the inhospitable desert hills, camp out in the open, and fend for themselves and their flocks and livestock for days or weeks at a time. They are a hybrid sort. They are accustomed to surviving out-of-doors in quasi-desert terrain, to fending off lions, bears, snakes, jackals and human predators. But they also are civilized Hebrew family men who live peaceably as nomads, and hew to the beliefs of the One God. They are self-reliant, physically and spiritually courageous young men, raised in the bosom of a wealthy nomadic family.

They have just walked into their home camp, Shimon carrying his sister, Dinah, in his arms, wrapped completely in his capacious saddle blanket. The two brothers silently and gently deposit Dinah in their mother's tent, instruct the women to "take care with her," and then present themselves at their father's tent. The two are covered in sweat, and stained with blood up to their shoulders. They do not dare to enter their father's sanctum in such a state. So Jacob comes out to them. The nine other brothers stand supportively behind and around Shimon and Levi. The other brothers, who had looted the city after Shimon and Levi had dispatched the Shechemite men, stand together, ready to hear whatever their father has to say. Perhaps they expect their father to acknowledge their bravery and express his gratitude for bringing Dinah home.

But as we have seen, Jacob does not thank them. He does not even acknowledge the rescue of his raped and battered only daughter. Instead, he admonishes the two ringleaders, exhibiting worry for his honor and fearing Canaanite retaliation.

The brothers must be breathing hard. They have been clever tacticians and valiant in battle, and now, their adrenaline still pumping, they stand silent as their father calls them to task. They do not waste their breath as they respond. Their four-word answer — *ha-kezonah ya'aseh et achoteinu?!* — eloquently lays out the motive and explanation for the massacre of the men of Shechem.[239] In effect they are answering Jacob, "She is our only sister, gentle-born, and not a harlot. We were right to avenge her humiliation. When the inhabitants of the land will consider all that has occurred here, they will *not* be inclined to attack us.[240] Let our action serve notice on the Emorites and the Perizzites that they cannot take liberties with our family. Let all the Canaanites be forewarned — we shall *not* let our sister be treated like a harlot!"[241]

Such bravery and spirit, such focus and familial devotion are noble and indispensable qualities for the family that Jacob is building. The brothers' motivation is correct and laudable. But it is in the *means*, say some critics,[242] not in the *motivation*, that the brothers erred. Shimon and Levi went too far, they say, and as such, Jacob was right to chastise them. Jacob's goal was to tame their sword-arms, with the aim of molding them into a family worthy of becoming the chosen people.

But because the Torah ends this episode with the brothers' words ringing in our ears, **the better inference is that the scripture upholds their conduct**.[243] Robert Alter uses this precise biblical exchange to illustrate the exegetical "rule of thumb that when biblical dialogue is entirely one-sided *or when an expected response is cut off*, we are invited to draw inferences about the characters. . . ."[244] Because Jacob's detailed remonstrance of Shimon and Levi is followed by their response (*Shall he treat our sister like a harlot?*) and then by Jacob's silence, this "final silence"[245] is eloquent. The thoughtful reader is invited to conclude not only that Jacob is powerless against his sons' actions, but also that the Scripture approves of their rescue of Dinah and of its means.

The *midrash* agrees, and embellishes Shimon and Levi's reasoning in their own words. We can envision the two brothers explaining their actions to the other members of their extended household:

"We went into the city to rescue our sister. It was a risky business, and there was a better-than-even chance that we would not make it out of there alive. But an honorable death—on a mission to save Dinah—is preferable to a lifetime of shame.[246] And we could not live with the shame of *not* trying to extricate her; that shame, heaped upon the disgrace that our sister had been violated by an uncircumcised Canaanite, would be very great indeed. Our sister was an innocent, and was forced to submit to that monster's abuse. He stole her happiness and her future life from her. If we had not avenged her and put her rapist and his cohorts to death, then the surrounding nations would have thought her a harlot,[247] and would have treated us as if we all were common property.[248] How could she—and we—continue to live among them under that cloud?"

And so the word went out among the surrounding peoples that *just two* of Jacob's sons were able to overcome all the males in the city of Shechem and rescue their sister. The Canaanites were awed and fearful, and whispered one to the other to take heed! They feared that if *all* the sons of Jacob were to band together they would certainly have the strength to destroy the entire world![249] In this way was Jacob's fear unrealized; the Canaanites did *not* raise arms against him. Instead, Shimon and Levi's infamy secured safe passage for Jacob and his family as they continued their nomadic wanderings,[250] and not a word was uttered against their sister Dinah.

CONCLUSION

Dinah's story ends here. She is mentioned only once more in the Bible, and that is when, years hence, she is named as Jacob's daughter who emigrates with the entire family into Egypt at the time of the great famine.[251] It is apparently sufficient, from a textual standpoint, to know that Dinah's brothers avenge her, that she is returned to her parents' tent, that her rapist and his cohorts have been destroyed, and that she is incorporated back into the family. But the reader is anxious to know what becomes of Dinah *after* her rescue. The many authors of the *midrash* must have felt similarly, as they do not abandon her story just yet.

We assume that Dinah's mother[252] and the entire household treat her with care, never pressing her about her night in

Shechem's palace. Their erstwhile-vibrant young daughter, sister and niece has become, overnight, introspective and taciturn. Now that the family is pulling up stakes, leaving this nightmarish place behind and traveling to Beit El,[253] her mother Leah and her aunt Rachel are hoping that Dinah will come back to herself with the natural resilience of youth. They watch her carefully to gauge her progress.

But in a matter of weeks it becomes apparent that fate is not done with Dinah just yet. Her violent sexual initiation has left her pregnant, and the news rocks her family. Her mother is distraught, seeing that hopes for the girl's return to maidenly pursuits are now dashed. Her brothers are sick at heart, and view the pregnancy as Shechem reaching out from his bloody grave to mock her and them. Her father is predictably angry, and the family tip-toes around him.

Our *midrashic* imagination allows us to envision a courageous and still-beautiful Dinah who approaches her father when she is about to give birth.

"My father, I know that I have made your last months a misery. I am about to enter the women's birthing tent to give birth to my child, a dangerous time for a woman. Before I go I must request a boon of you."

Jacob, his heart softened to his lovely, troubled and tragic only daughter, nods his head in consent. Dinah continues:

"I seek your oath that if I am delivered of a healthy, live baby, you will not allow it to be killed. Yes, I know that that would be the easy solution; for the babe to be stillborn, or to cease to breathe in its swaddling clothes. But I beg you, father, on the strength of all my suffering, to protect my baby and your grandchild. If the Lord wills it, it will be born innocent of the sin of its uncircumcised father and the agony of its violated mother. Promise me that you will protect it."

Dinah, who has not shed a tear since her return to her mother's tent nine months before, cannot now stop the tears from welling out of her expressive eyes and rolling down her cheeks. Jacob—a distant father who ordinarily spares no patience for womanly moods—grants Dinah her request. The girl kisses his hand and backs out of his tent.

So Dinah gives birth to a healthy girl.[254] Jacob's sons would just as soon allow the infant to die,[255] as they see it as provoking talk among the peoples of the land that Jacob is harboring living proof of harlotry in his tents. But surprisingly, Jacob intervenes, remembering his promise to Dinah. He causes a golden amulet to be fashioned, onto which is carved the story of Shechem's rape of Dinah, and identifying the bearer of the amulet as kin of Jacob, believer in the One God. He attaches it by a delicate golden chain to the baby's neck to serve as an order of protection from all who would do her harm, and he orders the infant to be placed under a thorn-bush, consigning her fate to God.[256]

Thus Dinah's baby girl is named Asnat, after the Hebrew word *sneh*, meaning "thorn-bush."[257] It is God's providence that the angel Michael watches over Asnat, so that she is discovered and carried off to Egypt by caravan, landing eventually in the house of Potifar, a member of Pharaoh's cabinet. We see that the *midrash* has Dinah's daughter paving the path that Dinah's brother, Joseph, will follow some years into the future!

Potifar's wife is childless, and adopts and raises Asnat as her own. God's wondrous plans spin out, and in a few years' time Joseph, favored son of Jacob, is sold as a slave and eventually becomes the Pharaoh's advisor and viceroy. When it comes time for Joseph to marry, among the beautiful Egyptian maidens presented to him at court is Asnat, adopted daughter of Potifar. She holds out her amulet for Joseph to see, and when he recognizes her provenance he selects his niece as his bride.

So Dinah's daughter Asnat weds her uncle Joseph in Egypt, and gives birth to two sons, Ephraim and Menashe.

In the meantime, after Dinah has given up her baby, Shimon offers her a place in his household. While some say she weds Shimon[258] and might even have borne his son,[259] the likeliest scenario is that Shimon — Dinah's older brother and warrior-protector, who avenged her rape and carried her from Shechem's palace — comes to her aid once again, offering her a home and a haven. We see that Dinah's youthful ebullience is long gone; she now wears her air of secret tragedy like a veil. She has endured so much personal terror and misery that she feels disconnected from her family, but manages to find distraction and solace in the midst of her young nieces and nephews. Dinah is resigned to the fact that God has not meant her to have a family of her own.

The Talmud[260] and the *midrash*[261] are mindful of Dinah's suffering, and so they wed her to Job, the righteous man who — blameless as is Dinah — suffers greatly before God sees fit to reinstate his life and fortune. There is a legend that Job lived in the time of Jacob, and that the years of his life exactly coincide with the number of years the children of Israel were enslaved in Egypt; that he was righteous as well as wise, and that, like Dinah's brother, Joseph, Job served as an advisor in the court of the Pharaoh.[262] The *midrash* sees Job as a fit mate for Dinah.

Clearly the *midrashists* wish to alleviate Dinah's undeserved misery. They want her to have found comfort, meaning, respect, fulfillment, pride, even happiness as time passes. As we know, the Bible specifically mentions that Dinah entered Egypt with her parents and family.[263] It is therefore not a stretch of the reader's credulity to imagine that Dinah comes face-to-face with her own daughter, Asnat — by now a grown woman — when Jacob's family is reunited with Joseph in Egypt. What a joyful reunion that would be! And what a validation for Dinah and her years of profound suffering. It is logical that we are meant to infer this closure from the biblical reference to her — she is highlighted later on in the text as "his [Jacob's] daughter Dinah" — one of the few named women singled out for mention among the seventy souls who migrate into Egypt from Canaan to escape the famine. Curiously, though perhaps understandably, in light of our analysis, the other female named with some verbal panoply five verses later[264] is "Asnat, daughter of Potifera, priest of On."

Surely mother and daughter meet in Egypt; Asnat, a grown young woman with two sons of her own, is still wearing her golden amulet. Recognizing the necklace, the aging Dinah weeps tears of relief and of gratitude to God. All these long years she has imagined the girl as dead; now she is blessed with the flesh-and-blood proof that her suffering has borne fruit. She is beholding her own beautiful, grown daughter. Asnat is moved by the meeting and weeps, too. By some miracle she has come face-to-face with a birth mother she never thought to see.

Perhaps Egypt will be the site of Dinah's transformation from tragic victim to triumphant survivor. This is surely the reason for her presence in the text and *midrash* as the family of Jacob becomes the Children of Israel: *her* story mirrors *theirs*. They will suffer unspeakable tortures (her suffering at Shechem's hand is called *inuy*, and the same Hebrew word is used to describe the miseries of the Hebrews at the hands of the Egyptians), and yet even *they* are eventually redeemed. Dinah is connected *midrashically* to the redemption from Egypt via her daughter Asnat, her brother Joseph, and her husband Job.

But the reader is impelled to ask, If Dinah dies of old age *before* the exodus from Egypt hundreds of years hence, where is *her* redemption?

The *midrash* has laid out these tantalizing tales about Dinah, Asnat, Joseph and Job as the trail we must follow to Dinah's biblical reward. And for the *midrash*, the answer is simple. Dinah's daughter, Asnat, the "daughter of the thorn-bush" and of Dinah's bitter tears, is fated to be the mother of Ephraim and Menashe, whom the aged Jacob blesses and adopts as his own.[265] Thus, **Dinah's grandsons are *midrashically* rewarded with a double portion of her father's legacy.**

⚔ ⚔ ⚔

This chapter has retold and examined the story of Dinah, innocent only daughter of Leah and Jacob. The girl Dinah steps outside her mother's tent and is snatched away in an instant, kidnapped, raped, and abused by Shechem, the local prince. In that instant, her world is irretrievably shattered.

Is this the story of unleashed evil that found and destroyed an innocent victim? Or is it a love story cut short by over-zealous avengers? Biblical evidence reveals that Dinah was targeted by an evil and lustful foe, against whom she was powerless. And the literature concludes that Dinah survived her ordeal to live out her life among her family, receiving and dispensing comfort and hope during a time of famine, slavery and terror.

Dinah, the nomad-princess, went out to see the daughters of the land. A wretched and powerless victim, she eventually also became Dinah-the-survivor. But she did not do it alone. Dinah was the first sibling in the book of Genesis who had the help of her brothers. Standing up for — and with — one's sister and brothers to oppose a tyranny and avenge a wrong is a prime lesson of her story.

PART

THREE

Judah

Tamar

THREE

Judah & Tamar

GENESIS 38:14-18

*So she removed her widow's garments from her person, and
she covered herself in a veil, and she wrapped herself and sat
at Petach Enayim, which was on the road to Timnah, because
she realized that Shelah had grown, and she was not given to
him as a wife.*

*And Judah saw her and thought her a harlot, for she had
covered her face.*

*So he turned toward her by the wayside, and he said,
"Here, I would come unto you." For he did not know she was
his daughter-in-law. And she said, "What would you give me
if you came unto me?"*

*And he said, "I will send you a kid-goat from the flock."
And she said, "Will you give me a pledge until you send it?"*

*And he said, "What pledge shall I give you?" And she
said, "Your signet, your sash and your staff that is in your
hand." So he gave them to her, and he came unto her, and she
became pregnant by him.*

The rich and complex story of Judah and Tamar should be read
as if viewed through a stereoscope. The stereoscope is a device

that allows a viewer to see two separate, flat pictures as if they are one multi-layered scene. The two pictures are laid out closely side-by-side; one on the left, the other on the right. The stereoscope is mounted above them so that as we peer through its lenses the two flat pictures blend in our mind's eye, and through the magic of optics it appears as if there is only *one* picture. But it is no longer flat; the resulting picture is a *three-dimensional*, stereoscopic and unified whole.

Applying this concept to chapter 38 of Genesis, the first picture I will present hews closely to the simple or literal reading of the Torah text but is told from Tamar's point of view. The second version of this story will be the Bible's telling of this same chapter of Genesis, translated and unembellished. My "stereoscope," if you will, will be the lenses of the Talmud and *midrash*, and in this way the stories of Tamar and of Judah will emerge as a three-dimensional whole, with depth and fresh perspective.

TAMAR'S STORY

This is the story of the tragedy and transformation of a young Canaanite maiden named Tamar. She begins her journey as a compliant victim of doomed marriages and manipulations, but by dint of her desperate, audacious sexual act she emerges a vindicated and victorious mother of a royal dynasty.

We meet her in verse 6 of chapter 38, when Judah selects her to wed his eldest son, Er. She is filled with hope, and is optimistic at the promise of a productive wedded life to the son of an important Hebrew nomadic family. But Tamar's dreams quickly turn nightmarish. Her young husband, for reasons we will explore, is deemed evil in God's eyes, and he dies very soon after they are married. The young, childless widow, still reeling from her husband's death, is given by Judah to his second son, Onan, in compliance with the custom of levirate law.[1] But Onan resents his duty to produce an heir to perpetuate his dead brother's name, so he spills his seed on the ground and shuns not only his duty to his brother's memory but also his duty to Tamar, Er's widow. Onan's behavior angers God, and he, too, dies soon after the marriage to Tamar.

Unfulfilled and now twice widowed, Tamar is sent back to her father's house by Judah, her father-in-law. He tells her that his third son, Shelah, is as yet too young to take her in levirate marriage, and that she should wait in her father's house until the boy comes of age and he sends for her.

The young widow waits dutifully in her father's house, but as time passes she comes to realize that Judah has deceived her. He will *not* be sending his third son to take her in marriage as the law demands, for he fears that Shelah will die, also. Tamar is trapped; she is no longer a girl — in fact she has already been given away twice in marriage — yet she must live shut-in in her father's house as if she were unwed. Nor is she a bride, as she has been banned from the house of her two dead husbands. And miserably, neither is she a mother, for neither Er nor Onan had planted his seed in her before meeting his death. Yet the guiltless Tamar must now subsist as a hybrid creature who dresses in widow's weeds but in reality is something less than a widow, for by law she may not marry anyone but Shelah, or the closest male kin to her dead husband. She is bereft of a husband and a husband's protection, she is without heirs, and she is very nearly without hope of acquiring either.

One day, Tamar is told that her father-in-law, who has not set eyes on her for at least one year's time, will be passing by on his way from the annual sheep-shearing. So she removes her widow's garments, veils her face and drapes herself in everyday clothing. She sits at the open crossroads — at Petach Enayim — where Judah must pass, and she waits. Tamar has learned patience throughout her ordeal of death and exile. Perhaps she thinks that just seeing her will remind Judah of his levirate duty to give her to Shelah as a wife.

As Judah passes by he sees a woman at the crossroads with her face veiled, and, thinking her a harlot, he turns from the path and asks if he may lay with her; he does not recognize the veiled woman as his daughter-in-law. Tamar is stymied for a moment, but recovers quickly and asks what he will give her as a price for laying with him. Judah offers a kid-goat, but as he does not have it with him, Tamar suggests that he leave a pledge with her until the morrow. She suggests his signet ring, his sash and his staff, all of which Judah has readily at-hand and are uniquely his.

Judah agrees, and he comes to her and lays with her, and Tamar becomes pregnant by him.

Immediately afterwards, Tamar arises and departs, sheds her veil, and dresses herself once more in widow's garments.

Judah soon sends the pledged kid-goat to Tamar via his friend Hirah the Adullamite, intending to redeem his pledged articles from the woman with whom he had lain, but she is nowhere to be found! His Adullamite friend inquires of the men of her place, asking, "Where is the sacred prostitute from Enayim who had been seated by the road?" And he is told, "There never was such a prostitute there." Hirah returns to Judah explaining that he could not find the woman, and also that the men of the place denied that there had ever been a harlot there. So Judah says, "Let her keep the pledge; we tried our best to find her to give her the promised kid-goat, but you could not. Let us not persist in this lest we draw attention to ourselves and be shamed."

After the passage of about three months, it is told to Judah that Tamar, his daughter-in-law, has prostituted herself, for she is obviously pregnant and, as she is a levirate widow—that peculiar creature who is intended and betrothed but technically still unwed—if she is pregnant she must surely have engaged in an act of harlotry. And Judah says, "Bring her out and burn her!"

The pregnant Tamar, wearing widow's weeds, is brought out. She calmly sends a message to her father-in-law, saying: "From the man to whom these articles belong, am I with child. Do you recognize this signet, this sash and this staff?" And Tamar waits for Judah's response.

Judah recognizes the items as his, and he says, "She is more righteous than I am! For it is because I refrained from giving her as a wife to my son, Shelah, that this has come to pass."

So Tamar was saved and not burnt. Nor was Judah ever again intimate with Tamar.

Months pass, and when Tamar's birthing time arrives, behold! there are twins in her womb. And at the birthing, a tiny hand emerged. So the midwife took the hand and tied a scarlet cord around it saying as she did so, "This one emerged first." And after he pulled his hand back inside, his brother came forth, so she said, "See how you have burst forth!" Therefore he was named Peretz (meaning, "burst forth"). And afterwards his brother emerged, with the scarlet cord tied upon his hand, and he was named Zerach.

✠ ✠ ✠

Questions abound just from this first telling of the drama: Who is Tamar and what is her provenance? Why do Er and Onan die so suddenly? What does the levirate law require? Is it a boon or a bane to Tamar? Why does Judah send her back to her father's house, and what is Tamar's status there? Does Judah have any intention of giving her to his third son as the law requires? Had Tamar intended to appear as a harlot? Had she planned to seduce Judah? Was her seduction a permissible act? Was it permissible for Judah? Why was Judah the one to pronounce sentence upon her? Should he not have recused himself? Do the births of Tamar's twin sons by Judah vindicate her and justify her life?

Let us now examine the entire chapter text itself, incident by incident *and in its biblical context*, with the aid of the *midrash* and Talmud, so that the story can emerge in stereoscope. Our understanding of the events and their implications will become clearer in the process.

GENESIS 38:1–10

And it happened at that time that Judah went down from before his brothers and turned away to a certain Adullamite, whose name was Hirah.

There Judah saw the daughter of a Canaanite man whose name was Shuah; and he took her [in marriage] and he lay with her. And she conceived and bore a son, and he called his name Er. And she conceived again, and she bore a son, and she called his name Onan. And yet again she bore a son and she called his name Shelah; and it was in Cheziv that she bore him.

Judah took a wife for his firstborn; her name was Tamar.

But Er, firstborn of Judah, was evil in God's eyes, so God caused him to die.

Then Judah said to Onan, "Come lay with your [dead] brother's wife and marry her according to the levirate law; and you will [thereby] establish offspring for your brother."

But Onan knew that the offspring would not be his; so that whenever he came unto his brother's wife, he wasted his seed on the ground so as to prevent giving offspring to his brother. And what he did was evil in God's eyes, so He caused him to die also.

JUDAH SEPARATES FROM HIS BROTHERS

And it was at that time that Judah went down from before his brothers and turned away to a certain Adullamite, whose name was Hirah. . . . Gen. 38:1

The story begins with the verbal knell of doom: the Hebrew word *Vayehi,* meaning "and it came to pass," or "and it happened . . ." This word often prefaces trials and unfortunate events in the biblical narrative,[2] and the word's use here is no exception, as we already know that Judah will experience, very soon in the chapter, the deaths of two of his sons as well as the death of his wife.[3] Even in the chapter's opening verse, the biblical narrator tells us that **Judah went down** *from before his brothers.* Of course, the phrase can mean, on its most basic level, that Judah actually descended from the hill town of Dotan, where chapter 37 ends with the sale of Joseph, to the Adullamite lowlands,[4] where Judah presently makes his home. Dotan is located on a higher topographical plane than is Adullam, which is situated in the hilly and rocky land that is the backdrop to this story in Genesis.[5]

But given the portentous word *Vayehi,* it is likely that while the land's topography might lend Judah to actually "going down" to Adullam, the complete phrase *Judah went down* **from before his brothers** is referring to Judah's altered status within his own family.[6] It is probable that Judah had lost face and standing among his brothers because of the events immediately preceding this chapter and verse. In chapter 37 Judah — perceived by his brothers as their titular leader — had pulled them back from the brink of murdering their seventeen-year-old brother, Joseph, by advising them to sell him instead. Judah had argued, "What will it profit us if we kill him and cover up his blood? Rather, let us sell him to the Ishmaelites; let *our* hand not touch him! For after all, he is our brother."[7] The brothers had heeded his words, and they sold their brother Joseph for twenty pieces of silver to a prosperous caravan of spice traders heading for Egypt.[8]

But neither Judah nor his brothers had reckoned on their father's profound grief when he was presented with the forged evidence that his favored son, Joseph, had been torn to bits by a wild animal. The brothers had cast lots to determine which of them would present their father with the boy's torn and bloody cloak, and the macabre and fraudulent task had fallen to Judah.[9]

Thereupon, their father had sunk into a chasm of mourning and depression that became deeper and more impenetrable by the day. The brothers came to rue their agreement to Judah's plan. The *midrash* tells us that their own guilty anger for causing their father's despair and depression was vented on Judah.[10] For this reason the brothers emotionally and physically effected a separation from Judah, demoting him from his place of leadership and blaming him for the miserable state of their family. "You were our leader; we listened to you. If you had told us to return Joseph to our father whole and intact instead of to sell him, we would have done as you said. But because we heeded you, our father will mourn Joseph until the end of his days."[11]

In fact, aside from the brothers' childish and irresponsible need to divert blame and responsibility from themselves, there is empirical truth to what they say. Of the ten brothers who greeted the young Joseph at Dotan that fateful day, nine were present when they decided to sell him rather than kill him outright (Reuben was not present on the day Joseph was sold; it had been his turn to stay at home and tend to their father, which duty the brothers took in turns.[12] Reuben also had opposed killing Joseph and had planned to return after nightfall to rescue him[13]). Five of those brothers present, including Judah, were sons of Leah, and the other four were the sons of Bilhah and Zilpah, the concubines.

The nine brothers were ranged against Joseph, son of Rachel, their father's favored wife.

The moment of decision about Joseph's fate is presented in the *midrash* as if it were a political caucus.[14] The brothers were divided down the middle and along "party" lines: Leah's four sons voted to sell him; the concubines' four sons voted to return him to their father. *Judah's was the swing vote.* In Reuben's absence Judah was their leader, and they would carry out the course of action he sanctioned. So when Judah voted to sell Joseph, in effect *he* decided the boy's fate. He conceived of the plan to sell the boy, and then cast the deciding vote. For this reason the brothers later blamed Judah, saying, "Had you voted to return him to our father, we would have done so. It is because of *you* that we sold our brother and have brought our father lasting despair."

The opening verse's phrase, *and it happened **at that time**,* also connects this story of Judah and Tamar to the story of the sale of Joseph that immediately precedes it.[15] The two incidents are linked by their contiguous proximity in the Bible text as well as by common "descent" language.

For instance, the phrase *and Judah **went down** — Vayered Yehudah* — in verse 1 of this story (chapter 38) echoes a virtually identical phrase in verse 1 of the very next story (chapter 39): *And Joseph **was brought down** to Egypt — Veyosef **hurad**.*[16] The descent language common to both Judah and Joseph links the two brothers; both are in exile from their family. Joseph had been sold into exile by his brothers, and Judah is in a self-imposed exile in Adullam resulting from his guilt, shame, and his brothers' rejection of him.

But the Bible's descent language also serves the purpose of framing the story of Judah and Tamar. The common words that open chapters 38 and 39 act as a set of brackets, highlighting for the reader that *this* story that appears in chapter 38 contains Judah's make-or-break moment; something important is about to happen that will somehow connect Judah and the brother he sold.[17]

The primary question for the Bible reader is: What will happen in this story to bring Judah back from his personal exile? We are alerted by the strategic positioning of this chapter that this story will be a pivot-point for Judah. His behavior here is not only the *result* of his complicity in the sale of his younger brother, it is also the *catalyst* for the action stories that follow. Why is Judah in Adullam? Why does he marry a Canaanite woman? What will occur in this story that will alter Judah's *downward* path away from his family, and set him once more on the path toward family leadership? As the story unwinds, we will see how Judah's behavior here — *and the all-important behavior of the girl named Tamar* — will radically change him, and will propel him forward into the saga of the Children of Israel.

JUDAH MARRIES A CANAANITE

Because he was shunned by his brothers and could not bear to witness his father's misery, Judah exiled himself from the family compound and made his way to Adullam.[18] Judah, about twenty years old at the time,[19] is friendless, temporarily fatherless, and is without family, a wife, or business prospects.[20] So Judah, alone and on his own for the first time in his life, befriends an honorable Adullamite man by the name of Hirah, and becomes partners with him[21] in the business of raising sheep and selling the wool.

> *There Judah saw the daughter of a Canaanite man whose name was Shuah; and he took her [in marriage] . . .* Gen. 38:2

Judah is flexing his independent muscles and forging a life for himself. Having already made a friend and acquired a business partner, it is not surprising that he should also have his eye out for a wife. The *midrash*[22] tells us that when Judah was still living at home after the sale of Joseph, he and his brothers had been concerned about their marriage prospects. Ordinarily, in their society, their father, Jacob, would have gone about scouting and arranging appropriate marriage partners for his sons.[23] But the brothers saw that their father was drowning in sorrow for Joseph and was neglecting their futures.[24] So they turned to Judah saying, "Are you not our leader? Arise, and go and obtain a bride for yourself." They hoped Judah would pave the way for the rest of them. Either Judah's act of selecting a wife would jolt Jacob into acting on their behalf, or they would be empowered to seek out their own brides as Judah did.

While settling and working in Adullam, Judah admired and befriended another local, this time a prominent[25] merchant[26] named Shuah. The affinity between Shuah and Judah was mutual, and Shuah, a respected Canaanite man of means, kept his eye on this son of the legendary Jacob. He saw that Judah was a keen shepherd and wool trader, and sought to keep him in Adullam as a close associate. For his part, Judah was accustomed to being mentored by his father, Jacob, and, missing him, he fell into a comfortable relationship with the older Adullamite man.

Shuah, a generous and kind-hearted soul,[27] was intent on keeping Judah close, and as he had a daughter of marriageable age, he made sure that whenever Judah was a guest in his home, during discussions about the price of wool or the state of the flocks, his eligible daughter was nearby. Soon enough, Bat-Shuah — the daughter of Shuah — caught Judah's eye. She was physically attractive and Judah desired her.[28] Also, in Judah's eyes, Shuah's daughter seemed to be a moral[29] maiden, and he took her in marriage. Their wedding was a grand affair,[30] as befitted both Shuah and Judah, two of Adullam's important men, and Bat-Shuah brought Judah a rich dowry.[31]

Of course, none of Judah's family were in attendance; Judah had broken with them, and the wedding was a Canaanite feast. Judah must surely have been lonely on some elemental level; after all, for all of his twenty years he had not taken a step without at least two or three of his brothers at his side, and his father's presence had at all times loomed large over the household.

The reader must be wondering when, if ever, Judah will reconcile with his family. Because the present story precedes this reconciliation, we pay close attention to Judah's every step.

The Bible text does not mention the name of Judah's wife; we are told only that she is "Bat-Shuah," meaning the daughter of Shuah, the Canaanite merchant.[32] There are several possible reasons for this seeming omission. The first is that her role is not important to the story; that perhaps, as I have just described, Judah's affinity was primarily for Shuah, the father, and his marriage to the daughter was meant as a means of cementing his alliance with a business partner and mentor. While there is no doubt that Judah desired a union with her,[33] the girl's name is absent from the text because she is of no lasting significance; two of her three children are termed "evil" and are killed, and she herself is fated to die within several verses. Neither she nor her issue will be of lasting import in Judah's story.

A second, related reason might be that precisely because she was "the daughter of Shuah" in Judah's eyes, Judah did not take due care to examine the girl's personal qualities, to consider whether she would be a fit mother to their future children. The text leaves her nameless and without any clue to her appearance, her personality or her deeds.[34] We are not told whether she is pretty or plain, kind or cruel, wise or foolish. When she dies in verse 12 her passing leaves no hole in the text;[35] except, of course, it clears the way for Judah to unite with another.

We are left with doubts about Bat-Shuah because she names her second and third sons "mournfulness" and "error," respectively. Do these names reflect her own state-of-mind? Judah's? And also, her first two sons meet untimely death at God's hand. Was it entirely because of their own behaviors? Was it because of something she did, or did not do? Was it because she was a Canaanite?

This latter query leads to the third possible reason for her namelessness. Consistent with the earlier story line of Genesis when Esav took Canaanite brides, Judah's taking of the daughter of a Canaanite as a wife is considered a bad move, contrary to the wishes of his father, grandfather and great-grandfather before him,[36] as Canaanites bore the curse of Noah.[37] In fact, this provenance could explain, suggests the Ramban, why Judah's first two sons with Bat-Shuah are fated to be characterized as *ra*, or "wicked," by the Torah. But as for the nameless woman who bore them, we know nothing about her other than that she is a Canaanite and generally would not be wed to a Hebrew. One *midrash* goes so far as to call Judah "unfaithful" to his father and to himself; that by marrying the Bat-Shuah he had "married the daughter of an alien god."[38]

It is certainly an insult to Judah's wife that she is nameless in the text when every other character appears to be identified and counted. Even Hirah, Judah's friend, is named. Perhaps the literary burden she shoulders—being a non-Hebrew Canaanite as well as bearing two doomed sons fated to be sentenced to death by God Himself—is too great, and she simply disappears from the narrative without a trace.

And yet, one *midrash* rescues Judah's wife from anonymity. Abarbanel says that her name could very well be Bat Sheva—a recognizable name and a very close version of the text's Bat-Shuah—and that, like her father, the girl is a decent Canaanite soul who unfortunately is not long-lived or important in our story.

We will see that the critical female figure in this story is Tamar, and her name will be explicated in detail.

JUDAH'S WIFE BEARS THREE SONS

. . . and he [Judah] lay with her. And she conceived and bore a son, and he called his name Er. And she conceived again, and she bore a son, and she called his name Onan. And yet again she bore a son and she called his name Shelah; and it was in Cheziv that she bore him. Gen. 38:2–5

Judah's three sons are named here, and, as in a Dickens novel, knowing their names and nothing else we can still almost predict their fates and future character traits.

The first son is named by Judah, as it might have been the custom of that time and place for a father to name his firstborn.[39] He names the boy Er, which has two meanings. The optimistic meaning of "Er" is "to awaken."[40] Perhaps Judah named the boy Er in order to—consciously or subconsciously—awaken his own inner strength and resolve, causing him in future years to step forward and acknowledge his responsibility to Tamar later on in this story. But it is the gloomy reading of the name Er—meaning "barrenness,"[41]—which resonates for Bible readers. In naming his firstborn, Judah has highlighted his own emptiness and existential loneliness. He is confessing to missing his brothers.

Also, we will soon see that the name Er predicts and describes the boy's fate precisely.

Bat-Shuah names their second son Onan. Because the name means "sorrow" or "grief,"[42] the *midrash* tells us first, that Bat-Shuah is fated to mourn this son's premature death,[43] and second, that Judah probably presented a mournful countenance,[44] caused by an abiding guilt and regret over his part in the sale of his brother. Whether or not Bat-Shuah was aware of the reason for her husband's overlay of sadness, this reading affords us a window into Judah's state of mind at the time.

Their third son is born in a place called Cheziv, which means "failure." And the birth is a difficult one, injuring the mother's womb so that the assisting midwife tells Bat-Shuah that she will henceforth be unable to conceive.[45] Bat-Shuah names the third baby Shelah, meaning "error." The names Cheziv and Shelah presage, respectively, future infertility for Judah's wife, and a constant reminder of Judah's past and future errors in judgement. Not only had he seriously erred in advising his brothers to sell Joseph, but we also expect to witness Judah's future mistakes as the story develops.

The mention here of the names of Judah's sons born during his exile from his family is another subtle connection between Judah and his brother Joseph, whom he sold to the merchant caravan. The two brothers unwittingly share similar life experiences: In years to come Joseph also will marry while he is in exile, and he will have two sons. He also names his sons to reflect his inner exile. They are named Menashe, meaning "forgetfulness," and Ephraim, meaning both "fruitfulness" and "disintegration, separation, or nothingness." The Bible reader is expected to take the not-so-subtle hint that in naming his first son Joseph wishes only to forget the family that sold him, dismissed him and feigned his death. By the time of his second son's naming, though he is grateful for his fertility, he has no hope or desire of reuniting with his family. His sons' names reflect that Joseph is resigned to a life spent among strangers, separated from his family, and so names his sons accordingly.

In naming their sons after their depressing and bleak experiences, both brothers unknowingly are forging an experiential link with one another across time and distance.

Frymer-Kensky[46] makes a point of juxtaposing the optimistic meaning of Judah's sons' names with their negative meanings. We are meant to see that one's name is not necessarily one's destiny, whether for good or ill. She acknowledges that Er means both "energetic one" as well as "evil one." The weight comes down on the side of the negative meaning of Er's name, and this is because of his future actions, not simply because in Hebrew the name Er happens to be an anagram for the Hebrew word *ra*, meaning "evil." Similarly, continuing the explanation of the duality of their names' meanings, the name of Judah's second son, Onan, can mean "vigor" as well as "nothingness." Onan's future actions seal his destiny and confirm the darker meaning of his name.

And as regards the third son, Bat-Shuah named him Shelah, which in Hebrew means "belonging to her." We might ask, to which woman does this name refer? It could refer to Bat-Shuah, as this was apparently the last son she would bear for Judah; or it could refer to Tamar, Judah's future daughter-in-law, who in future years waits in vain to be given to Shelah as a wife. When Judah fails to give Shelah "to her" he fails to live up to his obligations to his own family and to Tamar.

Frymer-Kensky implies that one can tread the straight path and so live up to the optimistic vision of one's name, or one can do evil and in this way give vent to the dark equivalence of oneself. Judah's three sons' names are at once a reflection of Judah's state-of-mind at the time of their births, and also an unknowing prediction about their fates.[47]

A person almost always has the choice to act either properly or improperly; our story is about to reveal which choices Er and Onan — and Judah — will make.

EIGHTEEN YEARS LATER

Eighteen years have passed since Joseph was sold to the Ishmaelite merchant caravan. In Bible terms, "the sale of Joseph" is a watershed event, and it is the point of reference for the events in the Judah story. This is because the sale of Joseph occurs at the end of chapter 37 of Genesis, where the Bible abruptly stops its

Joseph narrative, not picking it up again until chapter 39. Sandwiched in between the sale of Joseph and the story of Joseph in Egypt we find Chapter 38, consisting of the story of Judah and Tamar. Our free-standing story makes no mention at all of Joseph's plight. But as we already have seen, the sale of Joseph underlies and even motivates much of Judah's behavior, and it is the lodestar for determining the ages of our story's players.

Using biblical reference points that mention Joseph's age at the time of his sale and thereafter, Bible commentator Umberto Cassuto[48] has constructed a definitive chronology of events in the story of Judah and Tamar. It is an important tool to understanding and visualizing Judah's separate life among the Adullamites, and the life-altering drama that occurs at the crossroads on the way back from Timnah.

Let us, then, briefly step back in time and follow Cassuto's chronology.

The Bible tells us that Joseph was seventeen years old when his brothers sold him to the Ishmaelites.[49] Judah, fourth-born son of Jacob and Leah, was about three years older than Joseph[50] at the time he advised his brothers not to kill the boy, saying, "For what will it profit us?" The Bible tells us that "immediately"[51] after the sale of Joseph, seeing that his father is inconsolable and suffering his brothers' scorn, Judah "goes down" to Adullam and—still at age twenty—marries Bat-Shuah the Adullamite.[52] She swiftly becomes pregnant and gives birth to three sons in as many years. Er is the firstborn; Onan is born the next year, and Shelah the year after that. So Judah is the father of three sons by the third year from the sale of Joseph. Judah's age is twenty-three (and Joseph, sold into Egypt, is twenty).

Cassuto says that the Bible text implies that "Judah did not delay" finding a wife for Er once the boy attained the proper marriageable age, and that at that time "it was customary to marry at the age of eighteen."[53] So when we read in our chapter that Judah brings Tamar to be a wife for Er, we know that the boy is eighteen, Judah is about thirty-nine, and Joseph, by now viceroy to the Pharaoh in Egypt, is thirty-six years of age. It is, also, the sixth year of the seven predicted years of plenty.

We are poised to read in our story about the deaths of Judah's first two sons. The Bible gives the impression that Er dies immediately after his marriage to Tamar (Gen. 38:6–7), and that Onan marries her (in a levirate marriage[54]) that same year, when he is seventeen years old. Onan, too, dies right after his marriage (Gen. 38:8–10). This leaves Shelah, aged sixteen. But Judah is afraid to give Tamar to Shelah, his third and remaining son, lest he die, too. So he sends Tamar back to her father's house to wait "until Shelah will be grown" (Gen. 38:11).

The Bible tells us that "the days multiplied" (Gen. 38:12), from which we infer that twelve months pass, and the situation remains status quo: Tamar is living as a widow in her father's house and Shelah grows to age seventeen. Judah's wife dies, and another year passes. Shelah is now eighteen, but the Bible tells us (Gen. 38:14) that Tamar sees that though Shelah is grown to marriageable age, Judah has made no move to give her to Shelah as a wife.

So it is at that time — when Judah is himself a forty-one-year-old widower, and twenty-one years have passed since the sale of Joseph — that Tamar removes her widow's weeds and, appearing to be a harlot, she waits at the crossroads, seduces Judah, and becomes pregnant from him (Gen. 38:14, 18). Incidentally, Joseph, the lost brother and viceroy of Egypt, is by now thirty-eight years old, and the entire country is in year-one of the predicted seven years of famine.

Tamar gives birth to twin sons in the second year of the great famine, and that same year (Gen. 45:6) Jacob and his entire family, *including Judah [and Tamar] and their infant sons* (Gen. 46:12), go down to Egypt to purchase food. Glimpsing ahead of our story, we see that Judah becomes reconciled with his father and brothers soon after Tamar bears him twin sons, and that the infants are suckling babes when the entire family migrates down to Egypt during the great famine.

Knowing all this enhances our fascination with the drama of Judah and Tamar. We are eager to learn more about the extraordinary events that occur in chapter 38 leading to Tamar's near-canonization and to the end of Judah's exile.

WHO IS TAMAR?

Judah took a wife for his firstborn; her name was Tamar.
Gen. 38:6

Tamar's origin is a mystery. Because the Torah text does not tell us Tamar's provenance, the *midrash* and Talmud, along with modern scholars, minutely examine her name and the textual references to her in chapter 38, in order to give face and form to the audacious heroine of this chapter. So mysterious is Tamar that we are told "she could have been a Canaanite or an Aramean; she could have come from Mesopotamia."[55] It will soon become evident that the Torah text is telling us, by the mystery that shrouds her, that more important than where Tamar comes from is what she will make of herself.

We first meet Tamar when she is taken by the hand and led from her father's house to Judah's compound and presented to Er as his bride. We can presume that Judah has had his eye on Tamar for a while, as he knew from personal experience as well as from family and local tradition that it fell to the head of the family to scout out and obtain a suitable maiden to wed his son. In this way, when Er, his firstborn son, turned eighteen[56] and was of age to marry and start his own family, Judah readily presented him with Tamar, the girl he had hand-picked.

The prevailing opinion is that Tamar was descended from priests and royalty.[57] The *midrash*[58] tells us that she is the daughter of Malki-Zedek, son of Shem, the righteous eldest son of Noah. The name Malki-Zedek means "king of justice," and he is introduced earlier in the book of Genesis[59] as the king of Shalem who brought bread and wine to an exhausted Abraham after he had fought a fierce battle to rescue his nephew, Lot. The Torah also identifies Malki-Zedek as priest of "the most high God," and we are told that he blesses Abraham (at that time his name was Abram) as well as the God who delivered his foes into his hand,[60] and that Abraham gives Malki-Zedek a tithe of everything.

These royal, compassionate and spiritual qualities of the non-Hebrew "king of justice" are imputed retrospectively to the non-Hebrew Tamar by the *midrash*. We will see that the young girl

Tamar grows into her lineage over the course of the story. We note that the priest/king's name is *Zedek*, meaning **righteousness** or justice; at the denouement of our story and about three years after he first brings Tamar into his house, Judah will use this precise root-word, *zdk*, and will pronounce Tamar "more **righteous** than I." In addition, the biblical psalmist writes that "the righteous person flourishes like a date palm."[61] The quality of *zdk* or righteousness associated with Tamar's name and provenance (in Hebrew *tamar* means "date palm") is fated to become her own biblical hallmark.

At the outset, the fact that the Bible text names the girl who will wed Judah's son, while it has obviously and specifically omitted naming his wife and the mother of his sons, arouses our interest. The *midrash*[62] implies that even without knowing the story's end (that a heroic Tamar is fated to be the mother of future kings in Israel), when Tamar is introduced by name in verse 6 — *her name was Tamar* — the reader should sit up and take notice. This girl Tamar must be of some importance in her own right to be mentioned by name in this story, especially when we contrast her naming with Bat-Shuah's anonymity.

So Tamar was the daughter, not of an ordinary Canaanite, as was Bat-Shuah, but of a righteous convert who believed in and acclaimed "the One God." The Talmud[63] tells us that her father had died and that she was an orphan at the time of her marriage to Judah's son, Er. Some are of the opinion that she was still a minor at the time of her father's death, others that Tamar was of marriageable age.[64] It is also thought that, like her father, Tamar already had been converted to the One God.[65]

As we have seen, the names — or the anonymities — of the biblical characters in our story are significant. The girl whom the Torah text introduces in verse 6 is named after the date palm tree, or *tamar*. The Bible wants us to associate the girl with the image her name evokes. The date palm grows tall and straight in the arid desert climate, and we are expected to infer that the young girl named Tamar is tall, lovely to look at, straight of stature and of true moral fiber. The commentaries infer other qualities about the girl Tamar. One *midrash* terms her "beautiful, fine and exceedingly comely;"[66] another says that "she was by nature chaste and modest,"[67] and still another says that her manner was as pleasing and as delightful as incense.[68] It appears that in selecting a bride for his eldest son, Judah made a better choice than he did for himself.[69] At the very least the girl has a name, and by inference she has admirable qualities.

The date palm also bears copious and precious fruit, but interestingly, without human pollination its fertility is not assured.[70] We recall that the name of the place where Judah's wife had given birth for the last time was Cheziv, meaning "an end to giving forth fruit,"[71] signaling that it was unlikely she would be able to bear more children. Tamar appears on the scene in the very next verse, her name evoking a fertile and beautiful desert plant. Perhaps the contrast is set up in order to signal a subtle passing of the childbearing mantle from Bat-Shuah to Tamar. And this is highly ironic, given early events in our story where Tamar is *prevented* from bearing children by her first two husbands.

The agricultural idiosyncrasies of the date palm's fertility inject another aspect of suspense into our story. Tamar has the *potential* to be the mother of kings; but as we witness the deaths of her two husbands one after the other in upcoming verses, we experience a sense of foreboding. We fear, justifiably, that "the woman who bears this name is in danger of disappearing."[72] Fertility is no sure thing to the date palm. Likewise, Tamar's potential for productivity, or for greatness, remains inchoate given the deaths of her two husbands.

As it is with many of the Bible's heroines, the text omits any reference to Tamar's provenance; it is the *midrash* which fills in the blanks. It is as if the Torah text is telling us that the girl Tamar is strong enough to stand on her own. There is no need to refer to her as "daughter of . . ." The Bible says simply, almost proudly, *her name is Tamar*. So we read on, waiting to see how Tamar develops, and by what means she wrests a fertile future from a barren beginning.

TAMAR MARRIES ER

But Er, firstborn of Judah, was evil in God's eyes, so God caused him to die. Gen. 38:7

Er is a strapping young man of eighteen.[73] He has inherited his father's skill with the sheep, and he had taken over much of the business of shepherding, shearing and selling the wool. He is full of the knowledge that he will one day be a wealthy man in his own right, and that the girls of the town consider him prime as a marriage prospect. He and his brother, Onan, spend many hours discussing the attributes of each marriageable young woman in Adullam. We can imagine their conversation might have sounded something like this:

"I am the eldest, and this is my year to marry. Surely father already has decided on a girl to be my mate. And she needs to be special! But I haven't seen him talking with any of the other fathers, nor has he invited any of them into his tent to drink wine or share a pipe. I am burning with curiosity to know who it will be!"

Onan, only a year Er's junior, grunts his agreement. Onan resents the fact that Er will be getting the pick of the crop of local girls. He has come a close second to his older brother for his entire life — with his father, the family sheep business, and the locals. He has an easy, lusty desire for the females, and he tamps down a fierce envy that Er will be wed first, and to the choicest specimen.

Onan has just had an idea, so he addresses his brother. "You know, the girl Tamar is an orphan. She's also the best-looking girl in all of Adullam: tall, and slender as a reed. Not much to say for herself, but definitely choice. So if father is thinking of *her* for your mate we would not have seen him in negotiations with any of the other men! He would have asked permission only of her *mother*, and the deal would have been done fast and without anyone being the wiser. And you could do worse! Not only is she beautiful, but her father left them that house, and the family seems comfortable. I'll bet you Tamar is the one he's chosen for you."

And so it was. Judah took Tamar, the orphaned beauty from the priestly house, granddaughter of Shem,[74] the righteous son of Noah, to be a wife for Er, his eldest son.

But what should have been the beginning of a blessed and fruitful new marriage ends in tragedy almost immediately. The same ominous word portending misfortune that began this chapter — *Vayehi* — also opens *this* verse. And, true to form, we read in the very next verse that Er, Judah's firstborn, was *evil in God's eyes*, and that *God slew him*. Instead of announcing a pregnancy and birth — as the Torah did at the opening of the chapter after announcing Judah's marriage — the text here begins by announcing the marriage, but follows it immediately with the bride groom's death.

What went wrong? The Bible clearly says that Er *was evil in God's eyes*. What was Er's sin?

We are primed to expect bad news about Er, as his name in Hebrew letters, when inverted, is the word *ra*, meaning evil or wicked[75] — the precise word that verse 7 uses to describe the reason for God's judgement of him.[76] The *midrash* and the Talmud explain that Er took advantage of Tamar's sexual inexperience. Er wanted to keep Tamar slim and lovely and he decided, after consulting with his brother, Onan, that the best way to do this was to keep her from becoming pregnant.[77] So instead of engaging in natural sexual relations with his young bride, Er took Tamar to his bed but engaged only in sodomy, or sex acts with no potential for impregnating her.[78] Tamar submitted to this sexual treatment because she did not know any better, nor did she have a father or brother to speak up on her behalf.

Er's spilling his seed in a way that was calculated to prevent Tamar from conceiving was adjudged by God to be an evil act perpetrated against Tamar.[79] It also was a rebellious act directed against God Himself, who had issued the command to "be fruitful and multiply."[80] Even non-Hebrews considered the duty to procreate to be a primary function of married life, so that there was no need to give advance warning of the severe penalty for transgressing this universally-recognized duty.[81] So wicked was Er's act of withholding children from Tamar that God slew him, making certain that Er would *never* sire children.[82]

Part One of this book described the reasons the Torah and the Almighty had termed the people of Sodom "evil," using the same one-word description the text assigns to Er (and to Onan after him) in our story: *ra*. The reader will also recall that a singular element of their wickedness was acts of sexual depredation, and of course we recognize that the word "sodomy" has its origin in the city's name. An earlier story in Genesis (10:22) also links some of these textual elements. We read of a mysterious sexual act involving Noah and his son, Ham, the father of Canaan. This is followed swiftly by Noah's severe curse of Canaan for whatever had been done to Noah as he lay drunk and naked in his tent. In this way the Bible reader is alert that such "unnatural," fruitless sexual behavior is frowned upon by God, and that death by divine decree may be the inevitable punishment. We also have seen that Canaanites feature prominently in this forbidden sexual behavior.

Here, in the early verses of the story of Judah and Tamar, we see recurrence of these same elements. We see Judah marrying a Canaanite woman who bears him three sons; we see the sons described as *ra* or evil in the text, and we see divine death or destruction as the response. The logical inference of the *midrash* is that Er's sin involved sodomy, as that is the single missing link that is present in both the Noah story and in Sodom. And when we continue our tale, we see in the coming verses that Judah's second son follows the pattern of his brother, so there are *two* incidents of unproductive sex followed by divine punishment.

ONAN MARRIES TAMAR
UNDER THE LEVIRATE LAW

> . . . *Then Judah said to Onan, "Come lay with your [dead] brother's wife and marry her **according to the levirate law**; and you will [thereby] establish offspring for your brother."*
>
> *But Onan knew that the offspring would not be his; so that whenever he came unto his brother's wife, he wasted his seed on the ground so as to prevent giving offspring to his brother.*
>
> *And what he did was evil in God's eyes, so He caused him to die also.* Gen. 38:8–10

The levirate law, or *yibum* in Hebrew, is a special suspension of the incest taboo.[83] Incest taboos prohibit sexual relations and marriage among close relatives, including a marriage between a surviving brother and his deceased brother's widow,[84] or sexual relations between a father-in-law and his daughter-in-law.

But custom among the Canaanites in the ancient Near East,[85] and certainly among the Israelites both before and under Mosaic law (Deut. 25:5–10),[86] carved out an *exception* to these strict taboos. When a brother died childless, leaving a widow of childbearing age, in order to keep the deceased brother's landed portion in his name,[87] the deceased's brother (or his closest male relative[88]) was *permitted* (actually, he is *obligated*) to marry his sister-in-law for the purpose of siring a child. In the best-case scenario such a levirate marriage also served to "redeem" the deceased's widow from her childlessness and from a "chained"[89] widowhood. Absent a levirate marriage the widow was forbidden to wed a "stranger," defined as anyone from outside the family unit.

Under levirate law the widow and her brother-in-law joined in a union *for the express and sole purpose of having a child* who would stand in the shoes of his deceased father. Such a child would be the heir to the *deceased* brother, and not to the brother who contributed his seed via *yibum*. As such, it was forbidden for the *yavam* to have intercourse with his brother's widow *for his pleasure*, or if he loved her, or because of her beauty. The levirate union needed to be consummated strictly with the intent of inseminating the widow, thus fulfilling the obligation to keep alive the name and portion of his deceased brother.

The Talmud[90] explains that such a levirate union occurs only with the consent of the widow; she is never forced to accept *yibum* against her will, and does not forfeit the terms of her *ketubah*, or marriage contract, if she refuses such a marriage for a valid reason (such as a displeasing odor or a defect in the *yavam*, the relative she is expected to wed).[91] But once wed, she is her new husband's wife for all purposes, and cannot be sent away without payment according to terms of a *get* or proper divorce.[92]

Here, in verse 8, close upon the sudden death of Er, we see Judah advising his second son, seventeen-year-old Onan, to take his brother's widow in levirate marriage. It is the first documented act of *yibum* among the Children of Israel.[93] Judah is clear that the purpose of their union is "to give seed to your [deceased] brother." We note that Tamar's name is not mentioned in Judah's instructions. The essence of the act of *yibum* is that Onan beget a child with his dead brother's widow, not with Tamar *qua* Tamar. It is not so much a sexual act as it is a dutiful, if intimate, trans-action;[94] a final and essential filial responsibility owed to his deceased brother.[95] The resulting child would be a "resurrection," for purposes of inheritance, of Er; he would be considered *Er's son.*[96]

> **But Onan knew that the offspring would not be his**; *so whenever he lay with his brother's wife he wasted his seed on the ground so as to prevent giving offspring to his brother.*
> *And what he did was evil in God's eyes, so He caused him to die also.* Gen. 38:9–10

Judah's attempt at preserving the name and portion of his firstborn son ends in more tragedy. Apparently Onan has no intention of giving over any child he might eventually sire with Tamar to be his dead brother's heir. Also, Onan desires Tamar sexually,[97] and as we know, the levirate union must be motivated not by a prurient desire for one's sister-in-law, but by duty to the dead brother. So Onan's sin is, first, that he selfishly refuses to "donate" his seed for the purpose of begetting an heir for his dead brother. And second, but related to the first, is his sin of commit-ting an incestuous act with Tamar. By laying with her *out of desire* rather than duty, Onan transformed the permissible into the forbidden. Only the permitted act of *yibum* suspends the incest taboo. Once his desire trumped his duty, Onan was engaging in an unlawful union.

Furthermore, the text tells us that Onan's "evil" act was that he spilled his seed and engaged in unproductive intercourse with his brother's widow. Knowing his mission—to sire a child for Er via a levirate union—still Onan flouted both his father's request and God's law. Onan destroyed his seed, as did Er, but Onan's reason was that he did not want any offspring of his to be credited to his older brother.[98]

One *midrash* puts a spin on Onan's forbidden behavior. The *Netziv* agrees that Onan spilled his seed because of his base selfishness in not wishing to perpetuate his dead brother's name and inherited portion. But the commentary adds that Onan did *not* find Tamar to his liking;[99] perhaps he did not wish to marry his brother's "used goods." Onan felt forced by his father to take Tamar to his bed and so, in a passive-aggressive way, while he ostensibly consented to wed her in levirate fashion, he secretly and without his father's knowledge spilled his seed on the ground insuring that she would not conceive. His plan was that after a time, when Tamar remained without child, he would divorce her, and take another girl to be his wife. He would give his seed only to a virgin whom he had consented to wed, who had not first belonged to his brother.

Onan's behavior is contrasted with Er's. While Er spilled his seed because he wished to keep Tamar un-pregnant, slender and virginally beautiful *so that he could continue to enjoy her sexually*, Onan's behavior was the direct opposite (*i.e.*, he did *not* wish to enjoy her sexually) but just as abhorrent. According to Kass, "rightly understood, the sin of Onan is not . . . simply spilling one's seed . . . but rather *the sin of pretending but failing to perform the levirate duty to the deceased.*"[100]

The Talmud[101] says that Onan's wasting of his seed *in these circumstances* was the equivalent of spilling the blood of the unborn children he could have "given" to Er. His act was also akin to worshipping false gods, as he flouted God's directive to "be fruitful and multiply." Both of these acts commanded the death penalty, which explains Onan's premature death.

The tiny Hebrew word *gam*, meaning "also," at the end of verse 10, indicates that *both* of Judah's sons acted wickedly by calculatedly spilling their seeds. Just as Er is struck dead by God as punishment, Onan is killed *also*.[102]

ER AND ONAN'S SEXUAL SINS

The Babylonian Talmud[103] discusses Er and Onan's sexual acts with Tamar. Did the brothers engage in ordinary sexual intercourse but ejaculate onto the ground? Or did they never penetrate Tamar's virginal membranes, choosing instead to sodomize her?

These questions and attendant discussion become important later on in our story, when Tamar has sexual intercourse with Judah and becomes pregnant immediately. Was she a virgin at that encounter?

As we examine Er and Onan's sins and swift deaths, the Talmud cites *Breishit Rabbah*[104] for the proposition that Onan, at least, had "natural" sex with Tamar, and that he withdrew before ejaculation, deliberately spilling his seed onto the ground. But the Talmud and some *midrashim*[105] still sense a hint in the Torah text that *both* Er and Onan's sexual acts with Tamar were "unnatural," and in this way she remained virginal as well as unpregnant. Either way, "discharging [one's] seed in vain" was considered a great sin for the brothers to have committed.[106]

In fact, the manner in which Judah's sons treat Tamar — selfishly, with sexual carelessness, considering only their own pleasure — resembles the manner in which they might have treated a harlot. And we empathize with the young bride, Tamar, who has no say in the matter. How ironic, then — even measure-for-measure — that in years to come Judah mistakes Tamar for a harlot and she cleverly play-acts the role with momentous consequences. We will see how the widowed and passive bride grows into a deliberative and wise woman,[107] turning misfortune into triumph.

By the time of her marriage to Judah's second son and his sudden death, Tamar had intuited her husbands' sins, realizing not only how they had wronged her, but also that they were struck down by God because of it. Judah, on the other hand, has no inkling of their sins, and in fact suspects that his sons died because of *her*.[108] Not only that, but he erroneously thinks Tamar protected herself from becoming pregnant for her own reasons. In his grief and because of his understandable inability to perceive his sons' faults, Judah has turned the truth on its head and paints Tamar as the villain in the story, somehow responsible for his sons' deaths. He thinks of her as "the killer wife"[109] and secretly resolves not to give her to Shelah, his youngest son.

The Bible has set up a dramatic irony: The reader knows that Judah's sons have sinned; we even know their motivations and what they were thinking at the time. But Judah has no clue, and by his actions condemns the innocent party, and actually mistreats

Tamar throughout the story until the denouement.[110] It is important that the reader see Judah *as he is* when chapter 38 opens, so that by the end of the chapter, when we read of his public confession and acknowledgement of Tamar, we appreciate how far Judah has traveled in his journey on the road to his restitution as leader of Jacob's family.

Right now, however, we encounter Judah close on the heels of the sale of Joseph, a sale that Judah had instigated. In the words of Professor Jeansonne, the biblical narrator "reveals Judah as a scheming and corrupt man."[111] His plan to sell his younger brother to a merchant caravan was certain to give the boy a worse fate than Reuben's planned rescue would have done. It is *this* Judah who holds the young Tamar's future in his hands. We wait to see what Judah does next, and we wonder, What will become of Tamar?

JUDAH SENDS TAMAR AWAY

Then Judah said to Tamar, his daughter-in-law, "Remain as a widow in your father's house until Shelah my son grows of age." Because he said to himself, "Lest he will also die, like his brothers." And Tamar went and dwelled in her father's house. Gen. 38:11

Judah has no intention of giving Tamar to his third son. So he banishes her to her father's house and "humiliates her by keeping Tamar, a twice-married woman, confined" as a widow in the home of her childhood.[112]

The verse is contradictory,[113] which only highlights for the reader Judah's intent to deceive Tamar. First he tells her to go to her pre-marriage home *until* Shelah is of age, implying that he will give her to Shelah *after* the appropriate time interval. Next we are made privy to his secret intentions[114] as he thinks "there's no way I'll be giving Shelah to her; what if *all* her husbands are fated to die?" This is a prime instance in the story where Judah acts deceitfully toward Tamar. He only *lets Tamar believe* that he will do his levirate duty by her in the future.[115] And the Bible will not forget Judah's deceit; later on in the story we will see that, measure-for-measure, it is Judah who is deceived, when he is unwittingly drawn by Tamar into fulfilling the very obligation he is now evading.

Understandably, Judah seeks to preserve his third son from Tamar's "bad luck,"[116] and secretly resolves *not* to give her to him in levirate marriage. The rabbis of the Talmud and *midrash* disagree about whether Judah was justified to assume that because his first two sons died while married briefly to Tamar that this created a presumption that the third would meet the same fate. The Talmud[117] says that there is no such presumption; that the deaths of Judah's two sons at most created a *potential* danger, implying that Judah should have risked it. Others raise the argument that even *two* deaths create, if not the presumption of "mortal danger," then perhaps the portent of it.[118] Such a negative portent would have been irresistible for Judah *not* to consider, and we can appreciate why he withheld Shelah from Tamar.

But in the scheme of our story and in the eyes of the biblical narrator, Judah is making a wrong choice. He is ignoring both the duty he owes to his eldest son, and the right of his daughter-in-law to a levirate union. One clue we have is that the text in this verse identifies Tamar by her relationship to Judah *as well as* by her name (*Then Judah said to Tamar, his daughter-in-law . . .*). This is a subtle hint to the reader that Judah is betraying *both* the woman *and* the widow. By banishing her from his house and his protection, Judah is condemning Tamar to the limbo of levirate widowhood; she is not free to marry another as long as Judah's third son is alive. Tamar remains "chained"[119] or "bound"[120] to Judah's family, albeit from a distance, and she awaits his whim.

JUDAH GOES UP TO THE SHEEP-SHEARING

And the days multiplied, and Bat-Shuah, wife of Judah, died; and Judah was comforted, so he went up to Timnah to his sheep-shearing with his comrade, Hirah the Adullamite. Gen. 38:12

Twelve months pass[121] and misfortune visits Judah yet again. His wife, the daughter of Shuah, dies. It is quite possible she never recovered from the one-two blow of losing her sons, Er and Onan, within weeks of each other. We recall that after the birth of Shelah, Bat-Shuah was told she would never again become pregnant. So with two of her sons gone perhaps she lost her reason for being, and thereafter, her will to live.[122]

The Talmud suggests that Judah's suffering was to a certain extent brought upon himself. Nineteen years before, Judah had interceded to prevent his brothers from killing Joseph. We recall that Judah appealed to them saying, "What would it profit us? Let us sell him to the passing caravan." To the rabbis of the Talmud, Judah's act—however twisted his motivation at the time—*began* the process of saving Joseph's life. But because Judah did not follow through—and in fact aided the boy's sale as well as the subsequent deception of their father—the Heavenly scales remained unbalanced. It was only a matter of time before Judah would be made to pay the price for selling his brother Joseph, and that time is now. The Talmud states that a person who begins a righteous deed but does not see it to its end will be fated to bury his wife and sons as punishment.[123] For had Judah not interceded those many years ago, Reuben's plan to return at night, rescue Joseph from the pit and return him to his father, would have achieved the better result. Instead, years later, Judah has buried two sons and a wife, and has mourned them for at least a year's time.

Because the text says "the days multiplied" without specifying the exact passage of time, it also is possible that *less* than a year's time has passed. Judah and his wife had been living through a period of intense grief, and time would have passed on leaden feet,[124] so that it might only have *seemed* as if twelve months had come and gone.

But the better view is that Judah's miserable situation—and by inference Tamar's, too—has remained unchanged not only for the complete year that has passed after Onan's death, but even for longer. According to Cassuto,[125] one year of mourning passed for Judah's sons, and then another was spent mourning his wife. This would explain why the text states *both* that "the days multiplied" in verse 12 *and* "she saw that Shelah was grown" in verse 14; *two* years are implied.

Tamar gives Judah the benefit of the doubt and waits not only until the first mourning period ends, but also until Shelah reaches age eighteen, to see if Judah will do his duty and free her.

We read that with the passage of time Judah became comforted after his wife's death. We are meant to understand that Judah is comforted after his sons' deaths, too.[126] He is emerging from under a cloud of depression during which he stayed inside his house and expressed no interest even in his prized sheep business, let alone in the welfare of his daughter-in-law Tamar. His father-in-law, Shuah, his friend and business partner, Hirah, and even his third son, Shelah, all have worked together to keep the family business alive and thriving notwithstanding Judah's absence.

So it is after two years' time, and with a mixture of personal reawakening and recognition of his own economic success, that Judah agrees to attend the annual sheep-shearing festival in Timnah. The occasion will serve as a kind of "coming-out" party for Judah after his mourning periods. The shepherds and townspeople all congregate at Timnah to celebrate Judah's wool harvest. The party is sumptuous, akin to a king's feast,[127] with Judah filling the role of ceremonial overseer.[128] Judah is recognized as the undisputed boss of the thriving business, from which the Adullamites know their own good fortunes stem. It is hoped that Judah will take some satisfaction from watching over the sheep shearers as they harvest his flocks' fine wooly coats. The mountains of fluffy white wool will translate into a fortune when traded at the wool exchange. Perhaps, seeing all this, Judah will be moved to feel that the new season will be the harbinger of better events to come for him and for his family.

The Bible features a sheep-shearing ceremony only twice in the Five Books of Moses, and twice more in the books of Samuel. Each time it appears, the sheep-shearing marks a momentous turn of plot.[129] This time is no exception.

Hirah, the first friend Judah had cultivated in Adullam nineteen years before, accompanies him up to Timnah to partake in the celebration. It is the first time Judah is appearing in public in at least a year, and as such, this is an important day for Judah and for Hirah, Shelah, Shuah and all the men who support and surround him. They must be relieved that their friend and *padrone* is returning to life after experiencing such bleak and tragic happenings. His men await him in Timnah.

Importantly for our story line, the passage of time noted in the text also clues the reader that Shelah is growing closer to marriageable age.[130] After the first year of mourning passes, Shelah is seventeen, the age at which Judah gave Onan in levirate marriage to Tamar. It is certain that Tamar, in the exile and isolation of her father's house, also is counting the time, and that she expects that her levirate widowhood will soon end. Unfortunately, Tamar is fated to be ignored, as Judah does not come for her.

Still another year passes; Shelah has turned eighteen, and Tamar is hopeful that surely *now* Judah will marry her to Shelah. But again Tamar's hopes are dashed, as Judah still does not come for her or contact her.

Judah is now forty-one years old and is in the prime of his life. Actually, Judah has, in essence, already lived *two* lives. His youth and formative years were spent in Jacob's house as a son of the unfavored wife. There, he learned how to tend and manage enormous flocks of sheep. He also learned how to live and work with and among other men: his full- and half-brothers as well as his father's shepherds. Unfortunately, in the first twenty years of his life Judah also learned to nurture hatred for his younger half-brother, Joseph, son of the favored wife. This misguided hatred culminated in Judah's suggestion to his brothers that they sell the boy. It was Judah's intense feelings of guilt stemming from this sale and the subsequent deception that propelled him to exile himself from his family.

Thus began the second phase of Judah's life. Estranged from the ones he had wronged, Judah's next twenty-one years have been spent among strangers. Judah created a new identity for himself, married, and cultivated a new "family." He also took his shepherding skills to a new level by creating a small wool industry in Adullam.

Unfortunately, now, two decades after arriving in Adullam, Judah finds himself bereft of his wife and two of his three sons. He has divested himself of his daughter-in-law, Tamar, the physical reminder of much of what he has lost, by hiding her away in her father's house in the town. He has done his best to forget his outstanding duty to wed her to Shelah and beget heirs for, now, his *two* dead and childless sons.

Judah has buried himself in grief and denial for the past two years, and only now, in response to the urgings of his friends and partners, is he responding to the need to return to the business of life. What better time to do this than the festival of the sheep-shearing, which signals a seasonal turningpoint and a new beginning?

But other needs are churning beneath the surface. The *midrash* wants the Torah reader to extrapolate from the spare Bible text that Judah is first and foremost a flesh-and-blood character and a virile man. True, he is deeply troubled and flawed, and has left the blameless Tamar in a cruel limbo, but the text is weaving its story inexorably to the point where, in order to appreciate Judah's coming behavior, we must first see *him*.

And the Bible is not done with Judah yet. He still has a third facet of his life ahead of him. How will it take shape? What will fill the next twenty-plus years of his life and beyond? What propels Judah to stop on his way back home from the sheep-shearing festival at Timnah? And how will Tamar figure into this equation?

The *midrash* supplies the answer. In their commentaries on verse 12, Abarbanel and the *Netziv* state the extraordinary truth that *Judah is gripped by intense sexual urgings after his two years of mourning and abstinence.* As a result, he sees a woman whom he assumes is a harlot and he takes his pleasure with her.

TAMAR READIES HERSELF FOR A SEDUCTION

[Now] it had been told to Tamar as follows: "Behold, your father-in-law is coming up to Timnah to shear his sheep."

So she removed her widow's garments from her person, and she covered herself in a veil, and she wrapped herself and sat at Petach Enayim, which was on the road to Timnah, because she realized that Shelah had grown, and she was not given to him as a wife. Gen. 38:13–14

We learned two important things from verse 12: that Judah's mourning period for his wife had ended, and that he was comforted. The Bible relates these facts so that we are mentally prepared for Judah to end both his celibacy and his isolation.[131] It is necessary for us to know this because in the ancient Near East, even in a culture of polygamy, a married man or one who was still in mourning would not do what Judah is about to do in the coming verses.[132]

When we read in verse 13 that Tamar is told that Judah will be attending the sheep-shearing festival at Timnah, the reader must assume that Tamar also is aware of the implications of that news. She now knows that Judah has emerged from mourning and is enjoying a liberated status. For if Judah were still in mourning, propriety would have dictated that he forego attending such a public celebration.

We take note of the parallelism set out for us in verse14. After Tamar is told that her father-in-law is no longer in mourning and will be attending the sheep-shearing, we read that *she, too,* sheds her mourning garments and goes out of her house. The Bible takes the unusual further step of detailing Tamar's toilette: *she shed her widow's clothes, covered herself in a veil, and she wrapped herself.*

The reader should be excited by this news. We applaud Tamar's activity, thinking that, finally, Tamar is emerging from her chrysalis. But questions abound. What does Tamar intend? When she sheds her widow's clothing, dons a veil and wraps herself, is her intent to disguise herself, or to return to a normal life as Judah is doing? Is she bent on a seduction or a confrontation?

The past two years have been difficult ones for Tamar. Her return to her father's house had reversed her status by placing her back with her mother in a public and shamed manner. The Adullamite community was doubtless as superstitious about Tamar's role in the deaths of Er and Onan as Judah was.[133] They looked upon her as having "a bad karma." It mattered little that Tamar was probably still in her teens as well as an innocent bride of only a matter of weeks when she was banished from Judah's house. In the eyes of her neighbors she was a pariah. She encountered stares, whispers, and likely outright shunning when she made her daily trip to the town well. Perhaps the locals reacted something like this as they watched her walk past:

"There goes Tamar, the girl who has just buried two husbands! Is it any wonder that Judah has sent her away and will have nothing to do with her? He refuses to adhere to the levirate law and marry her to Shelah because his first two sons died suddenly after marrying her. Who knows but that she is possessed of some killer poison — or that she is diseased?[134] We, too, should keep our distance."

Fortunately for Tamar, she still has a friend or two from her girlhood who visit her clandestinely and keep her abreast of the local goings-on. Surely it is one of these friends who hurries, breathless, into her house, intent on being the first to reveal what must be good news.

"Tamar, Tamar! You are saved! Your father-in-law has at long last emerged from his period of mourning! He has left his house and gone with Hirah and Shuah and his son, Shelah, to the sheep-shearing at Timnah! I was told this by my mother, who heard it from the kitchen maid, who heard it from her sister, who works for Hirah, your father-in-law's close friend and partner. It was she who saw them leaving Adullam as they wended their way up the mountainside to Timnah.[135]

"Tamar, this is wonderful news! For if Judah has shed his mourning then surely you are next!"

So Tamar, who has had two lonely years to contemplate her chained state as a levirate widow, stands up from her habitual seat by the window where she has been weaving cloth. She is still tall, slender, and as lovely and seemingly untouched as she was when Judah first brought her into his house more than two years ago. She does not smile, as her faithful friend perhaps expected. Instead, wordlessly and with deliberation, Tamar begins to unwind the black headdress, neck scarf, shawl and tunic that have enveloped her for twenty-four months, until she stands unclothed in front of her loyal friend.

"Tamar, what are you doing?" her friend asks in amazement.

And Tamar turns to the girl. This young bride and widow who has worn a shapeless shroud of dreary sackcloth for two years is reveling in her unclad freedom. She answers in a firm, but soft voice, "Why, now I, too, will shed my mourning clothes. I will wash, purify myself in the ritual bath,[136] and prepare to enter society once more. I will don colorful clothing[137] from my trousseau that has been packed away these many months. I will be waiting by the road for my father-in-law when he passes by on his return trip. I will be ready to return with him to his house, for surely he will be reminded when he sees me[138] that it is time he gave me to Shelah as a wife. Let me make haste to bathe and dress, my friend, and get myself to the crossroads,[139] where I will sit and wait. In that way my father-in-law will be sure to see me when he passes on his way home[140] with Hirah."

Verse 14 is a turning point. Up until now Judah has been the focal point of chapter 38, and events have revolved around *his* life in Adullam. Tamar has appeared in Judah's dramatic story only as another silent woman, at most as a bit player and a tragic catalyst. While the text did mention her by name—thus hinting to us of her coming importance—for all intents and purposes Tamar disappeared from the story without a murmur of protest when Judah banished her back to her father's house.

Now, midway through the chapter, Tamar reappears and we see the change. The biblical spotlight has shifted its focus *to Tamar*. We watch as this passive girl from prior verses comes to life and becomes an initiator. The verse contains five action verbs describing Tamar's behavior, including one that explains the motivation for her present activity. She *removes* her widow's garments; she *covers herself* with a veil; she *wraps herself*; and she *sits* at Petach Enayim. She is propelled into action *because she saw* that Shelah had grown to maturity but that Judah had not given her to him as a wife.

What does Tamar intend to do?

By shedding her widow's garments and positioning herself at the crossroads, Tamar is bracing for a confrontation with her father-in-law, Judah. There are several possible reasons for her behavior. Shedding her mourning clothes could indicate that Tamar intends to push Judah to do his duty; she plans to request that he end her waiting period and give Shelah to her in marriage according to the levirate law. Or, alternatively, it could signal that she is done waiting for Judah to do his duty and give her to Shelah as the law requires;[141] that she *no longer* desires the levirate union with Shelah, that she wishes to be freed of the levirate limbo and get on with her life. That she now intends to make her wishes known to Judah. A third possibility is that Tamar, despairing of being given to Shelah,[142] has decided, instead, to attempt one final strategy. She will make herself desirable to attract her father-in-law,[143] who also is a possible candidate for levirate marriage.[144]

Based on Tamar's silent appearance as a background character in the story up until now, any of these possible courses of action might seem unlikely. Yet here she is, stripping herself of the widow's weeds and, symbolically, of her former passivity. She realizes after a futile two-years' wait for Judah to act, that *she* must be the one to take the action that will secure her future.[145] So she determinedly veils herself, dons colorful "woman's armour," and positions herself on the roadway to intercept Judah.

Let us pay close attention to Judah's upcoming behavior and Tamar's responses, so that we can draw our own conclusions as to her reasons for waiting at the crossroads.

We must appreciate that Tamar's transformation from background-figure into action-figure is a hard-won personal battle. The *midrash* appreciates her effort. When the Bible tells us that first she veiled herself, and then *she wrapped herself*, we are meant to understand that the first verb means that Tamar changed her *physical* clothing; the second verb is adding that she "wrapped herself" *in courage*.[146] She needed to fortify herself before she was able to abandon her comfortable and familiar — albeit stifling — levirate widow's limbo.

While Tamar may have understood intellectually that she *had* to take action or remain in that untenable state forever, still it required an enormous psychological girding to propel herself to act out-of-character. Tamar was accustomed to being *acted upon*, not to acting. First she was *brought* from her childhood home to the home of her groom; then she was *given* in levirate marriage to her dead husband's brother. Now, in contrast, in verse 14, Tamar acts completely on her own initiative.

Actually, Tamar is terrified. It was audacious for her to remove her mourning clothes and adorn herself[147] in colorful, everyday garments *on her own initiative*. She was still, in the eyes of the law of that time, a levirate widow-in-waiting, required to await the whim of her dead husband's nearest male relative. Because she knew this was only her first unauthorized step in her unprecedented personal journey, Tamar was *covered in trembling*.[148]

Even more than shedding her widow's status without authorization, Tamar was about to act in a way that was utterly alien to her character. She would have had to talk to herself, to give herself false courage, to rationalize in the strongest possible terms her upcoming behavior. She might have thought the following: *Judah has no intention of marrying me to Shelah. If I don't force his hand I will molder away in my widow's weeds until I am old and ugly. I will die without ever having had a man hold me in real passion, without having borne and held my own child to my breast. Make the move, Tamar! What have you got to lose? Make the move!*

It is not surprising, then, that the *midrash* understands that Tamar was shaken to her core, was quivering in panic; was, in fact, in the throes of an anxiety attack. Tamar is at her essence a modest woman. After throwing off her widow's weeds she became momentarily weak with fear and anxiety at the thought of "going out" of her comfortable, traditional role. *Midrash* Sechel Tov reads the Hebrew root *alf*, meaning "to wrap oneself," in its alternate definition: *chlf*, meaning "to change, to come anew." Tamar is, truly, emerging from her chrysalis, shedding the passive girl-persona and replacing it with the new, assertive, grown woman: Tamar. And she is doing this right before our eyes.

So prepared is the *midrash* to see Tamar in a heroic light that it says that she had heard the news that Judah was traveling to Timnah *via a divine inspiration*, a flash of divine insight.[149] Whichever it was—the words of a flesh-and-blood messenger, or of a gossip-mongerer,[150] or via a spark of intuition—we are expected to marvel at the speed and decisiveness with which Tamar processes the information and resolves to take action.

The reader is on tenterhooks now, and asks, Will Judah see her? Will he stop to speak to her? Will he take her back to his house and marry her to Shelah?

"SEEING" IMAGERY

The story of Judah and Tamar is threaded through with "seeing" imagery.

The chapter begins with the words *and Judah saw* the daughter of Shuah in verse 2, and next it tells us that Judah's sons were *evil in God's eyes* in verses 7 and 10.

Then here, in verse 14, the Bible names the crossroads where Tamar waits for Judah *Petach Enayim*, meaning "the opening of the **eyes**," and the story picks up momentum.

Seeing, finding and recognizing language appears thirteen times between verses 2 and 26! I will outline the instances here, and in the coming pages the words will serve as progress points as the drama develops and builds to a crescendo. The reader will watch as Judah's eyes are literally "opened" over the course of the story. What Tamar initiates at the place called *Petach Enayim* — "the opening of the eyes" — will reverberate through this chapter as well as for years into the biblical future.

In verse 14 Tamar *sees* that Shelah has grown but that Judah has not given her to him.

In verse 15 Judah *sees* her and thinks her a harlot.

In verse 20 Hirah returns to pay the prostitute but *does not find* her.

In verse 21 Hirah inquires of the locals, "Where is the sacred prostitute who was *ba-enayim* — at the **eye** — of the path?"

In verse 22 Hirah returns to Judah and says, "I **have not found** her."

In verse 23 Judah replies to Hirah, "Behold, I have sent this kid goat [in payment] but **you cannot find** her."

In verse 25 Tamar **is found**.

In verse 25 Tamar asks her father-in-law, "Do you **recognize** to whom these [pledged items] belong?"

And finally, in verse 26 the Bible tells us, "Judah **recognized**" the pledged articles.

In verse 14 the reader is poised to examine the text so that we perceive what Judah "sees" at the crossroads. We already know that Judah's vision is flawed; that he "cannot see straight." After all, he *saw* the Adullamite woman, desired her and took the Canaanite as a wife; he *perceived* Er and Onan's behavior as correct and Tamar's as suspect; in his *view* the best course was to banish Tamar from his house and allow her to languish as a levirate widow. All these were misperceptions and failures of judgement. Now we watch in suspense as Tamar waits by the crossroads. Will he "see" *her*? Will he recognize his daughter-in-law and do the right thing? What drastic steps will Tamar take at *Petach Enayim* in order to "opens Judah's eyes?"

TAMAR WAITS AT THE CROSSROADS

So she removed her widow's garments from her person, and she covered herself in a veil, and she wrapped herself and sat at Petach Enayim, which was on the road to Timnah, because she realized that Shelah had grown, and she was not given to him as a wife. Gen. 38:14

Where does Tamar sit and wait? Verse 14 tells us that she sat at *Petach Enayim* which was on the road to Timnah.

The Bible's naming of this crucial waiting-spot is a wonderful bit of irony. Taken literally, as I mentioned above, it means "the opening of the eyes." But it also can mean, simply, that she sat at a crossroads.[151] The term can signify the place in the roadway where several paths converge, and where the traveler must be vigilant — that is, he must "open his eyes" — lest he take the wrong road by mistake.[152]

Petach Enayim also could have indicated the twin stone plinths that were placed as road markers for all "eyes" to see and read.[153] It was customary to mark each stone with the word *ayin*, meaning "eye" or "marker." The plural of the word gave the place its name after an open road, or *petach*, was beaten between the two plinths, or *enayim*.

So *Petach Enayim* was the spot in the mountain road to Timnah where several roads converged. It is obvious why Tamar sat and waited at that place; she wanted to be certain to intercept Judah when he returned from the sheep-shearing festival. *Petach Enayim* could also have been the actual name of the small settlement that had sprung up on the shepherd's road to Timnah. One *midrash*[154] explains that the settlement was called by that name because it was marked by two wells of water — termed *enayim* in Hebrew — situated right on the mountain path, creating a natural opening, or roadway, between them. It was through the worn path between the wells that Judah would, of necessity, pass on his return from Timnah.[155]

The crossroads at *Petach Enayim* was a place not-too-distant[156] from the town of Adullam, allowing Tamar to walk there and back relatively swiftly. But it also was far enough away from town that she would not attract the attention of the Adullamites as she sat and waited. And this is borne out by later events, when Hirah will ask the locals if they have seen a woman at the crossroads, and all will reply that they have not. Tamar chose her spot strategically and well.

Tamar went alone to the crossroads.[157] She neither asked nor expected her friend to accompany her. This is evidence of her courage and confidence. Even Judah, a grown and respected man who was known in the town and surroundings, did not travel the road alone; he traveled with his friend, Hirah, and probably with at least one other man, as well. For a lone girl such as herself, waiting for and intercepting a man on a public road is audacious, even risky. But if Tamar has in mind to intercept Judah either for a confrontation or for a seduction, it is understandable that she would have wanted to act on her own. Her business is personal, between her father-in-law and herself.

We cannot ignore the symbolism of the meaning of *Petach Enayim* as it applies to Tamar herself. *Her* eyes were opened, too.[158] The Torah says (in verse 14) she wrapped herself and sat at the crossroads at *Petach Enayim* **because she saw** that Judah was not making the move to give her to Shelah, who had by now come of marriageable age. She finally realized, after waiting for two years, that she would die alone if she did not take matters into her own hands. So the veiled Tamar sat at the crossroads of a town named "the opening of the eyes."[159]

Tamar is at a literal as well as a personal crossroads. Does she take the path of least resistance, which will lead her straight into her old age, still wearing her widow's weeds and leading a barren existence in her father's house? Or does she take the other path, the one that winds and is fraught with unknown pitfalls? Does she dare take the risky, frightening road? Does she dare *not* take it?

The Talmud[160] says that in addition to being a crossroads town, *Petach Enayim* was a destination for travelers and pilgrims who were experiencing personal difficulties. The legend was that *Petach Enayim* was situated on the very spot of the famous shade tree of the patriarch Abraham. At that very spot, years before, he had offered hospitality to the three angel/wayfarers[161] and miraculous tidings had been revealed to him. It was said that *the eyes of God* still watched over all who passed through *Petach Enayim*. So passers-by came there *to raise their eyes* in prayer to the Almighty.

We might expect Tamar to whisper a prayer of her own as she waits at *Petach Enayim*. In fact, the Talmud sets out Tamar's own desperate prayer at the crossroads. She prays: "Master of the Universe, let it be Your will that I do not leave this place empty." We will see if her gamble pays off, and if her prayer is answered in the place where God watches closely.

WHAT DOES JUDAH SEE?

And Judah saw her and thought her a harlot, for she had covered her face. Gen. 38:15

We described that Tamar had stripped off her widow's weeds, and veiled and wrapped herself. It is important that we have a mental picture of Tamar at the crossroads in order to appreciate how Judah could misperceive her.

The Bible tells us that *she veiled herself*. Did she veil her entire body, or only her face? According to the Talmud,[162] Tamar veiled her face only, as this was the traditional mode of dress for a modest woman.[163] But if a veiled face signified modesty, how, then, could Judah have thought her a harlot? The answer, according to the Talmud, is that her lone placement in the roadway at the crossroads at *Petach Enayim* would have labeled her a harlot.

Some *midrashists*[164] state the opposite: that ordinary women going about their business did *not* cover their faces; that only a harlot kept her face covered, out of shame. It is said that they veiled their faces to cover the actual brand of harlotry that was seared into their foreheads.[165] It would have been Tamar's placement by the side of the road together with the fact of her veiled face that would have signaled "harlot" to Judah.

There has been much discussion through the ages about how Judah could *not* have recognized his own daughter-in-law, even though she veiled her face. Surely one is familiar with the appearance of one's own family and in-laws, especially if they lived in the same house! And if the mode of conduct and dress for modest women at the time was to veil one's face, as the Talmud says, then surely Judah *should* have recognized the veiled Tamar, as that is how she had appeared when she lived in his house.[166]

But the *midrash*[167] suggests an alternate possibility. Perhaps the Torah's phrase should be read with an implied addition at the end: *And Judah saw her and thought her to be a harlot because she covered her face **while she was in his house***. The suggestion is *not* that Tamar's face was veiled when she sat at the crossroads, but that her *body* was veiled, while her *face* remained exposed. Because Tamar was exceedingly modest,[168] while in Judah's home she never appeared before him — or before anyone except for the women of the house and her own husband — without veiling her face. This would explain why he did not recognize her that evening at the crossroads; he was looking at a face he had seen only once, years before!

Still, the best, text-based reason for Judah's *non*recognition of Tamar as she sat at the crossroads is that her face was veiled. There are also other explanations for Judah's misperception.

First and perhaps foremost, as Judah stood at the crossroads he saw precisely *what he expected to see*. If it was the practice for harlots to situate themselves by the crossroads in order to avail themselves of passing trade, then simply the fact of the figure of a woman *at that place* would have indicated to Judah that she was a harlot. He would not have examined her face minutely under those circumstances. Also, it is likely that harlots typically posted themselves by the roadsides on festival days in order to intercept willing, homeward-bound shepherds whose hearts were already merry by reason of overindulgence in wine. Judah was expecting to see a harlot positioned at the side of the road on that day, and so this is what he saw.

Which brings us back to the question of whether Judah could have recognized Tamar in any event. Recognition would have been highly improbable for several practical reasons. To begin with, Tamar had been in Judah's house for a matter of only a few short weeks. He took her from her father's house when she was, at most, in her late teens. Her face was uncovered then, surely, and her hair unbound, as typified a maiden. But that was perhaps the last time he would have seen her face.

Thereafter, when she was wed first to Er and then to Onan and living in Judah's household, she remained there for a total of, at most, a matter of a few weeks before each was struck down. Allowing for the public period of the funerals, when Judah was so distracted with grief that he would not only not have looked at Tamar, it is likely their paths never crossed. And, as he had already begun to suspect Tamar's "bad karma" of having struck down his two sons, Judah—blinded by his grief and his trans-ferred anger—banished Tamar from his sight even before eventually banning her from his very home. There would have been no opportunity for him to view her face.

Added to this, for the past two years Tamar has been living a completely separate and cloistered existence in the home of her youth by the time Judah sees the seated figure at *Petach Enayim*. Tamar is by now out of her teens, has been widowed twice, and is no longer the girl he would have remembered. It is even possible that *nobody* outside of her own house has seen Tamar unveiled since she was banished there. Any venturing from her house would have been limited to the business of everyday living, such as routine trips to the town well, when she was not only veiled, but also shrouded in mourning clothes and shunned by the other Adullamites. Nobody was looking closely at Tamar.

One *midrash*[169] even says that swathed in scarves as she was, with only her eyes exposed, Tamar looked like a fortune-teller sitting by the crossroads! Judah would never have seen that veiled, seated woman and associated her with Tamar. Other *midrashim* say that Tamar's veil was long and diaphanous;[170] that she tightly wound it 'round her neck and shoulders and did not remove it, even during the coming sexual intimacy, so that she retained a veiled and erotic mystery. Her face and neck were never fully visible.[171]

So not only is it credible that Judah did *not* recognize his daughter-in-law as she sat at *Petach Enayim* and thereafter; it would have been surprising had he done so!

JUDAH TRANSACTS WITH "A HARLOT"

So he turned toward her by the wayside, and he said, "If you please, I would come unto you." For he did not know she was his daughter-in-law . . . Gen. 38:16

That evening, as he walks with Hirah back home to Adullam, Judah passes the crossroads at *Petach Enayim*. He sees a female figure, her lithe form swathed in veils from head to toe.[172]

Judah has spent the day among the reveling shepherds, all of whom he has known for two decades and who are, in essence, his family-in-exile. The men had been glad to see Judah take his rightful place as master of ceremonies of the important sheep-shearing festival.

We can envision the sheep-shearing scene at Timnah:

The men had begun their hot and gritty work at sunup. By the time the sun was setting, the crush of bleating sheep, men with sleeves rolled bearing wickedly honed shearing knives, hundreds of shorn and subdued animals, and tired workmen, had become an ordered field of tied and counted bundles of raw wool. Tables were set up off to the side for the celebratory meal, and undiluted wine was poured and drunk freely as the men toasted Judah, their partner and boss, the man who had brought them all such prosperity.

The trek up to Timnah was Judah's first happy outing in two years, since the death of his first son. Judah was exhausted by it. He longed for his own bed, and he surprised himself by pining for a woman to warm it. His celibate mourning period was at an end; his frozen desires had thawed, and the natural urges of a man in the prime of his life surfaced within him.

It is at this point, as Judah and his friend and partner, Hirah, wend their way back down the mountainside as evening closes in, that Judah sees the veiled vision of a woman sitting at the crossroads.

The Torah tells us that Judah thought her a harlot. One *midrash*[173] says that he kept walking past the veiled, seated figure, as it was not his practice to visit prostitutes. But the angel Michael[174] had been sent by the Almighty — perhaps in answer to Tamar's prayer — and he turned Judah back. This is the reason verse 16 says, *So he **turned toward her** by the wayside* . . . The Hebrew word indicates Judah *turned aside*[175] from his homeward path especially to address the woman he mistook for a harlot.

It might not even have been necessary for the angel Michael to have turned Judah back toward Tamar. A fascinating commentary[176] explains that a person's strengths, desires, or inclinations are also called "angels" in *midrashic* literature. In the present situation Judah began to walk past the "harlot" by the roadside; but the strength of his own long-dormant sexual desire turned him back.

> *So he turned toward her by the wayside, and he said, "Here, I would come unto you."* **For he did not know she was his daughter-in-law.** *And she said, "What would you give me if you came unto me?"* Gen. 38:16

Judah's physical needs overcame his initial reticence. He turned from the path and approached "the harlot," asking — perhaps even demanding — to lie with her. The Torah text interrupts what will be a detailed negotiation of terms, and explains to the reader in an aside, *For he did not know she was his daughter-in-law.* This is a critical piece of information because Judah, arguably Adullam's most respected patriarch, is about to behave in the manner of a commoner, by soliciting sex with a roadside "prostitute." He also is about to violate the incest taboo, albeit unknowingly, by being intimate with his daughter-in-law.

While neither Judah nor Tamar is married and one would think each is free to engage in this sexual encounter, there are actually serious social and quasi-legal complications surrounding such a liaison.

True, Judah is a widower and done with his mourning period, but nevertheless association with a prostitute—while not forbidden—carries a "social stigma."[177] Proof that this stigma is widely known appears in verse 23. There, after Judah has had relations with "the harlot," he sends Hirah searching in vain for her in order to tender payment. Judah is embarrassed by his own behavior, and it is his long-standing friend who goes looking for the harlot, and not Judah himself. Also, it is Judah who calls off the search, saying, *let her keep the pledges, lest we be **shamed***. He did not wish to draw attention or ridicule[178] upon himself for being with a prostitute. Years into the future Mosaic Law (Deut. 23:18) will codify the prohibition against harlotry. But for now, open knowledge that he had consorted with a harlot would have shamed Judah.

But the most significant deterrent to this liaison is that Tamar is *not* actually free to cohabit with any man she wishes. Under the social laws in place at the time, she is an unreleased levirate widow "whose status is equal to that of a wife"[179] for purposes of being forbidden to another, even though she remains technically unmarried. It is a difficult, Gordian limbo into which Judah has placed her. She must comport herself chastely, as a wife would, though she is not *truly* married; she was banished as a young widow to an exile in her childhood home, while at the same time she is bound by strong social tradition to wed only a male from her deceased husband's family—a mate whom Judah is deliberately withholding from her!

As a result, because Tamar is considered a *de facto* wife, if she has sexual relations with a man other than her levirate redeemer she is considered an adulterer, and dire consequences would flow from that, as we will see later on in our story.

Judah turns from his homeward path and approaches "the harlot," saying, "here, let me come unto you." It is striking how forthright Judah's words are.[180] It is stunning that, unbeknownst to him, his first words in more than two years to Tamar, his daughter-in-law, are requesting a sexual liaison! Tamar is astonished, too. She had been intent on accosting Judah on his route home either to demand that she be given to Shelah in levirate marriage, or that he set her free from her levirate widowhood. But Judah's words and his assumption that she is a harlot push her to decide to play the role that he has assigned her.[181]

Judah is saying to her, in effect, "Excuse me, miss, but if you're free for the next hour I would like to hire your sexual services." A moment after he poses the question—once she absorbs the shock of his mistaken assumption—Tamar makes her decision. She *will* lay with Judah, Er's father; she *will* use him to fulfill the levirate obligation to her dead husband.

And if her intent in waiting at the crossroads had been not to *confront* Judah into doing his levirate duty, but to *seduce* him as her levirate mate, even so Tamar would have had only a moment to register surprise that her hastily-conceived and -executed plan was apparently working. Judah had not recognized her!

The Talmud[182] is aware that there exists some sort of critical pause, an interstice, between Judah's request and Tamar's response. There *has* to be one. So it posits an unwritten verbal exchange between Judah and "the harlot," which might have taken place during the pause between the asking and the negotiation. The Torah text presents a clear instance of a proposition for transactional sex. But the *midrash* is bothered by the idea of Judah having a chance sexual encounter by the side of the road, so we will see that it reads a detailed proposal of marriage into the Bible's fact pattern.

Judah turns off the road to Adullam and approaches the comely woman waiting by the crossroads. He is taken with her form and bearing, and in the haste of the moment he decides to ask her to be his wife.[183] He has had enough of the solitary life and is more than ready to reenter the world of the living. So he asks her, "Excuse me, madam, but perchance may I claim you for myself and lay with you? But first, pray, tell me, what gods do you worship?"

"You may be at ease, Sir," Tamar replied. "I am a convert, and do not worship false gods. I am a worthy partner," Her eyes are cast downward, her heart beating wildly, out of fear that her true identity will be discovered — or out of fear that it will *not*, and that she will have to go through with the charade that has already begun.

"But are you married to another?"

"No, sir, I am unmarried."

"But perhaps your father has accepted a betrothal on your behalf and you are already promised to another?"

"Sir, my father died when I was still a girl. My mother and brothers gave me away to my first husband. I am an orphan, with no father from whom we must seek permission before marrying."

Then Judah *midrashically* poses his final question. "And is this the right time for us to mate?"

Tamar understands that Judah is inquiring if it is the right time of the month for this encounter. He must know before taking her if she is ritually clean and thus free to engage in sexual activity with him immediately. Judah would rather not put off the physical part of the union and he is hoping that this lovely woman is ritually permitted to him. Tamar is pleased to be able to respond, "Sir, I am pure and ritually clean and am permitted to you."

Now that the preliminaries are out of the way, Judah is more at ease. This mysterious woman who has attracted him mightily is available to him as a bed partner as well as a potential mate. He is eager to follow her[184] to the roadside visitors' kiosk when her query stops him.

> And she said, "What would you give me if you came unto me?"
>
> And he said, "I will send you a kid-goat from the flock." And she said, "Will you give me a pledge until you send it?"
>
> And he said, "What pledge shall I give you?" And she said, "Your signet, your sash and your staff that is in your hand."

So he gave them to her, and he came unto her, and she became pregnant by him. Gen. 38:16–18

Judah does not appear fazed when "the harlot" asks him, *What would you give me if you came unto me?* Their exchange sounds like any other business deal, with "buyer" and "seller" discussing and agreeing upon price and terms. Their interaction takes place hundreds of years before the giving of the Mosaic Laws at Sinai, when harlotry is made categorically forbidden. In Judah's time, it was not yet prohibited. In fact, at that time it was not uncommon for a man to encounter a woman in the market-place, and, if both were free and willing, for them to agree upon a price in advance, conduct their intimate business discreetly,[185] and then go their separate ways.[186] Still, notwithstanding all this, contracting for sex with a harlot has a negative valence even in Judah's time; it is not a neutral activity, and it will become clear from the text that Judah is embarrassed about his behavior.

The Torah presents Judah and Tamar's negotiation in detail: Tamar asks, *What will you give me, so that you will come unto me?* Judah figuratively pats down his pockets, and says, "I don't have any money on me right now,[187] but *I will send you a kid goat from the flock* tomorrow, if that is acceptable to you." Like any good businesswoman, Tamar rejoinds, "But *surely you will give me a pledge as a guarantee until you send* the kid-goat?" To wit, Judah responds, *What pledge should I give you?*

TAMAR REQUESTS A PLEDGE

And she said, "Your signet, your sash and your staff that is in your hand." So he gave them to her, and he came unto her . . .
Gen. 38:18

It is at this juncture that Tamar's presence of mind and cool head come to the fore. She speaks up and responds to his proposition, asking, *What will you give to me if I agree to allow you to come unto me?* **These are the first words Tamar speaks in the Bible**. As such, and given that she will have more to say before the story's end, her words are significant. We will deal with their subject matter presently; but for now, there should be a small gasp from the intent reader. We might ask, What if Judah recognizes Tamar's voice? In fact, the *midrash*[188] suggests that this was her intent! Tamar's "plan A" was to position herself at the crossroads in order to confront her father-in-law and push him to take her back into his household, to wed her to Shelah in levirate marriage. She spoke up to him expecting that he would recognize her voice. It was when Judah fell prey to his own desires as well as to his own assumptions that she was a harlot, that Tamar resorted to her hastily-crafted "plan B." She resolved to play along with Judah's assumption. She would be intimate with her dead husband's father in order to perpetuate Er's name.

Tamar knows that it is possible that she could become pregnant from the coming sexual encounter with Judah. She knows, too, that as a "chained widow" she is forbidden from being intimate with any man *except* one who stands in levirate relationship to her deceased husband; that she would be considered an adulteress otherwise. So she asks that Judah give her — as a surety that he will proffer the agreed payment the next day, but in reality so that she will have proof-positive of his identity — the three objects he is wearing that identify him. *Tamar has no intention of returning Judah's identifying pledges to him.* She is, instead, preparing against the day when she might have a need to prove unequivocally the identity of the father of her unborn child.[189] She will need to prove that he stood in proper levirate relationship to her and that her sexual union with him was therefore permissible.

From her specific request that Judah's identifiers serve as his pledge we see that Tamar intends to become pregnant *by Judah*, Er's (and Onan's) next closest male relative,[190] so that her dead husband's name would be sustained, and his inheritance share secured. It is vital that her intention be pure and her motivation proper, otherwise her imminent act of sexual intercourse with her father-in-law would bring the death sentence upon both of them.[191]

The Talmud[192] unambiguously states that Tamar's seduction of Judah was motivated by noble intentions: to perpetuate her dead husband's name. Therefore, her intimate coupling with Judah was permissible and even praiseworthy. Her pure intentions are key.[193] The Torah is clear that she did not lay with Judah for prurient pleasure, but *because she saw that Shelah had grown but that Judah did not give her to him* in levirate marriage. This is the reason that Tamar merited not only that she would become pregnant from this one-time intimacy by the crossroads, but also that she would bear Judah twin sons to make up for the two sons who had died, and that kings and prophets—even the Messiah—would descend from them. The Talmud is explicit that this reward would *not* have devolved to a woman who had engaged in actual harlotry, where death to both the harlot and her male partner is the expected end.[194]

So Tamar asks Judah to leave as a pledge of future payment his signet ring, his sash, and his staff. Judah agrees, and one-at-a-time he gives the pledged items to Tamar, who keeps them with her own garments. It is curious that Judah agrees so readily to part—albeit temporarily—with his indicia of power and authority.[195] *Ibn Ezra*[196] explains that the three items of collateral that Judah ceded to Tamar were tremendously overvalued relative to the agreed-upon price of the kid-goat. The *midrash* concludes that Judah's desire overwhelmed him and so he agreed to give her the three items she requested. The fact that he eagerly parted with such valuable pledges might have contributed to his embarrassment the next day, when his friend, Hirah, could not find "the harlot" to exchange the kid-goat for the pledges. We will see that Judah calls off the search, as he does not want word to get out that a canny businessman such as he, had been bested in the transaction by a harlot.

Judah must have been very certain the items would be returned when he proffered payment. It probably never crossed his mind that his pledged items would *not* be returned, for of what use would they be to a harlot or to anyone other than their true owner? The price of a kid-goat perhaps holds a higher "street value" than the pledged items, as it can be sold at market, kept for its milk, or slaughtered and used for food; while the pledged items are of great value to their owner only. Or perhaps it was common practice to pledge such items in a transaction such as this. Their unique and recognizable nature would actually have shielded them from theft; whoever found them would be obliged to return them to their owner.

Judah's signet ring bore the image of the head of a lion,[197] and served double duty as a branding tool for identifying his sheep and his wool;[198] it probably had never before left Judah's hand, for fear of its duplication and use in forging Judah's unique signature.[199] His sash, or tunic, bore the unique design worn by him and his brothers, recognizable to all as belonging to a person of consequence;[200] and the staff was irreplaceable, as it was the very staff that his father, Jacob, had used when he ran away from home half a lifetime ago.[201]

There is much lore assigning special powers to Judah's staff. The *midrash*[202] explains that this staff, inherited from his father, Jacob, is the staff that Moses will use in years to come when he is standing in the Pharaoh's court. This same staff will match—and best—the king's necromancers when it morphs into a serpent. It will turn the Nile's waters into blood and will perform all manner of signs and wonders, the most dramatic of which will be that in Moses' hand it will split the Sea of Reeds allowing the Children of Israel to walk through to the other side as they flee Egypt.

It is *this* staff that Judah entrusts to the veiled woman who is Tamar. It is momentous that the commentaries elevate Judah's workaday, wooden staff into the legendary one that is fated to perform wonders. They place this same staff into Tamar's hands as one-third of Judah's pledge of payment. They want the reader to appreciate that Tamar's status and character are unblemished by her masquerade by the crossroads and that she is worthy of wielding it. One might say that the staff will save Tamar from death when she produces it in future verses. Or one might just as well say that it is Tamar's extraordinary grace under intense pressure and fear of imminent death by burning that brings the staff to yet another level. Tamar's behavior will "work the magic" of turning Judah from exiled son into family leader and forefather of kings and prophets. Does she infuse the staff with her own strength or is it the other way around? Perhaps it is both. The *midrash* is saying that the staff finds its way into the hands of the worthy. Tamar is in heady company!

The three items Tamar names as pledges actually point to some measure of divinely-inspired intuition on her part.[203] Not only are they signs of Judah's present status, they also are destined to become the hallmarks of future kings, prophets and judges of Israel. The signet ring is a direct reference to royalty, as it is will be worn by unborn kings of the Kingdom of Judah on their right hands; the sash—*p'til* in Hebrew—is an allusion to the judges on the high court of the Sanhedrin, who will tie their robes with a *p'til*—a sash or cord of blue; and the staff points not only to Moses the redeemer, as we have just seen, but also to the future Messiah, who is referred to as God's "staff of strength."

Judah would not have consented to part with these three possessions as collateral if he had had any doubt that when presented with the kid-goat "the harlot" would return them without qualm.

WAS IT LEGAL?

Was Judah's act of paying for and laying with "a harlot" permissible?

At the time of this story—that is, in the pre-biblical period before the giving of the Mosaic Law at Sinai—such extramarital, temporary or "companionship sex" was legally permitted. Even after the giving of the Torah and much later, the Nachmanides (Ramban) did not prohibit "faithful sexual companionship" even though he considered it "unwise." But the codes of Maimonides (Rambam) and Rabbi Joseph Karo did prohibit such nonmarital sexual relationships, and normative Jewish law has evolved in this vein.[204]

Still, even though sex with a prostitute was not actually forbidden, because of the pressure of pre-biblical societal norms, the Talmud[205] explains that Judah did feel shame for his rendezvous with "a harlot," and Rashi[206] also felt that there was a shameful or negative cast to Judah's behavior. But there is more than meets the eye to the conversation between Judah and Tamar. Let us see how Judah dealt with his desire for the veiled woman at the crossroads.

A "MARRIAGE" AT THE CROSSROADS

There is a fascinating *midrash*[207] that Tamar intended to be intimate with Judah *only under the auspices of a proper marriage,* or *kiddushin.* This is providential, as absent some sort of legal sanction the union of Judah and Tamar, his daughter-in-law, violates the incest taboo. When she asked Judah for a surety of payment, as we know, Tamar's first request was that he remove his signet ring. *Midrashically,* she said to him, "This is the ring that you use to stamp your possessions. If you want me, you must use it now to take me in marriage according to the law of the God of Abraham."

Judah was powerfully attracted to the tall and mysterious veiled woman.[208] His great desire for her is reflected in the language of the verses: First the Torah says that *he saw her*; then that *he turned from his path*; and third, that *he requested of her,* "*Pray, tell, will you allow me to come unto you?*" There is a flavor of haste[209] about the verbs. Judah is making up his mind right in front of the reader's eyes. It is possible that he had experienced a moment of clarity, or a *coup de foudre*, or a rush of unbridled, uncontrollable lust for the veiled woman by the road. Whatever the impetus, the *midrash* says that Judah asked the woman for an exclusive sexual relationship.[210] He might have asked her, "Will you refrain from harlotry and dedicate yourself *to me alone*?" By any other name, he was requesting a marriage commitment.

As Judah was a nobleman, he never traveled without at least one, and usually two, *aides-de-camp*. His trip to the sheep-shearing at Timnah was no exception. This particular evening, Judah was accompanied by Hirah, his longtime friend and business partner, and also by at least one other friend or servant, as was the custom of the day.[211] Tamar saw that his two aides were standing by the crossroads at a polite distance, watching their friend and master as he approached her and began the dialogue. Tamar held out her hand in full view of the two witnesses, and as Judah placed his signet ring onto her forefinger the marriage deal was struck. It met the bare-bones requirements of an Israelite union.[212] In the presence of two male witnesses, an object of value—here a ring— was tendered by the man with intent to take the woman as his wife, and it was accepted freely by the woman. Immediately afterwards, as night was falling,[213] the couple secluded themselves in a shack[214] at the side of the crossroads and consummated the union.

Another *midrash* supports this suggestion that Judah took the veiled woman in marriage. The opening word in verse 16 is *vayet*, meaning **And he [Judah] turned aside** to her. . . . The *midrash*[215] examines that simple word and sees a hint to what transpired between Judah and the veiled woman by the roadside. We are told that the word hints that Judah *turned aside* to hand her a *ketubah*, a marriage certificate. The *gematria*, or arithmetic value of the letters of the tiny word *vayet*, is twenty-five, hinting that he offered the woman twenty-five *dinar*, the bride-price for a virgin. He offered this high cash amount as the price of the marriage agreement, over and above the price of the kid-goat.

Aside from the question of whether Judah took the roadside woman in marriage, Tamar's intimacy with her father-in-law fulfilled the requirements of a levirate marriage.[216] She had not comported herself as a harlot; neither had she violated her status as an unreleased widow. Rather, she acted honorably, and engaged in an eyes-open, sanctioned sexual union *for the intended purpose of producing an heir for her deceased husband.*[217]

Of course, the problem persists that Judah *did not know that she was his daughter-in-law.* Even if the negotiation by the roadside at *Petach Enayim* produced a marriage and not merely a sexual dalliance, we have a situation where the woman Judah took to bed was not the woman he thought she was; he did not intend to wed and bed *his daughter-in-law.* The reader will recall that a similar situation had presented itself to Jacob, Judah's father, about half-a-century before. Then, Jacob had thought he was marrying Rachel, his true love, when in fact he was wed to Leah, her older sister. He lay with Leah all that night, consummating the marriage, believing her to be Rachel, *and in the morning, behold, it was Leah!*[218] Still, the marriage to Leah was not dissolved, notwithstanding the absence of a meeting of the minds of both parties. When the situation was ultimately exposed, the deed had been done, so-to-speak, and presumably to protect the woman and her status, the union held. The same principle could be at work here, but we will see that there is much drama and terror first.

An interesting word-play in the Torah text hints at Tamar's dual role in the story vis-a-vis Judah: she is both his daughter-in-law and also his "bride" and mother of his twin sons. In verse 16 the text says *for he did not know she was **his daughter-in-law***. The Hebrew word for "daughter-in-law" — *kalah* — has a dual definition. It means both daughter-in-law and also bride![219] Given that Judah does not know either that "the harlot" is his *kalah*, his daughter-in-law, or that his new *kalah*, his bride, is Tamar, the implication of the text is highly ironic. Here, at the crossroads town by the name of *Petach Enayim* — at the place where one's eyes should be open — Judah fails to see, and *does not know*.

TAMAR BECOMES PREGNANT

*. . . So he gave them [the pledges] to her, and he came unto her, **and she became pregnant by him.*** Gen. 38:18

The deal having been struck, the "marriage" between Judah and the veiled woman having been effected with the gift of his signet ring, all that remained was that they complete the transaction via sexual consummation. This sexual consummation was, after all, what Judah had desired from the moment he caught sight of the veiled woman at the crossroads. And from a practical standpoint this was also what Tamar had sought: a levirate marriage that would plant within her the seed of her dead husband, Er, and allow her to give birth to the next generation of Judah's family.

The Torah does not leave us in suspense. It tells us straight-out that immediately after Tamar received the pledges from Judah he lay with her and impregnated her. We are certain that it is Judah's seed that impregnated Tamar because the Torah is careful to depart from its usual form, which is to state "and she became pregnant." Here, at the end of verse 18, the Torah adds the seemingly superfluous two-letter Hebrew word that holds the key to this drama: it is the word *lo*, meaning "to him," "by him," or even "belonging to him." The text leaves no room for doubt that Tamar has become pregnant *by Judah*.[220]

The same *midrash* interprets the word *lo* to mean that Tamar became pregnant *by him* — specifically by Judah — with sons that would be progenitors of kings, as befits the man who is to be known as the lion of Judah, the mighty and righteous leader of his brothers and of half the Israelite kingdom.[221]

The *Netziv*[222] says that the extra word *lo* (*by him*) is a textual allusion to the fact that Tamar's pregnancy *by Judah* — a closely-related male relation of Er — means the end of her levirate widowhood. Once she has conceived a child with the redeemer or *yavam*, she — and the redeemer — have done their duty to her deceased husband and she is free to get on with her life.

There is some *midrashic* discussion about whether Tamar was a virgin when Judah *came unto her* in the hut at the crossroads. The Talmud[223] states that she was, indeed, a virgin at that time, and that she conceived from her first-ever act of sexual intimacy. This may strike Bible readers as impossible, given that Tamar had been married twice, both times to young, virile men who surely did not fail to have sex with her. And Rashi agrees, saying that Onan, whom Tamar wed in levirate marriage, *did* initially engage in natural sexual relations with Tamar, although he spilled his seed onto the ground.

But the Talmud explains that it *was* possible for Tamar to have remained a virgin notwithstanding her marriages. This is because, as I discussed earlier, both Er and Onan wasted their seed by cohabiting with Tamar "unnaturally." Er sodomized her to prevent impregnating her, so intent was he on keeping her slim and lovely for his enjoyment. And Onan, the Torah states explicitly, deliberately "spilled his seed onto the ground" in order to avoid his levirate duty to impregnate her with his seed and sustain his brother's memory and inheritance share.

The same Talmudic discussion explains that Tamar had deliberately broken her own hymen just moments preceding her intimacy with Judah, thus easing the way for a possible pregnancy.

Why is it so important that Tamar is a virgin when she shares a bed with Judah? It strains credulity to think that this was so, and even Rashi weighs in on the side of her having been sexually initiated by Onan, if not by Er. Clearly the rabbis of the Talmud want an indisputable provenance for the twin sons that Tamar will bear. If Tamar is a virgin when she has her sexual encounter at the crossroads, then there is no doubt that Judah is the father of her sons. What remains unsaid is if she is not a virgin, there is the finite possibility that her pregnancy is not Judah's. Such a situation would be intolerable, as the Davidic dynasty has its roots in Tamar's sons, and must originate with Judah.

There is no intimation in the *midrash* that Tamar's pregnancy is not precisely what it appears to be: that she is pregnant for the first time and by Judah's seed. And the reason for this is most probably, as I discussed above, that the Torah text ends verse 18 with the words *vatahar lo*: *she became pregnant by him*. There is absolutely no ambiguity in the Bible text as to who impregnated Tamar.

TAMAR DISAPPEARS

GENESIS 38:19–23

Then she arose, and went away, and removed her veil from upon her; and she [again] dressed herself in her widow's garments.

And Judah sent the kid-goat by the hand of his friend, the Adullamite, in order to retrieve the pledge from the hand of the woman; but he could not find her.

So he asked the people of her place as follows: "Where is the kedeisha *who [sat] at the opening of the crossroads?" And they said, "There was no* kedeisha *in this place."*

And he returned to Judah and said, "I could not find her. And also the people of the place said there was no kedeisha *in this place."*

And Judah said, "Let her keep it, lest we will be shamed; for I have sent this kid-goat, yet you have not found her."

What does Tamar do next?

Then she arose, and went away, and removed her veil from upon her; and she [again] dressed herself in her widow's garments. Gen. 38:19

This verse presents four verbs, one on the heels of the other, so that Tamar once again is a blur of action.[224] After their sexual interlude, and perhaps as Judah lies sleeping, Tamar rises quickly from their bed, exits the hut of their assignation, and under cover of darkness she hastily makes her way, unseen, back to Adullam and her father's house.

We must assume that the faithful Hirah and his companion, both loyal to Judah, are still waiting for him to conclude his business. Perhaps they moved across the road, perhaps there was a public house where they could drink a glass of wine and exchange stories while they passed the time. Tamar easily eluded their and anyone else's curious eyes. She passed silently and swiftly through the dark crossroads like a wraith, leaving no trace.

Upon arriving at her home, and in the privacy of her room, Tamar unwinds the veil from her face and neck, sheds her colorful clothing, folds them and puts them away. There is no sentimentality attendant to any of her actions. The veil and clothing have served their purpose, and she packs them out-of-sight. She then dons her despised widow's black, and if there were anyone to observe her, she would have once again appeared as the passive, compliant, and tragic young widow. By no outward sign could it have been detected that Tamar had, not an hour before, played the harlot, and fooled and lain with her father-in-law.

The Torah is precise in its descriptions of Tamar's undressing and dressing both in verse 14 and here, in verse 19, when it narrates her pre- and post-crossroads wardrobe changes. In fact, the text twice uses the identical word, *vatasar*, meaning *and she removed,* when it describes the earlier removal of her widow's weeds, and here her veil of secrecy and seduction. Both her widow's black and her veil were cloth coverings, but there ends the similarity; for Tamar was enshrouded by the former and liberated by the latter. Also, the Bible twice relates her undressing and dressing. She is, after two years of being silent and passive, at long last in charge of her "identity." Like a magician who deftly covers and uncovers his tricks with scarves and dramatic sleight-of-hand, Tamar is becoming, at least outwardly and right before our eyes, the widow woman she had been five verses previously.

Judah *does not know* what really transpired in the hut that night[225] at the crossroads, but Tamar and the reader do. We have watched her in both her identities. This dramatic irony heightens our anticipation. What will happen next? Will Tamar be found out?

The fact that Tamar once again dons her widow's black can have but one meaning. Her widow's clothing shields her from the eyes and the prurient desires of other men. The widow's black is a signal to all that the woman within is unavailable for either casual or permanent liaison or remarriage.[226] Tamar's widow's black affirms for the reader that what she did at the crossroads was a one-time event. She "played the harlot" solely for the purpose of becoming pregnant by Judah, the levirate redeemer, and in order to perpetuate Judah's seed. She has neither the intention nor the desire to take another man to her bed for as long as she lives.[227]

The woman who dresses herself in black in verse 19 is not the same woman who shed it in verse 14. *This* Tamar is legally free to shed her widow's clothing now that she has been intimate with her *yavam*, or levirate redeemer.[228] For the past two years she has had no choice but to wear those clothes—an eloquent symbol of her unavailability; but now she dresses herself in black voluntarily, using those same garments to shield herself from the eyes of the village men. She is secretly happy[229] in the hope that she has just become pregnant from Judah, and that her audacious sexual gamble will pay off.

SEARCHING FOR "THE WOMAN"
AT THE CROSSROADS

Keeping to his agreement with "the harlot," the next day Judah sends his friend, Hirah, to the prearranged spot to tender the kid-goat as payment for his sexual liaison. At the time that he had negotiated the fee with her, Judah had inquired of the woman where he could find her to effect the exchange and redeem his pledges. She had specified the particular passageway and lane in the village of *Petach Enayim* where she could be found.[230] But though he leads the kid-goat by a tether, walks through *Petach Enayim* and follows Judah's specific instructions, Hirah can find neither the address nor the woman.

So Hirah diligently inquires of the people who are in the lane, "Where is the sacred prostitute who sat at the crossroads?" And he is met with genuine puzzlement when they respond, "Why, there never was a sacred prostitute in this place."

The *Netziv* slows down the action and says there is more than a casual reason that the Torah text explains in detail that Hirah searched in vain for the woman, and that it also recounts the seemingly trivial interchange between Hirah and the locals. The commentator explains that, unbeknownst to Judah, he is being taught a lesson. The double iteration of the words "there never was a prostitute in this place" should echo in his mind so that when, in the near future, fingers will point to Tamar calling her a prostitute, he should pause and consider the accusation rather than accepting it outright. And when Tamar forces him publicly to confront the truth — that it was *he* who impregnated her — the Torah wants Judah to understand that she had not prostituted herself with others at the crossroads or elsewhere. Hirah and the locals at the crossroads tell Judah in these verses that "there never was a sacred prostitute in this place," and they speak the truth. There was only Tamar, seducing Judah, the *yavam*, so that he would do his duty by her.

We note that the Bible uses varying nouns to refer to Tamar in this episode. When Judah first glimpses her, in verse 15, he mistakenly thinks her a *zonah*, or a harlot. In the same verse we are told he did not know that she was his *kalah*, his daughter-in-law (the word *kalah* also means "bride"). In verse 19 he sends the Adullamite to retrieve his pledges from *ha-isha*, the woman; and in verse 20 Hirah asks about *ha-kedeisha*, the cultic prostitute. As the Torah text is deliberately precise in its word-use, we should explore this word-switch as it refers to Tamar.

As far as Judah's perceptions are concerned, Tamar is, in truth, the first three: a harlot, his daughter-in-law (his bride, as well, according to the *midrash*), and the woman. By the time we encounter Judah walking down the mountainside from Timnah to Adullam, we can be sure he has not given even as much as a fleeting thought to his daughter-in-law Tamar in months, if not years. He had bundled her away to her father's house and banished her from his sight and his presence, so that even as he automatically labels the woman sitting by the roadside a harlot, there is no connecting her to his daughter-in-law Tamar.

It is fascinating that only *after* Judah has been sexually intimate with the harlot does the Torah refer to her in verse 20 as "the woman." Judah has related to her as a man relates to a desirable woman; perhaps he was so attracted to her that he sought an exclusive sexual arrangement or even marriage, as the *midrash* suggests. Either way, as wife or as bed partner, she is described more sympathetically — as "the woman" — when he is seeking to redeem his pledges, than she was previously.

But why does Hirah refer to her as the *kedeisha* or sacred prostitute in verse 19? Apparently a subtle difference in mode of dress distinguished the *zonah* from the *kedeisha*. The commercial prostitute, or *zonah*, did not cover her face, while the cultic prostitute, or *kedeisha*, did.[231] Frymer-Kensky[232] discusses the *zonah* versus *kedeisha* issue, and concludes that because *zonah* is a less desirable epithet than is *kedeisha*, both Hirah and Judah attempt to save Judah's reputation by searching for a *kedeisha*.[233] "Even though it was not illegal to sleep with a prostitute, it appears that Judah nevertheless preferred to keep it quiet."[234] Judah cared about his reputation, and for that reason Hirah toned down the search. Judah did not wish "to seem needy or foolish"[235] in the eyes of his neighbors.

The *midrash*[236] will not let the irony of the coincidence of a kid-goat, a deception, and Judah rest. It reminds the reader that The Almighty "laughs at men" as their destinies spin out. Here is Judah, left holding the kid-goat, searching in vain for the woman who has taken his seed. Twenty years before, Judah had dipped his brother's many-colored cloak in the blood of a kid-goat, thereby deceiving his father into thinking his son — his seed — was dead. Now, by a twist of the same strand of fate, Tamar has deceived Judah through the medium of a kid-goat, she has taken his seed, and now she has vanished, too. In both incidents the primary underlying issue is continuation of family and the destructive unwillingness of brother to stand for brother. The difference is that in our story Tamar is the wildcard. We will see how her presence alters the outcome.

Hirah returns to Adullam still leading the kid goat. He reports back to Judah that the woman has vanished, and that everyone he asked said that there had never been a *kedeisha* in that place.[237] Judah is in a bit of a bind. He badly wants the return of his signet ring, his sash and his staff, but it seems the harlot has kept the pledge and has disappeared. So he sends Hirah back to the crossroads to try again.[238] When his friend returns a second time, again leading the hapless kid-goat, Judah decides to call off the search, telling Hirah, "Let the woman keep the pledges. If we keep searching for her we will only draw attention to ourselves, and I will become a laughingstock.[239] It is obvious that I have done my best to find her, bringing a fat, fine[240] specimen of a kid-goat as I promised. Let this be an end to it."

TAMAR'S PREGNANCY IS FOUND OUT

And it happened, after about three months, it was told to Judah as follows: "Tamar, your daughter-in-law, has whored, and now, behold, she is pregnant from her whoring." And Judah said, "Take her out and burn her!" Gen. 38:24

About three months have passed since Judah's intimacy with "the harlot" at the crossroads. He has put the incident out of his mind as he resumed his busy life as town father and prominent businessman in Adullam.

The familiar portentous word *Vayehi — And it happened —* opens this verse, hinting to us once again that bad news is coming; and so it is. Just as Judah emerges from his years of mourning the decimation of his family, he is hit with the news that his nearly-forgotten daughter-in-law is brazenly pregnant.

For a levirate widow still wearing widow's black to be found pregnant was a serious matter. The reader will recall from our earlier discussions that the status of a levirate widow was a peculiar hybrid of widowhood combined with an ersatz betrothal-cum-marriage. The levirate or unreleased widow (*i.e.*, a woman whose husband has died without issue and who awaits marriage to his next-closest male relative for the sole purpose of producing an heir to carry on his name and secure his inheritance share[241]) is *not free* to marry just anyone. She is, in effect, a widow-in-waiting, and if she violates her "unreleased" state by being intimate with a man who is not in levirate line to her husband, she is considered an adulterer.[242] In the eyes of the law it is *as if* she were already the wife of the levirate redeemer.[243] And as such, the penalty for a levirate adulteress was that she be put to death.[244]

This levirate prohibition was added onto the common legal restriction against "seclusion with an unmarried woman." This social limitation was codified as prohibited behavior but not until later times.[245] At the time of our story, as we already have seen, cohabiting with a strange woman was seriously frowned upon in Judah's social circle. These two verboten behaviors — one addressing the female and the other the male — scorched the very threads of the society's social fabric, and generated communal anger and instant scandal.

Which is another reason why it is fascinating that the *midrash*[246] is so staunchly supportive of Tamar. It even advances the argument that the fact of her pregnancy actually proves she could *not* possibly have been a harlot! A true harlot would have taken appropriate precautions against pregnancy. A true harlot would either have drunk an herbal contraceptive, or, if perchance that had failed, she would have aborted the fetus.[247] The fact that Tamar was openly pregnant at just three months, when perhaps she could have hidden the fact underneath her black robes for a bit longer, is proof, according to the *midrash*, that not only did she do no wrong, but that she knew that what she was doing was not only not forbidden, but was juridically correct. The *midrash*, if not Judah and his fellow Adullamites, is in Tamar's corner as this round plays out.

Another *midrash*[248] explains that Tamar was seen to be pregnant, but not because she flaunted her belly at three months. On the contrary, even doing her best to conceal the pregnancy, she was, as we know, carrying twins, and at three months gestation there was no way she could hide that fact. According to Rashi,[249] Tamar felt the movement within her womb, and instinctively knew she was carrying more than one child. It is even thought that Tamar's pregnancy lasted shorter than the usual nine months because of textual hints in the Bible. For instance, instead of saying (in upcoming verse 28) "and in the fullness of her term," as the Torah said earlier about Rebecca's twin births (Gen. 25:24), it will say *and it happened, at the time she gave birth.* The *midrash* does not characterize Tamar as brazen; merely that her pregnancy was visible, and that it was inevitable she would be found out, bringing this episode to a head.

JUDAH JUDGES TAMAR:
"TAKE HER OUT AND BURN HER!"

And Judah said, "Take her out and burn her!" Gen. 38:24

This phrase should send shivers up and down the reader's spine. For one thing, why is Judah pronouncing sentence at all, and second, why is he judging his own daughter-in-law, and so quickly?[250] What has become of the universal requirement for objective judges and measured justice, especially in a capital case? Judah had risen in importance over the two decades of his settlement in Adullam. He is a respected prominent businessman and an employer of many locals, even sustaining entire families. Not insignificantly, he also is known as the son of Jacob, the legendary Hebrew tribal patriarch. All this attaches much prestige to Judah, and he is called upon to sit as a town judge as incidents arise.[251] He was an officer of the law,[252] and may even have been the chief judge of the local assize.[253] So even absent a connection to the accused, it is virtually certain that this case would have been brought before him to adjudicate.

This incident of "a whoring adulteress" brings to the fore a primitive feature of ancient Near East justice. It was the custom of the time to allow the wronged husband to decide the woman's fate.[254] Presumably this allowed him to mitigate the intense public embarrassment of being cuckolded, by permitting the "wronged man" to vent his spleen under color of law and pronounce his wife's sentence. Here we see that Judah, sitting judge of Adullam, also wears the "hat" of the wronged next-of-kin. He summarily announces, even before he views the evidence of Tamar's pregnancy with his own eyes, that she should be "brought out and burnt!"

In a prescient reference to Nathaniel Hawthorne's *The Scarlet Letter*, one *midrash* suggests that in those times it was customary to brand a harlot by burning a mark on her forehead.[255] It was in order to conceal this defacing mark that harlots veiled their faces! This fact solves two puzzles in this episode. First, it explains why, at the crossroads, when Judah saw that the woman's face was covered, he immediately thought her a harlot. And second, it is the reason Judah summarily orders the townsmen to take Tamar outside and "burn her;" she is *ipso facto* a harlot if, as a levirate widow, she has become pregnant by someone other than the levirate redeemer.

Tamar is being made to pay not only for her "adultery," but also for shaming Judah. We recall from the recent incident with the kid-goat that Judah is acutely concerned with his public image and was even willing to give up his signet ring, his sash and his staff to avoid appearing as a fool in the eyes of his neighbors. Yet here is a pregnant Tamar, bringing public ridicule upon him and his house.

Judah almost certainly perceived Tamar as a plague upon him, and he longed to make her disappear. Upon hearing that she was found out to be pregnant, his thinking ran perhaps along these lines: "Oh, for Heaven's sake, this girl has brought me nothing but trouble from the first moment I brought her into my house. And she was such a quiet and lovely thing, wouldn't even say 'boo' to a goose. I can't figure it. My two sons were married to her for a week or two apiece and wham! both boys died on the spot. There was no way I ever was going to let her near Shelah, my third boy. I thought sending her away was a good solution. I figured she'd sit out the years quietly in her father's house. And my plan was working — not a peep has been heard out of her for over two years. And now this! Well, she's brought this sentence on herself. There's nothing for it but for her to be judged an adulteress. *Take her out and burn her!* Perhaps now I'll finally have some peace. "

As I discussed above, Tamar was thought to have been the daughter of Malki-Tzedek or granddaughter of Shem, son of Noah. This provenance would have made Tamar a descendant of pre-biblical Hebrew priesthood, which would have brought her an elevated social status and also would have held her to a stricter code of acceptable behavior.[256] As such, even though the sentence for adultery or for *de jure* levirate adultery was death, if the woman were a daughter of the priesthood her sentence was the more horrible death of being burnt at the stake[257] instead of death by stoning.[258] There is even some *midrashic* reference[259] that Judah, too, would have been due the punishment of burning for having violated the incest taboo by sleeping with his daughter-in-law.

Clearly this entire incident — ostensible harlotry by a local highborn woman who violated levirate widowhood, coupled with a possible breaching of the incest taboo by one of the town's aristocrats — is an electric and incendiary situation. Various important familial and societal rules have been broken, and the community is riled to punish and purge the wrongdoer. Judah's quick pronouncement — *take her out and burn her!* — in fact smacks of overzealous vigilante justice. All the actors in this biblical drama are males — except for Tamar herself — with their attendant prejudices about meting out swift punishment to an adulteress. The deck is stacked against her, and the verbal knell of *vayehi* is ringing a dirge. Surely the situation is hopeless and Tamar is doomed. She already has been judged and sentenced, and by none other than her father-in-law, the man who has "done her wrong" at every turn. We think, Is there no justice for Tamar?!

A SILENT TAMAR IS TAKEN OUT TO BE BURNT

And she was brought outside; and she sent to her father-in-law saying, "By the man to whom these [items] belong, [from him] I am with child!" And she said, "Recognize, please, to whom these belong: this signet ring, and the cords and the staff!" Gen. 38:25

The men of the town, dispatched by Judah to *take her out and burn her!* enter Tamar's house without knocking. In an ancient version of the "perp walk," they strong-arm her[260] through the streets to the town square, where the public burning will take place.[261]

Throughout this ordeal Tamar stands straight and tall, her rounded belly visible under her widow's black, and she keeps her silence.[262]

But Tamar had been expecting them, and unbeknownst to the men who came for her, she already had prepared her trump card. Tamar had taken Judah's pledges—which she earlier had wrapped and tied in a large cloth—from their concealed hiding place. She then sent the unwieldy bundle to Judah's house in the hands of her two trusted household servants,[263] with specific instructions: "Give this bundle and this note to Judah alone; not to one of his servants or even to his son. You are to wait while he unwraps it and you must watch him read my note. Then come find me immediately to tell me his reply. Now go quickly, as they will be coming for me. And remember, make haste, for my life hangs in the balance!"

The Bible text (in verse 25) tells us *hi mutzayt*, meaning *she is taken out* or even *she is found*. But the Torah spells the Hebrew word for "she" with a *vav* instead of with a *yud*, so that the unvowelized word, *hu*, can mean that **he** *is taken out* or **he** *is found out*—not "she!" The *midrash*[264] interprets this biblical double entendre to mean that the Torah is acknowledging the obvious: *both* he and she—both Judah and Tamar—were responsible for her pregnancy and must share the burden of it. One implication of this reading is that Tamar should not be the only one burned at the stake for adultery; her partner must step up and share in the gruesome repercussions. Another implication is that if both actors in this drama were permitted to one another under the levirate law, then both are innocent of punishment, and neither should be burnt.

Tamar's extraordinary strength of character is brought under the spotlight at this precise point in our story. She has been dragged from her house, manhandled nothwithstanding her delicate condition (one could even say *because* of it), propped up in the town square and tied to a stake. The twigs are assembled at her feet and the man with the lit torch is standing by, ready to kindle the death pyre at the judge's signal. **And still Tamar holds her peace!**[265] She alone is in possession of the knowledge that could stop these proceedings in their tracks. She knows that she did not commit levirate adultery for the reason that the man who impregnated her was *permitted* to her as a levirate redeemer!²⁶⁶

So why does Tamar keep silent?

The Talmud²⁶⁷ supplies the answer and in the process extolls Tamar. It teaches that exposing another person to public humiliation or embarrassment is so grave a sin that one should allow oneself to be thrown into a fiery furnace rather than do such a thing. Exposing another to public calumny is such a weighty sin that transgression will cause the sinner to forfeit his portion in the world-to-come.²⁶⁸ The rationale is that public humiliation is akin to murder,²⁶⁹ and one must allow oneself to perish rather than "kill" another. The Talmud points to our story as proof of this principle, citing Tamar's silence in the face of the imminent threat that she will be burned at the stake rather than point her finger at Judah.

The Talmud and *midrash* imagine Tamar's thoughts: "If it comes to light without my saying so that Judah is the father of my unborn child, so be it, I will be saved. But if it is God's will that it is *not* disclosed, still I must go to my fiery grave before humiliating him."²⁷⁰ Tamar resolves that any disclosure of Judah's role in this scandal must come from his own lips, and not from hers.²⁷¹ She keeps her silence until she can maneuver Judah into admitting *in public* that the child she carries is his.

So Tamar marshals her courage and, using her wits, relies on a more subtle means to prod Judah to speak up on her behalf. She secretly sends him his three pledges from the night of their sexual encounter, along with a cryptic note that only he can interpret. Tamar is careful in her wording lest the items and note fall into the wrong hands. Her note says, "*From the man to whom these items belong, am I with child. Please, won't you recognize whose signet ring, cords, and staff these are?*" The unexpressed finale to her last-ditch plea is "*. . . and thereby save my life and the life of my unborn child?*"

The *midrash*²⁷² is in awe of Tamar's tenacity and determination to save herself against all odds while still "protecting" Judah. After all, given how Judah has behaved towards her thus far, the chances are slim indeed that he will do a *volte face* and help establish her innocence, especially when that would entail bringing shame upon his own head.

The tension is palpable. We wonder, will Tamar be spared?

TAMAR'S GUARDIAN ANGEL

The rationale that threads through the Talmud and the *midrash* is that Tamar's audacious act of seducing Judah is justified not only on its face, but also because we know that its direct result is that she thereby gives birth to the ancestors of King David.

But what if there were forces at work *other* than societal ones that were operating to foil Tamar's unorthodox plan? What if it were not only Judah's monolithic rejection of his daughter-in-law that Tamar needed to overcome? As a flesh-and-blood heroine Tamar could not get much better or more virtuous: an innocent, reticent girl who is abused by her husbands and is ignored by the man responsible for her welfare, grows to womanhood and proves to be smart, articulate, proactive, pious and audacious, in addition to being beautiful. We have seen that Tamar has taken every possible action short of humiliating Judah to, first, conceive children, and second, to save her own life and the lives growing within her. But her best might not be good enough if the forces ranged against her are dark and powerful. In order to defeat such harmful forces — be they real or imagined — Tamar will need the help of the Almighty.

The Talmud[273] weaves a tale of Satan, and of the dark angel's obsession with foiling the birth of the future Davidic line of Israelite kings. It is terrifying to imagine Tamar standing alone against not only the mortal Judah, who has pronounced her death sentence, but also against a powerful and determinedly evil supernatural force. The Talmud's story is told against the backdrop of verse 25, where we are told that Tamar is *mutzayt*, meaning she is *brought out* or that she is *found*. Because of the nuanced meaning of the word, the *midrash* takes flight with the notion that *something* is lost and then "is found" at about the same time that Tamar is at the point of execution.[274]

The Talmudic tale is that Satan, ever-vigilant for an opportunity to thwart God's plans for a glorious Israelite destiny, waylaid Tamar's two messengers and stole the three items that comprised Judah's pledge. Satan knew that without them Judah would have no opportunity to confess his responsibility for Tamar's pregnancy, and that she would perish, confounding, *ab initio*, the birth of the ancestors of King David. So the dark angel secreted the pledges under a cloud, and planned to lift the cloud, if ever, only after Tamar was burned to death.

But Satan had not considered that the Almighty had been watching and guiding the course of events, and that God would shield Tamar from real harm.

God had been observing the unfolding drama, and watched as Tamar stood, outwardly stoic but inwardly terrified, innocently hopeful that her messengers would reach Judah with his pledges in time to save her. God's compassion and sense of justice are aroused by the display of Tamar's courage and righteousness, and he sends the angel Gabriel to foil Satan's plot. The Talmud[275] teaches that God often functions through the agency of an angel when redeeming an individual who is in dire straits. And Gabriel, known as the "angel of fire," appears on the human proscenium at God's behest whenever fire is in play or is required.[276] Here, with the threat of Tamar's death by fire looming, God sends Gabriel to undo the Satan's mischief by finding the secreted pledges and restoring them to Tamar's messengers.

It is interesting that the Hebrew word for "angel" and "messenger" — *mal'ach* — is identical. In the end, Tamar's messengers successfully do her bidding, handing over the pledges to Judah in time. Who is to know whether God aided Tamar through the intercession of the angel Gabriel, as the Talmud proposes, or through the success of the human messengers? Either way, the dark forces opposing Tamar and seeking her destruction are defeated. The Almighty is easing the way for Tamar's ingenuity to win the day.

TAMAR'S PLEA

Tamar's cryptic message to Judah is in two parts. The first part is the bombshell, so-to-speak, revealing, in a coded manner, the identity of the father of her unborn children.[277] She says, *To the man to whom these [pledges] belong, it is by him that I am with child.* The second part of her message contains a plea in addition to an inventory of the identifying objects. She says, *Recognize, please, to whom these belong: this signet ring, and the cords and the staff!*

We must assume that the town fathers and virtually the entire town of Adullam are congregated in the town square to witness Tamar's punishment. They have no inkling of what is about to unfold before their eyes. We can envision the tableau almost as a freeze-frame, with Tamar awaiting execution, the crowd surrounding the pyre, but with Judah nowhere to be seen. Suddenly the hum of voices dies down and the crowd parts as Judah strides forward with Tamar's messengers trotting close behind. In Judah's hands are his long-lost pledges and Tamar's coded note. Judah stops to stand opposite Tamar, staring at her as if seeing her for the first time. She is standing tall, dressed in her mourning clothes, but her face and cascading black hair are uncovered, her head-covering having been dislodged as she was dragged from her father's house. Tamar's eyes are watching Judah intently, as she attempts to gauge whether her gambit was successful, or whether he will give the signal to light the pyre.

Or it could have happened slightly differently. Tamar is tied to the stake, the kindling is awaiting the torch, the crowd is standing by in horror and in expectation. Suddenly the crowd parts, a hush descends on the square, and Tamar turns to see her two messengers hurrying toward her. But their faces are tear-stained. Tamar's heart—until that moment hopeful of reprieve—sinks. She barely hears their voices as they explain. "Mistress, we had your bundle and your message, but we stumbled on the way to Judah's house. The bundle flew out of our hands and just disappeared! Mistress, believe us, we searched for it everywhere. It is as if it vanished into thin air! We are heartsick to have failed you. Forgive us." Tamar realizes in that instant that a dark force has taken hold of her destiny, and that her desperate plan to goad Judah into admitting paternity of her unborn children was hopeless in the face of this sinister power.

Tamar is on the brink of death, yet she does not waver in her faith in God. Nor does she wonder in vain what evil she might have done to merit such a brief and miserable existence; instead she thinks of the lives she has felt quicken within her, and sends up a silent plea to God to save her and them. The *midrash*[278] tells us the content of her prayer: "Creator of the Universe, it is known to you that my intention was pure and good; that my wish was only to bear children of the house of Judah, children fit to be prophets and kings. If it be Your wish, I beg you to save my life that I may fulfill my destiny."

In answer to Tamar's prayer, the Almighty sends the angel Gabriel to wrest the pledges from Satan and deliver them to Judah.

Within moments the figure of Judah is seen striding toward the pyre. All eyes turn to him, including Tamar's. She can see only one thing: in his hands he holds her draped bundle containing his three pledges, and also her note.

It is crucial that the reader appreciate that at no point does Tamar explicitly point to Judah and say, "**You are the man** who is the father of my unborn child!" What strength of mind and purpose, what faith she must have possessed to keep silent! Who knows but that she might even have been justified in identifying the father and saving her own life, as she alone possessed the knowledge that if she were allowed to die Judah would also be condemning to death the unborn children she was carrying. Yet she is silent, relying instead on God and the trump card she has played. She has sent the pledges with her coded note, and now it is Judah's turn to accept responsibility for siring the child (or children) she is carrying. Judah is responsible not only because she is pregnant by his seed, but also because it is *his failure* to give her to Shelah despite his assurances to the contrary; *his failure* to set her free of her levirate obligation, that caused Tamar to take the desperate step of sitting and waiting for him sat at the crossroads.

The signet ring, sash and staff are in Judah's hands. The *midrash*[279] tells us that they are so uniquely his, bearing his identifying marks, that it was as if his name was inscribed on each of the items. Still, he could have kept silent, and, since no one was privy to the contents of her note, no one would have been the wiser. And in fact, Judah hesitated[280] at the moment he held the pledges and note in his hands, facing Tamar moments before she is to be burned. Even at this point Judah wished to deny paternity of Tamar's child! How despicable, how cowardly, but then, again, how predictably "Judah," and how entirely human. In an instant, if he were to admit responsibility for Tamar's pregnancy, his present life, reputation, future lifetime trajectory, would all be altered. There would be no going back. Certainly Judah "recognizes" the pledges themselves. And together with Tamar's note, he also "recognizes" his fault in the entire series of past incidents. But will Judah *publicly admit* to this recognition? Will he recognize his duty to the future?

Tamar's note had said, *Recognize, please* . . . Her simple and unadorned plea penetrates decades of Judah's callous self-interest. When he had been presented with evidence that his daughter-in-law was an adulteress, Judah did not falter. Like the Queen of Hearts in *Alice Through the Looking Glass* who doggedly repeated, "Off with her head!" Judah stood on his command: *Take her out and burn her!* That is, until he saw his pledges, held them in his hands, and read Tamar's note. Tamar's words, *Recognize, please* . . . caused him to falter, to consider, to *re*consider, to remember, to shudder at the recollection of his own, earlier identity he thought he had outrun.

Her words, *Recognize, please* . . . resonate primally in Judah's mind and heart. Judah recalls his words to his father two decades earlier, when, as a young man, Judah had presented Jacob with Joseph's tattered coat-of-many-colors dipped in the blood of a kid-goat. *Recognize, please, is this your son's tunic, or not?*[281] His father had blanched, recognizing the distinctive tunic, and was deceived by Judah and his brothers into believing Joseph had been devoured by a wild beast.

The Hebrew phrase *haker-na*, meaning *recognize, please*, is repeated precisely in our story, in Tamar's coded plea. The Torah does not intend that Tamar's use of this precise phrase should be viewed as a coincidence.[282] Rather, it is an inspired request meant to jog Judah's memory and shock him out of his complacency, hopefully forcing him to remember his paternal, his filial, and his moral duty.

Recognize, please . . . that the pledges you hold in your hands are the ones you gave to the woman you lay with on your way home from Timnah. *Recognize, please* . . . that I am that woman! *Recognize, please* . . . that you have an unfulfilled obligation to your firstborn son. *Recognize, please* . . . that you had promised to release me from my levirate widowhood; that I waited in vain for two years for you to do this. *Recognize, please* . . . that *you* are my *yavam*, my levirate redeemer, and that our union was permitted under custom and law. *Recognize, please* . . . that the children in my womb are *yours*, and that you cannot—you *must* not—allow all three of us[283] to be burned here unjustly! *Recognize, please* . . . that the Creator has brought these pledges before you as "witnesses"[284] to my righteousness; that the Creator has brought us to this day to give you the chance to overcome your pride; do not allow yourself to feel humiliated by the opinions of flesh-and-blood judges.[285] *Recognize, please* . . . that if you do *not* openly recognize all this now, and you allow me to be burned, then know that you *will* be held to account for *three* souls when the Almighty brings judgement upon you![286]

Tamar is portrayed as fiercely eloquent, steadfastly righteous, highly intelligent and frighteningly audacious. Her cryptic words—*Recognize, please*—are laden with meaning and, as we will see, they find their mark.

JUDAH ADMITS TAMAR
"IS MORE RIGHTEOUS THAN I!"

And Judah recognized [them], and he said, "She is more righteous than I, because I did not give her to my son Shelah." . . . Gen. 38:26

We can imagine the scene. A hush has fallen over the crowd in the square. Tamar already has been pronounced guilty of adultery, the sentence issued by none other than her own father-in-law. She is tied to the stake, the kindling awaits the torch, and yet she stands stoically silent. In the words of the *Sforno*, Tamar possesses the "heart of a lion."[287] She does not weep, she does not cry out at the base injustice of having to bear the stain of her husbands' deaths, she does not point her finger at Judah and name him as her levirate redeemer and father of her unborn children. She has prayed to God, and she also has appealed unambiguously to Judah. There is nothing more for her to do but wait.

The dramatic irony is nearly overwhelming. Judah stands in the crowded market square, holding—unbeknownst to all who are watching except for Tamar, Judah and the Almighty—proof of her innocence. We hold our collective breath; will Judah own up and save her?

The verse states *vayaker Yehudah*, meaning *and Judah did recognize . . .* The biblical narrator is telling the reader that Judah has put together the pieces of the puzzle. He recognizes his pledged items, he recognizes that Tamar is "the woman at the crossroads," and he recognizes that he is culpable for her plight. The Bible's words echo, for a second time, Judah's father's recognition of his son's bloody coat two decades earlier in Gen. 37:33. The recognitions indicate an inevitable acceptance by the actor that he has brought this fate upon himself. In Jacob's situation, faced as he was with his favored son's death, he could do nothing to rectify it, and so he sank into mourning and a pit of despair that lasted years. But here Judah has the option of admitting to the recognition, thus sparing Tamar and any children she carries within her. But we have yet to hear from him.

Judah is holding his pledged items and Tamar's note; he is staring at Tamar when he says the words that alter the fates of Tamar, of Judah himself, and of the line of kings and prophets that will descend from them. Judah announces aloud, *She is more righteous than I! Because I did not give her to my son Shelah.*

The crowd must have gasped in unison; Tamar must have closed her eyes in relief and gratitude and sent up a silent "thank-you" to God. The reader surely says, Halleluya! The *midrashim* concur, and offer their opinions as to the subtleties inherent in Judah's words, *She is more righteous than I!*

The fact that Judah recognizes the totality of what he has done to Tamar and publicly owns up to it, saving Tamar's life, is held to Judah's credit. Judah's name in Hebrew, *Yehudah*, is from the same root-word as *hudah*, meaning "to be known," and *hivad'ut*, meaning "recognition." This is still another instance in our story where the character's name mirrors his behavior, his nature or his fate. While Judah's mother, Leah, named him for her gratitude to God for giving her another son,[288] it is *this* meaning— his knowledge or recognition of his responsibility—in all its nuances, that marks him as a man and potential leader.

The *midrash*[289] tells us that a distant consequence of Judah's admission is that in future years, in the lifetime of Daniel, after the destruction of the Temple in Jerusalem and the exile to Babylon, God will reciprocate Judah's having saved Tamar and her unborn twin sons from a fiery death. Judah's descendants, the Hebrew lads Chanania, Mishael and Azariah, will be miraculously unscathed by the flames of Nebuchadnezzar's furnace.[290] The Almighty will reward Judah for having saved these three souls[291] in our story, by rescuing three of his descendants years hence.

Rashi interprets Judah's words mean that he is announcing to all, "She is right! It is from *me* that she is pregnant." The Talmud[292] agrees that the first part of the announcement (*She is right!*) comes from Judah's mouth, but it explains that the second part (*it is from me . . .*) is a voice from the heavens, echoing like a thunderclap over the heads of all who are assembled in the square. The voice belongs to the Almighty, coming to Tamar's defense in a dramatic and unambiguous way, only *after* Judah steps up and acknowledges her righteousness himself. God is bearing witness for the crowd and also for untold future generations that "It is *I* who have allowed Tamar to become pregnant from Judah!" The *midrash*[293] is adding divine imprimatur to the provenance of Tamar's pregnancy; for even if Judah acknowledges her pregnancy as his, how can he be absolutely sure that this is so?

The *Netziv* raises an important philosophical issue. What does Judah mean when he labels Tamar *more righteous than I*? If Judah lay with a woman he thought was a prostitute, with no inkling that she was his daughter-in-law, then he did not commit either adultery or incest. In theory, then, Tamar would be the one to bear the shame of those wrongs since *she knew* she was seducing her own father-in-law. So how could Tamar be "more righteous" than Judah in the *Netziv*'s construct?

His solution crystallizes the reason that rabbinic writings over the centuries support Tamar and her seduction of Judah. The key is Tamar's *intention*. Not only is Tamar blameless, she also is righteous, because her intention—stated unambiguously in the Torah—is pure. She sought to preserve the name and inheritance of her dead husband, Er. She saw no alternative but to become pregnant from Judah because *she saw that Shelah had reached marriageable age and Judah did not give her to him as a wife*[294] (Gen. 38:14).

The Torah tells us that over time Tamar lost hope that Judah would give her to Shelah, and this fact released her from the *de facto* bond between her and Judah's third son.[295] At that moment Judah became her next-best levirate redeemer after Shelah.[296] Not only that, but in becoming pregnant by Judah, Tamar has endangered her life.[297] By not publicly exposing Judah as the man who impregnated her, she has acted heroically twice-over. Once in persevering to fulfill her levirate duty, and a second time when saving face for Judah brings her to the brink of death.[298]

Judah acknowledges that he is in the wrong and that Tamar, having acted with proper intentions in seducing him, is "more righteous" than he; that even her deception at the crossroads was the right thing for her to do, as he had driven her to take desperate measures.[299]

Judah acknowledges his blindness not only at the crossroads but in his mishandling of the levirate marriage, as well. He acknowledges that Tamar acted more honorably than he, as she faithfully kept her part of the bargain and waited for Shelah in her father's house for two years; whereas he failed to keep his promise to redeem her.[300] Judah acknowledges that it was his sons, Er and Onan, who had been at fault while married to Tamar; that their own sins — and nothing Tamar did — caused their premature deaths.[301] Judah admits that he kept Shelah from her because he feared he would lose his third and remaining son;[302] but now he is humbled sufficiently to see that Tamar's courageous act has, ironically, saved his seed from extinction.[303]

And finally, Judah admits publicly that he was wrong to pronounce the judgement of death-by-burning upon Tamar; that her pregnancy is *his*,[304] and that she committed no wrong. Judah admits that Tamar is the blameless one and that *he* is the sinner![305]

This is quite an admission from a man who has fled filial responsibility and has held a guilty deception in his heart for more than twenty years. He was not courageous enough *then* to save his brother Joseph from forces he helped put into play; now, faced with intense internal and social pressure to keep silent, Judah makes up for his youthful sins and shoulders the blame. While it is certainly true that Tamar saved her own life by her audacious sexual gamble, unquestionably Judah's belated recognition and admission saved her from the fiery death to which he had condemned her.

AFTER JUDAH'S CONFESSION

> *. . . and he did not cease from/continue knowing her.* Gen. 38:26

After her apotheosis in the marketplace, Tamar was cut loose from the bonds that tied her to the stake. Figuratively, but just as real for her, she also was set free from the levirate widowhood that imprisoned her. We can envision that Judah — now publicly acknowledged as father of her unborn children — had Tamar carefully escorted to his house, where she was cosseted and cared for throughout the duration of her pregnancy. We can only imagine Tamar's inner satisfaction. It might have been like the emotions felt by a wrongly-disgraced warrior returning home, years later, now publicly vindicated by the people who had reviled him. She would never forget the pain and abuse, but she was wise enough to turn her face to the future and focus on the gift of her pregnancy by Judah's seed. Her time of misery was at an end.

Still and all, absorbing Tamar into Judah's family via motherhood of Judah's twin sons feels comfortable and right. This is because the union of Tamar and Judah "repairs the social fabric"[306] that had been rent when Judah sent Tamar back to her father's house. He had condemned her, first, to the anomie of non-wife and non-mother. Later, he condemned her to death. Tamar had suffered this abuse and exile at Judah's hand. By accepting the role of levirate husband and father, Judah has now, in one move, rebuilt his moribund family and rescued Tamar. He has also, at last, modeled the correct behavior for a tribal leader.

But the Torah is not yet through with its description of the relationship between Tamar and Judah. The end of verse 26 plants a tiny bombshell. Depending on how one interprets the Hebrew phrase *v'lo yasaf od*, it can mean *either* "and Judah did not *continue* to know her [sexually],"[307] *or* "and Judah did not *cease* from knowing her [sexually]."[308] The reader is intensely curious. What is the Torah telling us?

The Talmud[309] is of the opinion that the phrase means Judah *did not cease* from sexual intimacy with Tamar, and Rashi concurs.[310] But the Talmud and Rashi base their interpretations on the Bible's consistent usage of the term *v'lo yasaf* elsewhere in Scripture. They do not attach any psychological rationale to their readings. Chizkuni's and the *Netziv's*[311] preferred reading of the phrase *v'lo yasaf od* — agreeing with The Talmud and Rashi that Judah did not cease from his sexual intimacy with Tamar — is based on the reason that since she was permitted to him under the levirate law as a true wife, Judah gave in to his desires and *did not cease* from knowing her.

On the other hand, Ramban, the Tosefta,[312] the Sifrei[313] and Radak interpret the phrase to mean that Judah *did not continue* to be sexually intimate with Tamar after her public vindication. They ignore the fact that their reading of the phrase is the exact *opposite* of the Torah's prior use of the same term. According to the Sifrei and even Chizkuni, Judah had a difficult time overcoming the intense embarrassment that Tamar was, still-and-all, his daughter-in-law. The pall of committing incest hung low over him, and this could have overshadowed any lust he still felt towards her. This interpretation would explain Hirsch's translation of the phrase as "and not again did he know her." For while Judah's impregnating her was technically allowable, at the time he lay with her he did so without knowledge of who she was.[314] And according to the Talmud,[315] the intent of the *yavam* or levirate redeemer can determine the legitimacy of the sexual union. Now, even after Tamar has become Judah's lawful wife according to the levirate law,[316] her erstwhile status as wife of his two sons continued to loom large and perhaps quashed his desire for her.

A final reason that Judah might have *ceased to know her* could have been that Judah considered that once he had made Tamar pregnant pursuant to the levirate law, his job was done; the levirate obligation ended at that moment. According to Frymer-Kensky, the law did not specify that Tamar was obligated to continue to act as Judah's wife.[317] Judah could well have felt that the incest factor made any continued intimacy with Tamar forbidden.

The book of Genesis is preoccupied with the large themes that the Bible has illustrated here in chapter 38 in a dramatic and compressed fashion: marriage to the right person; fertility; birthing and raising honorable, God-fearing offspring; relations with one's father and brothers; sexual attraction and its consequences. It is the story of the universal cycle of life, made more urgent by the characters' movement toward a confrontation with and acceptance of God. So we must ask, which interpretation of *v'lo yasaf od* at the end of verse 26 makes the most sense both as we understand the man Judah, and in the context of the grand story of the family of Jacob on its route to nationhood?

As concerns the man Judah, I would read verse 26 as meaning Judah *did not cease from knowing* Tamar. As the Bible has presented Judah, he would not have stopped himself from being sexually intimate with a woman who stirred his desire and who was permitted to him legally. After all, the chapter opens with Judah seeing the Canaanite daughter of Shuah and swiftly thereafter taking her in marriage and becoming intimate with her. We also saw that later on Judah cast his eyes upon a woman he thought was a harlot, and without hesitating he turned off the path, propositioned her, gave her her price, and was intimate with her, as well. This is not a man who curbs his sexual impulses.

We are meant to connect these two incidents to one another because both encounters involve the unique Hebrew word *vayet*, meaning "and he turned aside." Judah is a man who has twice before "turned aside" any misgivings based on familial or societal convention in order to satisfy his physical desire for a particular woman. It is likely he would do so again with Tamar.

Extrapolating from the picture of Judah the Bible has drawn for us, then, it is likely that if the woman at the crossroads pleased him sexually, Judah would have been secretly ecstatic to continue his physical relationship with her under imprimatur of the levirate law. Also, as we already explained, this is true because once Tamar was permitted to Judah as a levirate wife, in the eyes of the law she was permitted to him in every way.

Also, the phrase *v'lo yasaf od* appears at the end of the verse where Judah makes his extraordinary confession admitting responsibility for failing to give Tamar in marriage to his remaining son. We could ask, why is the phrase here? Why doesn't it occupy its own, discrete sentence? We conclude that it must derive meaning from the verse's earlier phrases. After acknowledging Tamar's righteousness in the verse's opening words, and her innocence of wrongdoing via the second phrase, Judah is in the clear. He can now resume intimacy with her with a clear conscience. Tamar is even a worthy mate for him, as she is now and forever publicly cleansed of the taint of harlotry. She was clever and sufficiently clear-headed to see what everyone else had missed: that once Shelah was withheld from her, it was Judah—and not Shelah—who became the correct and proper sire under the levirate law for purposes of family continuity. What's more, she acted heroically by preferring to be burned at the stake rather than embarrass Judah in the court of public opinion. She has met the personal and legal qualifications of a mate for Judah, a prince of Adullam and son of the patriarch Jacob. All these reasons point to Judah's continuing sexual relationship with Tamar.

But if we were to consider this question within the larger context of the development of the children of Jacob into the nation of Israel, the answer would likely be different. Considering the bigger picture, the phrase *v'lo yasaf od* in verse 26 probably means that Judah *did **not** continue to [sexually] know* Tamar. This is because their shared sexual act at the crossroads already has yielded the pregnancy Judah needed and Tamar was seeking. For purposes of family continuity Tamar's twin sons from Judah will serve to perpetuate Judah's family, tribe and legacy. Her twins will be the progenitors of prophets, kings and even the Messiah.[318]

This may well be the reason that Tamar's twins, Peretz and Zerach, are listed among those who accompany Jacob and his family from Canaan into Egypt mere months in the future, in the second year of the great famine (Gen. 45:6 and 46:12). In 46:12 the Bible names Peretz and Zerach and specifically reminds the reader that they stand in the shoes of Er and Onan, Judah's sons who died in Adullam. The Bible thereby puts the reader on notice that Judah's twin sons from Tamar have been expressly incorporated and counted into the Children of Israel as seed of Judah. As such, from the point of view of family survival, there was no need for further sexual activity or offspring between Judah and Tamar. Both had done their duty to posterity.

TAMAR GIVES BIRTH TO TWIN SONS

And it came to pass, at her time for giving birth, that behold, twins were in her womb!

And it came to pass as she was giving birth that [the one] put out his hand; and the midwife took it and tied upon his hand a red thread saying, "This one emerged first."

And it came to pass when he pulled back his hand, behold his brother emerged. And she said, "Why do you burst forth!" And his name was called "Peretz."

And afterwards his brother emerged, upon whose hand was [tied] the red thread; and his name was called "Zarach."
Gen. 38:27–30

Several months pass and, probably at the end of seven months' gestation,[319] Tamar gives birth to Judah's twin sons. In the book of Genesis this twin birth gives Tamar entry into the pantheon of the biblical matriarchs. For in this biblical volume where single births are prayed for, cherished and enumerated, twin sons are exceedingly rare. Only the matriarch Rebecca, married to Abraham's son, Isaac, gives birth to twin sons (Gen. 25:24). Inevitably, the verses describing Rebecca's and Tamar's birthings are scrutinized by the *midrash*. Attention to the Torah's wording in both birthings will yield some clues as to the sons' fates and allow us to better appreciate Tamar's place in the larger story.

Most striking is the spelling of the Hebrew word *te'omim*, meaning "twins." The same word is used in both birthing stories, but in the first telling the word is spelled *missing* two letters, and in the present story the word is spelled in its *complete* form, missing no letters.[320]

Also, there is an inversion of sorts in the two twin birthing stories. The first set of twins in Genesis is born to Rebecca, hand-picked wife of Isaac, covenantal son of Abraham, after twenty barren years. The parents are God's chosen ones, and one would expect the birth of their twins to be a double blessing. But this is not to be. When Rebecca's sons are still in her womb her twins struggle actively within her, causing her much pain and tribulation, and portending their future conflicts.

The second set of twins is born to Tamar — a woman who was mistaken for a harlot, and who had to resort to subterfuge in order to conceive — and Judah, exiled son of the patriarch Jacob who had sold his younger brother for twenty pieces of silver. He also is, incidentally, grandson of Rebecca and Isaac. One would not be faulted for expecting the children born of this union to be problematic.

But the plot inversion takes the reader by surprise.

Rebecca has the difficult prenatal experience, while Tamar apparently carries and births her twins with no trouble. In both Rebecca's and Tamar's birthings there is a small in-womb shoving match to determine which twin will emerge first.

We might have expected that the sons born of Rebecca and Isaac to have been exemplars of righteousness and brotherly love, and the ones born to Tamar and Judah to have been troublesome. In fact, the reverse is true.

The twins born to Rebecca and Isaac — a covenantal union — are a mixed blessing. The elder — Esav — grows up to be a hunter and is beloved by his father, while the other — Jacob — is a homebody who is favored by his mother. Jacob is in constant struggle against his older twin, and when later on Jacob tricks Esav out of his father's blessing, he is forced to flee his brother's enraged blood-oath to kill him.

Tamar's twins, on the other hand, born of a morally ambiguous union, grow up righteous and live side-by-side harmoniously.

Rebecca's *te'omim* — twins — mirror the "missing" Hebrew spelling of the word in their birthing story, as they are *lacking* in brotherly love and mutuality, and one twin grows up wicked. On the other hand, Tamar's *te'omim* mirror the *complete* or full spelling of the word as it is written in their birthing story. They grow up as brothers and to be honorable men, forebears of prophets and kings in Israel.[321] In fact, Tamar's giving birth to twin sons, Peretz and Zerach, is considered one of the three places in the book of Genesis where brothers coexist in harmony.[322] This is quite a biblical endorsement of her behavior.

There is still one more instance of a reversal of expectation in the birthing story.[323] Tamar's twin son, whose tiny hand had emerged first from the birth canal, was expected to be the firstborn, and was marked "first" by the midwife. But to the midwife's surprise, it was his "younger" twin who burst forth and was born first. The firstborn's name identifies the manner of his birth: Judah names him Peretz,[324] meaning "burst forth." And his brother, the one marked with the red string,[325] is also named by Judah.[326] He is called Zerach, meaning reddish-gold, after the color of the thread that marked him, and reminiscent of a shining sunrise.[327] His naming is an optimistic augur, also heralding the dawning of a revived future for his mother, Tamar.

In yet another instance of the character's name reflecting his nature or destiny,[328] Peretz means one who jumps fences or hurdles barriers.[329] The twin who pushed his way into the world against the odds was named for this quality, perhaps unconsciously mirroring Tamar's hurdling the barriers she herself faced as an abandoned levirate widow. Peretz also means "a ready strength,"[330] and one who places himself at risk in war;[331] fitting traits for the ancestor of future Israelite warrior-kings.[332]

※ ※ ※

A word should be said about the "reincarnation"[333] of Er and Onan's souls via the births of Tamar and Judah's twin sons. By operation of the levirate law, Peretz and Zerach are stand-ins for Er and Onan, respectively.[334] Tamar's pregnancy and the near-miraculous birth of her twins restores Judah's house to life. This is not a trivial matter, as Judah's self-imposed exile from his father and brothers coupled with his marriage to a Canaanite woman and the deaths of his two sons spelled the imminent extinction of his line. It is Tamar who is the instrumentality of his revival.

Alschich[335] explains that such "transmigration" or substitution of one life for another through the fiction of levirate marriage

and conception is not without its price. There are severe afflictions that must be experienced by all parties before such a
substitution is effected, and we certainly have witnessed them in
chapter 38 of Genesis. Betrayal, disaffection, guilt, exile, death and
more death, grief, undeserved banishment, risky sexual behaviors,
existential terror coupled with last-minute reprieve; all these are
experienced in sequence first by Judah and later by Tamar over
the course of Judah's years in Adullam. Ultimately it is Peretz's
and Zerach's births that salve Judah's wounds and even Judah —
not known up until now in the Bible for his clarity of vision —
recognizes that through Tamar God has given him a second
chance at family and at eternal life itself.

TAMAR AS A MATRIARCH

In the book of Genesis, the matriarchs — Sarah, Rebecca, Rachel
and Leah — reign as the embodiment of female drive, vision,
desire, attraction, and motherhood.[336] They partnered the Hebrew
patriarchs (Abraham, Isaac and Jacob), and bore the children who
would carry God's covenant of ethical monotheism into future
generations. In short, they *were* the future.

The Tamar of our story and of chapter 38 of Genesis is an
impressive amalgam of the qualities and experiences of the
biblical matriarchs who preceded her, and as such she qualifies to
be named the *de facto* fifth matriarch. The title of "matriarch" is
not merely an affectation. The woman who bears it has shown
herself to "have the stuff," in the words of E. A. Speiser.[337] Tamar
most definitely took inspired, risky and independent action to
secure the future,[338] at potentially great cost to herself. And,
importantly, by dint of her own heroism (and divine providence)
she was successful! This is true matriarchal behavior.

For these reasons, as we conclude our analysis of the Tamar
of Genesis, it is worthwhile to view her through the lens of the
matriarchs,[339] because, as we have seen, her goal matched theirs
precisely: Tamar and the matriarchs were driven to bear the
children of the covenant, the ones who would become the
underpinnings of the Children of Israel and the ancestors of kings
and prophets.

Tamar's life bears an undeniable resemblance to Sarah's. Both Tamar and Sarah are bereft of their fathers[340] when we first encounter them in the Bible. Tamar is "rescued" from her orphaned state by Judah just as Sarah was by Abraham, via the vehicle of marriage. Next, we see that the young and lovely Tamar was handed off by Judah to his eldest son, Er, and after his sudden death she was once again given away, this time to his second son, Onan. This two-time "bestowing and taking" of the prized Hebrew female echoes Sarah's experience when Abraham gave her away first to Pharaoh and then to Avimelech (Gen. 12 and 20, respectively). Tamar's experiences at the hands of Er and Onan involve some measure of sexual abuse and terror, as was the case when Sarah was forcibly abducted by the two kings. Also, Judah wrongly thought that Tamar was a threat to his third son's life, which echoed Abraham's fear of death at the kings' hands on account of Sarah. And most importantly, Tamar conceived a plan and acted audaciously — she played the harlot — in order to bear a child from Judah's line. Her bold act is reminiscent of Sarah's plan to bear Abraham's child through a surrogate.

We see that Tamar's actions *also* eerily channel Rebecca's. Tamar veiled herself before facing Judah, as Rebecca did before coming face-to-face with Isaac for the first time (Gen. 24). Importantly, Tamar bore twin sons as did Rebecca (Gen. 25), and she used disguise and deception to achieve her end, also as did Rebecca, who helped her favored son Jacob disguise himself as Esav in order to secure Isaac's blessing (Gen. 27).

Leah, too, is a template for Tamar. Tamar's signal sexual encounter with Judah came about because she disguised herself as a harlot, reminding us how Leah earlier had used disguise to achieve marriage to Jacob, impersonating her sister Rachel on her wedding night and in her nuptial bed (Gen. 29). Both Leah and Tamar contrived to conceive sons from the covenantal sire via use of a sexual deception. These acts of deception against both Jacob and Judah, respectively, were understood *midrashically* to be a justified comeuppance to the two men, each of whom had used trickery in the past to achieve their own ends. Finally, the commercial negotiation that Tamar engaged in so that she could lay with Judah at the crossroads recalls Leah's bartering of her mandrakes for a night in Jacob's bed (Gen. 30:14–15).

Tamar's life even bears a resemblance to Rachel's. When Er chose to keep his lovely wife unpregnant we are reminded that the *midrash* had accused Jacob of similar behavior after Rachel accosted him and demanded a child (Gen. 30). And importantly, Tamar is viewed as the mother of future Israelite prophets, kings, King David and the Messiah. Likewise Rachel's immortality also is linked to her status as a mother, one who comforts her exiled children and offers them hope of redemption. Immortality, hope and redemption are thus the commonalities shared by Tamar and Rachel.

In reflecting on the similarities of Tamar's life experiences to those of the matriarchs of Genesis, we are able to appreciate that while she is not of their blood, Tamar is their spiritual daughter and sister. "The great-grandmother, the grandmother, and the mother of Judah overcame vulnerability and powerlessness to give birth to and determine the success of the grandfather and father of Judah and to Judah himself."[341] We have seen that Tamar grasped the matriarchal baton and, overcoming the obstacles of abuse, vilification, abandonment and near-death, she heroically bore Judah's twin sons, securing the covenantal line in perpetuity.

CONCLUSION

Tamar's story ends with the birth of her twin sons; she does not appear again in the Bible.[342] We can infer from later events that very soon after her twins are born she turns her back on Adullam and accompanies Judah back to his father's compound in the Valley of Hebron. If Adullam was hard-hit by the widespread drought, this would have provided the impetus for Judah to migrate southward and rejoin his father and brothers. He would have been on a desperate quest for grazing land for his flocks and food for his new family. The Torah text does not tell us of Judah's reunion with his estranged father and brothers, but we know it occurred because the upcoming stories of Jacob's family refer to Judah implicitly (Gen. 42:3) and explicitly (Gen. 43:3 *et seq.*). We find Judah back in the bosom of his family, once more the titular spokesman for his brothers, conferring with his father about the famine that has a choke-hold on the land.

We also know that the infants Peretz and Zerach, Judah's twin sons, are listed among Jacob's family that migrates into Egypt during year-two of the famine (Gen. 46:12). It is virtually certain that the boys are carried into Egypt in the arms of Tamar, their doting and protective mother.

Tamar has single-handedly effected an amazing turnaround in the storyline of Genesis. She is the woman who had been mistreated by Judah's two sons and who was shunted aside by Judah, and by all rights should have quietly faded from the story. Instead she defied convention when, as a pious and modest widow,[343] out of desperation she seduced Judah and become pregnant by him, thus perpetuating her dead husband's name.

Until Tamar's risky sexual gamble is won, Judah's family line is moribund; the continuity of his name and tribe is by no means a sure thing. It is highly ironic that by stepping out-of-character and boldly and successfully imitating a harlot—that fringe female shadow-figure—Tamar breathes life into Judah's family. Not only that, but her audacity also jolts Judah into behaving in a responsible and moral fashion, setting him on the road to reconciliation with his father and brothers. When Judah proclaims *She is more righteous than I!* the Bible reader is able, through the clear lens of hindsight, to detect that *this* is the moment Judah begins to act like a leader.

Tamar has provided the biblical reader with *two* heroes: First, of course, is Tamar herself, the beautiful orphaned girl who breached sexual convention and was rewarded with the pregnancy she so passionately desired. Second, her act allows the Bible to reclaim Judah, who had grievously betrayed his kin in chapter 37 and who had treated Tamar shamefully in chapter 38 until she forced his hand. Judah became a hero-in-the-making when he left off acting selfishly, and began acting Tamar-like, placing loyalty and filial responsibility above self-interest. Judah took the first step toward personal redemption when he found his spine and publicly admitted responsibility for Tamar's pregnancy. When confronted with the real potential of more blood on his hands, Judah could not deny this truth.

And it is Tamar who did it! It is Tamar who showed Judah the way back to tribal pre-eminence through her "unorthodox and hazardous"[344] seduction. It is Tamar who had the "right stuff," and who took heroic measures to see to the future when Judah was morally paralyzed and unable to see clearly. It is Tamar, the desperate, lone and brilliant tactician, who orchestrated a public vindication and who mothers an unprecedented line of future prophets and kings.

Are we surprised that God selected Tamar to be the ancestor of King David, and ultimately of the Messiah?[345] Not at all. We applaud Tamar, the victim-turned-victor, "harlot"-turned-heroine.

PART

FOUR

David

&

Batsheva

FOUR

David & Batsheva

II SAMUEL 11:1–5

And it happened, at the return of the year, at the time that kings go out [to war], that David sent Yoav with his servants and all Israel to raid the Ammonites. They laid siege to Rabbah while David remained in Jerusalem.

And it happened, at the time of nightfall, that David rose from his bed and he strolled on the roof of the palace. He saw a woman bathing from the roof, and the woman was extremely beautiful.

And David sent to inquire about the woman. And he said, "Is this not Batsheva, daughter of Eliam, the wife of Uriah the Hittite?"

So David sent messengers and he took her and she came to him and he lay with her (and she had just cleansed herself from her impurity); then she returned to her house.

And the woman conceived; and she sent word to David saying, "I am pregnant."

The story of David and Batsheva is the story of a forbidden physical attraction that spirals out of control, culminating in a murder. It is complicated by the fact that David is the king of Israel when he sees and takes Batsheva. So it is also a story about monarchy. For these reasons alone it was a story destined inevitably for the biblical headlines. And in fact loose versions of this ancient plot resound in twentieth-century literature and film noir[1] and also before our eyes on the evening news.

The modern reader expects serious consequences to flow from the spare story of the taking by the king of another man's wife, and this does come to pass. Batsheva becomes pregnant and David reacts to the news by plotting and ordering the murder of her husband, Uriah, on the battlefield. Batsheva mourns her husband, but is taken by David to be his wife immediately after she arises from her mourning. Her son from the adulterous union sickens and dies within days of his birth, and David is severely chastised and cursed by God because of his sins.

In fact, this story marks the beginning of the end of David's monarchy, although he retains his crown for twenty-two more years. His sons will rise up and rebel against him, and four of his sons and heirs will die in David's lifetime; his house will never know peace, the kingdom of Israel will be irrevocably split in two, and David—the charismatic, flawed, rash, warrior-poet king—will labor under the burden of his sins until his death.

But as is the case with the other stories presented in this book, because of the sleight-of-hand of the author of the book of Samuel there is more here than meets the eye. There is the story of the woman Batsheva, victim of her beauty and at the mercy of the king; a woman forced to violate her marriage vows. She buries her husband and weeps over him, and soon thereafter she gives birth to a son and then buries him, as well. We are reeling from this woman's plight. Yet the Torah is not done with Batsheva; she is destined to survive as a queen in Israel. We are told that as David's wife she becomes pregnant once again and this time her son grows to manhood and is beloved by God. Her son's name is Solomon, and he is groomed by God for immortality. Batsheva herself will outlive David and will be a revered and beloved queen mother and confidant to a prophet.

Still, questions abound. Why is David in Jerusalem in the first place, if his armies and countrymen are at war? Why is

David napping during the day, pacing the palace roof at nightfall? Who is this exquisite woman Batsheva, "daughter of Eliam, wife of Uriah?" Does she come to David voluntarily? What does Uriah know or suspect about David's adulterous affair with his wife? Is Batsheva complicit in David's plot to kill her husband? Does God punish David for his sins of adultery, abuse of power and murder? Has God punished Batsheva by proxy with the deaths of her husband and infant son? Is she an innocent caught up in the backwash of David's temptation, sin and punishment? Is Batsheva's ultimate role of mother to king Solomon in the nature of a divine reward?

Technically, the opening verses of the story of David and Batsheva are closer in kind to the story of Dinah and Shechem than they are to any of the other stories yet examined in this book. Batsheva is no more seduced by David than Dinah was seduced by Shechem; Batsheva, too, is "taken." The "seduction" in this chapter might instead refer to David's own personal seduction into temptation and descent into immorality. Also, it might refer to David's efforts to seduce Uriah into spending the night with his wife in his own bed. The kaleidoscope shifts minutely and we view the biblical narrative in a different light. All in good time we will examine the verses that narrate Batsheva's abduction by the king's "messengers" and all that flows from it. First we will examine the opening verse and its back story.

DAVID FIGHTS THE AMMONITES

The story immediately preceding the incident of David and Batsheva is of the ongoing war between the Israelites and the Ammonites (chapter 10 of II Samuel). It is this conflict that provides the crucial backdrop to our story. The active and vibrant King David, who has personally led his troops to previous military victories, becomes, midway through chapter 10, a "sedentary king"[2] who has delegated his military duties to Yoav, his fearless general. We are treated, in chapter 10, to a glimpse of Yoav's brilliant military tactics. He evades a pincer maneuver and executes a successful counterstrategy, vanquishing the enemy.

The reader is left in no doubt of Yoav's utter competence to handle the troops even in David's absence.[3] We will see how David will come to rely on Yoav's loyalty not only in military matters, but in matters of intrigue as well. We also will see, in the opening verses of chapter 11, how David's new, sedentary, non-fighting persona affords him much idle time, which he fills with nonmilitary mischief.

There could be a legitimate reason for David's surprising switch from indefatigable fighting man to one who naps in the daytime while his troops wage a protracted military campaign. In a later account of a fierce, earlier battle between the Israelites and the Philistines (II Sam. 21), we see that the aging David already is slowing down. The Bible specifically says that "David grew weary,"[4] and that as a consequence he had fallen back as his troops and aides surged forward.[5] But-for the quick intervention of Avishai, son of Zeruyah, David would have been slain by a giant Philistine warrior. This account of David's exhaustion should resonate with the reader, as we recall the story of its polar opposite years earlier. Then, the youthful and energetic David, armed only with a slingshot, killed another Philistine giant named Goliath. That earlier famed incident *began* David's legendary career as a warrior-king; years later, this statement of his weariness effectively *ends* it. Afterwards, David's own troops, terrified at the near-miss, swear that David, their king, will no longer march with them into battle.[6]

Chapter 10 also serves as a second foil for David's behavior in chapter 11. In chapter 10 when David learns that Nachash, the king of Ammon has died, he sends emissaries to the court of the new king Hanun, Nachash's son, to express condolences, because King Nachash had "kept faith with" or "showed kindness to" David in the past, when he was on the run from King Saul. In striking contrast, we should pay special attention to the David of chapter 11, who ironically and tragically will break faith with Eliam and Uriah, officers in David's army and father and husband of Batsheva. We will see the consequences that result when David remains faithful to an enemy king, but betrays himself, his crown, and his own officers.

THE KING REMAINS IN JERUSALEM

The story of David and Batsheva opens with the Hebrew word *Vayehi*, meaning *And it happened that . . .*[7] The reader will recall from our discussion of Judah and Tamar in Part Two that when the word *vayehi* opens a biblical narrative, often it is a verbal clue portending misfortune.[8] We will see that this is borne out multiple times in the present story, as well, as we analyze chapters 11 and 12 in II Samuel.

It is the seventeenth year of David's reign.[9] One full year has passed[10] since David heroically assisted Yoav in the defeat of the Arameans in the Israelites' drawn-out war against Ammon. The season is springtime, warming into summer — the grasses are tall in the fields, the trees heavy with fruit. The Bible explicitly tells us that it is the perfect time for kings to lead their armies into war. The rainy season has ended, the ground is fit for both infantry and horse soldiers, and because the growing season is well progressed, military beasts are able to graze effortlessly and troops can literally eat of the fat of the land.[11]

The Bible is preparing the reader to expect that David will be out on the battlefield with his troops on this first anniversary of his rout of the Arameans. In fact, the Bible has already told us that *All Israel and Judah loved David* **because he went out and came back in front of them.**[12] The Ammonites are still at large, and in fact are barricaded within the walls of Rabbah, their capital city.[13]

But instead we read that David sends Yoav and his troops to lay siege against Rabbah while he, himself, remains in Jerusalem.

The *midrash*[14] is prepared for readers to be disappointed and shocked that David remains at leisure while his army is in a pitched battle, and so it expects that they will attempt to advance excuses for the king's lassitude. The *midrash* presents the three excuses and counters them *seriatim*. Lest you say that David was tired or weakened from the prior battles, thus justifying his remaining at home, verse 1 tells us that this chapter takes place *at the return of the year*, signifying that David has had a full year within which to recover his energies from his last military action. Lest you say that the inclement weather kept David at home, the verse tells us it was *the proper time* for kings to go out into battle, as the season was warm and dry. And lest you say it was only a small battle and there was no need to trouble the great king to join in the campaign, the verse also says that David sent Yoav, his storied general, as well as *Israel's entire army* to fight the Ammonites.

The wording is unambiguous; the battle was sufficiently serious to have warranted David's presence alongside his bravest and most skilled troops.[15] It was the custom of kings — David especially — to accompany their troops into battle;[16] in fact, military prowess was a main reason the Israelites demanded a king in the first place, replacing the ages-old system of judges.[17] Therefore, David's absence from the battlefield is strange and even derelict.[18] Indeed, it is tantamount to David having violated the social contract of his monarchy.[19]

At the outset of chapter 11, after chapter 10's detailed battlefield descriptions, we are expecting another chapter in the same vein. But chapters 11 and 12 will present a story-within-a-story:[20] the unexpected story of David and Batsheva is superimposed upon the story of the ongoing military campaign against the Ammonites, taking urgent precedence.[21] But the two tales will converge repeatedly, the one informing the other, as the lives of the stories' actors straddle the worlds of both the battlefield in Ammon and the palace in Jerusalem, with messengers dashing back and forth between the two.

A WALK ON THE PALACE ROOF

And it happened, at the time of nightfall, that David rose from his bed and he strolled on the roof of the palace . . . II Sam. 11:2

Further evidence of the Bible's story-within-a-story is verse 2, which actually begins the telling of the Batsheva episode. This verse *also* opens with the ominous word *Vayehi* (*And it happened*) as did verse 1! The word's repetition foretells trouble twice-over: first, because David did not act in the manner of kings and personally lead his troops into battle, and second because David was napping during the day and walking on his roof in the evening.

On the evening of the same day[22] that David had dispatched Yoav and his warriors into battle against Ammon, he took an afternoon siesta[23] and slept away the day from noontime until the evening. The Bible expects us to conclude that "this recumbent king has been in bed an inordinately long time."[24] The reader should be thinking that not only is David remiss as warrior-king because of his absence from the battlefield, he also is lax concerning his palace duties. Why is David not busy with affairs of state during the daytime? One would think that he certainly should be concerned and engaged with the needs of his subjects. Daytimes are for business. Yet verse 2 says *at nightfall David rose from his bed*.

The *midrash*[25] actually details for us this warrior-king's at-home schedule. It is astonishing in its indolence: When King David ate his meals in solitude, afterwards he was wont to sleep until 9 PM. When the king ate state meals during the daytime, afterwards he would generally nap until evening. After arising from his nap David would attend various nighttime state functions, and still later on that same day he would withdraw from affairs of state entirely, choosing instead to take a leisurely stroll around his palace roof.

Apparently David's peripatetic wanderings were watched and commented upon among his Israelite subjects. They were able to see their king atop his palace roof or on its parapets as readily as he could see them.[26] The *midrash* views this transparency as an indication of David's callousness; the Bible had told us in verse 1 that *all of Israel* was fighting Ammon, so it is fair to assume that virtually every Israelite household had contributed at least one male member to the king's army. The Israelite monarchy was a relatively recent phenomenon, with David only their second king. The people were accustomed to their king fighting alongside his soldiers. It could not have sat well with the Israelites that David had altered his *modus operandi* and was seen taking his leisure during an ongoing military campaign.

So it is likely that King David's afternoon nap and his rooftop stroll are a new, first-time occurrence. The people are surprised and shocked to see him walking about up there. They fully expected him to be fighting the Ammonites. The text's description of David's relaxed behavior draws a chastisement of him by the *midrash*.[27] Because the Bible's verse referring to David's nap comes on the heels of the verse that sends his warriors out to defend the Israelite flag, there is no question that the context implies a condemnation of David. His troops are fighting and dying while he naps. The image presented is the opposite of a conscientious monarch. It is the *midrashic* version, perhaps, of "idle hands breed mischief," telling us that had David busied himself with legitimate pursuits and been less self-indulgent, the entire Batsheva incident might never have occurred.[28]

DAVID SEES A WOMAN BATHING

David arose from his bed . . . He saw a woman bathing from the roof, and the woman was extremely beautiful. II Sam. 11:2

David's palace was situated atop a prominent hill in Jerusalem, and as such his palace roof was higher than those of the surrounding homes, giving him a unique vantage point.[29] The idle, bored or sexually needy king has chosen for this particular evening's entertainment to stand on his rooftop, lean on its parapet and look out upon his neighbors. It was the royal version of the present-day urban summer pastime of stoop-sitting. Whether or not David knew in advance what he would see because he had gazed from his roof on other evenings is an unanswerable question. But after the sun has set and evening is fallen, absent electric lights it is unlikely that he would have been able to see the bathing woman clearly unless he knew beforehand what he was looking at and where to look.

David has just arisen from his bed and it is physiologically possible that he was in a post-slumber state of arousal. He is gazing out over the neighboring rooftops, where the water cisterns for gathering and heating rainwater are located, now brimming over with the winter's rains.[30] On any given evening it might have been common for the neighbors to head up to their rooftops or bathing chambers to enjoy a cooling bath to rinse off the day's dust and sweat. Living in close proximity to others requires a certain modicum of civility, and the nearby residents had every reason to believe that their monarch would not be spending his time in voyeurism. It is reasonable to assume that everyone bathed, many atop their roofs or with open windows. So, too, they employed what modest covering they could engineer, and the neighbors averted their eyes to afford one another privacy.

But the *midrash*[31] tells us that David most emphatically did *not* avert his eyes from the sight of Batsheva at her bath. On the contrary, Abarbanel explains that once David caught sight of her washing herself, the picture of her nakedness became imprinted on his mind and heart.[32] The *midrash* paints the picture of a man in the throes of a sexual obsession. The *Malbim* says that David had to have strained his eyes to see Batsheva. Her house was some distance away from the palace, and was not in David's direct line of sight. Other *midrashim* agree, explicating further that instead of being situated outside and in full view of other rooftops, Batsheva's bath was private, located *within* her house.[33] This means that David had to have concentrated on peering *into* Batsheva's bathing chamber, through an open window,[34] for instance. While her window would have been on a straight trajectory from the palace roof, it was still not a casual sighting.

The Bible text nowhere states that Batsheva's bath was upon *her* roof; only that *from **his** roof* David was able to see a woman bathing. From the logistics, then, it is even possible that not only did David know in advance toward which house to direct his eyes, but also that in order to watch Batsheva as she washed herself he had to peer *into* her lighted window or *through* her doorway.

The Talmud[35] explains its own version of how this sighting came about. David was walking about on his roof that evening because he had altered his domestic sleeping schedule. That day he had slept with one of his wives during his afternoon siesta instead of waiting until their usual nighttime tryst. This is the reason he was awake and pacing his roof that evening. The Talmud says that quite possibly David was in a state of arousal;

notwithstanding that he had already had sexual relations with his wife earlier in the day, as it approached nighttime — the time David ordinarily was accustomed to sexual intimacy — his body was primed and ready.

The Talmud continues its depiction of the scene at nightfall. From the vantage point of his roof David saw indistinctly in the evening gloom that a woman in a nearby house was at her bath. He boldly watched her from a distance as she washed her hair, an enterprise which took some time. The king's view of the woman was obscured, however, by a modesty canopy[36] which was spread out over her rooftop bathing area. As David strained to watch, the Satan appeared to him in the form of a bird, and David — unable to resist his years-old habit — shot at the bird with his slingshot. In the poor light David's shot missed its mark and instead it hit the woman's protective canopy, tearing it. It was then, when the woman became exposed to his view, that David saw that she was exceedingly beautiful.

If we credit the Talmud's scenario about how David came to see the woman at her bath, the reader will want to consider whether "the Satan" was a dark angel doing the bidding of the Almighty, or whether it represented David's own *yetzer ha-ra* — his passionate inclination. Either way, the implication is clear. David, sadly and tragically, was not strong enough to resist giving in to the pull of the dark side. He yielded to his desires and failed the Almighty's test of sexual temptation.[37] David was seduced by the vision of the beautiful bathing woman, and we will see how this first yielding — he watched her at her bath instead of turning away — devolved into baser and then still baser transgressions.

"AND THE WOMAN WAS VERY BEAUTIFUL"

The Bible describes the woman David watched at her bath as *tovat-mar'eh me'od*, meaning *very beautiful to behold*. Extreme beauty is rarely mentioned in the Bible, and when it is, it often operates as a curse rather than a blessing to the one so described, as it leads to "takings" or abductions, rape or near-rape, seductions, marital misery and even death.

The two women in the Bible who are described as *tovat-mar'eh me'od* (*very beautiful to behold*), are Batsheva in our story, and Rebecca in Genesis.[38] There are some striking coincidences of fact and theme between the two women's stories. Both Batsheva and Rebecca face the threat and terror of being taken against their will by powerful kings. In Batsheva's story, her husband is away at war and so cannot stand up for her and protect her honor when David views her beauty, desires and takes her. In Genesis, Rebecca and her husband Isaac have just ventured into the Philistine city of Gerar during a famine, and Rebecca's beauty has aroused the lust of the Philistine men as well as the lascivious interest of Avimelech, their king. By use of the wife/sister ruse Isaac forestalls a forcible taking of Rebecca, but it is a close call.

In the Batsheva story the king acts like a Peeping Tom, observing the bathing woman unbeknownst to her, leading to her forcible "taking." In Rebecca's story the king also is a Peeping Tom, observing through a window as Rebecca and Isaac are "at play" with one another, watching them behave not as brother and sister, but as sexually intimate husband and wife.[39] The Philistine king's voyeurism leads to the couple's expulsion from Gerar.

There is a special category of biblical "beauty" that meets and exceeds the *very beautiful* description of Batsheva and Rebecca. In three places the Bible describes a person as *yefat mar'eh*, meaning *fair of face*, **along with** the companion description *yefat to'ar*, meaning *of beautiful form*. Who are the biblical characters described as possessing **both** a beautiful face and a beautiful figure? They are Rachel,[40] Joseph,[41] and Esther.[42] Rachel suffers humiliation and misery for years as the exquisite but barren wife of Jacob. Joseph, her long-awaited son who is sold by his brothers into slavery, is the object of the sexual predations of the wife of his master, Potifar, and he ends up in prison. And Esther is "taken" by the Persian king's soldiers in a nationwide round-up of beautiful virgins, and is eventually wed to the king.

Then there are the biblical characters who are called simply *yafah, yefat mar'eh* **or** *tovat mar'eh* (*yefeh mar'eh* for the male), sister expressions to the ones already described, but standing alone without augmentation. Who is described as *beautiful* or *fair to look upon*, and what befalls them? Sarah,[43] princess Tamar, daughter of

King David,[44] Tamar, the daughter of Avshalom,[45] and Vashti[46] have the distinction of being labeled *yafah* (princess Tamar) or *yefat mar'eh*.[47] True to our pattern, Sarah is forcibly abducted on two occasions by lawless kings who are mesmerized by her beauty and seek to possess her. First she is "taken" by the Egyptian Pharaoh, and some years later she is "taken" by the Philistine king. Princess Tamar, beautiful only-daughter of King David, is violently raped by her half-brother Amnon, who had become consumed with desire for her, and who then abandons her on his doorstep after abusing her. Tamar, daughter of prince Avshalom, is mentioned once in the text and never heard from again. Finally, queen Vashti, predecessor to Queen Esther, refuses king Achashverosh's summons to publicly display her beauty to his drunken court, and she is banished or possibly killed in retaliation.

Interestingly, David[48] also is described in the Bible as *yefeh mar'eh*, meaning "handsome." But David is the one "beautiful" character who is *not* "taken" — forcibly or otherwise — on account of his beauty. One might argue convincingly that his beauty, charisma, and lust for power are instruments of his eventual downfall, but for purposes of this analysis we will simply describe one of the two scenes where his beauty is mentioned.[49] In David's first heroic appearance in the Bible he is mocked by Goliath, the Philistine giant, as youthful, ruddy and *beautiful to look upon*. To his detriment Goliath takes David, quite literally, at face value, underestimating his skill and courage as a warrior on account of his looks; a deadly mistake. Of course, David goes on to kill Goliath and become king, and thereafter twice in his life is attracted to women whom the Bible similarly describes as "beautiful."

Avigayil[50] is the wife of Naval when she comes to David's attention. The Bible describes her uniquely as *tovat sechel v'yefat to'ar*; she is a woman *of good mind **and** lovely looks*. Displaying her keen intelligence, Avigayil defies her husband and feeds David's hungry army. Predictably, David is stirred by her physical beauty and takes her as his wife immediately after her husband's sudden death.

Finally, there is the young virgin by the name of Avishag the Shunamite[51] whom the Bible describes as *yafah ad me'od*, meaning *very beautiful*. In both an imperfect echoing of the earlier Batsheva story and a foreshadowing of the later Esther narrative, this *very beautiful* virgin — the result of a countrywide search — is found and brought to king David's bed chamber when he is old and cold and near death. Avishag, plucked from obscurity because of her beauty in order to service the king, later becomes the hapless object of desire of David's son Adoniyah, who seeks to usurp his half-brother Solomon as David's successor. Adoniyah is soon put to death for his desire to appropriate Avishag, David's concubine, and seize the crown.

In the Bible, then, we see that great beauty or proximity to it is not necessarily a great blessing for those who posses it; oftentimes it brings abuse, misery and even death. At the very least it brings with it peril and fear. Coming to the story of David and Batsheva with this knowledge arms the reader and readies us for what is to befall the *exceedingly beautiful* woman whom David watches at her *toilette*.

WHO IS "THE WOMAN?"

And David sent and inquired about the woman. And he said, "Is this not Batsheva, daughter of Eliam, wife of Uriah the Hittite?" II Sam. 11:3

Immediately after he sees the "very beautiful woman" from his rooftop vantage point, David asks the members of her household who she is.[52] Then in the same verse, practically in the same breath, he answers his own question.[53] David identifies her formally as the *daughter of Eliam and the wife of Uriah the Hittite*. He is, in effect, announcing that she is the property of not one, but *two* other men whose "rights" over her supersede his.[54] Yet still David has no compunction about seeing and taking her.

Because there is no doubt from the Bible text that David knows the identity of the bathing woman he has been ogling, it is possible that he might have intended, *ab initio*, specifically to watch Batsheva at her *toilette* when he went out on his roof that evening. While it is theoretically possible that David only discovers her identity after the fact, verse 3 indicates that at the very least he recognizes her sufficiently that he can name her and even recite her lineage. This alone would imply that he had known who she was *previous* to this viewing.

The woman is called Batsheva, and her father, Eliam, is the son of Achitofel HaGiloni, who is David's own political adviser.[55] It is worth noting that unbeknownst to David, when he states her father's name he is calling into play possible future events. For Batsheva is the granddaughter of Achitofel, David's secretary of state, the man who, in future years, will abandon David and mastermind David's son, Avshalom's, treasonous rebellion against his father![56] As this story progresses the reader will consider whether there is a causal connection between Achitofel's support of David's rival for the crown, and David's abduction and rape of Achitofel's married granddaughter and the murder of her husband years before. Had Achitofel, a seasoned and patient man of state, secretly nurtured his animosity for David all this time? Had he been cleverly biding his time until he could pay David back in kind, one betrayal for another? He certainly would have had a very strong motive to do so.

As for Eliam, Batsheva's father, he was a soldier, as was Uriah, her husband, and both were members of the king's elite corps of warriors.[57] In modern parlance they were two of David's Green Berets.

David also identifies Batsheva as *wife of Uriah the Hittite*. It is well established that Uriah is numbered among Yoav's mightiest fighting men and is one of David's most valued battlefield officers.[58] Other than that, he is something of a mystery, as his name is Hebrew, with an exalted meaning – *God is my light* – yet his provenance is apparently Hittite. Is Uriah Israelite, or is he "other?"[59] Perhaps Uriah's name refers to the Hittite district he governed as one of David's military officers.[60] Perhaps he was descended from the native Canaanite tribe of Hittites that inhabited the land before the Israelites conquered it, or he might have just been an Israelite who lived among the Hittite tribe.[61] Uriah as a character will become more transparent and developed as we listen in on his conversations with his king, and as we observe his forthright and admirable behavior when he is called home from the front. For now, it is sufficient that he is a soldier who is known to David as Batsheva's husband.

As granddaughter of the king's secretary of state and as wife of one of the king's elite officers, it stands to reason that while Batsheva is not a member of the nascent Israelite nobility, she is certainly a member of David's court. It is even likely that the king knew her by sight, and that at the very least he had observed her — clothed — as a member of the court retinue. Perhaps they had exchanged words in polite conversation. Batsheva's place in Israelite society — as granddaughter of a cabinet minister and daughter and wife of distinguished military men — would explain the proximity of her house to the king's palace. Surely members of court had homes that ringed the royal dwelling. Their houses or roofs would have been visible to anyone standing atop the palace. This also would support the notion that David knew precisely what — or whom — he was about to observe that fateful evening.

In this vein, Shmuel Herzfeld[62] suggests that David, fully aware that the woman he has been watching at her bath is from a politically connected and powerful family, deliberately sets out to "take" her in order to strengthen himself politically. After all, there is precedent for this in the book of Samuel, where David has pursued specific women for reason, *inter alia*, of their political value to him. He did this with Avigayil, wife of Naval, and again with Michal, daughter of Saul. "There is a sense that David is becoming . . . powerful through his marital alliances."[63] Herzfeld considers that "the sin with Batsheva is not only one of lust, but there may be an element of cold, premeditated ambition on the part of David as he tries to strengthen his kingdom through another alliance with a very powerful woman, the daughter of Eli'am, and granddaughter of Achitofel."[64]

Supporting this reading is the simple textual fact that while David *sees* Batsheva in verse 2, he only *takes her* in verse 4. In verse 3, in between the seeing and taking, David inquires as to the woman's identity; only *after* he ascertains her politically lofty provenance does he proceed with the abduction, notwithstanding that she is in fact "unavailable" to him, as she is linked to a husband and father with prior, stronger claims. David is nevertheless determined to take Batsheva.

David is behaving in a reckless and unlawful manner. Batsheva's married status should have ended David's interest in her. We have seen that in the earlier biblical incidents of royal abductions of Hebrew beauties both Pharaoh and Avimelech were horrified when they learned of the married state of their sexual quarry. They may have backed off reluctantly and with righteous excuses, but they backed away from Sarah and Rebecca once their married status became known (and after divine interventions). Frymer-Kensky explains that "even in his worst nightmare, Abram never expected the Egyptians to take his wife without killing him first."[65] Hence the wife/sister ruse. "In the social order of Israel and the ancient world, adultery was a serious transgression."[66] Even among pagan and Canaanite kings such a "taking" of a married woman was considered verboten. That David does not hesitate to send for and take the married Batsheva — in fact the spate of verbs implies haste — tells the reader volumes about his moral code, his mental state, his inflated sense of entitlement, his hubristic and lustful nature.

WAS BATSHEVA FORBIDDEN OR AVAILABLE?

The Talmud[67] expounds on the phrase in verse 3 *and he inquired about the woman.* In answering the question "What was the nature of David's inquiry about Batsheva?" the Talmud says that David's question to members of Batsheva's household was whether or not their mistress was a free woman and thus available to him. We see that the rabbis of the Talmud, clear-sighted and quick to denounce David for this shameful episode, nevertheless ironically and somewhat incompatibly proceed to devise legal arguments that will exonerate their beloved poet-warrior-king from the shame and sanction that cling to him as a consequence of his illicit acts. One of their devices is known as the "battlefield writ of divorce."

The famous opening line from this Talmudic discussion leaves no doubt as to the rabbinic predilection: "Whoever says that David sinned is simply in error." We are stunned. What can this mean? Surely David sinned! He took Batsheva, a married woman; he had Uriah, her husband, killed in battle, and he engaged in all manner of abhorrent behaviors including rape, adultery, abuse of power, fraud in the inducement, conspiracy to murder and the collateral killing of innocent others. How can the Talmud issue such a statement and still retain credibility?

Leaving aside, for argument's sake, the plot to murder and the killing of Uriah, at issue here in the Talmud is whether Batsheva was married and thus forbidden to David at the time he took her. It sets out two possible versions of a legal technicality that might be the loophole through which David can slip.

The first Talmudic possibility is what is known as a *conditional* bill of divorce. In David's time it was customary for a soldier going into battle to give such a document to his wife either before he left for war or to send it back home if the battle became protracted or fierce. This writ of divorce became operational only in the event the husband-soldier failed to return. In this way, if the husband met his death in battle or was missing, his wife would be divorced *retroactively* from the time her husband left her. This mechanism was instituted to avoid tragedies such as the *agunah*, which is the Hebrew term for a woman who is chained to her husband, unable to remarry even though he is missing in action and presumed dead, because she lacks the definitive proof that she is a widow.

At the time of the Batsheva incident Israel is at war with the nation of Ammon in a protracted campaign, and Batsheva's husband, Uriah, is fighting in that war. The instant he dies in battle (in 11:17) his conditional writ of divorce takes effect *retroactively*, leaving Batsheva unmarried, and permitting David to have taken her to his bed. This is because—by operation of the retroactive divorce—she was an unmarried woman at the time David took her.

The second possible Talmudic loophole is a variant of the first. David's soldiers customarily gave their wives a secret, *unconditional* bill of divorce before they went off to war. The women were expected to remain faithful to their soldier husbands, however, notwithstanding the secret divorces, and upon the men's safe return they remarried their "wives."

The serious problem with the conditional divorce argument is that it practically begs for David to have Uriah killed in battle in order to legitimize his adultery. Such an untenable situation would never be supported societally or communally. All civilized communities should at all times work toward and fiercely support the safe return of their troops from battle.

The rabbis of the Talmud do not present a monolithic face in support of David's exoneration for taking Batsheva. Some commentaries[68] have quite properly faulted David for taking her notwithstanding the possibility that Uriah had given her a battlefield writ of divorce such as the ones the Talmud describes. At the very least, they say, David should have held back until it became clear that Batsheva was not a married woman *at the time that he took her*.

This concept of the wartime or battlefield writ of divorce is an ancient one that predates the Bible.[69] We can appreciate that in the ancient world, where battles often were conducted in far-distant locales, communication was slow at best and there was no technology for identifying bodily remains, communities developed a routine for officers, at least, to give their wives a wartime bill of divorce *before* they left for war. Their military service often took them away from their homes and families for months or years at a time, and the divorce certificate, while cold comfort for the wife, was brought into play in the event the woman sought to remarry after her husband's absence of more than two years and lacking a formal confirmation of his death. The certificate was the *sine qua non* for a remarriage, because in the ancient Near East a woman did not have a legal right to remarry until her (presumed living) husband provided her with a certificate stating that he relinquished his claim to her. In the second millennium BCE, in the time of the Middle-Assyrian Law, this certificate was known as a "widow's tablet." It allowed the woman to remarry and it removed the rights of the soldier-husband to reclaim her.

Even if Uriah, an officer in David's army, had given Batsheva a certificate of divorce before going off to war, it is inherently obvious that it was *the woman* who called the document into play when she wished to remarry after her soldier-husband's prolonged absence. Batsheva did not do this in our story. In fact, the wording of the text flies in the face of an argument that Batsheva was divorced from Uriah. In II Sam. chapters 11 and 12, the text repeatedly refers to Batsheva as *wife of Uriah* before, during and after David sees and takes and sleeps with her (she is called "Uriah's wife" three times in II Sam. 11:26 alone). What's more, David himself sought to reinstate the husband-wife intimacy between Batsheva and Uriah in order to legitimize her pregnancy in 11:8. David knew that Batsheva was at all times married to Uriah until his documented death on the battlefield in verse 11:17.

David and the Talmudists cannot have it both ways. Either Batsheva was divorced from Uriah when he went off to war, in which case she was free to be intimate with another, or she remained the lawful *wife of Uriah* as the text emphasizes, in which case David committed the sin of adultery when he took her from her house, brought her to his palace and slept with her.

DAVID "TAKES" BATSHEVA

*And David sent messengers **and he took her** and she came to him and he lay with her (and she had purified herself from her uncleanliness); and she returned to her house.* II Sam. 11:4

Once David confirmed the identity of the very beautiful woman he had watched at her bath, he wasted no time. He already knew that both her father and her husband were away at war, fighting with Yoav in the fierce Ammonite campaign, so he made his move when she was alone and unprotected. David dispatched two members of his armed palace guards to Batsheva's house with orders to bring her to him. We can imagine the guards knocking perfunctorily on the door. It is nighttime, when an unexpected knocking is more ominous than it might be by day. Batsheva or a servant could not very well have refused entry to the king's imposing palace guards. Furthermore, she had no reason to do so. Her father and husband were well-placed members of David's elite fighting unit, and her grandfather was a member of the king's cabinet. Batsheva had no reason to feel threatened or to fear from the guards.

But all this changed in an instant. The Bible reader must infer the dramatic action of this critical scene because, as Sternberg says, the narrator has "slyly" left enormous gaps in the story, pointing up "what has *not* been communicated."[70] So we judiciously fill in the gap here. Perhaps the king's men stood in Batsheva's entryway, looking boldly about in a proprietary manner, leering at her and demanding, "Come with us!" Perhaps they even manhandle Batsheva as she steps away from their grasping hands asking them, "What is the meaning of this, and what do you want?" Perhaps they volunteer the phrase, "It is the King's orders!" as they hold her between them and march her out the door to their waiting chariot, not even giving her a moment to catch her breath. Perhaps the guards had danced this same pavane other times on other nights, at other addresses, doing the king's bidding and plucking a woman from her home in order to slake the lust of the king. They knew the purpose of their mission was to bring Batsheva to the king, and not to engage in polite conversation. So they remained mute, with a terrified Batsheva held fast between them.

We can imagine Batsheva's fear. It is terrifying to be accosted in one's own home at night with no one present to stand up for her against the king's men. At the time David's "messengers" come to fetch her she is a woman alone, helpless to resist, at the mercy of her society regardless of her place at court. Will the king and his guards treat her with respect, or will they treat her with disdain?

The Torah text does not embellish Batsheva's "taking," it only states that it occurred. Did Batsheva try to block the guards' entry? Did they carry her outside against her will? Did she scream and fight in protest? Other than the word *vayikacheha*, meaning *and he took her*, the text is silent and so is Batsheva. There is no textual evidence that Batsheva protested or resisted her "taking." There is no textual evidence that she did *not* resist it, either.

The Bible does give the reader a clue, however. In similar contexts the word *vayikacheha*, meaning *and he took her*, is one we have seen before. Recall that Shechem, Prince of his city, saw Dinah, then **he took her** and lay with her and abused her (Gen.

34:2).[71] This echoes the seeing and subsequent **taking** of the matriarch Sarah by the Pharaoh earlier still in Genesis (12:14–15), and a later sending-for and **taking** of Sarah once again, this time by Avimelech, king of Gerar (Gen. 20:2). In this context, Bible readers recognize this sequence for what it is: *vayikacheha* signals an abduction bent on rape.[72]

It should be emphasized that even in the episodes of the abduction and rape of Sarah and Dinah the Torah text is silent on what occurs in the woman's mind as well as on what occurs in the abductor's bedroom.[73] It is the *midrash* that "speaks in the voice of the woman,"[74] telling of the pain, the tears, the courage, the miracles, the humiliation and the shame of violation these women felt, having been "taken" by the kings.

There is even an earlier description of "seeing" and "taking" of beautiful women in the Bible, though the episode's characters remain anonymous. It occurs early in Genesis (6:1–2), when we are told that man is beginning to increase and multiply on the earth, and that daughters are born to them. The Bible continues: *The sons of the rulers saw that the daughters of man were good, and they took themselves wives from whomever they chose.* The Bible is readying the reader for the upcoming story of the depraved generation of the Flood, and this verse is the opening salvo. We are told that the sons of the princes and judges of that generation were wont to *see* and *take* the beautiful daughters of the lower classes, young women who were not in a position to resist the rapacious behavior of their superiors.[75] Even married women were not safe from the "takings" by the ruling males of the pre-Flood generation.[76] In this way the next generation resulting from these "takings" became a polluted one, sown from the seeds of a godless and degenerated society where the weak innocents were forced to submit to those who were more powerful but lawless.

The similarity to the David and Batsheva incident is striking. The main defect of the generation of the Flood was the sexual sin of *seeing* and *taking*, or of an urgent desire followed by an immediate "snatching away" to the bed of "the great one."[77] Zornberg says this behavior highlights the "barbarity" of the arrogant ruler "who simply enters the intimate domains of others and expresses his mastery. He ignores the sacredness of thresholds, the dangers, . . . the temptations, the respect due" others.[78] It was this generation of sinners that was swept away in its entirety by the Flood.

This brief allusion to the pre-Flood sin and punishment sets up a template for our story. We can see that, in biblical terms, King David's arrogant assertion of his sexual desire of Batsheva, whom he knew to be wife of another, and his employment of the power of his position to assert his will over one who was powerless and unprotected, bespeaks great sin sufficient to bring about his downfall.

In our story, in addition to the laden word *vayikacheha* (*and he took her*), the chapter's first four verses are filled with action verbs describing David's movements. We see the king *staying* in Jerusalem; *arising* from his bed; *pacing* his roof; *seeing* the woman bathing; *sending* and *inquiring* about the woman's identity; *sending* royal messengers; *taking* and *sleeping with* the woman. In verse 4 alone we can feel the fast pace: *David sent messengers and he took her and she came to him and he lay with her*. It is a verse that speaks of haste.[79]

The king was so aroused by the sight of this woman at her bath that he could not wait to possess her, so he summoned his palace guards and dispatched them to Batsheva's house with instructions to bring her to him without delay. The verse leaves no breathing space between its action phrases either in the *p'shat*— the simple reading of the verse — or in the trope, its musical cantillation. *And David sent messengers and he took her and she came to him and he lay with her* is a run-on sentence. The Torah reader cannot catch his or her breath until after the next phrase, *she cleansed herself from her impurity*, where the Torah trope signals a pause. The phrase *And David sent messengers* is followed immediately by *and **he took her***, because that is precisely how it happened.

In verse 2 David ***saw*** the *very beautiful* Batsheva at her bath and lusted after her; in verse 3 he *sent to inquire* about her; in verse 4 he *sent messengers and **he took her.*** The power of the sovereign is enormous and unquestioned. It is not surprising that all the actors in the text jump to the king's command; his messenger/guards as well as the unfortunate Batsheva.

Not only is the verse's wording reminiscent of other biblical "takings," it also is a dramatic signpost to the reader that David, second king of Israel, is behaving in the same degenerated manner as the pagan kings who, when they see something they want, they abduct and ravish it. When David sees and takes Batsheva he is acting like the Pharaoh did when he saw and took Sarah. David also imitates Avimelech, the Philistine king, who saw, sent for and took Sarah.[80] Bible readers familiar with David's story are aware of the extended time he spent among the Philistines when he was on the run from Saul. It is not unreasonable to conclude that the Philistines' dissolute morals inhered in the young David. In the adult David's moral rubric, passion and desire are not sublimated; they are fed immediately with no supervening brake.

Verse 4 continues: . . . *and she came to him and he lay with her* **(and she had cleansed herself from her impurity)**; *then she returned to her house.*

Verse 4 supplies the reason that the woman is bathing. It states in a by-the-way remark that the woman *had cleansed herself from her impurity.* Rashi and others[81] understand this to mean — in conjunction with the reference in verse 2 to her *washing herself* — that she had been cleansing herself after the end of her menstrual cycle. This parenthetical remark by the biblical narrator will become significant because such a ritual cleansing signifies that the woman is not only not pregnant when David "takes" her, but according to the Talmud[82] she also is likely to be at a fertile point in her cycle, increasing her chances of conceiving.[83]

But another reading of the phrase does *not* have this "cleansing" refer back to the bathing that David observed in verse 2. In biblical times, it was prescribed that a Hebrew woman bathe herself after having any manner of carnal relations (licit or illicit), and that both parties remain impure until the evening.[84] So it is possible that in verse 4 when Batsheva cleanses herself she is engaging in "postcoital purification,"[85] not in a ritual, post-menstrual bath.

Then she returned to her house. This is such an ordinary, prosaic ending to this dramatic section of chapter 11 that sets in motion a series of willful acts that will escalate to a murder and alter the destiny of kings. Batsheva *returns to her house*, but only after a spate of action verbs: *and he sent . . . and he took her . . . and she came . . . and he lay with her . . . and she had purified herself . . . and she returned to her house.* As was explained earlier, the entire verse bespeaks haste.[86] We can only wonder whether the king kept Batsheva overnight, with the same palace guards escorting her back to her house before daybreak. Or did the king leave her to her own devices, so that *she returned to her house* on her own, so as not to draw attention to the nature of her nocturnal adventure?

COULD BATSHEVA HAVE BEEN WILLING?

We cannot leave off discussing verse 4 without revisiting the phrase *and she came to him*. It has been suggested that that phrase is redundant here. Had the verse gone directly from *and he took her* to *and he lay with her* without this intervening statement it would have made seamless sense. David's abduction would thus have fit the pattern set in other such biblical "takings." Perhaps the phrase is inserted here in order to indicate that Batsheva "is not utterly passive" when she "comes to" David.[87] Batsheva certainly starts out as the *object* of male actions: she *is seen* at her bath, she *is taken* by the king. But if this phrase whispers of Batsheva's complicity—because it perhaps hints at her willingness to *come to him* [*sexually*]—we must ask *why* Batsheva would *come to* David, seemingly compliant?

The first answer is one we already have mentioned: the woman simply was not given any choice in the matter. She submitted or faced dire consequences. "The king does not entice Bathsheba with seductive words; he 'sends' for her and 'takes' her. David's actions presume the privileges of power, which depend upon subordinates being intimidated by that power . . . [query] whether a woman can refuse the king—if she wants to—even if the order is sexual and immoral."[88]

The answer is of course she could not. Batsheva was one lone, unprotected woman pitted against the power and force of David's majesty.

The second answer is at once practical and problematical. The text makes no mention of Batsheva and Uriah having any children; rather, the implication is quite the opposite. Which points to still other unanswerable questions: How old is Batsheva? How long have she and Uriah been married? Is this a barren marriage?

Batsheva is a young woman, most probably in her late teens,[89] at most twenty years old, and at the peak of her lush beauty at the time of this incident. She is a prize mate for Uriah, and likewise he is a prized catch. Uriah is an "alpha" male, a scion in a family of soldiers, an older man,[90] a handsome and heroic officer in the king's elite fighting brigade. One *midrash*[91] says that Batsheva had come to be cared for in Uriah's house while she was still a young girl; that when she came of age Uriah, a widower,[92] took her to be his lawful, wedded wife, and that his love for her was very great. In these circumstances it is fair to assume they engaged in intimate sexual relations with one another after their marriage ceremony and whenever Uriah was home on leave. If Batsheva is still childless at the time of our story, the societal presumption is that *she* is the source of the infertility problem, not Uriah.[93] If, in fact, Batsheva were Uriah's second wife, and he already had sons from his previous marriage,[94] this would explain the presumption that Batsheva was unable to conceive.

In biblical society the childless state is of grave concern to the woman. Batsheva is aware that to survive in her society she *must* become a mother. Clearly her union to Uriah has not produced the child she desires, and she is not certain whether the fault lies within her or within Uriah. It is even possible, of course, that the problem is mechanical, as Uriah is absent more than he is present, and that the times he has been home on leave may not have been fertile times for Batsheva. Regardless of whether the problem is infertility or a lack of proximity, the result is the same: Uriah is away, and Batsheva is alone and childless. She longs to test her fertility, but her dilemma is that she is a married woman and "cannot test her capacity for reproduction outside her marital bonds."[95]

There is one solution, however. If the king "takes" her at the time of the month when she is most fertile, she can (blamelessly) test her ability to conceive, and also, potentially, fulfill her own maternal destiny and bear sons. This rationale might be at work behind the seemingly unnecessary phrase in verse 4, *and she came unto him*, suggesting, according to Klein, a non-resistant compliance.

Supporting this line of inquiry is verse 2's description of Batsheva's bath. Klein calls it provocatively ambiguous.[96] The inevitable question is whether Batsheva deliberately took her purifying bath on that evening and at that particular time, in the king's line-of-sight, in order to catch his eye and provoke the "taking." Did Batsheva engineer the "taking" in order to become pregnant by David in circumstances that would have allowed her to retain her personal honor? Was Batsheva riskily trading her lonely, motherless state for the *potential* of achieving the desired, even honored state of motherhood? If so, she would not be the first biblical woman to audaciously trade sexual morality for motherhood.[97]

Other than the suggestion of different voice and tone in verse 4 described above, the text does not definitively answer these questions. Despite the Talmud's vigorous, sometimes far-fetched defense of David's immoral and inexcusable abduction of the married Batsheva,[98] thoughtful and learned modern-day Bible scholars[99] and traditional commentators such as the Abarbanel have stated emphatically that **nowhere in the text is there any support for the notion that Batsheva is at all to blame or responsible for her "taking" by David**. Frymer-Kensky is outspoken on this point: "To say that Bathsheba set out to entice the king is to say that violated women 'were asking for it' because they smiled, or wore tight clothes, or went to a club. Bathsheba is enjoying a private moment—she thinks—and [David] violate[s] it" and her.[100]

We will explore these various opinions over the course of this analysis. In the meantime, let us return to the story so we can draw our own conclusions.

AND SHE SAID TO DAVID, "I AM PREGNANT"

And the woman conceived; and she sent word to David saying, "I am pregnant." II Sam. 11:5

Three months have passed since David's abduction of Batsheva. We do not know whether he continued to be intimate with her after that fateful night, or whether, as the text implies, she *returned to her home* after the king slaked his lust, and she never returned to the palace. Perhaps the king's close advisors warned him afterwards that he was playing with fire; that it was insupportable to abduct and lay with the wife of one of his military officers; that his one night with her had to be the end of the affair. Perhaps the king heeded their politic advice. Or perhaps he gave in to Batsheva's pleas to be returned to her house when he had finished with her. Perhaps with the passage of days and weeks David even conveniently ignored his lustful liason, thinking, "Might that not be the end of it?"[101]

But of course this was not fated to be so. There were "fundamental"[102] human consequences to his unlawful act.

Batsheva sends a message to David consisting of two Hebrew words: *Hara anochi. I am pregnant.* **These are the only words spoken by Batsheva throughout this entire incident, and they are explosive**. We can imagine, given the analysis above, that Batsheva's words might be spoken somewhat triumphantly (*I am pregnant; I am not barren; I am to be a mother!*). But at the same time they surely are spoken warily. She knows that the king cannot blithely accept such an unstable state of affairs. The monarch must acknowledge his sired children, and as regards an Israelite monarch, his issue must be born within the sacrament of a lawful marriage. Batsheva must have spoken these words with some trepidation, then. What would this headstrong king do when he found out she was carrying his child, proof of his adulterous affair with the wife of a prized officer?

Perhaps Batsheva announced her pregnancy to David at this time for another reason. She knew that she would soon begin to show, and that it was public knowledge both that she had been taken to the palace that night, and that Uriah had not slept in her bed since the Ammonite military campaign had begun months before. In biblical times adultery was a capital offense. Given the circumstances, Batsheva could therefore have feared for her life. Her pregnancy during Uriah's absence is proof that she has been unfaithful, and she would be liable for the death penalty.[103] So quite possibly Batsheva's sending word to the king of her pregnancy is a request for his protection. She knows she is at grave risk and she is terrified.

Perhaps Batsheva's words were in the nature of a plea to David. One *midrash*[104] has her begging the king to return her husband, Uriah, from the front so that he could sleep with her, thus putting an end to her "shame," ending the gossip about whose child she could be carrying.

In the text, however, the idea to implicitly renounce this unborn baby and the act of calling Uriah home from the front is entirely David's. The twist is that David's calculated plan is "all business," while Batsheva's *midrashic* plea is personal. David cold-bloodedly plots to have Uriah furloughed home from the battlefield on a pretext of reporting about the war's progress directly to the king. The weary soldier would then spend the night in his own bed in the arms of his wife, thus legitimizing any future child she would bear, and letting David off the hook. Of course, David's plan does not work out quite that way.

WHO IS THE SEDUCER?

Let us issue a freeze-frame at this juncture in the story in order to revisit the notion of an alternative reading of verses 1 through 5. In a Rashomon-type of analysis, it has been suggested by Mia Diamond that Batsheva — and not David — initiates, or at least catalyzes, her own "taking." That instead of David being the primary, initiating actor here, it is Batsheva. That Batsheva's act of bathing herself is "the first direct action taken" in this story; that David's actions in these verses are purely reactive, and that David is not the one who is in control. This reading casts Batsheva not as a passive woman to whom things *are done* (notwithstanding that she *is seen; is sent for; is taken; is lain with*), but as an "active agent" who performed and displayed; and though she *is taken* by the king, she *comes into* him volitionally.[105]

The primary proof-text advanced for this reading is verse 5 itself. The literal reading of the verse is stilted: *And the woman conceived; and she sent and she **told** David and **said**, 'I am pregnant.'* Diamond suggests that because the verse contains two similar words meaning "and she spoke" — *vataged* and *vatomer*, meaning *she told* and *she said* — without a change in speaker and with but a single message, something is missing from the text. There should be two messages if there are two verbs signifying speech. Because the only "message" in the verse is the laconic "I am pregnant," Diamond sees a gap in the text.[106] What could have been said, or should have been said, or was said in the space or gap left by the first "she told" in verse 4? Diamond suggests that this is "the space in which Batsheva tells David something of her plan"[107] to attract him and to conceive a child with him. Diamond goes further, positing that within that textual gap "[Batsheva] and David decided on the Uriah plan together,"[108] referring to the idea of recalling Uriah from the front and having him spend the night in his own bed.

Diamond's reading is fascinating and provocative, and at first blush seems tantalizingly possible. An important textual difficulty with it is that in the books of Samuel, where any suspect or negative behavior by the book's characters is almost gleefully described by the narrator in acid prose,[109] there is absolutely nothing explicitly linking Batsheva to the seductive behavior posited by Diamond. Had Batsheva deliberately instigated the seduction it is certain the narrator would have said so, in order to mitigate the hero's guilt, if not simply to state the truth of the matter.

But let us hew to the text and examine it in light of Diamond's proposition. The sequence is first, that David is at home and at leisure in Jerusalem while his army and all of Israel are fighting a fierce war. In fact, the Israelite army has run the enemy to ground and is besieging it as the story opens. The narrator tells us all this, precisely in order to present David as he is: a warrior-king who for reasons of his own has chosen *not* to fight alongside his troops, but to remain in his palace in Jerusalem. Already in verse 1 the narrator is preparing the reader for a tale of David's leisure-time activity.

Next we read that David is recently gotten up from his afternoon nap—more odd behavior by a soldier-king—and that he is pacing atop his palace roof. *Only then* are we told that David beholds a very beautiful woman bathing herself. David is the only "active agent" in the story thus far. *He* is the subject of the reader's lens *until* we begin to imagine what the narrator tells us *David sees.*

And importantly, the narrator does not say that Batsheva's act of bathing was outside on *her* roof; **the only person who is explicitly out on a rooftop is the king**. If the narrator had wanted to present a situation where the woman was intent on seducing the king, it would have been a simple matter for the text to have said that her bathing was out in the open. But it did not say this, although readers mistakenly assume this fact. Legitimately, the reader can only infer from the text that David watched from *his* rooftop while a woman bathed herself *inside* her own — perhaps windowed — bathing chamber.[110]

The text only tells us of the woman's bath *after* it narrates David's rooftop stroll as evening is falling. As readers of the text we must take the text as we find it. It is *David's* behavior that takes precedence in the narrative, literally and temporally. If Batsheva has calculated this display in advance, it is news to the narrator.

And as regards Diamond's perceived gap in verse 5, she acknowledges that Bible scholar Meir Sternberg "misses" it, and also that doubling of verbs is common in the Torah.[111] Yet her assumption is that the *vataged* and *vatomer* verbs (*she told* and *she said*) are *not* the same for purposes of Batsheva's *I am pregnant* message. Her contention is that each verb signals a separate *and different* communication from Batsheva to David.

But this is not so. The two verbs — *vatishlach vataged* — are two side-by-side verbs that signify one action.[112] The verb *vataged* is in fact joined to the immediately prior verb, *vatishlach* (*and she sent*), **and** to its object word that follows: *to David*. The phrase properly reads *vatishlach vataged l'David*, meaning *and she sent word to David*.

What's more, Diamond's "second verb," the word *vatomer*, which immediately follows *and she sent word to David*, should not be translated literally as *and she said*. Rather, it is the indicator of the direct quotation that follows it: Batsheva's announcement, "*I am pregnant.*" The word *vatomer* functions as the open quote. *Vataged* explains *what* Batsheva did (*she told* David), and *vatomer* explains *how* she tells David (via a direct quotation, Batsheva's only spoken words in this entire episode).[113] If the text belabors the Hebrew verbs in verse 5 it is because the words act as a trumpet trill, a *ta-da!* blast to announce Batsheva's fateful and damning words that climax the verse. For all these reasons, the verse is properly translated as, *The woman conceived, and she sent word to David: "I am pregnant."*

To be sure, Diamond's thesis—that the childless Batsheva could have initiated the seduction of David for her own purposes—may still be a possibility. But reliance on a "gap" in verse 5 for that proposition is probably misplaced.

Along similar lines, Klein has suggested that "Bathsheba may well have been purifying herself on her roof with the hope of seducing King David into 'seducing' her."[114] Klein engages in the misreading I described above, and so takes more liberty with the text than does Diamond. Klein improperly assumes a critical fact not in evidence: that Batsheva was outside on *her* roof. As I discussed above, not only is this fact absent from the text, but its absence is striking and possibly deliberate when contrasted with the clear and detailed narrative of verse 2 stating that David is pacing *on the roof of the palace of the king.* **David was out on his roof; Batsheva was *not* out on hers**.

Notwithstanding this important flaw, Klein's "gap" is more convincing and supportive of her argument than is Diamond's. This is because Klein suggests that verse 4 (not verse 5) holds the key to this puzzle. Verse 4 says, *So David sent messengers and he took her and she came to him and he lay with her . . .* David's behavior is associated with action verbs, with the exception of the phrase *and she came to him.* This phrase is interposed in the abduction verse almost as a redundancy. For if we were to delete just that phrase for the purpose of illustration, the verse would read, . . . *and he took her and he lay with her . . .* The meaning remains clear: David sent for, took and lay with Batsheva. There is no need for the narrator to shift his lens from David to Batsheva with the words *and she came to him,* **unless** the text is hinting something to the reader. Klein's point is that the Bible reader, "alerted to [the] excess verbiage," would conclude from the phrase that Batsheva is "complicit in the sexual adventure."[115]

At most, as Klein concedes, Batsheva's bathing "presents a subtle *opportunity for enticement* rather than an overt sexual invitation."[116] The reins to this story's action remain firmly in

King David's hands. What we see is what the biblical narrator intends us to see:

> The thick procession of verbal actions gives texture to the picture of the potentate who unwisely assumes that his power places him above the Torah. It is the king who *sends* armies and messengers, *inquires* after the identity of the vision of loveliness sighted from his rooftop, *takes* another's wife, *interrogates* and *orders*. Responses to this autocratic figure are servile and shielded.[117]

Diamond's and Klein's theses do fit neatly into this book's point of inquiry. For *if* (and I use the word cautiously and *arguendo*, only) Batsheva were complicit in her own taking, then she would fit precisely our category of women who engage in sexually audacious behavior (*i.e.,* aggressive seduction, incest, and/or adultery) yet who are not condemned in the Bible text. Instead, these women are rewarded with sons who are prophets and kings, who continue the Davidic dynasty, and who even become forebears of the Messiah. A seductive Batsheva would fit this template.

But interestingly, even absent any complicity on the part of Batsheva in her own sexual abduction by the king, Batsheva's story could still fit our pattern. For the shadow of adultery hangs over her eventual marriage to the king. Batsheva has — albeit not initially of her own free will — been a party to David's audacious sexual behavior. And looking ahead, she will give birth to Solomon, whom the Bible will call "beloved of God." It is Batsheva and David's son Solomon who will inherit David's throne and rule as king over Israel.

The answer to why the Bible rewards such audacious sexual behavior is beginning to take shape. Batsheva, and perhaps all the biblical women presented in this volume who fit this category, are pursuing a destiny that is consonant with the divine purpose of moving the Israelite family toward immortal nationhood. This cannot be done without a steady line of sons and attendant succession. When we meet the woman Batsheva she is childless.

Perhaps she chose to accept the king's forced sexual ministrations for reasons of her own. We will never know, and the text does not tell us what went on in the king's bed that fateful night.

Absent clear textual support, then, I am uncomfortable assigning complicity or partial blame to a woman who is the object of a forcible abduction. Such a reading, however fascinating it might be, has insidious implications for the victims of abductions when, as here, the reading is not supported by the Torah text.[118] And because of the absence of any textual support for the notion that Batsheva is even partially responsible for her "taking," I must side with the *p'shat*, or straightforward reading of the verses. We are told that King David saw Batsheva at her bath; that he sent for and took her; and that he lay with her. David is the primary actor.

As I discussed above, in the earlier stories of Sarah and Dinah, Bible readers witnessed eerily similar *seeing-sending-taking* stories that echo each other as well as our present incident. And because the Bible has laid out this verbal and behavioral pattern at least thrice before, the Bible reader is primed to recognize the typology of a royal abduction of a beautiful woman here. Absent divine intervention (as with Sarah), the woman/victim is helplessly at the mercy of her more powerful abductor (as with Dinah). As any experienced rape counselor will confirm, when faced with a willful, arrogantly entitled, and powerfully aroused male aggressor, Batsheva could not very well have politely declined and walked away unscathed. The upcoming chapter discussing prince Amnon's violent rape of the beautiful and eloquent Tamar will illustrate the truth of this statement.

For all these reasons, then, however existentially lonesome, yearning for a child and temptingly lovely the young Batsheva is, the text tells us only that she was "taken" by the king, and *not* that she instigated her own abduction. It is unsupported speculation to suggest that the woman had any voluntary say in the matter. And the reader should bear in mind that even Batsheva's possible ambivalence would not have mitigated David's arrogant and sinful act of adultery.

"SEND ME URIAH THE HITTITE!"

And David sent to Yoav, "Send me Uriah the Hittite!" And Yoav sent Uriah to David.

And Uriah came to him, and David inquired about the welfare of Yoav and the peace of the people, and the welfare of the war.

And David said to Uriah, "Go down to your house and wash your feet." And Uriah departed from the king's house, and the king's provisions followed after him.

And Uriah slept at the entrance of the king's house with all the servants of his lord, and he did not go down to his house.

And they told David, saying, "Uriah did not go down to his house." And David said to Uriah, "Have you not come from a journey? Why did you not go down to your house?"

And Uriah said to David, "The ark and Israel and Judah dwell in huts, and my lord Yoav and the servants of my lord are encamped in the open field; and shall I come to my house to eat and to drink and to lie with my wife? By your life and by the life of your soul, if I would do this thing!" II Sam. 11:6–11

Verse 3 begins as David *sends — vayishlach —* to inquire about the very beautiful woman he saw at her bath. Verse 4 begins with the same exact verb, as David *sends* messengers to take Batsheva and bring her to his bed. The action shifts momentarily to Batsheva in verse 5, when it is *she* who *sends* — again using the same Hebrew word — a message to David announcing *I am pregnant!* And verse 6 opens this section of the story with two additional incidents of *vayishlach,* or sendings, plus yet a third variant of the verb. David *sends* a message to Yoav, his general, demanding that Uriah the Hittite, Batsheva's husband, be *sent* home from the front to appear before the king; Yoav complies with his king's request, and dutifully *sends* Uriah to David.

As we noted earlier, these verbs indicate action on David's part, and their sequence and repetition bespeak haste. Certainly David's *sending* a message and Yoav's responsive *sending* of Uriah in the same verse and using the same verb leave the reader with no doubt that events are moving very quickly. We can understand the reason for David's haste. He wants Uriah to sleep in his own bed, with his own wife, on this very night, so that her pregnancy—which is about to become obvious—can legitimately be attributed to her husband and not to the king himself,[119] or at least that the child's provenance will at least be confused.[120]

All this *sending* to and fro of persons, messengers and messages into and out of David's palace also tells the reader that "the adultery can scarcely [have been] a secret within the court."[121] This fact becomes a primary piece of evidence when we examine the question of whether Uriah had any inkling that David had abducted and sexually violated his wife.

At the moment, however, we are witnessing an ostensibly legitimate inquiry about the state of the battle between a commander-in-chief and a decorated active officer. Uriah comes into the king's court and David inquires about the welfare of Yoav, his general, and of the troops, and also Uriah's opinion about the war itself.

But after this perfunctory inquiry about the business of the war, the conversation rapidly devolves into the personal. In a kind of hail-fellow, just-between-us-guys fashion, the Bible tells us that David tells Uriah to go down to his home and "wash his feet." Imagine the king draping his powerful arm over Uriah's muscled shoulders and in the universally male manner of boss to subordinate saying to him, in effect, "Now, Uriah, why don't you take a well-deserved night off and go on home to your lovely wife. Take a hot shower, wash off all that battlefield grime, and have a drink and a good night's sleep." David's latter comment might even have been uttered with a little wink. Boys will be boys, after all.

In fact, in the Bible the expression "wash your feet" is often a euphemism for the sex act,[122] and the word "feet" has been used as a euphemism for the male genitals.[123] The reader must also recognize that David's suggestion to Uriah to "wash your feet" is an ironic subtle reference to David's having witnessed Batsheva's bathing of her entire body, an act of voyeurism that led to the illicit sexual behavior that began this incident. Uriah's sanctioned act of sex with his own wife could neutralize the king's illicit taking of her.

The meaning of verse 8 is no doubt crystal-clear to Uriah. The king is granting him a boon not offered to his fellow soldiers who still fight and sleep on the rocky battlefield. The text even mentions at the end of verse 8 that the king sent his palace staff after Uriah with a prepared meal.[124] What else is David doing but unsubtly suggesting to Uriah that he head home for a night of sex? David is providing the romantic trappings of a dinner *à deux*: wine and good food.[125] David is engineering what he hopes will be an irresistible invitation for Uriah to be intimate with Batsheva and thereby silence any wagging tongues on the issue of her pregnancy. David is attempting to seduce Uriah into sleeping with Batsheva, Uriah's own wife!

URIAH DOES NOT SLEEP IN HIS HOUSE

Had Uriah been anyone else, he would have bowed gratefully and thanked the king, made his way to his home, and followed the not unpleasant blueprint laid out for him by David. But Uriah is unique. The man is a straight-arrow, true to his name, which means "God is my light." He is the Bible's foil for David in this story. Where David is portrayed as lustful, immoral and housebound, Uriah is asexual, honorable, perhaps even naive, and he is portrayed as rejecting conventional shelter. Uriah is the single-minded warrior that David once was. He is a man who is at-one with his fellow soldiers, whose battlefield bivouac—not his palace—is his real home, and, other than coming to the palace in response to the king's summons, he does not set foot in a "house" in our chapter.

The Torah text wants us to appreciate the Uriah-David contrast, so it repeats and alternates the phrases *your house* and *the king's house* seven times in verses 8 through 11 (and once again in verse 13). Each time David thrusts the phrase *go to your house* at Uriah, either Uriah or the narrator parries with *and Uriah did **not** return to his house*. In a move that is surely incomprehensible to the lustful king—and also, perhaps, to the reader—instead of going to his own house Uriah chooses instead to spend the night on a pallet of straw[126] on the stone floor of the servants' hall of the palace.

The drama intensifies with the coming interchange between David and Uriah. Their conversation of the day before was nothing unusual, an appropriate exchange of greetings and a report on the state of the battle followed by a suggestion that the officer sleep in his own bed before returning to the front. But in verse 10 we are told that the palace whisperers — or the king's own house spies — have informed him that Uriah never went home. He slept on the palace floor instead of in his own bed with his wife, Batsheva! In fact, the verb *vayishkav*, meaning *and he lay*, which appears at three pivotal times in our story (once in verse 4 when David abducts and then *lays with* Batsheva, again in verse 9 when the text tells us that Uriah *lay down* for the night with the servants), will appear for the third time in Uriah's long speech in verse 11 when he responds to the king about where he can and cannot properly *lay down*.

In a case of dramatic irony, these two men, who would ordinarily share a common purpose — love for and defense of their country — are in point of fact adversaries, fencing here with words and morals, dueling over the same woman. But of course, the reader is only certain that one of them — David, the king — is aware of the facts and the true stakes of his meetings with Uriah. Uriah's level of awareness of the fraught situation is ambiguous.

We overhear the king as he accosts Uriah the next morning:[127]

"But you have journeyed far. Why did you not go down to your house?"

Would Uriah have bristled at this inquiry? Is it common practice for the king to express such an avid interest in where a soldier sleeps when he is on leave? Could the king's intrusive inquiry have set off alarm bells in Uriah's head? Or perhaps Uriah had been tipped off some time *before* that morning conversation with David, and comes to David on day-two knowing or suspecting about the king's affair with Batsheva.

We must consider that Uriah did not sleep in his own house on the first night of his leave *because* he either knew of or suspected the king's sexual affair with his wife. Uriah was silent during his first meeting with David perhaps because he was taking the king's measure. Uriah, an experienced, lifelong soldier, was nothing if not thoughtful and circumspect. He was determined not to set foot in his own house—notwithstanding his own physical desires and needs—until he has gotten to the bottom of the rumors of the sexual goings-on.

By the same token, it is also possible that Uriah as yet had *no* suspicions at all. He has just hours before come from a bloody battlefield. An elite soldier fights "in a zone" of intense focus and concentration. It has been suggested that as a commando soldier on active duty he was expected to remain celibate.[128] Under such constraints Uriah makes the best of the situation, transitioning from his battlefield sleeping bag to a pallet in the servants' hall.

Recall that in verse 1 the king's soldiers are referred to as "servants." The words "servants" and "soldiers" are thus interchangeable for our purposes. Uriah has been sleeping alongside his fellow "servants"—his fellow soldiers—on the fields of battle for months. Here, in verse 9, we see that Uriah again makes his bed with the king's "servants." He has chosen to bed down near a warm hearth on the floor of the servants' hall of the palace with his former comrades, the king's palace guards,[129] before he heads back to the front. He is no doubt plied with food from the kitchen, treated with affectionate care by the king's cooks and maids who have sons, grandsons and lovers on the front and are eager to hear news of them.

We must also consider that David's palace guards, Uriah's former buddies, might have taken advantage of their night all together on the palace floor to put Uriah in the picture about the king's sexual escapade with Batsheva. We will consider this possibility in coming pages.

The contrast between David and Uriah is brought into sharp relief by Uriah's response to David in verse 11:

> *"The Holy Ark and Israel and Judah are sitting in huts, and my master Yoav and the servants of my master are camped out on the open field. Should I then come to my house to eat and to drink and to lay with my wife? By your life and by your soul, I will not do this thing!"*

Uriah is taking the dangerous step of teaching the king a lesson in manners. We already have learned in verses 1 and 2 that David was napping in Jerusalem while his troops and all of Israel were fighting a fierce war. The contrast of king to subjects is stark and deliberate. A similar play is at work in Uriah's response in verse 11. He has painted a word-picture for the king and for the reader that shows Uriah in a pure light of morality and righteousness. Uriah "gets it" while the king does not; Uriah refuses to rest comfortably while his comrades and God's Holy Ark are precariously at risk. He knows they cannot rest on a perilous battlefield; baked by the sun by day, and freezing on the ground by night.[130] Uriah—not David—exhibits unity with his comrades and with the ark of God. Uriah is absolutely in the right and the king, not surprisingly, is in the wrong.

Tragically, though a warrior's might as well as the moral right are on Uriah's side, this "perfect soldier" is no match for the sovereign power behind "the treacherous king"[131] who is bent on legitimizing Batsheva's pregnancy. Uriah's obdurate behavior will presage his death warrant.

We should revisit briefly the concept of the "battlefield divorce" suggested by the Talmud.[132] Within that construct, discussed at length earlier in this chapter, if Uriah had accepted David's offer of "home leave" and had spent the night with his wife, his behavior would have invalidated any such divorce.[133] If his divorce from Batsheva had been an unconditional or absolute one, then neither David nor Batsheva committed adultery, as she was not married to Uriah at the time David abducted her. In such circumstance Uriah might have escaped death had he accepted the king's offer of "home leave," as Batsheva's baby would have been "his." Also, at the end of his home visit Uriah could easily have presented his wife with a second bill of divorce, and left her a free woman once again.[134] So there would have been no motive for David to kill off Uriah if the bill of divorce already was in effect.

We must assume, then, either that Uriah had *not* issued Batsheva such a bill before he went off to war, or if he did, that it was a *conditional* divorce, which would only come into play if Uriah were to die in battle or go missing. But even if Uriah had issued Batsheva an *un*conditional divorce, it would still have been grossly unseemly for David to have taken Uriah's wife while the officer was at war.[135]

DAVID TRIES AGAIN

David said to Uriah, "Stay here today and tomorrow I will
send you off." So Uriah remained in Jerusalem that day and
the next day.

And David called him, and [Uriah] ate and drank with
him, and David made him drunk. And [Uriah] went out in
the evening to lie on his bed with the servants of his lord, but
he did not go down to his house. II Sam. 11:12–13

David is determined and resilient. He sees that Uriah did not fall
in with his initial plan to take a "home leave" in his own house
and in his own bed. So he resorts to "plan B." The king's "last
desperate attempt"[136] at an alibi[137] for Batsheva's pregnancy is to
ply Uriah with good food, wine and spirits, to get him drunk, and
to point him toward his house, his wife and his bed, leaving the
rest to nature. All the king needs to legitimize Batsheva's
pregnancy is that Uriah spend one night in his wife's bed. He is
hopeful that this time he will successfully subvert Uriah's
inhibition, slide beneath the soldier's scruples, and achieve his
end. Because if not, David will not shrink from engineering the
unthinkable.

Uriah has been chafing to return to the front.[138] Now that the
king has promised him a quick return to the battle after a leave of
a day or two, Uriah believes his return to the king's table that
night[139] will be in the nature of a farewell meal. He has not slept
with his wife nor has he even seen her. He is determined to keep
faith with his warrior's sexual abstinence,[140] not only for his own
honor, but also as a bond with his fellow elite corpsmen still on
the battlefield. It is not easy being a soldier, nor is it easy being a
soldier's wife. But for Uriah it is the only life; it is the best life; it is
what he has been expertly trained for, and for him soldiering is
God's work: defending his country, his Ark, and his home. He
would disregard the irritation of the swirling rumors and spend
one more night at the palace. By this time tomorrow he would be
back in the thick of battle with his comrades. Private time with
Batsheva would wait until his next appointed leave.

Uriah, perhaps a bit awed at the honor David was bestowing
upon him, eats and drinks in the palace with the king.[141] So much

so, that he becomes intoxicated from the unaccustomed quantity of undiluted liquor. But drunk or sober Uriah remains true to himself. After the meal, instead of heading down to his house Uriah makes it only as far as the familiar servants' hall, where he beds down once more with the palace guards.

FOILED, DAVID PLOTS URIAH'S MURDER

And it came to pass in the morning that David wrote a letter to Yoav and sent it with Uriah.

In the letter he wrote as follows: "Place Uriah in the front line where the battle is heaviest; then withdraw so that he will be hit and die."

And it came to pass, when Yoav kept watch upon the city, that he assigned Uriah to the place where he knew there were brave warriors.

And the men of the city went out and fought with Yoav, and some of David's troops fell, and Uriah the Hittite also died. II Sam. 11:14–17

David's plans to cover up his adultery with Batsheva have come to naught. His night of unchecked passion, abuse of his office, betrayal of his vows to God and to the people he serves, and his ravishment of Batsheva, have led him to this point of no return. He had calculated the best way to deal with Batsheva's unexpected pregnancy, and after the benign methods fail, the king has his back against the wall, so-to-speak, and he sees only one way out. He must have Uriah killed. In the words of Robert Alter, "David now gravely compounds the original crime of adultery by plotting to get Uriah out of the way entirely by having him killed. What follows in the story makes it clear that bloodshed, far more than adultery, is David's indelible transgression."[142]

The reader's eyes widen, our stomachs clench with tension and nausea as we read of David's perfidy. David was through trying to entice Uriah into sleeping with Batsheva. Uriah was now the problem, and David's gloves—and mask—are now off. He pens a message to Yoav, his general, a practiced *modus operandi* when communicating with the battlefield commander. The king begins the letter with military instructions, and interspersed with the battle plans he instructs Yoav on the subject of Uriah.[143] David's letter leaves no room for doubt; it is Uriah's death warrant.

In a dramatically ironic and underhanded move, David seals this poisoned letter and places it *into Uriah's hand* with instructions to deliver it personally to Yoav. We think, the king's treachery is fathomless. He counts on Uriah to carry his own death writ! Moreover, David is confirming for posterity that Uriah is as honorable as he, David, is corrupt. By this important detail the Torah text "emphasize[s] the monstrous requirements and hypertrophied passions of the king, or of kingship itself."[144] David trusts Uriah to behave in the loyal manner of his calling. The reader is screaming silently at Uriah to open the letter, read it, and outmaneuver David. But of course Uriah delivers the letter intact.

The king commands Yoav to place Uriah at the front-most lines, face-to-face with the Ammonites' bravest warriors at the wall of the Ammonite city. The other Israelite commandos, all thirty-seven members of Uriah's troop,[145] are to beat a retreat, leaving Uriah exposed and alone. David not only wants Uriah slain; he wants him to die an ignominious death at the hands of Israel's Ammonite enemy. For a soldier of Uriah's pride and competence to perish in a foolish military maneuver such as David is outlining, is to die a humiliating—not a hero's—death.

David is striking two blows at Uriah, one of the bravest among the elite soldiers of the realm.[146] First, David cuckolds Uriah, forcibly abducting Uriah's wife and then impregnating her. Now, in an intricate coverup murder plot worthy of a classic gangster film, David is having Uriah killed so that the king's name will not be smeared as an adulterer. If it sounds like a Byzantine maneuver, it is: plotting a murder in order to cover up an act of adultery. It is akin to putting out a small kitchen hearth fire by dynamiting the entire house.

The murder of Uriah will leave the field clear for David. If, as we have discussed earlier, Uriah had given Batsheva a divorce decree when he went off to fight the Ammonites, with his death

Batsheva is free to remarry, and the divorce might even have been retroactive to Uriah's first leave-taking. With Uriah's death David would technically be in the clear, since, under this theory, Batsheva was *not technically married at the time David abducted and bedded her*. All that would remain is for the king to see to it that Batsheva's pregnancy does not become public until after he has married her. It would be a simple matter for him to confine the woman to her house until it suited him to publicize her pregnancy.

As it happened, Yoav implemented David's command with slight variations, and many members of the elite Israelite fighting force were slain in the maneuver along with Uriah.[147]

There is some *midrashic* opinion that Uriah was liable for the death penalty on three counts of disloyalty to the crown.[148] First, because Uriah refused David's order to go down to his house on the first night of his home leave, publicly flouting the king's order and sleeping instead on the palace floor. It was the king's intention to keep Uriah in Jerusalem, but Uriah disobeyed the king and sought to return to the front. Second, because Uriah publicly spurned the royal feast the king sent after him, making light of the honor that the king was granting him. Third, because Uriah referred to Yoav, the king's general and subordinate, as "my lord" while addressing the king. Royal etiquette required that only the king be referred to in that exalted language.[149]

Even if this line of argument presented technical just cause for charging Uriah with treason against the king, it is seems an unduly harsh *ex post facto* excuse for ordering Uriah's execution. While "insubordination in time of war can be tantamount to treason, punishable by immediate execution, . . . David's handling of Uriah's case was hardly within the bounds of due process."[150] David engineered Uriah's death for David's own selfish and corrupt purposes. Hanging Uriah's death on his "treason" was a bogus, after-the-fact attempt to excuse the king's sin.

DID URIAH KNOW?

Meir Sternberg's now-iconic, classic biblical enigma is "Does Uriah know?"[151] Paradoxically, one of the reasons for the enduring drama of the biblical narrative is that the reader is kept eternally pondering and hypothesizing about the motives and thoughts of the Bible's actors. We project assumptions onto the characters, injecting "passions, fears and scheming"[152] precisely because the spare Bible text tells us only the facts. The biblical narrator "leaves his agents' inner lives opaque."[153] And through close reading of the text — and, for me, interweaving *midrashic* opinions — we attempt to clarify these characters' motives and thoughts. The answer, then, to Sternberg's eternal question is a maddening "perhaps."[154]

Considering the multiple messengers and messages that were dispatched from the palace to Batsheva's house and to and from the battlefield — at least twelve incidents of *sending* or *telling* in chapter 11 alone — and the sheer number of open conversations between David and Uriah, David and the messengers, and even the one between Batsheva and David, it is likely that the king's adulterous relationship with Batsheva was an open secret.

A better inquiry might be, therefore, when did Uriah find out? To this query we have an answer, based on Uriah's own behavior and speech. It is likely that Uriah was told about the king's abduction of his wife, Batsheva, on the first night of his home leave.[155]

In the first conversation David has with Uriah (verses 7 and 8) upon his arrival from the front, Uriah is silent. Only David speaks in the text. One gets the impression that Uriah, only recently arrived from the battlefield and with the dust of the journey still on his feet, is slightly awed by the majesty of the king. He has no inkling of the reason he was called back to Jerusalem.

After spending the night on the floor of the servants' hall with other soldiers who are members of the palace guard, Uriah has undergone a small transformation. His response the next morning to the king's pressure to spend the night in his own bed (verse 11) is lengthy and sharp; in fact, it is just this side of discourteous. Our silent soldier has grown teeth overnight.

A logical inference is that overnight Uriah's soldier comrades have put him in the picture and told him of the swirling rumors concerning the king and his beautiful wife. The tone and content of Uriah's riposte to the king's query the next morning — *"But you have journeyed far; why did you not spend the night in your home?!"* — indicates that *this time* Uriah exhibits suspicion and hostility when he meets with the king.[156] He begins to see David's insistence that he spend the night in his own bed for what it is: an attempt to maneuver him in order to give the king a way out of his adulterous predicament. And Uriah has no desire to do this.

But we must consider another scenario. It is possible that Uriah may *already have suspected or known of* David's affair with his wife even *before* his first audience with the king. This is a logical inference if we employ common sense and walk, for argument's sake, in a soldier's shoes. It is simply unnatural for a soldier on furlough from active duty *not* to take advantage of the opportunity to engage in available sexual relations. Uriah's "extremely beautiful" young wife was available to him just a short distance away. Added to this, the king had issued Uriah a friendly order saying "go down to your house and wash your feet," a royal warrant entitling him to spend the night in his wife's arms. Furthermore, the king also sends along a catered meal to accompany Uriah on his expected reunion with his wife.

So it is reasonable to conclude that had Uriah *not* suspected his wife and the king, he would certainly have slept in his own bed in his own home when he was on furlough.

Contrarily, though, Uriah, for reasons of his own, chooses *not* to go home to his wife and their marriage bed. He spends the night on the palace floor with the other servants of the king. It is logical, fair and inevitable to infer that Uriah is determined not to touch his wife. And why is that? If Uriah suspects the goings-on between David and Batsheva no doubt this proud man is deeply hurt, feeling betrayed by his king as well as by his wife. He is a thoughtful, logical soldier, accustomed to considering actions and reactions, and is not prepared as yet to confront his wife about his suspicions. Perhaps he does not even know what his course of action will be. Perhaps Uriah is not prepared to accuse his wife of adultery and subject her to the public calumny and punishment that would bring. If, as the *midrash* indicates, Uriah had been Batsheva's ward before he became her husband, then it is probable that Uriah is still accustomed to protecting her. He was not prepared to challenge Batsheva openly about the rumors he had heard. Nor was he prepared to ignore them and share her bed.

All this thoughtful indecision might explain Uriah's *silence* during his first meeting with David. Thereafter, Uriah spends that night at the palace because he has not yet decided what he will do. If what he suspects is true, this is not a mere dalliance. His wife's partner in the adultery is the king himself! And after all, Uriah cannot very well challenge the king to a duel.

So it is logical to assume that had Uriah *not* already suspected the adultery he would have gone to his home on his first night of home-leave.

Another neutral reason that Uriah might have stayed away from his house on this furlough is that perhaps Uriah's accustomed short-furlough behavior was *not* to spend the night in his home. If so, this would explain Batsheva's childless state.

Uriah's sharp response to David on the next morning gives us the key to the puzzle. In verse 11 Uriah tells the king, *"The ark and Israel and Judah dwell in huts, and my lord Yoav and the servants of my lord are encamped in the open field; and shall I come to my house to eat and to drink and to lie with my wife?"* . . . Eating, drinking, and lying down are the three points of conflict between Uriah and David. On the first night of Uriah's leave David gives him a royal meal which Uriah scorns; Uriah also expressly ignores the king's suggestion that he go to his home and lie down with his own wife. On the second night David plies Uriah with food and intoxicating drink but still Uriah sleeps with the soldiers rather than in his own bed.

In fact, in verse 13 Uriah's words to David come back to plague the soldier. David takes Uriah's three objections and tries to turn them against him. David summons Uriah and pressures him *to eat* with the king and *to drink* until he is drunk. But as for the third and essential component, it is Uriah who wins the battle of wills — but tragically he will lose the "war" — when he *lays down* on the second night — not with his wife, but in the servants' hall once again.

The inference is that even if on day-one Uriah likely did *not* know of the adultery, by the morning of day-two Uriah surely *knew*. And David's behavior toward Uriah on the second night —

his last-ditch effort to get Uriah *drunk* so that he would sleep at home with his wife—illustrates that David was *aware* that Uriah knew. David knew that a sober Uriah would not yield to his maneuvering. Of course, even drunk Uriah remained true to himself, and when David saw this, he did not hesitate to plan Uriah's murder. According to Bal, David the king was by this time royally—if irrationally—peeved that his prized soldier would not "roll over" at the king's bidding. David viewed Uriah as having breached a code of "negative solidarity" by refusing to eat, drink, and sleep where the king willed it. For this reason, and of course to suit his own purposes, David plots a vendetta[157] against Uriah.

URIAH'S DEATH

Verses 18–24 describe Yoav's instructions to his runner and the messenger's recounting the manner of Uriah's death to David. According to Alter, Sternberg and others have noted that this entire story, rife as it is with messengers and messages, is a "vivid demonstration of the . . . effecting of ends through the agency of others."[158] An important element in these verses is the message-within-the-message that Yoav lays out for his messenger. He creates the seeming "red herring" that the king might become angry at the messenger's news, asking why the army foolishly approached so near to the city wall during the battle. "He might even remind you," Yoav tells his messenger, "of how king Abimelech was killed in such a battle when a woman threw a millstone down from the wall upon him. If the king says this, you are to tell him 'Uriah the Hittite is dead.' "

This is yet another irony: Yoav is either anticipating or feigning anticipation that out of David's own mouth might come a battlefield tale of a "Warrior King Laid Low by Woman."[159] In our present iteration it is David's own star that began to dim the moment he sent for the *very beautiful* and married woman whom he had watched at her bath. Yoav is incorporating a veiled jibe within his messenger's speech for the king: a king must beware of the seemingly innocuous woman who can bring him to destruction. And the reader is keenly aware that Yoav's hinted reference is an imperfect one. In Batsheva's case the woman was the passive instrumentality of the actor-king's downfall. The king at all times engineered his own "demise." Whereas in the case of the woman who killed Abimelech by dropping a millstone on his head, it was absolutely the woman whose action felled that king. The main thrust of the reference to the Abimelech story is to point out that everyone now knows that coming too close to the city wall during a siege courts death.

Back at the palace, the only news David waits to hear is that Batsheva's husband has died.

Yoav's messenger tells David that after a fierce hand-to-hand battle the Ammonites retreated into their besieged city of Rabbah where their archers rained arrows down upon Uriah and his squad. The enemy killed not only Uriah the Hittite, acknowledged far and wide as "the bravest of the brave,"[160] but also many of the king's troops besides. The king learns that eighteen[161] of his elite corps of thirty-seven valiant fighting men[162] perished in the maneuver to murder Uriah.

If Yoav's runner expected an outbreak of anger or an expression of sadness from the king when he heard the news, he must have been surprised. The king exhibited only an eerie *sang froid*, saying, "Go and tell Yoav, 'Let this thing not seem evil in your eyes, for the sword devours sometimes one way and sometimes another. Battle even more fiercely against the city and destroy it.' In this way shall you strengthen his spirits." King David, the passionate, red-headed warrior-of-old, now offers tepid, clichéd words in lieu of the lives of the lost men: *Such is the way of war,* says David. *The killing sword is indiscriminate.* By any measure, David's conduct is reprehensible, his verbal response flat and disinterested. But we must ask ourselves, is this perhaps business-as-usual for a king?

BATSHEVA MOURNS URIAH

And Uriah's wife heard that Uriah, her husband, had died; and she mourned over her husband. II Sam. 11:26

If there existed any doubt that Batsheva was a married woman at the time that David forcibly took her and lay with her, it should be dispelled by verse 26. Of the ten words in this verse, four of the Bible's words are dedicated to underlining Batsheva's relationship to Uriah.[163] Her name is never mentioned, only her status. She was *isha*, the *woman*, in verses 2, 3 and 5 when David saw, sent for and took her. Likewise here, using the same Hebrew word, *isha*, she is first, *Uriah's wife*, and second, Uriah is identified as *her husband (ishah)*. And third, the verse ends with the unambiguous term *ba'alah*, stating that she mourned *her husband*.

We can imagine the scene. The pregnant Batsheva is in her house attending to ordinary housekeeping duties when there is a loud knocking at her door. Recalling, perhaps, another such unexpected tattoo on a fateful night three months before, Batsheva suffers an existential moment of panic. Surely the king would not be coming for her once again!

The beautiful Batsheva is a tormented woman. She has heard that her husband, Uriah, had been summoned to the palace by the king and she had expected him to appear at their doorstep at any time. She waited in fearful anticipation for two days, but Uriah did not come. He had returned to the front without even a farewell wave to her. She was making herself sick with guilt and worry; true, she had had no choice but to submit when the king had taken her to his bed, but to a man as proud as Uriah she knew that would make no difference. She feared that either he would attempt to avenge her with the king—in which case her husband was surely a dead man—or else he would abandon their marriage altogether, which would spell public shame and personal disaster for her.

Now, pregnant with the king's baby, she resignedly opens her door. She faces two powerful military men whom she vaguely recognizes as Uriah's fellow corpsmen. Their faces are stricken, and as directly and gently as they can they tell her that her husband has perished on the battlefield at the hands of the enemy. Batsheva faints at their feet.

The *midrash* explains that this verse's multiple references to Batsheva as *wife of Uriah* is a badge of honor for her.[164] She was not at fault when David "took" her; now the biblical reader is told conclusively — thrice-over — that she conducted herself properly *as Uriah's wife*. At the news of his death she prostrates herself, rends her garments, lays upon the ground and grieves for *her husband*, as befits a true *wife*. Batsheva's tears, mourning and misery for her lost husband are spontaneous and genuine.[165]

One *midrash* even suggests that the repetition of the wife/ husband motif in 11:26 is in the nature of an elegiacal poem.[166] Rashi would agree, noting elsewhere that the word *isha* implies intimacy as well as the sweet poignancy of youthful first-love.[167] Unambiguously, then, Batsheva here genuinely mourns her lost husband. Probably, too, she mourns her lost opportunity to speak to him in her own defense, explaining the circumstances of her abduction. But if Rashi's reading of the word *isha* is credited, perhaps Batsheva was able to comfort herself with the thought that Uriah did not need or even seek her explanation; he knew at whose feet the fault lay.

The woman Batsheva, wife of Uriah and compromised object of the passion of David, is nothing more and nothing less than *wife of Uriah* when she mourns his death and their forfeited life together.

DAVID WEDS BATSHEVA

After the passing of the mourning period David sent and gathered her to his house, and she became his wife, and she bore him a son; and the thing that David did was evil in God's eyes. II Sam. 11:27

David allows Batsheva to weep and to mourn for Uriah for seven days, the accepted mourning period after the loss of a close family member.[168] At the end of the seven days the king reverts to type, once again *sending for* Batsheva, but this time he *takes her in marriage*. We note that there are no words exchanged between David and Batsheva as he relieves her of her mourning and takes her immediately as a wife. This contrasts with David's earlier taking of the widow Avigayil as a wife, where first he spoke with her *and then* he wed her.[169] The *midrash* explains the lack of conversation here — perhaps the absence of a request for consent — with a play on the word *davar*, meaning both *word* and *thing* or *matter*. David and Batsheva exchanged no *words* this time around because they already had many *matters* or experiences between the two of them. Presumably words were unnecessary in the mind of the king. He cared only that Batsheva was pregnant with his child. The issue of succession and legitimate royal issue was his concern and his province. Batsheva was but a vehicle.

But there is an additional verb in verse 27 that bears noting. The text says that David *gathered her* into his house. He effectively arranged to scoop Batsheva off the floor of her house and ensconce her in the palace; he ordered that she be washed and pampered, that her widow's garments be replaced with finery. Was David, in his way, rewarding Batsheva for Uriah's valiant service? Was his marriage to her a kind of posthumous "gold watch" for the very beautiful widow of one of the king's elite soldiers? Given the king's self-centered nature, more likely the expression *he gathered* is an echo of the universal plea of a husbandless pregnant woman: that her "shame" *be gathered* or ended via a marriage.

After the seven days of mourning have passed the king weds Batsheva properly, presenting her with a *ketubah*, or marriage document, and sanctifying the union through *kiddushin*, the marriage ceremony.[170] Verse 27 emphasizes this, stating unambiguously that she was wed *to him*, and that she bore *him* a son.

Does the story end here? We have seen so far that the very beautiful woman Batsheva, wife of another, was taken by the king and became pregnant by him. One sin leads to another and to cover up his adultery the king arranges the murder of the woman's husband, and afterwards he marries the widow. After all this treachery, we read that the king achieves his goal. We are told that it is *the king* whom she marries, and it is *the king's son* whom she bears. This entire sordid and bloody affair ends, it would seem, with a literal whimper. The Torah text tells us that Batsheva mourns twice: once for her husband, Uriah, in 11:26, and again for her newborn son in chapter 12, as we will soon see. David, too, will weep for his doomed newborn son, as he failed to mourn either for Uriah, whom he murdered by proxy,[171] or for the soldiers who died alongside him. We can imagine a trail of weeping wives, mothers and lovers across the Israelite kingdom in the wake of David's crimes.

No, the story does not end here. David does not get away with it. Tacked on to the verse that tells the reader that he achieved his goal of a new wife and infant son is the phrase, *and the thing that David did was **evil in God's eyes**.*

DAVID'S SINS

Readers of the book of Samuel must acknowledge that David, the book's deeply flawed hero, is a seducer. His pattern of seduction is clear. As a young warrior his charisma and military exploits seduced the women of Israel so that they sang of David's battlefield victories over King Saul's, they fell in love with the beautiful young hero, and inadvertently fueled Saul's anger and paranoia.[172] The beautiful and wise Avigayil, wife of Naval, also fell under David's thrall, shifting her fealty from her husband to the young warrior-king.[173] Michal, daughter of King Saul, "loved David,"[174] was married to him, was demeaned and verbally abused by him, was ignored and shunted aside by him. Pitiably, David eventually forced her to return to him even after her marriage to another. And in what has been termed David's "greatest seduction,"[175] he seduced Jonathan, King Saul's son and crown prince. Jonathan "loved David as himself,"[176] ceding the throne and his filial loyalty to David, and indirectly, some might say, ultimately his life.

David seduced with his physical beauty, his personal charm, his velvet tongue, his warrior's — and later, his royal — power. People were drawn to David, a vortex of energy and potential. He cut an unheeding swath through his life, laying low his enemies as well as those who loved and trusted him to the extent he seemed unstoppable — until Batsheva. This time David has gone too far. His sins with Batsheva and Uriah signal the beginning of the end of David's glory and ascendancy.

Don Isaac Abarbanel, one of the great, late-medieval Torah commentaries, in a fearless move, catalogued David's sins from

the Batsheva incident. After reading the cruelly ironic pantomime
of an unknowing Uriah carrying his own death warrant to Yoav,
followed by the statement in verse 17 that *Uriah the Hittite also
died*, Abarbanel seemingly can no longer restrain himself. He
writes in his commentary that David's actions comprise five
despicable offenses:

First, David sinned by taking a married woman. Not only
that, but he lay with the wife of a soldier and comrade! This is one
of the lowest forms of betrayal, says Abarbanel, as the woman's
husband was a loyal and conscientious warrior, trusting in and
serving his king at the time of the king's adultery.

Second, David sinned when he attempted to seduce Uriah
into sleeping with Batsheva in order to deceive him about the
provenance of her unborn son. For a mighty king such as David
to stoop so low is an insult and an indignity to his own issue.
That David would deny royal provenance to his own son just to
spare his own embarrassment is an abrogation of paternal
responsibility.

Third, David sinned when he commanded Yoav to place
Uriah in a dangerous and untenable military position specifically
in order to have him killed. It is a grave sin especially in light of
the fact that this elite soldier not only bore David no malice, but he
also fought to the death for his king and country. Yet David
repaid Uriah with treachery. Abarbanel suggests that David
would have done better to have kept Uriah occupied on the
battlefield throughout the nine months of Batsheva's pregnancy.
Then, after the baby's birth—which could have been kept secret—
the baby could have been handed over to an Israelite wet-nurse
and raised in the palace. In this way David could have avoided
compounding the sin of forbidden sexual relations with that of
murder.

Fourth, David sinned in the manner that he had Uriah killed:
by the hands of his—and God's—enemy, the Ammonites, and on
foreign soil. For an elite and fearless warrior such as Uriah to be
entrapped and laid low in a battlefield grave by such an enemy is
a betrayal. "Are there insufficient graves in Israel?" asks Abarbanel, that Uriah was forced to meet his ignominious death on a
foreign battlefield? And did Uriah not merit beholding the face of

the enemy who was to slay him? Was the distant bow-and-arrow of the Ammonite archer a fitting death for such a warrior? David's sin is gravely compounded by the fact that Uriah was joined in battle by numerous other elite corpsmen. David plotted, entrapped and murdered not only Uriah, but also many of Israel's bravest fighting men. Their deaths were outright murders as was Uriah's.

Fifth, David sinned by his hasty taking of the widow Batsheva as a wife. Was David so besotted with lust and passion that he could not wait a decent interval before sending for Batsheva and ordering the marriage? Was David's desire not satisfied by his first night with her, so that he had to rush her into an unseemly marriage? Abarbanel is disgusted with David's haste to take Batsheva so soon after the end of her seven-day mourning period. "At the very least, the king should have waited ninety days."

Abarbanel's litany is articulate, merciless and powerful. He takes on the Talmud's apologetics (in *Shabbat* 56a) and other traditional commentaries who irrationally refuse to look at David's actions objectively and label them sins. Abarbanel, fully aware that he is taking an outlier's position, asks rhetorically, "If [these other commentaries are correct and] David did *not* sin, then why does David respond to the prophet's condemnation by saying, 'I have sinned before God!'? And why, if he had not sinned so greatly here, would David have needed to repent, as he did, for the rest of his life?!" The commentary points to Psalm 51:5, where David admits he daily repents his sins against Batsheva and Uriah: *For I recognize my transgressions and am ever-conscious of my sin.*

The *Malbim*, responding to Abarbanel's indictment of David, presents one text-based argument in David's favor.[177] It is, incidentally, one of the thematic inquiries of this book: In light of David's numerous and grave sins, why, then, does God select and anoint David's son from Batsheva to be "God's beloved?" Why does an illustrious line of kings emerge from Batsheva? Must we not conclude from this that Batsheva *was not forbidden* to David?

My response is that even though Batsheva and David's future son (this is Solomon) will be called "beloved by God" and will become a legendary king of Israel, this does not wipe David's slate clean of his iniquities. Solomon will not be the son who will pay for David's sin with Batsheva; tragically, the "tainted" fruit of their adulterous coupling, their first, unnamed son, will pay the ultimate price for that sin. And the Bible details David's prayers and tears as well as Batsheva's grief over this death.

We will see in coming verses that David is, indeed, made to pay for his sins, that he will never fully recover from them, and that their reverberations and tremors shake the Israelite monarchy and wreak havoc on David's own family. Moreover, who is to say when payment for one's iniquities is complete? If David sinned *in God's eyes*, it stands to reason that any forgiveness must likewise fall within divine providence.

The author of the book of Samuel does not leave the David and Batsheva incident without a parting shot. The final words of the final verse of chapter 11 are *And the thing that David did was* **evil in the eyes of God**. This is an allusion to the earlier fact that while Yoav, David's general, thought the set-up and murder of Uriah was "evil in his eyes," (11:25) David's actions were not common knowledge *among the people of Israel*.[178] While perhaps the king was able to conceal the entire affair from the masses, we are told that *God knew*, and that God saw it as it was: "evil." Whether the people really did not know, or whether they were primed to overlook the doings of royalty, the phrase *evil in the eyes of God* tells us that David's doings will not be overlooked by the Almighty.

NATHAN'S PARABLE

And we see that this is so. Chapter 12 will function as the epilogue to the Batsheva incident. In light of chapter 11's final words, the reader is not surprised that chapter 12 will outline God's punishment of David.

As the chapter opens we are told that *The Lord sends Nathan [the prophet] to David*. Even with the dozen-odd "sendings" of people and messages back and forth in chapter 11, none of those sendings involved God. Here, God is taking charge. *God sends* His prophet to David, "to read him the riot act." And in the way of the prophet, Nathan speaks to David, the corrupt poet-king, in a parable:

> *There were two men in a certain city, the one rich and the other poor.*
>
> *The rich man had very many sheep and cattle;*
>
> *But the poor man had nothing but one little ewe lamb that he had bought. He tended it and she grew up together with him and his children: it ate from his bread, drank from his cup, lay in his lap, and was like a daughter to him.*
>
> *One day, a traveler came to the rich man, but he was loath to take anything from his own flocks or herds to prepare a meal for the guest that had come to him. So he took the poor man's lamb and prepared it for the man who had come to him.*
> II Sam. 12:1–4

The Bible reader surely had expected God Himself to step in to indict and punish David (after all, that has been God's role in the Bible). Instead, in a bit of irony and in high literary style, God has sent the prophet to set a verbal trap to ensnare the royal manipulator. We see that David takes the bait.

Upon hearing this story, which Nathan presented as if it were a real case awaiting the king's judgement,[179] David flies into a rage, pronouncing sentence on the rich man. He shouts to Nathan, *"As the Lord lives, the man who did this deserves to die! He shall pay for the lamb four times over, because he did such a thing and because he had no compassion!"* (II Sam. 12:5–6)

David falls in with God's intention, unknowingly indicting and convicting himself. God had wanted David to objectively view his own behavior, and to condemn it. And David does so, issuing from his own mouth yet another death sentence, this time against "the man." Moreover, David levies a stiff fine, ordering that the man must pay for the ewe lamb four times over. It is interesting that David still appears to have a moral compass; unfortunately, it is not trained on himself.

Expertly, Nathan springs the trap. Dramatically, the prophet points his finger at David and pronounces, *"You are 'the man!' "* (12:7)

One might ask, given the obvious and somewhat simplistic analogy to himself and his own recent reprehensible behavior, how could David *not* have seen through Nathan's parable? The man David, whose mental process functioned comfortably within the symbolic language of the psalmist, failed to intuit past Nathan's words. Had he stopped to think for just a moment, surely he would not immediately, indignantly and righteously have pronounced sentence on himself. Nathan's parable is relatively transparent. The animal was adopted into the family, which reminds us of the *midrash* that told of Batsheva's adoption as a foundling by Uriah. There is also "a powerful erotic valence to the word-picture of the man sharing his bed with the ewe,"[180] reminiscent of Uriah cherishing his young and beautiful wife, Batsheva. The rich man's taking the ewe lamb was clearly a reference to David's "taking" of Batsheva. But David did not see this; he did not catch on. In an impulse born of anger at the injustice, David does not take a moment to calmly consider the "case." Had he considered the matter for just that extra moment, imperious and impulsive David would not have been the man he was.

Paradoxically, David embodied the qualities of warrior, poet, opportunist, king, judge, heartbreaker, philanderer, strategist, lover, and murderer. And Nathan knew his man. With his parable Nathan appealed to David-the-judge, who desired "to do the right thing" and to protect his (albeit fictitious) disadvantaged subject.[181] But while David slips into judicial mode and pronounces sentence for the theft of the sheep, we are struck that he does not exhibit any of the "sobriety and patient discrimination" that are the prime qualities of a judge. On the contrary, David reacts immediately and in anger, swearing an oath for good measure. David's reaction exposes his deeper subconscious involvement with the elements of the "case" before him. His outburst is "evidence of his plagued conscience."[182]

But this is not obvious to David. He is the king of the Israelites, and pronounces sentence on the fictitious thief. No matter that in his own recent life David has behaved in precisely the opposite manner from what is right. His idealization of himself remains the underestimated and unsullied youngest son of Jesse, and his knee-jerk reaction is to rule in favor of Nathan's wronged "poor man."

Fokkelman has said, "because a parable is not a *comparison*, we need *not* look fanatically for a counterpart in David's reality to each of its elements."[183] Still, as was shown, the counterparts are readily discernible. The rich man of the parable is David, wealthy king possessed of many wives. The poor man is Uriah, who had but one young and beautiful wife whom he had cherished from the time she was a girl. And the poor man's ewe lamb is Batsheva, who is stolen away by the rich man.[184] David, in his instant condemnation of the rich man for his rapacious and merciless act, is pronouncing judgement upon none other than *himself* for his abduction and "taking" of Batsheva, Uriah's wife.

Robert Alter explains that when David pronounced sentence on the "rich man," his angry words were literally "he is the son of death!" meaning the man was *deserving* of death. This was David's spontaneous, outraged opinion, but it was not the law of the land. The penalty in biblical Israel for unlawfully taking the property of another was not death, but four-fold restitution. David's outburst "reflects the way that the parable conflates the sexual 'taking' of Bathsheba with the murder of Uriah."[185] Nathan's parable smoothly fits David's "taking" of Batsheva, who is the ewe lamb in his parable; but the same ewe lamb also morphs into Uriah once Nathan's rich man slaughters it. The implicit image of the blood of the slaughtered lamb is meant to evoke Uriah's murder. Such is the mastery of Nathan's parable that it fits both of David's carnal sins: the adultery and the murder.

Of course, the reason Nathan's parable rings true is that it is patently unjust for one who has much to take that which belongs to one who possesses nearly nothing. The outrage the reader feels is matched by David's instinctive rush to judgement based on reaction to the parable's facts.

Nathan is God's mouthpiece. Before pronouncing the Lord's punishments for David's crimes (verses 10–12), Nathan explains God's erstwhile relationship with David.

> So says the Lord God of Israel: "It was I who anointed you king over Israel, and I who delivered you from the hand of Saul.

> *"And I gave to you your master's house and possession of your master's wives; and I gave you the House of Israel and of Judah; and if that were not enough, I would give you twice as much more."* II Sam. 12:7–8

God is reviewing, for rhetorical purposes, his generosity toward and his championship of David. God not only made him king and saved him from the murderous King Saul, but He also gave David Saul's wife and daughter to possess. God bestowed the kingship of Israel and Judah and all its perquisites upon David, so He is "incredulous" that David would have had a need to take it upon himself to take Batsheva, wife of Uriah, and then to have Uriah murdered. *"Why did you then despise the word of the Lord, and do what is evil in His eyes? You have slain Uriah the Hittite with the sword, and you have taken his wife for yourself as a wife, and you have slain him with the sword of the children of Ammon."* (II Sam. 12:9)

DAVID'S PUNISHMENT

After outlining David's sins, Nathan continues, detailing in graphic and terrifying simplicity what David will be facing in the future as a consequence of his lawless behavior:

> *"Therefore, the sword shall never depart from your house, because you spurned Me by taking the wife of Uriah the Hittite and making her your wife.*
>
> *"Thus says the Lord: 'I will make a calamity rise against you from within your own house; I will take your wives and give them to another man before your very eyes and he shall sleep with your wives under this very sun.*
>
> *'"You acted in secret, but I will make this happen in the sight of all Israel and in broad daylight.'"* II Sam. 12:10–12

David's life as God's protégé is passing before both David and the reader through Nathan's damning words. We are treated, along with David, to an object lesson of "measure-for-measure."[186] David has forfeited his charmed spot, and his punishments not only will fit his crimes, they also will be amplified, to reflect the requirement that the offender pay additional damages to expiate his sins. The reader should watch for and note the amplification.

Nathan previews David's punishments:

Because David sent Uriah into battle with the specific object and orders to have him killed, the killing sword will *forever* hover over David's house. This is quite a fall for David who, in his debut act of public heroism, slew Goliath with a slingshot. The text there twice said that "David had no sword,"[187] highlighting that he audaciously cut off Goliath's head with the giant's own sword. Now, tragically, David's punishment and fall from grace will be marked by the constant presence and surfeit of swords, wars, rebellions and bloodshed.

Because David stole Uriah's wife, God will likewise give David's wives to another, and also will bring David public disgrace. This comes to pass in future chapters of the book of Samuel as Avshalom, David's favored son and chosen successor, stages a revolt and seizes control of Jerusalem, David's capital city. *David's son* will publicly usurp his father's power and potency by forcibly sleeping with his father's *ten* wife/concubines on the very palace roof from which David watched Batsheva at her bath! Perhaps this aspect of the punishment is a hint that David's betrayal of Uriah, one of his chosen military elite, is akin to a father's betrayal of his son. We see the measure-for-measure punishment *plus* its exponential intensification when David's beloved son betrays *him*, rebels against him and humiliates both David and his helpless wives.

A heightened irony is that Achitofel, David's close advisor at the time of the incident with Batsheva—and Batsheva's grand-father—will switch his allegiance from David to the treasonous Avshalom during the coming rebellion. As we have suggested, Achitofel certainly has a compelling personal motive to shame and replace the man who raped his granddaughter and had her husband murdered.

It is not lost on the Lord that what David tried to hide under cover of darkness and through secret missives and messengers will be avenged out in the open "under the sun" when God wreaks punishment on David. David's kingship and privileged status will be sullied irretrievably, and this will be done by none other than David's own blood kin. Avshalom engages in a "rooftop orgy,"[188] violating his father's harem in the eyes of *all Israel* in broad daylight. The phrase "all Israel" echoes the same "all Israel" who were fighting the war against the Ammonites in 11:1 while David was abducting Batsheva. "All Israel," who were kept in the dark about David's sins of adultery and murder, will be eyewitnesses to this punishment.

How will David pay "four-fold" for his taking of Uriah's wife (the penalty David himself pronounced on the rich man for his taking and slaughtering of the poor man's ewe lamb)? The Talmud[189] explains David's awful four-fold punishment: David will suffer the deaths or near-death of four of his children. First, his infant son conceived with Batsheva, wife of Uriah, will die shortly after its birth. Second, David's daughter, Tamar, will be violently raped by his son, Amnon, and becomes a "ruin"[190] in the king's house. Third, two years after Tamar's rape, Avshalom, Tamar's brother, will avenge her honor and kill her rapist—his half-brother, Amnon, David's son. And fourth, David's son, Avshalom, will himself be killed during his revolt against his father.[191]

Despite David's pronouncement to Nathan that the rich man who took the poor man's ewe lamb was "deserving of death," David is not killed. The Talmud goes on to recount a little-known legend that in lieu of suffering "the ultimate punishment" of death, David was afflicted with *tzora'at*, or leprosy, for a period of about six months.[192] The Bible has elsewhere equated *tzora'at* with a "living death,"[193] and also has likened the person stricken with *tzora'at* to a stillborn baby. It is said that David's *tzora'at* took the place of the death penalty that he deserved.[194] If David did, indeed, suffer the punishment of *tzora'at*, then he came as close to the precipice of death as a living person could. His flesh turned white as snow,[195] and he was like a walking corpse, humiliated and exiled from the community of the living. That he resembled a stillborn is even a veiled reference to his newborn son's death.

So we—and David—have glimpsed the future, where David is fated to pay four-fold-*plus* for his sins. Now we await David's reaction.

"I HAVE SINNED AGAINST GOD!"

And David said to Nathan, "I have sinned against God."
And Nathan said to David, "The Lord has also remitted your
offense; you shall not die. But since you have surely spurned
the Lord by this deed, even the child about to be born to you is
doomed to die." II Sam. 13–14

It is widely understood that the death sentence that David
pronounced on himself in 12:5 (*By the life of the Lord, the man who
did this deserves to die!*) was commuted because of his quick
admission of guilt and his simultaneous repentance.[196] David did
not offer up any excuses to Nathan or to God, instead taking the
prophet's indictment and the Lord's punishment full-force,
acknowledging his guilt. David said simply: *I have sinned against
God*. There follows no qualifying "but " or a request for clemency.
David's statement *I have sinned* contrasts starkly with the same
statement by Saul, his predecessor. After the victory over Amalek
Saul had violated God's express command to spare no living
thing. When the prophet Samuel confronted him, Saul offered a
raft of excuses and even attempted to shift blame to the people of
Israel. Only then, tragically and too late, did Saul say, *I have
sinned*.[197] But God did not forgive him. Saul's disobedience and
his belated and inept admission of his sin forfeited his kingdom.

   David's statement is a bit strange. Why was it necessary for
him to have added the words *against God*? Would it have sufficed
if he had said simply *I have sinned*? Aren't *all* sins sins *against God*?
And finally, it was not only God whom David "sinned against;"
what about the violated woman Batsheva? What about the
murdered Uriah? And what of the Israelite soldiers who perished
alongside Uriah? What about David's own infant son who dies on
account of David's sin? David's sins are many and far-reaching.

   It seems that with the addendum *against God* David is
seeking expiation from God for his sin of "taking" Batsheva, wife
of Uriah.[198] David knew that his murder of Uriah was so grave
that it could never be forgiven. An-eye-for-an-eye, or one life in
place of another, was the strict law code of the ancient Near East.
Taking a life was also a sin against God. According to the *midrash*,

it was beyond question that David deserved death for engineering Uriah's murder. But the abduction and adultery of Batsheva were possibly in a different category; they were moral sins against the Israelite God, who held His chosen people to a higher standard of conduct. That a king of Israel should flagrantly commit such sins made God a laughingstock among the other nations, and therefore only the jealous and merciful God of the Israelites could forgive him those sins.

Hirsch offers a slightly different view. He is commenting on David's words in Psalm 51, where David admits to the sins of Batsheva and Uriah, and expresses contrition. In verse 4 David says, "Against Thee, Thee only, have I sinned." In Hirsch's view *both* the sins against Batsheva and the sin against Uriah "were violations of the spirit rather than the letter of the legal code of the *land*.[199] But in the sight of *God* both these acts of David were grievous crimes."[200] Therefore, as Hirsch understands it, by his words *I have sinned **against God*** David is saying, "Because I have sinned against You, Oh Lord, You are justified in any sentence You will pronounce against me. I admit my guilt, I accept my punishment."

Another possibility is that with Uriah's death David is foreclosed from approaching the wronged and slain man and begging his forgiveness for both sins.[201] That avenue of repentance is closed to him because of the nature of his sin. Therefore God stands in for the slain Uriah, and David must voice his admission of guilt *to God*; he must seek expiation *from God* and no other.

It is this immediate and absolute admission of guilt and acceptance of the consequences that causes God to spare David's life. The same verse 13 that opens with David's admission closes with God's remission of the death sentence David had pronounced on himself: *And Nathan replied to David, "The Lord has remitted your sin; you shall not die."* But of course David lives to dread and to experience consequences even more dire, perhaps, than his own immediate death would have been. Nathan continues in verse 14: *"Nevertheless, because you have greatly blasphemed the Lord by this thing, the son that is born to you is doomed to die."* The reader is expected to recognize and accept the obscene symmetry of the grave punishments David has brought upon his own head. "He has killed, therefore the infant of Batsheva dies. He has betrayed, therefore his own house and blood [will] rise against him. He has spoken glibly about the sword and those who fall by it, therefore the sword will never depart from his house."[202]

BATSHEVA'S INFANT SON SICKENS AND DIES

What of Batsheva? She suffered deep emotional trauma after being taken by the king. In this state of guilt and terror of being discovered and exposed—perhaps stoned—as an adulteress, she bore her pregnancy. And we must make no mistake, Batsheva wanted that baby. Not only and not even primarily for the reason that she could bear a sovereign heir; but also because with this baby she was to become a mother in Israel.

We are told in chapter 12 verses 15–20 that immediately upon[203] Nathan's departure from David after pronouncing sentence, the baby born to Batsheva, *wife of Uriah*, is stricken by God and becomes mortally ill. The *midrash* explains the text's puzzling reference to Batsheva as *wife of Uriah* at the moment that it is discussing her son with David. This is the final time that she will be linked to Uriah in the text. It is because there is no escaping this baby's genesis; it was when she was still wed to Uriah that he was conceived.[204] Hereafter, when the sin has been atoned, Batsheva will be called "David's wife,"[205] or, years in the future, "mother of the king."[206]

David slips into beseeching mode in these verses. Notwith-standing Nathan's prophecy that his infant son would "surely die," David pleads with God to spare the infant's life. David also fasts and spends seven nights lying on the ground in abject supplication and misery. It is worth noting the continuation of the symmetry here: just as Uriah slept on the floor of the palace instead of in his bed, so, too, David prostrates himself and spends the nights upon the floor.

There is no mention of Batsheva's beseeching God or fasting on behalf of her baby. Perhaps this is because it was David who initiated and promulgated the sins, and God's punishments are primarily directed against him. Also, from a practical standpoint,

Batsheva was surely sleepless with anxiety and helplessness, alternatively nursing the baby and bathing him with cool water to douse its fever. There is no need for the text to diagram her frantic behavior; the reader appreciates that it is unlikely she ever let the infant out of her arms for the duration of its brief life.

Surely, too, Batsheva felt the weight of her responsibility for her baby's suffering. Perhaps she thought, "*can* this baby, conceived in sin, be permitted to live and thrive?" The reader has no inkling of whether she was privy to Nathan's prophecy and God's promise of punishment to David. We can assume that the prophecy and prediction of punishment were enacted in open court, and that Batsheva knew what had been forecast for her newborn son. She did the simple calculus connecting God's anger with the son of David's (and her) adultery when her infant son — born healthy — immediately after Nathan's departure becomes gravely ill.

But all David's prayers and prostrations are to no avail. David's infant son born to Batsheva dies seven days after it is born.[207]

How can we reconcile that this innocent infant is sentenced to death on account of his father's sins? What sense can we make of the divine retribution that is exquisitely outlined for David beginning in verse 14? In verse 13 Nathan decrees that God will spare David's life: "**you shall not die.**" Immediately afterward, in verse 14, the prophet declares that "because you have greatly spurned the Lord by this deed **the child** that is born to you **will surely die.**" We note the symmetry of the verses, which makes it clear that the first part of David's punishment is a life for a life. His lust aside, David desires nothing more than to sire a healthy son; succession is always of prime concern to a king. David is spared, but the price for David's life is his son, who was conceived via his father's sinful act with Batsheva. But this is not a chess piece that will disappear from the chessboard; it is a human life.

The Torah makes diverging statements about the sins of the father being visited upon his son. In Ex. 34:7 Moses first says that "God . . . visits the iniquity of parents upon children and children's children," a statement that would ratify David's punishment here. But later on, in Deut. 24:16, Moses does an about-face, saying "Each person shall be put to death only for his own sin," and not for the sin of his parent or child. The law appears to be evolving. The Talmud[208] cites Ezekiel for the reconciling proposition that "the person who sins, he alone shall die." (Ezek. 18:4, 20) This is quite a legal correction, one which fits our sense of justice and our sensibilities that children are born in innocence, representing a brand-new life, and that the child is born free of the sins of his parent.

Which brings us back to the pressing question at-hand. How can we reconcile God's exacting the death penalty on a newborn baby? Several responses come to mind. None is perfect ("perfect justice" would have God punishing David for his sins and allowing his infant son to live), but we take the Bible as it is written, and try to make sense of it in its context.

According to Radak and the Mahar"i,[209] there is some degree of God looking over His shoulder, so-to-speak, at the surrounding lawless nations when He pronounces this punishment. The theory is that David, divinely anointed king over Israel, has made God into a laughingstock by his sins of adultery and murder, two of the three iniquities that call for the death penalty. If God in His mercy is sparing David on account of his immediate and profound contrition, that still leaves the matter of retribution. God *must* exact it against the newborn. David must not be permitted both to live *and* to enjoy the fruit of his sinfulness.

Metzudat David[210] adds that David's adultery with Batsheva was a shameless flouting of God's laws, and that left unpunished David's behavior would teach an immoral lesson. Payment is required, notwithstanding David's admission and contrition. The commentary considers that it is fitting that David's infant son, born of this shameful sin, should be exacted in payment. Perhaps this is a measure of retribution that the surrounding nations (Ammonites and Philistines) will fathom and fear.

At that time in Israel a newborn was not considered viable until it had lived outside its mother's womb for thirty days.[211] There is discussion in the commentaries about whether a parent is even required to mourn a child who is alive for fewer than eight days.[212] The hapless newborn son of David and Batsheva met his death before he was able to hold his own. "Though David himself is spared, his folly [led] to the death of his child, as restitution begins."[213] We might consider that this is a snapshot of the nature of a monarchy: others are made to pay the price for the king's sins. This scenario will be repeated later on in David's reign when, in punishment for his folly of counting the people without God's permission, God brings a pestilence on Israel killing 70,000 of David's subjects.[214]

✠ ✠ ✠

David's servants were afraid to tell him that the baby had died, so distraught had David been during the seven days of its illness. When the king discerned that the child had died he arose from the ground, shed his dusty clothes,[215] washed and anointed himself, and went to the House of the Lord to bow down. David had had hopes that his prayers to God would reverse the judgement sufficient to allow the child to live, but now, upon its death, he presents himself to the Lord as if to say, "For both the good *and the bad* will I give thanks to the Lord."[216] Afterwards, David ate his first meal in a week. His courtiers expressed their surprise at his ability to pick himself up, eat, drink and function normally. So David said to them, *"When the child was still alive I fasted and wept because I thought, 'Who knows but that the Lord may have pity on me and the child may live.' But now that he is dead, why should I fast? Can I bring him back again? I shall go to him but he shall never come back to me."* (II Sam. 12:22–23)

It is stark and chilling how swiftly Nathan's prophecy is coming true. Here, in brutal present-tense, the first part of David's punishment is meted out in the death of his infant son. David's "haunting words are the pivotal moment"[217] in this story, because they are the first words he speaks in this episode that are candidly personal instead of cannily political. *"Can I bring him back again? I shall go to him but he shall never come back to me."* Here, we see David speaking "for the first time . . . in his existential nakedness."[218] We glimpse the king not in his imperious majesty, but as a wounded man acknowledging his own mortality. For what was his infant son's death if not an *akeidah*, a sacrificial substitution for his own death? David is staring this reality right in the face.

David will never again be the cocky and confident shepherd with a slingshot. He will never again be the libidinous upstart or the "rock star" charismatic warrior dancing in the streets. He will never again be the rapacious "taker" of women. The David we hear uttering the heart-splitting words *I shall go to him but he will never come back to me!*" is on the far side of his personal mountain and is on the decline. The next time he "will see" his son will be when he has left this life.[219] Ironically, David, the "invincible" and fearless warrior who has spent his adult life taking with both hands, has never before encountered the immediacy of his own death. This, then, is the grim first phase of his punishment. "In place of David the seeker and wielder of power, we now see a vulnerable David, and this is how he will chiefly appear"[220] for the rest of his life.

DAVID COMFORTS BATSHEVA

And David consoled Batsheva his wife, and he came to her and he lay with her, and she bore a son and called his name Solomon, and the Lord loved him.

And He sent by the hand of Nathan the prophet and called his name Yedidya, for the Lord's sake. II Sam. 12:24–25

As this episode winds to a close, we note the contrast between the verbs describing David's behavior here, and the verbs that described him when he first saw Batsheva from his roof about two years earlier. At the outset of the story David *saw* her, he *sent* for her, he *took* her, and he *lay* with her. Here, after all that has occurred, we see that David *consoles* her, then he *comes unto* her, and finally he *lays* with her. This is the soft language of permission, a far cry from the earlier language describing David the plunderer.

We note that Batsheva is described in this verse as "David's wife" for the very first time. She is no longer *wife of Uriah*. The first time David had lifted Batsheva up from her mourning was after her husband, Uriah had been killed. At that time David had shown no forbearance, marrying and bedding Batsheva in haste, right after the seven-day mourning period had passed. Now, once again Batsheva is in mourning, this time for the death of her long-awaited baby. David knows that he is the instrumentality of Batsheva's grief. He does not know if Batsheva is aware of the depth of his responsibility for these two deaths that are devastating to her. So he treads softly.

David's newest wife is still very beautiful and she remains desirable to him, but he knows he must change his tactics if he expects to enjoy the woman whom he has acquired at such a high personal price. The *midrash* points to a subtle redundancy in verse 24, and infers that Batsheva has serious reservations about welcoming her husband, David, to her bed. The verse states first that David *came unto her*, and then that *he lay with her*. Both phrases mean the same thing: that David was intimate with Batsheva. Surely only *one* of those phrases would have sufficed? There must be a reason for the text's use of *both* synonymous phrases.

The doubling of the phrase is a clue to how Batsheva, now wife to the king, reacts to this "new" David. Apparently she had no taste or desire for sex after her baby's death.[221] Indeed, it is inferred from the fact that David consoles Batsheva *and then* "comes unto her" that while a person is in a state of mourning it is appropriate for her to refrain from having sexual relations.[222] Here, David resorts to soft words,[223] cajoling and pleading with Batsheva, so opposed is she to resuming intimate relations with him. One *midrash*[224] explains that she held David responsible for the baby's death, as it was *his sin* (the *seeing* and *taking*) that brought the tragedy about. Also, Batsheva was genuinely fearful that if she were to have a son with David, the sons from his other wives would hold *her* son up to humiliation and ridicule. They would despise him and brand him as the son whose origins were in his parents' sinful behavior.

What Batsheva did not reckon was that perhaps she, too, would be made to "pay" four-fold for her part — however passive — in the adultery. The Bible tells us[225] that Batsheva gave birth to four more sons after the unnamed infant in our story, named Shimea, Shobab, Nathan and Solomon. All but Solomon died, so including the unnamed baby Batsheva birthed and buried four sons.[226] Her reluctance to engage in intimate relations with David might have been prescient.

The reader might recall the Bible's language when Batsheva was abducted by David two years earlier. In 11:4 the parallel phrases were *and **she** came to him, and he slept with her.* Here, in 12:24, the language is nearly identical: *and **he** came to her, and he slept with her.* The earlier phrase was part of a forced and forbidden "taking;" Batsheva had no choice, she came to the king and was forced to lay with him. This later phrase illustrates by subtle contrast that now, as lawful wife of the king, their physical union is permitted;[227] now David comes *to her.* Paradoxically, Batsheva is now in a position to hold David off.

The *midrash* supplies David's reaction to Batsheva's refusal to lay with him.[228] He swears an oath to Batsheva: "Be consoled; God has pardoned my sin. I swear to you that the son you and I will have together will rule Israel after my death. God has disclosed this to me through Nathan's prophecy."

David was careful to frame the oath so that it would reach Batsheva's heart. She relents, but still she waits three months[229] before accepting David into her bed. She is recovering from childbirth as well as from the infant's death. This is another explanation, perhaps, for the text's doubling of the phrases *and he came to her, and he lay with her.* There was a time gap of several months between *he came to her* and *he lay with her.* Moreover, *this time* Batsheva does not become pregnant as easily as she did the first time; she does not conceive from their first sexual encounter after her mourning period for the first baby.[230] Eventually, though, she does conceive, and it is in the nature of a victory for Batsheva that she gives birth to another son.[231]

BATSHEVA'S SON IS NAMED SOLOMON

And the boy born to Batsheva and David is named Solomon, but true to this story's multiple ambiguities, it is unclear who named him; was it Batsheva? Was it David? Was it God? The text states *and **he** named him,* indicating that David named the boy. But when the Torah is read aloud the word is read *and **she** named him,* crediting Batsheva with naming him Solomon.[232] And in truth, many biblical mothers have named their sons. We need only consider Leah, Jacob's wife and mother of half the tribes of Israel. Not only did she name her six sons, but she also explained each naming. Her sons' names reflected her yearnings.

In the book of Chronicles[233] it is said that *God* named the boy Solomon. In a section of the text written in first-person, David says, "And God's word appeared to me, and He said, 'Behold! a son will be born to you. He will be a man of peace, and I will elevate him above all his surrounding enemies, and Solomon will be his name, for peace and tranquility will I give to Israel in his lifetime.'"

In fact, the name "Solomon" comes from the root-word *shalom*, meaning "peace." If Batsheva named him it was surely in the nature of a prayer that her son's life not follow the fraught pattern of his parents' lives. We can imagine Batsheva's thought process: "If it please the Lord, let this baby live; let him grow and thrive in peace in his own house and in Israel." What greater blessing could she aspire to for him than peace, considering that her own life thus far has been marked by its antithesis? She was orphaned at a young age, was married first to a professional soldier and later to a soldier-turned-king-turned-murderer. She has suffered loneliness, widowhood, abduction and rape; she has buried one husband and mourned him, then buried her long-awaited infant son and mourned him, too.

Batsheva's new son's name also comes from the root-word *shalem*, meaning "complete." With this son Batsheva meets her destiny as a mother in Israel, and much later, as a queen mother. God has gifted her with a new son to substitute for the one she lost, thus making her *shalem*, complete. Her new baby Solomon is vested with her overarching cosmic hopes: for peace and for completeness. Who would gainsay Batsheva her dreams?

More precisely, the Hebrew name *Shlomo*, for Solomon, means "*his* peace." So the name could mean, dually, God's peace with David, and David making his peace with God's judgement. If it was David who named the boy Solomon, perhaps he was naming it for *his* hopes: that through his new son he could make peace with the Lord.[234] Or it could very well still have been Batsheva who named him[235] praying this baby would bring an end to her husband's torment, allowing her and her baby to live in peace. Perhaps Solomon will grow up to heal the rift between David and his God that David had caused by his awful sins. This is more than just wishful thinking; the last words of verse 24 after *and he called his name Solomon* are *and God loved him.* The *midrash*[236] explains that *this* son is not like their first baby. *This* boy is "beloved by God," an indication that God will keep this baby alive.

No sooner is the baby named Solomon in verse 24, than God, through the prophet Nathan, gives him another name in verse 25: Yedidya, meaning "beloved of God" or "God's friend." This is a logical addendum to the final words in verse 24, an expression of what the text has just told us. Rashi and others say[237] that the extra name demonstrates that God truly loved the boy. God knew Batsheva's terrors about this baby's survival were real and great. Would God take this baby's life as a penance, too? Abarbanel explains that God named him Yedidya as a consolation and a promise that He would love and shelter him from the moment he exited Batsheva's womb.[238] The Hebrew word for womb is *rechem,* which is the same root as the Hebrew word for mercy. In reading the verse to mean that God named the baby "beloved of God," the *midrash* suggests this new baby's name could be a symbol of God's capacity for mercy, and a promise of life.

It is fascinating that the name Yedidya and the name David have virtually the same meaning: beloved. When the prophet Samuel clandestinely anointed the ruddy-cheeked shepherd boy named David king in his father's farmhouse a lifetime ago, the Bible said that "the spirit of the Lord gripped David from that day on."[239] By God's naming David's son Yedidya here, years removed from that hopeful moment, we must consider that God is perhaps transferring His special attention and affection from David to his newborn son. Yedidya/Solomon will step into the young David's shoes with God and with Israel.

From a practical standpoint, it is thought that Yedidya was Solomon's "official throne name"[240] when in future years he reigned over Israel. It was also a political move on Nathan's part to bestow the second name on the baby, thus indicating to the Israelite people that *this* heir to the throne would have special access to God's favor.

Despite his double naming, Batsheva's son will henceforth popularly be known only as Solomon, meaning "peace," for the reason that an era of peace will be ushered in with his future kingship. This gift of *shalom* or peace is an expression of God's love for Solomon *and for Israel.*

DAVID JOINS THE BATTLE AT RABBAH

Yoav, David's formidable general, defeats the Ammonites and is poised to capture their royal city of Rabbah after a two-year siege. But Yoav is also politically clever, and he dutifully serves the monarchy. So he sends word to David notifying him of the impending victory, suggesting to David that he gather more troops and join them at the front so that the king himself can take credit for the victory. The reader appreciates that Yoav is literally poised on a double-edged sword. He is a terrifically powerful general who serves David, his king. By "inviting" the king to the battlefield—now Yoav's home turf, not David's—Yoav is subtly sharing the power with David rather than the other way around. One must wonder: How long will David allow this imbalance to persist?

David follows Yoav's advice and marches into the city of Rabbah to capture it. Dramatically, David takes the heavy, solid-gold, bejeweled crown from the head of the Ammonite king, and places it upon his own head for all to see. David also loots the city and the royal storehouses and brings the booty home to Israel. David forces the surviving Ammonites to take apart their city brick by brick and he impresses them into labor in the rock quarries[241] as an example of what befalls the enemies of Israel.

The episode ends in poetic opposition to its opening verse. In 11:1 David sent Yoav and the army to fight Ammon and besiege Rabbah. The phrase *and David remained in Jerusalem* began his slide into abduction, adultery and murder. Here, two years later, in 12:31, *David and all the troops return to Jerusalem.* David, the king, is at the head of his army, where he should have been from the beginning.

BATSHEVA AS KINGMAKER

What becomes of Batsheva? It seems at first glance that she disappears from the story after giving birth to Solomon. Was her story—a disturbing, tumultuous, and depraved tale told in fifty-eight verses in the book of Samuel—simply a vehicle demonstrating the precipitous fall of the second monarch in the kingdom of Israel? Is the woman Batsheva of any lasting import? What of *her* continuing story?

We have teased out the bare bones of Batsheva's life from the text and *midrash*. Significantly, her biology was her destiny, and her fate was set while she was still in her girlhood. She was "exceedingly beautiful," and after she was orphaned (her father had been a soldier in the king's army) she came to live under the protection of Uriah the Hittite, her ward. It is likely that Batsheva ran Uriah's household, as Uriah, an officer in the king's elite special forces brigade, was absent from Jerusalem for months at a time. When she reached womanhood Batsheva, probably about eighteen years old and at the height of her beauty, was wed to Uriah, a widower with several sons. Batsheva was comfortable in the house of Uriah, having grown up there. It is certain she knew no fear, cosseted as she was, first by her soldier father, and now by her warrior husband. Only one sadness marked Batsheva's existence: she was childless.

The backdrop of Batsheva's story-within-a-story is the narrative of the books of Samuel, which describe the faltering steps of a fledgling Israelite monarchy. The reader is regaled with details of wars, sieges, ambushes and clever offensive maneuvers. Interwoven is David's own quest for a monarchic dynasty. These narratives of battlefield violence and political intrigue are interrupted with the Batsheva episode: a frightening tale of sexual violence, lawlessness and retribution. Batsheva's personal nightmare of abduction and rape, pregnancy and murder is brought center-stage because the prime actor, the "taker," initiator and plotter is none other than David, the king of Israel.

This narrative tension between the military and the monarchic, the political and the deeply personal escalates when Batsheva is swept into David's sphere. "These are not separate spheres, public and private . . . [T]he private acts of David have public consequences; . . . [his] politics and sexuality are so deeply and complexly integrated as to be *one*."[242]

Nowhere is this more true than in this episode of David's abduction and rape of Batsheva. The consequences of Batsheva's personal tragedy cross personal, political and military lines. Everyone is involved, comprising a cross-section of Israelite life: servants, messengers, palace guards, elite soldiers, a general, a minister of state, the wife of a special forces officer, the Ammonite enemy, the king, a prophet, and God.

When David saw and took Batsheva—daughter of a soldier in his army, granddaughter of his privy councilor, and wife of a special forces officer—David was committing an unlawful violation upon Batsheva, of course, but he also was asserting his power, stealing "sexual rights to a woman"[243] who belonged to another. Even Nathan's parable stresses that "the king's adultery is a violation of a property right,"[244] comparing Batsheva's abduction and rape to the theft and slaughter of a ewe lamb. It is no accident that in the parable the lamb is likened to the poor man's *bat*, Hebrew for "daughter." The word-play with the name *Bat*sheva is obvious.

So our question persists, but has some color now: What of Batsheva the queen, mother of a son who is in line to inherit David's throne? Batsheva now embodies the intersection of political and sexual power. Will she have another scene to play in the drama of the Davidic monarchy, or will she fade from the biblical proscenium?

Batsheva does not disappear from the story of David. In fact, she reappears twenty years later, in I Kings chapter 1, to play a crucial role in the succession intrigue when David is old and on his deathbed.

David is seventy years old and the years have not been kind to him. The once-vital young warrior and lusty king of boiling passions is depicted, ironically, as pitifully weak and cold. A countrywide search is launched for a beautiful virgin who will warm the king's bed and ward off the inevitable chills of impending death. Avishag the Shunamite is the "very beautiful" young woman who is brought before the king, and we are told that while she tried to warm him, he did not — or could not — engage her in sexual activity.

With this as background, we are told that Adoniyah, spoiled fourth son of David and his wife Chagit, proclaims himself king even though his father still lives, while publicly spurning his younger brother Solomon and the prophet Nathan.

Nathan, the prophet whose parable and punishment forecast David's downfall after the incident with Batsheva twenty-two years earlier, also prophesied that Solomon would reign after David.[245] So Nathan seeks out Batsheva, mother of seventeen-year-old Solomon, and urgently advises her as follows: "Allow me to give you counsel so that you might act now to save your own life and the life of your son Solomon. Go before King David and say to him, 'My lord, O king, did you not swear to your maidservant, saying, "assuredly Solomon your son will reign after me, and he shall sit upon my throne?" Why, then, does Adoniyah reign?'"

Nathan continues instructing Batsheva: "And behold, while your are speaking with the king I will also come in after you and confirm your words."

The reader will recall that Nathan, acting as God's emissary, had given Solomon the name Yedidya right after his birth, thereby proclaiming God's love for the boy. He therefore favors Solomon as God's choice for David's successor. We can imagine that on a personal level he has invested sufficient time and energy in the young Solomon so that he feels proprietary about him, having had a hand in educating the lad as he grew up in David's court. The prophet knows Solomon, trusts him, and probably loves him.

Batsheva enters the king's bedchamber, bows, and prostrates herself before her husband, the king. And from his bed the king invites her to address him saying, "What can I do for you?" It was highly unusual and not according to protocol for a queen to bow her head and prostrate herself before the king *unless* she had a special personal request.[246] David appreciates this and under-stands the import of Batsheva's actions, and he immediately asks her her wish.

Up until now Batsheva's only words in the Torah text were "I am pregnant." In the intervening two decades at court and in

David's bed as his favored wife[247] and confidant, Batsheva has had an education. She has learned how to speak to the king in a way to arouse his various passions. Here, operating under the imprimatur and instructions of the prophet of God, she activates the old king's passion for power and for pulling the political puppet strings in his own kingdom. We see that she has learned how to present an appealing case to David, Israel's monarch and judge.

Rather than criticizing David for failing to publicly name Solomon his successor earlier and with attendant ceremony, Batsheva takes the tack of focusing on Adoniyah's perfidy. Batsheva reminds David that he had sworn to her in the name of the Lord that Solomon, their son, would reign after him and sit upon his throne. She also tells him straight-out that Adoniyah has fomented a rebellion, and has seized the reigns of power unbeknownst to the king. She adds, "And Adoniyah has slain many oxen and sheep, and he has called all the king's sons, and Evyatar the priest, and Yoav, captain of the army, to feast with him. But Adoniyah has spurned your servant Solomon."

As she expected, David became incensed when he heard that his son Adoniyah had seized the reigns without his permission and was already holding coronation parties as the king lay in his sick bed. Perhaps David thought, "While there is still breath within me, and I am still king, *I* will proclaim my successor! I will not suffer another rebellion."

Batsheva continues her articulate plea to David, saying: "Now, my lord king, the eyes of all Israel are upon you, and *you* should tell them who shall sit on your throne after you. If you do not do this thing, then it will come to pass when you sleep with your fathers that I and our son Solomon will be counted among the new king's opposition, and we will surely be killed."

Batsheva is pleading for her life, and for the life of her son. What a sense of déja vu she must be battling! Having lost her husband Uriah and then her newborn son because of David, she must be determined not to allow another bloodbath to claim both her and her other son. Nathan had explained to her that if Adoniyah's plot to usurp David were successful, his first act as king would be to kill Solomon, his chief rival for their father's throne, and to murder her. It was a *modus operandi* for a successor to the crown to put the old king's widow to death upon accession to the throne.[248] The only chance for survival for Batsheva and her son is to mobilize David to oppose Adoniyah's rebellion and to name Solomon king.[249]

It is also likely that Batsheva feared that Adoniyah would seize on David's earlier affair with her, and use it as an excuse to have her put to death as an adulteress. Solomon, the issue of the king's affair, would also meet his death. By proclaiming both mother and son as "sinners" Adoniyah the usurper could kill or banish them[250] with "clean hands," thus freeing himself from any perceived threat to his succession to the throne.[251]

Enter Nathan the prophet. His approach differs a bit from Batsheva's. He tells the king he assumed Adoniyah had received the king's blessing, but that the king had neglected to inform the prophet for reasons of his own. The one-two punch of first Batsheva's and now Nathan's accounts of Adoniyah's self-coronation and snubbing of David's intimates spurs David into action.

"Call Batsheva to me!" he commands from his bed. When Batsheva is standing before the king he addresses her and swears an oath saying, "As the Lord lives — the Lord who redeemed my soul from calamity — truly as I swore to you before in God's name, Solomon your son shall reign after me — *he* shall sit upon my throne in my stead. So will I do this very day!"

Batsheva bows low, her face to the earth, and prostrates herself to David saying, "Let my lord king David live forever!"

And David does as he has promised. He commands Solomon to be publicly paraded on the king's donkey, and anointed with holy oil by the king's priests, attended by Nathan the prophet and the king's ministers, royal archers and marksmen. The ceremonial shofar horn is blasted, announcing the elevation of a new king over Israel and Judah, and all the people acknowledge it, crying out, "Long live king Solomon!" And there are banquets and celebrations.

CONCLUSION: BATSHEVA AS QUEEN MOTHER

So we see, Batsheva did not fade away after her nightmare of abduction and death in II Samuel chapter 11. She has incubated, perhaps healed, certainly listened and learned, and she has carefully nurtured her cherished son, Solomon, along with her relationship with his father, king David. She helped assure that after David's death (I Kings 2:10) her son Solomon would sit upon David's throne and that the kingdom was firmly established for his reign.

Batsheva is acknowledged by Solomon's court and the people of Israel as the *gevira* or "queen mother," a position of respect, importance and influence. As a political figure, the *gevira* was second in station only to the king himself.[252] We are told[253] that king Solomon arose from his throne to give public honor to his mother, and that he even bowed before her. Solomon also prepared a seat near to his own throne for Batsheva, so that she was able to sit by his right hand whenever he held court.

❈ ❈ ❈

It is evident that Batsheva has more than merely survived her personal tragedies. Unlike Dinah, whom the text ignores after she is abducted and raped by Shechem and rescued by her brothers, Batsheva's later life is documented. To this end, there is one more incident that should be noted before we leave the story of Batsheva. It involves Avishag the Shunamite, the young virgin who was brought into the palace to warm David's bed.

The incident is briefly told (in I Kings 2:13 *et seq.*), but has shattering consequences. To appreciate it, we must recall that after Adoniyah's rebellion was quashed and Solomon publicly anointed, Solomon surprisingly allowed Adoniyah to live, restricting him to house arrest for as long as he maintained good conduct (I Kings 1:51–53). Soon after David's death, however, Adoniyah boldly presents himself at the palace and seeks an audience with Batsheva. Batsheva's first query of him is "Do you come in peace?" to wit Adoniyah replies "In peace."

Adoniyah makes an appeal to Batsheva: "You know that the kingdom was mine, and that all Israel had set their sights on me to be king. But as the Lord willed it the kingdom has become my brother's. Now I ask but one petition of you, do not refuse me.

I beg of you, say to Solomon the king—for he will not refuse *you*—that he give me Avishag the Shunamite as a wife."

And Batsheva agrees to speak to the king on Adoniyah's behalf.

But when Batsheva presents Adoniyah's request, Solomon sees his half-brother's "simple" request for what it is: a toe in the door to usurp the kingdom and monarchy. Batsheva incorrectly interpreted Adoniyah's request at its face value: he wanted the lovely Avishag as a wife.[254] Given Batsheva's own traumatic experience as a young and "very beautiful" woman, this is an understandable interpretation. But Solomon has been coached in the ways of politics by his father, David, before his death. He instantly grasps that by taking the old king's concubine for himself Adoniyah intends it as the first step to acquiring the throne. In Rashi's words, "from the moment he uses the scepter of the king, that is the beginning of his seizure of sovereignty."[255]

Solomon responds to his mother with mild irony, saying, "Why do you ask only for Avishag for Adoniyah? You might just as well ask for the kingdom, for he is my elder brother!"

Adoniyah has brought a death sentence upon his own head by approaching Batsheva in this way. His attempt to use *two* women of the royal house—Avishag the Shunamite, David's concubine, and Batsheva, David's widow and the queen mother—was a reckless, insolent and thinly veiled attempt to subvert Solomon's authority. Solomon sends his trusted aide to put Adoniyah to death.

※ ※ ※

In the end, Batsheva's life was a success. Her hasty marriage to the king before her tears had quite dried for her husband Uriah lasted more than two decades, until David's death. What's more, she was widely considered the favored of his eight wives. Batsheva commanded the loyalty and assistance of Nathan, God's prophet, who spurred her to make the eloquent and successful case for her son Solomon to inherit the crown of Israel and Judah. Finally and importantly, Batsheva retained the affection and respect of her son Solomon even after he ascended the throne.

Thus was Batsheva, an innocent victim of the king's unbridled lust and murderous plotting, eventually rewarded: She became a mother in Israel and a respected *gevira*, a queen mother. Batsheva bore the son from David's loins who was "beloved of God," who grew to be a near-mythic king gifted with legendary wisdom, and who was himself the ancestor of kings.

PART

FIVE

Amnon

&

Tamar

FIVE

Amnon & Tamar

II SAMUEL 13:1–18

And it happened sometime afterwards: Avshalom, son of David, had a beautiful sister named Tamar. And Amnon, son of David, became infatuated with her.

Amnon was distraught and ill with longing for his sister Tamar, because she was an untouched virgin, and Amnon thought it was impossible to do anything to her.

And Amnon had a friend named Yonadav, the son of David's brother Shimah; Yonadav was a very clever man.

He asked him, "Why are you so dejected and sickly, O prince, morning after morning, pray, tell me." So Amnon replied, "I am in love with Tamar, the sister of my brother Avshalom!"

And Yonadav said to him, "Lie down in your bed and pretend you are sick. When your father comes to see you, say to him, 'Let my sister Tamar come and give me something to eat. Let her prepare the food in front of me, so that I may look on, and let her serve it to me.'"

So Amnon lay down and feigned sickness, and the king came to see him, and Amnon said to the king, "Let my sister Tamar come and prepare a couple of pancakes in front of me, and let her feed them to me."

And David sent a message to Tamar in the palace commanding her, "Go, now, to your brother Amnon's house and prepare some food for him."

So Tamar went to her brother Amnon's house, and he was lying down. And she took the dough, and she kneaded it into cakes before his eyes, and she cooked the pancakes.

She took the pan and poured them out before him, but he refused to eat. And Amnon ordered everyone [else] out of his presence, and everyone left him.

Amnon said to Tamar, "Bring the food into the bed chamber so that I may eat from your hand." And Tamar took the pancakes that she had made and she brought them into the bed chamber of Amnon her brother.

When she served them to him, he caught hold of her and said to her, "Come lie with me, my sister!"

And she pleaded with him, "Don't, my brother! Don't force me! Such things are not done in Israel! Do not do such a vile thing!

"And I, where will I carry my shame? And as for you, you will be like any of the dissolute men in Israel! Now I beg you, speak to the king, for he will not withhold me from you!"

But [Amnon] would not heed her voice. He overpowered her and he took her by force and lay with her.

[Afterward] Amnon loathed her with a loathing that was very great; his hatred for her exceeded the love that he had felt for her; and Amnon said to her, "Get up and go!"

And she said to him, "Please don't commit this wrong; to send me away would be even worse than the first wrong you committed against me!" But he would not listen to her.

And he summoned his young attendant and said, "Get that [female thing] away from me, outside, and bolt the door behind her!"

T he story of Amnon and Tamar can break your heart. It is the brief tale of the beautiful daughter of king David, who — unbeknownst to her — is the object of her half-brother's sexual obsessions. Tamar, the innocent princess, is lured into her brother Amnon's bedroom where, once they are alone, he overpowers and violently rapes her. What happens next — Amnon's outright hatred and heartless rejection of Tamar — seals this episode as a dark tale of cruel family betrayals, palace politics, manipulation by men in power, rape, incest, and ultimately, revenge and fratricide.

The reader is familiar with the story's background. It is found in II Samuel 11 and 12, the chapters that narrated the story of David and Batsheva — this book's Part Four — and that immediately precede this coldly terrifying tale. The Bible expects the reader to connect that prior story to this one, as chapter 13 begins with the words *And it happened after all this* . . . So the template of battle, palace intrigue, sexual transgression and murder is one we have recently examined. The reader asks, Can it be true? Is this about to happen again? The answer is Yes, and in spades. But this time it is David's *children* who are the story's actors. David's sins have, tragically, accreted to the next generation, and sadly, we will see that they embroider the familiar pattern and take the king's behavior to a new nadir.

There is an important difference in this story, however. Here, Tamar, the virginal victim of the rapacious Amnon, *speaks* to her attacker! This differs markedly from the two previous abduction scenes we have examined and the reader will want to cheer for her. In our earlier discussion of Dinah's rape in Part Two we saw that Dinah was utterly silent before, during and after her attack in the Bible text. Similarly in Part Four, Batsheva was also silent before and during her abduction. She spoke only two words to David as the incident unfolded, and those only months afterward to announce her pregnancy. The Bible's progression from, first, presenting a *silent* rape victim, then to an *almost* silent victim, and now to two eloquent attempts by the rape victim at deflecting her attacker, is fascinating, and we will explore it in upcoming pages. We will see that Tamar's voice as well as her actions distinguish her as heroic among the palace royals.

Let us meet the players.

WHO IS TAMAR?

This chapter in the book of Samuel opens, familiarly, with the word *Vayehi*, meaning *and it happened* . . . , indicating, yet again, that we are about to encounter a tragic and troubling episode. It is the biblical code-word equivalent of the cautionary phrase "fasten your seat belts!" and readers will, indeed, need to gird themselves.

Tamar is introduced as *the beautiful sister of Avshalom, son of David*. She is about twenty-two years old at the time of this incident,[1] and, as the Bible specifies, she is a virgin. A Bible reader who is sensitive to verbal clues will note that the text announces our tragic heroine with the verbal flourish "and her name is . . ." The Hebrew word *ushemah* (*and her name is*) or *ushemo* (*and his name is*) oftentimes precedes the introduction of a righteous person in the biblical narrative.[2] So from chapter 13's economical first verse we already know a bit about Tamar. We know that she is beautiful; that she is a princess, as she is the sister of Avshalom, the king's third son; and also, perhaps mirroring her biblical namesake in Genesis, that she is righteous.

Tamar is identified, firstly, as *Avshalom's* sister. So we must take a step back and outline the provenance of both Avshalom and Tamar. The two are full siblings, having the same father — king David — and mother. Their mother's name is Maacah, who was herself a princess, daughter of Talmai, king of Geshur.[3] David took the beautiful princess Maacah as spoils during a battle, and married her early in his reign.[4] It is likely that David's marriage to Maacah was another of his expedient politico-sexual alliances, some of which we mentioned in Part Four.

Tamar is not the only character in this drama who is described as "beautiful." Her full brother, Avshalom, well-known for his thick and luxurious mane of hair, is identified later on as a "beautiful man."[5] So we see that the offspring of the "beautiful" David[6] and his captive princess Maacah are both beautiful and, as we will also see, they are doomed. Of course this reminds the reader of Batsheva, who was "*very* beautiful"[7] and who was at the vortex of an abduction, an act of adultery, and eventually a murder, all committed by David, king of Israel. David's actions in the prior two chapters with Batsheva and Uriah are at the genesis of this present incident with Amnon, Tamar and Avshalom. Our present chapter 13 of II Samuel is called David's "book of punishment" — *torat onesh*[8] — as it outlines the behavior of three of his offspring who are entwined in a scenario that leads to their destruction. We will see that while being "beautiful" in the books of Samuel is clearly less than a blessing, it is still a recognizable common thread in these stories and is a catalyst for Amnon's present attack on Tamar.

The Talmud[9] explains that Maacah was a "beautiful captive" whom David "took" and was intimate with before she converted to belief in the Hebrew God and married him.[10] At issue for the Talmud is whether Tamar is therefore a "true" daughter of David. Perhaps the rabbis of the Talmud, disgusted and overwhelmed with Amnon's coming sins of incest and violent rape, are seeking to blunt his incest offense. Their theory is that if Maacah was not a converted Israelite and proper wife of David at the time she *conceived* Tamar, then Tamar is not a full-rights sister to Amnon and thus was not truly forbidden to him.

Abarbanel addresses the Talmud's hypothesis in his logical and articulate fashion.[11] He says that it is impossible even for physicians to say when, precisely, a fetus was conceived; so in the case of Tamar, it is simply not credible to say that she was conceived before Maacah was properly wife of the king. It is more than sufficient that at the time that Maacah *gave birth* to both Tamar and Avshalom Maacah already was a convert and lawfully married to David. Therefore, reasons the commentator, any daughter or son born thereafter is legitimate and royal. Amnon is still on the hook. Tamar was absolutely Amnon's half-sister and therefore forbidden to him sexually.

And if Tamar were only Maacah's daughter and not David's issue at all,[12] the fact that the girl was raised in the palace, was called "princess" or "daughter of the king," and was treated as royal by David, by the members of David's family and by the palace servants, all makes her a *de facto* sister to David's blood offspring. Tamar was therefore "forbidden" to Amnon.

WHO IS AMNON?

Amnon is David's firstborn son, born in Hebron, and his mother is David's wife, Achinoam of Jezreel.[13] He is about twenty-five years old and is crown prince, the treasured heir to David's throne. Amnon occupies this privileged, exalted, unitary space in the royal household, and it will become evident from his speech and the way he is treated by Yonadav, David, the servants and others that while the willful Amnon is either pandered to or feared, he is never chastened or disciplined. This story will give us "a glimpse into the ways and standards of these . . . stripling warlords or regal thugs or restless, indulged princes"[14] who heedlessly and intentionally plan and then execute a vile crime against their innocent sister and cousin.

The same first verse that identifies Amnon as "son of David" identifies Avshalom not only as "son of David" but *also* says that Tamar is Avshalom's sister. We can speculate at the absence of a sibling identifier annexed to *Amnon*. In fact, this is curious, considering that it might have been more fitting for the text to have identified Tamar as "sister of *Amnon*" than as "sister of *Avshalom*" since other than Tamar, Amnon is the primary actor in the first 17 verses of this fraught chapter. The answer must be that it is Avshalom who is worthy of being known as "brother of the beautiful Tamar" for the reason that he — and not Amnon — behaves in the true manner of a brother to her. In the second half of this chapter it will be her brother Avshalom who will give the battered Tamar shelter and a home, advise her, and ultimately, avenge her by murdering her rapist.[15]

The other distinctive fact we are told about Amnon is that "he loves" the beautiful girl Tamar who is sister to Avshalom and is, implicitly, his sister, too, as he is identified here as "David's son." It is this illicit "love" that will rule Amnon and ruin Tamar.

AMNON IS OBSESSED

Amnon is so mad with longing for the beautiful and innocent Tamar that he actually makes himself sick.[16] His face is thin and wan, his pallor grayish in cast.[17] The Bible tells us twice that Ammon *loves* Tamar: in its narration in verse 1, and in verse 4 where Amnon confesses his "love" to his friend and cousin. Already, then, the reader is clued that this "love" is an unholy emotion, as earlier we read that Tamar is Amnon's half-sister. Israelite law handed down at Sinai prohibits a man from sleeping with his half-sister. Any "love" Amnon has for Tamar should be strictly platonic, but we are told in verse 2 that he loves Tamar *because she is a virgin*. Amnon is presented, then, as a man caught in the throes of a taboo sexual obsession.

The Mishnah[18] has a strong philosophical opinion about Amnon's "love." In a terse exposition on the subject of ideal love the *mishna* says: "All love that is dependent on a [physical] cause will pass away once the cause has disappeared; but love that is *not* dependent on a [physical] cause will never pass away." The *mishna* offers our present story as an example of selfish pleasure: "Which love is dependent on a [physical] cause?" asks the *mishna*. "The love of Amnon for Tamar." The *mishna* can think of no more perfect example of a fleeting and shallow imitation of "love"than Amnon's attraction to Tamar in the story before us. Amnon's strong and forbidden feelings are based in large part on Tamar's untouched status and as we will see, his "love" lasts only until he has rid her of that virgin condition.

Verse 2 opens with the Hebrew word *vayetzer*, meaning *Amnon became **distressed** and ill with longing for his sister Tamar, because she was an untouched virgin*. The Hebrew word has the same root as *yetzer*, as in the expression *yetzer ha-ra*, or "the evil inclination." *Yetzer* can also mean an uncontrolled desire. Another derivation is the word *tsar*, meaning "narrow." Amnon's sexual obsession for Tamar has caused his focus to shrink to a narrow corridor of desire. He has blotted out his family obligations, his human responsibilities, society's moral expectations; all he sees and feels and thinks about is his own forbidden lust. How eloquent is this description of Amnon's "distress." In using this precise word to describe Amnon's emotional and physical lust for Tamar, the Bible deliberately allows Amnon's distress and desire to commingle in language and in life.

Amnon's *yetzer* most likely also includes a power-lust. As firstborn son next-in-line to succeed David, Amnon must be ever-vigilant lest his younger brothers grow in power or attempt to usurp him. Within the royal household the jostling for preeminence is a constant. Amnon knows that dominating Avshalom's sister would serve two purposes: it would slake his lust for the beautiful maiden, and incidentally it would show Avshalom that he — Amnon — is superior, that he is the almost-monarch; that as such, he can see and take at his will, even to violating this virgin princess, Avshalom's sister. This could also explain why chapter 13 opens with the words that *Avshalom had a beautiful sister named Tamar, . . . and Amnon became infatuated with her.* Amnon desired Tamar *precisely because* she was Avshalom's sister! Raping her is a display of power as well as a political act.[19]

There might also be an element of bored privilege in Amnon's love-sickness, a variant of his father David's indolent stroll on the palace roof. "Like father, like son" might be the watchword here.[20] Amnon's father David could not control his inappropriate lust for the very beautiful *and married* Batsheva; neither will Amnon even attempt to curb his unholy desire for the beautiful girl Tamar, *his younger sister.* Perhaps if Amnon had been gainfully occupied in a worthwhile enterprise of state, or in horseback riding or weapons practice, he would have been too busy to pander to his own forbidden sexual fantasies.

Amnon is aware that moral convention restricts his uncurbed passion for his sister. The Bible says that *he loved her **because** she was a virgin*, and that he therefore thought it was *impossible to do anything to her.* The Hebrew word for "because" can also mean "but," so the text could also read *Amnon loved her **but** she was a virgin.* Perhaps the fact of Tamar's virginity gave Amnon fleeting pause. Perhaps he thought, "Could I take her **even though** she is a virgin?" It is more than likely that the girl's untouched state acted as catnip to Amnon, inflaming his desire to bed her.[21] Furthermore, the fact that she was his half-sister did not douse his desire or quell his determination to have her.

If anything, the fact of Tamar's virgin status poses only a tactical impediment for Amnon. It was traditional for the virginal Israelite girls and young women to remain cloistered within their family house or palace compound so as not to exhibit themselves before men or outsiders.[22] Not only that, but verse 1 introduced Tamar to the reader as "beautiful." It is virtually certain that this beautiful virgin princess is being held in abeyance in the royal house of the women while David arranges a tactical, dynastic marriage for her.[23] So Tamar is trebly off-limits to Amnon: she is his half-sister, she is a virgin, and she is destined for an important and expedient marriage to another.

For these reasons Amnon is racking his brain trying to figure out a way to entrap and sleep with the protected Tamar.[24] If she had been allowed outside the palace he could have engineered any number of "accidental" trysts. But restricted as she was within the house of the women he cannot for the life of him come up with a viable plan. For this reason he is sick with a combination of anxiety and lust.

THE PLOT TO LURE TAMAR

Enter Yonadav, Amnon's "friend," the son of Shimah, David's brother. This episode of palace intrigue is all in the family; Amnon's "friend," his advisor in the brewing imbroglio, is none other than his exceedingly clever first-cousin. Yonadav is Amnon's soul-mate. He is known within the family as the best tactician; able to unravel the most complex games, the most inventive trickster among all the cousins.[25] The Talmud says that Yonadav is an evil genius[26] who appears on the scene just when Amnon is most receptive to his plotting.

It is telling that the Bible uses the word *re'ah* to describe Yonadav as Amnon's "friend." In Hebrew the word *re'ah* and the word for evil are spelled identically: *ra*.[27] So Yonadav is called *re'ah*, the word that appears simply as *ra* or "evil one" in the unvowelized Torah text. Surely the author of Samuel is offering us his opinion of Amnon's "friend" and his coming advice. The *midrash* tells us that Yonadav did not use his natural wisdom for good and productive ends; he turned his mind instead to plots and intrigues.[28] In fact, the word *re'ah* in the context of "friend to a royal" might have meant that Yonadav was a cousin-cum-counselor,[29] filling a semi-official role in service to the prince. As such, Yonadav was in a unique, trusted position to advise Amnon to the good or, as here, to pander to his base desires.

Yonadav inquires about the prince's dejected mood. *"Why are you so depressed and sickly, O prince, morning after morning, pray, tell me."* The reader is accustomed to the Bible's precision with words, and the word it uses here for "sickly" — *dal* — has been used earlier in the Bible in Genesis, in the narrator's description of Pharaoh's "lean, sickly" cows.[30] There the "sickly" cows were contrasted to the "beautiful" animals in the prior verse. The image there portended famine and tragedy coming to those once-beautiful and cherished. The use of the same words in our story brings the same cast to the narrative. We will see that Amnon's self-induced love-sickness will translate into terror and misfortune for the beautiful Tamar. In the story of Pharaoh's cows, the sickly ones consume the beautiful healthy ones, but amazingly, the sickly cows remain sickly; they are not sated after their meal. So, too, here, where the "sickly" Amnon will prey upon the beautiful Princess Tamar, but he will remain unsated.

How irresistible it must have been to Amnon to have a comrade in whom to confide his illicit obsession. As his younger half-sister, Tamar, grew in beauty from girl into young woman, Amnon's desires have grown exponentially. He has been spending sleepless nights, kept awake by his overactive imagination fueled by his libido.[31] Hence his haggard appearance come morning.[32] In response to Yonadav's query, Amnon admits his secret to Yonadav saying, *"I am in love with Tamar, sister of my brother Avshalom!"* It is curious that Amnon refers to Tamar here as *Avshalom's* sister, not as *his*. Perhaps Amnon is so deeply immersed in a mixture of desire and compulsion that he refuses to allow his conscious mind to admit that the object of his obsession is, indeed, his sister. He has rationalized his incestuous compulsion. Or perhaps, simply, Amnon is about to treat Tamar to the antithesis of brotherly love, so he describes her as *Avshalom's* sister, not as his.

Yonadav does not exhibit the smallest hint of horror or disapproval at Amnon's revealing confession. To the contrary, Yonadav will sow trouble and will facilitate a rape. His scheming nature had been nurtured by his father's and uncles' seething resentment of their younger brother, David's, brash success. David's "superseded" brothers[33] held no love for or pride in their red-headed sibling. Even though David took his nephews into the palace and situated them at court, his brothers' bitterness had been passed on to their sons—to Yonadav in our story. While he appears to all to be a counselor and friend to Amnon the crown prince, he is in truth the sly snake in Eden, the patient agent-in-place within the king's court. Yonadav's plot will play on Amnon's incestuous sexual obsession. It will lead to Tamar's destruction and, ultimately, to Amnon's murder. It would be difficult to imagine a more successful agency for the implosion of David's monarchy.

To this end, Yonadav's plan emerges full-blown. In David's palace, because appearances are everything and reality is hidden behind a subterfuge, Yonadav counsels Amnon to **pretend** that he is sick. *"Stay in your bed and feign illness. When your father comes to visit you say to him, 'Perhaps my sister Tamar can come visit me and bake me bread and make it fresh in my presence while I watch her, and she will feed it to me.'"*

We can imagine Yonadav's plot taking shape as he speaks to Amnon: "Be sure your face appears sickly, so that you arouse your father's concern and so that he is anxious to grant you whatever you request to help you recover your strength. You should appear so thin and wan that your request that your sister Tamar prepare hot pancakes at your bedside will not seem strange. Having her fry the cakes in front of you might stimulate your appetite, and the king will know this and will surely grant your request.[34] Understand, cousin, that if the king does *not* command Tamar to leave her quarters and come to your chambers, she will not be permitted to leave the house of the virgins. Your only hope to get her alone[35] is to trick your father."

So the contemptible Amnon follows his cousin's plan to first trick his father, the king, into issuing an express command that his virgin sister be permitted to leave her quarters and enter Amnon's house.[36] Amnon has settled on "a subterfuge that in its way echoes David's deviousness regarding Uriah."[37] Once David falls into the trap and issues the command, Amnon's main objective— to get the innocent Tamar alone in his bed—should be easy enough to achieve, as the young woman has no inkling of the threat that her brother poses and will not be on her guard.

Amnon lays on his bed and feigns illness. As expected, the king comes to visit him and Amnon asks him, *"Please let my sister*

*Tamar come and prepare a couple of pancakes right here in my presence,
and let her feed them to me from her own hand."*

There is some fascinating word-play in this verse. Twice
Amnon uses the word *levivot*, meaning fried pancakes. The
conflation here of love (or Amnon's imitation-love) and food as
the cure for what ails Amnon is evident in this verse. The Hebrew
word for heart is *lev*, and *levivot* are the "hearty"[38] or perhaps
heart-shaped[39] pancakes he bids Tamar to prepare — *telabev* — and
cook for him.[40] Also, Amnon's obsession for Tamar is "fed" by his
watching her hands knead the dough and fry the cakes, pour them
out and bring them to him with her own fingers. The *midrash*
explains the reaction at work saying, "what the eye beholds, the
heart desires."[41] Here we even see a doubling of the intensity of
Amnon's "love"-obsession, signified by his request for **two** *levivot*
to be hand-made by Tamar while he watches. Nouns and verbs
all play on the word "heart" and on the loving or desiring it
ostensibly represents.

Amnon actually out-thinks Yonadav when he specifies to his
father that Tamar should cook the pancakes on-the-spot. He
specifically requests hot pancakes fried in oil, which are at their
peak of flavor when consumed immediately. Had he only asked
for a hot meal cooked by his sister, she could easily have prepared
the food elsewhere and had a servant convey it to Amnon's
bedside while it was still warm. But Amnon had only one chance
to convince David that his health required that his sister cook his
food *in his presence,* and this meant that he had to request special
hot, fried pancakes that would be eaten immediately.

The *mis-en-scène* is steeped in forbidden sensuality not only
because of the "love" and food imagery, but especially because the
action takes place in Amnon's private quarters and, as we will see,
he sends away all his servants. He is alone with the object of his
desire with there is no one and nothing to stand in his way. The
tension for the reader is almost unbearable.

A word about the continued intrusion of the account of
David and Batsheva into this present plot; an intrusion that will
echo throughout this story. Food and seduction as set props and
themes are used in both narratives. In the earlier story we recall
how David tried to set the seduction scene between Uriah and

Batsheva by sending along food and drink on Uriah's first night of home-leave. We note that that romantic set-up was a charade, too, a perversion of a true romantic "love" scene, as Batsheva had already been violated by David, was in fact pregnant by him, and David sought to cover it up by seducing Uriah into sleeping with his wife. As we know, David's plan was unsuccessful, which led him to plot Uriah's murder. The similarity of the plots in both stories lends a sense of dark inevitability to the present tale.

Both David and his son and heir, Amnon, employ food to set a false seduction scene. Both men violate the objects of their unchecked and illicit desires, and in both situations murders will be committed as a result of their selfish compulsions.

DAVID IS DUPED

All the heart, love, food and seduction imagery is lost on David.[42] He is completely fooled by Amnon's charade. Once before — when Nathan the prophet presented his parable after the incident involving David, Batsheva and Uriah — was David, the master-manipulator, himself caught in a "sting." The common element in both stories is David's strong emotion. Listening to Nathan's parable, as we've discussed at length, David-the-judge became wroth and outraged, pronouncing sentence without appreciating that *he* was the culprit, "the man" in the parable. And here, the powerful emotion that blinds David is his love for Amnon, his firstborn son and heir to the throne.

Therein lies the irony of the text's express "seeing" imagery, which appears seven times in verses 2 through 8. It is not only David who fails to see clearly here. Amnon cannot **see** his way clear to fulfilling his desire with Tamar; Yonadav advises Amnon to appear ill when his father comes **to see** him, and to request that Tamar his sister prepare the food before his **eyes** so that he can **watch** her as she cooks it and eat from her hand. The seeing imagery *repeats* as Amnon plays the part. He acts sickly when his father comes **to see** him; he requests that the king command Tamar to cook the food before his **eyes**. And it repeats yet again when Tamar arrives at Amnon's house and in real-time cooks the pancakes while Amnon **watches** her.

Yet even this abudant textual language is an understatement, as it fails to include the *implicit* "seeing" imagery that underlies the story line. There is quite a bit of "pulling the wool over the eyes" play-acting that is emphasized and repeated here. For example, Yonadav advises Amnon only to **appear** to be ill, and Amnon easily manages to trick the king's **eye**. Then the king, who fails **to read** the signs of obsessive "love" that are right in front of **his eyes**, acts unwittingly as Amnon's accomplice[43] and sends his own daughter into Amnon's lair so that she can **appear** in front of him while he lusts after her, unbeknownst either to David or to Tamar. Amnon's servants **see** or certainly appreciate what is happening in their master's bedroom, but they turn a **blind eye** to his behavior even to the extent of ushering the abused and weeping princess from Amnon's house and locking the door behind her.

The actual and the pretend are interwoven. The reader is struck by David's capacity to be gulled, and his failure "to see" and protect his beautiful and innocent daughter Tamar. Of course with the objectivity of readers we can appreciate that David is incapable of "seeing" Amnon for what he is because his son Amnon is a reflection of none other than David himself! By extension, then, Amnon is doomed. We will later witness the extreme consequences to Tamar, to David — and ultimately to the kingdom — that will flow from David's blindness.

DAVID SENDS TAMAR TO AMNON

The imperious David is acting in a familiar way: he **sends a message** to his daughter Tamar at her house saying, "*Go, now, to the house of your brother Amnon and prepare food for him.*" (II Sam. 13:7) This repeats the "sending" and "house" imagery of chapter 11, and the reader cringes at the eerie similarity to the Batsheva story. David is once again sending a message to the house of the female quarry; she is given no choice but to answer *two* royal commands:[44] David commands Tamar *to go to the house of Amnon your brother* and *to cook him healing food.* So she enters the house of the predator where tragically, her fate is written.

While David was obviously the main character of the prior episode of the taking of Batsheva and the murder of Uriah, here David remains mostly a secondary player. It is Amnon who loves, plans and acts, Yonadav who advises, Tamar who responds and speaks and suffers. Much later it is Avshalom who avenges. As we have seen, the shadow of David's prior acts is cast over Amnon's behavior, but it is the generation *after* David's that is moving the story forward into tragedy by its "new deeds."[45]

Even so, David's single act of sending Tamar to the house of Amnon is the critical piece that Yonadav and Amnon's plot had to successfully maneuver in order for the rape to occur. It is the *sine qua non* of the plot that David be tricked and chivvied into doing precisely what Amnon wants: David instructs Tamar to leave the safety of the women's compound and enter Amnon's lair. It is David who delivers his beautiful, virgin daughter into Amnon's power.

TAMAR COOKS WHILE THE PRINCE WATCHES

Tamar obeys her father's commands and ventures out of her cloistered residence, making her way to the house of her brother Amnon. Once there, she finds Amnon reclining on his bed. She wastes no time, unpacks her baking and cooking utensils and supplies, and begins kneading the dough and preparing the *levivot* Amnon has requested.

The reader must appreciate the cherished position Amnon holds in the royal family. He is first in line to succeed David the king. While a beautiful princess such as Tamar was also of some value to the king for purposes of securing a political alliance, for instance, it is certain that she was expected to be subservient to her father and brothers, with the crown prince holding pride of place. She was expected to do the king's bidding, and in this instance perhaps she even worried that her father the king would hold her responsible if her *levivot* failed to revive the sickly prince. So she is intent on her cooking mission, and is eager to please Amnon and by extension her father the king.

Tamar fries the pancakes as Amnon watches her. She tips the hot *levivot* out of the pan to serve to her brother, but he refuses to

take even a bite. True to his plan Amnon acts the cranky, moody
prince and orders the room emptied saying, *"Clear out, everyone!"*
The prince's rooms consist of an outer chamber, where Tamar was
cooking the *levivot* and where the servants and perhaps even
Yonadav had congregated, and the more private inner bed
chamber. Amnon was reclining on his bed located in the adjoin-
ing chamber—a room-within-a-room[46]—where he could watch
Tamar through the open doorway.

In a matter of moments Amnon and Tamar are utterly alone.
Perhaps she is worried; not for her personal safety, as she has no
reason to fear being alone with her brother at this point, but
because he is not compliant about eating the food that she has
been commanded to provide. She sees that the cakes are cooling
with every second of delay. Tamar is concerned and distracted,
and is perhaps even engaged in cutting the fresh pancake ready to
feed to Amnon if he would only stop frowning.

Amnon says to Tamar, *"Bring the healing food further into the
bed chamber so that I may eat from your hand."* *So Tamar took the
pancakes that she had made and she brought them to her brother Amnon
in his room.* (II Sam. 13:10)

We watch, helpless, as Tamar is reeled in, ever-closer to her
predator. Her brother is reclining on his bed at the far end of his
bed chamber. The palace room is spacious and utterly private; all
the servants have been banished, and Tamar ventures further
inside and sets down the tray carrying the pan, the fresh pancakes
and her utensils. The text here refers to Amnon as "her brother"
because that is precisely how Tamar perceives him. She looks
upon Amnon strictly as a sibling, and her innocence highlights
Amnon's perfidy. He *knows* Tamar will enter his bed chamber at
his request *precisely because* she thinks of him only as her brother.
Only Amnon and Yonadav (and the reader) know of his *un*filial
and obsessively carnal designs on her. The reader thinks, leave
the pancakes and run! But of course Tamar proceeds inexorably
to her brother's bedside[47] to feed him the freshly fried *levivot*, as
her father commanded her.

We can appreciate how well-choreographed Amnon's evil
plan is. Because his bed is located in his bed chamber that is itself
situated within his larger quarters, no sound can be heard outside

the thick walls of his room. Once the outer door has been shut by the retreating servants, his chambers are effectively sound-proofed. The trap is sprung! Amnon has planned his moves and speed is essential. First to surprise and overwhelm his prey, and second to overpower her before anyone outside would perchance hear her cry out in the course of his attack.[48]

THE RAPE OF TAMAR

If the pace of the Bible's story thus far has been painstaking and deliberate — detailing even Amnon's pallor and the frying of the pancakes — right here it takes off dramatically. When Tamar approaches Amnon's bedside the better to feed him, he grabs her saying, *Come! Lie with me, my sister!* Off balance and holding the food she had prepared, Tamar stumbles as Amnon pulls her on top of him. She drops what is in her hands and pushes Amnon away with all her strength.[49]

We will slow down the action to better reflect on the echoes, here, of other earlier biblical rape scenes.

We notice that Amnon's language — *Come lie with me* — has been used before in a forced seduction or near-rape scene. When Joseph was Potifar's trusted servant in Egypt Potifar's wife said, *Lie with me!* to the very handsome Joseph when she cornered him in her empty house.[50] Joseph was fortunate to evade the woman's physical predations (he suffered some scratches and a torn coat), but her venomous testimony landed him in prison where he languished, forgotten, for two years. Will Tamar be able to evade Amnon?

Amnon's prefatory word "Come" might signify request or softness in other contexts, but when coupled with his iron grip on Tamar's arm and around her waist, the word is belied by his use of force. This is no polite request; the erstwhile sickly Amnon surges up from the bed sheets like a sea monster from a placid lagoon. He seizes the shocked Tamar, catching her unaware. Amnon's grip is not a playful grab; it is an unambiguously aggressive move, overpowering Tamar so that he can have his way sexually.[51]

In the earlier biblical stories of Sarah's abduction by Pharaoh, Dinah's rape by Shechem, and David's abduction and violation of Batsheva, we analyzed the recurrence of the "seeing" and "taking" dyad as a pattern of violation by kings or princes of the innocent, beautiful or forbidden objects of their desire. Amnon's behavior here fits this pattern. We connect the earlier abundant "seeing" imagery in this chapter with Amnon's present "taking" and grabbing of Tamar. For instance, the text belabored Amnon's ogling of Tamar while she prepared his food. His perverse demands *to watch* the unaware, innocent Tamar were voyeuristic foreplay, a prelude to his brutish taking of her in verses 11 and 14.

TAMAR'S PLEA

A prime reason this story is so heart-rending is that the virtuous and violated female character speaks so eloquently — albeit futilely — on her own behalf. The reader does not need to rely solely on inference or even on *midrash* to appreciate the heroine's thoughts and feelings. Here, the text reveals Tamar pleading with all her might, trying to deflect Amnon from his intended purpose: ravishment of her, a theft of her innocence. We root for her to succeed, though her fate was written when she answered her father's summons and entered Amnon's house. Because speech by the Bible's women is not usual or extensive, Tamar's words in verses 12, 13 and 16 are especially significant and poignant. If the power of her speech could be translated into brawn Tamar would overpower Amnon. Instead, she wins the debate but loses the "war." Let us examine Tamar's words.

It is clear from Tamar's response that although she is an innocent she is still sufficiently mature to immediately understand what Amnon is about to do to her. Surely she knows "the facts of life;" doubtless the earlier accounts of abductions and violations of royal and ancestral women are told and retold by the Israelite mothers to their daughters as cautionary tales. And after all, the Talmud[52] has told us that Tamar's mother, Maacah, was both a princess and a wartime "beautiful captive" who had herself endured sexual domination. Tamar's birth was most probably the result of her mother's sexual initiation, so Tamar has heard about abductions and forced sexual encounters her whole life. Violent rape is every girl's nightmare. It is therefore a measure of Tamar's strength of mind and character that at the same time that she mightily resists Amnon physically, she retains the presence of mind to try to dissuade him with heartfelt, desperate words.

TAMAR RESISTS AMNON

*"**Don't**, my brother! **Don't** force me! Such things are not done in Israel! **Do not** do such a vile thing!"* II Sam. 13:12

Three times Tamar resists and refuses to yield to Amnon. Obviously she is no physical match for her older brother who is a trained warrior, but still Tamar resists him. This young woman is fighting for her life, temporarily fending off Amnon's physical domination while simultaneously doing her best to appeal to him on intellectual, emotional and political levels. In his aroused state, especially after having waited and plotted for this moment, it is a foregone outcome that Amnon will ignore Tamar's pleas and arguments. Still she tries desperately to convince Amnon that what he is poised to do to her will only bring tragedy down upon their heads.

First Tamar begs Amnon not to force her. She focuses her first protest on the act of forcible rape itself. The Hebrew term she uses is familiar to the reader from the story of the rape of Dinah; it is the word *te'aneni*, from the noun *inuy*, meaning oppression, suffering, force or torture. Just as the threads of the Batsheva episode are woven into this story, so, too, are the elements of Shechem's rape of Dinah.[53] In both stories we see the daughter of an Israelite tribal chief as the object of desire of a young and spoiled prince of the realm. We see a "going out" from her cloistered women's compound. We see a sexual attack, and we see the term *inuy*, meaning the girl was forced.[54] We also have the presence of the word "love" in both stories; in both situations the word is not unambiguous and is troublesome. If a man *truly* loved his sister he would not "uncover her nakedness" and lay with her as Amnon is doing here.

And, still to come, we have the element of the ravished girl's full brother (brothers in Dinah's case) avenging his sister's honor by murdering her rapist. This could be the meaning of her first words, *Don't, my brother!* She is telling Amnon that his behavior of grabbing and overpowering her, of forcing her to lay with him, is diametrically opposed to the behavior of a loving brother.[55] She is, in effect, attempting to verbally jolt him out of his sexual haze and bring him back to an ordered reality where *true* brothers protect (and avenge) their sisters.

Here, though *not* in the Dinah story, we have the added element that Amnon, Tamar's attacker, is her half-brother. Thus the element of incest, of being taken against her will by a member of her immediate family, intensifies the element of *inuy* or torture for Tamar.[56] Not only is she debased by the rape; but because of the act of transgressive sex, of crossing the incest taboo through no fault of her own, she instantly becomes tainted, shamed and "other," excluded from society's sympathy and protection. It is humiliation heaped on degradation, leading — we will see — to a punitive isolation or exile.

Tamar appeals to what she hopes might be Amnon's remaining shred of decency, pleading with him not to cross the line from the civilized to the savage. *Such things are not done in Israel! Do not do such **a vile thing!*** This plea repeats another element in common with the Dinah story, the word *nevalah,* "a vile thing." She points out that *such a thing is not done in Israel!* Of course, laced as this episode is with ironies, Amnon's savage behavior is precisely the way the king of Israel *has* recently behaved. Amnon is even poised to out-do his father by further degrading himself and Tamar by violating the incest taboo.

> *"And I, where will I carry my shame? And as for you, you will be like any of the dissolute men in Israel! Now I beg you, speak to the king, for he will not withhold me from you!"* II Sam. 13:13

Tamar's second plea centers on Amnon's assault on *her honor.* In her naïveté she thinks she might have some success getting Amnon to shift his focus from the horror of the act itself to its consequences to *her*. She is not sufficiently worldly to appreciate that Amnon has not spared a whit of thought or feeling for her or her sensibilities or for the consequences the rape will have on the rest of her life. She appeals to a brother's concern for his sister's humiliation and degradation. Of course this argument falls on deaf ears.

Tamar's third plea is more to the mark. She shifts her argument to the fact that Amnon's violent act is sure to impair *his* own standing in the royal court as well as in the court of public opinion among the Israelite people. In effect she says to him, "Do not do this act, for if you do you will be the same as the dissolute and hopelessly depraved men who are at the bottom of the social ladder.[57] Do you want to be counted among them?! You will be the same as the person who cannot discern between what is true and what is a lie; one who cannot distinguish between good and evil, between fantasy and reality."[58]

Tamar is describing a disturbed personality. Tragically for her, this unheeding person is Amnon, her attacker. He is unresponsive to her eloquent pleas. He is too far gone; he has already forsaken his inhibitions and his social and filial responsibilities, and is focused solely on satisfying his obsessive prurient needs, to her eternal detriment.

One textual marker subtly pointing out Tamar's powerlessness is that her eloquent speeches are nowhere preceded by her name.[59] This contrasts with the speeches by the male actors in this episode, each of which carries the typical pattern of introduction: "Jonadab said, Amnon said, David said and Absalom said. Such a pattern occurs even where the pronoun *he* would suffice."[60] Yet Tamar's speeches are only preceded by the pronoun *she*. As powerful and *right* as her words are, she might as well be invisible as a speaker; she is only a body to Amnon. He does not hear her. Still, she keeps trying.

What can Tamar mean by her parting shot? She says, *"Now I beg you, speak to the king, for he will not withhold me from you."* Some interpret this to mean that Tamar must not be Amnon's half-sister after all.[61] Perhaps her mother Maacah was already pregnant by another man when David bedded and then wed her. Or perhaps this means that marriage to a half-sibling was permitted in Israel and Amnon had only to ask his father's permission so as to acquire Tamar legally.

The best understanding of Tamar's last argument is expressed by Don Isaac Abarbanel, writing in the 16th century. The commentator understood that what Tamar was doing was grasping at whatever straw she could. A frantic Tamar is about to be ravished. She understands that what Amnon is poised to do will end her life as effectively as if he were to run a sword through her heart. She has only seconds at most and there is no real hope of reprieve. For this reason she will promise anything, concoct any possible argument that might give her attacker pause and just perhaps save herself. "There can be no stone left unturned when a person's life is at stake," says Abarbanel.[62]

So a desperate Tamar says to Amnon, "If you are determined to have me, wait a bit and get permission to do this. For the king will grant you whatever you request, even to the extent of giving me to you in marriage. Only don't force me!"

Professor Trible[63] points up both the pluck and the pathos inherent in Tamar's speech: "Her words are honest and poignant; [yet] they acknowledge female servitude. Tamar knows Amnon can have her but pleads that he do it properly," via a special license from the king. If she is to be taken by force, she pleads that Amnon at least allow her to retain her public dignity by taking her in a proper marriage. Sadly, now that she is at the sword's point, the princess knows better than to aspire to justice; she would settle for wedlock.

AMNON FORCES TAMAR

Tragically and inevitably, Tamar's efforts are not sufficient to deflect Amnon. His eyes are blinded, covered with a red haze of lust; his blood is heated by the fire of his desire. He has plotted and waited and finally he has gotten Tamar alone and at his mercy. He would not be stopped, and the text tells us as much: *But Amnon would not heed her voice; he overpowered her by force, abused her and lay with her.* (II Sam. 13:14)

The succession of the three verbs of violation — Amnon *overpowered her by force, abused her and lay with her* — should remind us, yet again, of Shechem's rape of Dinah.[64] There, the Bible set out the pattern of three verbs of violation: *And Shechem . . . saw her, lay with her and took her by force.* The narrator in Samuel wants the reader to understand that an unambiguous sexual violation of a virgin is taking place here, as well. Amnon will take his place among the Bible's unredeemable villains. But what will happen to Tamar?

The *midrash*[65] fills in the details. Tamar is done with words. She tried that to no avail. Out of time now, she switches seamlessly to actions, pushing Amnon away with every bit of strength she possesses.[66] She uses her voice: she screams at the top of her lungs, hurling curses at Amnon, shouting for help. She uses her fists: she pummels his chest, his shoulders, his back. She uses her teeth and her nails: she bites his hands and arms, scratches his face and any part of his body that is exposed to her. She uses her legs and her knees, kicking out and protecting herself in the only way a woman victim can do.

In the story of Shechem's rape of Dinah the text says, first, that Shechem *lay with* Dinah, and then that he *forced* her (using the word *inuy*). As we discussed in Part Two, this meant that first he *forcibly* lay with her in the manner of a man with a woman, and that afterwards he forced her in the manner of a man with a man. Here, the Hebrew words are in reverse order, indicating that at first Amnon seeks to satisfy his lust by forcing Tamar from behind; he follows this with raping her face-to-face. It is likely, says the *midrash*, that Amnon first sought to preserve Tamar's technical virginity, but that this was not sufficiently exciting for him, so he turned her around and raped her again.

The Bible's use of the language of *inuy* or force is textual evidence that Amnon's attack was resisted; that Tamar fought her attacker at every step.[67] She never softened to him, she never accepted him, she never grew weary of fighting him off; every moment was an *inuy*, a forced invasion, a physical torture and a mental torment.[68] The *midrash* is uncompromising in its graphic depiction of Amnon's animalistic abuse of Tamar, of her heroic struggle to repel him, and implicitly, of her suffering.

AFTERWARD, AMNON HATED TAMAR

Immediately after attacking, raping, beating and abusing his half-sister, the Bible tells us that Amnon *loathed her with a loathing that was very great; his hatred for her exceeded the love that he had felt for her; and Amnon said to her, "Get up and go!"* (II Sam. 13:15)

What is the reason for Amnon's *volte-face*, for the lightning shift from obsessive "love" to excessive hatred?

Posited explanations run the gamut from the psychological to the physical. One explanation is that after abusing her with bestiality Amnon experienced a rush of guilt so that in his perverse mind his attack of Tamar somehow *became* "her fault." After his passion was spent Amnon couldn't accept his own heinous behavior, so he blamed Tamar for causing him to sink so low.[69] Another explanation is that in the course of the struggle Tamar cursed and insulted him.[70] However improbable it may seem, Amnon's immature "feelings" were wounded by the invectives hurled at him by the victim of his assault. Or perhaps Amnon "hated" Tamar simply because she rejected him.[71] It is likely that Amnon suffered from feelings of grandiosity and narcissism, so that Tamar's utterly rational, angry and terrified rejection of him ignited his hostility towards her. Perhaps Amnon felt some shred of remorse after he took his pleasure and release with Tamar. In Amnon's twisted psyche his remorse *became* self-loathing, which he in turn projected onto Tamar.[72]

Another possibility that rings with authenticity is that in the course of Tamar's desperate struggle she kicked, punched or bit Amnon in such a way that she did damage to his sexual organ. It is not difficult to imagine such a "lucky shot" occurring in the course of the violent rape and her heroic resistance, leading, in turn, to Amnon's howl of pain and angry, spiteful retaliation. According to the Talmud and Rashi,[73] Tamar actually emasculates Amnon in the course of the rape. In the Talmud's version an entangled pubic hair does the grave damage. Whatever the cause, it is doubtful that he is able to have sexual relations from that day forward. As far as the reader's sensibilities are concerned Amnon gets what he deserves.

But whether Amnon was completely emasculated or whether Tamar just got a bit of her own back in the course of her nightmare experience, the *midrash* is sending two implicit messages. First, that Amnon is so reviled that the rabbis have woven a scornful scenario where a woman's pubic hairs are able to un-man him! Amnon is *midrashically* hoist with his own petard. And second, that the rabbinic tradition holds Tamar to the special standard of a warrior. She is vanquished by her foe, but she does not go quietly. On the contrary, she does him much damage before the battle is done, and her act is recorded in the Talmud for generations to read and consider.

I agree with the interpretation that Amnon's excessive loathing after the rape is mainly a reaction to Tamar's having done him physical damage during her struggles with him. There might also be a small dose of guilt and avoidance, followed by his rewriting events to twist truth and responsibility, but Amnon's post-event anger and hatred is directed against Tamar for the reason that Tamar fought back and inflicted injury where it hurt her attacker most.

Modern scholars also appreciate and interpret Amnon's fickle exhibition of temper here. Gunn notes the "violent fluctuation" in Amnon's emotions, emphasizing that he is unbalanced; that his present loathing of Tamar is as overpowering an emotion for Amnon as his love for her was just hours before. "There is excess of love at the beginning, excess of hate at the end."[74] According to Trible, the violence and the hatred exhibited by Amnon are kindred emotions. "Violence in turn discloses hatred, [which is] the underside of lust . . . All along [Amnon's] desire was *lust*, not *love*. Having gratified itself, [his] lust deepens into hatred."[75] Alter is in awe of the story's remarkable psychological insight. The text has led us inexorably from Amnon's long-nursed obsession for a beautiful, forbidden virgin sibling to her violent rape. Because Tamar resisted so strongly "perhaps it has hardly been the fulfillment he dreamed of . . . The result is an excess of revulsion against Tamar, a blaming of the victim for luring him with her charms into all this trouble."[76]

The *midrash*[77] wonders if Tamar's injuring of Amnon such that he howled *Get up, go!* and hated her wasn't a blessing in disguise. For in so doing, whether Tamar's defensive act was deliberate or inadvertent, she tapped Amnon's loathing (what Trible calls "the flip-side of lust") and he banished her. Had he still nursed a love-obsession for her even after the rape it is possible he would have sought to wed her, as marriage to one's rapist with no possibility of him ever divorcing her was one way the ancient Israelite society protected the violated virgin against societal spurning, isolation and unmarriageability.[78] In such a situation — assuming David would even have agreed to the marriage — it would *not* have been practicable for Tamar's brother, Avshalom, to later kill Amnon to avenge her rape, for then she would have been left a widow! Also, had Amnon married Tamar he would thereby have gotten away with the rape, something the *midrash* seemingly has no taste for at this point.

The story's literary symmetry continues with Amnon's cruel command to Tamar that she *Get up, go!* The Hebrew word *lechi*, meaning "go!" echoes her father David's earlier command to her in verse 7 to *lechi!* or "go!" to Amnon's house and fix him a hearty meal. Tamar is twice-over the powerless victim, sandwiched between her father, the king, and her half-brother, the rapist. Both act willfully, without considering the consequences to her. David acts in character, the imperial personality protecting his crown prince, maneuvering Tamar to suit his needs, unwittingly enabling one child to violate the other. And Amnon mirrors David's *modus operandi* when he orders everyone from his chambers, traps Tamar, and abuses her mercilessly. He further reveals his sadistic nature when, afterwards, he brutally throws Tamar out.

Amnon's command to Tamar — *Get up, go!* — in verse 15 eerily mirrors (using antonyms) the "imperative verbs of sexual invitation"[79] he used in verse 11: *Come, lie.* His unholy desire for Tamar, long nurtured and banked, has finally found expression, and now he cannot be rid of her quickly enough.

A BATTERED TAMAR SPEAKS ONCE AGAIN

The Bible text is not done with Tamar yet. "This abused woman will no more heed Amnon's order of dismissal than she consented to his demand for rape. Nor does she allow anger to cloud her vision."[80] We hear from her one more time.

> And she said to him, "Please don't commit this wrong; to send me away would be even worse than the first wrong you committed against me." But he would not listen to her. II Sam. 13:16

The reader must imagine Tamar's situation. She has just suffered a brutal rape, during which she fought back and landed some blows. She is reeling emotionally — from the shock of having been attacked and violated by her half-brother — as well as physically — she is sore, bleeding and bruised. We appreciated Tamar's eloquence earlier, *before* Amnon raped her, but we must stand in awe of her now, *afterwards*, that she is able to once again marshal her thoughts and make a final attempt to salvage her future.

Imagine the disheveled Tamar bracing herself against a wall in Amnon's bed chamber and raising her other hand in an eloquent expression of beseeching. She is addressing the brutal young man whose acts of sexual abuse have left him unsatisfied and surprisingly, bloodied as well. Tamar says to him, "Do not do this evil act of sending me away. If you send me away *now*, you will compound the first wrong of forcing me, with another, *greater* wrong. Do not send me away!"[81] We note that this time her sentences are a bit muddled, as if she is stammering,[82] but this is understandable. She would be superhuman if she were unaffected by what she has just been through. The *midrash* tells us that Tamar watches Amnon preparing to throw her out the door, and she desperately appeals to him to pause and reconsider.

Tamar is acutely aware that by sending her out of his house as a "used" woman Amnon would be subjecting her to *public* humiliation. Whereas his initial act of rape was known only to the two of them and could remain her own *private* shame.[83] While Tamar's first, bootless speech prior to the rape spoke in terms of justice, Tamar avoids that concept now and seeks damage control. Tamar does not ask much; she seeks only to remain in Amnon's house at least until nightfall, so that the people passing in the street will not see her returning to the women's quarters and witness her shame.[84]

But just as he had spurned her words the first time Tamar spoke to him (verse 14), so, too, here (in verse 16) the Bible repeats the refrain that Amnon *does not wish to hear her voice.*

Tamar's beseeching words are barely past her lips when Amnon cuts into her little speech and calls out to his young servant saying, *"Get that woman away from me! [Take her] outside now, and bolt the door behind her!"* (II Sam. 13:17)

According to Fokkelman, by his violent and brutal act of rape Amnon reveals himself as a bullying egoist who is incapable of an intimate relationship. He spurns Tamar now because Tamar is the single witness to his secret! "Therefore, Amnon pushes his half-sister as far away as he can with his hate. The acute observer perceives fear of a confrontation" behind Amnon's mask of indifference when he expels her from his house.[85] Amnon does not even address Tamar by name; he refers to her as "that woman," treating the young woman who was the erstwhile object of his "love" with unmasked contempt. "She has become for him solely a disposable object . . . For Amnon, Tamar is a thing, a 'this' he wants thrown out . . . with the door bolted after her."[86] Paradoxically, the man who was so agonized early in the story because he loved his sister from a distance "is now oppressed by the idea that she might stay near him even one minute longer."[87]

Amnon is an unmitigatedly detestable figure. Literarily, he is the evil foil to Tamar's courageous innocence. "Amnon's repulsiveness is defined with a sharper outline by Tamar's clarity."[88] The Bible wants the reader to simultaneously appreciate, mourn and cheer for Tamar as we revile and despise Amnon. We have witnessed this scenario before — an innocent young woman destroyed by an amoral and spoiled roué-prince — but this time the victim is outspoken on her own behalf. If even *she* is not fated to be rescued, then the reason must be that the Bible is graphically showing us that the society these characters inhabit is utterly corrupt. David's punishment is raining down upon him; his sins are coming home to roost. His family is self-destructing before his eyes.

TAMAR IS SHUT OUT OF AMNON'S HOUSE

She was wearing a kutonet passim, *for maiden princesses were customarily dressed in such robes. And his servant brought her outside, and barred the door after her.*

And Tamar put dust upon her head, and she rent the kutonet passim *that she was wearing. She put her hands on her head as she walked about, crying aloud as she went.* II Sam. 13:18–19

The very tunic Tamar was wearing announced her royal and virgin status.[89] A *kutonet passim* was a multi-colored, appliquéed striped tunic or cloak that maiden princesses wore over their other clothing.[90] This beautiful, finely flowing and identifiable garment generally functioned as a badge and a shield, and bore an implicit warning: "Here walks one of the king's beloved virgin daughters. Let no one touch or molest her in any way, for she is the property of and under the protection of the king himself."

The reader has encountered such a distinctive, striped coat of many colors once before; the only other time such a garment is mentioned in the Torah. It appears in Genesis 37:3, when Jacob gives his beloved son, Joseph, a *kutonet passim*. Much has been written about this special cloak that Joseph wore. It was a mark of Jacob's special love for the boy, his son from his beloved wife, Rachel. Jacob gifted the cloak to him because it was known in the ancient Near East as a princely garment.[91] The boy Joseph was born to Jacob in his old age, and was all-the-more precious to him because his favored wife, the boy's mother, had been barren for many years. The cloak singled the boy out above all his brothers and prompted envy and rage in them, and cockiness and braggadocio in Joseph himself.

Importantly, Joseph's bloody and torn *kutonet passim* was the final proof that his brothers brought to their aged father to demonstrate unequivocally that their brother "was no longer."

As one would expect, the *kutonet passim* links the Joseph and Tamar stories with other common elements. In both stories the cloak is considered "royal" raiment,[92] especially calculated to point out the wearer's special or favored status, differentiating him or her from non-wearers. In both stories the coats are torn, providing mute evidence of brutal violence perpetrated against the wearer,[93] and in both stories the violence was done to the wearer by his or her siblings. Also in both stories the wearer is exiled or outcast.

Another revealing common element is that in both stories the word "love" features prominently and is a proximate cause of the violence against the wearer. With Joseph, the Bible says *Now Israel loved Joseph more than all his children, . . . and he made him a coat of many colors.* (Gen. 37:3) Regarding Tamar, the Bible says (II Sam. 13:1, 4, and 15) that *Amnon, son of David, loved [Tamar] . . . and Amnon said to [Yonadav]: I love Tamar, sister of my brother Av-shalom!* and once again, *And Amnon loathed her greatly; and his hatred for her exceeded the love that he had loved her. . . .*

Jacob's excessive love for his young son fomented in the boy's older brothers a deep hatred of him. While Jacob's sons perhaps subconsciously resented their father for his favoritism and for his rejection of them, they directed their anger and violence against their younger brother by throwing him into a desert pit and eventually selling him to a passing caravan. As for Tamar, Amnon's perverse love for his half-sister led him to violate and abuse her. After the rape, his excessive love turned quickly to excessive loathing, and he continued his abuse by literally throwing her out of his house. Amnon was filled with self-loathing following his rape of his sister, and this emotion found expression in his sadistic dismissal of her afterwards.

The *Zohar*[94] says, "Observe the consequences that followed the excessive love shown to Joseph by his father! . . ." Indeed, violence of brother against brother was the consequence. Jacob's preferential love should have been kept in his own heart. Certainly he should not have made his son a moving target by dressing him in the multi-colored, striped royal cloak. Likewise, Amnon's obsessive love for his half-sister should never have been allowed to surface. When it was vented, the consequence this time was violence of brother against sister, and in future years, as we will see, violence of brother against brother.

❈ ❈ ❈

Amnon's servant brought her outside . . . II Sam. 13:18

The brutish and spoiled prince Amnon orders his servant to do his dirty-work. One can imagine the servant scurrying to escort the battered woman from the bedroom through the antechamber, from there to the entrance hall, and then to the door. His servile act of ejecting Tamar is delayed because it does not follow in the text immediately after Amnon's command to "get her out of my sight!" Instead, the narrator allows us first to "see" Tamar's royal clothing, mentioning the striped tunic she and the other virgin princesses wore. It is as if the servant is seeing Tamar at the same moment we are, and he has been reminded of her royal status.

Perhaps he hesitates. What should he do? On the one hand, Tamar is a royal princess, daughter of the king, worthy of his obeisance. But on the other hand, Amnon is his autocratic, fickle master, and he is standing by looking on, in a fine rage, besides. Any fleeting compassion the servant might have had for the young princess is eclipsed by his fear of the prince. One would like to imagine that once out of Amnon's sight he puts his hand beneath Tamar's elbow, supporting her as he slowly walks with her to the front door. But it is more likely that he imitates his master's brutishness and thrusts her forcefully out the door as he was commanded.[95]

It is worth considering that if Amnon's servant was able to hear Amnon's call in verse 17 to take the girl and throw her out, it would follow that his other servants also were within ear-shot.[96] They heard her cries and her near-mortal struggle as she pled for her freedom and fought off her attacker. Where were the household servants while the rape was in progress? If the servants of prince Shechem were held to be complicit in his rape of Dinah and thus worthy of destruction by Shimon and Levy because they heard Dinah's cries but did nothing,[97] should not

Amnon's servants be held to the same standard? Amnon's entire household, including his cousin Yonadav, must have been keenly aware of the violence Amnon was perpetrating on Tamar that afternoon, yet not one of them came to her aid. This silent collusion spells doom not only for Amnon, but for his household, for the monarchy, and by extension for the corrupt Israelite society that tolerated such callous immorality against a person it was obliged to protect.

TAMAR MOURNS IN PUBLIC

And Tamar put dust upon her head, and she rent the kutonet passim *that she was wearing. She put her hands on her head as she walked about, crying aloud as she went.* II Sam. 13:19

The scene shifts abruptly from indoors to outdoors; from private domain to public. Tamar, Amnon's door to her back, her hair disheveled and her garments askew and bloodied, chooses the heroic stance rather than the expedient one. She bends down, scooping dust and ashes from the courtyard fireplace onto her head in the accepted expression of public grief. It is fairly certain this sheltered princess had never before put anything on her hair other than soap or unguents, yet by her action she signals that she is no longer the sheltered maiden princess she had been. She is now a victim of a brutal, incestuous rape.

Tamar is still wearing the *kutonet passim*, the appliquéed and undulating striped tunic attesting to her royal[98] and virgin status. We have seen that her special cloak is a clear textual echo of the Joseph story.[99] "Is it not remarkable that each person appareled in the *kutonet passim* was authorized by his or her father to perform a service and, during the performance, each was abused by brothers then cast out?"[100] Here we see Tamar after an obscenely true enactment of Joseph's brothers' ruse in Genesis: she *has*, in actuality, been attacked by "a wild animal"[101] and "is no more."[102] Tamar the maiden princess has been attacked and torn apart by Amnon, a human predator. The erstwhile maiden princess is "dead;" in her place is a violated and stained Tamar, who—again likened to Joseph who was sold to a passing caravan and was considered as good as dead — will be cast out, exiled from her familiar society.

The *midrash*[103] tells us that Amnon had stripped Tamar, leaving only her striped tunic in one piece. When he threw her out on the street she was wearing *only* the tunic and nothing else. Amnon intended to continue to debase her by sending her out in public nearly naked, in the manner of a common prostitute. If anyone had inquired, he had planned to deny responsibility, point to her deshabille, and accuse her, saying that *she* had seduced *him!*[104]

There is another fascinating interpretation of the *kutonet passim* that connects Tamar (and Joseph) to an early, sacred, or quasi-priestly function of dream interpreter and healer.[105] In both the Joseph and Tamar narratives the wearer of the *kutonet passim* has a special, extraordinary skill or function. Joseph interprets dreams, and Tamar is sent to perform a healing ritual. This interpretation would explain why, in Tamar's case, when Amnon proposed that his sister cook the healing pancakes and feed them to him *in person and by her own hand*, his request was unquestioned. The king did not suggest that another woman in his household bring Amnon his healing food; Tamar's unique healing power was an accepted fact, a gift she alone could bestow on the ailing Amnon. It would also explain why Amnon might have left her cloak intact, while ravishing Tamar and tearing everything else: the *kutonet passim* was the symbol of a princess, a "royal priestess whose duties included some sort of divine inquiry/ritual purification for ill members of the royal house."[106] Perversely, while he could ravish *her*, Amnon would not do violence to her royal healer's garment.

This exciting interpretation suggests that Tamar, daughter of David, was commissioned by the king as a "woman healer."[107] She was "an intermediary between an ill member of the royal family and YHWH [the Israelite God]."[108] She was permitted to venture from the house of the women, attired in her distinctively identifying *kutonet passim*, when specifically requested to make a house call, bringing her specially-prepared food to an ailing royal at his bedside. This would explain Yonadav's knee-jerk instruction to Amnon (13:5) *to feign illness*. He knew the pretense of illness was the only way Amnon would be permitted to be alone with the beautiful royal virgin. This also would explain Amnon's commanded "Leave us!" to his servants and hangers-on, and their immediate compliance. While they were no doubt anxious to remain and watch the ritual, at the prince's command for privacy they did not demur, and significantly, they did not hesitate to leave Tamar alone in a virile man's presence. She was a princess and a healer, and thus was an exception to the strict rules of cloister.

Tamar knows the proper way to display mourning and agony, and she embraces it. She cries out for her lost maiden self and for her lost future. She will never be a virgin bride; she fears no Israelite man will wed her now; she may never bear children, might never be a mother in Israel. She has been violated and shamed. With the dust trickling down her beautiful, stained face, she stands tall and crosses her arms, grasping the neckline of her striped tunic and tearing it apart in one pull. "This tearing up is a heavily charged gesture and especially symbolizes the violent loss of her virginity."[109] This, too, is an act of public mourning. Tamar hears the sound of the rent cloth and once again feels the pain of her rent maidenhood. In the words of the *midrash*,[110] she has been stripped of her honor as she now strips herself of her cloak. She places her bruised hands upon her soiled head and cries out in misery. In such a state "of her utter despair and defeatedness"[111] Tamar puts one foot in front of the other and walks back and forth on the public street.

Tamar's cry in verse 19 is called a *za'akah*. This word is special in the Bible, and is usually reserved for an anguished, hopeless, and primeval crying out. As we discussed in Part One, the hapless maiden of the Talmud issued the Bible's *za'akah*[112] after she had been tortured and brutalized by the Sodomites and left to die. This same *za'akah* appeared in the Bible when the Children of Israel were slaves in Egypt.[113] It was this *za'akah* that God finally heard and heeded after centuries of crushing bondage. It is said that such a cry, or *za'akah*, is an elemental, profound cry that catches God's ear.[114] God responded to the maiden in Sodom and to the Children of Israel in Egypt by bringing wholesale destruction upon Sodom and Egypt. Significantly, the offenses of both Sodom and Egypt included sexual transgression, a situation that is the centerpiece of our present story of Amnon's rape of Tamar. As we will see, the kingdom of David will be met with death and destruction as punishment for David's sins of abduction, adultery and murder; sins his sons are repeating in this story.

Fymer-Kensky suggests that Tamar's "crying out" is a brilliant tactical move. By making a public spectacle of herself immediately after the rape and with the gruesome physical evidence of the act still manifestly obvious on her person, Tamar consciously or subconsciously was saving herself *post hoc* in the only way she could. Under Middle Assyrian Law governing Israel's neighbors (this law was certainly known to the Israelites), a married woman who had been the object of a forced fornication could only be considered free of blame if she publicly declared that she had been forced.

Here, Tamar was a *betulah*, a maiden who owed her unblemished chastity to her father. If she had left the scene of the rape and silently returned to her house, washed herself off and said nothing, she could well have suffered future humiliation if her secret ever became known. For instance, what if Amnon were to announce that Tamar had seduced *him*, or that she had consented to the sexual liaison (something the *midrash* has suggested he planned to do)? What if nothing was revealed, but on her wedding night her groom discovered that she was not a virgin? Or failing that, what if she became pregnant from the forced encounter (it had happened to Batsheva, after all)? In all those potential scenarios a silent rape victim would be considered the wrongdoer rather than the wronged. Her only hope for societal survival (however liminal) was to "cry rape" *immediately*, exposing the rapist as well as her own physical fragility and shame to public scrutiny. For "the Bible does not condemn the victim of a rape. A girl who cries out when she is attacked is considered innocent of sexual wrongdoing."[115]

Tamar's *za'akah* announces and displays her as a victim. Her disheveled self is the best evidence of Amnon's crime against her.

Tamar's other action, her tearing of the *kutonet passim*, functions as a portent here. We have read with horror that crown prince Amnon raped and brutalized his virgin half-sister. The Bible now narrates loud and clear that this violated princess is left standing, ruined and wounded, clad in the *kutonet passim*, a recognized sign of royalty. When Tamar rends the royal tunic in public in verse 19 she is more than a tragic figure; she is the articulate, weeping prefiguring of the rending of the Davidic kingdom.

In diametric opposition to Amnon's behavior toward Tamar after he had abused her, we can cite Judah's redemptive public admission when the Tamar of Genesis was about to be burnt as a harlot at his command.[116] Judah announced, "She is more righteous than I!" and not only saved the earlier Tamar from further humiliation and death, but also reclaimed his place as progenitor of the monarchy. Not so Amnon, who never admits his sin or accepts responsibility for ruining his sister's life. With his outrageous, sadistic and unrepentant actions he forfeits both the monarchy and his own life.[117]

The Talmud[118] and *midrash* tell us that members of David's royal court witnessed Tamar's *za'akah* and keening grief and exclaimed one to the other, "If such a thing could happen to the king's daughter, surely it could happen to a commoner! And if it could happen to a modest girl like Tamar, how much more so could it happen to an immodest one?!" Realizing they had a duty to try to prevent such obscenities from occurring in the future, the courtiers arose at once and issued a decree that a man must not be closeted alone with an unmarried woman. To modern sensibilities this is not an ideal solution, as it skirts the presumption inherent in a society of laws that both men and women are expected to act in a civilized manner regardless of how many people are present in the room. The ancient Israelite ruling places the onus subtly on the shoulders of the woman, implicitly cautioning: Do not be alone with a man, as men cannot be expected to control themselves when in the presence of a woman.

Still, while the court's insight and legislation were too late to help Tamar, the ruling is perhaps one positive note in this symphony of perfidy and pain.

Tamar's brave public display of her own personal devastation and abuse has shut Amnon's mouth. His plan to turn the story around and say that she had seduced him was foiled *ab initio*. By walking out in public half-clad and with the caking blood, bruises and authentic shock evident on her face and in her gait, she made a heroic decision to repress her modesty and exhibit her humiliation; this was an unheard-of display. She deliberately chose to reveal to all Israel not only Amnon's evil deeds, but also the fact that she was forced.[119]

Tamar is centuries ahead of her time. It is only a relatively modern practice among police and forensic law enforcement personnel to encourage the rape victim to phone the police immediately after the attack, and to present herself at a hospital while evidence of the brutalization is still on her clothes and on her body. It is understandable and almost instinctual for the victimized woman to wish to throw away her torn and bloodied clothing and to shower off the evidence of her nightmare. But these days such a cleansing could destroy critical DNA evidence that could otherwise help to put the rapist behind bars.

We must recognize Tamar's prescient heroism. She is older than Dinah was, less cowed than Batsheva. She is a princess in Israel. She closes her eyes on her pain and shame and stands near the palace in public testimony against the crown prince. What will happen next?

AVSHALOM GIVES HIS SISTER SHELTER

And Avshalom her brother said to her, "Has Aminon [sic] your brother been with you?! For now, my sister, keep silent, for he is your brother. Don't eat your heart out over this thing." And Tamar remained alone and desolate in the house of Avshalom her brother. II Sam. 13:20

Almost immediately, Tamar's brother Avshalom hears his sister's cries, and sees her standing outside bereft, in her torn tunic. Avshalom is horrified, and instantaneously grasps the situation. It must have been known within the palace that Amnon was sickening for something and that the king had ordered Tamar to visit him to prepare him heartening food. Avshalom takes one look at his sister and puts two-and-two together. *Has Aminon [sic] your brother been with you?!* he asks her. Tamar's response is not recorded in the Bible text, but the reader can assume she nods or gives an assenting signal, because Avshalom hushes her, saying, *Now be silent, my sister, because he is your brother!* Avshalom probably enfolds Tamar in his own cloak to cover her shame, attempts to calm her, and brings her to safety within his own house.

We might infer from Avshalom's query that he came upon Tamar *before* she had had the chance to reveal to anyone the identity of her rapist.[120] Avshalom has two problems on his hands now. First is his beautiful, violated sister, and second is his willful and spoiled half-brother Amnon, who because of his position as crown prince is able to act with impunity. What is to be done?

The Bible allows the reader to appreciate Avshalom's thought process. Once the truth of what has happened dawns on Avshalom, he cannot bear to speak his brother Amnon's name, using, instead, a derogatory, pidginized version of it in verse 20. He asks Tamar, *Has your brother **Aminon** been with you?!* He cannot refer to Amnon without belittling his name and holding him in contempt. A petty affectation, perhaps, but understandable. Uttering someone's name gives that person dignity and consciousness. Avshalom refuses to vest Amnon with either.

Avshalom ensconces Tamar safely within his household with orders to bathe and pamper her, and for her to make his home her own. There is no question that she can never return to the house of the virgins. His immediate plan is that it would be better all-around for her to keep her silence and remain under his protection, for several reasons. First, she retains her royal dignity by keeping out of the public eye while she is in such a fragile post-traumatic state. Second, by keeping silent she keeps her brother Amnon's name out of the gossip mill.[121] Third, how could her "going public" with the rape in any way repair what has already been done to her?[122] And fourth, in counseling silence Avshalom is tacitly admitting that Tamar would have a valid legal claim. He also seems to be anticipating that his father, the king and judge, will fail in his duty to handle the matter juridically. This gives Tamar and the reader a hint of Avshalom's as-yet-unformed vigilante plans.[123] In brief, Avshalom reasons that no good will come to anyone if Tamar were to stand on a soapbox and reveal what Amnon has done to her.

It appears that Avshalom is implicitly tolerating his sister's rape by counseling her silence. He seems to be favoring the façade of family unity over facing down Amnon and bringing him to public justice. But Professor Trible reads the structure and substance of the entire story and comes to a different conclusion. To the contrary, she says; "in contrast to each of the other male characters [in this story], **Absalom is the *advocate* of Tamar**."[124]

First, Avshalom is Tamar's advisor, counseling silence. We must consider that his advice is an effective smokescreen for his plans for revenge. He counsels that Tamar not take the attack "to heart." That is, he counsels pretense, a course calculated to buy him time to achieve his unexplained purpose. Avshalom would lull Amnon into thinking he has gotten away with his crime.

We can infer Avshalom's state of mind from his speech. Avshalom employs euphemisms in his conversation with Tamar (*has Amnon **been with** you?* and *do not take **this deed** to heart*), speaking to his sister with a certain delicacy.[125] Rather than minimizing the crime, Avshalom's careful words actually "underscore the horror; [they] cover the unspeakable, even as Jonadab's innocent vocabulary [earlier] promoted rape."[126] We can see Avshalom as the counterpoint to the sinister Yonadav, who had earlier counseled Amnon and promoted pretense, thereby enabling the crime. Avshalom uses Yonadav's methodology to pay Amnon back in his own coin. Following Yonadav's counsel, Amnon employed planning, aforethought, pretense and manipulation; Avshalom takes a page from their playbook and bides his time.

Second, verse 20 opens and closes with the words *Avshalom, her brother*. This true "fraternal language" is an obvious antidote to the perversion of the word "your brother" used to identify Amnon the rapist in the same verse and earlier. Avshalom is literally surrounding, supporting and protecting Tamar where Amnon seduced Tamar into entering his bed chamber and then raped her. It is Avshalom's tenderness for his sister, according to Trible, that motivates his advice that Tamar keep her silence. We can appreciate that Avshalom seeks time to plan his revenge.

Modern sensibilities generally reject this reaction to a violent rape. While closing one's mouth and closing ranks may be a common reaction of family members of victims of abuse and rape, criminal and psychological experts believe that serious consequences will almost certainly redound if such a course is followed.[127] From a criminal standpoint the unpunished perpetrator could become emboldened and might repeat his violent act, or even escalate his behavior with other victims. And from the standpoint of the psyche of the victim, nowadays she is counseled with sensitivity and encouraged to work through her fear, shame and rage, with the goal of eventually becoming healed sufficiently to re-enter society.

Unfortunately, as regards the specific subset of victims of *familial* rape and other victims of domestic sexual abuse, the destructive conspiracy of silence is mostly the norm, regardless of modernity or socioeconomic position. Tamar appears to be caught between the horrific rape by one brother and the stubborn silence of the other brother. She is as helpless to countermand Avshalom's order as she was to prevent Amnon's abuse. Looking at Tamar from twenty-first century hindsight, we see that "Tamar is trapped by family. Raped by a close family member, she is denied her right of reaction . . . To Amnon she was an object of lust and then hate; to Absalom, she is a crisis that has to be contained."[128]

But in biblical times, the practical method of dealing with any rape victim was for the woman's closest male relation to open his home and heart to her. We recall that Dinah's brother, Shimon, took her into his home and gave her lifelong protection, familial love and society. And here, Avshalom is doing the same for his sister, Tamar.

Avshalom is the only character who speaks in the narrative after Amnon has thrown Tamar out of his house. Tamar has run out of words, she is all raw emotion. David will grow angry, but he does not speak. And Avshalom will never again exchange a word with his brother Amnon, who himself is mute in the text. After nineteen verses of dialogue and action, we are met only with silence from the main characters for two years after Amnon's brutal crime! The only voice we hear is Avshalom speaking carefully and protectively to his sister Tamar in verse 20.

It is a great relief that Avshalom takes charge. Throughout this chapter Tamar has been acted *upon* to sinister ends by the other royal men in her life, with her father, the king, playing the pivotal role of unwitting but imperious enabler to the evil prince Amnon. David twice *ordered* Tamar: first, to go to Amnon's house, and second, to prepare food before his eyes. Then, it was the rapacious Amnon who lured the obedient and unsuspecting Tamar into his bed chamber and attacked and raped her, afterwards rejecting her.

Finally, with Avshalom's speech in verse 20, we have a male actor who uses his princely power and prerogative in order to protect Tamar. It is this behavior that distinguishes Avshalom from his father and brother. He comforts and shelters his sister, "even though he cannot reverse [her] desolation."[129]

Of course, there is one additional mode of behavior that the biblical rape victim's closest brothers also engage in: they plot and execute revenge. Avshalom may have cautioned his sister to be silent; he may in fact hold his own tongue for the next two years, as we will see. But he is by no means done with the matter. We will examine Avshalom's response in coming pages.

TAMAR IS SILENT AND DESOLATE

And Tamar remained alone and desolate in the house of Avshalom her brother. II Sam. 13:20

Tamar is the beautiful princess who up to now has been seen moving with ease from one house to another. She bakes, cooks, heals, speaks eloquently, and she acts heroically. Yet the reader watches as, swiftly and tragically and right before our eyes, Tamar literally and psychologically becomes "locked-in." The Bible uses the word *vateshev*, meaning "she settled in" when it tells us that Tamar *remained alone and desolate in the house of Avshalom*. This house of refuge appears to be her last stop. She has been transformed from a traveling healer-of-the-sick to one who never leaves her own small space within her brother's house just outside the city.[130] Tamar's world has shrunk to the size of the four cubits comprising her personal space. No one attempts to enter her private universe of agony, betrayal, loneliness, and shame, nor does she invite anyone in.

Zornberg has written that the "dark image of desire [is] feminine, helpless, wordless."[131] In this, a third retelling of a story of biblical rape (Parts 2 and 4 of this book have dealt with Dinah's and Batsheva's stories, respectively), we see that even Tamar, the one victim who speaks up to deflect her rapist, is eventually struck silent, as were her two biblical predecessors *ab initio*. Zornberg's statement rings true this third time, as well. We have seen Amnon's brutal and violent desire, lust, and putative "love" render Tamar—the feminine object of his forcible taking— "helpless and wordless."

The Torah laconically tells us that Tamar is *shomemah*: this single word tells the reader that she is empty, alone, desolate, depressed.[132] It is used here to describe her existential state of being, but more typically it is used to describe empty, burned-out cities where nothing is left standing; not a single tower, nor even a fruit tree; a place that is bereft of all signs of life.[133] This chapter opened with the statement of Tamar's beauty, a gift that others could behold. Yet through no fault of her own it was her innocent beauty that became the trigger of her downfall once the dissolute and evil Amnon beheld her. Ironically and tragically, her story is drawing to a close with the image of her beautiful face locked away from society or from anyone outside Avshalom's household.

Amnon has "ruined" Tamar more than just in a sexual sense, as heinous as that is. By manipulating Tamar's own sisterly feelings for him (she was, after all, vising a sickbed, cooking for her brother specifically to bring him back to health), he *used the victim* to pave the way for her own degradation! Amnon thus has shattered Tamar's trust in her family, undermining her social scaffold. Every time she relives the events of that day, she must relive her own innocent compliance with her father's and brother's requests. How deep the betrayal must cut! Amnon ignored their filial bond and his role as brother-protector. He manipulated their father into leading his beautiful daughter to her defilement. Amnon scorned societal taboos, and brutalized Tamar ruthlessly. He has literally slammed the door on his trusting, innocent sister and left behind an emotional and physical "ruin."[134] This, too, is the meaning of the word *shomemah*.

If all that were not enough for one person to bear, one *midrash*[135] suggests that Tamar's neighbors are whispering that perhaps Tamar was responsible for her own defilement; or that her misfortune was a divine punishment and that she never was as pure as she had appeared. These unjust rumors (the "blame-the-victim" phenomenon), perhaps put into play by Amnon himself, unfortunately tend to bedevil victims of abuse and rape, causing or exacerbating intense feelings of worthlessness and shame.

Tamar is *shomemah*. She sits alone, ruined, while palace life and Israelite life continue to swirl around her. She is apart from it all, shamed, shunned and "other." In Trible's words, "she lives in death."[136] One *midrash* interprets *shomemah* to include the fact that Tamar remains alone and *unmarried* for the rest of her life.[137] This unmarried state is in itself a desolation, because Tamar will never become a mother in Israel. Amnon has sentenced her to the societal purgatory of non-virgin and non-wife.

The Bible has shown us how quickly a life — and by extension, a society — can be ruined. In the space of less than a day we saw Tamar inhabiting the **house** of the women, where she was a beautiful virgin princess and *daughter*; then she was commanded to enter the **house** of Amnon, where "she became a violated *thing*."[138] And finally, she is taken to the **house** of Avshalom, where "she is a desolate *sister*."[139] She is a woman who has done violence to no one yet has herself become a victim of violence. Tamar is *shomemah* because her "selves," her identities, have been betrayed, and with bewildering swiftness.

Is it any wonder, then, that Tamar is willing herself to disappear! Tamar cloisters herself in Avshalom's house and becomes a recluse.

THE AFTERMATH: DAVID'S REACTION

And David, the king, heard about all these things and he became very angry.
  And Avshalom did not speak with Amnon either about good things or bad, because Avshalom hated Amnon for the reason that he forced his sister, Tamar. II Sam. 13:21–22

We are in a topsy-turvy palace world where the king can take to his bed the wife of one of his prized soldiers, plot and arrange the murder of the unsuspecting husband, and remain in power. We are in a palace universe where a prince can rape his sister, the princess, in broad daylight and nobody speaks of the matter or brings the offender to justice. After reading of these things one might presume that we will be inured to news of the king's apathy.

But no, reading verse 21 *(and David became very angry)* we are hopeful that the king has learned from his own chastisement at the hands of the prophet Nathan in chapter 12. We are hopeful that the very next verse will outline David's further reaction; surely it will describe the punishment that he has meted out to Amnon, or at a minimum will disclose his comforting words to his suffering daughter. And the reader is disappointed when not a word is spoken or any action taken against Amnon.

The reader is disappointed, but not really surprised, for several reasons. First, in Part Two of this book we encountered a similar paternal reaction when we read of Jacob's reaction after the rape of his daughter, Dinah.[140] Second, after our analysis of David's taking of Batsheva and the king's cold-blooded murder of her husband in Part Four, we have taken the measure of this man, David. We measure his present behavior against his own prior immoral actions. We don't expect him to come to the defense of a ravished girl or take to task the royal who ravished her; it cuts too close to the bone. It is not likely that he will now censure or punish his firstborn son for acting as he himself has done. And third, the crown prince has modeled the behavior he has learned from his father. David will surely make excuses for his heir.

The *midrash* is troubled by David's silence and, dissatisfied, it fills in the gap itself. Abarbanel posits that David did, perhaps, admonish Amnon, but that his reason for not meting out punishment was a practical one: there were no witnesses (other than the victim) who would come forward to testify against him.[141] Punishment in such a situation and at that time would not have been possible. Astonishing as it may seem to modern readers, it is only in very recent years — within the last quarter-century in Anglo-American jurisprudence and not by any means in all jurisdictions — that a rape victim's testimony is sufficient to convict the accused aggressor without corroboration by additional witnesses. Tragically but plausibly, a rapist in biblical Israel could have walked away from his crime if no witnesses existed to the act or if none came forward to corroborate the victim's accusation.

The verse says that *King David* **heard about all these things** *and he was very angry*. What precisely did David hear? In chapter 11 we saw that the king's surveillance network must have been extremely efficient, as he knew almost to the moment where Uriah slept and where he went. The king's "messengers" — read "informers" — were ubiquitous and active in that story. Can we assume that here, several years later, David still has that measure of control over his palace? Probably not. On the contrary, we had best acknowledge that the king's power over his staff as well as over his offspring is weakened. The Torah has just allowed us to witness how Yonadav and Amnon were able to manipulate and trick David with ease. So it is not merely academic to be curious about what the king "heard."

There are several opinions about *what David heard* that would have elicited such anger in him. The *p'shat*, or straightforward explanation of the text, is that David heard about Amnon's rape of Tamar, and he was "appalled"[142] that his son had done such a thing.

The reader begins to appreciate that David the king "hears" what he wishes to hear. If he is blinded by the fact that Amnon is heir-apparent,[143] he will not hear the truth: that crown prince Amnon plotted and executed the vile and lawless act against princess Tamar and he must be brought to justice. That David does not "hear" this truth elicits outrage among modern scholars. Trible writes that because David is blinded by his love for his firstborn, he has "complete sympathy for Amnon and total disregard for Tamar."[144] Or perhaps David saw that his own hands were far from clean in similar circumstances; that for this reason he did not see himself as worthy of meting out punishment or reprimand to Amnon.[145] Indeed, Gunn says that David's own "sin has come home to roost."[146] In Trible's words, "The father identifies with the son; the adulterer supports the rapist; male has joined male to deny justice for the female."[147]

Alter sounds the knell of doom, echoing yet again the Dinah story. "In all this, the rape of Tamar plays exactly the same pivotal role in the story of David as does the rape of Dinah in the story of Jacob. *Jacob, too, 'hears' of the violation and does nothing*, setting the stage for the bloody act of vengeance carried out by his sons Simeon and Levi."[148]

Perhaps David "hears" and heeds the twisted, false rumors that it was Tamar who enticed Amnon. If David blinds himself to the truth and favors this mendacious version of reality, it might explain why, other than exhibiting anger, David takes no action either to punish Amnon or to comfort Tamar.[149]

David hears . . . and **becomes very angry**. As we have seen, depending upon what David allows himself to hear and to believe, his anger could variously have been directed at Amnon, at Tamar, at himself, at Nathan the Prophet, or even at God. Perhaps David's anger was directed *inward*, at himself. David is aware, on some level, that *he* bears responsibility for the downfall of two more of his children in the aftermath of his sins of taking Batsheva and killing Uriah. He appreciates that *his* deeds began this tragic spiral. The *midrash* interprets the king's anger as signaling that he sees the rape by Amnon and the devastation of Tamar as part of the inevitable fulfillment of *his* fourfold punishment predicted by the prophet Nathan.[150] A third interpretation is that David's anger is kindled after he hears the twisted and fabricated version of events: that his daughter Tamar had initiated the sexual encounter with Amnon![151]

But still David takes no action. This king and father takes no action, makes no remonstrance, gives no comfort. His anger goes nowhere. We will see that David's "imponderable silence"[152] will lead to even more violence and tragedy for his family and his monarchy.

The reader is therefore unsatisfied with verse 21 and is disgusted with the king. "Hearing" followed by unspecified and undirected "anger" are unjust responses of a father to stories of his daughter's rape at the hands of his firstborn son. The last time we witnessed David's anger was in response to Nathan's parable in 12:5 (Part Four above). There, David exploded with knee-jerk anger (in the same language as he does here in 13:21) upon hearing of the injustice of the rich man's having taken the poor man's only ewe lamb. There, David-the-judge responded instinctively and correctly as to gravitas of sin and rectitude of punishment. The reader is therefore entitled to assume that this selfsame David, king and judge, exhibits anger here because he likewise perceives the situation as it is: his crown prince has grievously sinned against his daughter, ruining and shaming her, himself, the monarchy, and David's family entity.

A heinous injustice has been perpetrated. That the Torah reflects David's failure to act in response to this knowledge tells us that David is wrongly constrained by other, supervening needs. The most obvious supervening drive, as we discussed above, is probably David's blind love for Amnon, his firstborn son.

The *midrash* also is unsatisfied with David's reaction. That he was *very angry* is mere empty emotion if it is not followed by the administration of justice. So the *midrash* tells us that the reason David did not act against Amnon is that he knew Amnon was subject to *God's justice* for his sin against Tamar.[153] David ignores his daughter's distress, but as for Amnon David knew that he was due the mandatory penalty of *mitat karet*,[154] the divine punishment of excision or premature death for raping his half-sister. David must be thinking that nothing he could mete out to Amnon could equal or exceed the impending punishment of *karet*. So David does nothing. This rationale is weak and unsatisfying. It is the duty of citizens of a law-abiding society to hold every member of that society accountable for their actions, be he king or commoner. David, as king of Israel, has a sworn obligation to execute justice even as against his son. For what use are laws if they fail to protect the weak against the aggressor? David owed his daughter Tamar the full protection of his rank. He failed her and his kingdom by doing nothing.

The reader is aware that David's own sins are destroying his children and his "house." The reader as well as David will have counted two-down, and we wait for the other shoes to fall. Will Amnon be next? If so, how will he meet his fate?

THE AFTERMATH: AVSHALOM'S SILENCE

And Avshalom did not utter a word to Amnon, good or bad, for Avshalom hated Amnon because he had [sexually] violated his sister Tamar. II Sam. 13:22

After she is locked out of Amnon's house, Tamar speaks no more. The only sound we hear is her keening *za'akah* or cry. Neither does David the king speak; we are told only of his great anger. Likewise Avshalom, who we learn in verse 22 speaks not a word to Amnon, feeling only hatred towards him. David and Avshalom are literally choking on their emotions. The Bible does not tell us who or what is the object of David's anger, but it positively identifies the object of Avshalom's hatred: it is Amnon, *because he [sexually] violated his sister Tamar.*

There is a curious inverse symmetry in this episode's description of its main characters' speech and emotions. Unusual for the Bible narratives, the first half of chapter 13 is largely dialogue and monologue between and by the main characters. Curiously, though, the characters' emotions are monochromatic, either black or white, love or hate. In contrast, in the second half of the chapter the characters are silent; oddly, the only person who speaks after the rape scene is not one of the actors in the rape drama itself. Examining this asymmetry of speech and silence, of emotion and action, could give us a clue to what is coming next.

At the beginning of this incident, **Amnon** did much **speaking** as he misdirected David and prepared to trap Tamar. David heard him but did not perceive the trick that lay beneath Amnon's words. **David** also spoke, but only to Tamar, issuing the fateful commands to prepare the healing food and go to Amnon's house. Then, when Amnon sprang his trap, **Tamar** did quite a lot of speaking—she tried to dissuade Amnon from committing incest and rape—but Amnon deliberately would not listen to her. This sequence is repeated after the rape when Tamar again speaks to Amnon, pleading with him not to send her away. Again Amnon refuses to hear her words. Amnon speaks again, this time to his servants: first to dismiss them, and then to command one of them to throw Tamar out and lock the door behind her.

Regarding **emotions**, the Bible tells us only of "love" and its polar opposite. We are told that "**love**" was the reason Amnon planned and executed the rape of his beautiful virgin sister; and that after he raped her he "**hated** her even more than he had loved her." And we are told that when David hears of all this, he is "very **angry**."

There is a serious flaw, an emotional and moral disconnect in David and his family, that is tragically manifest in the rape of Tamar and in David's non-reaction to it, as we have just discussed. This flaw also is evidenced in the crescendo of words followed by the crash of silence among the characters in chapter 13.

In fact, here, on the "other side" of the action, words have become *scarce*. The Bible tells us that **Tamar**, the eloquent one, is done with speaking; her words have fallen on deaf ears and have dried up; instead she cries out in existential anguish and desolation. Without words, she is all raw agony. **Avshalom**, a silent brother until that moment, is the only character who speaks now. He addresses Tamar, ironically counseling *silence*. As for **David**, when he hears what happened, this father of the three actor-siblings is himself *all feeling*—he is "greatly incensed"[155]—but he remains mum; he is utterly silent. From **Amnon**, the evil brother,

we likewise hear not a word. As for **Avshalom**, verse 22 reinforces the characters' deafening silence by telling us that he, too,
like the other main characters, is silent, choking on a surfeit of
hatred. He cannot speak a word to Amnon *because he hates Amnon,
on account of [Amnon's] sexual violation of his sister Tamar.*

Amnon's atrocious act has created a vacuum, where it seems
words cannot breathe. The articulate, tragic heroine can only cry
out in pain; the evil brother who refused to heed his victim's pleas
is himself given the silent treatment; and the king, so accustomed
to giving orders, is struck dumb. Only the internal "sound" of
roiling passions — in modern idiom, the "sounds of silence" — are
given voice in the text: pain, betrayal, desolation, anger, love and
loathing.

This reversal — silence now replaces words — perhaps
embodies the calm before the storm, signaling a coming retribution. The characters are in waiting; perhaps they wait for
comfort, or for forgetfulness; surely they await punishment and
justice, inevitably they wait and plot revenge when none of the
others are forthcoming.

Verse 22 says *Avshalom did not utter a word to Amnon, good or
bad.* The next verse tells us this state of limbo, of silence and
inaction, persists for two years! The *midrash* tells us that Avshalom's failure to speak to his brother causes Avshalom's hatred
of his brother and anger and resentment of his father to grow and
mushroom within him, paving the way for future tragedy.[156] We
can contrast Avshalom's silence with the earlier biblical tale of
brotherly strife between Joseph and his older brothers. In Gen.
37:4 we learned that the brothers *hated him; so they **could not speak
a friendly word to him.*** The elements of hatred and silence are
common to both narratives, but with a difference. In Genesis,
Joseph's brothers have not yet reached the stage of cutting off *all*
communication with Joseph. They still speak to him, even if it is
in angry exchanges; via even hostile words Joseph's brothers give
vent to some of their pent-up resentment. But Avshalom does not
allow himself this outlet; he hoards and suppresses his hatred.
Maimonides[157] and the *midrash*[158] perceive an important psychological consequence from this difference in anger management.

Perhaps the brothers were able to pull back at that last moment from killing Joseph because some of their hatred had been released by their speech. In contrast, perhaps Avshalom's volcanic hatred of Amnon—however justified—allowed of only one solution: fratricide.

TWO YEARS PASS

And it came to pass after two full years, that Avshalom had sheepshearers in Ba'al Hazor, which is near Ephraim. And Avshalom invited all the king's sons. II Sam. 13:23

Avshalom is careful and patient. He has waited daily, weekly, monthly for his father the king to seek out Amnon and mete out punishment for the rape of Tamar, but no punishment has been forthcoming. Nor has the king sent word to Tamar inquiring about her health; nor has he even spoken of the incident to Avshalom. The incident is simply ignored. Avshalom returns to his house every night and visits his sister Tamar in her chambers; he asks after her health, and watches as her youthful beauty settles into sadness and resignation. He knows she looks at him with only one unarticulated question in her eyes: Has Amnon been punished? Avshalom is sick with impotence; he cannot give her the answer she seeks, and he cannot act against Amnon as long as the king, his father, still protects his crown prince from harm.

So Avshalom banks his anger and resentment against his father the king, and he hides his deep hatred for his half-brother Amnon, both of whom he must see frequently at court occasions. Avshalom keeps his personal contact with Amnon to a minimum; he does not trust himself to speak to Amnon and not give away his true feelings of abhorrence.[159] Avshalom has a half-formed plan in his mind. He intends to wait until the time is right and then he will strike. Avshalom is prepared to be as cunning as his cousin Yonadav and as dissembling as his brother Amnon.

For months after the rape Amnon was on his guard against Avshalom; he fully expected that his half-brother would retaliate against him for the rape of his sister.[160] As a result, Amnon went nowhere unescorted and did not shut his eyes at night without a bodyguard camped nearby.

Avshalom trained himself to smile at his hated brother, even to flatter him when the need arose.[161] And inevitably, as no backlash occurred and no reprisal was forthcoming, Amnon let down his guard. Amnon faced no admonishment from the king and no attempt at retribution from Avshalom, so he came to believe that he had gotten away with the rape. All this played into Avshalom's plan.

AN INVITATION TO THE SHEEP-SHEARING

> *And Avshalom came to the king and said, "Behold now, your servant has sheep-shearers; let the king, I beseech you, and his servants, go with your servant."*
>
> *And the king said to Avshalom, "No, my son, let us not all go now, lest we be a burden to you." And he pressed him, but he would not go, but he blessed him.*
>
> *Then Avshalom said, "If not, I pray you, let my brother Amnon go with us." And the king said to him, "Why should he go with you?"*
>
> *But Avshalom pressed him, so that he let Amnon and all the kin's sons go with him.* II Sam. 13:24–27

Avshalom set his sights on the annual spring rite of the sheep-shearing festival as the perfect time to make his move. It was "a grand occasion,"[162] the traditional time of drinking and celebration[163] following the hot and dirty work of the wool-harvest. It was a festival which everyone attended, from high-born to servant.[164] Avshalom allowed the event to pass by without incident the *first* year after the rape, but was looking to the festival marking the *second* anniversary of the rape as his time to strike. It was critical to Avshalom's plan that Amnon feel secure and unthreatened, that no one suspect that Avshalom still harbored a grudge against him, and that the king not feel the need to protect his crown prince from Avshalom's hostility. So Avshalom wore a smile and kept his hatred secret.

As preparations by Avshalom's sheep shearers in Ba'al Hazor crescendoed, he sent out invitations to all the king's sons—his fellow princes—to join him at his table during the festivities.[165] Avshalom's shepherds had enjoyed a bumper season, and his lavish feast was an anticipated event. As a smokescreen, Avshalom extended a personal invitation to the king himself, asking David to bring along his royal retinue and to grace his table at Ba'al Hazor. By the act of extending a sincere invitation to the king, Avshalom intended to put both the king *and Amnon* at ease. Certainly if Avshalom invited his father, the king, to attend the festival along with his guards and all the princes, it was to be a jolly gathering, and no one would have cause to suspect that he intended any harm.[166]

In fact, as we read in Part Three, attendance at the sheep-shearing festival can mark the end of a mourning period,[167] as it did for Judah. There was every reason for David, Amnon and the princes to perceive Avshalom's invitation to attend his sheep-shearing festival as an indication that he was prepared to let bygones be bygones and repair relations with his father and brother.

Avshalom was counting on the king *declining* the invitation. It was not typical or even appropriate for the king and his court to sit at the revelers' table during the sheep-shearing feasts.[168] Also, Avshalom had observed David's "increasingly sedentary habits"[169] and assumed he would stay in Jerusalem rather than bestir himself to make the trip all the way to the mountains of Ephraim.[170] Still, when the king declined, saying he did not wish to burden Avshalom with his royal retinue, Avshalom played the game, pressing his father to change his mind and come along to the festival. Fortunately for Avshalom's scheme, the king still refused to attend, but he gave Avshalom his blessing of godspeed.

This was the moment Avshalom had waited for these two long years. Keeping his face free of expression, his eyes level with the king's, and his roiling emotions hidden behind his cool manner, Avshalom asks, "Well then, if your majesty cannot come with us, please allow Amnon my brother to attend." To wit the king snaps a reply, "Why should Amnon go with you?"

From the standpoint of protocol, it is wholly legitimate for Avshalom to request Amnon's presence at the festival. As the crown prince, Amnon is not included in a general invitation with the rest of the princes; he stands in a place of honor second only to the king.[171] If David elects to stay in Jerusalem, Amnon can properly stand in for the king at the festival.[172] Still, we can detect, from the king's quick, challenging response, that he might have had an inkling of suspicion of Avshalom's motive for pressing for Amnon's presence.[173] But David brushes his hesitation aside and allows Amnon and all the princes to go to the sheep-shearing in Ba'al Hazor. Really, nothing is amiss. After all, the king has swept Amnon's vile act against Tamar under the proverbial palace rug, and Avshalom has given no sign that he still holds a grudge two years later against his half-brother. Avshalom's plan is working perfectly.

The clever David, who in chapter 11 manipulated people and events to suit his purposes even to the plotting and killing of Uriah, is himself *twice* duped and manipulated by his own sons in chapter 13. First he is easily fooled by the malingering Amnon, and now he is gulled by the vengeful Avshalom. **Twice, then, David "sends" his children to be killed.** First he commanded or sent Tamar to Amnon's house, where Tamar was effectively "murdered" by Amnon. While her corporeal self remains in Avshalom's house, her soul, her spirit, her trusting nature, her future life, have been snuffed out.[174] And as we are about to see, the rapacious and evil Amnon will in turn be slain while carousing at Avshalom's sheep-shearing, where he is sent by his father, David.

David's warrior instincts have become dulled. Both times he never saw the trickery coming. Now his sons are champing at the bit, poised to take the lead, anxious for succession. If they follow in their father's footsteps — and the present incident tells us that they have learned how to behave from watching their father at work — it does not bode well for the monarchy or for Israel.

AVSHALOM AVENGES TAMAR

Now Avshalom had commanded his servants, saying, "Mark you now when Amnon's heart is merry with wine, and when I

*say to you, 'Smite Amnon!' then kill him! Fear not; have not
I commanded you? Be courageous, and be valiant!"*

*And Avshalom's servants did unto Amnon as Avshalom
had commanded. Then all the king's sons arose, and every
man got himself up on his mule and fled.* II Sam. 13:28–29

Avshalom is in his tent at Ba'al Hazor. As he watches the
controlled chaos of the business of the sheep-shearing and the
hubub of his servants' festival preparations, he reflects momentarily on the ease with which he has come to the verge of
achieving his goal. The king as well as Amnon have fallen for his
play-acting. His father really was "over the hill," he thought. The
fearless young man who slew Goliath bore no resemblance to the
father and king he knew. It was time for the next generation to
take over the throne of Israel. Not only that, but the man was
spineless, letting his daughter's rapist go unpunished. And all
because Amnon was next-in-line to be king. For heaven's sake,
the king had a raft of princes ready to succeed him! Amnon was
dissolute, rash, and a bully. Not only that, but Amnon, too, was
losing his edge. Two years ago Amnon would not have given
Avshalom the time of day, so afraid was the crown prince of
reprisal or of being caught off-guard by the brother of the girl he
had attacked and raped. But time has caused Amnon to forget,
and the wine at tonight's party would further dull his reflexes.[175]
Amnon's hours are numbered.

Tonight, thought Avshalom. Tonight he would strike a blow
for his sister Tamar. Perhaps then she would be able to smile, to
speak, to walk with her head up outside in the open square. He
had not heard her utter a word since the day he had followed the
almost-inhuman sound of her cry, and had found her wandering
up and back in front of the palace with her clothes in tatters and
her fingernails torn. Since that day she had sat by the window in
her spacious bedroom in his house, and other than submitting to
the gentle ministrations of her servant and allowing *him* to check
on her well-being, she could not tolerate human company.
Tonight, thought Avshalom, Amnon would pay the price for
Tamar.

Avshalom is brought out of his reverie by the voice of one of his personal guards. "You sent for us, O Prince." The charismatic prince Avshalom had known and fought alongside these six men since they had first picked up swords as young lads over a dozen years ago. He trusts them with his life, and they reciprocate with unwavering fealty. Avshalom fastened the tent flaps behind them and the men closed rank in a huddle around him.

"Tonight is the night," he told them. "Tonight we avenge my sister. You must drink sparingly, but do not allow anyone to be the wiser. Sit close to prince Amnon, keep watch and be ready. I have instructed the wine steward to keep Amnon's cup filled throughout the festivities. You will know when he has drunk too much wine because that is when he will begin grabbing at the serving girls. They will not smile, for we all have seen how he deliberately hurts them, but neither will they cry out in pain. He will shout lewd comments, and he might even knock over a few wine goblets. He disgraces the monarchy.[176]

"One of you will be watching *me*, and when I give the agreed-upon signal,[177] the man I have selected from among you will wield my personal sword that I have entrusted to you. You will make certain you are closest to Amnon, and you will run my sword[178] through Amnon's heart, killing him. The others of you will guard me, watching all of our backs. We will all of us stand up and calmly but quickly back out of the tent. The place will be in an uproar, but no one will raise a finger against us. The other princes despise Amnon as we do, and they are selfish and weak. They will fear for their own lives. But you will fear nothing, my comrades. You are acting at my command.[179] Comport yourselves as brave and fierce fighting men, and bring credit to our regiment and our honor. We will not fail."

And Avshalom's soldiers follow his orders precisely. As Amnon slumps in his throne-chair at the head of the long table, his lifeblood staining his tunic and the tablecloth, the king's other sons jump up in shock, knocking over their chairs in their haste to escape. It was as Avshalom had predicted: all the princes scattered like frightened geese, and in a matter of minutes the festival tent was deserted. The other princes are so unfilial that their flight is every man for himself! Each prince jumps onto his own donkey, raising dust in their stampede down the mountain, as the night falls over Ba'al Hazor.

DAVID HEARS A RUMOR OF A MASS KILLING

And it came to pass, while they were on the way, that news came to David, saying, "Avshalom has slain all the king's sons, and there is not one of them left."

Then the king arose, and tore his garments, and lay on the earth; and all his servants stood by with their clothes rent.

And Yonadav, the son of Shimah, David's brother, answered and said, "Let not my lord suppose that they have slain all the young men, the king's sons; for only Amnon is dead. For at the command of Avshalom this has been determined from the day that he defiled his sister Tamar.

"Now therefore let now my lord the king take not this thing to his heart, thinking that all the king's sons are dead; for Amnon alone is dead."

But Avshalom had fled. And the young man that kept the watch lifted up his eyes and looked, and behold! many people were coming from the road behind him, from the side of the hill.

And Yonadav said to the king, "Behold! the king's sons are coming! As your servant said, so it is."

And it came to pass, as soon as he had finished speaking, that behold, the king's sons came, and lifted up their voices and wept; and the king also, and all his servants wept bitterly. II Sam. 13:30–36

At the time of the princes' panicked flight, but before their return to Jerusalem,[180] their father David hears that *Avshalom has slain **all** the king's sons, and there is not one of them left*. This unsubstantiated rumor is apparently sufficiently credible that the king arises from his throne, tears his clothing and lays prostrate on the ground in abject mourning. All the king's servants stand by, also with rent garments.

This biblical description of David's reaction to a "phantom event, a massacre that does not happen,"[181] shifts the story's focus from Tamar, Amnon and the rape, back to David. How telling of David's blood-thirsty character that he "can not only imagine such a mass fratricide, [he can also] believe it!"[182] David is haunted by the sinister specter of the prophet Nathan's censure and punishment in chapter 12. The king's mourning described here even echoes his long-ago behavior when "phase 1" of his punishment was effected: we recall that David had lain prostrate on the ground for the entire night (12:16–17) when his week-old infant son with Batsheva was stricken with a mortal illness. The reason David now readily believes the truth of the rumor of the massacre of all his sons is that Nathan had foretold (in 12:9–10) that *because you have put Uriah the Hittite to the sword; [because] you took his wife and made her your wife and had him killed . . . Therefore, **the sword will never depart from your house**.* The death now of all his sons – by David's own reckoning – would be the next horrible phase of his ongoing punishment for his sins with Batsheva and Uriah.

Another reason David believes the rumor that *all* his sons have been killed is because it would have been consistent with the template of the aftermath of the rape of Dinah when her brothers avenged her by killing her rapist and massacring "the entire town." David has not reckoned on Avshalom, however, the most "kingly" of his sons, and a better man than he. For Avshalom does *not* kill *all* the king's sons; he kills only the guilty party – Amnon, the evil schemer who raped his sister and would be king. And Avshalom did not rush to judgement. He gave David two years to chastise Amnon or bring him to justice himself, and only when David failed to act did Avshalom step in. He avenged his sister and exacted the death penalty by killing the guilty man, the single person who richly deserved death.[183] Avshalom administered a rough justice.

Rearing his scheming head, we encounter cousin Yonadav once more. After two years he is still a hanger-on in the king's court, though not a close enough confidant to Amnon to have accompanied him to Avshalom's party at Ba'al Hazor. It is Yonadav who, once again in this story, has much to say. He tells his prostrate uncle: "My lord the king must not give credence to the rumor[184] that **all** the king's sons have been killed! Only Amnon alone has died. For this has been Avshalom's intention from the day Amnon forced his sister Tamar!"

The *midrash*, having no affection for Yonadav, "the cool-of-mouth, enterprising young manipulator,"[185] is struck by his sure knowledge of the true facts of the killing. Did Yonadav somehow know of Avshalom's plans in advance of Amnon's fateful attendance at the sheep-shearing festival? If so, why did he not forewarn his "friend" and cousin that he was walking into a trap?[186] Unless, as Rashi says, Yonadav was simply voicing what was common knowledge among the cousins: that Avshalom's "standing order" to his officers was to strike Amnon dead at the first opportunity.[187] Alternatively, Yonadav could have been expressing to the king what Yonadav knew instinctively: that since the day that Amnon had raped his sister Tamar, Avshalom's constant animating desire was to avenge her, and the sheep-shearing festival was the perfect set-up for an ambush.[188]

No sooner had Yonadav finished speaking than the palace lookout raised his eyes and saw a large crowd converging on the palace from the hillside. It is Yonadav who announces their arrival to the king: "Behold, the king's sons have come! It is just as your servant said — Amnon alone has died!" The *midrash*[189] suggests that Yonadav was eager to be the one to announce the news to the king, thinking that his stock would rise thereby, as he had predicted exactly this.

But the king and his sons are too devastated to register Yonadav's posturing. The princes raised their voices and wept, and the king and all his courtiers wept copiously also.

AVSHALOM FLEES

And Avshalom fled, and went to Talmai, son of Ammihud, king of Geshur. And David mourned for his son for many days.

So Avshalom fled, and went to Geshur, and remained there for three years. II Sam. 13: 37–38

Avshalom knew, when he meticulously planned his revenge against Amnon, that he would either be slain himself or he would become a fugitive. Either way, even if his mission were successful, he knew he would not be returning to his home. So before he left for Ba'al Hazor he had said goodbye to his silent sister Tamar, and as he looked into her eyes that very morning he had allowed Tamar to read his intent. She returned his stare, and, comprehending, she had gripped his hands. Then he had left her safely in the care of his household, one loyal soldier-at-arms her constant protector ever since that horrible day of her rape two years before. Avshalom was confident no further harm would come to Tamar; she posed no threat to his father and brothers.

After the killing, while the other princes scattered in panic, Avshalom and his comrades fled to Geshur, to the palace of King Talmai, his maternal grandfather.[190] It is fair to assume that Talmai was not expecting him. Avshalom would not have endangered his plan by sending messengers far and wide with his travel itinerary. But though unexpected, his grandfather would not have turned him away, even at the risk of angering David. His own daughter, Maacah, had a quarter-century before been ravished by David, and taken as spoils of battle. True, she had become David's queen, but Talmai's granddaughter, Tamar, was not so fortunate. Tamar was Talmai's favorite, the beautiful and wise young princess who so resembled her mother. Talmai burned with hatred for Amnon, and seethed with resentment against David, who had not raised a royal finger to punish Tamar's rapist. His grandson, Avshalom, however, had acted like the prince and soldier he was. He had taken in his ruined sister, and patiently planned Amnon's execution. Talmai would have held the killing sword himself if he had been in Avshalom's shoes, but the young had their own ways of getting things done.

So Talmai opened his palace gates to Avshalom and his six comrades, and gave them refuge.

There were no secrets even in Talmai's palace, and Avshalom assumed that his father, David, would soon discover his whereabouts. He expected a reprisal, and assumed that David would dispatch his strongmen to hunt him down and fetch him back to Jerusalem to face justice for killing the crown prince. So

Avshalom's days in Talmai's palace were not peaceful ones. Neither Talmai nor Avshalom were taking chances, and Avshalom was hidden in a series of safe houses within the city, the better to confound any of David's spies.[191]

Avshalom remained in Geshur for three years, for as long as David mourned for Amnon. During that time Avshalom accompanied his grandfather, King Talmai, on his various campaigns, both as a distraction and also to keep safely out of reach of David's soldiers.

It is curious that the Bible says *three times* that "Avshalom flees" (in verses 34, 37 and 38), when only *one* time would have sufficed. Perhaps the first "flight," which immediately precedes the phrase that the princes and their retinue were returning to Jerusalem, indicated that the princes waited until Avshalom had left Ba'al Hazor before they ventured back to the palace,[192] fearing an ambush. The *second* mention explains Avshalom's flight for refuge to the palace of Talmai, his grandfather. And the *third* "flight," immediately after the Bible's phrase about David's many days of mourning for "his son," could juxtapose father and son, illustrating the gulf between them. David is in Jerusalem in deep mourning, longing for a son he will never see again, while Avshalom is in Geshur, seeking only distance from his father.[193] The prophet Nathan's prediction is coming true right before our eyes. Three of David's children are dead or ruined, and a fourth is in exile. Swords are raised within David's household, and treason is in the air.

DAVID MOURNS FOR AMNON
AND LONGS FOR AVSHALOM

And this caused king David to long for Avshalom; for he was comforted concerning the death of Amnon. II Sam. 13: 39

David mourned for Amnon for three years,[194] after which he ceased his pursuit of Avshalom.[195] Over time, David became reconciled to and gradually comforted about Amnon's death, so that eventually he came to pine for Avshalom, his son-in-exile.[196]

But out of pride and guilt David refused to send for Avshalom to return to Jerusalem.[197]

There is a gap in the last verse of this fraught chapter. The verb that opens verse 39 is in the *feminine* gender; but because David is the subject — and requires a matching *masculine* verb — Torah scholars question if a feminine word could be missing from the text. The phrase reads *And King David longed to go forth to Avshalom.* It appears to make sense, but not if read in the Hebrew. For this reason some translations insert the words "the soul of" into the phrase, because the Hebrew word for "soul" is feminine. The verse would then read: *And **the soul of** King David longed to go forth to Avshalom.*

But because the verb refers to a feminine subject, this solution still does not satisfy. The important question for students of the Bible text remains unresolved: **Who** — not *what* — is longing to go forth to Avshalom in verse 39?

The answer proposed by Radak, citing *Ibn Ezra*, is emphatically *not* "David." According to these commentaries, the feminine verb *vatechal* — meaning "something or someone *feminine* related to or belonging to King David longed to go forth to Avshalom" — refers to **David's wife**, Maacah, Avshalom's and Tamar's mother![198] Maacah so yearns for her son Avshalom's safe return after three years of self-exile that she courts the king's impatience and anger and implores him to send messengers to her father's palace to guarantee Avshalom safe passage back to Jerusalem.

The commentaries' reasoning even allows for **David's daughter**, Tamar, to have come out of seclusion specifically to petition her father to assure her brother Avshalom's safe return.[199] In this way the unmentioned grief and longing suffered by *the women* in David's and Avshalom's life are given voice *by inference*.

Such alternative and highly plausible readings of verse 39, far from being confusing, are thrilling to this Bible reader. I wonder about Maacah's emotions and influence on David, and I am especially loath to part with Tamar. I can see why Rashi and Ralbag, *et al.*, favor the more common interpretation that "the *soul* of David longed to go forth to Avshalom." Their reading is supported by the very next verse, which begins a new chapter in II Samuel. While the story of Amnon and Tamar ends here in chapter 13, verse 39, chapter 14, verse 1 tells us that Yoav, David's general, "knew that the king's *heart* longed for Avshalom." In the upcoming chapter Yoav engineers Avshalom's return to Jeru-salem.

Perhaps both interpretations of verse 39 can coexist. It is certainly possible, knowing that David's soul longs for a reconci-liation with Avshalom after three years (verse 39), that his wife, also missing her son, senses David's nascent receptivity and intercedes with David on Avshalom's behalf. As for Tamar's part in bringing Avshalom home, we will explore that *midrash* in the upcoming coda. Already we can see that the *midrash* reads Maacah's and Tamar's presence, as well as their voices, into the last verses of our story.

CONCLUSION

Once Tamar is brought under Avshalom's protection in 13:20 she disappears from the Bible text.

We ache for this beautiful, articulate and ruined princess. The broad pattern of her life is eerily like that of her ancestral sister, Dinah. We are familiar with the stories' common template. She is the innocent daughter of the ruler of her people, privileged and ostensibly protected by her status. Notwithstanding—or because of—who she is, she is forcibly raped by a young prince who "loves" her, and she suffers the afflictions of the attack. After the rape, her father is inexplicably silent, and offers not a word of comfort to her or admonishment to her rapist. She is taken into the home of her full brother for care and protection, and it is this same brother (in Dinah's case her *two* brothers) who risks his life to avenge her, killing her rapist.

We have explored the similarities of the two stories in detail in Part Five. But the most significant difference, from the standpoint of character development of the female biblical actor, is that Tamar is an older young woman who speaks up, while Dinah was but a girl barely into her teens, without a voice. As such, the Bible allows us to know David's daughter Tamar rather well, while Jacob's daughter Dinah remains a silent and inchoate victim in the text. [200]

Not only does Tamar speak eloquently and at length in II Samuel 13, but we also see her in action. She is a go-er and a do-er. Tamar is summoned to her brother's house in order to heal him, and *she goes*. The Bible's word, in II Sam. 13:8, is *vatelech*, "and Tamar *went* to the house of her brother Amnon." Students of the text will recall this special word and its grammatical cousins as it was applied to two primary actors in the book of Genesis who were charged with recognizing, accepting and passing on the divine covenant. Abraham famously picks himself up and goes — *vayelech* — in response to God's *lech lecha* summonses,[201] and Rebecca echoes this action by emphatically agreeing to go — *elech!* — to a strange land to marry Isaac.[202] So at the very outset of Tamar's story, before she utters a word, we are alerted by the verb *vatelech* to a hint of covenantal element in her character, perhaps to her mission.

We next see Tamar in a spate of verbs, also a pattern we associate with Abraham, also associated with preparation and serving of food, and also touching on healing or recovering from illness.[203] Tamar *goes, takes* the dough, *kneads* it, *prepares* it, *cooks* the pancakes, *takes* the pan, *pours* them out, once again *takes* the healing pancakes, *brings* them to Amnon, and *approaches* him. All this action occurs *before* she speaks, attempting, futilely, to fend off her attacker. Her impassioned words spill out of her and onto the biblical page in verses 12 and 13. And after the brutal attack, with her broken body aching, with Amnon's loathing evident in his abrupt and cruel dismissal of her — *Get up and get out!* — a perversion of her original "going in" — Tamar speaks fervently to Amnon once again in verse 16, also to no avail.

After Amnon has his servant slam and bolt the door after ejecting Tamar onto the street, the Bible allots one more bout of verbs to our victim-heroine, so that she is associated with no fewer than *fifteen* action words altogether. She *takes* dust and ashes onto her head, *tears* her striped tunic, *places* her hands over her head, and — in a bookend to her first action earlier in the chapter — she *walks* back and forth — *vatelech* — as she *cries out* in anguish.

The reader is breathless, indignant and ineffably sad after reading Tamar's story, having watched her in action, listened to her plead, imagined her violent struggle, felt her pain, and watched her descend into mourning and desolation. We note that the very last verb attributed to Tamar is the word *vateshev*, "and she sat or remained," a verb which signifies the direct opposite of *vatelech*. Tamar began the story as a young woman in motion, Abraham- and Rebecca-like, and ends it, tragically, in stasis.

We ask, is this the end? What ultimately becomes of Tamar?

To answer this question we must first acknowledge and appreciate Tamar's literary and moral purpose in II Samuel. Tamar is Amnon's foil. She is a virginal princess, daughter of king David, one of the specially-designated "beautiful" women in the Bible. She is also recognized as a healer within the royal family. There is no shadow on her character; she is "goodness" and loveliness personified. This story pits Tamar against Amnon, *her half-brother*, the eldest son of king David, the spoiled and privileged crown prince, a young man of leisure and lusts who has fixated his sexual fantasies on the unattainable virgin princess. Amnon plots, entraps and violently rapes Tamar when she comes to feed him healing food *at David's command*. Amnon is as unremittingly evil as Tamar is unblemished and good.

If Tamar exists literarily as the antithesis of Amnon, and the two characters effectively cancel each other out—she is ruined and he is killed—there are only two main actors left on the biblical proscenium: David and Avshalom. We recall that chapter 13 opened with the statement that the beautiful Tamar was *sister to Avshalom*, and we commented that the reader might have thought that filial emphasis was out-of-place. We see now that it was not; it was deliberate and literarily important. This is because Avshalom, a non-actor in the book of Samuel until he comes upon his sister post-rape, functions as the foil for his father, David! David is infuriatingly silent, neither comforting Tamar nor censuring Amnon. **It is Avshalom who acts in David's stead,** speaking to Tamar, comforting her, protecting her, sheltering her and avenging her. The Torah is telling us that but-for Avshalom's vainglorious and treasonous behavior in coming chapters,[204] rebelling against the father he cannot forgive, Avshalom could have stepped into his father's shoes and been another David![205] His behavior in the Tamar episode was both brotherly and kingly, and marked the moral high point of his life.

Literarily, then, Tamar is sacrificed. The royal house that has engendered and allowed this sexual crime to go unpunished will itself be torn and bloodied, betrayed and embattled as Tamar is. As "ugly" and "calculated as David's murderous betrayal of Uriah, **this** familial rape tears the fabric of lives apart in a widening, accelerating gash."[206] Measure-for-measure the kingdom of Israel will become *shomemah,* desolate. Even the pure and good will not be left standing.

The *midrash* and commentaries — both traditional and modern — respond to Tamar on a personal, not solely a metaphorical, level. They love Tamar, admire her cool head, decry her violation, and are reluctant to let her disappear from the biblical narrative. We will see that it is the commentary Abarbanel who *midrashically* brings Tamar out of her self-imposed isolation.[207] Let us envision what might have occurred.

When we last encountered Tamar in verse 20 she was in a post-traumatic state, sitting desolate and cloistered in her brother Avshalom's house, under his protection. Two years pass before Avshalom kills Amnon, and, as we know, Avshalom immediately flees to Geshur and has been *persona non grata* in Jerusalem ever since. For the ensuing three years of Amnon's absence the king has mourned Amnon's death.

Tamar and her mother, Maacah, along with Avshalom's wife and children, are missing Avshalom sorely. It is only at the end of three years, when they see that the king appears at last to be comforted after Amnon's death, and that he has begun pining for Avshalom, that Avshalom's loved ones cast about for a way of appealing to the king to permit Avshalom to return to his home safely. Their task is delicate, as David has had his soldiers searching for Avshalom all this time. Avshalom's family fears that in their eagerness to welcome him home they might be playing into the king's hands, unwittingly baiting a trap for him. Maacah tries appealing to her husband, but he will not relent. The family is in despair, and they fear that this will be the pattern of their lives, sidelined and shunned in the royal household and bereft of their beloved champion — son, brother, husband and father.[208]

Tamar has watched this domestic drama unfold. Rationally or not, she feels a responsibility to her brother's household. Had it not been for her, she reasons, Avshalom would not have felt compelled to take revenge by killing Amnon, and Avshalom would still be a prince in Israel, living peaceably among them. So focusing on her gratitude and filial love for her brother, Tamar prepares to approach her father, the king. This is an enormous undertaking, as she has been in seclusion and has not spoken to her father since that fateful day five years before when her life was changed cataclysmically.

We can imagine Tamar's courage and resolve. She is battling traumatic demons and primal feelings of betrayal and abandonment. After all, it was her father who sent her to her fate, via his royal command to "go" to Amnon's house in order to heal him. But she girds herself, telling herself it is the least she can do for her brother Avshalom.

Tamar dresses in proper court clothing and presents herself before her father, the king. She has the element of surprise on her side. David is stunned to see her. The last time he beheld Tamar she was in the flower of young adulthood: her skin shone with vitality, her eyes flashed with humor and wisdom, her lithe form was graceful and her movements efficient, her thick black hair was plaited in a glossy coronet. In contrast, the woman standing before him is no longer young. He recognizes her as Tamar, for her features and bearing are much the same, but she has aged. His beautiful daughter has disappeared, and this woman standing calmly before him is a shadow of her former self. Her skin is sallow, having been sheltered from the sun; her eyes, when not downcast, are too knowing; thin-to-fragile now, she walks with deliberation, as if she were unaccustomed to the movement; her hair, while neatly plaited beneath a pristine head-veil, is white as snow.

In the pause during which her father beholds and registers her presence, Tamar bows low before him and begins to speak:

"Revered king, please forgive a daughter's audacity in appearing before you unannounced. I have come to appeal to you not for myself, but on behalf of another. It is known in the royal palace that you have accepted comfort from your courtiers and ministers and that you have shed your mourning for your first-born son.

"My appeal to you today is on behalf of your living son, Avshalom, my brother who has been absent from this palace and from your presence for lo these past three years. I beg you, o king, to hear a daughter's plea and to let my words fall upon your heart. Let my request appeal to a father's love and mercy, understanding and forgiveness.

"I plead with you, o king, dispenser of justice, to rescind your orders to seek out and pursue Avshalom. I beseech you, o merciful king, to send out your couriers to my grandfather, Talmai, king of Geshur, and let it be known that king David welcomes Avshalom back to Jerusalem. Let it be known that your majesty guarantees him safe passage and safe haven, and that no one may harm a hair on his head by order of David the king.

"O king, allow your thirst for vengeance to be quenched by the rain of relieved tears that will be shed by your loyal servants, Maacah, mother of your son Avshalom, and by myself when you have welcomed Avshalom home. Perform this one act so that by your mercy shall you be called 'great.' "

Abarbanel says that in response to Tamar's eloquent plea, king David relented, and sought revenge against Avshalom no longer. This paved the way for Yoav's intervention to bring Avshalom back to Jerusalem, a story told in II Sam. 14.

Modern Bible scholar Adrien Janis Bledstein, picking up on Tamar's long and heartfelt (though futile) passages in chapter 13 in which she had appealed to Amnon, suggests, in parallel to Abarbanel, that Tamar eventually used her gift with words to become an author and poet in Israel.

> I cannot believe that this learned, gifted woman shriveled up and died in her brother Absalom's house. We are not told what happened to Tamar thereafter, as the Court History focuses on David and the demise of Absalom. I like to imagine that Tamar, like Joseph, came to understand her trauma and to use her gifts to benefit all Israel. The [*kutonet passim*] garment distinguished her [commission] . . . to perform a ceremony to bring about healing. Bereft of the garment, she was free from the illusions woven into it by her father. Perhaps she wrote stories and poetry.[209]

The Bible text does give us a hint to Tamar's endurance and immortality. In chapter 14 of Samuel (verse 25) the narrator will describe Avshalom's "beauty," which is an echo of Tamar's, mentioned at the introduction of the story of her defilement in 13:1. Next (in 14:27), continuing the echo of our Tamar of chapter 13, the narrator mentions Avshalom's children: "three sons and **one daughter whose name was Tamar, and she was a woman beautiful to behold.**" The reader does a double-take. Can it be that there exists *another* girl named Tamar in the house of David who is also known to be "beautiful?" What can this mean?

It is extraordinary that the Bible names Avshalom's lone daughter. When a daughter is named in the course of a list of biblical begats, especially to the exclusion of the sons, this denotes her importance.[210] The *midrash*[211] tells us that Avshalom intentionally named his one daughter after his living sister, whom he had risked so much to avenge. Avshalom hoped by this seeming small act of naming to ensure that Tamar and her hallmark beauty and royalty would be honored and carried forward into future generations. How poignant is Avshalom's tribute! He cannot bear to leave his sister, Tamar, desolate and barren, so he confers her stature and heroic qualities onto his own young daughter. "In *her* Absalom has created a living memorial for his sister ... From aunt to niece have passed name and beauty so that rape and desolation have not the final word in the story of Tamar."[212]

Tamar's future, stolen by one brother, was retrieved by another. We have seen that biblical brothers hold the keys to both destruction and also to survival and immortality. Avshalom, Tamar's brother, named his only daughter "Tamar" in order to ensure generational memory. Tamar's story has been told and retold for millennia, her name and mantle passing into legend and, as well, into readers' hearts and minds.

PART

SIX

Ruth

&

Boaz

SIX

Ruth & Boaz

RUTH 3:6–14

And [Ruth] went down to the threshing-floor, and she did all that her mother-in-law bade her.

And Boaz ate and drank, and his heart was merry, and he went to lie down at the edge of his grain-pile. And she came silently and uncovered his feet and lay down.

And it came to pass at midnight, and the man gave a start and was taken aback, for behold! there was a woman lying at his feet!

"Who are you?" he asked. And she said, "I am Ruth, your handmaid. Spread your skirt over your handmaid, for you are a redeeming kinsman."

And he said, "May you be blessed of the Lord, my daughter; your latest act of kindness is greater than the first, for you have not turned to younger men, whether poor or rich.

"And now, my daughter, have no fear. All that you have asked I will do on your behalf, for all the elders at the gate of my people know that you are a valiant woman.

"But while it is true that I am a redeeming kinsman, there is a kinsman closer than I.

*"Stay for the night. Then in the morning, if Tov will act as
a redeemer, well, let him redeem you.[1] But if he does not wish
to redeem you, I will redeem you, as the Lord lives! Lie down
until morning."*

*So she lay at his feet until dawn. And she rose before one
person could distinguish his fellow, for he thought, "Let it not
be known that the woman came to the threshing-floor."*

This is the story of a journey. From famine to abundant harvest,
from death and mourning to joy and redemption, from barrenness
to birth. It is the story of Ruth, an impoverished and childless
Moabite widow who burns her bridges and follows her Israelite
mother-in-law into Judah, to live among a people who scorn and
revile Moabites. It is the story of Ruth's immersion into a strange
culture that allows her to glean at the edges of a rich man's field,
and to marry her dead husband's nearest kinsman. It is the story
of Ruth's journey from Moabite princess to mother of the Israelite
monarchy.

Questions clamor to be answered. What impels this young
Moabite woman to abandon the land of her birth and accompany
her mother-in-law, Naomi, to a place where she is not wanted?
Why do Naomi and her family travel to Moav in the first place?
Why is she now determined to return to Judah? What does
Naomi *really* want—Does she desire a Moabite companion, or
does she wish to be rid of the girl? How do the Israelites react to
Naomi's return, with Ruth in tow? How do the two destitute
women subsist? How does Ruth meet Boaz, a judge and tribal
chief, and how and why does she come to sleep at his feet on the
night of the harvest festival? Why does she seek a redeemer, and
who will assume this role?

And perhaps most important of all, we seek to answer the
question, Why would a Moabite woman's act of sexual audacity
merit her being the ancestor of King David and, ultimately, the
Messiah? The answer must lie in Ruth's journey from Moav to
Judah, seemingly only a mere matter of topographical miles, but
in reality a more arduous journey of the spirit, of one woman's
struggle against prejudice, a journey from idolatry into righteous-

ness. It is a fraught and tortuous trek, one we will analyze and experience along with her.

THERE WAS A FAMINE IN THE LAND

The Book of Ruth opens with the portentous words *Vayehi biymei — And it came to pass in the days of* . . . , urgently signaling, as we have seen in prior chapters, that trouble is on the horizon.[2] And so it is. The word *vayehi* even appears *twice* in the first verse, so the alert reader will expect the coming story to deliver a one-two punch, and this, too, comes to pass.

The story takes place *when the judges judged* — in the period of time between Joshua's death and the anointing of Saul as the first king of Israel[3] — when the nation is still ruled by appointed local magistrates. Because there was, as yet, no single, nationally-recognized leader exerting unified legal control over the people of Israel, it was a time of widespread corruption and judicial chaos during which "each man did what was right in his eyes."[4] Some say the judges were Deborah, Barak and Yael, some say they were Shamgar and Ehud,[5] and still others say one of the judges was named Ivtzan, whom the Talmud[6] suggests could have been Boaz. Some say the judges were honest and true, and others say some of them reflected the character of the people whom they judged, and were themselves dishonest.[7] The first *vayehi* points to this widespread corruption among the people of Judah.

Not only was it a time of fraud and irresponsibility, but verse 1 adds desperation and hunger into the mix, telling us *there was a famine in the land*. The scorching famine was seen as a divine punishment[8] for the people's iniquities, and is the reason for the second *vayehi*.[9]

Despite the privations attendant to the famine, the Bible tells us about only "one man" who leaves Judah for greener pastures. In fact, according to the *midrash*,[10] everyone else in Beit Lechem clung tenaciously to their land and homes and remained in Judah, suffering through the draught and starvation. Yet we are told that *a certain man from Beit Lechem of Judah went to sojourn in the fields of Moav; he, and his wife and his two sons*. Who is this "certain man," and what is the significance of his emigration to Moav?

"AND THE MAN'S NAME WAS ELIMELECH"

The man's name is Elimelech, and by its very meaning—"kingship is mine"[11]—we are enjoined to remember his name as well as what befalls him, his wife and his sons. His name is an early hint that the important subtext of the Book of Ruth is kingship and its provenance. In verse 3 Elimelech is referred to as *husband of Naomi*, which is an unusual addendum when referring to a male biblical character by name, and could be an indication that it is his wife who is of important merit in her own right.[12] The story will bear this out. We will see that although her husband will disappear from the narrative, Naomi will slip into his role of head-of-family and will initiate and plot much of the dramatic action.

Elimelech is an Israelite nobleman,[13] an Ephrathite or important[14] landed lord from Beit Lechem, a man of vast wealth[15] whose fields and enterprises sustain a great proportion of the people in Beit Lechem.[16] He is one of the four sons of Nachshon, the storied prince of the tribe of Judah who was a trusted aide to Moses.[17] It was Nachshon who, during the exodus from Egypt, waded up to his neck into the roiling waters of the Red Sea in full view of the entire company of terrified Israelites. Nachshon had unwavering faith that God would perform a miracle allowing the Israelites to escape Pharaoh's pursuing chariots,[18] and, perhaps in response to Nachshon's steadfast heroism, it was when the waters reached the level of his nostrils that God caused the Red Sea to split, allowing the Israelites to cross on a strip of dry land. Nachshon himself was son of Aminadav, a fifth-generation descendant of Judah, the fourth son of the patriarch Jacob. Nachshon also was brother-in-law to Aaron (who was brother of Moses and Miriam), as his sister, Elisheva, was Aaron's wife. We see, then, that Elimelech's father was an honored and beloved true hero in Israel.

Given Elimelech's impeccable provenance, it is a shock to read that in response to the famine in the land of Judah, Elimelech decamps with his family and travels across the Jordan River and east of the Dead Sea to relocate in the fields of Moav, Israel's enemy. This is compounded by the fact that it was considered a grave sin to abandon the land the Israelites had fought so valiantly to wrest from the Canaanites a mere generation before. As long as a person was able to feed his family, he was expected to remain within the land of Israel.[19]

The wealthy Elimelech possesses ample resources to withstand the famine. So we must ask, What could have motivated him to uproot his family and abandon his landed portion as well as his countrymen?

There are several possible reasons for Elimelech's turncoat behavior. The first involves his character. Apparently Elimelech was a parsimonious and miserly man,[20] but this quality had never before been tested in a protracted famine. When the famine hit Judah in full force the people naturally turned to Elimelech for both courage and sustenance. As a leader of the Beit Lechem community — it is richly ironic that Elimelech is fleeing a famine in the province whose name means "house of bread" — a positive attitude and words of encouragement from Elimelech to his fellow citizens would have gone far to boosting their morale. On a practical level, it was the custom in times of trouble for the local lord to take a leadership role, opening his storehouses or fields and sharing his bounty with the townspeople who worked for him throughout the year. This was expected of Elimelech, a tribal leader; the locals depended on him for welfare assistance to see them through famine and drought. It is said that when the drought first hit Judah, Elimelech's countrymen continued to rely on him as they had during past misfortunes. "Up until now they had been secure in his care, saying 'we will survive because he will shelter and feed us.' "[21] But when they saw Elimelech pack up and leave, his abandonment of the ancestral land brought home to the Beit Lechemites the stark terror of the famine, and they shuddered.

Despite the fact that Elimelech's vast wealth would have sufficed to sustain all of Beit Lechem for a period of ten years,[22] the *midrash* tells us that "when the famine came [Elimelech] said, 'Now all Israel will come knocking at my door [for help], each one with his basket.' He therefore arose and fled from them."[23]

As his name suggests, the second reason Elimelech turned his back on his countrymen involves his pretensions to future kingship.[24] Elimelech was preoccupied with the possibility that one of his sons should fulfill the prediction that the royal and messianic line was destined to emerge from the tribe of Judah through a marriage with a descendant of Lot.[25] The famine in Judah provided the perfect excuse to flee Beit Lechem and ensconce himself and his family in Moav (Moav and Ammon were Lot's sons[26]). His intention was that one of his two sons, Machlon or Chilyon, would marry a Moabite girl, bringing his family that much closer to fulfilling the monarchic prophecy.

So Elimelech left his country and countrymen and settled with his wife and two sons in Moav, initially intending only to remain there temporarily, until one of his sons found a mate. But life was comfortable in Moav; the famine had not spread across the river from Judah. Elimelech's sons were in no hurry to marry, the weeks turned into years, and he settled in Moav permanently. It is this change of intention — from sojourner to permanent resident — that was his undoing in God's eyes.[27]

The *midrash* would introduce a note of ambiguity into our portrait of Elimelech. While the reader is not expected to react sympathetically to this man who abandons his fellows and hoards his riches in a time of dire straits, still even Elimelech's actions have a destiny all their own, and the reader should be aware of their duality.

Only twice in the Bible does the phrase *vayelech ish mibeit . . .* ("and a man went out from the house of . . .") appear.[28] The first time is in Ex. 2:1, introducing Amram, who returns to his wife Yocheved and eventually fathers Moses.[29] The second time is here, in Ruth 1:3, introducing Elimelech, husband of Naomi, his flight to Moav, and his death. The *midrash* notes the verbal connection between the two men (the Hebrew phrases are identical) and makes a fascinating link between these two "fathers." The first man who "goes out" will introduce us to Israel's *first* redeemer; while the second man who "goes out" sets in motion events that will eventually lead to Israel's *ultimate* redeemer. Amram will father Moses, while Elimelech's flight to Moav will lead, in a roundabout way, to Ruth, who is destined to be great-grandmother to king David and ancestor of the Messiah. The reader anticipates that perhaps some good will come of Elimelech's "going out," and we eagerly follow the story line to see how this develops.

HIS WIFE, NAOMI, AND HIS SONS,
MACHLON AND CHILYON

Elimelech's wife's name is Naomi, which means "pleasantness." She is presented in the text in direct counterpoint to her husband's less-than-honorable behavior. We will see, as the story unfolds, that Naomi renounces her name as an ironic and mocking banner when fate deals her blow after harsh blow and she is despondent.

His two sons are named Machlon and Chilyon, meaning, respectively, illness (*machala*) and annihilation (*chilaya*).[30] In light of their upcoming actions and sudden death, the dark interpretations of their names take on predictive import. It is possible they were both taken **ill** and died suddenly; and because neither of the young men had fathered children, their name and portion in Israel were fated to be **annihilated**. The singsong, rhyming sound of the two names—Machlon and Chilyon appear almost as a single name-form[31]—is a biblical hint that the two operate as one indistinguishable "character" in the narrative.[32] Their single purpose is to show that Elimelech's dishonorable character traits devolved to his sons, and they echo his punishment. The two remain in self-exile in Moav even after their father's death, they marry Moabite sisters,[33] and they die prematurely and childless, thus rendering themselves and their father's name extinct. They live as one and die as one, disappearing from the text together. The singular distinguishing difference is that Machlon marries Ruth, who, unbeknownst to everyone in the narrative, is destined to lift the name of Elimelech out of the dustbin of history and into immortality, foiling the "prediction" of annihilation.

Their names could also have benign meanings: dance (*machol*) and fullness (*chelil*), and could likewise be distantly prophetic to the ending of our story. Machlon's name could also come from the word *mechilah*, meaning "forgiveness," hinting to Ruth's eventual redemption of Machlon's name. But for now, we are told only that the two boys accompanied their father and mother as they left their homeland of Judah and emigrated to the fields of Moav.

ELIMELECH AND HIS SONS DIE SUDDENLY

Ironically, it is in the land that famine has not ravaged, in this alien place where Elimelech has sought refuge—from drought as well as from his responsibilities as a leader—that *Elimelech, husband of Naomi, dies.* Elimelech's sudden death in verse 3, unexplained in the Bible text, is discussed at length in the *midrash.* It is widely believed that his death was a punishment. It came about primarily because Elimelech lacked a charitable heart. He is punished for failing to act benevolently and generously toward his impoverished countrymen as behooved him, a leader of his generation.[34] Neither did he importune God on their behalf, which was also his role. Another reason he is struck down is that he physically abandoned the land of Israel and cast his lot with the Moabites and settled down in enemy territory. His temporary sojourn in Moav would not have led to a death sentence; it was only when his visit became permanent that God's anger overflowed and Elimelech's craven behavior sealed his fate.

Also, Elimelech's flight specifically to Moav was calculated and intentional on his part. The Moabites, more than any other surrounding nation, were known for their stinginess, a trait he shared. The Torah exhorts the Children of Israel to shun the Moabites because they failed to greet the exhausted Israelites with bread and water when they passed by their land after the exodus from Egypt.[35] It is partially for this act of unfeeling cruelty to the newly-freed slaves that the Children of Israel were prohibited from marrying a Moabite unto the tenth generation. Elimelech's abandonment of Judah for Moav, then, struck a near-atavistic chord of abhorrence among his countrymen, which will make it doubly hard for Naomi when she seeks to return to her home.

We are told that *Elimelech,* **Naomi's husband,** *died.* It is telling that the text emphasizes that the loss is primarily *Naomi's.* There is one other place in the Torah text where we learn that a spouse's death weighs most heavily on the one who survives; this is when the patriarch Jacob says *When I came from Padan,* **Rachel died unto me.**[36] The *midrash*[37] points out this similarity, implicitly alerting the reader that Naomi and the patriarch Jacob share this signal moment and may share others. And in fact, Naomi's life will eerily echo first, Jacob's, and then his son Judah's experiences. First, the unexpected and mourned deaths of their spouses; Elimelech's death echoes Rachel's. Next, as readers will recall from Part Three of this book, we recognize key elements of the Judah story, as well: there is a self-imposed exile from his family and homeland; he settles elsewhere; marries a foreign woman; his spouse and two sons die. The inescapable inference is that the Torah is inviting us to compare Naomi with the patriarchs in the Jacob and Judah stories. We must ask, will Naomi step up, assume a patriarchal role, and control her destiny? We will pay close attention as her story unfolds.

After their father's death and over their mother's objection,[38] Machlon and Chilyon marry Moabite women, one of whom is named Orpah and the other is named Ruth. The text does not disclose until the last chapter of the Book of Ruth[39] which son married which woman, when we learn that Ruth was married to Machlon,[40] the elder son. The girls were sisters and royal princesses, daughters of Eglon, the deceased king of Moav.[41] Chilyon, the younger son, was first to marry, and took Orpah, the elder sister, as his wife. Machlon's marriage to Ruth followed afterwards.[42] The fact that Elimelech's sons marry Moabite women is the first step toward their downfall, according to *midrash*.[43] It is an indication that they have no intention of returning to Judah and are settling in Moav permanently, thus ratifying and adopting their father's self-exile. In fact, verse 4 tells us *they lived there for about ten years* after their marriages,[44] and by inference we learn that their marriages were barren.[45]

MARRIAGE TO A MOABITESS

The Bible prohibits intermarriage between an Israelite and a Moabite in Deut. 23:4–5: *No Ammononite or Moabite shall be admitted into the congregation of the Lord; none of their descendants, even in the tenth generation, shall ever be admitted into the congregation of the Lord, because they did not meet you with food and on your journey after you left Egypt . . .*

So the inevitable question is, were Machlon and Chilyon permitted to marry Ruth and Orpah, Moabite princesses? In light of the above Torah prohibition it would seem that an Israelite was expressly forbidden to marry a Moabite or an Ammonite even if there had been a conversion to the one God. The Torah even supplies the reason: those nations' unfeeling and uncharitable conduct to the exhausted and hungry Israelites, refusing them food and water after they had emerged from slavery in Egypt. But oral tradition authenticated by the court of Samuel the prophet[46] ultimately establishes that the Torah prohibits inter-marriage only with *males* from Moav and Ammon. *Female* Moabites or Ammonites were *not* forbidden to Israelites and were in fact *sub silencio excluded* from the Bible's prohibition.[47] The reason for this is that *it was only the men*—and not the women—of Moav and Ammon who had acted uncharitably and cruelly to Israel.[48]

Still, at the time the events of this story take place, Machlon and Chilyon are not aware when they take Moabite brides that the Torah law's prohibition does not apply to females.[49] What's more, neither Orpah nor Ruth was converted to the Hebrew religion prior to their marriage,[50] which is why the text in verse 4 refers to them as "Moabites" when it tells of the marriages.[51] Elimelech's sons will pay the price for remaining in Moav and for taking Moabite brides.

ONE WAS ORPAH AND THE OTHER RUTH

We already have established that Orpah and Ruth are sisters and princesses, either daughters or granddaughters of Eglon, recently-deceased king of Moab. But we can intuit more about these young women if we explore the meanings of their names, as we have done with the other biblical characters in this book. For as the Talmud tells us, "one's name can cause future occurrences."[52]

Orpah's name (*orf*) means "the back of the neck" or "to turn one's back on." And as we will see in coming verses, this is what Orpah does when she is standing with Naomi and Ruth at the crossroads of Moav and Judah; she turns away and heads back to Moav and her mother's house, leaving Naomi to return to Judah without her.[53] Also, it is said Orpah turned her back on Chilyon's

God and engaged in sorcery and idolatry.⁵⁴ The *midrash* frowns
on Orpah's behavior and takes her to task for it in future generations, saying that at the moment she turned her back on Naomi
and returned to her alien ways it was decreed in the Heavenly
Court that Orpah's descendants would fall by the hand of Ruth's
descendants. In fact, the Philistine giant Goliath is said to be a
descendant of Orpah, and he is destined to be slain by none other
than David, the Israelite shepherd,⁵⁵ Ruth's great-grandson.⁵⁶

Ruth's name has numerous meanings. The Talmud inter-
prets her name (*rvt*) to mean "saturated" (*revah*, from *rvh*), because
based on Ruth's merit David will descend from her line and will
"saturate" God with his songs or psalms of praise.⁵⁷ Ruth can also
be derived from the Hebrew word *re'uth*, meaning "friendship."⁵⁸
We will see in coming verses how Ruth's friendship with Naomi
blossoms and deepens into a legendary bond that eventually
welcomes Ruth into the Israelite nation and keeps alive the name
of Naomi's deceased son. Others say that her name comes from
the Aramaic word *re'ut*, which in Hebrew is *retzon*, meaning
"desire,"⁵⁹ an indication that God desired her good works.
Another Aramaic derivation of Ruth is *yeret*, meaning "inheritance,"⁶⁰ because as a reward for holding fast to Naomi and to her
people Ruth is fated to "inherit" the royal house of David. And a
lovely *midrash* relates Ruth's name to the Hebrew word for "dove"
(*tor*) because the Hebrew spellings are mirror reflections of each
other.⁶¹ The dove is a blessed messenger of peace or refuge and is
considered a pure bird, and Ruth's future behavior toward both
Naomi and Boaz is characterized as pure and free of sin.

Some say that Ruth's Moabite name was Gilit or Palnitah,
and that it was changed to Ruth either before her marriage to
Machlon or that Naomi renamed her at the time of her roadside
conversion.⁶² Thus, Ruth symbolically shed her Moabite name
and origins, and ultimately *became* "Ruth."

And finally, summing up the *midrashic* beatification of Ruth's
name is the *gematria* or mathematical equivalence of the letters of
the name Ruth. They equal 606, seven short of 613, the number of
commandments incumbent upon every Jew. It is said that Ruth
had already adhered to the seven universal Noahide laws
required of every civilized person, and that she then voluntarily

took upon herself the 606 additional laws when she converted to Naomi's religion.[63]

The reader is aware that the young woman Ruth will face some difficult tests and that her road will not be an easy one. But by the explication of her name we are primed to expect great things from her. Let us see what the text has in store.

MACHLON AND CHILYON ALSO DIE, LEAVING NAOMI ALONE

Life is good for Machlon and Chilyon. They have married well, and are important members of Moabite court society. They have no intention of returning to famine-ravaged Judah.[64] They remain in Moav for another ten years after their father's death, signaling their own decision to settle there permanently. For this sin of abandonment of their land and starving brethren, Machlon and Chilyon will experience *escalating degrees* of divine punishment. The theory is that perhaps by a *gradual* loss of their material wealth they will be prompted into an understanding that their obligation is to share their bounty rather than hoard it, even with the poor in Moav.

But Machlon and Chilyon fail to take the hint. They watch as first, their inheritance is depleted before their eyes, but still they do not repent their uncharitable ways. They then lose their material wealth, in the form of their horses and donkeys, then their cattle, sheep and camels. They are forced to sell the ten fields that their father had acquired in Moav[65] so that they can raise money to purchase grain. Still unrepentant, they are finally stricken with a terminal illness that claims their lives.[66]

Both Machlon and Chilyon die on the same day.[67] They pay the ultimate price for remaining aloof from their suffering countrymen, for taking Moabite wives, and for settling in Moav and remaining there for ten years, ignoring the poor even in a foreign land. What's more, they die childless, so that their names are essentially erased from the face of the earth.[68]

Verse 5 says, *Both Machlon and Chilyon **also** died . . .* The word "also" could simply indicate that the text first told us about

Elimelech's death, and now it is telling us that his two sons *also* suffer the same fate. But the *midrash* reads the rest of verse 5, which says, *and the woman was left bereft of her two children and her husband*, and adds a dimension to Naomi's loss. Apparently Naomi was pregnant when her husband uprooted her from Beit Lechem and caused her to settle with their small family in the fields of Moav.[69] In the course of this upheaval of her life and her own opposition to the move, she miscarried the unborn baby. Shortly thereafter her husband Elimelech died, and gradually, her property and possessions dwindled and disappeared. Now, years later, she *also* loses her two sons, Machlon and Chilyon.

Naomi has lost everything, and faces a future without physical or emotional compensations. After losing a pregnancy and then her husband, she mourns the losses and feels the deep loneliness after her decades of marriage. But still she was comforted by the presence of her two sons. Now, however, Naomi is felled by this further double blow of personal disaster, the deaths of both her sons cut down in the prime of their manhood, premature deaths that fall outside the natural order of things. Following on the heels of the depletion of their fortune, this God-fearing woman sees these deaths for what they are; she understands that her family has been singled-out for divine punishment.

The *midrash*[70] is sensitive to Naomi's feeling of oppression that follows her personal calamity. Essentially, as the verse makes clear, she is *a woman left behind*. Her sons' deaths are the heaviest blow she has had to bear, their deaths unexpected. She is alone, a widow and, now, childless as well as penniless. She has neither sustenance nor physical protection. She is at the very bottom of society's ladder. And in the society of Moav, a place known for its indifference to the plight of the needy and unfortunate, it would be only a matter of time before she would succumb to illness or starvation and suffer the same fate as her husband and sons. In fact, the *midrash* tells us that Naomi was weak, ill and shattered after the death of her husband;[71] after ten years pass, an older, frailer Naomi would have been a pitiable person, indeed.

One *midrash* delves deeper into Naomi's psyche and suggests her illness and depression might have their origin in her own behavior years earlier, when the famine struck Judah. It suggests that perhaps it was Naomi who advised Elimelech to leave Beit Lechem![72] Either that, or she felt in hindsight that she had acquiesced to the move too readily. She did not protest loudly enough, or stand her ground against Elimelech. If that had been the case, then she was surely burdened with the guilt that *she* was to blame for starting her family down the road to ruin. Her misery weighed upon her heart because she felt partly responsible for her husband's and sons' deaths, and she could not forgive herself.

In Moav Naomi lacks the familial or societal safety net she would have had in Beit Lechem of Judah. Ironically, because of her husband's faults and pretensions, she is now worse-off than she would have been had she remained in drought-stricken Judah. At least in Judah she would have suffered through the famine with her family around her, sharing her wealth and resources with the less-fortunate. But alone in Moav, without kith, kin or coin, it would seem that Naomi's fate is sealed.

NAOMI LEAVES MOAV - THE JOURNEY

Now she arose with her daughters-in-law and returned from the fields of Moav, for she had heard in the field of Moav that the Lord had remembered His people to give them bread.
Ruth 1:6

God and fate have other plans for Naomi. After her seven days of mourning are ended she lifts herself up from her place on the earthen floor of her tiny home.[73] Word reaches her that the famine in Judah is ended, and she makes a plan. Apparently Naomi knew of the end of the famine in Judah before the news had become public knowledge. This almost prescient awareness is attributed to a flash of keen intuition, or to a vision. It is said that while Naomi was standing in a field in Moav an angel approached her saying, "Leave this land and return to the land of your birth. Go quickly, do not waste a minute, lest you perish here in Moav like the rest of your family!"[74] Whether Naomi learned the news in a dream, a vision, or from itinerant peddlers,[75] we see that though she is very nearly sinking under the weight of her despair, she rouses herself and makes a final push to escape what she now perceives will be, inevitably, a moribund existence. Naomi does not want to die in Moav.

Let us imagine the morning of her leaving Moav. Naomi rises before dawn on the eighth day after her sons' burials and packs her meager belongings into the saddlebags of her one remaining donkey. She has determined to leave Moav that very morning, before her neighbors awaken to delay her with vain promises of food for her journey. Naomi also intends to leave her two Moabite daughters-in-law behind, and to return to her birthplace alone. Her plan is to be on the dirt road back to Judah by the time the sun is up. Perhaps she would just have left not even having taken leave of Orpah and Ruth; we will never know. Her daughters-in-law are awakened early by the sounds of her departure, and hurry to dress and accompany her, at least as far as the Moav-Judah border.[76]

Verse 6's statement about the cessation of the famine contains the first mention of the name of God in the Book of Ruth. The Lord's merciful face had been intentionally turned away during the years of famine in Judah and Naomi's troubles in Moav. But it would seem that the ten-plus harsh years of aridity and famine have allowed the Judean earth to rest. *God has remembered his people* and out of mercy for their suffering[77] brings the blessing of rain. The ready ground has quickly sprouted, and the workers at the granaries and threshing-floors are anticipating a plentiful growing season.[78] The famine is ended and likewise Naomi's exile in Moav. She is on a return journey to her birthplace: Beit Lechem, the *house of bread*.

So Naomi leaves Moav, *and her two daughters-in-law accompany her on the road*. Verse 7's reiteration that "the two" women go with her suggests that each has a different motivation for starting the journey. Orpah escorts Naomi out of courtesy, while Ruth yearns to stay with her.[79] Or perhaps the two young women are anxious to leave behind the scene of their barren marriages and their own misfortune.[80] Or it may be that their intention is only to travel alongside Naomi until the border with Judah, out of honor and affection for their mother-in-law.[81] Regardless of their reasons or intentions, the young women attend Naomi on her way homeward.

The first leg of the journey takes place within Moav, giving the women a taste of what lies ahead. Because they left in haste and without preparation, they have no stores of food or water, and are forced to live off the land, drinking from streams and eating whatever fruit they can forage. The desert sun is unrelenting and the rock-strewn path makes it slow going. Their clothing hampers their every step, as it was made for housework and short trips, and not for arduous foot-travel. Their flimsy sandals quickly give way, and they are reduced to walking barefoot[82] over spiny grasses, slate and baking earth. Though their feet are blistered and bloodied they ignore their wounds by day, soaking them in the cold streams when they make camp at nightfall. By common assent the aged Naomi rides the beleaguered donkey for most of the day, but she takes pity on the tired beast and takes her turn at walking, too.

Aside from the physical rigors of the trip, three women on their own face very real danger from roving Moabite bandits and from lone men bent on molestation or worse, who prey on hapless travelers. So Naomi, Orpah and Ruth stay close together every moment of the journey, day and night.[83] They hope for a measure of safety in numbers. Ordinarily one of the young women would have gone ahead to scout the terrain, choose the best path, point out the streams and edible plants. But because of their fears, they travel abreast. This is why verse 7 tells us that her two daughters-in-law were **with her**, and **they** traveled on the return road to Judah. They took their lives in their hands by traveling alone in Moav,[84] but at least they stayed together and buoyed one another.

The three women exist in a private bubble of time, shared grief, and real concerns for the future. As they walk through the Moabite wilderness they care for each other, help one another as they stumble and grow thirsty and weary, and the younger women no doubt encourage the older woman's faltering steps. If they were wary co-travelers when the journey began, the rigors of the trip bring them to a better understanding of one another as individual women reaching for a better life. This difficult migration from one homeland to another pushes them into a physical dependency on each other and into a closer, more constant proximity than when they had lived together as in-laws in Moav.

As they walk, to pass the time and perhaps to whistle at the danger, Naomi talks to Orpah and Ruth about her homeland of Beit Lechem of Judah, of her youth, of her God, and of Israelite laws relating to daily life, including the laws for proselytes. The *midrash* derives this latter interpretation from the word *vatelachna* in verse 7 — meaning they walked or they went — and which has the same root as *halacha*, meaning both "law" and "going."[85] The *midrash* says they walked and talked, listened and learned, and all the time the Moabite women were being prepared for conversion by a wise Israelite mother-in-law.

THE FIRST ROADSIDE CONVERSATION

And Naomi said to her two daughters-in-law: "Go, please return, each woman to her mother's house. And may God deal kindly with you as you have dealt with the dead, and with me.

"May God grant that you find rest, each woman in her husband's house." And she kissed them, and they raised their voices and wept. Ruth 1:8–9

The tiny caravan reaches the border with Judah after about a week's trek.[86] The Torah text does not specify their route, but it is likely that Naomi deliberately chose the path that veered off the king's road onto the Moabite Road, headed northwest. She did not wish to travel long distances on the king's highway, thinking that three tattered women would attract too much attention. Perhaps she might even have feared some reprisal from the king's soldiers, if they recognized the girls and considered that perhaps she was enticing the two princesses to abandon their homeland against their will. No, Naomi planned to travel most of the way on the tributary Moabite Road, and then to cross over into Judah where it intersected with the narrowest and shallowest point of the Dead Sea, a simple matter to ford on foot. Once through that salty body of water she would be in home territory, and could follow the beaten road northward into Beit Lechem. She estimates that another week of travel once she enters Judah will bring her to her old home.

We can envision the scene. The time has come for Naomi to send her daughters-in-law back, and to venture into Judah alone. She is sorrowful but determined. Somewhat surprisingly, she has enjoyed their time together, even come to rely on the resourceful young women. They made the rigorous trip bearable. They had foraged for fruit and berries so that their hunger was somewhat assuaged, and they had proved attentive listeners as she talked about her home, her country and the ways of her God. But Naomi never forgot that neither of the two women had been granted a child that would link them to her and to the line of Elimelech. They really had no reason to remain with her. They were young and beautiful, and their lives stretched before them like an unfurled ribbon.[87] In cruel contrast, she, Naomi, had lived her life, buried her husband and sons, and forfeited her future. She was heading home to die. She could not bear having these young women tied to her out of an obligation they would live to regret.

So at the end of the Moabite Road she turns to Orpah and Ruth and says, *Lech-na, shov-na* — **Go, please return**, *each of you to the house of your mother.*

The double language she employs — *Go, please return!* — when certainly just one of those words would have sufficed, indicates Naomi's double meaning. First, she wants Ruth and Orpah *to go* to their mother's home and *not* come along with her to her home across the river. And second, she emphasizes that the "road" to Judah is long and tough, both physically and spiritually. She is giving them permission to *return* to their nation and, more specifically, to their Moabite gods.[88]

Naomi expects her job to be an easy one. Surely the young women only accompanied her this far out of kindness and courtesy to their old mother-in-law. But the girls surprise her; they are apparently of one mind,[89] and she can see by the look on their faces that they intend to come with her all the way to Beit Lechem![90] So in a commanding voice[91] she tells them to *Go, please return* . . . They are young, childless widows, and they properly belong with their mother, who will eventually arrange second marriages for each of them.[92]

Also, despite her best intentions, Naomi is bitter.[93] She looks at the young Moabite women and sees the instruments of her sons' sinfulness. Her uncharitable but all-too-human emotion should remind us of Judah's behavior when he banished Tamar to her father's house after his two sons, Er and Onan, died suddenly while married to her.[94] Then, Judah had viewed Tamar as the source of his misfortune, so he put her out of his sight. Here, we can appreciate that on some level Naomi wants to be rid of her two Moabite daughters-in-law. They are childless and thus have no lasting connection to her. In fact, they pose a real hindrance to her if she wishes to live out her life in Judah, among Israelites who view Moav as the enemy. Naomi wishes them gone.

Naomi reveals some of these suppressed feelings in verse 13, when she cries to Orpah and Ruth, *for I am extremely embittered on your account!* It is an ambiguous cry, for Naomi could mean either that she is embittered **on their behalf**, or that **because of them** her life has been embittered.[95] Either way, Naomi would prefer to enter Judah alone. She knows that returning to Beit Lechem will be difficult enough, given that a decade earlier she and her husband had forsaken their countrymen in their hour of darkness. It is an understatement that she was not expecting a hero's welcome, and even hoped to reenter the town unnoticed. If she returned to Beit Lechem with two Moabite daughters-in-law, she knew she — and they — would likely be shunned as outcasts.

But Naomi is stunned to see that as they stand poised to leave Moav and enter Judah, the two Moabite girls unhitch their long skirts that they had hiked up every morning at the start of the day's trek. They dust off their bodices, and drape their shawls about their heads and shoulders instead of about their waists. In deference to Naomi's God and countrymen, they are endeavoring to make their travel-worn clothing appear as modest as possible.[96] They have been listening intently as Naomi has told them about her people and her laws. She is surprised to see that they are taking their positions as her widowed daughters-in-law to-heart. The two women are preparing to cross over into Judah along with her, and they are desirous of blending into her culture. Naomi is touched and a bit alarmed. So she tries again to convince them to stay.

We will see that Naomi tries *three times* to convince Ruth and Orpah to return to their mother's house and not to accompany her to Judah. Three times she employs the word *shov-na*, meaning "please return," in verses 8, 11 and 12. The *midrash*[97] tells us that this presages the number of times a prospective proselyte must be turned away when he or she expresses a desire to convert to Judaism. If the intended proselyte persists even after the third rebuff, she must be accepted as a sincere convert. We will see that this will come to pass with one of Naomi's daughters-in-law. Also, the *midrash*[98] tells us that the use of two expressions, *Go* and *please return*, is a hint that Naomi was vested with a flash of divine intuition about the Moabite women. She intuited that one would "go" back to Moav and her people, and the other would "return" with her to Judah.

Naomi addresses Orpah and Ruth: "You both have shown me much courtesy by escorting me this far. Return now to your homes, where your *true* mother will treat you even better than I have treated you. For if you follow me into Judah you will eat the bread of sadness and poverty; I haven't even got a house in which to shelter you.[99] Go, return to your home. Whether you choose to keep faith with my God or return to your own gods, be assured that my God will still look favorably upon you. He will clothe your souls in the purest raiment and you will find husbands worthy of each of you, for you have behaved graciously toward me and toward the dead. These kindnesses will not be forgotten."[100]

The *midrash*[101] presents a marvelous reading of verse 8 that directly connects Naomi, Ruth and Orpah and the drama of their parting scene to the cave scene in the story of Lot and his daughters (discussed in Part One of this book). From the words *lech-na, shov-na — Go, please return, each woman to her mother's house* — the *midrash* detects a biblical hint and a prediction. First, the mention of *her mother's house* is a veiled reference to Ruth and Orpah's **Hebrew** — not Moabite — roots, as Lot and his daughter are their distant forebears! When Naomi tells the young women to *go, return!* she is issuing a subtle hint that they should return not to the fields of Moav, but earlier, to their spiritual beginnings.

Readers will recall that Moav was the son born of the union between Lot and his eldest daughter generations before. The *midrash* does not bring up this morally difficult incident idly. Rather, it recalls Lot's daughters' motivation in plotting and executing the intimate coupling with their father. Their world had been burned to cinders before their eyes, their mother turned to a pillar of salt, their sisters and brothers-in-law and betrothed young men annihilated. At the moment that they thought they were the lone survivors of this holocaust, their one thought was to "live through our father's seed."[102] Ruth and Orpah's distant foremother was terrified, audacious, and consumed with a need to perpetuate her father's line.

But we must remember that this same distant foremother, the nameless eldest surviving daughter of Lot—mother of Moav—was *also* Abraham's and Sarah's grand-niece! So Ruth and Orpah's legacy includes powerful Hebrew bloodlines, too.

Back to the present story, the two young Moabite widows are trembling on the brink between Moav and Judah ancestrally, physically, and spiritually. They are descended from both Hebrew and Moabite ancestors, and both bloodlines converge at the border crossing. Will the two women return to their *recent* past and stay Moabite? Or will they return to their *distant* past and act heroically, revert to their Hebrew roots, even perpetuate them? Naomi presents them with the choice.

RUTH AND ORPAH'S KINDNESS

*"God will do **chesed** with you, just as you have done with the dead and with me."* Ruth 1:8

What have these two young women done to merit Naomi's heartfelt blessing? The *midrash*[103] enlarges on Naomi's reference to the young women's kindnesses, or *chesed*. Because *chesed*—meaning acts of lovingkindness—is a central theme in this story, we are curious. To what acts of kindness or *chesed* is Naomi referring?

We are told their kindness is fourfold: First, Orpah and Ruth provided the burial shrouds for Chilyon and Machlon. Second, *they* paid for their husbands' burials, although widows are not obligated to clothe and bury their husbands under Israelite law. Third, the two young women mourned for their husbands, and cried tears of grief alongside Naomi. And fourth, they voluntarily gave up their marriage settlements, which would have entitled them to some portion of the family's landed holdings in Beit Lechem. Instead, they ceded all their property rights to Naomi. In a variation of this last kindness we are told that at their husbands' deaths Orpah and Ruth could have sought the alimony owed them as widows under their *ketubot*, or wedding contracts, *from Naomi*, who had co-signed the documents. But they did not do so; instead they chose to live with Naomi, sharing their "fortune" with her until it ran out.

These four kindnesses are known in Judaic tradition as *chesed shel emet*, or "truest kindness," because these acts — performed on behalf of the dead or destitute — are performed without any hope of reciprocation and out of the goodness of the giver's heart.[104] In recognition of these acts of *chesed* Naomi calls upon the name of her God three times; once each in verses 8 and 9, and later on in verse 13. She is seeking to confer God's blessing of providence, kindness and grace upon Orpah and Ruth, reciprocating those same gifts that they have unselfishly given to her.[105]

In addition to these acts of *chesed*, the *midrash* tells us that Orpah and Ruth continued to show their respect and love to Naomi even after Chilyon and Machlon's deaths.[106] Their affection for Naomi, the product of ten years of living together, did not dissipate when the catalysts for their emotion were gone. This tenacity of affection demonstrated the women's fidelity. In verses 8 and 9 Naomi addresses Ruth and Orpah in the *masculine* gender, and the *midrash* explains this textual oddity in a pre-feminist way, seeking to sincerely compliment the women. It says that the two young women had displayed "a manly fortitude and strength of character"[107] throughout the trials that beset them: the deaths of husbands and sons, their burials, the mourning period, the unaccustomed hardship and rigors of foot travel over long distances, and their steadfast loyalty to Naomi. This *midrash* points out these verbal clues, suggesting to the reader that this is a story where the women will step into the shoes of the absent males.

Naomi's farewell blessing to Ruth and Orpah (found in verses 8 and 9) is that God should grant them first, divine *chesed* or kindness, and second, that they should experience personal tranquility — *menuchah* — in worthy remarriages,[108] and in wealth and security. The *midrash* even connects Naomi's second blessing of *menuchah* to the hopeful blessing of a peaceful, unified monarchy — in direct contrast to the period of chaotic regional judges presently in place in Judah. This is still another hinted reference that this blessing of kingship is destined to arise from one of the daughters of Lot, who will be the ancestor of king David, and of his son, Solomon.

Naomi has come to identify with her daughters-in-law. She suffered an additional measure of grief as she watched the young Moabite women's lives unravel along with her own.[109] They had done nothing more than be themselves, yet they were saddled with an old Israelite mother-in-law, plus they were shouldering poverty, childlessness and widowhood — a staggering burden. Naomi could not remain aloof from this nor from the women's kindness to her.

So after she confers upon the two women the generous blessings of *chesed* and *menuchah*, the text tells us *Naomi kissed them.* Such a kiss after the bestowing of a blessing is said to bind together the souls of the one who blesses and of the recipient.[110] Not only the souls are bound by the kiss; the *midrash* says that Naomi's maternal spirit, combined with a measure of divine intuition, are conferred by her kiss onto the one daughter-in-law whose soul was prepared to accept it.[111] Later on, when we read that Ruth "cleaves" to Naomi (verse 14), we will have the answer to whom this special spirit has devolved.

This first goodbye kiss is followed in the text by a flood of tears (another kiss and cry will be found in verse 14). . . . *And they raised their voice and wept.* The *midrash* tells us that Naomi suspected that perhaps the two sisters were weeping for their lost life as princesses, and for the easy life of the king's palace.[112] Naomi is not convinced that the two women are up to the psychological as well as the physical rigors of traveling to Judah.

Have they really left Moav behind? Also, the word "voice" is in the singular form in verse 9, indicating that the two young women weep for separate, individual reasons. Orpah weeps over all she has lost; she does not wholeheartedly desire to travel to Judah and accept Naomi's God. Ruth weeps out of longing; for a righteous life, for a home and children in Judah, for a mother like Naomi. Or perhaps all three women wept,[113] their arms about each other, tears of shared grief and tears of an imminent parting of the ways.

The two Moabite women do not but know it, but their tears are for one another, too. After all they have shared, the two sisters are about to part forever.

RUTH AND ORPAH WISH TO STAY WITH NAOMI

And they say to her, "[No,] for we will return with you to your people." Ruth 1:10

Ruth and Orpah's response is a testament to Naomi's successful mothering of the two young Moabites notwithstanding her own deep ambivalence about them.[114] They tell her that regardless of her arguments, still they wish to return with her to her home and her people in Judah. Some interpret this as a keen desire for Israelite husbands, perhaps to duplicate, as much as possible, the ones they lost.[115] Some say it is a genuine wish not to be parted from Naomi,[116] who has been a surrogate mother to them. Still others say the two want wholeheartedly to become Israelite, to convert to the God of Naomi and of their deceased husbands.[117] The combined force of Naomi's kindness to them, coupled with her own strong belief in her God and the Commandments, have made a tremendous impression on Ruth and Orpah. On some level they want *to be like* Naomi,[118] who is not only a powerful mother-figure, but also a female role model for them to emulate. She is dignified in sorrow, self-reliant, and courageous in her desperate attempt to balance the scales by facing the people she and Elimelech had abandoned a decade earlier.

NAOMI SAYS, "RETURN, MY DAUGHTERS"

But Naomi said, "Return, my daughters; why should you go
with me? Have I yet sons in my womb that could be your
husbands?

"Turn back, my daughters, go, for I have become too old to
be with a man. Even if I thought there was hope for me, even
if I were to be with a man tonight and also gave birth to sons,
should you wait for them until they are grown?

"Should you tie yourselves down for them, unable to marry
another? Do not do it, my daughters! I am far more
embittered than you, for the hand of God has gone forth
against me." Ruth 1: 11–13

For the first time, Naomi calls Ruth and Orpah *benotai* — *my*
daughters — three times in these verses, instead of the previous
kaloteha, or daughters-*in-law*. The circumstances of their difficult
journey, and their sincere intention to return with Naomi to Judah
and to convert to her God, have brought the three women closer.
Naomi's hostility has faded, and her compassion has been aroused
on their behalf.[119] So Naomi warns "her daughters" that they face
enormous obstacles if they accompany her into Judah. They have,
essentially, three strikes against them already. Not only will an
Israelite man be leery of marrying a Moabite woman, but the two
are also childless widows.[120]

Furthermore, adds Naomi, it would be absurd to hope that
Ruth and Orpah could wait for her to conceive, bear and grow
sons that would be eligible as husbands. And what if these
hypothetical children were females? Ruth and Orpah would have
waited in vain. Not only that, but *yibum* or levirate marriage
(where a living brother marries his deceased brother's widow in
order to perpetuate her dead husband's name and legacy through
their offspring) would not apply to such a union with as-yet-
unborn brothers even if it were feasible.[121]

"No," says Naomi, "You are young women, and should not
tie yourselves to me. I am old and not likely to marry again, and
returning to my home in Beit Lechem will not rejuvenate me.
Even if you were to come with me to Judah and find husbands

there by some great good fortune, we would gradually become estranged, because you would be immersed in your new family. Eventually we would have no connection with one another. It is better that you return home to Moav straightaway and make new lives for yourselves. There is nothing ahead but hardship if you follow me into Judah.

"Watching you waste your lives out of the goodness of your hearts will only add to my misery and worry. God's hand has struck out at me in Moav. First He took my husband, and then He took my two sons; if you refrain from marrying again you, too, will be casualties of God's anger at my family. I beg you not to add to my heavy burden of guilt. I am not simply wretched; I am not simply old; I am *both*.[122] There is no need for you to suffer additionally because of me.[123] Go, return to your home, seek out husbands and make new lives for yourselves."

Though the Bible's narrator does not say so, Naomi understands that her family's misfortune is a punishment for their having left Judah in its time of need and relocated in Moav. The *midrash* is certain that Naomi has made this inference because of her precise words in verse 13: *For **the hand of God** has gone out against me*. Whenever the Bible speaks about "the hand of God" it refers to some sort of divine plague or punishment,[124] as in the plagues of Egypt, which the text refers to repeatedly as brought on by "God's hand."[125] Naomi does not wish to visit more of her punishment on Orpah and Ruth, so she urges them to return to their mother's house. Naomi sets Ruth and Orpah free to marry again.[126]

This permission to remarry is not a trivial gesture. The law of the land had not yet been promulgated that would permit an Israelite man to marry a Moabite woman.[127] As such, if Naomi had not thus released the two women, under Israelite law they would be considered *agunot*, or "chained women," required to remain widows forever, living a husbandless and childless limbo-life that the *midrash* likens to a living death.

Naomi's statement is apparently sufficient impetus for Orpah.

ORPAH RETURNS TO MOAV

And they raised their voices and wept again; and Orpah kissed her mother-in-law, but Ruth clung to her. Ruth 1:14

Naomi's speech is done. There are no more words to be spoken; it is the moment of truth. The *midrash* tells us that words failed the two young women, and this is the reason the Torah tells us only that they raised their voices and cried.[128] They had been weeping silently since Naomi's first attempted leavetaking in verse 9, when they had raised their voices in sorrow together. But now, after walking, talking and weeping, thinking and remembering, the three women are weakened and quite depressed. They are aware that the moment of parting is upon them. Their tears flow, but their voices, says the *midrash*, are hoarse.[129]

The Hebrew word for **raised** *their voices* is spelled without the requisite letter *aleph* here, and the *midrash* sees that missing letter as a hint that all is not what it seems at the parting. It is thought, given what is about to occur — one woman will leave, the other will stay — that only one of the young women raises her weakened voice in a cry of farewell. It is said that Orpah's farewell cry is insincere and that she cries "crocodile tears," giving lip service to her regret at parting, while in reality she is anxious to be gone. She is a daughter of kings, and will return to her place in Moabite society, marrying some important person in the royal court.[130] Another *midrash*[131] counts the four tears that fall from Orpah's eyes as genuine tears of sadness and regret at parting from her mother-in-law. Because she shed those four true tears Orpah is destined to be the ancestor of four great warriors, among them the Philistine giant, Goliath.[132] My thought is that both *midrashim* could be correct. Orpah's tears are real, but she also is anxious to take up the reigns and resume the rest of her life.

Orpah embraces Naomi and kisses her farewell, and though the text does not say so, we can imagine that she does the same to Ruth. Then she quickly[133] turns away[134] from the two women with whom she has shared years of her life and much sorrow, and she begins her slow but determined trek back to her mother's house in Sedei Moav.

The *midrash*[135] flashes forward several hours, and tells us that Orpah will meet with violent misfortune as she travels afoot on the Moabite road. A lone traveler, she will be ambushed and attacked by a band of ruffians, and she will suffer the tortures of rape throughout that first long night. Despite this horror, Orpah makes her way back to her mother's house, and lives out her life as a Moabite princess. Had Orpah remained with Naomi and Ruth, would she have had to endure such misery and physical trauma? The question is unanswerable. Further, it is unthinkable that Orpah or any woman traveling alone should be held responsible for her own rape. By telling the tale of violent consequences befalling Orpah because of her choice to turn back, the *midrash* is reminding the reader that in the blink of an eye, the decision to turn back versus the decision to go forward can have momentous consequences.

We note that Orpah's parting kiss is one-sided; she kisses her mother-in-law, but no reciprocity is indicated in the text. It would seem that once Orpah made up her mind to return home, there was no time for tears or for delay. She kissed, she turned and she departed.

Ruth and Naomi watch Orpah's back until she disappears behind the rise of a sandy hillock. It is only Ruth's soft cries that we hear now in the clear desert air, but it is two cameos we imagine outlined against the clear desert light: one young, and one older. And we read, *But Ruth clung to her*. Ruth's sister is returning home, but Ruth is clinging to Naomi. Ruth is plighting her troth to this older woman who has tried her best to discourage her from accompanying her into Judah. But as we will see, Ruth is complex. She, like all of us, has multiple needs. She is in need of a mother, of a comrade, of a link to her dead husband, of a family and of a future. This older woman, who is bent on returning to a land that she had forsaken and has nothing material to offer, is Ruth's only emotional lifeline, so she reaches for it. She sees in Naomi the answer to her unarticulated prayers.

Naomi turns to Ruth in verse 15 and says to her, *Behold, your sister-in-law is returning to her people and to her god; return [likewise] after your sister-in-law!* The *midrash*[136] adds that Naomi is practically turning Ruth around bodily and gently pushing her in the direction of her sister's retreating figure. "Go with her! This way neither of you will have to travel alone. Return to Moav together." Still, we see that Ruth clings to Naomi.

RUTH'S TURNING POINT

The *midrash*[137] waxes eloquent about the real and raw emotion that is inherent in the three Hebrew words in verse 14, *Rut davkah-bah — Ruth clung to her*. We are witnessing a rare and precious relationship unfolding before our eyes.

Contrary to lore and practice, this mother-in-law and daughter-in-law exhibit an unselfish recognition and love for one another. In a selflessness reminiscent of the newlyweds in O. Henry's 1906 short story "The Gift of the Magi," each of these two women in the Book of Ruth is trying to press on the other a choice that would mean hardship for herself. Naomi is trying to send Ruth back to Moav, which would leave Naomi — an impoverished and weakened old woman — to face a long and rugged journey alone. She does this because she sees that it is the best course of action *for Ruth* — a young widow who can easily remarry among her own people, unencumbered by an Israelite mother-in-law. And as we will see in coming verses, Ruth beseeches Naomi not to push her away, despite the very real physical, social and spiritual difficulties she will encounter as a Moabite woman in Judah if she follows Naomi there. Ruth presses her argument because it will be best *for Naomi* to have a true companion to help shoulder the burdens of her return to Beit Lechem.

As this story progresses, we will see that the two women will come to appreciate that the most valuable asset that each possesses is not material in nature, but is the fresh and enduring love[138] and loyalty each feels for the other. Let us see how Ruth convinces Naomi that the two should return to Judah *together*.

And Ruth replied, "Entreat me not to leave you, to turn back and not to follow you. For wherever you go, I will go, and wherever you lodge, I will lodge; your people shall be my people and your God my God.

"Where you die, I will die, and there I will be buried. This and more may the Lord do to me if anything but death separates me from you." Ruth 1:16–17

Verses 16 and 17 are arguably the most renowned words in the entire Book of Ruth, if not in the Bible. Her words bind her to Naomi as securely as Jonathan's similar words of fealty will bind him to David in coming years.[139] Frymer-Kensky notes that Ruth's evocative and poetic phrases "resonate with the Bible's cadences of covenant and contract."[140] This is the manner in which serious and credible promises of fidelity and allegiance are made between biblical characters.[141] By her words, Ruth is adopting Naomi's journey, her homeland, her God, and her future burial place. She is voluntarily handing over her life into Naomi's keeping, forsaking all that she had and was before this moment.

We must envision Ruth, her tears drying on her cheeks, speaking earnestly to Naomi as the two stand at the crossroads of Moav and Judah. She is making the equivalent of her summation to the judge in a capital case. She has one chance to make her words count, or she will be sent back to Moav to an empty existence that has ceased to have meaning for her. She is pleading for her very life. Perhaps she grasps Naomi's shoulders as she speaks, seeking to infuse her intensity and her probity into the older woman's consciousness. Naomi *must* believe her; she *must* be moved to actually adopt her as her daughter.

And Ruth succeeds. Her final phrase, *This and more may the Lord do to me if anything but death separates me from you!* is said after she tells Naomi that she intends to be buried in the same hallowed ground as her mother-in-law. Swearing on the death of a loved one, or here, on her own future grave in the name of Naomi's God,[142] is the final note of sincerity in her bid to Naomi. For a young and beautiful woman to turn away from the familiar and adopt the uncertain and the dangerous with no possible thought of a future boon to herself, is unusual and, here, is touchingly genuine.

In fact, Ruth's pledge to Naomi is interpreted by the Talmud and *midrash* as Ruth's sincere conversion from Moabite to Israelite. The Talmud[143] parses each of the clauses in Ruth's two-verse speech, understanding each as a response to a discouraging argument posed by Naomi. Let us consider each argument and clause in turn.

When Ruth "cleaved to" Naomi after Orpah had turned and headed back into Moav, Naomi knew she had to try one last time to discourage Ruth from laying her own young life down on the ruined pyre that had been Naomi's. She had to explain to Ruth what she would be facing if she agreed to accompany Naomi into Judah, into the Israelite society, putting herself under the rule of the laws laid down at Sinai.

It is at this point that Ruth interjects the words *Entreat me not to leave you*. The essence of the Hebrew words *al **tifge'i-bi***, translated as "entreat me not," comes from the root *pgh*, meaning "to wound." The *midrash* says that Naomi's words (*go, return!*) wound Ruth like arrows piercing tender flesh.[144] We can imagine Ruth holding her hand up as if to halt Naomi's words of discouragement. "Do not wound me so by pressing me to leave you!" she tells her mother-in-law.

But Naomi persists. She wants to be absolutely sure of Ruth. She says to her, "My dear, being a Hebrew is not an easy thing. Every aspect of our lives is prescribed. For instance, on the Sabbath and festivals it is forbidden for us to walk more than two thousand *amot* from his home. If you convert to the Hebrew faith you would have to obey this walking boundary and restrict your movements. Also, it is forbidden for us to be in seclusion with a prohibited member of the opposite sex. This means you will not be permitted to attend theatres and circuses, where lewd behavior is commonplace." Ruth accepts these restrictions, saying, *Wherever you go, I will go*.

Next Naomi says, "It is the custom of the daughter of Israel to dwell only in a house which has a *mezuzah* affixed to the doorpost." We see that Ruth has no intention of leaving Naomi to travel the road to Judah alone. She has resolved to stay with the older woman so that Naomi will not be alone in an isolated desert inn, or come to harm on the way to Beit Lechem.[145] This is another reason Ruth accepts Naomi's latest commandment saying, *Wherever you lodge, I will lodge*.

Naomi persists, saying, "We are commanded as a people to observe six hundred and thirteen commandments! And many of these commandments govern how we Hebrews must behave toward one another."[146] After listening closely, Ruth replies, *Your people shall be my people.*

Naomi's next argument is, "Understand that we are forbidden to worship idols." And here Naomi explains some of the precepts Israelite people are expected to follow when relating not to one another, but to the One God.[147] To which Ruth the Moabitess replies, *And your God shall be my God.*

Naomi continues her explanation: "There are four types of punishments that our *beit din*, or supreme court, will administer in the event a capital crime is committed. A Hebrew faces these punishments if he disobeys our laws. They are execution by stoning, by burning, by beheading and by strangulation." Ruth listens closely, and responds, *Where you die, I will die.*

Naomi's final argument is a last attempt to impress upon Ruth the severity of the penalties for certain acts, to the extent that even *after death* the offender will bear the mark of sinner: "We maintain two categories of cemeteries administered by our *beit din*: One cemetery is for criminals executed by stoning and burning — the most heinous of offenses — and the other cemetery is for those criminals executed by beheading or strangulation. Would you be prepared to hew to our laws and, God-forbid, face death for capital offenses?" To wit Ruth agrees, responding, *And there I will be buried.*

As we follow this Talmudic and *midrashic* conversation we are witnessing Ruth's acceptance of Naomi's interposed conditions to becoming a Jew,[148] and her determination to be sponsored in her conversion by Naomi and no other.[149]

And in fact, the Talmud and *midrash*[150] understand Ruth's two-verse speech to be an eloquent declaration of her sincere desire to share Naomi's life, including the consequences of Naomi's misfortunes; to share her poverty, her future travails, and the strict laws governing her everyday life *under the banner of Judaism*. The imagined dialectic is meant to show that Naomi carefully unfolds for Ruth a sampling of the variety and gravity of the rules and laws governing a Jewish life so that Ruth can make a true and reasoned choice whether to follow her into Judah or to return to Moav.

There is a *midrashic* difference of opinion about whether Ruth and Orpah had already been converted from paganism to Judaism by Machlon and Chilyon prior to their marriages,[151] or whether there had *not* been earlier, proper conversions.[152]

The view that Ruth and Orpah had *not* yet been converted to Judaism makes the most logical sense for several reasons. First, if Machlon and Chilyon had converted Ruth and Orpah, it was done without authority of a *beit din* or Jewish court, and did not follow the proper legal requirements, so it would have been invalid. Second, had the two been converted to Judaism, Machlon and Chilyon would probably not have been due the punishment of death. Third, even if Machlon and Chilyon did their best to convert them, it is possible that the two women accepted conversion only out of fear of or out of desire for their husbands, and not because of their genuine beliefs, so that the conversion would not have been effective. This is borne out by Orpah's return to Moav. Had she been truly converted from idolatry it is unlikely Orpah would have turned her back on Naomi, Ruth and Judah and returned to Moav to settle down and marry a Moabite.

This might explain why in verse 15 Naomi says that Orpah has returned to her people *and her gods*, while she urges Ruth only to *return with your sister-in-law*. Naomi is aware that the two women had never properly converted to Judaism, and that upon her return to Moav Orpah would almost certainly revert to idol-worship. But implicit in her exhortation to Ruth *to return with her sister-in-law* is Naomi's confidence that even if Ruth accompanied Orpah to Moav, still *she* would *not* revert to idol-worship, because her heart was already ripe to accept the Israelite God.[153] And this is borne out, of course, by Ruth's speech in these verses.

It would seem that the Talmud[154] also assumes there had been *no* earlier conversion, which explains its detailed exposition of the dialogue between Naomi and Ruth—half *midrashic*, half textual—touching on selected Torah laws and penalties. In the opinion of the Talmud, Naomi was laying the groundwork for Ruth's conversion in a deliberate and legally acceptable way so that when they arrived in Judah a *beit din* would be able to give Ruth's conversion its imprimatur. It is also likely that Naomi had been testing Ruth,[155] to see if she would flinch from accompanying

Naomi into Judah, where such stringent laws governing every facet of one's life were the norm.

TESTING RUTH'S METTLE

A word here about testing Ruth's determination and sincerity. Important biblical characters are often tested. In Genesis Abraham is tested repeatedly, some say with ten trials.[156] His first and his tenth trials are bracketed by God's explicit command to him to *lech lecha*, or to "go forth."[157] God is acutely interested in Abraham's willingness to "go forth" into a future that is indistinct, to a land that is unfamiliar, to face even more demanding trials whose nature Abraham can only imagine.

Abraham's first test is to "go forth" from his birthplace, from his father's house, to a land to which God will direct him. And for his last trial (the *Akeida* or binding of Isaac), God again commands Abraham to "go forth" to the land of Moriah, "to the place I will point out to you." For our purposes we should focus on the requirement that Abraham "go forth" from the familiar to the unknown, from the profane, perhaps, to the blessed, all because he is answering a summons he perceives is divine.

Abraham is not the only biblical character to be so tested. The next time it is a female who is summoned to "go forth." A more subtle version of the *lech lecha* test occurs two chapters after the *Akeida* trial. In Gen. 24 Abraham is swearing-in his trusted servant before he departs on the quest for the proper wife for Abraham's son, Isaac. It is critical to Abraham that the chosen girl be prepared to leave her homeland and her family and "go forth" with the servant to come to Isaac and marry and settle in *his* home turf. The familiar *lech lecha* root repeats no fewer than *ten times* in that dramatic chapter!

There is no doubt whatever that Rebecca is the chosen wife for Abraham's son and heir when she stands up before her family and declares *elech!* — "I will go!"[158] — away from her birthplace, away from her mother's tent, with Abraham's servant, to a strange land and to a future that even her brother recognizes may be divinely blessed.

The willingness to "go forth," whether in response to God's summons or in response to a tug of conscience, of instinct, of trust in another, is a critically important test for biblical strangers. And was not Abraham a stranger at the outset of his story? Abraham was just a nomadic shepherd, son of an idol-worshiper, when he heeded the first summons to "go forth." Rebecca, while kin of Abraham and Sarah, was also a stranger, a girl from the other side of the family, the unredeemed side that still worshipped idols. First Abraham and then Rebecca, strangers to God and to the land God had selected, were tapped to take the test. And as Bible readers know, each of them passed it; each left their birthplace and their family, *went forth* into the unknown, found the land to which God was leading them, and ultimately became part of the covenantal family.

At this point in our study of the story of Ruth, Abraham and Rebecca's "going forth" should echo with familiarity. From our vantage point as students of the biblical text we can recognize the Torah's method. Ruth the Moabitess is likewise being tested for greatness. Will she "go forth" with Naomi, forsaking her birthplace, leaving her mother's house, to travel to an unknown land and to adopt the ways of a strict and invisible God? Or will Naomi succeed in discouraging her, sending her back to Moav?

RUTH GOES WITH NAOMI TO JUDAH

When [Naomi] saw how determined she was to go with her, she ceased to argue with her; and the two went on until they reached Beit Lechem . . . Ruth 1:18–19

After Ruth delivers her impassioned speech, Naomi is momentarily struck silent. She is wise enough to realize that she has witnessed a true transformation of the spirit. Ruth has boldly, touchingly and steadfastly declared her willingness to become a daughter to Naomi and a sister of Judah . By deed and word Ruth is cleaving to Naomi and to her God.[159] According to the *midrash*, Ruth also exhibited a flash of fiery spirit and an infusion of faith by speaking so to Naomi. The *midrashists* give Ruth another voice:

"All your predictions of doom will not come to pass, my mother. I am with you now, and I am confident that *our* people and *our* God will not abandon us. Your attempts to discourage me are in vain. For even if you do not wish to bring me to your country so that I can convert to be one of you, I will enter Judah nonetheless, and will become a Jew another way."[160] *Wherever you go, I will go. Your people shall be my people, and your god, my God.*

The reader recognizes that Ruth has passed the critical test.

It would seem Ruth has raised the bar with her words in verses 16 and 17. She has done something unprecedented. She has committed herself utterly to an old Israelite woman who is not her blood kin! The Bible has never before recorded such an act. It is for this unique and important reason that Professor Trible elevates Ruth's courage a notch above Abraham's: "Not only has Ruth broken with family, country, and faith [as Abraham did], but *she has also reversed sexual allegiance*. A young woman has committed herself to the life of an old *woman* rather that to the search for a husband, and she has made this commitment not 'until death us do part' but *beyond* death. One female has chosen another female in a world where life depends upon men."[161]

This statement of commitment is a complete literary surprise. In the Bible a woman will cleave to a man, whether she loves him or not; a man will pursue and cleave to a woman or women for convenience, love, or sex. But there is no cultural or economic advantage for a woman to cleave to another woman, especially when they are both in dire straits. "There is no more radical decision in all the memories of Israel."[162] It speaks of Ruth's hopelessness and resignation; as a barren widow of an Israelite, she realistically forsakes any prospect of a husband in Moav, and she has been warned that no Israelite will wish marry her in Judah. Yet still she cleaves to Naomi. She has nothing and hopes for nothing, yet her moral sense and her love for the older woman edge out her despair. She will cleave to her Israelite mother-in-law, accompany her back into Judah, and trust herself to her God. With everything else stripped away, we see that Ruth's love is the moving force here.

Naomi would have to be made of stone not to respond to this, and the text tells us that in Naomi's silence we can read her assent. A dumbstruck Naomi ceases her attempts to persuade Ruth to return to Moav.[163] For better or worse she has got herself a travel companion and a daughter.

It is from Naomi's silence (in verse 18) that the law emerges that if a prospective convert is not only not discouraged by the attempts to dissuade her, but on the contrary, she remains steadfast in her intentions, then it behooves one to cease from the attempt to dissuade and discourage. For it is forbidden to refuse or dismiss a potential convert more than three times, and Naomi has urged Ruth *shov-na — to return —* three times already.[164] As Naomi does, one must delicately balance a pushing away with the left hand and a pulling nearer with the right.[165]

We can detect a subtle mutuality here. Typically, the reader interprets the scenario depicted in verses 16 and 17 in one way: as a demonstration that Ruth's choice to accompany the weakened and older Naomi is an act of *chesed* or kindness. But with Naomi's silence we can infer that it is Naomi, too, who is performing an act of *chesed*. Her heart goes out to this earnest young woman who is determined to follow her into a strange land with unfamiliar and likely hostile customs. Naomi sees more than Ruth intends her to see. Naomi sees a single, lonesome and forlorn woman[166] without family or child, a sincere seeker who desperately needs a guiding hand. With her silence Naomi agrees to take Ruth under her wing.

RUTH AND NAOMI WALK TOGETHER INTO BEIT LECHEM

And so we read in verse 19 that **they both walk together** *until they arrive in Beit Lechem.* According to Rashi, the sage Rabi Abahu interprets this phrase to mean that the text now holds Naomi and Ruth on an equivalent plane.[167] "See how precious are converts in the eyes of the Almighty," quotes Rashi.[168] Once Ruth becomes determined to convert to Judaism she walks side-by-side with Naomi — a woman who can trace her lineage back to Jacob the Patriarch — into Judah. "The storyteller emphasizes Ruth's coming and her balanced relationship with Naomi. . . . Ruth is not an appendage; she has come by choice . . . so *the two of them* come back to Bethlehem."[169]

The two women are not taking "a walk in the park" as they make their way into Judah. They eat what berries or vegetation they find along the way. They not only walk together, they suffer the same hunger pangs.[170] They hike, probably barefoot or in flimsy makeshift sandals, over rocky, untrod ground. Their journey is approximately fifty kilometers from the point of their crossing into Judah until they arrive in Beit Lechem. It is treacherous not only because of its physical rigors, but also because road travel in a lawless time was a dangerous undertaking. For two women alone it would have been reckless if not for their desperate situation.

Curiously — and this occurs several times in the Book of Ruth — verse 19 refers to the two women with a *masculine* pronoun when it says that *they both walked onward*. The Hebrew word *shteyhem*, meaning "both of them," is written with a masculine ending — with a *mem* instead of a *nun*. The *midrash* explains, in a tribute to the women's ingenuity, that the two cleverly altered their clothing and headdresses so that from a distance they looked like *men* on the road! Their objective was not to appear vulnerable, and they achieved their aim. Between their quick thinking and divine providence, it is considered a small miracle that during the week or two of their journey the women were not approached or molested in any way by bandits or other human predators. The same *midrash* says that Ruth and Naomi were stalwart and dogged, and focused on their objective of reaching Beit Lechem. In an anachronistic expression of admiration it says "they acted like men, and not like women,"[171] and that for this reason the text uses the male pronoun.

All through the difficult journey to Beit Lechem Ruth remains at Naomi's side, lending a hand lest she lose her footing, hoisting her onto their scrawny donkey when the older woman can walk no further. The *midrash* explains the phrase *The two of them walked together **until** they arrived at Beit Lechem*. It tells us that Ruth held onto Naomi's hand throughout virtually their entire journey, whether on the road or when they were able to stay overnight at a tented inn. But as they approach Beit Lechem, and Ruth sees the settlement in the distance, she begins to walk *behind* Naomi. She wants Naomi to precede her into the town. She thinks, "Perhaps my mother-in-law will be embarrassed to return to her home with me by her side. Her old friends will see me and hold her in contempt for befriending a Moabitess."[172] But Naomi holds Ruth fast by her side, and for this reason the verse goes on to say *when they arrived in Beit Lechem . . .* The two women, Jewess and Moabitess, enter the town as a unit.

THE TOWN IS SHOCKED: CAN THIS BE NAOMI?

> *. . . And it came to pass when they arrived in Beit Lechem the entire city was abuzz on their account. And they asked, "Can this be Naomi?!"* Ruth 1:19

We can imagine Naomi's ambivalence about returning to her home town after a dozen years. She is relieved to return to her birthplace, to a town she never thought she would see again. But she is deeply ashamed, knowing that when she last walked these streets she was heading toward Moav, abandoning her friends and countrymen to a fierce famine. She is keenly aware that her entire life has done a somersault, and that this reversal is evident to everyone who sees her.

Naomi and Ruth had stopped just outside the city, and Ruth did her best with Naomi, dusting her off, rearranging her clothing, washing off her face and hands. But the years of sorrow, suffering and privation, plus the evidence of recent weeks of hard traveling, are impossible to erase. Two tattered, wretched and beggarly women with a swayback donkey enter the gates of Beit Lechem[173] on a market day, when virtually the entire population is out and about.

Some say it was the first day of the barley harvest,[174] explaining the ceremonial foregathering of all the people of Beit Lechem to be parceled out to work in designated fields. Others say it was the day that a great man's wife died and was buried, and that the entire town turned out to pay her homage.[175] The great man was Boaz, a judge and wealthy landowner, and cousin to Naomi, but of course Naomi is not to know this as she slowly walks into the town square. The townspeople, following the casket according to the mourning tradition, stare at the two lone women. Naomi and Ruth stand where they are and watch the procession. It is the women of Beit Lechem who step away from the cortege and approach the two strangers. The older women peer closely at the strangers and, approaching *Ruth*, exclaim, "Can *this* be Naomi?"

The *midrash*[176] tells us that the weeks of hard travel have not dimmed Ruth's loveliness. When Naomi left Beit Lechem she had been forty years of age, trim and straight with lustrous hair and eyes, a bloom to her complexion. This young woman whom they see before them reminds the women of Beit Lechem of the younger Naomi. None of the women of the town look remotely like Ruth, for they have all been baked by the Judean sun or ravaged by a decade of famine. Ruth's youthful, glowing beauty is both a magnet and an affront. This is why the townswomen's first reaction is an exclamation of disbelief: *Can **this** be Naomi?!* They are stunned that Naomi could have survived these dozen years and still look youthful and fresh. It is fascinating that the *midrash* sees Ruth as a mirror-image of the younger Naomi.[177] Perhaps this similarity of appearance helped soften Naomi's heart to the younger woman.

Or perhaps the women did recognize the wrinkled old "mother" by Ruth's side as Naomi, and were subtly chiding her by pretending disbelief that the wizened and wretched stranger could be the lovely woman they had known. The *midrashim* lay out the scene for us:

There is a ripple in the small crowd of townswomen as they surround Naomi and Ruth and stare at them from all sides. The women's refrain — *Can **this** be Naomi? Can this be **Naomi**?*[178] — is one of wonderment and surprise. Some women even point to the two strangers and whisper, "After all this time, can it be that Naomi has come home from the fields of Moav?"[179]

"Why, *this* must be Naomi!" the townswomen say as they turn and behold the older traveler. "Why have you chosen to return to Beit Lechem from the fields of Moav *now*? And what has happened to the woman we knew?" The townswomen turn to one another saying, "The Naomi we knew was a golden girl with rosy cheeks. Behold before us is a woman *resembling* Naomi, but *this* woman is so changed that we barely recognize her. Her face is pinched and lined,[180] and her skin is grey from hunger.[181]

"Can this be the Naomi we knew who used to go out and about in a shaded wagon with maids and camels and many mules? *This* woman is on foot and with one mule and but one companion. Is *this* Naomi, who used to wear decorated shoes? The woman before us is barefoot.[182] Can this be our Naomi, who used to wear embroidered silk robes? *This* woman is dressed in patched rags. What has happened to the Naomi-of-Beit Lechem whom we knew, whose jewelry we all used to borrow and whose beauty was more radiant than the sun? What has befallen Naomi, who, with her husband Elimelech, were two of the great people of Israel?"[183]

NAOMI RESPONDS
TO THE WOMEN OF BEIT LECHEM

And she said to them, "Do not call me Naomi; call me Marah, for the Almighty has dealt very bitterly with me.
"I went away [from here] full, and the Lord has brought me back empty. Why [then] should you call me Naomi, considering that God has testified against me and the Almighty has dealt harshly with me?" Ruth 1:20–21

Naomi endures the women's stares and their shocked comments, their hardly-concealed, instinctive tinge of *schadenfreude*. She understands that they are expressing nothing more than her own thoughts and regrets. The irony is palpable: they had all survived the ten-year famine by remaining in Judah, while Naomi's husband and sons, who fled to Moav to escape the famine, perished there. Naomi is the lone survivor. Ruth moves closer to Naomi and holds her arm protectively. There is a momentary hush, as if the small crowd waits for a reaction from the silent pair of tattered travelers, and in particular from this Naomi-ghost.

Naomi takes a breath and holds herself with dignity. She answers the women: "Yes, my old friends, it is I, Naomi. But do not call me "Naomi," or "pleasantness," as that name suited me only *before* I left Beit Lechem. Then, I was full with blessing and promise, and life's prospect was sweet for me. I was blessed with wealth, with land, with a husband and with two young sons and the promise of more.[184] But God saw fit to take all that away from me, and today I arrive back in Beit Lechem empty.[185] So now, old friends, I ask you to call me "Marah" or "bitterness" instead of Naomi. For truly the Almighty God has judged me,[186] and has punished me, leaving me with me much bitterness. God has taken away husband, sons and wealth, and left me the sole survivor, without bread to eat or a dress to wear.[187]

The crowd murmurs and then disperses, either to harvest the barley crop or to bury its dead. Naomi and Ruth make their way to Naomi's former house.

THE BARLEY HARVEST

Naomi and Ruth's arrival in Beit Lechem is on the eve of the Passover, midway into the month of Nissan, at the start of the season of the barley harvest. In the agricultural cycle the barley is the first sustaining crop to grow to maturity. This is also the time that the first-yield measure—the *omer* of barley—is brought to the priest as an offering to God. After this ceremonial offering is brought, it is the signal for the actual harvest to begin, and thereafter the people are permitted to enjoy the fruits of their labor and to eat freely of the barley crop.[188] This barley harvest lasts for fifty days, until such time that the second harvest—the more desirable wheat crop—is ripe and ready for reaping. Ordinarily, in non-famine years, the farmer's barley crop was used primarily as *animal fodder* for his livestock![189] It was the *second* harvest—the wheat crop—that was used for bread, cakes and staple table foods. The barley's claim to fame, then, is that it is the harbinger of the eventual wheat harvest.

In our story, however, the humble barley harvest comes after the Israelites have experienced a decade-long drought. So this first harvest is not only a time of joyous and reverent thanksgiving to God for bringing rain; it also enables the barley crop to feed a hungry population.

It behooves the curious Bible reader to ask why the Torah has set Ruth's story specifically at this moment in the agricultural cycle. As we will see, metaphorically Ruth shares a few key characteristics with the barley harvest. The barley is typically the crop that nobody gets particularly excited about. It is taken somewhat for granted until, of course, a famine ravages the land; then the humble barley crop comes into its own. So, too, Ruth. She is an impoverished, childless Moabite widow, not a particularly desirable person to Naomi or to her countrymen in biblical Judea. In an unexpected development Ruth's companionship turns out to be a life-saving blessing to her bereft and aged mother-in-law. What's more, we will see that Ruth—Naomi's potentially forgettable dependent—surprises us all. Because of her careful, loving and yes, audacious acts, she will become the forerunner of royalty!

So it is significant that our story takes place during the barley harvest. The onset of the first harvest in more than ten years is a momentous time for Naomi and Ruth to return to Beit Lechem; perhaps it heralds *their* return to life along with this land and its long-suffering inhabitants.

NAOMI HAS A POWERFUL KINSMAN

Now Naomi had a kinsman on her husband's side, a mighty man of substance, of the family of Elimelech, and his name was Boaz. Ruth 2:1

The first portion of the Book of Ruth told of leaving Judah for Moav, of the attendant deaths and trials, and of Naomi's return, with Ruth by her side. Central to this first segment of the story was the development of the strong bond between Naomi and Ruth, her Moabite daughter-in-law, and the evolution of Ruth's nascent spiritual awakening to the Israelite God. We are poised now to witness our heroine's further character development. How will she behave under the pressure of living in a strange and somewhat hostile—certainly skeptical—society? How do the two women survive day-to-day? How does Ruth meet up with Boaz? What input does Naomi have over the course of events? How does Ruth acclimate to the strict laws that govern Israelite society and her life with Naomi? We begin the second portion of the story, where some of our questions will be addressed.

WHO IS BOAZ?

In chapter 2, verse 1 the Bible introduces a new character, an *ish gibor chayil*, a "mighty man of valor," a powerful and wealthy man who also happens to be a known relative[190] of Naomi's dead husband Elimelech. This man's name is Boaz. The name Boaz literally means "with strength," so it is consistent with the verse's description of him. From the outset the reader is expected to appreciate this man's personal vigor. And this precise issue, as we will see, is very much on Boaz's mind, and will figure into Ruth's own story later on.

In the way of the Torah, the reader can detect a clue that "this man Boaz" will play a heroic role in the coming story. For he is announced with a stylistic trill: *and his name is Boaz* (such as "and his name was Mordechai"[191]). If the man had been a villain, the Torah text would have had his name *precede* his introduction (such as "Goliath was his name"[192]).[193]

The Talmud[194] explains that the very day that Naomi and Ruth enter Beit Lechem, Boaz buries his wife of many years. The *midrash* teaches us that even on such a sad day for Boaz, unbeknownst to him, Ruth is at that very moment entering the orbit of his life, walking through the city's gates with Naomi. "God prepares the cure before sending an affliction," the theory goes. For this reason, the Talmud teaches us, one must strive never to lose hope, even in the face of extreme personal misfortune; the solution to our problem might literally be right around the corner. This teaching would seem to apply to Naomi and Ruth as much as to Boaz.

And who is Boaz?

While the Bible text merely tells us that Boaz is "a known relation of Naomi's husband," this same section of Talmud lays out the details of Naomi's husband's genealogy, which will prove to be the essential fulcrum of this story later on. We learn that

Naomi's husband, Elimelech, was also her uncle, one of her father's three brothers. These four brothers — namely, Elimelech, Salmon, Tov (or Ploni-Almoni) and Naomi's father — were the four sons of Nachshon, son of Aminadav, hero of the Exodus. As we already have discussed, Aminadav was a fifth-generation descendant of Judah, the fourth son of the patriarch Jacob. Boaz's father was Salmon, brother of Elimelech; this makes Naomi and Boaz first cousins.

Boaz is a warrior, to be sure, but he also is an honored, honest and wealthy man,[195] learned[196] and respected in Beit Lechem.

Some say that the Boaz of our story is also called Ivtzan, who was a judge in Judah for seven years at the time of the unfolding drama.[197] Yet the Talmud[198] tells a disturbing story about Boaz/Ivtzan. It says that he had sixty children; thirty sons and thirty daughters. When it came time for each of these children to marry, Boaz made two enormous feasts, one in his own house and one in the house of his in-laws-to-be. Given the size of their community, Boaz invited all the locals. Only one man did Boaz exclude, and his name was Manoach, who at that time was childless.[199] Perhaps Boaz thought that he had no need to invite Manoach, as Manoach would not be reciprocating any such invitations to Boaz. Perhaps Boaz only sought to spare Manoach embarrassment, reasoning that surely Manoach would wish to reciprocate for Boaz's generous invitations, but that he would be unable to do so, having no wedding festivities to which he could invite Boaz in return. Perhaps Boaz thought that inviting Manoach would only hurt the man's feelings repeatedly, reminding him of his own childlessness.

Boaz's flawed thinking no doubt caused Manoach much hurt and embarrassment notwithstanding Boaz's intentions. And it is precisely because of this absence of *chesed* or kindness, the Talmud tells us, that all of Boaz/Ivtzan's children died in his lifetime.

At the time of this story, then, Boaz is childless and a widower, and notwithstanding his great wealth, he is suffering deep emotional loneliness and regret. As such, he is not unlike Naomi and Ruth. Perhaps that is the reason the Talmud tells us about Boaz/Ivtzan's punishment; it is thereby equalizing the emotional underpinnings of the three main characters, each of whom has lost all the people they held most dear. We will see how the Tanach brings Naomi, Ruth and Boaz—wounded characters, all—within one another's orbit, and also, perhaps, how they heal themselves and each other.

NAOMI IS EMBARRASSED

RUTH 2:1

Naomi and Ruth make their way to Naomi's old homestead. The abandoned house has long ago fallen to roofless ruin, and there is only a partial foundation left to mark its former size and grandeur. Instead, we can imagine that the two women make their bleak home in a tumbledown gardener's shack on the grounds. It has four walls, a semblance of a roof and a door with a lock, it is empty of all tools and is cool and welcoming. Naomi is grateful for this humble blessing, considering that her husband's lands and fields are being tilled by another. She feels fortunate that her old house and its grounds are still unoccupied. So destitute and desperate is she that Naomi actually sells off part of her husband's land[200] in order to buy food for herself and Ruth.

With such a close and illustrious relation as Boaz, it is curious that Naomi does not seek help from him. Beyond their family connection she is also a destitute widow with an extra mouth to feed, so objectively, if he were appealed to, surely he would willingly proffer aid. The *midrash*[201] tells us that still Naomi does not approach Boaz. She is deeply embarrassed by her reduced circumstances, certain that it marks her as a sinner. She reasons, why else would God have punished her so? Also, she feels uncomfortable turning to him for help because years ago, when Elimelech fled with his family to Moav to wait out the famine, it was Boaz who stayed behind and fed the poor of Beit Lechem.

Another reason Naomi remains aloof from Boaz is that her instinct tells her that Boaz deeply resents—might even hate—her for bringing a Moabitess into the midst of their tightly-knit community.[202] She would never accept assistance meant only for herself; she has come to love Ruth like a daughter and she is mindful that her household now has two mouths and souls to feed. Naomi knows that if she were to beg food from Boaz he would be obligated to provide food for Ruth, too, though he would deeply resent feeding a Moabite on principle.

So Boaz keeps his distance, and Naomi does not seek him out. And even though the two women do not have a piece of bread between them, still Naomi's heart recoils from asking Ruth — a daughter of kings, after all — to follow in the fields after the gleaners and pick up the leftover sheaves with the rest of the poor of Beit Lechem.[203]

RUTH RESOLVES TO GLEAN WITH THE POOR

And Ruth the Moabitess said to Naomi, "I will go now to the field, and I will glean among the ears of grain, behind someone in whose eyes I may find favor." And she said, "Go, my daughter." Ruth 2:2

Among the Israelite laws Naomi taught Ruth[204] was the requirement that during the harvest, the single sheaves that fall to the ground are not picked up by the harvesters. Those sheaves are left for the poor and the stranger, who are permitted to glean the leftover stalks.[205] Ruth has paid close attention to her mother-in-law. So when they find themselves with nothing to eat — ironically stranded in the midst of the season of abundant harvest in the place called "Beit Lechem" — Ruth recalls the law of *leket*, as it was known. She kneels down before Naomi and earnestly says to her:

"My mother, I am younger than you are, and I am strong. I am unknown in Beit Lechem, and it will not be difficult for me to glean in the fields, as I know no one. For you this would be a humiliation.[206] Also, I am poor and I am a stranger. The law of *leket* applies to me, does it not?[207] You have explained that usually a poor person would glean in the field of a relation or at least in the field of an acquaintance. But I have no relations or friends in Beit Lechem. So I will go out into the field of one of our neighbors. I will seek permission to glean. And if the owner does not scold me or send me away, I will glean there and I will bring back grain.[208] From this grain we will mill flour, and bake bread and cakes for our meals. We will not be wealthy, but thanks to your laws neither will we perish from hunger."

It is an indication of Ruth's humble but sensitive nature that she asks her mother-in-law's permission, or at least her advice, about gleaning after the harvesters.[209] There is trepidation on both sides. Ruth knows that Naomi will be protective of Ruth's sensibilities, and will shy away from asking the daughter of a king and widow of a once-wealthy man to publicly align herself with the poor and disenfranchised; actually to *become one* herself! Likewise, Naomi knows that despite Ruth's seeming carefree resolution to glean there must be a fear or unease about humbling herself and participating in such an alien welfare custom. It is one thing to come from humble roots and to have known nothing but gleaning with the poor year-in and year-out. It is quite another thing to have known palaces, privilege and plenty and then to tumble such a distance that gleaning with the poor is the only stopgap between sustenance and starvation. Naomi appreciates Ruth's willingness to do this.

After all the shadowboxing is done, Ruth steps up and prepares to do what she must to feed Naomi and herself. The alert Bible reader appreciates the wonderful, subtle righting of the Moabite wrong that is taking place in these verses. Ruth the Moabitess is single-handedly about to repair the sin that her ancestors had perpetrated against the Israelites after they had been liberated from servitude in Egypt. Where the Moabites had denied the exhausted Israelites bread and water, Ruth is now extending herself, unbidden, to secure grain to keep her her Israelite mother-in-law from starving. And there is a reciprocity at work. Naomi has come to admire and love this young woman like a daughter of her own blood. Moabitess and Jewess are united in affection and purpose.

Naomi is deeply touched by Ruth's determination and courage. Though it pains her to agree, she responds to Ruth, *Go, my daughter.*

BOAZ NOTICES RUTH

RUTH 2:3–5

Now it happens that Elimelech's fields abut his brothers' land-holdings. So when Ruth goes "out to the field" that morning, the first field she reaches — already busy with harvesters, foremen and at its fringes a clutch of female gleaners — actually belongs to Naomi's husband, Elimelech![210] Elimelech's brothers' families stepped in in his absence after the famine ended, sowing the barley crop on his land. Now, with the harvest upon them, Elimelech's brothers and nephews harvest *all* their fields, including what had once been Elimelech's, treating all their holdings as family property. They are intent on reaping the abundant harvest and making up for the lost years.

Ruth ventures out into the nearby fields, marking her way so she will be able to find her way back to Naomi at day's end.[211] Unbeknownst to Ruth, the field in which she has chosen to glean is being worked by Boaz's men. One *midrash* actually assigns Ruth a guardian angel who leads her to glean in Boaz's field, and assigns another guardian angel to Boaz, to direct him to oversee the specific field in which Ruth is gleaning. It is said that in the spot where the two angels meet, Ruth and Boaz also meet, and there the holy *shechinah*, or spirit of God, hovers.[212] The confluence of time and circumstance that brings Ruth to Boaz's attention is considered a manifestation of God's plan. And this may well be the case.

A week has gone by since Naomi and Ruth walked through the gates of Beit Lechem. Boaz is just risen from his seven-day mourning period for his wife, and is out in his fields overseeing and orchestrating the all-important barley harvest. Under Israelite laws of mourning, this is the first time in a week that Boaz is permitted to formally greet his friends and workers; it is also the first time in a week that they are permitted to greet him.[213] Here, in chapter 2, verse 4, on that fateful morning, Boaz calls out *God be with you!* to his harvesters, and they respond *God should bless you!*

And in the very next verse Boaz spots Ruth.

After greeting his men, as Boaz surveys both his harvesters and the poor who glean on the edges of the field, he notices a strange woman among the gleaners. Boaz points to her and asks his foreman, *To whom does this maiden belong?*

The Talmud[214] is curious. Surely Boaz does not bother himself to inquire about *every* poor gleaner in his fields! Why does he take note of Ruth? The first reason is perhaps the obvious one: Ruth is exceedingly beautiful. So much so, that she modestly swaths herself in shawls and loose clothing so as not to attract attention to herself. Notwithstanding her care, the *midrash* tells us that "whoever saw her became sexually excited."[215] Boaz also might notice Ruth because her garments are strange to his eye; they are not made from typical Israelite cloth,[216] so perhaps she stands out regardless of her looks and in spite of her modesty.

Another reason Boaz notices her, according to the Talmud,[217] is Ruth's demeanor while she works. She adopts a nearly seated position, her posture erect as she gathers the fallen sheaves, while the other women are bending over from the waist. She takes care as she gleans not to expose her legs, even though the other gleaners have hitched their skirts above their knees in order to move faster. She is reserved, even dignified, not speaking either to the other gleaners or to the foreman unless she is spoken to first, while the other gleaners are known to one another and chatter and jest aloud.[218] And importantly, at all times she remains *behind* the harvesters so that she will be out of their line of sight and not the object of their stares.[219]

But there is still another significant and telling reason Boaz singles out Ruth from among the forty-two gleaners[220] in that corner of the field. Boaz, who is a Judge in Judah, is well-versed in the law of *leket*. He watches the gleaners and is struck that only one of the women is gleaning precisely according to the letter of the law. Only one woman, dressed modestly and carrying herself like a young queen, is picking up one or two forgotten sheaves at a time.[221] The other gleaners scoop up the stalks from between the rows; they do not even wait for the harvesters to pass by before they pounce on the sheaves. Only this new woman waits and selects from the stalks left behind as she is permitted to do.[222]

Boaz had never before seen a stranger glean with such care not to exceed the lawful limits. And as for the poor gleaners, they usually lack the ability to restrain themselves from gathering the sheaves as fast as they can. Says the *midrash*, "In Ruth he sees a special measure of intelligence."[223] For all these reasons Boaz is curious enough to inquire, *Whose damsel is she?* Perhaps she is married, with a husband and family.[224]

"SHE IS A MOABITE!"

RUTH 2:6–7

Boaz's foreman responds:

> *"The maiden is a Moabite who returned with Naomi from the fields of Moav. She asked permission to glean after the reapers, and she works tirelessly from morning to night, spending but little time in the hut."* Ruth 2:6

The foreman is taken aback by Boaz's interest in Ruth. He has worked alongside Boaz for many years and cannot recall Boaz ever asking about a gleaner's bona fides. He suspects that Boaz is physically attracted to this lovely woman.[225] And in the familiar, even protective way that long-time associates have with each other, Boaz's foreman seeks to preempt his boss from an entanglement with the new gleaner. He stresses aloud[226] that *She is a Moabite*, implying that she is forbidden to an Israelite man, certainly to a man of Boaz's stature. In the foreman's mind, though he has never spoken to her and knows nothing other than what he relates to Boaz, Ruth is at her essence "a Moabite." He thinks her modesty is a charade, her manners merely tutored. He is hinting to his master that this vision of a converted woman is merely that: an illusion, and that as a Moabite she will always revert to idol-worshipping type.[227]

The foreman is thinking, "aren't there women enough among the Israelites to find favor in your eyes?"

But the foreman voices none of these suspicions; Boaz is his employer and his better, and there is a requisite measure of distance and respect due him. The man hopes that Boaz will intuit his meaning just from his words *She is a Moabite*.[228] And despite his hostility toward the Moabite stranger, the foreman states the objective facts as he answers Boaz: The woman is new to the gleaners, but she is focused and hardworking. She gleans the fallen ears of barley and she gathers the forgotten sheaves, and she barely stops to rest.

Or perhaps this is not the case at all. Perhaps the foreman seeks to encourage Boaz's interest? Another *midrash*[229] interprets the verse as part of a larger conversation between Boaz and his foreman. Boaz first inquires, "Who is this girl? Is she anybody's wife, daughter or betrothed?" And the foreman, after long and close acquaintance with his employer, seeing his master's interest in this lovely, eligible woman, thinks, "My master Boaz has lost his children and his wife, and is deeply unhappy. This is the first time I have ever seen him express any interest in a gleaner. Let me hint to him that she is eligible. The fact that she is a Moabitess is no longer an impediment, and the fact that she's the widowed daughter-in-law of Naomi, a kinswoman, should ease his mind." So he responds laconically, *She is a Moabite maiden*.

Boaz could interpret his foreman's words as warning him off "the Moabite." Or he could interpret them as tipping him off to a good thing, implicitly saying, "The girl is of a high station but has just arrived from Sedei Moav with Naomi. She has already been converted to Judaism and is eligible for marriage. But as it is early days, nobody has seen her yet or made her acquaintance."[230] The ambiguity of the foreman's statement might have given Boaz pause. For the woman before him is not a young maiden as the foreman's words imply; she is a beautiful woman of about thirty[231] or forty[232] years of age. Looking at her, Boaz sees that her goodness radiates from her face, lending her a young appearance.

Even if his foreman resents the Moabite stranger, apparently Boaz does not share the man's hostility. Contrarily — or perhaps he is so drawn to her that he cannot help himself — Boaz turns from his foreman and addresses Ruth directly. Boaz hopes to soften his foreman's derogatory epithet (*She is a Moabite!*). It is anathema to a man of Boaz's wealth and stature to humiliate a poor person who has come to glean in his fields. It is also against the intent of Israelite law, which provides this opportunity for the poor, the stranger, the orphan and the widow[233] to allow them to retain their pride as they glean behind the harvesters. The fallen or forgotten sheaves belong to the poor *by operation of law*. Once the sheaves of barley or wheat hit the ground they are, in essence, no longer the owner's property. They belong to the gleaners.[234]

Whether the foreman approves or disapproves, Boaz is his own man and is unheeding of the man's messages. Let us listen in on the conversation as he turns to Ruth.

BOAZ SPEAKS TO RUTH FOR THE FIRST TIME

RUTH 2:8–9

Boaz is an *ish gibor chayil*, a prosperous and respected man of action[235] who has lived his life and made many decisions, some deliberately and some instantaneously. In the span of a moment Boaz observes Ruth, takes in her looks and her demeanor, and processes all that he knows of her relationship to his cousin Naomi. He does all this in the instant of time it takes to blink an eye, and in that fraction of a second Boaz makes up his mind.[236] Neither he nor Ruth can know it, but his decision to speak to her in his field will have important repercussions, and his words will not only begin their love affair, they will reverberate for millennia. Boaz is either on foot or on horseback as he surveys his fields. So he is looking down at Ruth as she gleans. Surely she looks up at him, even stops her work and stands in his presence as would all the gleaners, thus according the master and owner of the field due respect.

Boaz is looking at Ruth as he speaks to her, and what might have begun as a simple request ends up as a commanding, coaxing argument.[237]

"Listen to me, my daughter!" he begins. Boaz's use of the familiar expression of affection is seen most commonly in an address by an older person to one who is much younger; by one a person of stature to one who is of lesser station. It implies that the speaker is acting in the listener's best interests, like a father to a daughter. We see that Boaz has gone immediately from treating Ruth as a stranger and a gleaner to addressing her as someone with whom he has a protective relationship.

Or Boaz could have verbalized the phrase in another way: "Listen *to me*, my daughter!" By merely shifting the emphasis Boaz is telling Ruth to disregard the negative words and prejudiced behavior that the ignorant foreman or the other gleaners or the harvesters may have directed her way. He is appointing *himself* her protector, asking her to trust *him*.

"I ask you not to wander from field to field in your quest for gleanings during this harvest. Do not glean even one sheaf in any field that does not belong to me. Instead, come each day to *this* field and follow behind my harvesters, working with the other female gleaners,[238] staying close to them. You are among us now, so do not worship any gods but the God of Israel,[239] and you will be treated with kindness. And when you grow thirsty throughout the long day you must drink from the water my men have drawn. Do not tire yourself by drawing your own water.

"I will instruct the harvesters to leave behind sufficient sheaves for your needs, so you will have no reason to go elsewhere. And you can rest assured that I will have commanded my men not to lay a hand on you. They can sometimes be boisterous, but I promise that they will do nothing to embarrass you, annoy you, or cause you harm."[240]

If it seems that Boaz is getting a little ahead of himself — after all, he has only just a few moments ago set eyes on Ruth and here he is all-but-requesting that she plight her troth to him — the *midrash*[241] provides an explanation. This entire tableau being enacted in the corner of Boaz's field takes Boaz completely by surprise. In a matter of days his life has been utterly altered. His wife, the mother of the many children he sired and then lost because of his heedlessness, is dead, and aside from his wealth he has nothing enduring and personal to leave to posterity. He is not a young man, and had essentially abandoned hope for a future as he rose up from his mourning period. Now, in a flash, he beholds a woman whom he desires and who may be free to marry him. In a moment of divine intuition, he even imagines that she is already his wife, and that through her he might redeem his barren existence.

Boaz is driving at ninety miles per hour, so-to-speak, while Ruth is still in "park." He imagines a future with Ruth, but of course Ruth sees only a tall and powerful man who is master of the fields and in whose hands, quite literally, her survival rests. After his speech he is figuratively holding his breath. How will Ruth respond?

RUTH RESPONDS: "BUT I AM A STRANGER!"

RUTH 2:10

Ruth is stunned that the padrone has noticed her.[242] That he speaks to one of the gleaners for any purpose other than pure business is highly unusual; but that he should offer her his protection is unheard-of. After all, she is but one of dozens of hardworking, hungry girls to be found toiling in his fields and vineyards.[243] The gleaners stop in their tracks, all eyes and ears trained on Boaz and Ruth. They and she have heard everything already said; the foreman's use of the derogatory epithet, and Boaz's gracious extension of much more than mere courtesy to a stranger. Everyone awaits Ruth's response.

Ruth prostrates herself in humble submission directly onto the ground and bows her head low.[244] Then she raises herself, and responds to Boaz, asking, *"Why have I found favor in your eyes that you should take notice of me, considering that I am a stranger?"* She cannot imagine why this great lord is paying special attention to her. In her forthright, surprised query Ruth twice uses one Hebrew word-root that, as sometimes happens, embodies two opposite meanings.[245] First she uses the word *hakireini*, meaning "recognize me." And immediately afterward she uses the word *nachriya*, meaning "stranger."[246] Ruth is genuinely stumped. "Why do you speak to me in terms of **recognition** and familiarity, as if I am known to you, a part of your world? For as you well know, I am a Moabite Gentile, a forbidden **stranger**."

By using the *hcr* root in both of its dichotomous meanings, the text is poetically and subtly sending a series of dual messages. Just as Ruth is *both* a relative-by-marriage and a Moabite stranger, a royal princess and an impoverished gleaner, a converted Jewess and a former idol-worshiper, the root-word *hcr* exquisitely embodies both recognition and estrangement. Boundaries are blurred here. Can it be that the master will wish to wed the lowly gleaner? Such a man as Boaz has both a summer and a winter palace,[247] while Ruth lives in a broken-down shed. In the reader's culture, where the Cinderella motif is ingrained, and virtuous young women do, indeed, rise from scullery maid to wed the prince, the paradox of *hcr* may not seem so strange. But the enduring quality of such plots rests on their improbability. By her words Ruth is expressing her genuine disbelief that she is being recognized, singled out to such a purpose.

Ruth is not vain; while there is no mention anywhere in the text that Ruth is beautiful, the commentaries assign her exceptional looks, as we have mentioned. Yet Ruth does not appreciate that this could be the reason for Boaz's attentions. Compared to the female unguents available to her growing up in the palace in Moav, Ruth has nothing on hand to make her *toilette*. We can imagine that she has no mirror in which to catch her reflection, so she does not know that her skin is still supple and unlined, her dark eyes thickly fringed and fine, her black hair glossy and so dark it is almost blue in the sun. Even her tattered shawls and layered skirts cannot completely mask her fine shape or conceal her dignified manner. And nothing could alter her soft, refined speech that belies her appearance. But Ruth does not see this.

Ruth is embarrassed[248] at the special attention. She would have preferred anonymity. In fact, she makes it a point not to disclose to anyone that her mother-in-law is widow to Elimelech. She assumes that Boaz is unaware of the misfortunes that have befallen Naomi's family and of her dire straits, because in the week since she has returned to Beit Lechem Naomi has been visited by no one.[249] She suspects Boaz might have an ulterior motive for his apparent kindness,[250] because surely she is mistaken about his nuanced message. How could he possibly desire to wed *her*, an impoverished Moabite stranger, forbidden to him by Israelite law?[251] Perhaps it is a case of mistaken identity.[252] Which is why she answers him with frank wonder: *"Why have I found favor in your eyes that you should take notice of me, considering that I am a stranger?"*

BOAZ PRAISES RUTH

RUTH 2:11–12

Boaz addresses Ruth saying, "You are wrong, my daughter. You are *not* just one of the crowd of gleaners; you have been brought to my special attention. A number of people have told me all about what you did for your mother-in-law after her husband died. Such behavior is praiseworthy.

"There are actually two reasons that your character and behavior stand out. First, of course, is your kindness to my cousin, the widow Naomi, who had nobody in Moav to whom she could turn for help. And second is your choice to become a Jew, which is a difficult decision to make and to adhere to. You decided to do this when you could easily have chosen to remain safe and secure in your parents' house, or at the very least to remain in the land of your birth. Instead, you chose to leave all that was familiar and safe, and you came to Judah to make your home among a people you do not know. All this speaks of the depth of your feeling for Naomi and for the Israelite God, and it speaks well of your motives and your character.

"Once you genuinely resolved to become a member of the Hebrew faith you quickly and forthrightly carried out your decision by following Naomi into Judah. You have stayed by her side and you have comported yourself in the manner of a righteous proselyte.[253]

"So you see, you are not as unknown to me as you thought, nor are you a stranger. Your acts of kindness and genuine faith make you one of us![254]

"Furthermore, in the Israelite religion one is repaid for such *chesed* as you have shown Naomi not only by human means, such as my kindness to you, a gleaner in my fields. Your deeds also will be requited by a reward from our God. So my blessing to you is that you should be rewarded in full by the Lord, God of Israel, under whose wings you have sought refuge!

"May you bear children who will become leaders in Israel, and may your **complete** reward include that you, yourself, will be the mother of royalty."[255]

Boaz's lengthy response in verses 11 and 12 is more than Ruth could have imagined, and is replete with obvious as well as implicit meaning. The two momentous decisions that Ruth has made in her life—to follow her mother-in-law Naomi into Judah, and to accept the Hebrew God—are here recognized, praised in a loud voice for all to hear,[256] and, if Boaz is to be believed, will be rewarded richly now and in years to come. The *midrash*[257] builds on Boaz's prayer for a "complete" reward for Ruth. The Hebrew word *shelema*, meaning "full or complete," is seen as a broad hint that Ruth will be the ancestor to King Solomon, whose name in Hebrew is *Shelomo*. The two words are spelled exactly the same in the unvoweled Torah text.

Boaz thus publicly predicts marriage, fertility, privilege and even royalty for Ruth! This is unbelievably heady stuff for a woman who is barefoot and in tatters, and is scratching along for her next meal among the leftover stalks of barley. Boaz is predicting that Ruth's time of trials is at an end; that she will not suffer for years like many converts do when they first commit to serving the One God.[258] He predicts that she will find respite and peace in her lifetime and beyond. Boaz's blessing is quite a boon, really too much to absorb; Ruth would be forgiven if she disbelieved him. How does she respond?

RUTH IS COMFORTED

RUTH 2:13

Ruth bows her head. Perhaps she shuts her eyes and offers a wordless prayer of thanks to her new God. It would seem that she is saved! She and Naomi will not go hungry. But Boaz and the small crowd within avid earshot in the corner of his field expect a response. So in verse 13 she answers Boaz gratefully and in all humility:

"I am fortunate to have found favor in your eyes, my lord, for your words have comforted me. You have spoken to the heart of your handmaid, though I am not even as worthy as one of your handmaidens."

One *midrash*[259] suggests that Ruth knew before she set out that morning not only that Boaz was a prince and a judge in Judah, but also that he was Naomi's close relation, and that he was the master of the field nearest to Naomi's house. It is highly improbable that during the ten years of her married life in Moav her husband and her mother-in-law never disclosed to her that they had been members of the elite class in Judah. Or that they never disclosed to her that their family was still prominent in Beit Lechem.

If Ruth knew all this, why, then, did she present herself to Boaz as "a stranger?" The answer is that Ruth was allowing Boaz to distance himself from her and from Naomi. She did not presume to trade on her mother-in-law's relations; she was beginning to appreciate that a Moabite relation was an undesirable albatross for an Israelite. And furthermore, Boaz had as yet made no overture to Naomi to send her food or to ease her repatriation in Beit Lechem. For all she knew, perhaps Boaz had no charity in his heart, or resented Elimelech's abandonment at the onset of the famine.

And in fact, as we see from her responses to Boaz's speeches, Ruth does not step out of her modest persona; she is genuinely humble. Coming as she does from royalty, she appreciates that in her destitute state she is worlds apart from Boaz. He is the lord, she the handmaiden.

By her words the reader understands that Ruth is aware that Boaz is courting her, intending to make her his wife.[260] She "has found favor" in Boaz's eyes, and she is subtly telling him she understands that he has a special interest in her, although she remains incredulous. The *midrash* says that Boaz is so enamored of Ruth that he corrects her saying, "No, my daughter, you are not like one of the *handmaidens*, you are like the *matriarchs*!"[261] Boaz tells her that she will be privileged to share in the world-to-come, to sit in the heavenly presence alongside the four matriarchs, Sarah, Rebecca, Rachel and Leah.

Boaz's astounding statement is tantamount to accepting Ruth as a Jewess by the Beit Din, or court of law. Ruth acknowledges this, but with reserve. Fate has dealt Ruth a mixed hand so far, and she is wary of allowing herself to become too hopeful too soon. So Ruth holds herself back.

BOAZ INVITES RUTH TO SHARE
THE AFTERNOON MEAL

RUTH 2:14–16

When it comes time for the afternoon meal, all the harvesters and gleaners gather to eat at a communal table that is set up in a long shed near the field. On this day, Boaz is seated at its head, and to one side of him sit his harvesters, ranging down to the end of the table. On his other side, where perhaps his foremen ordinarily sit, is an empty space. Boaz's eye seeks out Ruth standing at the very back[262] of the group of gleaners who have gathered for the meal. He calls out to her and invites her to step out of the "cafeteria que," motioning for her to sit next to him. In verse 14 Boaz invites her to *Come here and eat from the food and dip your bread in the vinegar.* But Ruth is shy of being so singled out, and besides, she has no wish to sit so near the head of the table facing the curious harvesters.

So she seats herself, instead, *on the same side* as the harvesters, all the way at the end of the table, far from Boaz[263] and near to the other gleaners. But still Boaz is solicitous of her. He passes Ruth a measure of parched grain from his own meal[264] for her to eat;[265] she eats her fill and even has some left over. Boaz also extends the invitation to Ruth to join his workers for *every noon meal* at his field shed. He does not want this to be a one-time occurrence; he wants Ruth to return to his field to glean and to eat of his food throughout the months of the barley harvest. He already is feeding one hundred mouths, it is no trouble at all for him to feed one-hundred-and-one.[266]

One *midrash* enlarges on Boaz's proffer of parched grain to Ruth. A plate of parched barley is such a humble thing to offer a woman. If Boaz had known that the Scripture would record for eternity his seemingly paltry gift, surely he would have offered her a fatted calf instead![267]

But no, another *midrash* explains that we look into Boaz's *heart*, not at the paucity of the gift. His intention was to feed Ruth, as she was obviously hungry. Had he showered her with foodstuffs he would have overwhelmed her, embarrassed her, and perhaps even frightened her away. Also, the field shed where the meals were taken was a public venue, and had he fed Ruth a different food than he fed the other workers, he and Ruth would have been the object of fierce gossip.[268] With his humble offer of a plate of parched grain Boaz revealed to her (and to the observers) his intention to feed and protect Ruth in an appropriate way.

And Ruth accepts Boaz's offered plate of parched barley. In fact, this is the first time in weeks that Ruth is able to eat to satiety. She and Naomi have been consuming barely enough to sustain themselves,[269] and it is likely that Ruth feels guilty that *her* hunger is satisfied, while her mother-in-law is at home alone and unfed. She does not forget Naomi for one moment. As soon as she eats her fill—but before the mealtime is ended—Ruth excuses herself and returns to the field to get on with her work, but not before making a "care package" for her mother-in-law with what was left from the plate Boaz had handed her. She ties the small packet into a fold of her skirt so that she will be sure to bring it home with her at day's end.[270]

After Ruth has gone from the table, Boaz leans over and commands his foremen, *Allow her to glean also among the sheaves, do not embarrass or hinder her. Also, you must pretend to forget some of the bundles of sheaves; leave them there for her to glean, and do not scold her.* "Whatever she picks up from the field, you will allow her to take with her."[271]

Clearly Boaz is enamored of the Moabite widow.[272] His generosity towards her is way beyond the ordinary kindness shown to the poor, the widow, and the orphan who glean at the corners of every Israelite field. There is an echo here of Genesis chapter 24, where the young Rebecca extends her *chesed* or graciousness to Abraham's servant *beyond* what he explicitly requests. Regarding Rebecca, the Bible told us it was a test of her worthiness. Here, perhaps Boaz's ability to genuinely offer *chesed* above and beyond what is required of him is also a test. We remember the Talmud's story of Boaz/Ivtzan's selfishness. If Boaz already paid the high price for his *lack* of *chesed*, then the manner in which he treats this poor Moabite widow might right the moral balance in his favor.

As far as Ruth is concerned, we have yet to see if she reciprocates Boaz's attraction.

AT NIGHTFALL, RUTH RETURNS HOME

RUTH 2:17–23

Ruth does not glean from the exaggerated leavings of Boaz's harvesters.[273] Naomi has taught her well, and she gleans only precisely what the law allows. But she is an assiduous worker, and *she gleans in the field until nightfall.* Her plan is to stop work just before the other field workers, and to beat her sheaves where all can see. She wants no one to accuse her of stealing grain that is not permitted to her, and she wishes to do the beating of the sheaves herself, sparing Naomi the task.[274] Ruth is also determined not to be left in the field alone, so she works with a will.[275] When she beats out the sheaves she has gathered, she is surprised to see that it comes to about an *ephah* of barley, a substantial amount of grain, sufficient to feed two people for five days. She secures it into a tight bundle and places it on her head. This is quite a heavy burden for her to lift and carry home, but she is determined. As the sun sets Ruth slowly makes her way over the fields to the edge of the city of Beit Lechem.[276]

Meanwhile, Naomi has watched the sun make its way across the sky during the course of this first long day without her daughter-in-law by her side. She is deeply anxious on Ruth's behalf, as she can imagine the physical difficulty of gleaning stalks in the baking heat. More than this, she is fearful of the reception Ruth will get from the owners and foremen of the fields she will visit, as well as from her fellow gleaners. Naomi never forgets for a moment that Ruth is a Moabite. She knows it will be distasteful to many Israelites to suffer her gleaning and to share with her the product of their hard work from this first harvest. And of course as Ruth is also a beautiful stranger and a poor gleaner, she will no doubt be considered fair game by some.

Ruth is late and Naomi frets.

As the daylight wanes and Ruth still has not returned, Naomi gathers up her long skirts and laboriously makes her way across the town to the spot that borders on the fields.[277] She stands at the gateway[278] where Ruth is sure to pass, and she continues to wait as the evening fades and the stars wink on in the night sky.[279] We can imagine a near-frantic Naomi. At that most lonesome and frightening moment, the *midrash*[280] tells us that Ruth comes into view, the bundle atop her proud head appearing first, drawing Naomi's attention. Naomi is weak from hunger and relief, and the two do not speak until Ruth has helped Naomi back home. Ruth unloads her grain and unwraps the additional small bundle that had been secured in the folds of her skirt. It is the food she has saved for Naomi from her noon meal.

Ruth ministers to Naomi right away, and the older woman eats her fill. After the meal, surveying the bountiful amount of barley Ruth has brought home, Naomi asks in wonderment,[281] *Where did you glean today, and where did you work? Blessed be he who took such generous notice of you!* Ruth has not drawn attention to her bundle of barley. She modestly put it aside while Naomi ate. But when Naomi notices its size, remarks on it and starts asking questions,[282] Ruth recounts the details of her adventure at the barley harvest, telling her mother-in-law of the kindness of the master of the field, and of his behavior towards her both in the field and in the shed. Only *after* Ruth describes her benefactor does she disclose his name. *The name of the man with whom I worked today is Boaz.*

And Naomi answers her daughter-in-law, issuing yet another blessing, but this time praising Boaz in God's name. *May he be blessed **by the Lord**, who has not left off acting benevolently with the living and the dead.*

Naomi, who had all but given up hope that God had any blessings in store for her, feels her spirit coming to life. She thinks, "Surely it is God's hand that has caused Ruth and Boaz to meet so fortuitously in his field today! This must be a sign that God in His grace has not forsaken the family of Elimelech. The Lord is watching over Ruth and me, and also has not forgotten my dead sons, Machlon and Chilyon. Perhaps there is a greater purpose in their meeting so. Dare I even hope that Boaz might love Ruth and between the two of them they will sustain the name of the dead?"[283]

Naomi has lived a long time and has seen much tragedy. Though she is deeply spiritual, she is not a fanciful woman. Even so, she detects a miracle in Ruth's encounter with Boaz.[284] For the first time since burying her husband and sons Naomi sees a glimmer of hope for the future. The thought is intoxicating: just perhaps Boaz should marry Ruth! This would solve their problems and also would be the ultimate act of *chesed* or kindness.

She mentally ticks off the criteria for *yibum*, or a levirate union.[285] "Ruth's husband has died, and has left no issue; his brother, Chilyon, who would have been next in line to step forward and marry Machlon's widow, also has died. Therefore, it would fall to a second cousin to Machlon, or even a grand-uncle— one of Elimelech's brothers—to take Ruth in marriage. In this way, their first child would inherit Machlon's and Elimelech's landed portion, and Elimelech's name would not be lost in Israel."

And Naomi concludes aloud to Ruth, *Boaz is a close relative of my husband Elimelech and of Machlon.* **He** *could be our redeemer!*

To wit Ruth continues, *And he also told me "Stay close to my workers until all my harvesting is finished."*

Naomi interprets Boaz's instructions to Ruth as boding well for her nascent plans for a possible match. Boaz has obviously become smitten with Ruth, even on just the one day's acquaintance. So much so that he is attempting to protect her and keep her within his purview. Naomi is not so doddering that she has forgotten that sometimes—especially when God takes an interest—one look is all it takes to light a fire between two people.

THE DANGER IN THE FIELDS

A repeated refrain in chapter 2 is the danger posed by predatory men to a woman working in the field; hence the need for protection. It is important for the modern Bible reader to appreciate this fact-of-life in Judea at the time of our story. It is also a thematic thread that has woven its way through every story in this book: the innocent, lone or disenfranchised biblical woman is at grave physical risk when she is unprotected by either a father, brothers, husband or other concerned kin. We must consider that the need for personal protection—in addition to the desire for family and continuity, even overshadowing the prospect of affection—will be a prime motivator of Ruth's behavior as the story moves forward. What is the nature of the threat Ruth faces? How have the dangers been manifest to her thus far?

We have seen that Boaz, who is described in the text as an *ish gibor chayil*—a valiant and mighty man[286]—warns Ruth against gleaning in strange fields. This wealthy strongman urges her to be sure to stay close to his girls; he commands his male harvesters not to touch, molest, embarrass or scold Ruth, and he assures her repeatedly of his intention and ability to protect her.[287] There has got to be good reason for Boaz, on first meeting Ruth, to issue such warnings and assurances. One must assume that in general the field hands are more than merely boisterous; the picture emerging is that they are potentially abusive. Boaz's physical strength, presence and authority are the only sure-fire bulwark Ruth would have against a physical attack. He stresses to her that he can control his own men, and that this is the reason she should return only to *his* field.

Ruth is not unaware or even ungrateful for Boaz's assurance of security, and she recounts this promise of protection to her mother-in-law.[288] Naomi is seriously concerned about the safety issue as it applies to Ruth, a single, beautiful stranger who is forced to glean among a rough element of Israelite society. She correctly interprets Boaz's assurances of protection to mean there is genuine danger if Ruth chooses to glean among complete strangers in *other* fields.[289]

Also, Naomi is an old woman who has lived on this land most of her life, and who has observed decades of harvests from the time of her girlhood. When she says to Ruth, *It would be good for you, my daughter, if you went out with Boaz's maidens, so that they [the men] do not molest you in another field*, she knows what she is talking about. The harvesting field is, generally speaking, not the place for a beautiful and high-born woman. Naomi also is breathing a sigh of relief that Ruth has found a champion. The reason to glean in the field of a known acquaintance is to be afforded just such protection as Boaz is offering Ruth. If their proximity breeds a romance between a potential levirate redeemer and the young widow, so much the better. But at this moment Naomi is thinking primarily of Ruth's physical safety.

Naomi immediately affirms, in verse 22, Boaz's suggestion that Ruth glean in his field, alongside his female gleaners. Naomi is hyper-aware that Ruth is exquisitely lovely, unwittingly posing a tantalizing danger to her own well-being if she ventures out into the fields without protection. Boaz's offer will effectively neutralize a potentially hostile and hazardous situation. *It is good, my daughter, that you go out with [Boaz's] maidens,* **so that [the men]** **will not molest you in another field.** The *midrash* sides with Boaz and Naomi, and elaborates on this state of vulnerability, defenselessness and peril that is present in the fields. It bluntly states that a poor stranger with Ruth's looks will attract men who will do more than merely annoy her.[290] They will assault her, they will not allow her to glean; they will prey on her, attack her, rape her, even possibly kill her.[291]

If this seems unduly paranoid or theatrical, the reader would do well to remember that our seemingly-bucolic story takes place during a lawless and violent period in biblical history. It is the period of the judges, a time "when there was no king in Israel, and every man did as he pleased."[292] It is the dark and fearful time during which the defenseless concubine from Giv'ah is horrifically raped and dismembered by Israelite men.[293] It is the season of the "wild west" of the Bible, when territories are struggling against one another for supremacy, and before states become unified under an overarching rule of law, enforced by a monarch. It is a bloody and bellicose place, where fierce and conscienceless men prey on weak men and on weaker women.

The *midrash* is acutely aware of this and has Naomi speaking plainly to her daughter-in-law: "My daughter, at least if you work in Boaz's field, even if he should desire you, he will not take you without the benefit of the proper marriage ritual. He is family, after all; he is my first-cousin, son of my dead husband's brother, and so he is also cousin to your dead husband Machlon. Boaz will do the right thing. But if you glean in *other* fields you will be on your own, without protection. You will instantly be marked as a vulnerable stranger. I advise you to take Boaz's offer of protection very seriously; it could well save your life. And stay close to his field girls; keep a safe distance from the men."[294]

Ruth heeds Naomi's and Boaz's cautionary words. She accepts Boaz's offer of protection, and gleans only in his fields. She works from sunup until dusk, heading home exhausted each night to eat the evening meal with Naomi. She entertains her mother-in-law with stories of the day's small dramas and of the new friends she has made among the female gleaners. We are told[295] that Ruth could have stayed overnight in the fields with most of the other girls, sparing herself the nightly trek back to Beit Lechem. But she refuses to do so out of her sense of propriety and because she knows Naomi, still bitter and depressed, looks forward to their nightly conversations. So Ruth "commutes" back and forth between the city and Boaz's fields for the duration of the barley harvest, a period of about three months.

Significantly, Ruth cleaves to Boaz's female gleaners at the end of chapter 2 (verse 23) in the same way and with the identical Hebrew root-word — *dbk* — that she clung to Naomi in chapter 1 (verse 14). This woman is loyal, reliable, admirable, and heroic. But she also is a widow and childless, and lives on the edge of subsistence. We wonder, what will become of her now that the harvest is done?

A THREE-MONTH WAIT

Over the past three months Naomi has watched her daughter-in-law rise at dawn, prepare Naomi's breakfast and lunch, see to her comfort, and then head out to glean in Boaz's fields. She has watched Ruth embrace the culture of Israel, tentatively open herself to friendships, and, importantly, hold the interest of a kind and important man. Naomi is hopeful.

That Boaz is interested in Ruth is obvious. He, too, has watched her. He has watched from the sidelines every day of the barley harvest, taking the time to appreciate her true character. A seasoned and experienced judge of men, Boaz has observed Ruth's industry and diligence as she gleans, and her meticulous adherence to the laws of *leket*.[296] He has observed her humble modesty, her dignity, her bone-deep kindness to others and faithful consideration for her mother-in-law. He has watched her interact cautiously with the female gleaners, and shy completely away from the strapping male harvesters who have vied for her attention. He has broken bread with her, and has watched as she halved her own lunch portion, bringing it home to Naomi night after night.

Importantly, from a legal standpoint, Boaz, a judge in Judah, has privately counted off the past ninety days one-at-a-time. Before a man of Judah can marry a convert or a widow there is a required prelude to sanctioned sexual relations; he must wait a full three months in order to rule out a possible pregnancy by another man.[297] Boaz keeps his own counsel as he orchestrates the post-famine harvest and runs his agricultural empire. Boaz also watches Ruth and bides his time.

LEVIRATE LAW AS APPLIED TO RUTH

As we discussed earlier in Part Three and also in this present chapter, the levirate law is an exception to the laws forbidding incest and sexual relations between close family members. Known in Hebrew as *yibum*, the levirate law comes into operation when a married man dies without children. In such a situation, the levirate law mandates that his surviving brother marry his widow for the purpose of producing an heir to sustain the name and landed portion of the dead man.[298] Any child the "levirate couple" have together does not "belong" to the surviving brother, however, but is a kind of reincarnation of the deceased for purposes of retaining *his* landed portion, and for sustaining *his* name in Israel.

The surviving brother is thus known as the levir or *yavam*, or "redeemer;" this is because he *redeems* his dead brother's name from extinction, and his landed portion for his heirs. And in fact it is at once a commandment and an act of *chesed* or kindness for the surviving brother to step up as a redeemer in such a situation. He also thereby frees his brother's widow from a limbo life where she awaits marriage to her husband's nearest kin. The widow is otherwise constrained from marrying another until she is either "redeemed" or set free.

In the event that a brother or a kinsman *refuses* to redeem under levirate law, he must renounce his right as a *yavam* through the vehicle known as the *chalitza*, or shoe ceremony.[299] This formal renunciation is done in the presence of ten tribal elders at the gate of the town, **at the instigation of the widow.**[300] The redeeming kinsman is given every chance to change his mind and agree to redeem, but if he categorically refuses his duty, he declares "I do not wish to marry her!" At which point, at least in the Deuteronomic version, the widow approaches him in full view of the convened legal panel, she strips his shoe from his foot, spits into his face, and declares aloud, "*Thus* shall it be done to the man who will not build up his brother's house!" The levirate *chalitza* ceremony is thus a ceremony of public disgrace,[301] and the unredeemed widow administers it.

It is significant that even the Deuteronomic *chalitza* is female-initiated. The reader should appreciate that this is but one aspect of Judaic law that had an eye out for the protection and empowerment of women, though not much "press" is given over to this aspect of it. In the words of Jacob Neusner,

> The rabbis of late antiquity, founders of Judaism as we know it [via the Oral Torah], . . . **liberated Israelite women** by according to them what Scripture had denied [them]. That is, the standing and powers of sentient beings, possessed of a role that was, if not entirely equal, then corresponding, to that of men in **critical transactions of their existence.**[302]

This entire concept and application of *yibum*, or levirate marriage — intended to perpetuate landed inheritance — certainly qualifies as one of Neusner's "critical transactions" in a woman's life. Importantly, *yibum* also safeguards the childless widow! This book's discussion of Tamar's bold action to effect *yibum* in Part Three, and now the drama of Ruth instigating the operation of the same law, proves the point. The audacity of Tamar and Ruth is praised by the rabbis of the Talmud and *midrash* for the reason that these women were appropriately "taking" what was already theirs by operation of law. The nearest consenting kinsman was *obligated* to wed them *if they so desired*. Tamar and Ruth were endowed by application of the *yibum* law with "the power of intentionality."[303] Because the Israelite woman is a sentient and important entity, to paraphrase Neusner she *must* take the concomitant responsibility for her own widowed condition and demand from the law what it is offering her: a second chance at motherhood, family and inheritance. In Tamar and Ruth the Bible has given us bona fide heroes who used the law and took the risks in order to save their own lives, incidentally also saving the Judaic line for future kingship.

❇ ❇ ❇

It might help us to further appreciate the *chalitza* shoe ceremony if we consider the following *midrash*, which explains — in kabbalistic terms — the origin and underlying meaning of the custom.[304] It is said that the soul of the childless husband finds no rest either in the hereafter or in the world we know. Instead, it is fated to hover restlessly in our world, until it finds "protection" in the physical body of the man who will stand in his place and sire a child in his name. In a prosaic way, a shoe is useless and "unfulfilled" until it finds *its* proper "resting" place; it is all potential, only coming into its own, in a manner of speaking, once it is worn, resting on the foot that it then protects from mud and other hazards of the road. The *midrash* explains that the soul of the childless husband can likewise "rest" only if his kinsman marries his widow, when thereafter his soul is then reincarnated in their child. Only then is the childless husband's potential realized.

But if the nearest kinsman refuses to do his duty, he formally frees the widow from her obligation to wed him via the *chalitza* ceremony. By removing his shoe he symbolically "releases" his brother's soul from its temporary resting place: the body of the nearest male kinsman. The widow is then free to marry another, but unless it is a kinsman, her dead husband's soul remains in a state of unrest.

Modern scholars understand the *chalitza* ceremony a bit differently. The ceremony involves not a shoe *per se*, but a sandal. And "on the basis of almost universal folk usage . . . the sandal [is] a **female** symbol."[305] When the nearest kinsman renounces his duty to redeem his brother's widow, it is *she* who draws the sandal — a symbol of the obligation to wed her — off his foot. She is now free to marry another.

The *chalitza* ceremony will become vitally important later on in our story, when the redeemer's first-right to wed Ruth comes into play. For now, we consider how the levirate law might apply to Ruth, a childless widow.

In Ruth's case, both her husband, Machlon, and his brother, Chilyon, have died, so a "true" version of levirate marriage (*i.e.*, where the *brother* redeems the widow) is not possible. But Israelite custom allowed an "extended version"[306] of levirate marriage, so that the *nearest male kinsman* was permitted to step into the shoes of the deceased and marry his widow in order to preserve his name and inheritance.[307] From Naomi's comments in 2:20 (*The man is related to us; he is one of our redeeming kinsmen!*), it is clear that she considers Boaz to be the proper *yavam* or redeemer for Machlon, and thus for Ruth.

But the careful reader will detect a possible spoiler: Naomi does not say that Boaz is *the* redeemer; she says he is *one of* our redeeming kinsmen. So the tension mounts. Will Boaz step up to redeem Ruth? Is he even the next in line? What will become of her?

NAOMI COUNSELS BOLDNESS

RUTH 3

Up until now Naomi has counseled conservatism and return, caution and safety. In contrast, Ruth has been the risk-taker, *decisor*, and do-er. She has gently defied her mother-in-law and mentor, friend and role model by refusing to turn back to Moav. Instead she embraced an unfamiliar God and accompanied Naomi into the unknown land of Judah. Once there, on her own initiative she ventured to glean among the poor in a field of hostile strangers. And Ruth will soon enough seize the baton of boldness once again. But right here, in the opening verses of chapter 3, we see a turnabout. It is Naomi who presents a bold plan:

> *And Naomi her mother-in-law said to her, "My daughter, shall I not seek a rest for you, so that it may be good for you?*
>
> *"And now, is not Boaz our kinsman, with whose maidens you were [gleaning]? Behold, he will be winnowing barley on the threshing-floor this very night.*
>
> *"You should bathe and anoint yourself and put on your clothes and go down to the threshing-floor. Do not make yourself known to the man until he has finished eating and drinking.*
>
> *"And it shall be when he lies down that you should note the place where he will lie down, and you should come and uncover his feet and lie down [also]; and he will tell you what you should do."* Ruth 3:1–4

Naomi is proposing a blueprint for forcing Boaz's hand. Both she and Ruth have been given to understand,[308] by Boaz's behavior toward Ruth over the course of the three-month harvest, that he finds her both desirable and worthy of being his wife.[309] Naomi remained patient during the harvest, both because the waiting period was prescribed, and also because Boaz's mind was primarily focused on the harvest and other business matters. But the barley harvest has ended, and Ruth has ceased to go out into the fields. Boaz has not seen her lately, and still, to Naomi's consternation, he has made no move to formally seek Ruth's hand in marriage. So Naomi conceives of a stratagem that will push Boaz to act.

She first plies Ruth with subtle words. *My daughter, shall I not seek **a rest** for you, so that it may be good for you?* To what kind of "rest" is Naomi referring? Perhaps the simple reading of the verse is that Ruth should rest up after three months of unrelenting work as a field hand. Or the reference to "rest" could allude to the issue of Ruth as an unresolved levirate widow. As we discussed above, Machlon's soul will not "rest" until his widow has been redeemed by his closest male kin, and they have produced a child to stand in Machlon's place.[310] Naomi could be hinting to Ruth that the time is come to find her a levir or *yavam* — a redeemer — in order to put to rest once and for all time the matter of Machlon's landed inheritance. "It is time for me to find 'rest' for you and for my dead son," says Naomi through the *midrash*.[311]

But Naomi could also mean simply that she is ready and willing to find a match or a husband for Ruth.[312] "The woman will not find 'rest' until she is wed," says *Ibn Ezra* about Ruth's predicament. In this vein, the *midrash*[313] puts more words into Naomi's mouth. She says to Ruth, "When you were living in my son's house you did not find 'rest,' for he died before you could build a family and you've had nothing but sadness. But now I will find you 'rest' and security that will be lasting and complete. I swear to you, this is my mission. With my whole heart I will seek a true mate for you who will suit you and be good to you."

Next, Naomi throws down the gauntlet; she is crystal-clear about whom she has selected for Ruth. Whatever has remained unsaid between the two women these last three months is now manifest. *And now, is not **Boaz** our kinsman, with whose maidens you were [gleaning]?* **"Boaz is the one** who can free you from your waiting period, and also redeem Machlon's landed portion. You need have no fear before him, nor should you feel shy or embarrassed with him.[314] By now you know his character, for you have seen that he is a kind and generous man[315] who protects you as you glean in his fields.

"There are several reasons Boaz could be your perfect mate.[316] First, his name and reputation are known and revered throughout the land. Second, as you are aware, he is a close relative and he could be our family's redeemer. Third, after all your work in Boaz's fields throughout the long harvest you are well-known to the members of his household; I have been told that they have come to love and respect you. And fourth, this is the season for lovers and for romance. The harvest has been bountiful, and Boaz's heart will be full, ready to settle on a mate.

"All things considered, he is the perfect choice, but only if he suits you. And if he suits you, *now* is the moment."

Boaz is not a hands-down favorite, however. This is because Boaz is not a young man;[317] we are told he is eighty years old![318] This revelation may shatter the Cinderella-image of the story, but we should remember that according to the same *midrash* Ruth is forty, so neither Boaz nor Ruth is in the first bloom of youth. As we have seen, Ruth is still reputed to be beautiful and has shown herself to be loyal, considerate, modest and courageous, and Boaz is an *ish gibor chayil*; mighty, respected, fearless, and kind. These all are heroic characteristics that defy age. Given the biblical culture and mores of that time, and Ruth's status as a childless widow, Boaz's age and unquestioned standing in Judah are even a potential boon to her. He is a redeeming kinsman for Ruth's deceased husband, which is the *sine qua non* before she can wed. Also, he has the status and clout to take on the problematic issue of a Moabite bride.

THE DILEMMA

Naomi knows precisely what is going on on the threshing-floor this day. The harvest is done, the sheaves are piled high. In the cool of the afternoon the grain is separated from the chaff in a laborious and primitive way. The sheaves are tossed into the air, catching the evening breezes while they are aloft; the chaff is blown away by the wind, and the grain then falls to the ground, where it is cleaned and sorted. Thus are hundreds of piles of grain accumulated all through the long day and afternoon. Night brings the winnowing or threshing ceremony, after which each landowner and his trusted foremen sleep nearby their own grain piles to guard against thievery.[319]

Naomi is telling Ruth that there will never be a better moment for her to approach Boaz than this night. She must approach him immediately, while her image is still fresh in his mind, and while the exuberance of an abundant harvest gladdens his heart. Ruth has been a part of this first post-famine harvest, and surely Boaz will feel tenderly towards her. Furthermore, time is fleeting and Ruth is in need of a redeemer.

The problem is that the threshing-floor is a male enclave during the hours spent winnowing, and after-hours the only women who enter the threshing-floor are prostitutes[320] who service the landowners and the harvesters. It is not a place for a "decent" woman to be found. How can Ruth approach Boaz in a way that will best ensure success?

What Naomi is about to propose is daring and immodest. She must have been worrying the problem and possible solution during the long, lonesome days when Ruth was out gleaning in Boaz's fields. And now her plan is full-blown. Her only hurdle is Ruth's natural modesty and caution. How can Naomi convince her daughter-in-law to temporarily abandon her ingrained and practiced humble persona, and behave in a sexually forward manner? After all, Naomi has spent the past three months tutoring Ruth in the ways of the Israelite woman, erasing any trace of the Moabite. Would this conduct she has in mind qualify as Hebrew or as Moabite; as proper or as brazen? Will Ruth go along with it? It all comes down to trust. How deeply does Ruth trust Naomi to advise her wisely? How securely does Naomi trust Boaz not to abuse Ruth?

NAOMI'S SEDUCTION PLAN

RUTH 3:3–4

We can envision Ruth and Naomi seated at the crude table in their hut. Naomi grasps Ruth's hand in both of hers, and tries to infuse the younger woman with her intensity, wisdom and sincerity. Naomi says to Ruth:[321] "You are as dear to me a daughter of my own blood. Just as I would not steer my own daughter in the wrong direction, I would never tell you to do something improper. So heed me, my daughter, as I advise you. Boaz is our kinsman, and he can be your redeemer. You know him and trust him, and I believe he has feelings for you. The three-month waiting period is at an end. It is time for you to free yourself of the heavy burden of my dead son's spirit and reach out for your own happiness.

"Behold, he will be winnowing barley on the threshing-floor this very night. Bathe yourself, washing off the dust of the fields, and cleansing yourself of any sin that is in your heart,[322] and *anoint yourself* with fragrant oils.[323] *Don your* Sabbath[324] dress, the only other garment you have, preparing yourself with care as a bride would do before her wedding,[325] and *go* softly *down to the threshing-floor. Allow no one to detect your presence,* especially not Boaz. *Wait until he has eaten and drunk his fill. Mark the place where he lays down, and* after all have gone to sleep beside their grain piles, *come and uncover Boaz's feet and lie down. He will tell you what you should do."*

It is fascinating that the Torah text presents three key words of Naomi's speech in the *first*-person rather than in the *second*-person. She tells Ruth *ve-samti*, "**I** will don" your dress, instead of "**you** will don" it. Then, in the same verse 3, she says *ve-yaradeti*, "**I** will go down" instead of "**you** will go down." And in verse 4 she says *ve-shachavti*, "**I** will lie down" instead of "**you** will lie down." The *midrash* notes these grammatical discrepancies[326] and explains that because of the unusual, brazen behavior that Naomi is urging on Ruth, she is hinting—by use of the first-person—that she, Naomi, takes responsibility for it.[327] Furthermore, that her own merit[328] will be added to Ruth's in order to tip the heavenly scales in favor of the success of Ruth's daring venture. After all, Naomi is "endangering Ruth's reputation in the most Moabite way imaginable, . . . coaching her for a role that unnervingly resembles the role of the harlots, the *zonot*, who haunt granary floors . . . "[329]

Zornberg interprets this unusual trio of first-person commands as a seminal moment in the evolving relationship between Naomi and Ruth. Until now the reader has seen Ruth cleaving to Naomi, adopting her, her God, and her ways. Here, in this all-important instruction scene, the reader appreciates that Ruth's essential goodness has had an effect on Naomi. Naomi's use of the first-person reveals that she loves her daughter-in-law sufficiently that she is identifying with Ruth! "In other words, Ruth does not go [to the threshing-floor] alone; Naomi is with her as she moves into her moment of greatest narrative suspense."[330]

Still, Ruth is unconvinced. In fact, her face becomes enflamed with embarrassment[331] as Naomi outlines her plan. She does not wish to go down to the threshing-floor by stealth at night; she has heard that it is not the place for proper girls and women.[332] Furthermore, she has never been sexually brazen and she is frightened and reluctant to act as Naomi has described. What if it backfires? The only man Ruth has ever lain with has been her husband, Machlon, and those physical encounters had been mutual, willing, and under the sanction of a lawful marriage.

What Naomi proposes is nothing less than a seduction. "Ruth's preparations are to be those of a woman before a sexual encounter: washing, scenting, dressing, and secrecy."[333] The danger for Ruth is that as a levirate widow, unless she is released from her levirate obligation, she is forbidden to every man *with the exception* of Machlon's nearest kinsman. But is Boaz that man?

Ruth sees that Naomi is confident and emphatic. Still Ruth hesitates. Should she risk everything and literally throw herself at Boaz's feet? Or should she wait for him to make his move — or not? She weighs her options. She is as far down on the societal ladder as she can go. She is destitute, reliant on the charity of others to eat. She is a stranger in a strange land and is chained to her dead husband's memory so that by Israelite law she cannot marry any but the nearest kinsman. She is a Moabite immigrant reliant on the charity of others. She reasons that really, she has nothing to lose but the fragile persona she has built up since she arrived in Judah and took on the mantle of Naomi's God. If she acts and is rebuffed, she is still on the bottom rung of Israelite society, this time, though, without any hope of redemption. But if by some miracle she were to succeed — well, then, her future would be made, she could perhaps conceive a child, and she and Naomi would never go hungry again.

Ruth resolves to take the risk.

RUTH AGREES TO THE PLAN

RUTH 3:5

And she said to her, "All that you tell me to do, I will do." Though Ruth agrees to Naomi's bold plan, she is unsure of the propriety of it, and with good reason. Naomi is counseling Ruth to transgress the custom among proper Israelites that an unmarried man and woman should not be alone with one another.[334] Ruth is troubled. Is it permissible to attempt to seduce Boaz if her objective — redemption through levirate marriage — is worthy? Or is such brazen behavior never warranted?

The *midrash*[335] examines this moral dilemma through imaginary conversations between Naomi and Ruth. Naomi explains, "My daughter, life has taught me that even the most holy and worthwhile of goals is not monolithic. The means to achieve it are often comprised of a slight admixture of the permissible and the ostensibly impermissible. Think of the situation of Judah and Tamar, which occurred years ago in my own family, and which also involved the issue of *yibum*, or levirate marriage. We must consider that perhaps the path to redemption in Israel is strewn with obstacles. Perhaps it is through *you*, a Moabite widow, that my husband's line will be revived, and the promise of kings will be fulfilled. Who knows but that you **must** take this risk, my daughter! And if you agree, you must act tonight!."[336]

The reader might note a tonal similarity between Naomi's *midrashic* speech urging Ruth to act, and Mordechai's exhortation to Esther.[337] In that story, far in the biblical future, Mordechai urges a hesitating Esther, "Who knows if you have attained a royal position for just such a moment as this!"

Both Naomi and Mordechai counsel behavior that could prove disastrous to the stories' younger female actors. Esther's response is to agree to go before the king even though he has not summoned her — putting herself at risk of death. She says to Mordechai, "And if I am to perish, I shall perish!" Similarly here, Naomi counsels Ruth to gamble with her reputation and possibly her very life, and to throw herself on the marital mercy of Boaz, a great man and a judge in Judah. We can envision Ruth weighing the situation and being convinced, ultimately — like Esther was — that she really has no true choice. For if she acts as Naomi counsels, she *might* be rejected or scorned by Boaz and fail in her seduction, dooming herself and her mother-in-law to a life of abject poverty and eventual death. But if she does *not* act, she *will surely* die a living death as an unredeemed levirate widow.

Naomi also counsels Ruth to wash herself *before* seeking out Boaz on the threshing-floor. This is interpreted as a kind of advance purification.[338] Ruth's cleansed state will lend an imprimatur of holiness or rectitude to her seduction. Esther, too, engages in a prelude purification, fasting for three days before presenting herself to the king. These personal cleansing rituals elevate the profane or the ordinary into the sanctioned, and might even summon the blessing of the deity. Neither Ruth nor Esther goes into her personal "lion's den" unescorted by God's *shechinah*.[339]

Still, one must ask, surely there must be another way to achieve Naomi's ends? Why could Naomi not have approached Boaz herself and proposed the match in an above-board manner? Frymer-Kensky[340] says it is possible that widows in Israel were not permitted to broker marriage contracts. Or that Naomi's hands might be further tied because she can provide no dowry for Ruth. A destitute woman could not seriously approach a great man — a judge of his people — and propose a match.

Perhaps Naomi could engage a middleman or marriage broker to present Ruth's case to Boaz. That would allow her to avoid exposing Ruth to possible charges of harlotry if she is found-out on the threshing-floor.[341] The arguments to convince any marriage broker are simple; one would say even straight-forward and almost ineluctable: Ruth is a levirate widow; Boaz, the widower, is a redeeming kinsman of Elimelech and Machlon. Ruth is acknowledged to be a virtuous and considerate woman, and is beautiful besides; Boaz recognizes all this and is attracted to her. If both parties are willing, and if it is destined, then with the minimum of outside intervention it could all be arranged.

Why, then, the need for the nighttime seduction?

The answer, according to the *midrash*,[342] is that Ruth is an active messenger of God, and it is her function to actualize this match *herself* in a heroic manner, allowing Boaz to respond accordingly. This scene is a pas-de-deux and must be played out between Ruth and Boaz.

The *midrash* offers an insightful psychological reason for the necessity of the in-person tryst. If the entire proposal were presented to Boaz on Ruth's behalf but through the medium of a third-party, Boaz's answer could quite possibly be short and disappointing: "Ruth doesn't need *me*; she can ask another, closer kinsman to redeem her." To avoid such a cursory rejection, a proposal/proposition such as Naomi envisions must be presented in person, face-to-face, "mouth-to-mouth," in the words of the *midrash*.[343] Naomi is banking on the fact that Boaz will not be inclined to refuse Ruth if he is looking into her eyes, contemplating her loveliness, and urgently desiring her. The nighttime seduction is therefore key to Naomi's plan.

And so, Naomi says to Ruth, "Take the risk! Have faith! Sometimes unconventional methods must be used to achieve even a holy objective." And Ruth says, "I will do it."

RUTH ALTERS THE PLAN

RUTH 3:6

Ruth does not accept Naomi's plan blindly; like Esther does with Mordechai's instructions, Ruth makes modifications calculated to ensure her success. Naomi told her *first* to wash, anoint herself, dress in special clothing, *and then* to go down to the threshing-floor. Ruth considers this sequence, and alters it.

Ruth knows she has a long walk ahead of her. The settlement of Beit Lechem is located at the top of a hill, and the threshing-floor is in the valley.[344] If she were to bathe and don her one Sabbath dress *before* trekking down to the threshing-floor, she would arrive all dusty, negating her careful preparations. Moreover, she fears she might draw attention to herself if she walks about in special clothing. But wearing her everyday clothes Ruth runs less of a risk; surely no one will pay the slightest attention to the usual sight of Ruth the threadbare gleaner. Also, Ruth supposes that for the seduction to have at least a chance at success, she must present herself to Boaz in the most attractive and alluring light. He is accustomed to seeing her in her dusty gleaner's garb; if she wishes to arouse him she must surprise him and appear as a clean, sweet-smelling and desirable woman.

The Talmud[345] tells us that Ruth's subtle, tactical change in the order[346] of Naomi's plan is an example of a wise person who receives an instruction and cleverly improves upon it. This is the reason the text in verse 6 says, *And she **went down** to the threshing-floor; and **she did everything** her mother-in-law commanded her.* First she goes down the hill; *then*, in a secluded spot so no one can see her,[347] Ruth bathes, anoints herself with fragrant oil, and dresses specially and with care. She finds a private hiding place[348] that offers her a vantage point onto the threshing-floor so she can observe and yet be unobserved.

THE SCENE ON THE THRESHING-FLOOR

Naomi explains to Ruth the custom of the post-harvest revelry,[349] painting the picture of the coming night's threshing festival: As evening falls, after all work has ceased in the fields, the workers initiate the harvest celebration. They gather some sheaves, tie them in a bundle, and present them as a ceremonial gift to the owner of the fields in which they have worked, a symbol of their gratitude for the bounty of the harvest. The master of the fields accepts the ceremonial sheaves, and hands the gift *back* to his workers in full view of all the assembled field workers, acknowledging the mutuality of their success.

After the ceremony, the night's festivities begin. All the field hands and harvesters, everyone who has aided in the harvest during the course of the past three months — including the gleaners — are expected to be on-hand to partake in the happiness of the harvest festival. Everyone dresses in their best clothing and celebrates with relief and abandon, eating, drinking and dancing. The *midrash*[350] reminds us that it is a time of rife immorality, and that some walled areas of the capacious threshing-floors are frequented by harlots, who service some of the men.

In the festival melée it is not difficult for Ruth to pass by in an unremarkable fashion. She was, after all, a part of the daily team of gleaners in Boaz's fields, and her presence at the party will in fact be expected. She is able to make her way from one end of the threshing-floor to the other, noting precisely where Boaz's grain pile is located, and where he will make his bed.

THE SEDUCTION

RUTH 3:7–9

Ruth watches the scene unfold just as Naomi said it would. She has conquered her doubts, overruled her reservations. She has washed, anointed her skin with sweet-smelling oils, unbraided her hair, dressed in her best dress, and prepared herself for the night's encounter. From her hidden spot she waits as Boaz eats and drinks his fill, matching the harvesters drink for drink as they toast him in gratitude. She is amazed at Boaz's vitality; he does not look or act like an eighty-year-old.[351]

We are told in verse 7 that *his heart was good*. This can be because of the wine he drank; it can be because God has heeded his prayer and has removed the famine from Judah; or because it has been years since he has eaten his fill like he has tonight;[352] it can be because three months have passed since he buried his wife, and he now feels ready to marry again.[353] This festival marks the end of his oppressive sadness, and his fresh resolution to build a new family.[354] The phrase can also mean what it says: that Boaz was a man possessed of a good heart, that even a surfeit of food and drink could not mask his decent character.

Eventually, the party winds down. One by one and in small groups the harvesters call it a night and retreat to their stacks of sheaves and piles of winnowed grain, spread their blankets and lie down to sleep off the effects of the wine, food and festivities. The night air, so recently echoing with shouts of revelry, is now cool and silent, the only sounds those of human snores and shuffles, and the chitterings of night birds and animals. Ruth is focused intently on the spot where she saw Boaz lay down his pallet. It is good that she does so, because the only light to reach that corner of the threshing-floor comes from a partial moon.[355] Otherwise the entire place is curtained in the unrelieved blackness of a rural night. She forces herself to wait still longer, to be certain no one remains awake.

Finally it is time for Ruth to make her move. She leaves the safety of her overlooked corner to do what she has girded herself to do. Softly,[356] soundlessly, she slowly[357] tip-toes around the perimeter of the threshing-floor and stops in front of Boaz's blankets. Even supine he is impressive, and Ruth suffers an instant's hesitation. Then she kneels down, gently uncovers Boaz's legs, and stretches out next to him.

What, precisely, does Ruth uncover in verse 7? The unusual and rare Hebrew word used in the text is *margelotav*, meaning, literally, his legs or feet (*regel* is the singular for foot). But in biblical parlance it is important to analyze the verb that partners *margelotav*; it is the word *va-tegal*, which means she uncovered or revealed. The word *gal* can also mean a "shaft." And the word *margaliyot* means "pearls" or "jewels." So the phrase *va-tegal margelotav* can mean that Ruth uncovered Boaz's legs, his lower body, or euphemistically, that she uncovered his genitals.[358] In a subtle way, the phrase *va-te**gal** marge**lotav*** intentionally mirrors itself, partners itself, in sound as well as action.

This is, after all, Ruth's "daring seduction of Boaz."[359] Given all we have learned about Ruth, what she is doing is utterly out-of-character, even against her very nature. Yet she does what needs to be done. As we will see, in a few moments Ruth will take the initiative and propose marriage to Boaz, something Naomi did not explicitly tell her to do! Though we must assume that Naomi's earlier instruction in verse 4, *ve-galit margelotav*, "and you should uncover his legs" — virtually the same expression as in verse 7 — is an implied sanction for Ruth's behavior here. Ruth's future hinges on her seduction leading to Boaz agreeing to a proper, legitimate levirate marriage; a mere one-time sexual encounter would spell shame, failure and death to her. "Revealing Boaz's legs" is therefore but a prelude to her main goal.

For all these reasons it is likely that it was not only Boaz's legs that Ruth uncovered that night on the threshing-floor; she probably also uncovered his more intimate body parts in the course of her seduction.

The *midrash* also suggests that in a less-literal sense, Ruth is "uncovering" Boaz's essential self when she uncovers *margelotav*.[360] We will see that this is not far from the truth when we read about Boaz's struggle with his reaction to finding Ruth lying next to him.

And it came to pass in the middle of the night, that the man quaked and was encircled — there was a woman lying at his feet! Ruth 3:8

It is in the middle of the night, and Boaz sleeps deeply, out of a combination of fatigue from his hard work that day, and his consumption of quantities of food and wine.[361] Yet something wakes him suddenly, and he raises himself up on his elbows, startled and fearful.[362] He is chilled by the night air, and is immediately aware that his body is uncovered. Simultaneously, he realizes that there is someone or something lying next to him!

Boaz thinks, "Am I dreaming? What has awakened me? Is it a night-demon?"[363] He is in pitch-darkness, so he stretches out his hand and feels the face and head of a person. He is poised to cry out for help when he moves his hand, feeling the softness of a woman's hair.[364] He is relieved that at least it is not a super-natural creature; demons are known to be bald,[365] after all.

Ruth, sensing Boaz's muscles clenching in fear, his adrenaline pumping and his readiness to call out, winds her arms about him in a comforting embrace[366] and whispers in his ear, "Hush now! I am no night-demon, I am a woman!"

"And he said, 'Who are you?' Are you maiden or married?" And she answers, "I am a maiden; *I am Ruth, your handmaid."* And the *midrash* continues, telling us, behold! a flesh-and-blood woman, purest of all women, lay at his feet![367]

Most men, if awakened by stealth in the middle of the night in this way, would be wont to curse the person who had raised such fear in them, at the very least calling the intruder a fool.[368] But Boaz does just the opposite; we will see that instead of cursing Ruth, he blesses her.

Ruth's arms are still around Boaz and she is gripping him tightly,[369] whether to keep him quiet or to impress him with her own intensity of purpose. He asks her, "Why are you here?" She responds softly, saying, *"Spread* the corner[370] of *your robe over your* **handmaid**, *for you are a redeeming kinsman."* Ruth's words are laden with meaning that reaches beyond the simple under-standing of her response. For instance, the Hebrew word for *handmaid* is *amah,* which is nearly identical to the word for mother or matriarch: *imah*. We are told that this verbal similarity hints of the strong feminine line that begat Ruth, and that can be said to have spiritually accompanied her down to the threshing-floor that night. The *midrash*[371] says that by virtue of her own merit *as well as her maternal ancestry*, Ruth is worthy of being protected and wed to the levirate redeemer.

Also, the word *amah* is closely related to the Hebrew word for "truth" — *emet*. Ruth is subtly hinting to Boaz that despite her Moabite roots she is a *true* and righteous convert, a woman worthy to join the community of Israel and to mother Elimelech and Machlon's line.[372]

Ruth has said what she has come to say. By the manner and words of the first half of her speech she is making a request. The first half of verse 9 is an unambiguous appeal for a proposal of marriage. The specific expression to *spread the corner of one's skirt over* a woman is a trademark or badge of protection and marriage.[373] Ruth is hopeful, willing, and vulnerable.

But interestingly, at the same time, the second half of the same verse containing Ruth's whispered plea, is not really a plea at all; it is a statement of Boaz's obligation. By adding *for you are a redeeming kinsman* Ruth might as well have said, "Please marry me; and by the way, you really have no choice in the matter; the law requires you to do this." Ruth couches a demand within her petition.

Was Ruth tactically wise to present her "case" so baldly? The *midrash* says that not only was she permitted to so present herself to Boaz as available and willing, it is to her credit that she did so.[374] This is because Ruth is in that special class of women known as a levirate widow, and just as it was permissible and right for **Tamar** to seek the levir or *yavam*,[375] so, too, it is wholly appropriate for **Ruth** to seek out her potential redeemer. She must fulfill herself as a woman in Israel now that she has become one by choice. This fulfillment will find actualization only if she marries and bears a child. And she can only do so with her dead husband's nearest kinsman.

So it is not unseemly or aggressive for the levirate widow to act in such a manner; viewed another way, by her proposal of marriage she is enabling the levir to act charitably and lawfully.

She is presenting him with an opportunity to perform an act of *chesed* or lovingkindness both for the living widow and for the memory of his dead kinsman. Ruth is saying that she and Boaz already are linked by the thread of the levirate law; all that is needed to seal the relationship is the act of sexual intimacy[376]

By her words *spread your skirt over your handmaid* — a broad reference to birds, who spread wings over their partners while in the act of mating — Ruth expects Boaz to be intimate with her right then, on the threshing-floor![377] This is because for "redemption" of the levirate widow to take place under the levirate law, a marriage ceremony was not necessary. The levirate marriage was accomplished *de facto* by the levir and the levirate widow engaging in sexual relations *with the intention* of redeeming the land and name of her childless husband. It was *at the moment of intimacy* that the marriage occurred by force of law. Because Ruth sought marriage to Boaz, the near-kinsman, she assumed they must be ritually intimate that same night.

Ruth may have "right" on her side, but she is still a vulnerable woman, and she has put herself in physical jeopardy by secreting herself on the threshing-floor overnight. More personally, she has come to admire Boaz and desires his good opinion. She is afraid that he will reject her brazen behavior.[378]

What does Boaz do and say?

BOAZ'S TEST

Boaz is a man, after all. It is the middle of the night, and he is wrapped in the arms of the beautiful and willing[379] woman he most desires. Ruth's seduction is successful, and the Talmud[380] and *midrash*[381] tell us that Boaz is strongly aroused and wants nothing more at that moment than to become intimate with Ruth. We can practically see his rational self warring with his passionate, physical self. The judge in Boaz knows that to take Ruth now, knowing as he does that he is *not* the nearest redeeming kinsman, would be an outright sin. For Ruth is offering herself to him *thinking* that she will thereby be consummating a levirate union. On the other hand, the man in Boaz has been imagining just such a moment of intimacy with Ruth for the past three months, and he is more than ready to consummate the act.[382]

And so, according to another *midrash*,[383] that precise moment in the middle of the night on the threshing-floor when Ruth seduces Boaz is the make-or-break test of Boaz as hero of our story. Had he succumbed to Ruth's seduction it is likely that he would have morally forfeited the end he most desired: to acquire Ruth in levirate marriage.[384] Let us see how Boaz meets this test.

Boaz is, at his core, a man of honor. This is where the text's description of him (in 2:1) as *ish **gibor** chayil*—a man of strength and valor—comes into play. We are taught in the *mishna*,[385] "Ben Zoma says . . . *Eizehu **gibor**?* Who is strong? One who subdues his own inclinations." Boaz's inner strength, sufficient for the Bible to immortalize him as *gibor*, will draw him back from the precipice, will allow him to do what is morally right and not what is merely expedient. As the text will bear out, only *he* knows that he is forbidden from being intimate with Ruth. Because he is *not* the true *yavam*, sexual intimacy with Ruth would turn her into an adulterer! Boaz cannot do this to her.

We watch as he lives up to his name, which, in Dickensian fashion, reveals his essence: "Boaz" is a conjunction of the words *bo oz*, meaning "strength is within him." Boaz breaks out in a sweat, and by exerting an enormous mental and physical effort he quashes his strong desire and *speaks* to Ruth instead of giving in to his urgent physical inclination.[386] His actualized moral and physical strength marks Boaz as *gibor*, and elevates him as the fitting forebear of kings and, potentially, of the Messiah.[387]

Boaz says:

> *"Blessed are you to God, my daughter; your latest act of kindness is greater than the first, not to follow the young men, whether poor or rich."* Ruth 3:10

Boaz does not identify Ruth's "first act" of *chesed*. Beyond the obvious—that Ruth's first *chesed* was that she followed Naomi into Judah,[388] and her second was that she did not pursue a younger man—there are various interpretations identifying that first act of *chesed* which Boaz is praising.

The most resonant is that Ruth's "first *chesed*" was her act of sincere conversion to the Israelite faith.[389] After all, her unsolicited decision to become a Jewess was the *sine qua non* for all the other essential elements of this drama to come into play. It also is the deepest-seated act that she could have performed. It bespeaks an acceptance of the moral laws laid down at Sinai and a fundamental transformation of the self — Moabite into Israelite. It is personally momentous.

There is a wonderful *midrash* that expressly connects Ruth's act of seduction of Boaz on the threshing-floor to her distant ancestress' act of seduction of Lot in the cave above the burning city of Sodom.[390] Boaz's words of blessing (*your latest act of kindness is greater than the first*) actually tell Ruth that her act of seducing him (the *latest* act) brings a perfect closure to her foremother's sexual act that begat the nation of Moav all those years ago (the *first act*).[391]

The two acts of *chesed* are symmetrical bookends that span about two hundred years. The first seduction in the cave — by a young woman of an older man, nobly intended though incestuous — is brought full-circle by the second seduction on the threshing-floor — also by a young woman of an older man, and also righteously intended though ordinarily verboten. The first seduction literally began the Moabite line through Lot, Abraham's seed; the second seduction transforms a Moabite back into an Israelite and perpetuates the Abrahamic seed.

Boaz recognizes both past and present sexual acts to be courageous — even righteous — acts of *chesed*, because their intention is identical: to perpetuate the familial line. But even Ruth's act of *chesed* cannot prevail in the face of the priority of the levirate law. After blessing Ruth for her kindness and raising her hopes, Boaz has some crushing news to impart. He must reveal to her why she might be barred from his life forever.

"THERE IS A KINSMAN CLOSER THAN I!"

RUTH 3:10–12

Ruth is about to be deeply disappointed. Boaz says to her:

*"And now, my daughter, **have no fear**, all that you say I will do for you, for all of my people at the [city] gate know that your are an 'eshet chayil.' "* Ruth 3:11

Ruth is concerned; surely she thinks, "Why is Boaz seeking to comfort me; what do I have to fear?" She is chilled with fore-boding as she waits to hear what Boaz is implicitly warning her against. And in fact, Boaz's reply "wavers between promise and postponement."[392]

Boaz says, *"And now, while I am indeed a near kinsman, **there is a kinsman closer than I!**"* Ruth's heart quails within her. On the one hand, Boaz blesses her for her kindness in seducing *him*, and not a younger man; but on the other hand he shatters her dream by revealing that he is *not* Machlon's closest kinsman! There is a closer *yavam* than he, who must be given the right of first refusal.

Ruth and the reader learn simultaneously in verse 12 that Elimelech's land and Machlon's widow may both potentially belong to another. This is devastating news. As in all great stories, the tension between our hero's perfect objective and obstacle-strewn reality creates unbearable suspense. Will Ruth and Boaz prevail? We must wait and see if they can bend circumstances to their will.

In the meantime, the consolation, as Boaz presents it, is that Ruth's reputation among the elders who sit at the town gates as well as among the people of Beit Lechem is considered impec-cable.[393] Boaz tells her that everyone considers her to be an *eshet chayil*, a woman of valor. This is not an empty or trivial compli-ment. A Moabite woman possessing a character different from Ruth's would likely never have won acceptance so quickly and completely — if ever — as Ruth has done by gleaning doggedly in the fields, caring meticulously for Naomi, and remaining modestly softspoken. In fact, notwithstanding Ruth's attributes, it is possible that her Moabite status could still prevent her from even participating in a levirate marriage![394]

But all is not lost. If Ruth can set aside her crushing disappointment, she will hear that Boaz is presenting her with a measure of hope.

"Do not despair. If the nearer kinsman does *not* wish to redeem you, then I promise to perform the rite of the levirate, as you have requested of me tonight. Tomorrow I will sit in counsel with the elders at the gate. Even if one of them may try to dissuade me from redeeming you because you are a Moabite woman, *Have no fear*; I will stand my ground. In everyone's eyes *you are a woman of valor.*"[395]

The alert reader will note that the text is implicitly matching up Boaz and Ruth. The man described earlier in the text as *a man of strength and valor* is here describing Ruth is those precise terms: *a woman of valor.* We will see if it is their destiny to come together as man and wife, and what part Boaz will play in bringing this about.

As we analyze the coming scenes, we should consider the possibility that Boaz channels his act of sexual abstention from Ruth that night to ignite his inclination to another, more productive end: he will act with speed and cleverness on the morrow to convince the *levir* to yield *to him* his claim of preference.[396]

WHO IS THE NEAREST KINSMAN?

Just as the reader thinks that fate has finally smiled on Ruth, Boaz drops the bombshell in 3:12 that he is not the nearest kinsman for purposes of redeeming her. Why is this news so dire?

Elimelech and his two sons have died leaving widows, and also, unfortunately, without leaving any heirs. In order to keep Elimelech's landed portion from being subsumed within his brothers' estates, Naomi or Ruth must produce an heir from their husbands' line. But Naomi is too old to have children, so the last chance for *yibum* falls to Ruth. Hence the search for the closest kinsman; only *he* can be the one to take Ruth in levirate marriage. Their union is solely for the purpose of producing an heir to stand in the place of the deceased.

Who is closer kin than Boaz?

Boaz's and Naomi's fathers were brothers, making Boaz and Naomi first cousins. Naomi was married to Elimelech, Boaz's uncle, who was also — in the way of the peoples of the ancient

Near East — *her* uncle.[397] But how does this affect the pressing question of *yibum*?

The nearest kinsman for levirate purposes is the dead man's brother. But in Machlon's case, because his brother is also deceased, the law will climb higher up the family tree — to Elimelech's branch — to find the nearest kinsman. We know from our earlier discussion of Boaz's provenance that Elimelech was one of four brothers: Elimelech, Salmon (Boaz's father), Tov and a fourth unnamed brother (Naomi's father).[398] Elimelech, Salmon and Naomi's father are all deceased, leaving Elimelech's last living brother, Tov[399] — Boaz's and Naomi's uncle — as the nearest kinsman for the purpose of redeeming Elimelech's/Naomi's land and Machlon's widow.

Elimelech's brother, Tov, is closer kin for purposes of redeeming Machlon's levirate widow than is his nephew, Boaz. And in ancient Israelite society, the law of the levirate followed the law of inheritance; the brother who performs *yibum* with the widow inherits the deceased's estate.[400] The closest kinsman takes precedence.[401]

As we will see, Tov, the nearest kinsman, is called "Ploni Almoni" in chapter 4 of the text. The reason for this is related to the greater theme in the book of Ruth, which is an individual's and a society's moral obligation to perform acts of *chesed* or human kindness, protecting the unfortunate or disenfranchised.

ACTS OF *CHESED* PERMEATE OUR STORY

Acts of *chesed* or special kindnesses suffuse this story, propelling the narrative. Let us review them here, as they provide a road map for the protagonists' characters.

In chapter 1 Naomi blessed Ruth and Orpah, calling upon God to show them *chesed* as they have shown their dead husbands and herself. The theory is that Ruth and Orpah should be paid back by the Almighty for their kindnesses: for having treated their dead husbands with respect by purchasing burial shrouds for them and burying them properly, and also for having accompanied their mother-in-law on her way back to Judah.

Only Ruth actually fulfills this latter act of *chesed* by clinging to Naomi and returning with her all the way to Judah and Beit Lechem after Orpah turns back to Moav. Ruth left her home and family permanently, to join Naomi in a land and with a people that were unknown, even hostile, to her. Despite serious obstacles, Ruth completed the acts of *chesed* that she and Orpah began together.

Maimonides (the Rambam) defines *chesed* as an act of extraordinary kindness.[402] Ruth and Orpah's acts of shrouding and burying their husbands qualify as acts of *chesed*, since the dead cannot repay the living for their kindness. Though one could well argue that a wife has a *de facto* if not a *de jure* obligation to bury her husband, Ruth and Orpah were Moabites and might not have felt the need to treat their dead in the same way as a Hebrew.

But the Rambam allows for another category of acts of *chesed*; those that are done to another out of kindness, but *over and above* what the recipient is due. Ruth's behaviors to Naomi and Boaz's generosity toward Ruth would fall into this second category.

And should we not also recognize Naomi's generosity of spirit towards Ruth as an act of *chesed*? It is all-the-more note-worthy because it is against her will, against her heart to welcome and embrace a Moabite woman. For Naomi believes on some buried level that this Moabite woman catalyzed her son's downfall, ending in his death at the hands of an angry God. It is perhaps nearly as difficult for Naomi to accept Ruth as it was for her to accept her sons' deaths. The Talmud[403] even takes judicial notice of the "ordinary" antipathy flowing from a mother-in-law to her daughter-in-law. Here, surely Naomi must be in an agony of conflict over Ruth, asking herself, "Am I taking a viper to my bosom?" For all these reasons, her ability to overcome this powerful negative inclination is an act of *chesed*.

In chapter 2 Ruth's *chesed* grows to include her care and feeding of Naomi. This former princess goes out to glean in the fields with the poor of Beit Lechem. This chapter also introduced us to Boaz and to *his* acts of *chesed* toward Ruth. He graciously invited her to remain as a gleaner in his field throughout the harvest; he offered her the protection of his female gleaners and of his harvesters. He personally offered her food at his table and water from his harvester's jugs. Unbeknownst to Ruth, Boaz instructed his men to leave more sheaves behind than they ordinarily would have done, so that she would be able to glean an abundant amount. Boaz also instructed his men not to annoy Ruth in any way.

Naomi recognizes Boaz's kindnesses to Ruth as having their origin in the Almighty, who is the ultimate source of both punishment and *chesed.*

In fact, the two primary legal underpinnings of this story are themselves founded in *chesed*, in care for and kindness toward others less fortunate. First is the law of *leket*, which allows Ruth to glean in the field of a prosperous landowner, enabling her to feed herself and Naomi by gathering and then beating the forgotten sheaves and milling the grain. Second is a version of the levirate law or *yibum*, which allows a barren widow to keep her dead husband's landed portion and family name from devolving to others via a marriage to his kinsman. Both *leket* and *yibum* are societally sanctioned acts of *chesed* in Judah, and are the backdrop of the actors' behaviors in our story.

In chapter 3 Ruth's *chesed* is both manifest and subtle. Boaz is quick to praise and bless Ruth for her obvious acts of kindness: for caring for Naomi, and also for proposing marriage to an older man such as himself, when she could have had the pick of the young men, be they poor or rich. By proposing to Boaz, Ruth perpetuated her *chesed* to her dead husband *and his family*, because by agreeing to marry the redeemer she will sustain her husband's inherited landed portion as well as his name.

But the more subtle *chesed* that Ruth performed is that she did not engage Boaz in an intimate act while he was either drunk with wine or in a deep sleep. Instead, she waited specifically until he had slept off his meal. She uncovered him, awakened him, and engaged him in conversation. She proceeded in a straightforward way, saying "I am Ruth your handmaid," and she forthrightly asked Boaz to take her in marriage. The reader will surely distinguish this behavior from that of her distant foremother, Lot's eldest daughter, who plied her father with wine, and while he was insensate, engaged in sexual intimacy.[404] While both women's motivations are laudable — Lot's daughter sought to perpetuate her father's seed after a cataclysm, and Ruth's goal is to sustain

her dead husband's inheritance — what a difference in methodology![405] Ruth's above-board "seduction" on the threshing-floor
was an interaction, not a trick. This was her act of kindness to
Boaz.

Implicit in chapter 3 is also the heroic act of kindness Boaz
shows to Ruth by *not* taking what she is offering, by *not* accepting
her seduction and by honestly admitting to her that another male
relative is closer kin than he is. He stops short of allowing them
both to sin. He also is careful not to allow Ruth to be seen as a
loose woman, encouraging her to return home before daylight.
This is bone-deep *chesed* that is in addition to his gift to her of six
sheaves of barley so that she would not return home to Naomi
empty-handed. The latter is a courtesy, while the former is
genuine consideration of Ruth as a woman. Boaz is not a man
who takes advantage of a woman in desperate circumstances, no
matter how acutely he desires her.

Coming up in chapter 4 is Boaz's negotiation with the closer
kinsman for Ruth's hand and for Elimelech and Naomi's land.
The speed and strategy with which Boaz acts to free Ruth from the
limbo of her levirate widowhood is another act of *chesed* on Boaz's
part. In stark contrast, we will see how the closest kinsman (this is
Tov, called "Ploni Almoni" in chapter 4) backs away from his
levirate duty, rejecting his obligation to redeem both Ruth and his
brother's land. He will stand in lone relief, the one character in
our drama who *fails to perform* the *chesed* that will allow his
brother's memory to live on in perpetuity, and he will be
implicitly censured for this.

As the story draws to a close, Ruth's *chesed* will continue with
her coming generosity toward Naomi. Ruth will generously
include her mother-in-law in her new family, allowing her to
serve as nurse to her baby son. The town elders will bless Ruth as
a matriarch in Israel, and the neighbor-women will praise her as a
mainstay for the aged Naomi.

❈ ❈ ❈

But as the story now stands, the two protagonists in this biblical
drama — the primary do-ers of *chesed* — are still on the threshing-

floor. Boaz is wrestling with his desire for Ruth, Ruth is tamping down her disappointment that Boaz is not the first redeemer, and she must now either make her way homeward or stay the night.

"STAY THE NIGHT . . ."

RUTH 3:13–15

Boaz is reluctant to let Ruth go. So he tells her:

> *"Stay over tonight, and if it comes to pass in the morning that Tov will redeem you, well, let him redeem you; but if he does **not** wish to redeem you, I will redeem you, as the Lord lives! Lie down until morning."* Ruth 3:13

The crisis will not be resolved until the morning. It is then that Boaz will speak to the other elders about Elimelech's fields and about redeeming Machlon's widow. It is then that Boaz will present the situation to his uncle Tov,[406] who will either agree to redeem the land and Ruth, or not.[407] But Boaz is constrained to remain by his grain piles overnight. So, conscious of Ruth's safety, he decides that until the morrow comes he would rather have Ruth remain with him—albeit platonically[408]—than worry about what might befall her in the dark on her way home.[409]

Boaz sees that Ruth is disheartened. Perhaps she doubts his deep feelings for her, or perhaps she thinks there is no chance that the closer kinsman will forfeit his levirate duty, and she despairs that she and Boaz will have a future together. So Boaz swears fervently in God's name—perhaps he even grasps Ruth's arms as he does so—and he promises Ruth that he will redeem her if Tov does not. "You will spend *this* night without a husband, but with God's help you will not be without a husband tomorrow night!"[410]

Rashi suggests another reading of Boaz's oath. Boaz is fighting mightily to overcome his physical reaction to Ruth. His body is clamoring for release, but he is forbidden by law from intimacy with the levirate widow *because he is not the closest kinsman*. All this intellectualizing notwithstanding, Boaz swears aloud as he grits his teeth and battles the strength of his desire. Says Rashi, "Boaz's desire is whispering to him, enticing him, saying, '*You* are free, and *she* is free—come unto her!' But Boaz swears aloud that he will *not* come unto her without the blessing of marriage!"[411]

✠ ✠ ✠

And she lay at his foot until morning . . . Ruth 3:14

Ruth is in a quandary; should she go, or should she stay? Recognizing and acceding to the strength of the man before whom she has humbled herself, Ruth agrees to his request and remains at Boaz's side for the rest of the short night.

The text tells us (3:14) that "she lay down [at] *margelotav.*" This would seem at first blush to repeat the posture she had been in when she first knelt at Boaz's bed in verse 7. But the first time the word *margelotav* appears—when Ruth "uncovers" *margelotav*—the word is spelled with the letter *yud*, signifying the plural possessive. That is, *And she uncovered his "margelot,"* meaning **his feet, his legs,** or **his genitals**. Whereas this second time the word appears, here in verse 14, it is spelled *without* the letter *yud*. This effectively changes the word's meaning to a singular noun. It is probably best translated as *And she lay down **at his foot*** or *at **its** foot.* The *midrash*[412] focuses on this important spelling difference, saying that when Boaz tells Ruth to "stay the night," she does; but she stays *by the foot of his bed,* putting as much distance between them as she can in the small space. And for the next few hours she does not move from her spot.

If we pay close attention to the text of verse 14, we note that it says "and **she** lay down," and then "and **she** arose." Ruth lays down *alone*; there is no indication that she lays down *with Boaz* in the intimate sense of the word. So, too, she arises alone, before anyone has stirred, even Boaz. Ruth's seduction, while successful at arousing Boaz and at sharpening his interest so that he is fired to "fight" for her levirate hand, was a chaste one. And because it was a chaste "laying down," Ruth once again distinguishes herself from her distant foremother, Lot's eldest daughter. Lot's eldest daughter "lay down" *sexually* with her father — albeit for the noble purpose of perpetuating humanity — thus violating a sexual taboo. Not so Ruth, thanks to Boaz's restraint. Had Ruth succeeded completely in her seduction, and had Boaz succumbed sexually, they would also, like Lot's daughters, have transgressed a sexual taboo. This is because Ruth, as a levirate widow, is not permitted to engage in sexual relations with anyone other than the redeeming nearest kinsman.[413] She is not a free woman in the same way that an ordinary widow would be.

Had Ruth been sexually intimate with Boaz that night, she could have been considered an adulteress, and serious legal penalties and consequences could have come into play! All because Boaz, the object of her seduction, was *not* the nearest kinsman to her deceased husband.

So the *midrash* lauds Ruth, saying that by her bold but chaste behavior that night on the threshing-floor she has substituted, generations later — via a fictional reincarnation — for Lot's eldest daughter; she has *atoned*, in effect, for her foremother's "sin."[414] It is understood that both Lot's daughter and Ruth had noble motives. But while the first woman had no alternative but to sin, the second woman was spared from having to do so. Thus did Ruth "pardon" her foremother, wiping the ancestral slate clean.

> . . . *and she rose before one could recognize his fellow, for he said, "Let it not be known that the woman came to the threshing-floor."* Ruth 3:14

Once he sees that Ruth has agreed to stay, Boaz, too, is excruciatingly careful. He faces away from the woman by his side, stretches out onto his stomach, and remains in that position until morning.[415] It was perhaps impossible to keep Boaz's and Ruth's tryst a secret, but Boaz tries. Boaz's most trusted servant, whose pallet was nearby, must have awakened when Boaz swore out loud. With Ruth laying low and her face burning with embarrassment, Boaz orders the curious man to keep silent, and to reveal to no one what he has seen: the Moabite woman who had gleaned in Boaz's fields was now on the threshing-floor and had remained there, on his master's bed, all night.[416]

Boaz thinks to himself[417] that if Ruth is seen leaving the threshing-floor, gossip would be rife, and the only conclusion people would draw would be that Ruth has compromised herself and that he has been the instrumentality. Given what Boaz is planning to do after sunrise — he faces difficult and delicate negotiation for the levirate rights — he knows such suspicions will complicate his task and will likely inure to his detriment. To have even a chance at prevailing before his judicial colleagues at the gate Boaz must come to the matter "with clean hands."

Ruth arises one hour before the first light,[418] before Boaz even stirs. She did not shut her eyes the entire night; she had been in a state of tension and awareness, replaying the scene and reviewing her options. "What if the closer kinsman will not release me?" must be the fear uppermost in her mind. So at the first graying of the horizon Ruth is up and in a hurry to be gone.[419]

Boaz awakens next and has a plan to save them both from embarrassment and mishap.[420] Out of extreme modesty Ruth wears an outsized shawl atop her clothing which also doubles as a head covering. Because it presents a slight hindrance to walking and working, none of the other poor gleaners possess or wear such a garment. For this reason, Ruth is recognizable even from afar among the people of Beit Lechem and especially among the harvesting community. So Boaz agrees with Ruth that before it is light enough for her to be recognized, she should be away from the threshing-floor. The *midrashim*[421] tell us that Boaz accompanies her all the way to Beit Lechem to assure himself that she arrives at Naomi's door safely. This is based on the wording of verse 15, which states "**he** came" to the city — in the *masculine* gender — rather than the expected "**she** came."

BOAZ'S GIFT TO RUTH

And he said, "Grasp the shawl you are wearing, and hold it out." And she held it out, and he measured out six barleys and he placed them onto her shoulders, and [s]he came to the city. Ruth 3:15

Before she leaves the threshing-floor, Boaz asks Ruth to hold out a corner of her shawl. He measures out a *kav* or one-sixth of a *seah* of barley into it. Boaz is mindful that under Israelite law it is customary to give a person in need who is traveling from one place to another at least half a *kav's*-worth of food. Boaz gives Ruth *double* that amount, sufficient for the morning meal for both Ruth and Naomi.[422] Some say that Boaz loads Ruth down with six *seah*, which would be quite a heavy burden and nearly impossible to carry.[423] Others say Boaz gave Ruth just six barleycorns, in the nature of a symbolic gift,[424] presaging a six-fold blessing that would emerge from her, and hinting that she is destined to bear a son who will possess six heroic character traits: a spirit of wisdom, understanding, good counsel, bravery, political knowledge and a fear of the Lord.[425] Or the six barleycorns could represent six righteous men, kings and prophets who are destined to emerge from her.[426]

On a more immediate level, it is also possible that Boaz does not wish Ruth to leave him empty-handed,[427] so he gifts her with the only thing he has at-the-ready and in abundance: winnowed barley from the harvest. It is, perhaps, a subtle earnest-gift so that even on "the morning-after" Ruth will appreciate that Boaz stands by his promise, given in the dark of night, to take her in levirate marriage if at all possible.

It is significant that Boaz has personally handed Ruth two gifts so far in the text, and both have consisted of barley. The first was a plate of toasted barley which he passed to her when she sat with his harvesters in the field shack on the first day of the barley harvest (2:14), and the second is the gift of six barleycorns at the conclusion of the threshing festival (3:15). The symmetry of the gifts, bookending Ruth and Boaz's first meeting and the meeting that might be their last, is important to the theme of *chesed* in the story.

Considering the wealth that Boaz possesses, his two gifts to Ruth are notably humble. The message for the reader is also two-fold. First, we must appreciate that after ten years of famine the modest gift of a plate of toasted barley can, paradoxically, be an abundant offering to a destitute and hungry person. Things are not always what they seem at first glance. A Moabite widow may not be the stranger, burden, or danger to the community she appears to be at face-value. She may be a blessing to her mother-in-law and even the future mother of kings.

And second, once the harvest is done and famine is no longer looming, the selfsame unassuming barleycorns represent not merely a reprieve from starvation, but also more: a promise of satiety, of fertility, and of a future. The simple and modest can actually be *transformed* into the momentous and life-giving. Ruth's act of *chesed* in following Naomi, plighting her troth to her and choosing to become a Hebrew (1:16–17) is the embodiment of such a transformation, of realizing one's inchoate potentiality. Hence the second gift to Ruth of the six barleycorns, which bear the seeds of new barley sprouts within their kernels. Boaz recognizes Ruth's potential, and this recognition — of seeing beyond the outer shell — is an act of *chesed*, too.

RUTH RETURNS TO NAOMI

> *And she came to her mother-in-law, and she said, "Who are you, my daughter?" And she told her all that the man had done to her.*
>
> *And she said, "He gave me these six barleys, for he said to me, 'Do not come empty-handed to your mother-in-law.' "*
>
> *And she said, "Stay here, my daughter, until you learn how the matter turns out. For the man will not rest until he has resolved the matter today."* Ruth 3:16–18

Boaz leaves Ruth at her door while it is not yet light. Ruth knocks, startling her mother-in-law, Naomi, who has spent a sleepless night worrying whether she has done the right thing by sending Ruth to the threshing-floor. And because Ruth is shrouded in her shawl, Naomi cannot discern her features in the grey-black of pre-dawn.[428] So she calls out, "Who is it? Is it you, my daughter?"

The verse is also interpreted as "**What** are you?" Perhaps Naomi was asking whether Ruth was by now wed in levirate marriage to Boaz, or whether she was still an unmarried woman.[429] Or she could have meant, "What's happened with you? Did it work out? Are you hopeful and happy or are you despondent and rejected?"[430]

To all of these implicit queries we can imagine Ruth responds not by saying "It is I, Ruth, your daughter-in-law," but by telling her, "I am still unwed," and recounting all that Boaz had said and done to her that night. And she adds, "And see, mother-in-law, how Boaz was concerned for you, also. He gave me six measures of barley *for you*. For he knew I would not be partaking in meals with you much longer; tomorrow at this time I will be wed in levirate marriage either to him or to Tov, the nearest kinsman. But even after I am married I will not abandon you or leave off caring for you. You need not worry."[431]

The reader is permitted to see Ruth's essential, caring nature coming to the fore. Even in the aftermath of her trying night and the truncated seduction, even in her disappointment that Boaz is not the closest kinsman, Ruth hastens to assure Naomi that *her* welfare is secure.

After hearing Ruth's account of the night's drama and of Boaz's heroic behavior and his promise to her, Naomi reverts to her motherly self and seeks to comfort her daughter-in-law. "Come, sit down next to me, my daughter. You must be exhausted, for surely you have not even shut your eyes this night. You will remain here, and will not so much as show your face outside this house today. You will see, things will move quickly now. The sun will not set again without Boaz resolving the matter once and for all."[432] Naomi must have read between the lines and understood that Boaz's restraint and his sworn promise to Ruth indicated — perhaps even more eloquently than sexual intimacy would have — the depth of his feeling for her and his commitment to fight to redeem her. Naomi is cautiously hopeful, in counterpoint to Ruth's adrenaline-shocked fatigue and her unexpressed worry. For it is Ruth's future that is in the balance.

One more matter is on Naomi's mind, though it is unlikely that she shares this with Ruth. Naomi knows that under the levirate law Ruth is as good as betrothed or, peculiar as it may seem, already "married." The legal fiction, explained in Part Three's "Judah & Tamar," is that the levirate widow is tied to her dead husband's closest paternal kinsman the moment her widowhood becomes fact. This tie is known as the "*zikah*-bond," so even if she is not acquainted with the nearest kinsman, she is already "his" but-for the acts of acceptance, redemption and consummation. This is the reason the levirate widow may not give herself to another man during her widowhood. She is attached to the *yavam* or levir "like a full-fledged wife."[433]

This special *zikah* status explains Tamar's earlier urgency in Genesis 38 to have the nearest kinsman lie with her. Until she—and he—produce an heir to stand in her dead husband's shoes for inheritance purposes, she will not be free. In Ruth's case, Naomi now knows that unless Boaz can get Tov to renounce his rights as the levir, Ruth is as good as married *to Tov* in the eyes of the law. And Naomi is aware that Ruth's happiness will be forfeit if she does not marry Boaz; she sees with the eyes of an older woman that there is a special personal connection between them.

This is the real drama that will be played out in chapter 4: whether Boaz can engineer a renunciation by Tov, the nearest kinsman, of his rights to Elimelech's land, and by extension, to Machlon's widow.

THE NEXT DAY,
BOAZ SITS IN WAIT FOR THE KINSMAN

And Boaz went up to the gate and sat down there, and behold! the kinsman of whom Boaz had spoken was passing, and he said, "Turn aside, sit down here, Ploni Almoni." And he turned aside and he sat down.

And he took ten men of the elders of the city and he said, "Sit down here." And they sat down. Ruth 4:1–2

The sun is just up and the business of the day is beginning. We see that Boaz has not forgotten his nighttime oath to Ruth.[434] It is early morning, and he has made his way up to the town from the threshing-floor. Already he is sitting at the town gate—the place where the elders sit in judgement and court is held—intending to assemble a quorum of his judicial peers. We are told that Boaz is actually the head of the *Sanhedrin*[435] or judicial court, and that he is within his prerogative to summon a quorum. Boaz intends to set out the facts of the levirate widow from Moav and to ask for a judicial ruling on the question of whether she is permitted entry into the community of Israel, and if so, whether he is permitted to redeem her.[436] Whatever the opinion of the court is, it will be made public for all to know.

Boaz is not waiting long when his uncle—the closer kinsman for purposes of redeeming Naomi's land and Machlon's widow—passes by! Boaz is quick to take advantage of such a fateful coincidence,[437] and he calls out, "Hey, *Ploni Almoni*, you old So-and-So, turn aside and take a seat." And the man sits down beside him.

The reader is introduced in verse 1 to the phrase "Ploni Almoni," a name-substitute. We are curious. Why, if Boaz's uncle is named Tov,[438] do Boaz and the text hereinafter refer to him as Ploni Almoni? What does this epithet mean?

Rashi makes no bones about it; the man is not referred to by his proper name henceforth in the text because he is soon to renege on his obligation to redeem his dead kinsman's land and widow. The word "ploni" means "to disappear," and "almoni" means "anonymous, unknown, a nameless someone."[439] This is a fitting name-substitute, then. Once the levirate law is called into play, the obligation to redeem one's close kinsman from childless extinction is a serious one. Endurance of the extended family is of paramount importance. We are given a textual hint to its gravitas when we read the subtly insulting non-name of "Ploni Almoni." We will soon see how Boaz's recalcitrant uncle disappears utterly from the story and becomes an unknown and nameless someone; his disappearance is a precise measure-for-measure consequence of his refusal to sustain the name and inheritance of his brother.

In an interesting word-play Boaz requests his uncle to *surah*, or *turn aside*. This is the same word Lot used in Gen. 19:2 when he greeted the two angels and asked them to turn aside and enter his house. We are meant to connect Lot's miraculous salvation from the fires of Sodom to this morning in Beit Lechem, generations later. Lot was saved from death not for his own merit, which we saw[440] was dubious at best, but in order that Ruth should emerge from his loins and fulfill her own destiny years later. We are about to see how this develops.

BOAZ ASKS HIM: "WILL YOU REDEEM?"

And he said to the redeemer, "Naomi, who has returned from the field of Moav, is selling the portion of the field that belonged to our brother, to Elimelech.

"And I said I would let you know, saying: Buy it in the presence of those who sit here [today] and before the elders of my people. If you would redeem, redeem; and if you would not redeem, tell me so, and I will know, for there is no one besides you to redeem [first], and I am after you." And he said, "I will redeem."

And Boaz said, "On the day that you buy the field from the hand of Naomi, you [also] have acquired Ruth the Moabitess, the wife of the deceased, in order to preserve the name of the deceased [along with] his inheritance."

And the redeemer replied, "I cannot redeem, lest I extinguish my own portion; why don't you redeem my redemption, for I cannot redeem [it]." Ruth 4:3–6

We can envision the scene at the gates to Beit Lechem. It is still early morning, and at least ten judges other than Boaz are gathered in the semicircular outdoor area that is designated for the local assizes near the town's entrance. Boaz is seated, too, and next to him is his uncle, the nearest kinsman. Some early-rising townspeople are passing by, casting curious eyes over the convened court. Perhaps they think, what important matter could have brought the judges out so early on the morning after the winnowing festival? Perhaps some of them even stop to watch and listen in.

Boaz is speaking to the kinsman, in a seemingly casual manner, but he does so in full hearing of the assembled judges, who are paying close attention. He tells him, "Uncle, you are familiar with that portion of the family fields that belongs to your brother Elimelech,[441] he should rest in peace? Well, it has come to my knowledge that his widow, Naomi, who has recently returned from Moav, is in desperate straits, and is selling it off.[442] Since you are Elimelech's only living brother, I thought to let you know about the situation. You are first in line to purchase the land, and have the right of first refusal. But you need to decide today, as her situation is dire. There is no one else to redeem the land, it is down to the two of us.[443] If you do decide to purchase the land, you can do so easily, in the presence of the witnesses gathered here this morning.[444] I tell you this because I think the land of your brother should not be sold to a stranger.[445]

And Ploni Almoni responds, "I *will* redeem."

There is a moment's pause after Boaz's uncle agrees to purchase Naomi's field. Is this the end, then? What of Ruth? No mention has been made as yet of the levirate marriage obligation. One could say that the purchase of Naomi's **land** was "part A;" Boaz now proceeds strategically with "part B."[446]

"That's fine, Uncle. But there is one stipulation. You understand that when you purchase the land *from Naomi* you also, in effect, are purchasing it *from Ruth* the Moabite, as she is the widow of Elimelech's son, Machlon, and she inherited the land from him."

Boaz intentionally left this bit of information until after the kinsman had expressed his interest in the land. The implication for the redeeming kinsman — and it is not lost on him — is that since he is essentially purchasing the **land** *from Ruth*, he *also* must redeem **Ruth**, herself! Boaz drops the bombshell:

"And as such, Uncle, you have not only purchased your brother's *field* just now; you also have agreed to redeem his son's *widow*."

The kinsman hears Boaz out and realizes that, unintentionally, he has just agreed to acquire a levirate wife! He was not expecting this. First, because the practice of *yibum* had fallen into disuse,[447] and second, because the situation with Elimelech, Naomi, Machlon and Ruth is not a typical *yibum* situation. Classical *yibum* circumstances arise when *a brother* of the childless deceased takes his brother's widow in levirate marriage. Their future child — the main purpose of the otherwise-forbidden union — will inherit his father's landed portion, and will thereby perpetuate his family's name.[448]

Elimelech's death years earlier would not have triggered *yibum* because at that time he was survived by two sons. Only years later, when both married brothers—Elimelech's heirs—died childless, did *yibum* come into play. And then it would have been *Naomi* who would have been the levirate widow; because Elimelech had one brother still alive who could theoretically redeem her. This scenario was impossible, however, because of Naomi's advanced age (and concomitant *in*ability to conceive).[449]

So the kinsman at the town gate on the morning after the threshing festival cannot be faulted for thinking the deal he agreed to was for the land only; he would not have been expected to redeem Naomi, and never thought his obligation would devolve to Ruth, Machlon's widow.

The present situation is an unusual case, an extended form of *yibum*, because **neither Boaz's uncle, nor Boaz himself, is the actual brother of Machlon, the childless dead man.**[450] This is why the kinsman pauses when Boaz tells him, in essence, "when you buy the land from the widow you also acquire a levirate wife." It catches him completely unaware.

THE REDEEMER RENEGES

The redeemer reconsiders his decision in light of this new information, and he changes his mind. He has no problem buying Elimelech's land, but has no interest in redeeming Ruth.[451] *Twice* he says to Boaz, in front of the ten sitting judges, "Then **I** *cannot* **redeem** the land, lest I extinguish my own inheritance in the process. For I already have a wife[452] and five children of my own!"[453] Ploni Almoni refuses buy Naomi/Ruth's land for the reason that acquiring Ruth is part of the deal. He categorically refuses to fulfill the *yibum* obligation with Ruth. What is Ploni Almoni afraid of?

Ploni Almoni thinks that taking Ruth in levirate marriage would "extinguish his inheritance." It is unclear why he thinks this. In fact, the law is quite to the contrary. The express purpose of *yibum* is to allow the child from the levirate union to inherit the *deceased's* landed portion. The child Ploni Almoni would have with Ruth would *not* inherit through Ploni Almoni, or decrease his prior children's inheritance shares; the new child would inherit only Elimelech and Machlon's portions!

The commentaries explain that Ploni Almoni has several fears, the first two of which are related, and are readily understandable given human nature and the biblical characters' track record.

First, he fears that taking a levirate wife and siring a child with her would inject pernicious and relentless rivalries among all his children, shattering his family dynamic.[454] His peaceful home would become a fractious and quarrelsome place.[455] Second, he fears that because he already has a wife, bringing a second wife into his home would bring a new dimension of trouble down onto his head.[456] And third, he fears that bringing a Moabite wife into his bed would be in contravention of the Deuteronomic prohibition against an Ammonite or Moabite entering the community of Israel.[457] As discussed above, we are told that the law only prohibited *male* Ammonites and Moabites; it did not apply to *females*. But apparently Ploni Almoni is not aware of this loophole, so he backs away from redeeming Ruth along with the land. He fears that marriage to a Moabite would bring his death at God's hands, as it did with Machlon.[458] Or worse, he fears that in punishment for wedding a Moabite woman his own children could die before their time.[459]

So in the same breath that he refuses to redeem, Ploni Almoni says to his nephew, "*You* should redeem the field and the widow for yourself! You have no wife and no children,[460] and you are the next in line to redeem. Redeem them for yourself in my stead."

THE SHOE CEREMONY
IN COMMERCIAL TRANSACTIONS

Now this was the custom in former times in Israel concerning redemption and exchange: in order to confirm all matters, one would remove his shoe and give it to his fellow; and this was the [method of] attestation in Israel.

And the near kinsman said to Boaz, "Buy it for yourself," and he removed his shoe. Ruth 4:7–8

At one time in ancient Israel, one's word was sufficient surety to seal a commercial sale or a barter transaction between buyer and seller.[461] Later on, the custom developed wherein the *seller* removed his shoe — or any garment[462] — and gave it to the buyer as a symbol of the transfer of goods from one to the other (the seller's shoe symbolized the item that he was selling or transferring to the buyer). There is also an alternative theory that it was the *buyer* who gave his shoe to the seller, symbolizing his promise to pay him for the goods ("you see how earnest and reliable I am; I will take the very shirt off my back or the shoe off my foot in order to pay you!").

Regarding our scene at the city gate, even the Talmud asks, "Who gave the shoe to whom?"[463]

Either way — whether the acquisition is via the shoe of the *acquirer* (Boaz here), or via the shoe of the *seller* (Ploni Almoni), in biblical Israel the removal of the shoe of *one* of the deal's participants became integral to a sale or a transfer. So much so that at first, witnesses were not even required for the matter to be enforceable. **The passing of the shoe from one to the other was the official signal that the sale or transfer had the force of law.**

At the time of our story, the act of the shoe exchange was the single act that witnesses were required to observe and attest to, in order that a commercial deal could be confirmed. Of course, the shoe exchange was purely symbolic, and the shoe was always returned to its owner after the ceremony was witnessed and noted. The person was not expected to walk away barefoot.

The exception to this latter practice was a marriage transaction. When "acquiring" a wife, it was not appropriate for the betrothed bride to return the shoe to the prospective bridegroom, lest it appear as if she rejected the betrothal. So the explicit law in Israel became that a woman may not be wedded with a *conditional* gift (such as a shoe that must be returned).[464] A bride's wedding gift is an unconditional gift which she can keep.

This wedding exception is a reason that some say the ordinary shoe removal ceremony described in the text pertains only to the acquisition of Elimelech's[465] *field*; not to the acquisition of Ruth as a levirate wife. The former was a commercial transaction, while the latter is not. But the prevailing opinion is that the shoe removal ceremony is integral to acquiring the rights to redeem the levirate widow.

THE *CHALITZA* CEREMONY

Boaz's acquisition of Ruth, while obviously connected to his purchase of "her" field, is in truth not a sale or purchase at all, but is more in the nature of an exchange or redemption. Known as *chalifin*,[466] from the Hebrew root *chlf*, meaning "exchange" or "replace" — possibly from thence to *chalitza*, meaning "to remove" — it is thought that Boaz removed *his* shoe[467] and gave it to the renouncing redeemer *in exchange* for receiving his uncle's right to redeem Machlon's widow.[468] This *chalifin* or exchange was a necessary condition precedent to Boaz's purchase of the field from Naomi/Ruth. Once the redeemer received Boaz's shoe, he could not go back on his refusal to redeem.

Thus, the order of the day for Boaz was, first, to exchange his shoe for the kinsman's first-right to redeem; second, to purchase the field; and third, to acquire Ruth as his levirate wife. He could not proceed to steps two and three without first exchanging his shoe for the right to redeem.

Others say that it was *the redeemer's* shoe[469] that passed *to Boaz*. The nearest-kinsman was in effect saying to Boaz, the second-in-line, "Just as I give you my shoe, so, too, am I giving you my right to redeem." As explained in Deut. 25:9–10 and discussed above, the person who cedes his shoe or sandal is the *brother of the deceased* who is renouncing his first-right to redeem both the land and the widow of his kinsman. In our story that would be Ploni Almoni. And in the Torah's description he would cede his sandal *to the spurned levirate widow* in a public ceremony censuring and shaming him[470] for his dereliction of an important familial duty. In such a Deuteronomic *chalitza* — termed a "ceremony of disgrace"[471] — the levirate widow spits into the nearest kinsman's face and declares "*Thus* shall it be done to the man who fails to build up his brother's house!"

But this is *not* the situation at the Beit Lechem town gate. Even though Ruth is absent from this impromptu judicial proceeding,[472] modern Bible scholar Calum Carmichael sees "a muted form of disgrace" directed at the nearest kinsman in our story.[473] This censure is delivered not by the levirate widow. Instead, the disgrace is more subtle, but it is longer-lived. We see that **the text itself stands-in for Ruth**. As we pointed out earlier, by referring to him as Ploni Almoni or "So-and-So" rather than by a personal and meaningful name, the text shows its contempt for the renouncing redeemer. He who refuses to sustain the name of his kinsman is fated to remain nameless himself.

So Ploni Almoni, the nameless nearest kinsman, says to Boaz before witnesses and before the town court or *beit din*,[474] "Buy the field for yourself!" And a secretly satisfied Boaz removes his own shoe[475] and hands it ceremoniously to his uncle.[476] Thus does Boaz acquire the right to redeem the field as well as the levirate widow Ruth.[477] Once the shoe ceremony — the *chalitza* — is effected, the substitution, or *chalifin*, of Boaz for the nearest kinsman is symbolically and legally complete. According to the law of *yibum* Boaz now stands "in the shoes" of Ploni Almoni,[478] who stood in the shoes of Machlon, who stood in the shoes of Elimelech.

"YOU ARE WITNESSES TODAY
TO WHAT I HAVE BOUGHT"

Boaz might as well be raising his arms in a gesture of victory, Rocky Balboa-style. He turns to the court and to the assembled townspeople and announces jubilantly:

> *"You are witnesses today that I have bought all that was Elimelech's and all that was Chilyon's and Machlon's from the hand of Naomi.*
>
> *"And also Ruth the Moabitess, Machlon's wife, have I acquired for myself as a wife, [so that I might] preserve the name of the deceased to his inheritance, so that the name of the deceased will not be obliterated from [the midst of] his brethren and from the gate of his place. You are witnesses today!"* Ruth 4:9–10

By the time Boaz makes his announcement that Naomi's field and also Ruth the Moabite are *his*, quite a standing-room-only crowd[479] has gathered at the town gate. Word had gotten out that law was being made that day and everyone wanted to be a witness to it. They watch and whisper to one another in wonder at the rare proceedings: the second-in-line kinsman acquires the right-of-redemption from the nearest kinsman. See, he gave him his sandal as proof of the transfer, and Boaz is not even Machlon's brother![480] And a converted Moabite woman is *not* forbidden from entering the congregation of Israel![481] See, Boaz, a great and wise judge of our people, is taking Ruth the Moabite in levirate marriage!

Boaz pauses after his euphoric announcement, allowing anyone who has objection to the transfer of the redemption rights, the sale of the land, and his levirate marriage to Ruth to speak *now*.[482] The crowd is hushed; the seated elders have acquiesced to the proceedings, and not even a murmur is heard from the crowd. It is a solemn moment; Boaz is smiling and the people are optimistic. The barley harvest has ended, their storehouses are filling up, and the wheat harvest is upon them. What better way to begin the new era than with a marriage? The Israelites of Beit Lechem have just witnessed history-in-the-making.

BOAZ MARRIES RUTH, THE LEVIRATE WIDOW

Someone — perhaps it was Naomi — has dispatched messengers to Naomi's house to fetch Ruth,[483] and Boaz turns to watch as she is escorted through the town square. The crowd parts respectfully, and Ruth is led before the seated *beit din* to stand beside Boaz. She is still wearing her Sabbath dress, and is clothed as befits a bride. The reader notes the literary symmetry of the text: while Ruth and Boaz's chaste promises to one another were uttered in whispers under cover of *night*, the official and sanctioned marriage of levir and levirate widow occurs *hayom* — in broad daylight[484] — open and above-board, for all to see,[485] to be recorded in communal memory for posterity.

Their union is doubly consecrated. First, it is real and binding in and of itself, for as we have just seen, it was sanctioned by the *beit din* in public session. And second, it is binding as an act of proxy. For by stepping up as Machlon's redeemer, Boaz acts *in his stead* as husband to Ruth. The prime intention of this levirate union is to produce offspring *for Machlon*. The over-arching purpose of *yibum* is continuity of the family line and preservation of the familial inheritance. And the broad definition of "inheritance" includes both land and offspring.

Though the reader is doubtless relieved at the outcome of the ceremony at the town gate, the tension is only partially resolved. Important questions persist. Will Ruth and Boaz's union be blessed? Will they próduce the offspring Ruth so passionately desires?

THE ELDERS BLESS BOAZ AND RUTH

All the people who are at the gate, as well as the elders, respond to Boaz and proclaim in unison, "We are witnesses!"[486] And the elders bless Boaz, saying:

> *"May the Lord make the woman who is entering your house be like Rachel and Leah, both of whom built up the house of Israel. [And may you] prosper in Ephrata and your name be known in Beit Lechem.*
>
> *"And may your house be like the house of Peretz, whom Tamar bore to Judah; from the seed that the Lord will give you from this maiden."* Ruth 4:11–12

We are witnessing an extraordinary turnabout. When we first met Ruth she was an impoverished, childless widow of an Israelite from the tribe of Judah. Worse, she was a Moabitess, and perhaps forbidden to enter the congregation of Israel. Certainly she was a suspect stranger, born and raised in a nation of longtime enemies of her husband's people. She was headed for anonymity.

This chapter has followed Ruth's spiritual and physical journey from Moabite princess and wife of Machlon to devoted companion to Naomi, to Israelite-by-choice, to this rarified and thrilling moment at the gates of Beit Lechem. The elders of this Judaite town, vested with the legal power of their people, are about to endorse Boaz's redemption and pronounce a blessing upon him and upon Ruth. They are publicly ratifying Boaz's marriage to Ruth by acting as witnesses to his redemption of both the fields and the widow of Machlon, and by their expansive blessing. They are "cleansing" Ruth of her Moabite origins and declaring that henceforth she will be known as "Ruth of Beit Lechem," and not by the epithet "Ruth the Moabitess."[487]

Ruth is being welcomed into the Israelite fold with open arms. So much so that the elders bless her with the special blessing of fertility that built the house of Jacob. They invoke the names of Rachel and Leah, the women who, respectively, held Jacob's heart and bore and raised the children who would go on to be the foundational families of the people of Israel.

By specifically referencing Rachel and Leah the text is subtly and powerfully sending its approval to Boaz's marriage to Ruth. The reader is expected to recall that these two matriarchs embodied two of Ruth's signal behaviors. Rachel — like Ruth — was born and raised in an idolatrous home but volitionally turned her back on her roots and embraced the One God. And Leah — also presaging Ruth's behavior — "went out" to greet Jacob, inviting and welcoming him into her bed. All three women acted with the noblest of intentions, with an eye to conceiving and mothering sons and daughters of Israel.

Rachel was also known for her extraordinary beauty, the woman who captured Jacob's heart with his first glimpse of her. And Leah is remembered for her modest, self-effacing nature. We can see why the elders have chosen Rachel and Leah as Ruth's matriarchal avatars; Ruth is the embodiment of these Israelite ancestors.

The precious blessing of family and continuity is pronounced by the elders, in direct reward for Ruth and Boaz's bold actions: Ruth put her reputation in jeopardy in order to acquire a levirate redeemer, and Boaz stood up and claimed Ruth in full view of the assemblage when the closest kin renounced his claim. Boaz and Ruth are co-heroes of this story, and the text sees to it that they are repaid measure-for-measure. They are granted the marriage they both seek, and they are here vested with the blessing of the Bible's golden fleece — the blessing of fertility.

The reader is delighted to learn that the vehicle for this blessing is **the woman Ruth**. At last, we think; a happy ending.

The reader is watching as the threads of this book's seduction stories are literarily caught and tied together. The issue of "seed" or generational continuity is explicitly invoked in this blessing, and should be seen as a bookend to the story of Lot's daughters which opened this volume. The reader will recall that Lot's elder daughter's rallying cry and preoccupation was to perpetuate her father's "seed,"[488] and so she initiated the incestuous union with her father that resulted in the birth of her son, Moav. How fitting that the elders should now, several centuries later, implicitly ratify that audacious act by echoing her words as applied to Ruth, a descendant of none other than Lot's son, Moav!

Next, we see that the elders expressly connect Boaz and Ruth's union to Tamar's levirate union with Judah, which resulted in the birth of twin sons, Peretz and Zerach. The elders invoke Peretz and bless Boaz and Ruth saying, "May you raise a family of royalty like that of Peretz, and establish the monarchy through **this woman who took the initiative — as Lot's daughters and Tamar had done** — and who came into your house."[489] As we discussed in Part Three, Tamar's intimacy with Judah was another morally ambiguous coupling, and it was initiated, as here, to perpetuate Tamar's dead husband's family. The elders of Beit Lechem include Tamar and Judah's son, Peretz, in their blessing — Peretz was the elder son of that "levirate" union — because Peretz signified bold action; his very name means "to burst forth." Peretz personified the strength and perpetuity of Judah's family.[490] He also was the forebear of Israelite kingship.[491]

When we read the names here of Tamar, Judah and Peretz, we are reminded that in similar circumstances nearly two centuries before our story, Judah's familial continuity was assured because of **the instrumentality of the woman** Tamar, mother of Peretz.

The numerous parallels between the stories of Tamar and Ruth[492] highlight the Torah's intention of drawing connections not only between Judah and Boaz, but also between Tamar and Ruth, the stories' heroines:

Tamar remained childless through her first marriages, as did Ruth,[493] thus calling into play the levirate law for both women.

Tamar wrapped herself and dressed especially for her seduction of Judah by the side of the road; so, too, Ruth changed her clothes and dressed up specially for her seduction of Boaz on the threshing-floor. Both Tamar and Ruth took enormous personal risks in seducing Judah and Boaz, respectively. When Tamar gave birth to twins, there was a small intra-uterine drama over which son was to be first, with Peretz eventually emerging as firstborn. This drama is echoed in Ruth's story, where it appears certain at first that a closer kin will redeem Ruth. Only after a dramatic turnabout does the closer kin renounce, allowing Boaz to emerge as the redeemer. In both Tamar's and Ruth's stories the newborn sons are named by women. This fact highlights the importance of the agency of these biblical women in perpetuating and ensuring family continuity. And finally, the text sanctions both women's audacious behaviors first, with Judah's words immortalizing Tamar as "more righteous" than he; and here, with the eloquent and expansive blessing of the elders, sanctioning Ruth as an Israelite matriarch.

Ironically, Boaz—Judah's direct descendant—is, throughout this story, on the brink of dying without an heir. Boaz—who enters this marriage childless according to the *midrash*—and Ruth—whose childlessness is a driving force of this story—will both vanish without a trace unless the elders' blessing comes to pass! In the blessing of the elders the Bible text is here foretelling for the reader that the Judaic line *will* survive; but only because of acts of prescient courage, a woman's sexual audacity to effect this continuity, and—a new element that was introduced in this story—multiple acts of *chesed*.

RUTH GIVES BIRTH TO A SON

In one short verse the miseries and punishments of the main characters' lives are righted. In 4:13 Ruth marries, is intimate with her husband Boaz, and is blessed by God with pregnancy and the birth of a son. The verse economically contains all the steps necessary for a proper marriage: *And Boaz took Ruth* refers to his acquisition of the right to redeem her; *and she became his wife* refers to the public marriage ceremony or *chupah*; *and he came unto her* refers to the marital intimacy they shared that night.[494]

This same verse also contains only the second textual reference in the Book of Ruth narrating an act of God (the first was in 1:6 where we were told *The Lord remembered his people and gave them food*). Here the text tell us, in the same narrative structure and cadence, *the Lord gave her conception and she bore a son*. All other mentions of God's name in this story are *requests* for divine blessing. Just as the first reference to an act of God disclosed the end to a prolonged drought and famine, this second reference bespeaks an end to Ruth's barrenness and Boaz's loneliness.

It is morally fitting as well as literarily satisfying that Boaz, the man introduced in chapter 2 as *gibor chayil* — valiant and fearless, possessed of heroic character — should take in marriage the woman Ruth, who in chapter 3 is renowned by one and all as *eshet chayil*, his heroic and valorous counterpart. These two do-ers of *chesed* are well-matched, and are themselves the objects of God's *chesed*; their wedding-night intimacy yields a pregnancy for Ruth. The speed of her conception after more than a decade of barrenness is a measure of God's approval of her and of the union between her and Boaz.

A wonderful *midrashic* interpretation of the phrase *The Lord gave her conception and she bore a son* teaches that God stepped in at this precise point in our story because Ruth had already done *her* part and Boaz had done *his*; whether their union would yield issue was in God's hands.[495] Paraphrasing the words of the Gr"ah (the Gaon of Vilna),[496] women and men must do all they can — both physically and spiritually — while they are on this earth, to actualize their potential. We might compare our behaviors to a farmer sowing his field; we are likened to the farmer, diligently plowing and seeding. Ultimately, notwithstanding all our efforts, we must rely on the Almighty to provide rain and dew to nourish what we have sown. So, too, in our story of Ruth and Boaz. Both heroes acted out their parts to the extent of their abilities; it was ultimately up to God whether their efforts bore fruit.

It is consistent with Tamar and Judah's story referenced in the elders' blessing that Ruth and Boaz's single act of intimacy also results in the birth of a son. In both stories the Almighty sanctions the pairings with a long-awaited heir.

BOAZ'S DEATH

Ruth's dream of marriage and a child is granted, but tragedy strikes her once again. There are hints in the text that Boaz, already about eighty years old and at least double Ruth's age, dies on his wedding night after his one episode of marital intimacy with Ruth. In contrast to the earlier, unambiguous statements of the deaths of Elimelech, Machlon and Chilyon, the text does not expressly tell us that Boaz dies. The *midrash* infers this because Boaz simply disappears from the narrative.

How does the text signal Boaz's death? The *midrash* highlights several textual hints. We read in 4:9–10 that Boaz *twice* tells the elders and the assembled townspeople, *You are witnesses today . . . that I have acquired Ruth the Moabitess . . .* This doubling of language functions as a boldface indicator of Boaz's feeling of urgency. For whatever reason—and perhaps he feels his time is about to run out—Boaz pushes to consummate the land deal as well as his marriage *hayom*—**today**. The *midrash*[497] detects in these verses a tinge of immediacy; it is as if Boaz suspects, presciently, that he has only *one day left*.

A faint *midrashic* voice sees a textual hint of Boaz's death in upcoming verse 4:17, where Naomi's neighbor-women name Ruth's newborn son. According to the *midrash*,[498] the women friends of Naomi and Ruth act *in lieu of Boaz*, who had died nine months before; absent the father, they step in and name the boy Obed. The theory is that had Boaz been alive and present they would not have been the ones naming the boy. The difficulty with this reading is that it is not especially unusual for biblical women to name children; in Genesis Rachel and Leah named all their sons.[499] Still, of course, we have seen that Abraham named Yishmael, his firstborn son, and Jacob renamed his youngest son Benjamin, substituting his name for Rachel's name for the newborn.[500] This *midrashic* interpretation works only if we focus on the fact that the neighbor-women were not kin to the baby they were naming. This would indicate that for whatever reason the newborn's parents were unavailable; Boaz had died nine months before, and Ruth was possibly in the throes of a depression and was unable to name her son.

In fact, one *midrash* suggests just that, saying that after Boaz's death Naomi and Ruth sank into an depression.[501] This is understandable; Naomi succumbs because she is reliving with Boaz's sudden death the deaths of the other men in her life whom she had loved: her husband and two sons. And Ruth, as well, might be experiencing a frightening sense of déja vu about having suddenly lost her husband Machlon twelve months before. Also, Ruth is overcome with a sadness that her son will not know his father, the kindly and powerful man who had redeemed her.

We are told that with the baby's father dead and the mother and grandmother plunged, paradoxically, perhaps, into sadness at its birth, the neighbor-women took to calling the newborn "son to Naomi." They were referring to the essence of *yibum*, wherein the baby born to the redeemer and the levirate wife is a spiritual reincarnation of the dead husband. This baby was, in their eyes, and for practical purposes of inheritance, Naomi's son, Ruth's first husband, Machlon! Hence their name, "son to Naomi." It was likely a stop-gap name, not unlike the British royal family referring to a newborn as "child" until it has been formally named.

Others say that Obed is short for Ovadya, meaning "one who serves the Lord,"[502] and that the women called the boy by the name that his parents had already chosen for him. From a practical standpoint, in the course of blessing Naomi and Ruth, the women needed to call the boy by its name, so it is *they* — the neighbor-women of Beit Lechem — who are the ones to first articulate the baby's name in the text.[503] By whatever measure, this latter fact reinforces this story's sub-theme of feminine strength.

This community of women possess not a small degree of power and influence over social behavior within Beit Lechem. The reader will recall that they greeted Naomi upon her re-entry into the city one year ago, and expressed their shock at her reduced circumstances. They also had closely observed Ruth's behavior from the moment of her arrival amongst them. They watched as she comported herself lovingly as a daughter-in-law, and diligently and modestly as a gleaner behind Boaz's harvesters. The women continued to watch as Boaz daily treated Ruth in the manner befitting the widow of his kinsman.

The neighbor-women were satisfied that Ruth's union with Boaz was consistent with the requirements of the levirate law: the couple's intent was to produce an heir who would "give life" to Machlon.[504] This is another reason that this community of women[505] name the grandson of their friend Naomi. The name Obed comes from the Hebrew word *oved*, meaning "one who serves." They perhaps intended the name as a blessing and a hope for the boy's future, but the reader appreciates the dramatic irony: their naming is in the nature of a prediction. This son of Ruth and Boaz, the son born of acts of *chesed*, is blessed to grow up to be a servant of God,[506] the grandfather of king David, and progenitor of the Messiah.

With so much attention paid in these few verses of the text to names and naming — Boaz acquires Ruth as a wife in order to preserve **the name** of the deceased; the elders bless Ruth to be like Rachel and Leah, two named matriarchs; they bless Boaz saying that his **name** should be famous in Beit Lechem and that his house should be like the house of Peretz, born to Tamar and Judah; the neighbor-women **name** Ruth's son Obed — we cannot help but notice the implicit slap to the nearest kinsman. Immediately after Ploni Almoni, the nameless so-and-so, renounces his obligation to redeem Machlon's land as well as his widow, he disappears from the scene utterly. But almost to reinforce for the reader that preserving, remembering and honoring one's family name is essential, the text plunges us into this torrent of names old and new. In contrast to his nameless uncle, Boaz — the man and the name — is preserved as an *ish gibor chayil* notwithstanding *his* disappearance from the text after his wedding night with Ruth. He is gone, but his name and his actions are immortalized.

❇ ❇ ❇

We should at least consider the possibility that Boaz's sudden death after but one night with Ruth was a punishment. Could it be that this sensitive and generous, judicious and principled man committed a wrong that called for him to pay the ultimate penalty? One *midrash*[507] considers whether his marriage to Ruth—born a Moabite—was in truth permissible, or whether, after all, it contravened the Torah prohibition. We ask, was Boaz struck down as were Machlon and Chilyon, for marrying a Moabite? Could the nearer kinsman have been correct when he backed away from redeeming Ruth?

The same *midrash* that raises this question also offers its response: To the contrary; not only is Boaz's death not a punishment, but we should consider that his life-span had actually had been *extended* so that he would live long enough to fulfill his own as well as Ruth's destiny! We recall that Boaz was not a young man by any means when Ruth walked into Beit Lechem with Naomi; in fact, he was eighty years old, and was at the very end of his allotted time on earth. He had been married for half a lifetime, had sired and lost his sons and daughters, and had buried his wife. It was not at all a sure thing that he would remarry and sire additional offspring. We should recognize the hand of God at work initiating worthwhile and productive activity at the sunset of Boaz's life. Not only does Boaz feel an instant connection with and compassion for the impoverished stranger Ruth, but he also merits *additional time* in which to redeem her and sire a son with her. That done, one could say that Boaz's appointed time (that is, his allotted life-span *plus* his extra, "borrowed time") was finally and truly up; he had completed the additional tasks that had been set before him. This is why Boaz disappears from the biblical proscenium *at this time*.

The reader would no doubt have preferred if the romance between Ruth and Boaz had had a different ending. If only Boaz had lived to see and hold his young son, also living long enough to bring pleasure to Ruth for years to come. But the fact is that Boaz disappears from the text after he redeems and marries Ruth and fathers her child. We cannot rewrite the Bible text to suit our contemporary yearnings. We must be satisfied with Ruth's redemption and with her fertility. It certainly seems that Naomi and Ruth eventually grew content with their reality of a healthy newborn, renewed status, and the reverence of the community.

THE BLESSING OF THE NEIGHBOR-WOMEN

As we have seen, it is after Ruth buries her husband and carries her pregnancy to term that she gives birth to a son. This intermingling of death and new life, of sadness and ecstasy, is seasoned with an outpouring of communal support for both Naomi and Ruth. The neighbor-women bless the newborn and praise Ruth, whom they have taken to their collective bosom as one of them:

> *And the women said to Naomi, "Blessed is the Lord, who did not deprive you of a redeemer today; and may his name be famous in Israel.*
> *"And may he be for you a restorer of life, and to sustain your old age; for your daughter-in-law, who loves you, bore him. And she is better to you than seven sons."* Ruth 4:14–15

These same women who had comforted Ruth and Naomi after Boaz's death, now nine months later offer sincere blessings to the new family. Legends surround the baby's birth. Some say it was widely known that forty-year-old Ruth had been childless for so long because she actually had no womb; this would explain the fulsome blessings of the neighbor-women, who saw her quick conception and healthy birth as a no less than a miracle.[508] Some say that the text hints that Ruth carried the baby to term plus one day (*i.e.,* 271 days). This is derived from the *gematria* or arithmetic value of the letters of the word *herayon*—"conception"—in verse 13 (*and the Lord gave her* **conception**), which equals 271.[509] This numerical coincidence serves to confirm her conception *from Boaz*. It was God's will that she easily conceived on her wedding night.

The women's blessing is fascinating because it focuses, in large part, on what Ruth's baby will bring *to Naomi* in future years. They see the boy as Naomi's rejuvenator; as her bulwark, a sustainer in her old age. But even with Naomi as the explicit object of much of the blessing, the *midrash*[510] sees strong and generous praise *of Ruth* implicit in the women's words. Ruth's tenacious love for Naomi will be transmitted to the boy, who will in turn also love his grandmother. Ruth's nurturing care of Naomi, to the extent that she went out to glean as a pauper in order to feed her, will become this boy's emotional legacy, and likewise he, too, will bond indelibly with Naomi. And in the same way that Ruth followed in Naomi's footsteps — literally and figuratively — and became transformed from Moabite into Israelite, so, too, will the boy follow in God's ways all the days of his life.

Perhaps the women focus on the blessing this baby will bring *to Naomi* because they understand that members of the older generation, to some extent, are always concerned that they will be shunted aside and forgotten. Perhaps this is why the women bless the baby as a *restorer of life*. In the simplest meaning of the text a new baby does just that: its new soul and being introduce new hope, spark and yes, life, to the world, in particular to its immediate family. But beyond that, the women are quieting the aged Naomi's unexpressed and universal fears:[511] "Will anyone pay heed to an old woman? Who will care for me now that Ruth is preoccupied with a newborn son? Ruth doesn't need me anymore now that she has been given her heart's desire. What will become of me?" And her fears are not altogether unfounded; after all, she and Boaz are first cousins and of the same generation; with Boaz's death she quite naturally must come to anticipate and dread her own.

The *midrash* understands an old woman's fears, and explains that Naomi's insecurities are even deeper-seated. It points out that Naomi only takes the baby to her bosom only *after* the neighbor-women's blessing. This is because in her heart-of-hearts she was beset with doubts.[512] The *midrash* tells us Naomi's thoughts: "Was the union between Ruth and Boaz truly for the purpose of *yibum*? If it was not, then this baby is not mine; it is not the reincarnation of the soul of my son Machlon. How can I be sure?" We are told that Naomi became so beset with fears that she even suspected that Ruth's love for her would not be strong enough to survive motherhood and her new-found wealth and status as wife of Boaz. The *midrash* teaches us that Naomi's friends' elation and affirmation of the birth of her grandson was the objective validation she needed to help her overcome her hesitation to draw close to the baby. That the text eventually says *a son is born to Naomi!* (4:17) demonstrates to the reader that Naomi overcame her fear and depression and literally and spiritually embraced the baby as her own flesh and blood.

Another interpretation of the term *restorer of life* is the *midrashic* one.[513] It could be an unwitting prediction that this boy — grandfather of king David — is also forebear of the Messiah, in whose time resurrection of the dead is expected to take place.

On a purely practical level, the neighbor-women appreciate that Ruth's second chance at life will likewise vivify Naomi.

Their blessing for their lifelong friend Naomi is a reflection of what they would wish for themselves: that after living a life that has been heartbreaking and hard, she will end her days steeped in the happiness, love and promise this new baby will bring her.

The women go on to glorify Ruth and also to comfort Naomi's fears: . . . *For your daughter-in-law who loves you — who is **better to you than seven sons** — has borne him* (Ruth 4:15). The women are giving a pep-talk-cum-blessing to the aged Naomi. The are saying, in effect, "Come now, Naomi, old friend. Arise and seize this second chance that the Lord has given you! You have been blessed with a loving daughter-in-law who has borne you a grandson to sustain your son's line. This baby is the hope for your future! Bestir yourself to care for him. Take him to your bosom and make him your own. For he embodies Ruth's steadfast and loving qualities as well as Boaz's august lineage. You are privileged that God has allowed you to see the future! Ruth is better to you than seven sons. She and her son will never leave you!"

Why do the women reference "seven sons?" The reader will recall that the elders' blessing expressly mentioned Peretz, elder son of the union of Tamar and Judah. We understood this to connect the common matriarchal experiences of Tamar and Ruth. But if we actually count from Peretz to Boaz we count *seven* generations! They are: Peretz, Chetzron, Ram, Aminadav, Nachshon, Salmon, and Boaz.[514] It was Tamar's inspired audacity that seven generations back first gave new life to Judah's line. Now it is Ruth's similar behavior that has yielded a similar result seven "sons" later. Ruth's son, Obed — the "eighth son" — carries

Boaz's Judaic seed into posterity, bearing Judah's monarchic crown. Because Ruth has given Naomi a grandson, the neighbor-women's refrain is factually true: Ruth is better to Naomi than seven sons would have been; she has assured the future.

RUTH DISAPPEARS FROM THE TEXT

Verses 16 and 17 tell us *Naomi took the child and placed him in her bosom and became his nurse* and that *a son has been born to Naomi.* While this is welcome news given Naomi's intense sadness after Boaz's death, the reader is missing something. From verse 16 onward until the end of the story — the book's last seven verses — there is no mention of Ruth! She disappears utterly from the text. How do we explain this?

A minority voice suggests[515] that the absence of Ruth from these final verses could be a veiled reference to Ruth's death shortly after giving birth, necessitating Naomi stepping in to mother the boy.

But the better view, and one that I wholeheartedly subscribe to, hews closely to the *p'shat* or straightforward reading of the text. It is that Naomi, existentially alone, is welcomed into Ruth's life in the role of nanny and grandmother. The text has shown us that Ruth and Naomi have become an effective, functioning dyad over the course of the past dozen years. Their shared tragic experiences in Moav, their enforced dependency in the wilderness on the road to Judah and as a discrete unit within Beit Lechem, their shared spiritual closeness, and their common objective of Ruth's levirate marriage, all have forged a sturdy bond between them. Now, with the advent of a long-awaited baby, Naomi — an "old hand" at mothering and child-rearing — comes into her own. Naomi can now give back to Ruth, who had shouldered the burden of caring for the older woman. And a grateful Ruth welcomes a hopeful and energized Naomi into her new life.

The majority opinion is — and absent textual evidence to the contrary I agree with it — that Ruth lives to a ripe old age, and with her own eyes witnesses her great, great-grandson, Solomon, sit on the Israelite throne.[516]

Ruth is not mentioned in the story's last seven verses because literarily there is no further need for her presence. "Like Tamar, the mother of Peretz, Ruth disappears . . ."[517] She has done her job, in fact exceeded expectations. Not only did Ruth seduce Boaz and galvanize him to outwit the nearer kinsman and redeem her for himself; but also, in the process of caring for Naomi and gleaning daily throughout the harvest, Ruth won over the city's elders and the women of Beit Lechem, perhaps the harshest social critics of all. In their eyes Ruth became a full-fledged Beit Lechemite.

Ruth's absence from these last verses does not mean that she has disappeared from the scene. In fact, the story's last five-and-a-half verses are a male roll call, a genealogy, and one does not expect her to be mentioned there.[518]

> . . . And they called his name Obed; he is the father of Jesse, the father of David.
>
> And these are the generations of Peretz; Peretz begot Hetzron.
>
> And Hetzron begot Ram, and Ram begot Aminadav.
>
> And Aminadav begot Nachshon, and Nachshon begot Salmah.
>
> And Salmon begot Boaz, and Boaz begot Obed.
>
> And Obed begot Jesse, and Jesse begot David.
> Ruth 4: 17–22

It is only in the two verses describing Naomi's mothering role that Ruth's absence is obvious. But on reflection, the reader will realize that those two verses (16 and 17) fittingly round out the story, and Ruth's presence is not called for.

This story began, nearly eighty verses earlier, with Naomi's journey of exile, the death of her husband Elimelech, and on the heels of that, the deaths of her sons; all occurring in a hostile and strange land. Now the text ties up Naomi's story, symmetrically closing with her living among neighbors and kin—ironically, the same people she had abandoned years ago. And most importantly, the story ends with the birth of Naomi's grandson, whom the reader recognizes *is*—notwithstanding his given name of Obed—"Eli-**melech**"—the embodiment of kingship. After all, we are told in 4:22 that Obed is destined to be the grandfather of King David. Naomi's husband's monarchic fantasy lives, appropriately, in the person of Ruth's son, her grandson. Naomi's circle of life is closing.

In the absence of his father, Ruth's son is to be raised among a community of women. Naomi showers her grandson with love and care, and together with Ruth (and possibly the neighbor-women) she mothers him. We learn from these very verses[519] that a person who takes an orphan[520] into his house, loves him, teaches him, and raises him as her own, is considered as if she is its *natural* mother.[521] The heart does not distinguish between natural or surrogate mothering. Certainly the reader has witnessed this over the course of the book of Ruth, even as Naomi mothered the adult Ruth. And as for the son of Ruth and Boaz, we expect that nurture will join forces with nature to form this baby into the progenitor of kings.[522]

Ruth's potential is realized as we read the story's final verses. Her son Obed begets Jesse, who is the father of David. And as we know, David begets Solomon. In the book of Kings (I Kings 2:19) we are told that in Solomon's throne room he had a seat placed to his right for his mother Batsheva. The Torah calls this *kiseh l'em ha-melech*, the seat for the mother of the king. The Talmud[523] and *midrash*,[524] loath to part with Ruth, add another seat to Solomon's left: one for Ruth, his great, great grandmother! Says the *midrash*, Ruth was privileged to live to be a very old woman. She did not die until she had seen her great, great grandson sit on the Israelite throne, thus exceeding her modest dream of becoming a mother in Israel.

CONCLUSION:
RUTH IS A "MOTHER OF KINGS"

This story of Ruth, so filled with the essential and practical issues of the lives of its biblical women—surviving starvation, burying the dead, leaving one's home, immigration to a strange and hostile land, committing to a friendship, caring for an aging family member, taking desperate measures to survive, deciding how to dress, how to behave, whom to love, finding a spouse, begetting children—raises issues as enduring and pressing as any we face today. The book of Ruth does not stop there; it layers on complexity. It is unabashedly concerned with the application of law, kindness to strangers, and belief in God and in providence. And because it is part of the canonized Bible narrative, its nuanced text and rich subtext are important and universally appealing.

What has Ruth taught us? She has taught us to be patient but to take risks; to be loving even in the face of suspicion and hostility; to heed the voice of experience but to leaven it with tactical good sense; to be independent but to welcome the support of others.

Importantly, given the theme of this volume, Ruth has re-taught us a biblical lesson that we are revisiting for the *third* time: that even for a modest woman there is a time and place for sexual audacity when all other means are closed to her. We first saw this when Lot's daughters seduced their father in the mountain cave; again, when Tamar seduced Judah by the roadside at *Petach Enayim*; and most recently, when Ruth put on her best dress, seduced Boaz on the threshing-floor in Beit Lechem, and proposed marriage to him.

Finally, with Ruth's marriage and motherhood, she has taught us that a stranger and convert *can* be *em malchut*—the mother of kings. That what is within one's heart is often more important and enduring than the label one wears.[525]

❈ ❈ ❈

Ruth's story began with the word *Vayehi*—a prediction of doom and suffering—and ends with the name of *David*—the promise of Ruth's great grandson, first in an eternal line of kings.

Was that the purpose of this story—to legitimize David's Moabite roots?[526] Undoubtedly it is one important reason Samuel the prophet[527] wrote down Ruth's story. But her story also has another important literary purpose: In addition to correcting and echoing the stories of Lot's daughters and of Tamar's levirate marriage, Ruth's story also "reverses the Dinah story."[528] Recall from Part Two that Dinah's "going out to see the *daughters* of the land" ended in tragedy. But biblically, a century-and-a-half later, Dinah "finds" the female companionship she dreamed of in this story of Ruth's true friendship with Naomi. In still another literary reversal, Ruth's story, one of "gracious family be-havior,"[529] undoes the anger and familial dysfunction displayed by Jacob's handling of Dinah and her brothers.[530]

This theme of inter-generational cooperation and family continuity is central to Ruth's story. To bring this point home, the dramatic tensions between and among the story's characters are resolved or "mediated by *human* worth."[531] The initial suspicion and dislike between Naomi and Ruth; the shock and distance exhibited by the people of Beit Lechem toward the two women; the threat of starvation; the anomie of the convert; the limbo of levirate widowhood; the misery of childlessness; the loneliness of an aging matriarch—every one of these conditions is alleviated by human intervention and acts of kindness, or *chesed*.

In addition, a close reader will detect *God's* hand even as we cheer the *human* characters' behaviors. Was it, after all, merely a coincidence that Ruth wandered onto Boaz's field that fateful day? Was the meeting of exquisite stranger and kindly but lonesome landowner only a matter of chance? Was the measured success of Ruth's sexually daring gambit a foregone outcome? Was the first redeemer's retraction of his agreement to redeem predictable? And most of all, was it an everyday occurrence for a forty-year-old, barren widow to conceive a child from a single act of intimacy with an eighty-year-old man who was on the brink of death? The answer to these questions is "most probably not."

In fact, in case we miss it, the Bible text makes it clear in Ruth 4:13 that **the Lord** *gave [Ruth] conception, and she gave birth to a son.*

So we see that the story of Ruth is a perfect and satisfying interaction of benevolent human behavior and divine blessing. In fact, according to Trible, "the human struggle itself *is* divine activity."[532] This observation is momentous. It can mean that an all-knowing, all-seeing God has watched over Ruth perhaps from the moment she plighted her troth to Naomi and said, *"Wherever you go, I will go; and wherever you lodge, I will lodge. Your people shall be my people, and your God, my God. Where you die I will die, and there I will be buried.*"[533] Once Ruth took the leap of faith forsaking her homeland and her parents for Naomi and her God, she became covenantal and divinely protected in the same manner as other iconic biblical personalities.

It fits the biblical template and stands to reason that God should at long last bless this barren-but-righteous woman with a special son who will be the forebear of great kings and even, according to prophecy, the Messiah. After all, Sarah, Rebecca, and Rachel each suffered heartbreaking years of childlessness before bearing sons. The reader recognizes other hallmarks of biblical greatness in Ruth's biography, too: She was born and raised the child of idolaters; she was visited with misfortune and thereafter chose to flee into the wilderness, wandering there on her way across the Jordan river into Judah. For a time she suffered privation and loneliness, relieved only by the mentorship and affection of an older in-law. When faced with a seemingly-intractable problem she acted in a brave and inspired manner at great personal risk, and ultimately she succeeded!

The bones of Ruth's story are familiar because they are present, to varying degrees, in the stories of Abraham, Rebecca, and Moses.

We have seen that Ruth also has much in common with Tamar of Genesis. Both women were widowed from their first husbands, and both took audacious sexual risks to become proper wives and mothers in Israel. Their courage and daring actually retrieved the Judaic line from obscurity. In the words of the *Zohar*: "From these two women, then, the seed of Judah was built up and brought to completion . . . [B]oth of them acted piously, . . . for their aim [was] to do kindness . . . and truth with the dead; and God aided them in that work, and all was done fittingly."[534]

Ruth — like Tamar and the biblical matriarchs before her — had heroic underpinnings. Her instincts were pitch-perfect as she matched her behaviors to her desired end. In fact, on two pivotal occasions — on the road from Moav to Judah, and again on the threshing-floor in Beit Lechem — she took bold action that literally transformed her and galvanized those around her. For taking these risks and for forging her own destiny, Ruth is glorified and beloved by centuries of readers and Torah commentators. This erstwhile Moabite stranger is the role model for us all. She showed us that at its bleakest moment life can do an about-face. Human intentionality can walk in step with the divine will.

And an impoverished Moabite stranger can become *em malchut*, the mother of royalty.

NOTES

INTRODUCTION

1   Margaret Bruzelius, *Romancing the Novel: Adventure from Scott to Sebald* (Lewisburg, Pa.: Bucknell University Press, 2007), pp. 150–151.

ONE
Lot & his Daughters

1   This story can be found in Gen. 13:5–14.

2   *Ramban* on Gen. 13:7.

3   Gen. 3:24. Rabbi David Silber, in his lectures on the Book of Genesis at the Drisha Institute in New York City, introduced this insight.

4   For ease of reference, Abraham is referred to by his better-known name throughout, unless, as in the story-within-a-story described here, the Bible calls him Abram. The same applies to my use of the names Sarah and Sarai.

5   Chizkuni on Gen. 12:5. Even though the text only says that Lot is Abraham's nephew, the commentary says that Sarah and Lot were both the children of Abraham's deceased brother, Haran.

6   S. R. Hirsch on Gen. 13:12.

7 For my definition of the term *midrash* as it is used throughout this volume, please refer to page xxiv.

8 Rashi on Gen. 13:13.

9 *Ibn Ezra* on Gen. 13:13.

10 *Akeidat Yitzchak* on Gen. 13:13.

11 Gur Aryeh on Gen. 13:13.

12 Radak on Gen. 13:13.

13 Ba'al HaTurim on Gen. 13:13.

14 *Sanhedrin* 109a.

15 "Sodom" is used in chapter 19 of Genesis and in the *midrash* as an umbrella term for the evil cities of Sodom and Gomorrah and the cities of the plain.

16 *Sanhedrin* 109a.

17 *Sanhedrin* 109a and 109b.

18 One legend names the maiden in the Talmud's story Pelotit, saying she was Lot's daughter. See H.N. Bialik and Y.H. Ravnitzky, ed., *The Book of Legends/Sefer Ha-Aggadah: The Book of Jewish Folklore and Legend* (New York: Schocken Books, 1992), p. 37. Another *midrash* names the girl Paltith (*Sefer HaYashar*, 19:24).

19 Nehama Leibowitz, *Studies in Bereishit/Genesis* (Jerusalem: World Zionist Organization, 1972), p. 174, emphasis added.

20 Dr. Diane M. Sharon, Bible scholar, in a private conversation with the author.

21 Rabbi Joseph B. Soloveitchik, as told to the author by Rabbi Haskel Lookstein in a private conversation. Also, this is the same quality of hopeless "crying out" that God responds to in Ex. 2:23, when we are told the Children of Israel sighed because of their bondage in Egypt, and their "outcry" rose up to God, and God heard it.

22 *Ramban* on Gen. 13:13; also Mizrachi on Gen. 13:13.

23 *Breishit Rabbah* 50:3.

24 *Bava Metzia* 86b.

25 *Midrash Tanchuma* on *Vayera*.

26 *Yoma* 37a; see also *Sforno* on Gen. 19:1.

27 *Breishit Rabbah* 50:3.

28 Rashi on Gen. 19:1.

29 *Midrash Tanchuma* on *Vayera*.

30 Gen. 18:2.

31 Gur Aryeh on Gen. 19:1.

32 Gur Aryeh on Gen. 19:1; also Louis Ginzberg, *The Legends of the Jews* (Philadelphia: The Jewish Publication Society, 1968), vol. 1, p. 253.

33 Mizrachi on Gen. 19:1.

34 Levush HaOrah on Gen. 19:1. It is possible that Lot's usefulness to the Sodomites was that he could present the appearance, at least, of a viable justice system. They allowed Lot to function as a judge, while they continued to pervert justice as it suited them. There is no indication that Lot was aware of this subterfuge.

35 *Zohar* vol. I, 107a.

36 Leibowitz, *Studies in Bereishit/Genesis*, p. 176.

37 *Netziv* on Gen. 19:2.

38 *Netziv* on Gen. 19:2.

39 *Akeidat Yitzchak* on Gen. 19:1.

40 Mizrachi on Gen. 19:1.

41 Gen. 17:17, 24.

42 *Bava Metzia* 87a.

43 Rashi on Gen. 18:7.

44 Rashbam on Gen. 18:7.

45 *Breishit Rabbah* 50:2; also *Zohar* vol. I, 107a.

46 *Alschich* on 19:1.

47 *Ramban* on Gen. 19:3.

48 *Breishit Rabbah* 50:4.

49 Gur Aryeh on Gen. 19:2.

50 S. R. Hirsch on Gen. 19:2.

51 Levush HaOrah on Gen. 19:2.

52 *Netziv* on Gen. 19:3.

53 Commentary on the *Netziv* on Gen. 19:2.

54 Mizrachi on Gen. 19:2 and 3.

55 Rashi on Gen. 19:3.

56 Rashi and Siftei Chachamim on Gen. 19:3.

57 *Midrash Tanchuma* on *Vayera*.

58 *Breishit Rabbah* 50:4 and 51:5.

59 *Sforno* on Gen. 19:3.

60 *Breishit Rabbah* 50:5; also Radak on Gen. 19:5.

61 *Ibn Ezra* on Gen. 19:5.
62 Rashi, Rashbam, Gur Aryeh, Siftei Chachamim.
63 Tikva Frymer-Kensky, *Reading the Women of the Bible: A New Interpretation of their Stories* (New York: Schocken Books, 2002), p. 124.
64 Frymer-Kensky is discussing the horrific incident of the rape of the concubine in Giv'ah recounted in Judges 19, but she acknowledges that the template is virtually identical to the Lot story here (*Women of the Bible*, p. 125). Also see Radak on the similarities between the two stories.
65 Sechel Tov on Gen. 19:4.
66 S. R. Hirsch on Gen. 19:4.
67 *Netziv* on Gen. 19:4.
68 S.R. Hirsch on Gen. 19:4.
69 *Akeidat Yitzchak* on *Vayera* ch. 20.
70 *Netziv* on Gen. 19:5.
71 *Midrash Tanchuma* on *Vayera*.
72 Mishna *Terumot* 8:12.
73 *Ramban* on Gen. 12:11–12.
74 Leibowitz, *Studies in Bereishit/Genesis*, p. 175.
75 Gur Aryeh on Gen. 19:14.
76 Rashi and Siftei Chachamim on Gen. 19:14.
77 Nowhere are we told the youngest daughters' ages, but we can extrapolate that the two youngest daughters were perhaps around fourteen and fifteen years old. We know from the Bible text that twenty-five years have passed from the time of Abram's sojourn in Egypt with Sarai and Lot, to the day of Abraham's circumcision, which takes place just days before Sodom is destroyed (Gen. 12:4 and 17:17, respectively). We also learn from *midrashim* discussed earlier that Lot has lived in Sodom for fifteen years. Assuming that Lot was already married with at least three daughters at the time that he parted from his uncle Abraham and settled in Sodom, these two youngest daughters could have been born while Lot was living in Sodom. Their virginal and unmarried state would also support this calculation of their ages. See Eliezer Shulman, *The Sequence of Events in the Old Testament* (Brooklyn, N.Y.: Lambda Publishers, Inc., 1987), p. 36.

78 *Sanhedrin* 74a states that one must allow oneself to be killed rather than to transgress certain laws. Rabbi Adin Steinsaltz, in his *Iyunim* commentary on *Sanhedrin* 74a, interprets the words of the rabbis to include protection of a betrothed virgin.

79 See the mention earlier in this chapter of Abram's treatment of Sarai upon their descent into Egypt (Gen. 11–13), and the reference to *Ramban*'s commentary on Abram's behavior.

80 *Ramban* on Gen. 19:8.

81 See also *Sforno* on Gen. 19:8.

82 *Sforno* on Gen. 19:8.

83 Sechel Tov on Gen. 19:7.

84 Gur Aryeh on Gen. 19:8.

85 Jonathan Kirsch, in his book *The Harlot By The Side of the Road* (New York, Ballentine Books, 1997), pp. 26–27, cites Patai, Clements and de Vaux.

86 See Ex. 21:7–8, Kings 24:1–7, and Neh. 5:1–5.

87 See Leila Leah Bronner, *From Eve to Esther: Rabbinic Reconstructions of Biblical Women* (Louisville, Ky.: Westminster/ John Knox Press, 1994), p. 112.

88 The notable exception is the daughters of Zelophchad, who appealed to Moses for justice and were granted their father's landed share. Their story is told in Num. 27.

89 Kirsch, *The Harlot by The Side of the Road*, p. 39.

90 Sumerian Code of Hammurabi, 18th century BCE, sec. 130, emphasis added.

91 Rashi, *Breishit Rabbah* 50:9, Mizrachi, Gur Aryeh, Siftei Chachamim.

92 Avivah Gottlieb Zornberg, *Genesis: The Beginning of Desire* (Philadelphia: The Jewish Publication Society, 1995), pp. 51–52.

93 Ibid., p. 53.

94 Phyllis Trible, *Texts of Terror: Literary-Feminist Readings of Biblical Narratives* (Philadelphia: Fortress Press, 1984), p. 75.

95 Ibid.

96 *Sforno* on Gen. 19:8.

97 See also *Ramban* and Abarbanel on Gen. 19:8.

98 Tanchuma on *Vayera* 12.

[99] Bronner, *From Eve to Esther*, p. 115.

[100] Kirsch, *The Harlot by The Side of the Road*, p. 40.

[101] S. R. Hirsch on Gen. 19:11.

[102] Rashi and *Torah Shlema* on Gen. 19:29.

[103] Tanchuma on *Vayera* 21.

[104] Rashi and Siftei Chachamim on Gen. 19:14. It is unclear whether Lot's sons-in-law were part of the mob. It would appear from the *midrash* that they were not.

[105] *Netziv* on Gen. 19:14.

[106] *Breishit Rabbah* 50:9.

[107] Gur Aryeh on Gen. 19:15.

[108] *Yevamot* 77a.

[109] Sechel Tov on Gen. 19:15.

[110] *Yevamot* 77a.

[111] *Breishit Rabbah* 41:4 and 50:10.

[112] Psalms 89:21: *I have **found** David my servant; with My holy oil I have anointed him.*

[113] Bryna Jocheved Levy, *Waiting for Rain: Reflections at the Turning of the Year* (Philadelphia: The Jewish Publication Society, 2008), pp. 122–123.

[114] *Breishit Rabbah* 41:4.

[115] *Bava Batra* 91b.

[116] *Breishit Rabbah* 50:10.

[117] Sharon Pace Jeansonne, *The Women of Genesis: From Sarah to Potiphar's Wife* (Minneapolis: Fortress Press, 1990), p. 36.

[118] The word for "he delayed" — *vayitmahmah* — used here in reference to Lot in its single use in the Pentateuch — is embellished with the cantillation or trope sign known as the *shalshelet*. One other famed biblical hesitation occurs further on in Gen.39:8, when Joseph is fending off Potifar's wife's sexual advances. There, the Torah says "Joseph refused" — *vayema'en* — and we note that the trope sign annotating Joseph's refusal is, once again, the rare and beautiful *shalshelet*.

Chief Rabbi Lord Jonathan Sacks observes, "While there is no single *word* in Hebrew meaning "ambivalence," we do have a *tune* or trope that indicates hesitation; that is the *shalshelet!*" So from the Torah's use of the word *vayitmahmah* in Gen. 19:16

we understand that **Lot delays because he is ambivalent** about leaving the doomed city of Sodom, ceding his social position, abandoning his wealth. The *shalshelet* tells us this, via its melodic notation above this unique word. Rabbi Sacks made this observation to the author in a conversation at Yeshiva University in New York City on March 16, 2010.

[119] *Breishit Rabbah* 50:11.

[120] *Torah Shlema* on Gen. 19:16.

[121] *Sforno* on Gen. 19:16.

[122] *Alschich* on Gen. 19:19.

[123] *Alschich* on Gen. 19:19.

[124] Mizrachi on Gen. 19:17.

[125] *Torah Shlema* on Gen. 19:17.

[126] Rashi on Gen. 19:20; also *Shabbos* 10b.

[127] Sechel Tov on Gen. 19:21.

[128] *Torah Shlema* on Gen. 19:15, 17.

[129] Rashi on Gen. 19:24 explains that the Almighty is the source of rain that *destroys* (God brought inundating rains and the Great Flood to destroy the world; God "rained" the fire and brimstone that eradicated Sodom; and God will "rain" fiery hail upon the Egyptians), as well as of rain that *preserves* life (God "rained" *mannah* in the desert to save the Israelites from starvation, Ex. 16).

[130] Gen. 19:2.

[131] Kirsch, *The Harlot by The Side of the Road*, pp. 28–29, describes the flight to Zoar.

[132] *Pirkei d'Rabi Eliezer* on Gen. 19:26.

[133] *Ibn Ezra*, also *Ramban* on Gen. 19:17; the angels warned Lot and any of his family within earshot. It is possible Lot's wife did not hear the warning.

[134] *Pirkei d'Rabi Eliezer* on Gen. 19:17.

[135] Sechel Tov on Gen. 19:26.

[136] *Zohar*, 108b.

[137] *Netziv* on Gen. 19:26.

[138] *Ramban* explains that in Genesis 19:24 the text specifies fire and sulphur, while the version in Deut. 29:22 specifies sulphur and salt.

[139] *Pirkei d'Rabi Eliezer* on Gen. 19:17 names Lot's wife, though the Bible text does not. She is also called Edith in *Sefer HaYashar* 19:24.

[140] *Alschich* on Gen. 19:26.

[141] *Alschich* on Gen. 19:27.

[142] *Ibn Ezra* on Gen. 19:25.

[143] *Breishit Rabbah* 51:8; also Rashi on Gen. 19:31.

[144] *Ibn Ezra* on Gen. 19:31.

[145] Rashbam on Gen. 19:31.

[146] *Ramban* on Gen. 19:30.

[147] The daughters' names are mentioned in *Sefer HaYashar*. There are no fewer than eight books of *midrash* by that name, and it is unclear which one assigns names to Lot's daughters (though it is clear that it is not the book of the same name that is mentioned in 2 Sam. 1:18). It is possible that the 12th-century commentator, Rabbi Abraham Ibn Ezra, named the girls in his commentary on the Pentateuch entitled *Sefer HaYashar*. Ibn Ezra would have based the names on Iraqi legend that had assigned the same names to two girls in about the year 2,000 BCE in Ur, Iraq. This coincides with the time that Sarah, Abraham and Lot wandered and settled the area. See "World Genealogy," web address, http://wc.rootsweb.ancestry.com. Accessed 7/26/10.

[148] *Netziv* and Rashbam on Gen. 19:30.

[149] *Sforno* on Gen. 19:30.

[150] *Breishit Rabbah* 51:9.

[151] *Horayot* 10b.

[152] *Torah Shlema* and Sechel Tov on Gen. 19:30.

[153] *Alschich* on Gen. 19:30.

[154] Sechel Tov on Gen. 19:30.

[155] Gur Aryeh on Gen. 19:36.

[156] Rashi on Gen. 19:33.

[157] Chizkuni on Gen. 19:8; Mizrachi on Gen. 19:33; also Levush HaOrah, Gur Aryeh.

[158] *Breishit Rabbah* 51:9; also S. R. Hirsch on Gen. 19:31 *et seq.*

[159] *Nazir* 23b.

[160] *Horayot* 10b.

[161] *Alschich* on Gen. 19:35.

[162] S. R. Hirsch on Gen. 19:31.

[163] S. R. Hirsch on Gen. 19:31.

[164] *Sforno* on Gen. 19:31–38; also *Torah Shlema*.

[165] *Torah Shlema* on Gen. 19:31.

[166] *Berachot* 63a.

[167] Frymer-Kensky, *Women of the Bible*, p. 261.

[168] *Nazir* 23a.

[169] *Alschich* on Gen. 19:34.

[170] *Nazir* 23a.

[171] *Nazir* 23a and 23b; Sifrei; *Breishit Rabbah* 51:8; S. R. Hirsch; Siftei Chachamim (also quoting the Maharsha"l and the Mahara"m).

[172] *Torah Shlema* on Gen. 19:36.

[173] Rashi on Gen. 19:36; also Radak.

[174] *Breishit Rabbah* 51:9; also see Rashi, Gur Aryeh, Chizkuni, Siftei Chachamim and Radak on Gen. 19:36.

[175] *Torah Shlema* on Gen. 19:36.

[176] *Netziv* on Gen. 19:34.

[177] Frymer-Kensky, *Women of the Bible*, p. 262, emphasis added.

[178] *Bava Kama* 38a and 38b.

[179] *Sforno* on Gen. 19:37–38.

[180] *Ramban* on Deut. 23:4 and 7.

[181] *Ramban* on Deut. 23:4.

[182] *Nazir* 24a.

[183] *Zohar* 110b.

[184] Recall the different biblical spelling of the Hebrew word for *when she rose up* (*ubekomah*, Gen.19:33) when referring to the **elder** daughter's incestuous act: it is spelled *with* the Hebrew letter *vav*; while when discussing the **younger** daughter's night with her father the same word *lacks* the *vav* (Gen. 19:35).

[185] Ginzberg, *The Legends of the Jews*, vol. 1, p. 257.

[186] *Nazir* 23b.

[187] In fact, Lot's name is mentioned only three times in the Scriptures after the conclusion of this episode. The first two are in the book of Deuteronomy (2:9 and 19), when Moses is cautioning Israel against waging war or provoking quarrels with Moav or Ammon, "the sons of Lot." The third mention is in Psalms 83:9, in a listing of those who are confederates with

God's enemies: "Thine enemies make a tumult . . . they have helped the children of Lot."

T W O
Dinah & Shechem

1. Rashi on Gen. 33:17.
2. *Torah Shlema* on Gen. 33:17.
3. *Breishit Rabbah* 77:3.
4. Rashi on Gen. 32:26.
5. Meshech Chachma on Gen. 33:18.
6. *Breishit Rabbah* 68:5.
7. *Shabbat* 33b.
8. *Sforno* at Gen. 33:18.
9. *Rosh Hashana* 26a.
10. *Shabbat* 33b and Midrash Lekach Tov on Gen. 33:18.
11. Rashi on Gen. 33:18.
12. *Breishit Rabbah* 79:6 suggests that Jacob and his sons and his flocks arrived at Shechem as the sun was setting on the sixth day of the week, in time to rest for the holy Sabbath.
13. *Torah Shlema* on Gen. 33:18.
14. *Torah Shlema* on Gen. 33:18.
15. *Netziv* on Gen. 33:19.
16. *Netziv*, citing Midrash Chemdat Yamim.
17. *Breishit Rabbah* 79:7; *Ramban* on Gen. 33:19; *Torah Shlema* on Gen. 33:19.
18. *Sanhedrin* 102a.
19. Gen. 37:13.
20. Abarbanel on Gen. 33.
21. Midrash Lekach Tov on Gen. 33:19.
22. *Mei HaShiluach* on Gen. 33:18.
23. *Netziv* on Gen. 33:18.
24. Radak on Gen. 33:19.
25. Rashbam on Gen. 33:18.
26. *Akeidat Yitzchak* on Gen. 33:18.
27. *Torah Shlema* on Gen. 33:19.

28 *Breishit Rabbah* 79:7.

29 *Breishit Rabbah* 79:7.

30 *Rosh Hashana* 26a.

31 Sapirstein's commentary on Rashi for Gen. 33:19.

32 Jacob's travail in Lavan's household is summarized in Gen. 30.

33 Gen. 30:21.

34 *Pirkei d'Rabi Eliezer*, ch. 36.

35 Adin Steinsaltz, *Biblical Images* (New York: Basic Books, 1984), p. 61.

36 *Brachot* 60a.

37 See Midrash Meshiv Nefesh on Ruth 4:11 for a discussion of the kabbalistic view of the birth of male and female children, Leah's judgement, and the birth of Dinah.

38 *Bava Batra* 123a.

39 Shulman, *The Sequence of Events in the Old Testament*, p. 28.

40 Leila Leah Bronner, *From Eve to Esther*, p. *xix*.

41 Ibid.

42 Abarbanel on Gen. 34.

43 Rashi on Gen. 34:1.

44 See Gen. 30:14–16 for the text of the episode of the *dudaim*. See, also, Shera Aranoff Tuchman and Sandra E. Rapoport, *The Passions of the Matriarchs* (Jersey City, N.J.: KTAV Publishing House, Inc., 2004), pp. 255–262, for an analysis of the incident.

45 *Ohr HaChayim* on Gen. 34:1.

46 *Akeidat Yitzchak* on Gen. 34:1 *et seq.*

47 Abarbanel on Gen. 34.

48 S. R. Hirsch on Gen. 34:1.

49 *Malbim* on Gen. 34:2.

50 Leon R. Kass, "Regarding Daughters and Sisters: The Rape of Dinah," *Commentary* (April, 1992), p. 31, emphasis added.

51 See Bronner, *From Eve to Esther*, p. 121; and Frymer-Kensky, *Women of the Bible*, pp. 187–188; see, also, Eliezer Shulman, *The Sequence of Events in the Old Testament*, p. 28.

52 Bronner, *From Eve to Esther*, p. 121.

53 Gen. 37:2.

54 Kass, "Regarding Daughters and Sisters," p. 31.

[55] Abarbanel on Gen. 34.

[56] In Gen. 12:14–15 Abraham and Sarah are barely through the gates of Egypt when they are accosted by Pharaoh's princes, their status evaluated, and the lovely Sarah is taken forcibly before the king.

[57] Abarbanel on Gen. 33.

[58] *Ohr HaChayim* on Gen. 34:1.

[59] Gen. 34:1.

[60] *Netziv* on Gen. 34:1.

[61] *Ramban* on Gen. 34:12.

[62] Rabbi David Silber, in his lectures at the Drisha Institute in New York City, described the "seeing-and-taking" propensity of certain peoples described in the Bible text (Sodomites, Egyptians, Canaanites) as a textual clue to their unbridled lawless and sinfully sexual natures. These lectures, beginning in the early 1980s, were attended by the author. See also *Ramban* on 34:7.

[63] Gen. 12:10–20 narrates this first wife/sister episode.

[64] Gen. 20 describes this second wife/sister episode.

[65] Gen. 20:9.

[66] Mizrachi, Gur Aryeh and Levush HaOrah on Gen. 26:8.

[67] Note King Achashverosh's directive to search the land far and wide for "virgin maidens of great beauty" in ch. 2 of *Megillat Esther*.

[68] Gen. 20:13.

[69] Gen. 20:16.

[70] Kass, "Regarding Daughters and Sisters," p. 31.

[71] Mizrachi on Gen. 34:2.

[72] Gur Aryeh on Gen. 34:2.

[73] Abarbanel on Gen. 33.

[74] Gen. 28:20–21.

[75] Zornberg, *Genesis*, p. 120.

[76] *Midrash Tanchuma* on Gen. 34:1; also Rashi on 35:1.

[77] *Breishit Rabbah* 76:9; see also Rashi and Radak on Gen. 32:23.

[78] Chatam Sofer on Gen. 34:1.

[79] Abarbanel on Gen. 34.

[80] Abarbanel on Gen. 34.

[81] *Mei HaShiluach* on Gen. 33:18.

82 Abarbanel on Gen. 34.
83 Yalkut Shimoni on Gen. 34:2.
84 Abarbanel on Gen. 34.
85 Abarbanel on Gen. 34.
86 Bronner, *From Eve to Esther*, p. 121, citing Avot d'Rabi Natan.
87 Abarbanel on Gen. 34.
88 *Breishit Rabbah* 80:5.
89 *Sforno* on Gen. 34:3.
90 *Ketubot* 48b.
91 Frymer-Kensky, *Women of the Bible*, p. 179.
92 Ibid.
93 Ibid., p. 186.
94 Wendy Amsellem, Bible scholar and Drisha Institute faculty member, in a private conversation with the author in New York City on March 25, 2010.
95 *Pirkei d'Rabi Eliezer* and Yalkut Shimoni on Gen. 34:2.
96 *Netziv* on Gen. 34:1.
97 *Torah Shlema* on Gen. 34:2.
98 S. R. Hirsch on Gen. 34:2.
99 Siftei Chachamim on Gen. 34:2.
100 *Ohr HaChayim* and Mizrachi on Gen. 34:2; Mizrachi quotes Rambam, the Maimonides, for the proposition of holding the entire Shechem community responsible.
101 *Torah Temima* and Sifrei on Bam. 15:24.
102 *Breishit Rabbah* 80:1.
103 *Torah Shlema* on Gen. 34:2.
104 *Breishit Rabbah* 80:5; see also Rashi on Gen. 34:2.
105 *Torah Shlema* on Gen. 34:2.
106 *Netziv* on Gen. 43:2.
107 Avot d'Rabi Natan, quoted in Bronner, *From Eve to Esther*, p. 121, fn. 43.
108 *Malbim* on Gen. 34:2.
109 *Kiddushin* 22b.
110 *Torah Shlema* on Gen. 34:2.
111 *Yoma* 77b.
112 Levush HaOrah on Gen. 34.
113 *Breishit Rabbah* 80:6; also Gur Aryeh on Gen. 34:2.

[114] Bronner, *From Eve to Esther*, p. 138, fn. 26, quoting D. N. Freedman.

[115] Ibid., p. 118.

[116] Abarbanel on Gen. 34.

[117] See Ex. 22:15–16 and Deut. 22:22–29.

[118] If the rape victim is not betrothed, the rapist must pay the girl's bride-price and marry her. If she does not wish to marry him (*i.e.*, if her father refuses to give her to him), the rapist must still pay over the bride-price for a virgin. Ex. 22:15–16.

[119] *Mei HaShiluach* on *Vayishlach*.

[120] S. R. Hirsch on Gen. 34:3.

[121] *Sforno* on Gen. 34:3.

[122] *Netziv* on Gen. 34:3.

[123] *Malbim* on Gen. 34:3.

[124] *Netziv* on Gen. 34:3.

[125] *Akeidat Yitzchak* on Gen. 34:3.

[126] *Ramban* on Gen. 34:3.

[127] Rashi on Gen. 34:3.

[128] Rashi on Gen. 34:3; see also, *Breishit Rabbah* 84:5, and Sechel Tov on Gen. 34:3.

[129] *Ohr HaChayim* on Gen. 34:3.

[130] Trible, *Texts of Terror*, pp. 67, 69.

[131] Yalkut Shimoni on Gen.34:7.

[132] Midrash Lekach Tov and Midrash Sechel Tov on Gen. 34.

[133] Midrash Lekach Tov and Midrash Sechel Tov on Gen. 34.

[134] Zornberg, *Genesis*, pp. 52–53.

[135] Ibid., p. 53.

[136] *Netziv* on Gen. 34:3.

[137] Deut. 22:22–29.

[138] Avivah Gottlieb Zornberg in lectures attended by the author in New York City in the late 1990s.

[139] *Ramban* on Gen. 34:12.

[140] Jeansonne, *The Women of Genesis*, p. 138, fn. 17.

[141] Sechel Tov on Gen. 34:3.

[142] Radak on Gen. 34:5.

[143] Bronner, *From Eve to Esther*, p. 113.

144 Alice Ogden Bellis, *Helpmates, Harlots, and Heroes: Women's Stories in the Hebrew Bible* (2d ed.; Louisville, Ky.: Westminster/John Knox Press, 2007) p. 76.

145 See Trible (*Texts of Terror*, p. 67), saying that the precise biblical phrase "to speak to the heart" indicates that there was an offended party — here, Dinah — needing to be placated.

146 Rabbi David Silber of The Drisha Institute In New York City, in a private conversation with the author on March 2, 2009.

147 *Breishit Rabbah* 80:11 and Commentary on *Torah Temima* on Gen. 34:2.

148 See essay by Dr. Nils Bejerot, coiner of the phrase "Stockholm Syndrome." Dr. Bejerot, Professor of Medicine at the Karolinska Institute, Stockholm, helped negotiate the release of the hostages and described the event in his essay entitled "The Six-Day War in Stockholm," *New Scientist* 61, no. 886 (1974): pp. 486–487.

149 *Breishit Rabbah* 80:11.

150 Deut. 22:28–29; see also Ex. 22:15–16.

151 *Breishit Rabbah* 80:11.

152 Frymer-Kensky, *Women of the Bible*, p. 189.

153 Ibid.

154 *Alschich* on Gen. 33:18.

155 Dr. Diane M. Sharon in conversation with the author in the fall of 2008.

156 Radak on Gen. 34:26.

157 *Pirkei d'Rabi Eliezer*, ch. 35, says that Jacob was 77 years old when he left his father's house; that he spent fourteen years running from his brother Esav, either wandering the land or in the study house of Shem and Ever; he then spent twenty years in Lavan's house. In other *midrashim* cited earlier we learned that he spent eighteen months in Sukkoth, and approximately five years in Shechem. This adds up to about 117 years of age.

158 Abarbanel on Gen. 34.

159 Abarbanel on Gen. 34.

160 *Breishit Rabbah* 80:6.

161 *Torah Shlema* and Sechel Tov on Gen. 34:5.

[162] *Torah Shlema* points out that the word for *he was silent* in the Bible text is *hecherish*. Normally this Hebrew word is spelled with the letter *yud*; but here, describing Jacob's silence, the *yud* is missing, turning the word "silent" into the Hebrew word meaning "deaf."

[163] *Torah Shlema* on Gen. 34:5.

[164] Abarbanel on Gen. 34.

[165] *Torah Shlema* on 34:6.

[166] Paul Ekman, *Telling Lies* (W. W. Norton & Company, New York, 2009), p. 41.

[167] Rashbam on Gen. 34:9; see also Sechel Tov on Gen. 34:9.

[168] Sechel Tov on Gen. 34:23.

[169] Abarbanel on Gen. 34.

[170] Lekach Tov on Gen. 34:10.

[171] *Torah Shlema* on Gen. 34:10, quoting the Yerushalmi.

[172] Chizkuni on Gen. 34:7.

[173] *Netziv* on Gen. 34:7.

[174] *Ramban* on Gen. 34:7.

[175] S. R. Hirsch on Gen. 34:7.

[176] S. R. Hirsch on Gen. 34:7.

[177] S. R. Hirsch on Gen. 34:7.

[178] Abarbanel on Gen. 34; also see Shulman, *The Sequence of Events in the Old Testament*, p 30.

[179] *Breishit Rabbah* 80:6 and Rashi on Gen. 34:7.

[180] *Ramban* on Gen. 34:7.

[181] Kass, "Regarding Daughters and Sisters," p. 32.

[182] *Ramban* on 34:7; see also Gur Aryeh on Gen. 34:7.

[183] Lekach Tov on Gen. 34:11.

[184] Sechel Tov on Gen. 34:11.

[185] Lekach Tov on Gen. 34:11.

[186] S. R. Hirsch on Gen. 34:8.

[187] S. R. Hirsch on Gen. 34:8–12.

[188] Naomi H. Rosenblatt and Joshua Horwitz, *Wrestling with Angels: What Genesis Teaches Us About Our Spiritual Identity, Sexuality, and Personal Relationships* (New York: Delta, 1996), p. 308.

[189] Ibid.

[190] Onkelos, Rashi, Mizrachi and *Ohr HaChayim* on Gen. 34:13.

[191] Radak on Gen. 34:13.

[192] Radak on Gen. 34:20.

[193] Readers will recall the earlier discussion that Jacob arrived "in peace" at the city of Shechem after having survived the potentially deadly meeting with his brother Esav and his army of four hundred soldiers. We note the bitter irony the perversion here of the root-word *sh-l-m*, meaning "peace." We saw that Jacob came to Shechem *shalem*, "in peace;" that instead of "peace" Jacob's only daughter endured rape at the hands of the prime Shechemite. And now Jacob and his sons are being promoted as *shlemim*, "men of peace" by the very Shechemite who committed this brutal act of violence. The author credits Benjamin I. Rapoport with this insight.

[194] "Circumcision," *Encyclopedia Judaica* (ed. Cecil Roth, et al.; Jerusalem: Keter Publishing House Ltd., 1966–1981), vol. 5, p. 567.

[195] Frymer-Kensky, *Women of the Bible*, p. 193.

[196] Chizkuni on Gen. 34:24.

[197] Chizkuni on Gen. 34:24.

[198] Abarbanel on Gen. 34, and *Breishit Rabbah* 80:8.

[199] Rosenblatt and Horwitz, *Wrestling with Angels*, p. 308.

[200] Abarbanel on Gen. 34; see also, *Netziv* on Gen. 34:2. The *Netziv* says that Dinah was held captive in Shechem's palace for those several days.

[201] Chizkuni and *Torah Shlema* on Gen. 34:25.

[202] Rav Sa'adia Gaon on Gen. 34:25.

[203] *Sforno* on Gen. 34:26.

[204] Abarbanel at Gen. 34.

[205] *Torah Shlema* on Gen. 34:25 describes in detail the calculation of their ages: Shimon, Jacob's second-born son, had been born in the second year after Lavan gave Jacob Leah to be his wife; and as Jacob had first labored for seven years before he wed her, Shimon was born in the ninth year of Jacob's twenty-year sojourn in Lavan's house. Levi, Shimon's brother by the same parents, was born one year later. So Shimon was about twelve and Levi about eleven years old when Jacob left Lavan's house. One *midrash* adds two years to their ages for the two years Jacob spent sacrificing at Beit El, bringing them to fourteen and

thirteen, respectively. Abarbanel at Gen. 34 adds that when Jacob and his family arrived in Shechem, Dinah was only seven years old, and he suggests that the family spent about five years there before the rape. So depending on the calculations, Shimon and Levi could have been nineteen and eighteen years old, respectively, when they exacted revenge on Shechem and Hamor.

[206] Abarbanel on Gen. 34.

[207] *Breishit Rabbah* 80:10 and Rashi on Gen. 34:25.

[208] *Mechilta Beshalach*; see also Rashi on Gen. 34:25, and *Netziv* on Gen. 34:17.

[209] Malcolm Gladwell, *Outliers* (New York: Little, Brown, 2008), pp. 161–170.

[210] S. R. Hirsch on Gen. 34:25.

[211] Gladwell, *Outliers*, p. 169.

[212] Abarbanel on Gen. 34.

[213] Rabbi Nathaniel Helfgot, of the Drisha Institute, New York City, in a lecture delivered on December 9, 2008 on *Parashat Vayishlach*, attended by the author.

[214] Abarbanel on Gen. 34.

[215] *Breishit Rabbah* 80:11.

[216] Radak and *Torah Shlema* on Gen. 34:26.

[217] Abarbanel on Gen. 34.

[218] S. R. Hirsch on Gen. 34:25.

[219] S. R. Hirsch on Gen. 34:25; see also *Ramban* on Gen. 34:13.

[220] *Ramban* on Gen. 34:13; citing the Rambam's Hilchot Melachim, IX, 14, for this proposition; see also Abarbanel on Gen. 34 and *Torah Shlema* on Gen. 34:26.

[221] Radak on Gen. 34:27–28.

[222] *Sanhedrin* 56b. See also Part One above for a discussion of the Noahide Laws and the city of Sodom's wholesale culpability for failure to administer justice.

[223] *Ramban* on Gen. 34:13; *Malbim* on Gen. 34:13 and 25–26.

[224] Abarbanel on Gen. 34.

[225] *Ohr HaChayim* on Gen. 34:21.

[226] *Netziv* on Gen. 34:25.

[227] As I write these words on April 14, 2009, the world is riveted by a hostage situation unfolding in the Indian Ocean. U.S. Navy SEALS just two days ago rescued the American captain of a cargo ship that had been hijacked six days before by Somali pirates. The captain had been held hostage, incommunicado and at gunpoint. Navy officials were conducting negotiations with one of the pirates **while at the same time** the SEALS kept a distant watch over the hostage's place of confinement. SEALS sharpshooters were able to shoot and kill three of the pirates from a distance, and in this way they freed the captain.

While the facts of this modern-day hijacking differ from those in the Dinah story, there are some essential parallels: an innocent person is kidnapped and held hostage; the kidnapper and the hostage's representatives engage in discussions; simultaneously the hostage's people plan a commando rescue; said rescue is executed amid bloodshed in "a hail of bullets."

A summary of the event is reported in *The Wall Street Journal* of April 13, 2009, p. 1.

Even after the daring modern-day rescue, one American Rear Admiral's words sound eerily like Jacob's articulated fears of retaliation. The Admiral said, "the rescue ending in the pirates' deaths could ramp up hostilities. . . [and] 'could escalate violence in this part of the world, no question about it.' " And likewise Dinah's brothers' argument is echoed in the *Wall Street Journal*'s editorial page (*Ibid.*, p. A14, emphasis added): The "rescue of cargo ship Captain Richard Phillips from Somali pirates is a tribute to his personal bravery and the skill and steel nerves of the U.S. Navy. . . The [U.S.] has **an obligation to punish and deter these lawless raiders so they'll never again** risk taking a U.S.-flagged ship or an American crew . . . The pirates **made themselves potential targets of deadly force** under the law of the sea the second they took Captain Phillips hostage."

[228] Rabbi Nathaniel Helfgot, faculty member at the Drisha Institute, in a lecture delivered on *Parashat Vayishlach* on December 9, 2008 in New York City, attended by the author.

229 See I Samuel 15.

230 Esther 9:16; see also *Akeidat Yitzchak* on *Vayishlach*.

231 *Sforno* on Gen. 34:27.

232 Radak on Gen. 34:29; also *Torah Shlema* on Gen. 34:29.

233 *Ibn Ezra* on Gen. 34:29.

234 Abarbanel on Gen. 34.

235 *Torah Shlema* on Gen. 34:27.

236 S. R. Hirsch on Gen. 49:5.

237 *Yoma* 52b.

238 Devora Steinmetz, *From Father to Son: Kinship, Conflict, and Continuity in Genesis* (Louisville, KY: Westminster/John Knox Press, 1991), p. 142.

239 S. R. Hirsch on Gen. 34:25.

240 *Sforno* on Gen. 34:31.

241 *Ohr HaChayim* on Gen. 34:30.

242 S. R. Hirsch on Gen. 34:25.

243 *Akeidat Yitzchak* on *Vayishlach*.

244 Robert Alter, *The Art of Biblical Narrative* (Basic Books, 1981), pp. 160–161, emphasis added.

245 Ibid., p. 161.

246 *Torah Shlema* on Gen. 34:31.

247 *Netziv* on Gen. 34:31.

248 *Breishit Rabbah* 80:12.

249 *Pirkei d'Rabi Eliezer*, ch. 38.

250 Gen. 35:5.

251 Gen. 46:15: *These are the sons of Leah, which she bore for Jacob in Padan-Aram, **including his daughter Dinah**; all the souls of his sons and his daughters were thirty and three.*

252 It is unclear from text and *midrash* whether Dinah's mother Leah was still alive by the time of Dinah's rape. For purposes of this chapter we have assumed that Leah is still alive. Mary Anna Bader, *Tracing the Evidence: Dinah in Post-Hebrew Bible Literature* (Studies in Biblical Literature 102; New York: Peter Lang, 2008), p. 178, n. 48.

253 Gen. 35:3.

254 This *midrash* can be found in the writings of *Pirkei d'Rabi Eliezer*, ch. 38.

255 Yalkut Shimoni on Gen. 34:31.

256 Though of course it is hard not to see Jacob's abandonment or exposure of Dinah's baby as an act of cruelty. Earlier in Genesis (21:15–16) Hagar leaves her teen-aged son under a thornbush, and her act is much-criticized in the *midrash*. Surely it is even worse to subject a helpless baby to this fate.

257 *Pirkei d'Rabi Eliezer*, chapter 38.

258 *Breishit Rabbah* 80:11.

259 See Gen. 46:10. Shimon's sons include "Shaul, the son of a Canaanitish woman." The *midrash* infers that this epithet refers to Dinah, who had been intimate with Shechem, a Canaanite. See Bader, *Tracing the Evidence*, p. 42.

260 *Bava Batra* 15b.

261 *Breishit Rabbah* 80:4 and 57:4.

262 *Shemot Rabbah* 21:7.

263 Gen. 46:15.

264 Gen. 46:20.

265 Gen. 48:12–20.

THREE
Judah & Tamar

1 The levirate law will be explained fully in coming pages.

2 *Sanhedrin* 102a. See also Tanhuma Yoshon, *Vayeshev* 13, as cited in *Torah Shlema* on Gen. 38:1. Also, I cannot help but note that "woe is me" and *vayehi* sound alike in diction and cadence.

3 *Breishit Rabbah* 85:2.

4 E. A. Speiser, *Genesis* (Anchor Bible 1; New York: Doubleday, 1986), p. 299.

5 Radak on Gen. 38:1.

6 Rashi on Gen. 38:1.

7 Gen. 37:26–27.

8 Jeansonne, *The Women of Genesis*, p. 99.

9 *Mei HaShiluach* on *Vayeshev*.

10 S. R. Hirsch on Gen. 38:1.

11 Rashi on 38:1 citing Tanhuma Yoshon 8.

[12] *Zohar* 185b.

[13] *Netziv* on Gen. 37:22.

[14] Meshech Chachma on Gen. 37:26.

[15] *Sforno* on Gen. 38:1.

[16] *Breishit Rabbah* 85:2.

[17] Gur Aryeh on Gen. 38:1.

[18] Chizkuni on Gen. 38:1.

[19] Umberto Cassuto, "The Story of Judah and Tamar," in *Biblical and Oriental Studies I* (Jerusalem: Magnes Press, 1973), p. 33. See also Eliezer Shulman, *The Sequence of Events in the Old Testament*, p. 28.

[20] Perush Yonatan on Gen. 38:1.

[21] Rashi on Gen. 38:1.

[22] *Breishit Rabbah* 85:2.

[23] Bible readers will recall that this precise issue preoccupied Abraham, Judah's great-grandfather, who sent his trusted servant to seek out a proper wife for his son, Isaac (Gen. 24).

[24] *Mei HaShiluach* on *Vayeshev*.

[25] *Netziv* on Gen. 38:2.

[26] *Pesachim* 50a, where Reish Lakish says that the description of Shuah as a Canaanite is a synonym for merchant. See also Rashi and Onkelos on Gen. 38:2.

[27] Abarbanel on Gen. 38.

[28] *Ramban* on Gen. 38:2.

[29] Radak on Gen. 38:2.

[30] *Netziv* on Gen. 38:2.

[31] Abarbanel on Gen. 38.

[32] *Ibn Ezra* on Gen. 38:2 says the Bible's term "Canaanite" here can mean *both* a merchant and a native of Canaan.

[33] *Ibn Ezra* on Gen. 38:2

[34] Except, as we will see, she births three sons and names two of them.

[35] Though in the same verse that tells of Bat-Shuah's passing we are told that Judah was comforted after the passage of time. So we know that Judah mourned for her.

[36] *Pesachim* 50a.

[37] Gen. 10:25.

[38] *Alschich* on Gen. 38:1.

[39] Mahara"m and Radak on Gen. 38:5.

[40] *Ramban* on Gen. 38:3.

[41] Tzror Hamor on Gen. 38:3.

[42] *Breishit Rabbah* 80:4.

[43] Abarbanel on Gen. 38.

[44] Tzror Hamor on Gen. 38:4.

[45] Rashi on 38:5.

[46] Frymer-Kensky, *Women of the Bible*, p. 266.

[47] Sechel Tov on Gen. 38:3.

[48] Cassuto, "The Story of Judah and Tamar," pp. 29–40.

[49] Gen. 37:2.

[50] Eliezer Shulman, *The Sequence of Events in the Old Testament*, p. 30; see also Cassuto, "The Story of Judah and Tamar," p. 33.

[51] Cassuto, "The Story of Judah and Tamar," p. 39.

[52] Frymer-Kensky agrees that "in the structure of Genesis" the Judah and Tamar story follows "right after the sale of Joseph" (*Women of the Bible*, p. 265).

[53] Cassuto, "The Story of Judah and Tamar," p. 39.

[54] Levirate marriage will be discussed in an upcoming section.

[55] Frymer-Kensky, *Women of the Bible*, p. 266.

[56] Cassuto, "The Story of Judah and Tamar," p. 39.

[57] *Alschich* on Gen. 38:13.

[58] Abarbanel on Gen. 38; see also *Zohar* 188b.

[59] Gen. 14:18–24.

[60] *Nedarim* 32b.

[61] Psalms 92:13.

[62] *Netziv* on Gen. 38:6.

[63] *Sotah* 10a.

[64] Rashi on *Sotah* 10a.

[65] Rashi on *Sotah* 10a.

[66] *Torah Shlema* citing *Midrash HaGadol* on Gen. 38:6.

[67] *Zohar* 188a.

[68] Lekach Tov on Gen. 38:6.

[69] *Akeidat Yitzchak* on *Vayeshev*.

[70] Frymer-Kensky, *Women of the Bible*, p. 266.

[71] *Netziv* on Gen. 38:5.

[72] Frymer-Kensky, *Women of the Bible*, p. 266.

[73] Many commentaries express difficulty with the timing of chapter 38 of Genesis. Instead of its present place in the Bible, the question is asked, Could the episode of Judah and Tamar (chapter 38) have taken place *before* the sale of Joseph (chapter 37)? They point to the fact that chapters 37 and 39 form a seamless whole if the story of Judah and Tamar is extracted.

Luckily, the early story of Joseph is circumscribed by two dates clearly set out in the Torah: We know that Joseph is seventeen years old when his brothers sell him to the Ishmaelites, and thirty-nine when his father and brothers come down to Egypt in the second year of the great famine (Gen. 37:2 and 41:46). Therefore, from the time that Joseph is sold until Jacob's family immigrates into Egypt, *twenty-two years pass*. Can the Judah and Tamar story fit into that time frame? Is the story of Judah and Tamar in its right place?

Umberto Cassuto, in his seminal 1929 article "The Story of Tamar and Judah," uses commonalities of language and theme in chapters 37 and 38 to show elegantly and conclusively that *the stories are in their correct order* in the Bible. Not only are the texts narrating the stories of Joseph and of Judah and Tamar interconnected, but chapter 38 is the precise *sequel* to chapter 37. (See my earlier discussion of the births of Judah's sons where I explain the chronology according to Cassuto's analysis.) Cassuto explains that *there is sufficient time* within the twenty-two years allotted in the Torah for Judah to marry; for his three sons to be born and to grow to manhood and to marry Tamar; for Tamar to carry out her plan; for her to bear twin sons for Judah; and for all of them to immigrate into Egypt along with Jacob during the famine. There is thus no need to assign very young ages to Judah's three sons when they are wed to Tamar (Er would be eight according to the *Netziv*!). Rather, according to Cassuto, Er is the traditional marriageable age of eighteen years old when Judah gives him Tamar as a bride, Onan is seventeen, and Shelah sixteen.

[74] *Torah Shlema* on Gen. 38:6.

[75] *Zohar* on *Bereishit* 58b.

[76] Lekach Tov on Gen. 38:7.

[77] Abarbanel on Gen. 38.

[78] *Yevamot* 34b; see also *Breishit Rabbah* 85:4 and Rashi on Gen. 38:7.

[79] *Torah Shlema* on Gen. 38:7.

[80] Gen. 1:28.

[81] *Akeidat Yitzchak* on *Vayeshev*.

[82] Lekach Tov on Gen. 38:7.

[83] Frymer-Kensky, *Women of the Bible*, p. 267.

[84] *Yevamot* 39b.

[85] Abarbanel on Gen. 38 and Lekach Tov on Gen. 38:8.

[86] Rambam's *Moreh Nevuchim* 8:3.

[87] Rashi and *Ibn Ezra* on Deut. 25:5–6.

[88] Abarbanel on Gen. 38.

[89] Abarbanel on Gen. 38.

[90] *Yevamot* 39b.

[91] In Part Six I will discuss the *chalitza*, a "shoe ceremony" whereby in biblical times the male relative next in line to redeem the widow of his childless kin formally declines to redeem her (and forfeits his shoe as a result). The *chalitza* ceremony frees the widow to marry whomever she wants; she is released from any levirate obligation.

[92] *Sforno* on Deut. 25:5.

[93] *Breishit Rabbah* 85:5.

[94] *Breishit Rabbah* 85:5.

[95] To modern readers the concept of *yibum*, or levirate marriage, may appear barbaric and anti-feminist. Actually, levirate marriage was an important way to protect the Israelite widow. In Tamar's case, lacking a father or brother and now without a husband or heir, she is an anomie, a figure belonging neither *to* her father's house nor *in* her father-in-law's house. She is absent true home or protection, as she lacks father, husband or sons. By marrying her immediately after her husband's death to her husband's brother, she is afforded the protection of her husband and his "house." *Ramban* on Gen. 38:8. Also, if she gives birth to a son she importantly preserves her dead husband's familial share for her offspring, incidentally also preserving it for herself during her lifetime.

As for the levirate requirement of intercourse out of duty and without desire, attraction or love, it was not as difficult as modern readers might think. The young widow has just lost a husband, the prospective *yavam* has lost his older brother, and the house is in deep mourning. Everyone involved expects the levirate union to take place, and neither party is in the mood for or contemplating a pleasant sexual interlude; the expectation is that the brother will perform the duty of begetting an heir to preserve his dead brother's share, and to "do right" by the widow. It is a communal and familial obligation performed when all parties are deeply depressed; it is not a prurient license.

96 Rashi on Gen. 38:18.

97 Abarbanel on Gen. 38.

98 Rashi on Gen. 38:8.

99 *Netziv* on Gen. 38:9.

100 Kass, *The Beginning of Wisdom: Reading Genesis* (2d ed.; Chicago: University of Chicago Press, 2006), p. 529, fn. 26, emphasis added.

101 *Niddah* 13a.

102 Rashi on Gen. 38:9.

103 *Niddah* 13a. All references to the Talmud in this volume are to the Babylonian Talmud unless otherwise stated.

104 *Breishit Rabbah* 85:4.

105 See, e.g., Rashbam on Gen. 38:8.

106 *Niddah* 13a.

107 Abarbanel on Gen. 38.

108 Abarbanel on Gen. 38.

109 Frymer-Kensky, *Women of the Bible*, p. 267.

110 Jeansonne, *The Women of Genesis*, pp. 140–141.

111 Ibid., p. 99.

112 Kass, *The Beginning of Wisdom*, p. 529.

113 Rashi on Gen. 38:11.

114 *Tosfot HaShalem* on Gen. 38:11.

115 Frymer-Kensky, *Women of the Bible*, p. 226.

116 Abarbanel on Gen. 38.

117 *Yevamot* 64b.

118 *Breishit Rabbah* 85:5; see also Rashi and *Netziv* on Gen. 38:11.

[119] Abarbanel on Gen. 38.

[120] Frymer-Kensky, *Women of the Bible*, p. 268.

[121] *Breishit Rabbah* 85:6.

[122] See *Netziv* on Gen. 38:12.

[123] *Sotah* 13b.

[124] *Sotah* 13b.

[125] Cassuto, "The Story of Judah and Tamar," p. 40.

[126] *Netziv* on Gen. 38:12.

[127] *Ramban* on Gen. 38:14.

[128] Rashi on Gen. 38:12.

[129] *Breishit Rabbah* 74:5 and 85:6. The first time a sheep-shearing occurred in the Bible was earlier in Genesis when Judah's father, Jacob, clandestinely took his wives, children, sheep and livestock and left Lavan's house. He chose the time that Lavan was at the sheep-shearing, at a distance of three-days' travel, to make his break (Gen. 31:19). The story of Judah and Tamar is the second mention; the third is when Naval, husband of Avigayil, and owner of three thousand sheep, shears his sheep at Carmel (I Sam. 25:2); and the fourth mention is when David's son, Absalom, invites all his brothers — all the princes — to his sheep-shearing festival in Ba'al Hazor (II Sam. 13:23,24) and secretly plans a murder.

[130] *Torah Shlema* on Gen. 38:12.

[131] *Torah Shlema* on Gen. 38:12.

[132] Abarbanel on Gen. 38.

[133] Abarbanel on Gen. 38; see also commentary on the *Netziv* for Gen. 38:14.

[134] *Yevamot* 64b.

[135] *Sotah* 10a.

[136] *Sotah* 10a.

[137] Radak on Gen. 38:14.

[138] See Sapirstein's commentary on Rashi for Gen. 38:14, fn. 4.

[139] Rashi on Gen. 38:14.

[140] *Sforno* on Gen. 38:14; see also Frymer-Kensky, *Women of the Bible*, p. 269.

[141] *Malbim* on Gen. 38:14.

[142] Meshech Chachma on Gen. 38:14.

[143] Abarbanel on Gen. 38.

144　*Malbim* on Gen. 38:12–14.

145　Frymer-Kensky, *Women of the Bible*, p. 269.

146　Lekach Tov on Gen. 38:14.

147　Onkelos on Gen. 38:14.

148　Sechel Tov on Gen. 38:14.

149　*Midrash HaGadol* on Gen. 38:13.

150　Sechel Tov on Gen. 38:12.

151　Rashi on Gen. 38:14.

152　Radak on Gen. 38:14.

153　*Sforno* on Gen. 38:14.

154　*Ibn Ezra* on Gen. 38:14.

155　Rashi on Gen. 38:14.

156　Abarbanel on Gen. 38.

157　Radak on Gen. 38:15.

158　*Torah Shlema* on Gen. 38:14.

159　Lekach Tov and *Ibn Ezra* on Gen. 38:14.

160　*Sotah* 10a.

161　Gen. 18:4.

162　*Sotah* 10b. See also Rashi on Gen. 38:14.

163　Bible readers will recall that Rebecca, en route to meeting her intended husband, Isaac, for the first time, quickly *veiled her face* when she saw him standing in the distance. Gen. 24:65.

164　*Ramban* on Gen. 38:14.

165　*Malbim* Gen. 38:15.

166　*Sotah* 10b. See also Rav Sa'adia Gaon on Gen. 38:14.

167　*Breishit Rabbah* 85:8.

168　*Ibn Ezra* on Gen. 38:15.

169　Abarbanel on Gen. 38.

170　Chizkuni on Gen. 38:14.

171　*Netziv* on Gen. 38:14.

172　Sechel Tov. on Gen. 38:14.

173　Sechel Tov on Gen. 38:15–16.

174　Readers will recall that earlier in Genesis the angel Michael had been sent by God to announce to the aged Sarah that she would give birth in a year's time. The angel's name means "who is like God!" and he is dispatched to intervene on God's behalf in seemingly impossible human situations.

175　Da'at Zekeinim on Gen. 38:16.

176 Hemdat Yamim on Gen. 38:16, quoting Rambam.
177 Athalya Brenner, *The Israelite Woman: Social Role and Literary Type in Biblical Narrative* (Sheffield: JSOT, 1985), p. 82.
178 Ibid.
179 Ibid.
180 Judah's words to Tamar in Gen. 38:16, *Hava-na avo elayich, Here, let me come unto you,* are blatantly crude. They are nearly identical to Jacob's words to Lavan in Gen. 29:21: *Hava et ishti . . . v'avo eleha, Deliver my wife . . . and I will consort with her* earlier in Genesis. This was pointed out by Wendy Amsellem of the Drisha Institute in a conversation with the author on June 17, 2010.

     Father and son, years apart, use remarkably similar language when they are intent on intimate relations. In Jacob's case, he had been in love with Rachel for seven years and had worked as an indentured servant for her hand; we certainly can understand his peremptory tone with the man who had tricked him out of his heart's desire. But here, Judah has only just glimpsed the "harlot" at the crossroads, yet he is intent on a sexual liaison and uses similarly vulgar and unambiguous phrases. We must conclude from his words that he is powerfully attracted to the veiled woman and will not be denied. This is borne out by Judah's behavior in future verses, where without demur he gives "the harlot" the surety she requests.

181 Abarbanel on Gen. 38.
182 *Sotah* 10a.
183 Mizrachi on Gen. 38:16.
184 Brenner, *The Israelite Woman*, p. 82.
185 Jeansonne, *The Women of Genesis*, p. 141, fn. 13.
186 *Midrash HaGadol* on Gen. 38:16.
187 *Torah Shlema* citing Da'at Zekenim on Gen. 38:18.
188 *Sforno* on Gen. 38:16.
189 Abarbanel on Gen. 38.
190 The *Malbim* (on Gen. 38:11) teaches that Shelah, Judah's remaining son, did not wish to marry Tamar, erroneously holding Tamar responsible for his brothers' premature deaths. In such a case — where the closest male relative refuses to be

the redeemer, or *yavam* — the next available male redeems the widow. In our story this meant that Judah was next in the levirate line to impregnate Tamar.

191 Abarbanel on Gen. 38; also Levush HaOrah on Gen. 38:16–18.

192 *Horayot* 10b.

193 *Sforno* on Gen. 38:26.

194 In fact, the Talmud (*Horayot* 10b) mentions Tamar's roadside act as the example of a purely-motivated seduction that will yield future glory as its due reward. It contrasts Tamar's behavior with that of Cozbi, the Midianite princess, who in future years illicitly and publicly cohabits with Zimri, a prince of the tribe of Shimon. Cozbi's behavior is deemed "harlotry" and both she and the Hebrew prince are killed (Num. 25:1–9).

195 *Sforno* on Gen. 38:18.

196 *Ibn Ezra* on Gen. 38:18.

197 *Torah Shlema* on Gen. 38:18.

198 *Torah Shlema* on Gen. 38:18.

199 *Malbim* on Gen. 38:20–23; see also *Bava Metzia* 27b (discussing that identifying marks on a lost object are evidence of ownership).

200 *Netziv* on Gen. 38:18; see also Radak on Gen. 38:18.

201 *Torah Shlema* on Gen. 38:18.

202 Mahara"m on Gen. 38:18.

203 *Breishit Rabbah* 85:9.

204 Michael J. Broyde, *Marriage, Sex, and Family in Judaism* (Lanham, Md.: Rowman & Littlefield, 2005), pp. 97–98.

205 *Sotah* 7b.

206 Rashi on Gen. 49:8.

207 *Torah Shlema* citing Da'at Zekenim on Gen. 38:18.

208 *Ibn Ezra* on Gen. 38:18.

209 Radak on Gen. 38:16.

210 Gur Aryeh on Gen. 38:18; see also *Alschich* on Gen. 38:16.

211 *Torah Shlema* citing Da'at Zekenim on Gen. 38:18; also *Alschich* on Gen. 38:16.

212 Earlier in this chapter I described how, according to the *midrash*, Tamar had immersed herself in the ritual bath after she shed her widow's clothing and before she wrapped herself

in veils and sat in wait at the crossroads. Thus, the requirement that a bride be ritually clean before consummation can take place was also met.

213 *Torah Shlema* on Gen. 38:16.

214 Radak on Gen. 38:16.

215 *Torah Shlema* on Gen. 38:16.

216 Levush HaOrah, on Gen. 38:16–18, explains that before the giving of the Mosaic law at Sinai, a levirate union with the deceased husband's *father* was an exception to the incest taboo and was, therefore, a permitted union.

217 *Zohar* 188b on *Vayeshev*.

218 Gen. 29:18–28.

219 Jeansonne, *The Women of Genesis*, p. 102; also Lekach Tov on Gen. 38:16.

220 Tanhuma Yoshon on *Vayeshev* 17, as cited in *Torah Shlema* for Gen. 38:18.

221 *Breishit Rabbah* 85:9.

222 *Netziv* on Gen. 38:18.

223 *Yevamot* 34b.

224 *Netziv* on Gen. 38:19.

225 *Torah Shlema* on Gen. 38:25.

226 *Sforno* on Gen. 38:18.

227 Radak on Gen. 38:19.

228 *Netziv* on Gen. 38:19.

229 *Netziv* on Gen. 38:19.

230 Radak on Gen. 20–21.

231 Bronner, *From Eve to Esther*, pp. 161–162.

232 Frymer-Kensky, *Women of the Bible*, pp. 271–2.

233 See Speiser, *Genesis*, pp. 299–230.

234 Frymer-Kensky, *Women of the Bible*, p. 272.

235 Ibid.

236 *Breishit Rabbah* 85:9.

237 Lekach Tov on Gen. 38:22.

238 *Torah Shlema* on Gen. 38:23.

239 *Torah Shlema* on Gen. 38:23.

240 Rambam on Gen. 38:23 as cited in *Torah Shlema*; also *Netziv* on Gen. 38:20.

241 *Yevamot* 17b and 24a.

[242] Abarbanel and S. R. Hirsch on Gen. 38.

[243] Radak on Gen. 38:24.

[244] Rashi on Gen.38:24 and 34:7.

[245] *Avodah Zarah* 36b.

[246] *Sforno* on Gen. 38:24.

[247] See Meshech Chachma on Gen. 38:24; also *Yevamot* 35a.

[248] Siftei Chachamim on Gen. 38:24.

[249] Rashi on Gen. 38:25.

[250] Abarbanel on Gen. 38 raises just these questions.

[251] Tanhuma Yoshon on *Vayeshev*.

[252] *Ramban* on Gen. 38:24.

[253] Chizkuni on Gen. 38:24.

[254] *Ramban* on Gen. 38:24; Abarbanel on Gen. 38.

[255] *Malbim* on Gen. 38:15.

[256] Chizkuni on Gen. 38:24.

[257] Abarbanel on Gen. 38.

[258] Deut. 22:24.

[259] Chizkuni on Gen. 38:24 and Abarbanel.

[260] Tanhuma Yoshon on *Vayeshev*.

[261] Rashi on Gen. 38:25.

[262] Rashbam on Gen. 38:25.

[263] *Sotah* 10b.

[264] *Breishit Rabbah* 85:11.

[265] *Torah Shlema* on Gen. 38:25.

[266] Radak on Gen. 38:25.

[267] *Sotah* 10b; see also *Ketubot* 67b, *Berachot* 43b, *Bava Metzia* 59a.

[268] *Sanhedrin* 107a.

[269] *Bava Metzia* 58b.

[270] Rashi on Gen. 38:25.

[271] Radak on Gen. 38:25.

[272] *Sforno* on Gen. 38:25.

[273] *Sotah* 10b.

[274] Rashi on *Sotah* 10b.

[275] *Pesachim* 118a.

[276] Steinsaltz on *Sotah* 10b. Also, the reader will recall that it was the angel Gabriel who was charged by the Almighty with the task of destroying the cities of Sodom and Gomorrah *by fire*.

277 As I noted above, Rashi explains that Tamar felt the children's movement within her and instinctively knew she was carrying twins. See also *Netziv* and *Sforno* on Gen. 38:27.

278 *Torah Shlema* on Gen. 38:25.

279 *Ramban* on Gen. 38:23.

280 *Breishit Rabbah* 85:11.

281 Gen. 37:32–33.

282 Radak on Gen. 38:25.

283 Rashi on Gen. 38:25.

284 *Midrash HaGadol* on Gen. 38:25 as cited in *Torah Shlema*.

285 *Torah Shlema* on Gen. 38:25.

286 *Sotah* 10b.

287 *Sforno* on Gen. 38: 25.

288 See Gen. 29:35.

289 Maharsha as cited in *Torah Shlema* for Gen. 38:26.

290 Daniel 1:5 and 3:18–26.

291 Meshech Chachma on *Vayeshev*.

292 Makot 23b.

293 Mizrachi on Gen. 38:26.

294 *Ibn Ezra* on Gen. 38:26.

295 *Ohr HaChayim* on Gen. 38:26 explains that the *zikah*, or moral bond of attachment or betrothal between Tamar and Shelah, dissolved because of Judah's delay and Tamar's eventual loss of hope that the union would be effected.

296 *Ramban* on Gen. 38:8 and 26; also Mizrachi on Gen. 38:8.

297 *Netziv* on Gen. 38:26.

298 See *Ohr HaChayim* on Gen. 38:26.

299 *Sforno* on Gen. 38:26.

300 Rashbam on Gen. 38:26.

301 Abarbanel on Gen. 38.

302 Perhaps Judah's eyes are opened once he realizes that he, too, engaged in sexual relations with Tamar *but he did not die!* All the time he had blamed Tamar for his two sons' deaths he had been wrong-headed. This realization blooms in Judah's mind and he admits, *She is more righteous than I!*

303 Chizkuni on Gen. 38:26.

304 Radak on Gen. 38:26.

305 *Ramban* on Gen. 38:26.

[306] Susan Niditch, "The Wronged Woman Righted: An Analysis of Genesis 38," *Harvard Theological Review* 72, nos. 1/2 (Jan./Apr. 1979), p. 149.

[307] *Ibn Ezra* and *Netziv* on Gen. 38:26.

[308] Rashi on Gen. 38:26.

[309] The Talmud (*Sotah* 10b) bases its interpretation on another usage of our phrase *v'lo yasaf* that appears in Deut. 5:19. There, the Torah describes the sound of the voice of God pronouncing the Ten Commandments. The text writes that *the great voice did not cease (lo yasaf)*.

[310] Rashi bases his interpretation on Num. 11:25. There the Torah says the spirit of the Lord descended upon Moses, and that Moses transferred some of God's spirit as well as some of his own prophesying ability onto the seventy Israelite elders, who *did not cease (lo yasafu)* from prophesying.

[311] Chizkuni and *Netziv* on Gen. 38:26.

[312] Tosefta *Sotah* 89.

[313] Sifrei for *Beha'alotcha* 88.

[314] Radak on Gen. 38:26.

[315] *Yevamot* 39b.

[316] *Ramban* on Gen. 38:26.

[317] Frymer-Kensky, *Women of the Bible*, p. 274.

[318] *Sotah* 10b.

[319] *Breishit Rabbah* 85:13.

[320] Rashi on Gen. 38:27.

[321] Radak on Gen. 38:27.

[322] Rabbi David Silber, in a lecture at the Drisha Institute in New York City attended by the author, November 22, 2009. According to Rabbi Silber, the other two incidents in Genesis that demonstrate the *promise* of filial coexistence are in Jacob's blessings to his twelve sons, and separately, in Jacob's blessing of Menashe and Ephraim.

[323] *Akeidat Yitzchak* on Gen. 38:29.

[324] Radak on Gen. 38:29.

[325] Rashbam on Gen. 38:30.

[326] Radak on Gen. 38:30.

[327] Chizkuni on Gen. 38:30.

[328] *Ramban* on Gen. 38:29.

329 *Ibn Ezra* on Gen. 38:29.

330 Rashi, Onkelos and *Ramban* on Gen. 38:29.

331 *Netziv* on Gen. 38:29.

332 Chizkuni on Gen. 38:29.

333 *Alschich* on Gen. 38:28.

334 *Malbim* on Gen. 38:27.

335 *Alschich* on Gen. 38:28.

336 See Tuchman and Rapoport, *The Passions of the Matriarchs.*

337 E. A. Speiser, *Genesis*, p. 300.

338 Frymer-Kensky, *Women of the Bible*, p. 269.

339 Frymer-Kensky discusses Tamar as matriarch in Ibid., pp. 276–277.

340 As I discussed early in this chapter, it is the *midrash* that explains Tamar's provenance and her orphaned status.

341 Frymer-Kensky, *Women of the Bible*, p. 276.

342 There are other women named Tamar in Scripture, one of whom I will be discussing at length in Part Five of this book. But the Tamar who seduced Judah and bore his twin sons does not appear again in the Hebrew Bible after chapter 38 of Genesis, except at the end of the Book of Ruth (Ruth 4:12), when the town elders invoke Tamar, Judah and Peretz in their blessing of Ruth and Boaz.

343 *Zohar* 188a.

344 E. A. Speiser, *Genesis*, p. 300; also Frymer-Kensky, *Women of the Bible*, p. 266.

345 *Sotah* 10b.

F O U R
David & Batsheva

1 Recall James M. Cain's *The Postman Always Rings Twice* (New York: Alfred A. Knopf, Inc., 1934), a story of desire for a married woman that leads inexorably to a plot to murder the husband. Cain, a journalist-turned-novelist, authored another wildly popular book on the same theme some years later: *Double Indemnity* (Avon Books, 1943). Both were made into popular films of the same era.

2   Alter, Robert, *The David Story: A Translation with Commentary of 1 and 2 Samuel* (New York: W. W. Norton & Company, 1999), p. 246.

3   David returns to lead his troops into the final successful battle against the Ammonites and the Arameans in 10:17 when news is brought to him of Yoav's struggles.

4   II Sam. 21:15.

5   Ralbag on II Sam. 21:15.

6   II Sam. 21:17.

7   *Vayehi* is the first word in II Sam. 21:11.

8   *Megilla* 10b.

9   Sefer Ha-Aggadah, p. 119, n. 8.

10 Radak on II Sam. 11:1.

11 Rashi and Ralbag on II Sam. 11:1.

12 I Sam. 18:16.

13 *Mossad HaRav Kook* on II Sam. 11:1.

14 *Malbim* on II Sam. 21:1.

15 *Mossad HaRav Kook* on II Sam. 11:1.

16 Radak on II Sam. 11:1.

17 I Sam. 8:19.

18 *Malbim* on II Sam. 11:1 says that not only should David have accompanied his troops into battle; he should have been *leading* them against the Ammonites. He was remiss in his duties as Israel's supreme military commander.

19 Meir Sternberg, *The Poetics of Biblical Narrative* (Indiana Studies in Biblical Literature; Bloomington, Ind.: Indiana University Press, 1987), p. 194.

20 Mossad HaRav Kook on II Sam. 11:1.

21 It should be noted that David's military campaign against Ammon and Moav might even be an illegal battle *ab initio*. As we discussed at the end of Part One of this volume after the birth of Moav and Ammon, Lot's sons with his two daughters, the Children of Israel are enjoined from initiating military hostilities against these two nations. *Ramban* on Deut. 23:4, 7.

22 *Mossad HaRav Kook* on II Sam. 11:2 notes the Bible's usage of the identifying letter *hay* prefixing the word *evening*. This indicates that it was on *that particular* day that David was walking on his roof.

23 *The Living Nach* (ed. by Yaakov Elman; New York: Moznaim Publishing Corporation, 1994), p. 317.

24 Alter, *The David Story*, p. 250.

25 *Malbim* on II Sam. 11:2.

26 *Mossad HaRav Kook* on II Sam. 11:2.

27 *The Living Nach*, p. 317.

28 *Malbim* on II Sam. 11:2.

29 Alter, *The David Story*, p. 250.

30 Frymer-Kensky, *Women of the Bible*, p. 144.

31 *Malbim* on II Sam. 11:2.

32 Abarbanel on II Sam. 11:2.

33 Abarbanel, Radak and Metzudat David on II Sam. 11:2.

34 Abarbanel on II Sam. 11:2.

35 *Sanhedrin* 107a.

36 Yad Ramah on II Sam. 11:2.

37 The Talmud (in *Sanhedrin* 107a) says that in his hubris, David had begged the Almighty to test him with a sexual impropriety, believing that he could rise above any test God would place before him. The story of the Satan, the bird, the slingshot and the canopy is told to warn human beings not to invite temptation. Even David was not strong enough to withstand a sexual lure. Says the Talmud, "One should never bring himself to the test, since David the king of Israel did so and fell."

38 Gen. 24:16.

39 Gen. 26:7–8.

40 Gen. 29:17.

41 Gen. 39:6.

42 As regards Esther, the text reverses the order and slightly alters the word-form, but the double description of her beauty echoes Rachel's and Joseph's. Esther is described as possessing a beautiful form **and** as being fair of face: *yefat to'ar v'tovat mar'eh. Megillat* Esther 2:7.

43 Gen. 12:11.

44 11 Sam. 13:1.

45 II Sam. 14:27.

46 *Megillat* Esther 1:11.

[47] It is fascinating that the seven fat cows in Pharaoh's famous dream follow our pattern exactly, though they are but female animals, not flesh-and-blood women. The Pharaoh's cows are alternately described in Genesis (41:2, 4, 18) as *yefot mar'eh*, handsome or beautiful animals, and *yefot to'ar*, of beautiful form. As we would expect, given our paradigm for beauty, even the doubly beautiful dream-cows meet a horrible fate: they are eaten alive, consumed by the scrawny, deformed and ugly cows.

[48] I Sam. 17:42.

[49] In I Sam. 16:13, the scene of David's clandestine anointing as king, the narrator describes David as Samuel first lays eyes upon him: he is ruddy-cheeked, bright-eyed and *tov ro'i*, meaning **handsome**.

[50] I Sam. 25:3.

[51] I Kings 1:3–4.

[52] Radak on II Sam. 11:3.

[53] Radak and *Alschich* on II Sam. 11:3.

[54] Regina M. Schwartz, "Adultery in the House of David: The Metanarrative of Biblical Scholarship and the Narratives of the Bible," in *Women in the Hebrew Bible* (ed. Alice Bach; New York: Routledge, 1999), p. 344.

[55] *Malbim* on II Sam. 11:3.

[56] *Sanhedrin* 107a.

[57] Alter, *The David Story*, p. 250.

[58] *Mossad HaRav Kook* on II Sam. 11:3.

[59] Radak on II Sam. 11:3 says that Uriah was possibly not an Israelite, but of Hittite origin.

[60] Da'at HaMikra to I Sam. 26:6.

[61] See Gen. 23:3–15; see also Radak on II Sam. 11:3.

[62] Shmuel Herzfeld, "David and Batsheva: Echoes of Saul and the Gift of Forgiveness, II Samuel 11–12," in *Tanakh Companion: The Book of Samuel* (ed. Nathaniel Helfgot; Teaneck, N.J.: Ben Yehuda Press, 2006).

[63] Ibid., p. 232.

[64] Ibid.

[65] Frymer-Kensky, *Women of the Bible*, p. 145.

[66] Ibid.

67 *Shabbat* 56a.

68 Rashi and Maharsha on *Shabbat* 56a.

69 David Instone-Brewer, *Divorce and Remarriage in the Bible: The Social and Literary Context* (Grand Rapids: Wm. B. Eerdmans, 2002), pp. 28–33.

70 Sternberg, *The Poetics of Biblical Narrative*, pp. 192, 194.

71 Describing and dissecting the story of Dinah's rape by Shechem is the subject of Part Two of this book.

72 It should be noted that in other contexts the same verb, *vayikach*, is used for taking a woman in marriage. *E.g.*, Abram and Nahor "take as wives" Sarai and Milcah (Gen. 11:29); Isaac "takes" Rebecca to be his wife (Gen. 24:67); and Judah "takes" Bat-Shuah as a wife (Gen. 38:2).

73 Though in Dinah's, case, as discussed in Part Two above, the Bible adds the word *vaya'aneha*, meaning *and he tortured her*, to the "seeing" and "taking" pattern, so the *midrash* takes flight describing the types of tortures Dinah suffered at Shechem's hand. But nowhere does the text hint at either Sarah or Dinah's mental states; readers rely on the *midrash* for this.

74 Avivah Gottlieb Zornberg in a public lecture in New York City attended by the author in the late 1990s.

75 Radak on Gen. 6:2.

76 Rashi on Gen. 6:2.

77 Zornberg, *Genesis*, pp. 51–53.

78 Ibid., p. 52.

79 See Rashi on Gen. 25:34, where the Torah narrates Esav's haste in satisfying his hunger with Jacob's lentil pottage. While the verbs differ from the ones in our story, the cadence is startlingly similar, as is the implication of arrogance and speed.

80 Da'at HaMikra on II Sam. 11:4.

81 Rashi, Ralbag, Radak, *Yalkut Me'am Lo'ez* on II Sam. 11:4.

82 *Niddah* 31b; see also Abarbanel on II Sam. 11:4.

83 It is also possible that the text belabors the fact of the woman's ritual purification and washing to stress that whatever David's other sins, he did not sleep with a menstruating woman. Radak on II Sam. 11:4. Because of the incongruity of the

phrase amidst David's action verbs, it is not impossible that the author inserted it as an afterthought for just the reason suggested by Radak.

[84] Lev. 15:18: "And if a man has carnal relations with a woman, they shall bathe in water and remain unclean until evening."

[85] Frymer-Kensky, *Women of the Bible*, p. 147.

[86] *Mossad HaRav Kook* on II Sam. 11:4.

[87] Lillian R. Klein, "Bathsheba Revealed," in *The Feminist Companion to Samuel and Kings* (ed. Athalya Brenner; Feminist Companion to the Bible; Second Series; Sheffield: Sheffield University Press, 2000), p. 49.

[88] Ibid., pp. 51–52.

[89] Abarbanel on II Sam. 12:1–2 says Batsheva was a *na'arah*, or young woman just past girlhood, when Uriah wed her.

[90] Abarbanel on II Sam. 12:1–2.

[91] *Malbim* on II Sam. 12:3.

[92] Abarbanel on II Sam. 12:1.

[93] Klein, "Bathsheba Revealed," p. 52.

[94] Abarbanel, Radak and *Malbim* on II Sam. 12:3.

[95] Klein, "Bathsheba Revealed," pp. 52–53.

[96] Ibid., p. 53.

[97] See Parts 1, 3 and 6 of this book; Lot's daughters, Tamar, and Ruth also were sufficiently desperate to do so, and with positive outcomes.

[98] *Shabbat* 56a.

[99] Rabbi David Silber and Dr. Diane M. Sharon, in public lectures and in conversations, respectively, with this author in New York City in 2009.

[100] Frymer-Kensky, *Women of the Bible*, pp. 144–145.

[101] Pinsky, Robert, *The Life of David* (New York: Schocken Books, 2005), p. 102.

[102] Ibid.

[103] Frymer-Kensky, *Women of the Bible*, pp. 148–149.

[104] Mahar"i on II Sam. 11:5.

[105] Mia Diamond, "A Roof with a View: Differing Perspectives on the Story of David and Batsheva" (B.A. thesis, Harvard University, 1992), pp. 27–28. Diamond's thesis was awarded the University's Thomas Temple Hoopes Prize, and as Mia

Diamond Padwa she went on to graduate from the Drisha Scholars Program. Ms. Diamond Padwa has graciously made her thesis available to me and I will endeavor to paraphrase or quote her faithfully.

Her provocative thesis is that an alternative reading of II Sam. 11–12 could creditably be supported by the text. She proposes that Batsheva initiated the seduction of the king (not vice versa), and that at the very least Batsheva was not only not passive when the king "took" her, but she could very well have controlled the sexual tryst, thereby making herself complicit in the illicit "taking." While Batsheva's non-passivity in this incident has been discussed by Lillian Klein in her essay, "Bathsheba Revealed," cited elsewhere in this chapter, Ms. Diamond's argument is based primarily on an interesting reading of verse 5, which I will explain and discuss here.

I am indebted to Ms. Wendy Amsellem of the Drisha Institute for pointing me to Ms. Diamond's work.

[106] Ibid., p. 33.

[107] Ibid.

[108] Ibid.

[109] Rabbi David Silber of the Drisha Institute has frequently commented, in his lectures on the Books of Samuel, that the author's pen was dipped in acid instead of ink. Lectures attended by the author during 2008–2009.

[110] Abarbanel, Radak on II Sam. 11:2.

[111] Diamond, "A Roof with a View," pp. 32–33.

[112] This technique of using two verbs to indicate one action is known as a *hendiadys*, meaning "one for two," and is used here for emphasis. Dr. Diane M. Sharon in conversation with the author, November, 2009.

[113] Dr. Diane M. Sharon explained the mechanics of the biblical grammar of this verse to this author in a private conversation in November, 2009.

[114] Klein, "Bathsheba Revealed," p. 53.

[115] Ibid., pp. 49 and 51.

[116] Ibid., p. 54, emphasis added.

[117] Carole R. Fontaine, "The Bearing of Wisdom on the Shape of 2 Samuel 11–12 and 1 Kings 3," in *The Feminist Companion to Samuel and Kings* (ed. Athalya Brenner; Feminist Companion to the Bible; First Series; Sheffield: Sheffield University Press, 1994), pp. 149–150.

[118] See Frymer-Kensky, *Women of the Bible*, p. 145.

[119] Rashi and Radak on II Samuel 11:6.

[120] *The Living Nach*, p. 318.

[121] Alter, *The David Story*, p. 251.

[122] Metzudat David on II Sam. 11:8.

[123] Alter, *The David Story*, p. 251.

[124] Ralbag and Metzudat Tzion on II Sam. 11:8.

[125] Mahar"i on II Sam. 11:8.

[126] Jan P. Fokkelman, *King David (II Sam. 9-20 and I Kings 1-2) (vol. 1 of Narrative Art and Poetry in the Books of Samuel*; Studia Semitica Neerlandica; Assen, the Netherlands: Van Gorcum, 1981), p. 56.

[127] *Mossad HaRav Kook* on II Sam. 11:13.

[128] Alter, *The David Story*, p. 252.

[129] *Mossad HaRav Kook* on II Sam. 11:9; Alter, *The David Story*, p. 253.

[130] *Malbim* on II Sam. 11:11.

[131] Alter, *The David Story*, p. 252.

[132] *Shabbat* 56a.

[133] Ri"f on II Sam. 12; *The Living Nach*, pp. 317–318.

[134] Although, according to the Ri"f on II Sam. 12, the matter of writing and securing a second writ of divorce on the morning after his home leave was not so simple, and it would have delayed Uriah's return to the battlefield unduly. According to the commentary Uriah stayed away from Batsheva so that he could remain free to promptly return to the front the moment his business at the palace was concluded.

[135] Malbim on II Sam. 11:27.

[136] Alter, *The David Story*, p. 253.

[137] Pinsky, *The Life of David*, p. 104.

[138] *Malbim* on II Sam. 11:12.

[139] *Mossad HaRav Kook* on II Sam. 11:13.

[140] Pinsky, *The Life of David*, p. 104.

141 Abarbanel on II Sam. 11:12–13.
142 Alter, *The David Story*, p. 253.
143 *Mossad HaRav Kook* on II Sam. 11:15.
144 Pinsky, *The Life of David*, p. 106.
145 *Malbim* on II Sam. 11:16.
146 *Mossad HaRav Kook* on II Sam. 11:17.
147 *Mossad HaRav Kook* on II Sam. 11:17.
148 *Shabbat* 56a; also *Malbim* on II Sam. 11:8.
149 *The Living Nach*, p. 318.
150 Ibid.
151 Meir Sternberg, *The Poetics of Biblical Narrative*, p. 191.
152 Ibid.
153 Ibid., p. 190.
154 Though modern-day Bible scholar Mieke Bal (*Lethal Love: Feminist Literary Readings of Biblical Love Stories* [Bloomington, Ind.: Indiana University Press, 1987], p. 31) says that Uriah did *not* know.
155 Alter, *The David Story*, pp. 252–253, citing Moshe Garsiel on the question of *when* Uriah discovered the king's betrayal.
156 *Mossad HaRav Kook* on II Sam. 11:13.
157 Bal, *Lethal Love*, p. 31.
158 Alter, *The David Story*, p. 254.
159 Sternberg, *The Poetics of Biblical Narrative*, p. 221.
160 Mahar"i on II Sam. 11:21.
161 *Mossad HaRav Kook* on II Sam. 11:24.
162 *Malbim* on II Sam. 11:16.
163 *Mossad HaRav Kook* on II Sam. 11:26.
164 *Mossad HaRav Kook* on II Sam. 11:26.
165 Abarbanel on II Sam. 11:26.
166 *Mossad HaRav Kook* on II Sam. 11:26.
167 Rashi on Hosea 2:18.
168 *Mossad HaRav Kook* on II Sam. 11:27.
169 I Sam. 25:39–40.
170 Abarbanel on II Sam. 11:27.
171 Alter, *The David Story*, p. 255.
172 I Sam. 18:7–8, 16.
173 I Sam. 25:3, 18, 24.
174 I Sam. 18:28.

[175] Herzfeld, "David and Batsheva," p. 233.

[176] I Sam. 20:17.

[177] *Malbim* on II Sam. 11:3.

[178] Abarbanel on II Sam. 11:27.

[179] *Mossad HaRav Kook* on II Sam. 12:1.

[180] Daniel Boyarin, *Carnal Israel: Reading Sex in Talmudic Literature* (Berkeley: University of California Press, 1993), p. 152.

[181] Abarbanel on II Sam. 12:1; Alter, *The David Story*, p. 257.

[182] Fokkelman, *King David*, p. 76.

[183] Ibid., p. 78, emphasis added.

[184] *Mossad HaRav Kook* on II Sam. 12:7.

[185] Alter, *The David Story*, p. 258.

[186] Frymer-Kensky, *Women of the Bible*, p. 155.

[187] I Sam. 17:39, 50.

[188] Jon D. Levenson and Baruch Halpern, "The Political Import of David's Marriages," *Journal of Biblical Literature* 99, no. 4 (1980), p. 514.

[189] *Yoma* 22b.

[190] Frymer-Kensky, *Women of the Bible*, p. 156.

[191] Ralbag on II Sam. 12:7 counts the four-fold payment differently, omitting David's daughter Tamar. According to Ralbag, David pays with the deaths of four of his sons: 1. the unnamed baby son; 2. Amnon; 3. Avshalom; and 4. Adoniyah. I also prefer Ralbag's count over the Talmud's for the reason that Tamar, while ruined, does not die.

[192] *Sanhedrin* 107a and b.

[193] See Num. 12:12, where Aaron pleads with Moses after Miriam is stricken with *tzora'at*, saying, "Pray, sir. . . do not commit her to a [living] death, so that she should be like a stillborn. . ." See also Shera Aranoff Tuchman and Sandra E. Rapoport, *Moses' Women* (Jersey City, N.J.: KTAV Publishing House, Inc., 2008), pp. 234–242, where the authors discussed the biblical punishment of *tzora'at*, "the living death."

[194] Iyun Yaakov on *Yoma* 22b.

[195] In David's Psalm 51 he admits his sin with Batsheva and expresses deep remorse for it, pleading with God for forgiveness. In verse 9 of the psalm he practically begs God to afflict

him with *tzora'at*, presumably so that afterwards he can be purged and purified, "whiter than snow." It is an interesting paradox that when a person is struck with *tzora'at* both the affliction and the purification, the guilt and the forgiveness, entail a snow-white allusion.

196 *Avodah Zarah* 5a; *Mossad HaRav Kook* on II Sam. 12:13; Frymer-Kensky, *Women of the Bible*, p. 156.

197 I Sam. 15:24.

198 Metzudat David on II Sam. 12:13.

199 Recall that the Talmud exonerates David via the legal device of a battlefield divorce and via the legal argument that Uriah had disobeyed the king's orders on three occasions, warranting a sentence of death.

200 S. R. Hirsch on Psalms 51 as quoted in Pinsky, *The Life of David*, pp. 112–113, emphasis added.

201 Abarbanel on II Sam. 12:13.

202 Pinsky, *The Life of David*, p. 114.

203 *Mossad HaRav Kook* on II Sam. 12:15.

204 *Mossad HaRav Kook* on II Sam. 12:15; *The Living Nach*, p. 323.

205 II Sam. 12:24.

206 I Kings 2:19.

207 Abarbanel and Ralbag on II Sam. 12:18.

208 *Makkot* 24a.

209 Radak and Mahar"i on II Sam. 12:14.

210 Metzudat David on II Sam. 12:14.

211 Radak on II Sam. 12:20.

212 Rambam, *Hilchot Evel* 1:2; Radak and Abarbanel on II Sam. 12:18.

213 Carole R. Fontaine, "The Bearing of Wisdom," p. 152.

214 See II Sam. 24:10–17.

215 Metzudat David on II Sam. 12:20.

216 Abarbanel on II Sam. 12:20; also Metzudat David.

217 Alter, *The David Story*, p. 262.

218 Ibid.

219 *Mossad HaRav Kook* on II Sam. 12:23.

220 Alter, *The David Story*, p. 262.

221 Abarbanel on II Sam. 12:24.

[222] Radak on II Sam. 12:20. Notwithstanding that mourning was perhaps not strictly required as the infant had lived only seven days, Batsheva is sick with misery at the loss of her baby. No doubt her mourning is compounded by the fact that this death came on the heels of Uriah's death.

[223] *Mossad HaRav Kook* on II Sam. 12:24.

[224] Radak on II Sam. 12:24.

[225] I Chron. 3:5, where Batsheva is referred to as Bat-Shuah.

[226] This is the teaching of Rav Yaakov Meidan, as told to the author by Rabbanit Chana Henkin in a lecture in New York City in November of 2008.

[227] *Mossad HaRav Kook* on II Sam. 12:24.

[228] Radak on II Sam. 12:24; see also Abarbanel on II Sam. 12:24.

[229] Alter, *The David Story*, p. 262.

[230] Abarbanel on II Sam. 12:24.

[231] Abarbanel on II Sam. 12:24.

[232] *Mossad HaRav Kook* on II Sam. 12:24.

[233] I Chron. 22:9.

[234] Abarbanel on II Sam. 12:24.

[235] Alter says "As a rule, it was the mother who exercised the privilege of naming the child." Alter, *The David Story*, p. 262.

[236] Radak and *Mossad HaRav Kook* on II Sam. 12:24.

[237] Rashi, Metzudat Tzion on II Sam. 12:25.

[238] Abarbanel on II Sam. 12:25.

[239] I Sam. 16:13.

[240] Alter, *The David Story*, p. 263.

[241] Radak on II Sam. 12:31.

[242] Schwartz, "Adultery in the House of David," p. 343, emphasis added.

[243] Ibid.

[244] Ibid., p. 344.

[245] I Chron. 22:9.

[246] *Malbim* on I Kings 1:16.

[247] Commentary of Dr. J. H. Hertz, *The Pentateuch and Haftorahs* (2d ed.; London: Soncino Press, 1994), p. 91, n. 11.

[248] *Malbim* on I Kings 1:11.

[249] Abarbanel on I Kings 1:12.

250 Rashi on I Kings 1:21. Rashi suggests that Batsheva and Solomon faced banishment, not necessarily outright murder.

251 Abarbanel on I Kings 1:21.

252 Zafrira Ben-Barak, "The Status and Right of the *Gebira*," in *The Feminist Companion to Samuel and Kings* (ed. Athalya Brenner; Feminist Companion to the Bible; First Series; Sheffield: Sheffield University Press, 1994), p. 171.

253 I Kings 2:19.

254 Abarbanel on I Kings 1:2:20.

255 Rashi on I Kings 2:22.

FIVE
Amnon & Tamar

1 Eliezer Shulman, *The Sequence of Events in the Old Testament*, pp. 116–119. David is 58 years old at the time of Amnon's rape of Tamar. David was between 30 and 33 years old when Amnon, his first son, was born; hence, Amnon is about 25 when he rapes Tamar. Tamar is born about three years after Amnon, and Avshalom is born about a year later. Hence, Tamar is about 22 and Avshalom 21 years old at the time of the rape.

2 Rabbi Aryeh Kaplan, *The Living Torah* (Brooklyn: Moznaim Publishing Corporation, 1981), p. 188, citing *Bamidbar Rabbah* 10 and *Esther Rabbah* 6:2.

3 II Sam. 3:3.

4 *Mishbatzot Zahav* on II Sam. 13:1.

5 II Sam. 14:25.

6 In Part Four we cited chapter and verse where David is identified as "beautiful" in the Bible text.

7 II Sam. 11:2.

8 *Mishbatzot Zahav* in introduction to II Sam. 13.

9 *Sanhedrin* 21a.

10 *Kiddushin* 22a.

11 Abarbanel on II Sam. 13:1.

12 *Mishbatzot Zahav* on II Sam. 13:1.

13 II Sam. 3:3.

14 Pinsky, *The Life of David*, p. 119.

15 These facts bring to mind the story of Dinah's rape discussed in Part Two of this book. Recall that Dinah, only daughter of Jacob and Leah, is abducted and raped by Shechem. Not only are Shimon and Levi—identified as Dinah's "brothers" in the Bible text—Dinah's *full* brothers from Leah, their mother, but these brothers defy their father and avenge her rape by killing her rapist. Some of the essential facts in the Dinah story are echoed here in the tale of Amnon and Tamar.

16 Rashi and Radak on II Sam. 13:2.

17 Metzudat David on II Sam. 13:2.

18 *Avot* 5:19.

19 Rabbi David Silber in a lecture at the Drisha Institute on June 30, 2008.

20 *Mishbatzot Zahav* on II Sam. 13:5.

21 Radak on II Sam. 13:2.

22 Tehillim 45: 14: "The glory of the princess is kept within;" and Abarbanel on II Sam. 13:2.

23 Frymer-Kensky, *Women of the Bible*, p. 158.

24 Radak on II Samuel 13:2.

25 *Mossad HaRav Kook* on II Sam. 13:3.

26 *Sanhedrin* 21a.

27 In the story of Judah and Tamar the Bible referred to Judah's "friend," Hirah the Adullamite, as "*his* friend." That word, *re'ehu*, was *not* spelled identically with the word for "evil." Gen. 38:12.

28 *Mossad HaRav Kook* on II Sam. 13:3.

29 Alter, *The David Story*, p. 265.

30 Gen. 41:19.

31 Radak on II Sam. 13:4.

32 *Malbim* on II Sam. 13:4.

33 Pinsky, *The Life of David*, p. 120.

34 *Mossad HaRav Kook* on II Sam. 13:5.

35 The Talmud, in *Avodah Zarah* 36b, discusses the biblical prohibition against seclusion with any of the specified forbidden persons (an *ervah*) in Lev. 18:6 ff. One of these forbidden persons (in Lev. 18:9) is "your father's daughter."

After Amnon rapes his half-sister, the law was changed to unambiguously forbid seclusion with an unmarried Jewish woman even if one were permitted to marry her. Moderate cloistering of unmarried women, even in advance of such a law, was intended to keep the girls out of harm's way. Clearly such efforts are not fool-proof, as this story reveals. See also *Sanhedrin* 21b.

36 *Mossad HaRav Kook* on II Sam. 13:6.

37 Pinsky, *The Life of David*, p. 119.

38 Alice Bach, *Women, Seduction, and Betrayal in Biblical Narrative* (Cambridge: Cambridge University Press, 1997), p. 185.

39 *Mossad HaRav Kook* on II Sam. 13:6.

40 The Bible uses the same verb *telabev* elsewhere to signify sexual arousal. Alter, *The David Story*, p. 267, citing Song of Songs imagery.

41 *Mishbatzot Zahav* on II Sam. 13:6.

42 *Mossad HaRav Kook* on II Sam. 13:6.

43 *Mossad HaRav Kook* on II Sam. 13:7.

44 Abarbanel on II Sam. 13:7; see also Trible, *Texts of Terror*, p. 42.

45 D.M. Gunn, *The Story of King David: Genre and Interpretation* (JSOT Supplement Series; Sheffield: University of Sheffield, 1978), p. 99.

46 *Mossad HaRav Kook* on II Sam. 13:10.

47 Metzudat David on II Sam. 13:10.

48 Ralbag on II Sam. 13:10.

49 Da'at HaMikra on II Sam. 13:12.

50 Gen. 39:7.

51 Abarbanel on II Sam. 13:11.

52 *Sanhedrin* 21a.

53 Gen. 34:2: *Now Shechem, prince of the country, . . . saw her, and took her and lay with her by force.*

54 *Inuy*, incorporating the root of the word *oneh*, meaning "to answer," could be a subtle hint both in the Dinah story and here that the malfeasor will be made *to answer* for his crime of force and torture.

55 *Mishbatzot Zahav* on II Sam. 13:12.

56 *Mishbatzot Zahav* on Sam. 13:12.

57 Metzudat Zion on II Sam. 13:13.

58 Abarbanel on II Sam. 13:13.

59 Trible, *Texts of Terror*, p. 46.

60 Ibid.

61 *Kiddushin* 68b.

62 Abarbanel on II Sam. 13: 13.

63 Trible, *Texts of Terror*, pp. 43–44.

64 Gen. 34:2.

65 *Mishbatzot Zahav* on II Sam. 13:14.

66 *Mossad HaRav Kook* on II Sam. 13:14.

67 Abarbanel on II Sam. 13:14.

68 *Mishbatzot Zahav* on II Sam. 13:14.

69 *Mishbatzot Zahav* on II Sam. 13:15.

70 Ralbag on II Sam. 13:15.

71 Ralbag on II Sam. 13:15.

72 *Malbim* on II Sam. 13:15.

73 *Sanhedrin* 21a and Rashi on II Sam. 13:15.

74 Gunn, *The Story of David*, p. 100.

75 Trible, *Texts of Terror*, pp. 46–47, emphasis added.

76 Alter, *The David Story*, p. 269.

77 *Mishbatzot Zahav* on II Sam. 13:15–16.

78 See Deut. 22:29, where the Torah enjoins the rapist from ever divorcing his victim in the event she consents to marry him.

79 Alter, *The David Story*, p. 269.

80 Trible, *Texts of Terror*, p. 47.

81 Rashi on II Sam. 13:16.

82 *Mossad HaRav Kook* on II Sam. 13:16.

83 Abarbanel on II Sam. 13:16.

84 *Mossad HaRav Kook* on II Sam. 13:16.

85 Fokkelman, *King David*, pp. 107–108.

86 Trible, *Texts of Terror*, p. 48.

87 Fokkelman, *King David*, p. 108.

88 Pinsky, *The Life of David*, p. 122.

89 Gunn, *The Story of David*, p. 32.

90 *Ramban* on Ex. 28:2.

91 *Ramban* on Ex. 28:2.

92 There is pictorial, archaeological evidence that an early, nameless god in Ancient Egypt with a ram's head and horns

wore a poncho-like garment with colorful stripes. The *kutonet passim* might well have been widely understood in the ancient Near-East to be a typical cloak for royals. Ottar Vendel, "The Spirits of Nature: Religion of the Egyptians," "Absolute Egyptology"web site, copyright 2001–2010, accessed 1/27/10.

93 Alter, *The David Story*, p. 270.

94 *Zohar* on Vayeshev, 182b.

95 *Mossad HaRav Kook* on II Sam. 13:18.

96 The *midrash* has depicted Amnon's bed chamber as a room-within-a-room; this effectively shielded any sounds made in his chamber from being heard outside his house. But *within* Amnon's house his servants were always within ear-shot.

97 See Part Two above.

98 *Ramban* on Ex. 28:2.

99 Gen. 37:31–32.

100 Adrien Janis Bledstein, "Tamar and the Coat of Many Colors," in *The Feminist Companion to Samuel and Kings* (ed. Athalya Brenner; Feminist Companion to the Bible; Second Series; Sheffield: Sheffield University Press, 2000), p. 65.

101 Gen. 37:33.

102 Gen. 42:13.

103 *Mishbatzot Zahav* on II Sam. 13:18.

104 Kli Yakar on II Sam. 13:18.

105 Bledstein, "Tamar and the Coat of Many Colors," pp. 65–83.

106 Ibid., p. 73.

107 Ibid.

108 Ibid., p. 78.

109 Fokkelman, *King David*, p. 110.

110 *Malbim* on II Sam. 13:18.

111 Fokkelman, *King David*, p. 110.

112 Gen. 18:20.

113 Ex. 2:23.

114 Rabbi Joseph B. Soloveitchik. See Part One, footnote 21.

115 Frymer-Kensky, *Women of the Bible*, pp. 165–166, citing Deut. 22:24.

116 Gen. 38:26.

117 *Mishbatzot Zahav* on II Sam. 13:17.

[118] *Sanhedrin* 21a; see also Abarbanel and Radak.

[119] Abarbanel on II Sam. 13:19.

[120] *Mishbatzot Zahav* on II Sam. 13:20.

[121] Ralbag on II Sam. 13:19.

[122] *Mishbatzot Zahav* on II Sam. 13:20.

[123] Fokkelman, *King David*, pp. 110–111.

[124] Trible, *Texts of Terror*, p. 51, emphasis added.

[125] Alter, *The David Story*, p. 270.

[126] Trible, *Texts of Terror*, p. 51.

[127] For a graphic literary rendering of this precise scenario the reader is referred to the novel *Prince of Tides* by Pat Conroy (Houghton Mifflin, 1986) dealing with a rape and family coverup and the lingering emotional and psychological damage that results.

[128] Frymer-Kensky, *Women of the Bible*, p. 167.

[129] Trible, *Texts of Terror*, p. 52.

[130] *Mossad HaRav Kook* on II Sam. 13:20.

[131] Avivah Gottlieb Zornberg, *The Murmuring Deep: Reflections on the Biblical Unconscious* (New York: Schocken Books, 2009), p. 3.

[132] *Mishbatzot Zahav* on II Sam. 13:20.

[133] *Mishbatzot Zahav* on II Sam. 13:20.

[134] Fokkelman, *King David*, p. 106.

[135] *Mishbatzot Zahav* on II Sam. 13:20.

[136] Trible, *Texts of Terror*, p. 52.

[137] Da'at HaMikra on II Sam. 13:20.

[138] Trible, *Texts of Terror*, p. 52, emphasis added.

[139] Ibid., emphasis added.

[140] Da'at HaMikra on II Sam. 13:21. The difference is that after Jacob learns of Dinah's rape, the reader is told in Gen. 34:5 that Jacob remains silent; whereas here the text tells us at II Sam. 13:21 "When king David heard of all these things he was very angry." Though David—like his progenitor, Jacob—does nothing about it.

[141] Abarbanel on II Sam. 13:21.

[142] *The Living Nach*, pp. 327–328.

[143] Ibid., p. 327.

[144] Trible, *Texts of Terror*, p. 53.

[145] *Mishbatzot Zahav* on II Sam. 13:21.

[146] Gunn, *The Story of David*, p. 99.

[147] Trible, *Texts of Terror*, pp. 55–56.

[148] Alter, *The David Story*, p. 271, emphasis added.

[149] Or perhaps David will "hear" about what Amnon has done and he will be sufficiently jolted by the news of the rape that he will correctly deduce, fatalistically, that thus far he has paid only *two*-fold for his sins with Batsheva and Uriah; that yet *two more* of his children are destined to pay the price for his sins before Nathan's prophecy will be fulfilled. In 12:6 David pronounced punishment on "the man" saying *he shall pay for the lamb four times over!* And in 12:11 the prophet outlined David's punishment saying, *I will make calamity rise against you from within your own family!* First, his infant son with Batsheva died; now Tamar has been ruined. One could ask, could David do anything to forestall these predicted tragedies, after all?

[150] *Mishbatzot Zahav* on II Sam. 13:21.

[151] *Mishbatzot Zahav* on II Sam. 13:21.

[152] Alter, *The David Story*, p. 271.

[153] *Mossad HaRav Kook* on II Sam. 13:21.

[154] Abarbanel on II Sam. 13:22; see also, Steinmetz, *Punishment & Freedom: The Rabbinic Construction of Criminal Law* (Philadelphia: University of Pennsylvania Press), pp. 43–44.

[155] Alter, *The David Story*, p. 271.

[156] Abarbanel on II Sam. 13:22.

[157] Rambam, Hilchot De'ot 5:6.

[158] *Mishbatzot Zahav* on II Sam. 13:22.

[159] Metzudat David and *Mishbatzot Zahav* on II Sam. 13:22.

[160] Abarbanel on II Sam. 13:23.

[161] Abarbanel on II Sam. 13:23.

[162] Alter, *The David Story*, p. 271.

[163] Rashi, Abarbanel, Metzudat David and Radak on II Sam. 13:23.

[164] The reader will recognize the sheep-shearing festival as the site for life-changing events in the Bible. See Part Three, Judah & Tamar, fn. 129, for a listing of the four biblical episodes involving sheep-shearings.

165 Abarbanel on II Sam. 13:23.

166 Abarbanel and *Alschich* on II Sam. 13:24.

167 *Mossad HaRav Kook* on II Sam. 13:23.

168 Ralbag on II Sam. 13:24.

169 Alter, *The David Story*, p. 272.

170 *Mossad HaRav Kook* on II Sam. 13:23.

171 Metzudat David on II Sam. 13:26.

172 Rashi on II Sam. 13:26.

173 *Alschich* on II Sam. 13:26.

174 *Mishbatzot Zahav* on II Sam. 13:28.

175 *Mossad HaRav Kook* on II Sam. 13:28.

176 *Mossad HaRav Kook* on II Sam. 13:28.

177 *Mossad HaRav Kook* on II Sam. 13:28.

178 Abarbanel on II Sam. 13:37.

179 Abarbanel and *Malbim* on II Sam. 13:28.

180 *Mossad HaRav Kook* on II Sam. 13:30.

181 Pinsky, *The Life of David*, p. 125.

182 Ibid., p. 125.

183 Rabbi David Silber in a lecture at the Drisha Institute, June 6, 2008, attended by the author.

184 *Mossad HaRav Kook* on II Sam. 13:33, noting that Yonadav unconsciously echoes Avshalom's words to Tamar when he comes upon her after the rape: "Do not take this thing to heart. . . "

185 Pinsky, *The Life of David*, p. 126.

186 *Mossad HaRav Kook* on II Sam. 13:32.

187 Rashi on II Sam. 13:32; see also Mahar"i and Radak.

188 Targum Yonatan on II Sam. 13:32.

189 *Mossad HaRav Kook* on II Sam. 13:35.

190 II Sam. 3:3; see also Radak on II Sam. 13:37.

191 Abarbanel on II Sam. 13:38.

192 *Mossad HaRav Kook* on II Sam. 13:34.

193 *Mossad HaRav Kook* on II Sam. 13:38.

194 Radak on II Sam. 13:38.

195 Abarbanel and *Malbim* on II Sam. 13:39.

196 This may remind the Bible reader of Rebecca's warning to Jacob in Gen. 27:45 when she counseled him to flee to the house of his uncle Lavan until his brother Esav's anger against

him cooled. Rebecca knew the consequences to the parent when two siblings fought each other to the death: "Let me not lose the both of you in one day!" she said. So it is with David. Amnon, his firstborn son, was killed by Avshalom to avenge Tamar's rape. Now Avshalom is a renegade, effectively lost to David, as well, which would explain why David pined for Avshalom.

[197] *Mossad HaRav Kook* on II Sam. 13:39.

[198] Abarbanel on II Sam. 13:39, citing "the wise man, my teacher, Abraham *Ibn Ezra*."

[199] Abarbanel on II Sam. 13:39, citing the Medieval commentary Ephod.

[200] In Part Two of this book we give Jacob's daughter Dinah a voice using Talmudic and *midrashic* interpretation of chapter 34 of Genesis.

[201] Gen. 12:1 and 4 and 22:2.

[202] Gen. 24:58.

[203] In Part One we described Abraham as a blur of action when the three angels visited his tent in Gen. 18:2–8. Though he had been recuperating from his painful self-circumcision, he eagerly got up and hastened to prepare a meal for his guests.

[204] In coming chapters of II Samuel we see the culmination of Nathan's prophecy of David's punishment. Already three of his sons (Chileab, not an actor in our stories and second-in-line after Amnon, also has died) have met premature death, and his daughter, Tamar, has been ruined. Avshalom, next in line for David's throne, will encounter both ruin and a horrible death in chapters 17 and 18. He undermines his father's monarchy, stages a treasonous coup, sleeps with his father's concubines upon the palace roof in view of all of Israel, and is ultimately tortured and slain for his sins. See *Sotah* 9b.

[205] Rabbi David Silber in a private conversation with the author in New York City on February 21, 2010.

[206] Pinsky, *The Life of David*, p. 123, emphasis added.

[207] Abarbanel on II Sam. 13: 37 ff.

[208] In II Sam. 14:27 we are told that Avshalom had four children: three sons and one daughter.

209 Bledstein, "Tamar and the Coat of Many Colors," p. 82.

210 See Tuchman and Rapoport, *The Passions of the Matriarchs*, p. 70. In Gen. 22:23, in the midst of a list of Nahor's begats, the only named grandchild is the girl Rebecca. Rashi explains that this singular listing exists in order to introduce and spotlight the girl Rebecca's future importance in the narrative.

211 *Malbim* on II Sam. 14:27. See also *Sotah* 11a, which tells us that two of Avshalom's sons were fated to die at young ages.

212 Trible, *Texts of Terror*, p. 55, emphasis added.

SIX
Ruth &; Boaz

1 Another reading of this phrase is: *Then in the morning, if he will act as a redeemer, good, he will redeem. . .*

2 *Megilla* 10b.

3 Rashi on Ruth 1:1.

4 Judges 17:6 and 21:25.

5 *Ruth Rabbah* 1:1.

6 *Bava Batra* 91a.

7 *Bava Batra* 15b.

8 *Ruth Rabbah* 1:4 and *Ibn Ezra* on Ruth 1:1.

9 Kitzur Alschich on Ruth 1:1.

10 Kitzur Alschich on Ruth 1:1.

11 *The Living Nach* p. 531. The name Elimelech could also mean "a king to me." Ruth Rabbah 2:5. For still another reading, it could mean "my God is king."

12 Likutei Anshei Shem on Ruth 1:3.

13 Rashi and *Malbim* on Ruth 1:2.

14 Rashi on Ruth 1:2.

15 Siftei Chachamim on Ruth 1:2.

16 Rashi on Ruth 1:1.

17 *Bava Batra* 91a; see also Ex. 6:23 and Num. 1:7.

18 *Sotah* 37a.

19 *Bava Batra* 91a.

20   Likutei Anshei Shem on Ruth 1:3.
21   Igeret Shmuel on Ruth 1:1.
22   *Ruth Rabbah* 1:4.
23   *Ruth Rabbah* 1:4 and *Malbim* on Ruth 1:1.
24   Torah Temima on Ruth 1:1.
25   Kitzur Alschich on Ruth 1:1.
26   See Part One of this book for the entire story of Lot and his daughters, including a discussion of the birth of Moav and Ammon.
27   Kitzur Alschich on Ruth 1:1.
28   Kitzur Alschich on Ruth 1:1.
29   Though in Exod. 2 neither Amram, Yocheved nor Moses is named. They are referred to only via pronouns, never by their proper names, until later in the biblical narrative.
30   The Book of Chronicles has two additional names for Elimelech's sons, calling them Yoash and Saraph, meaning, respectively, despair and burning. I Chron. 4:22.
31   *Me'am Loez* on Ruth 1:2.
32   The names Machlon and Chilyon are reminiscent of the names Bilhah and Zilpah, Rachel and Leah's handmaidens who were given as concubines to Joseph in Genesis. The handmaids' names are nearly indistinguishable rhymes of one another, signaling to the reader that the two fill the same role in the Genesis story. Their function was to augment their mistress' childbearing count in the competition to produce heirs for Jacob.
33   Me'am Loez on Ruth 1:4.
34   Kitzur Alschich on Ruth 1:1, and Likutei Anshei Shem on Ruth 1:3.
35   Deut. 23:4–7.
36   Gen. 48:7.
37   *Ruth Rabbah* 2:7.
38   Choter Yishai on Ruth 1:4.
39   See Ruth 4:10.
40   *Mossad HaRav Kook* on Ruth 1:4.
41   The sources agree that Ruth is royal, either a daughter or granddaughter of Moabite kings. *Sotah* 47a, *Sanhedrin* 105b and *Zohar* on Num. 190a all say that Ruth is *daughter* of Eglon,

King of Moab; *Sanhedrin* 105b adds that Eglon was grandson of King Balak; *Horayot* 10b and *Nazir* 23b say that Ruth is *grand*daughter of Eglon, who was either the son or grandson of King Balak.

42 *Me'am Loez* on Ruth 1:4.
43 *Me'am Loez* on Ruth 1:4.
44 *Mossad HaRav Kook* on Ruth 1:4.
45 Ralbag, Kitzur Alschich and *Mossad HaRav Kook* on Ruth 1:4.
46 *Kiddushin* 75a.
47 *Yevamot* 69a, 76b and 77a; see also *Midrash Zutah* on Ruth 4:5 and *Me'am Loez* on Ruth 1:4.
48 *Ramban*, the Nachmanides, even comments that the male Moabites *did* greet the Israelites with bread and water after the exodus from Egypt; he says that it was the Ammonites who did not do so. Moabites were prohibited from intermarriage with Israel because they had hired Bilaam the sorcerer to curse the Israelites. *Ramban* on Deut. 23:5.
49 *Me'am Loez* on Ruth 1:4.
50 Rashi and *Mossad HaRav Kook* on Ruth 1:4. I will discuss the question of Ruth and Orpah's conversions further on in this chapter.
51 Midrash Lekach Tov and *Me'am Loez* on Ruth 1:4.
52 *Berachot* 7b and *Zohar, Bereishit* 58b. Though it is also said that of course one's name will never preclude free will, nor can a name determine vice or virtue. One's name only contains within it *the potential* of its bearer, whether for good or for evil. The choice always resides with the individual.
53 *Mossad HaRav Kook* on Ruth 1:4.
54 Midrash Meshiv Nefesh on Ruth 1:4.
55 This story is told at I Sam. 17.
56 *Me'am Loez* on Ruth 1:4 and *Mossad HaRav Kook* on Ruth 1:2.
57 *Berachot* 7b.
58 *Mossad HaRav Kook* on Ruth 1:4.
59 *Mossad HaRav Kook* on Ruth 1:4.
60 *Me'am Loez* on Ruth 1:4.
61 The Gr"ah and *Me'am Loez* on Ruth 1:4.
62 Zohar Chadash on Ruth 1:4.
63 *Me'am Loez* on Ruth 1:4.

64 *Me'am Loez* on Ruth 1:5.

65 *Me'am Loez* on Ruth 1:6.

66 *Torah Temima* on Ruth 1:5.

67 Igeret Shmuel on Ruth 1:5.

68 Igeret Shmuel on Ruth 1:5.

69 *Me'am Loez* on Ruth 1:3 and 5.

70 *Mossad HaRav Kook* on Ruth 1:5.

71 Midrash Meshiv Nefesh on Ruth 1:5.

72 Midrash Meshiv Nefesh on Ruth 1:5.

73 Me'am Loez on Ruth 1:6.

74 Midrash Meshiv Nefesh on Ruth 1:6. See also Targum Yonatan.

75 *Ruth Rabbah* 2:11.

76 Kitzur Alschich on Ruth 1:7.

77 *Me'am Loez* on Ruth 1:6.

78 *Mossad HaRav Kook* on Ruth 1:6.

79 *Me'am Loez* on Ruth 1:7.

80 *The Living Nach* on Ruth 1:7.

81 *Malbim* on Ruth 1:7.

82 *Ruth Rabbah* 3:6 and *Me'am Loez* on Ruth 1:7.

83 *Me'am Loez* on Ruth 1:7.

84 Igeret Shmuel on Ruth 1:7.

85 *Ruth Rabbah* 2:12.

86 The journey from Sedei Moav to the Judean border is anywhere from twenty-five to forty kilometers. Once over the border, the distance to Beit Lechem from the shallowest point of the Dead Sea is about fifty-five kilometers. All-told, the journey is between fifty to sixty-five miles, depending on the route taken. Scaled map in *Mossad HaRav Kook* on Ruth 1.

87 *Mossad HaRav Kook* on Ruth 1:8.

88 Midrash Meshiv Nefesh on Ruth 1:8.

89 *Mossad HaRav Kook* on Ruth 1:8.

90 *Me'am Loez* on Ruth 1:8.

91 *Mossad HaRav Kook* on Ruth 1:8.

92 *Mossad HaRav Kook* on Ruth 1:8.

93 *Me'am Loez* on Ruth 1:8.

94 Gen. 38:11. See Part Three above, "Judah & Tamar."

95 *Mossad HaRav Kook* on Ruth 1:8.

[96] *Me'am Loez* on Ruth 1:8.

[97] *Ruth Rabbah* 2:16.

[98] *Me'am Loez* on Ruth 1:12.

[99] Midrash Meshiv Nefesh on Ruth 1:8.

[100] *Me'am Loez* on Ruth 1:8.

[101] Midrash Meshiv Nefesh on Ruth 1:8.

[102] Gen. 19:32.

[103] *Ruth Rabbah* 2:17.

[104] Midrash Meshiv Nefesh on Ruth 1:8.

[105] *Mossad HaRav Kook* on Ruth 1:8.

[106] *Me'am Loez* on Ruth 1:8.

[107] *Me'am Loez* on Ruth 1:8.

[108] Midrash Meshiv Nefesh on Ruth 1:9.

[109] *Me'am Loez* on Ruth 1:9.

[110] *Me'am Loez* on Ruth 1:9.

[111] Midrash Meshiv Nefesh on Ruth 1:9.

[112] *Me'am Loez* on Ruth 1:14.

[113] *Mossad HaRav Kook* on Ruth 1:9.

[114] *Mossad HaRav Kook* on Ruth 1:10.

[115] Eshkol HaKofer on Ruth 1:10.

[116] *Mossad HaRav Kook* on Ruth 1:10, fn. 8.

[117] Midrash Meshiv Nefesh on Ruth 1:10.

[118] Midrash Meshiv Nefesh on Ruth 1:10.

[119] *Mossad HaRav Kook* on Ruth 1:11 and 13.

[120] *Me'am Loez* on Ruth 1:11.

[121] Rashi on Ruth 1:12.

[122] *Mossad HaRav Kook* on Ruth 1:13.

[123] *Me'am Loez* on Ruth 1:13.

[124] Rashi on Ruth 1:13; see also *Ruth Rabbah* 2:19.

[125] See Exod. 7:4, 5, 17,27; 8:15; and 9:3, 15.

[126] Frymer-Kensky, *Women of the Bible*, p. 240.

[127] Midrash Meshiv Nefesh and *Me'am Loez* on Ruth 1:16.

[128] *Mossad HaRav Kook* on Ruth 1:14.

[129] *Me'am Loez* on Ruth 1:14.

[130] *Me'am Loez* on Ruth 1:14 and 15.

[131] *Me'am Loez* on Ruth 1:14; *Ruth Rabbah* 2:20 says the four warriors descend from Orpah as a reward for the four miles she walked alongside Naomi before parting from her.

[132] II Sam. 21:22.

[133] *Me'am Loez* on Ruth 1:14.

[134] See the earlier discussion of the etymology of Orpah's name. Its root is *oreph*, meaning "the back of the neck." When Orpah turns her face homeward, towards Moav, she is actually showing Naomi the back of her neck.

[135] *Ruth Rabbah* 2:20.

[136] Kitzur Alschich on Ruth 1:15.

[137] *Me'am Loez* on Ruth 1:14.

[138] *Me'am Loez* on Ruth 1:14.

[139] See I Sam. 21:42.

[140] Frymer-Kensky, *Women of the Bible*, p. 241.

[141] King Jehoshaphat of Judah, joining Israel's king in a war against the king of Aram, solemnly promises, "I will do what you do; my troops shall be your troops, my horses shall be your horses." I Kings 22:4. And later on, when king Jehoshaphat joins with Israel once again, this time—ironically for our story—against the king of Moav, Jehoshaphat uses his identical words in a second covenantal promise of loyalty. II Kings 3:7.

[142] *Mossad HaRav Kook* on Ruth 1:17.

[143] *Yevamot* 47b.

[144] *Me'am Loez* on Ruth 1:16.

[145] Midrash Meshiv Nefesh on Ruth 1:19.

[146] *Me'am Loez* on Ruth 1:16.

[147] *Me'am Loez* on Ruth 1:16.

[148] Though the term "Jew" is anachronistic when referring to the Israelites only two generations after the Exodus, for ease of reference the author uses the term in this chapter.

[149] *Torah Temima* on Ruth 1:16; *Ruth Rabbah* 2:22.

[150] *Ruth Rabbah* 2:22–24.

[151] *Ibn Ezra*, Zohar Chadash.

[152] Rashi, *Malbim*, Rabbi Meir, Midrash Meshiv Nefesh.

[153] *Me'am Loez* on Ruth 1:15.

[154] *Yevamot* 47b.

[155] *Me'am Loez* on Ruth 1:15.

[156] *Avot* 5:3. Rashi and Rambam differ somewhat on what Abraham's ten trials were, but they agree that he was tested by God ten times.

[157] Gen. 12:1 and Gen. 22:2.

[158] Gen. 24:58.

[159] Likutei Anshei Shem on Ruth 1:18.

[160] *Me'am Loez* on Ruth 1:16.

[161] Phyllis Trible, *God and the Rhetoric of Sexuality* (Philadelphia: Fortress Press, 1978), p. 173, emphasis added.

[162] Ibid.

[163] *Mossad HaRav Kook* on Ruth 1:18.

[164] Midrash Meshiv Nefesh on Ruth 1:15. Naomi used the same word, *shov-na*, please return, three times (in verses 8, 11 and 12) when trying to convince Ruth to return **to Moav** . Here, in verse 15, Naomi says *shuvi, return after your sister-in-law*, trying the new tack of convincing Ruth to keep the younger woman company on her return trip to her home. Naomi's three prior uses of *shov-na* prompt the *midrash's* statement about when to refrain from discouraging a sincere proselyte.

[165] *Ruth Rabbah* 3:5; *Me'am Loez* on Ruth 1:18.

[166] *Me'am Loez* on Ruth 1:18.

[167] In Gen. 22:6 and 8 we read that Abraham and Isaac, father and son, "walk together" toward Mount Moriah and the *Akeida*. The words are virtually identical to those here in Ruth 1:19, and, as here, the commonality of purpose and intention is noted by the commentaries in those verses, as well.

[168] Rashi on Ruth 1:19.

[169] Frymer-Kensky, *Women of the Bible*, pp. 241–242, emphasis added.

[170] Midrash Meshiv Nefesh on Ruth 1:23.

[171] *Me'am Loez* citing Midrash Dana Pashrah on Ruth 1:19.

[172] Midrash Meshiv Nefesh on Ruth 1:19.

[173] *Mossad HaRav Kook* on Ruth 1:19.

[174] See Ruth 1:22; *Ruth Rabbah* 3:6 and Siftei Chachamim on Ruth 1:19.

[175] Rashi on Ruth 1:19.

[176] *Ruth Rabbah* 4:2 and Midrash Meshiv Nefesh on Ruth 1:19.

[177] Midrash Meshiv Nefesh on Ruth 1:20.

[178] Midrash Meshiv Nefesh on Ruth 1:19.

[179] *Ruth Rabbah* 4:2.

[180] Kitzur Alschich on Ruth 1:19.

[181] Midrash Meshiv Nefesh on Ruth 1:19.

[182] Matnot Kehuna on Ruth 1:19.

[183] *Ibn Ezra* on Ruth 1:19.

[184] Rashi on Ruth 1:21, saying that Naomi had been pregnant when she left Judah for Moav.

[185] *Malbim* on Ruth 1:20.

[186] Rashi on Ruth 1:21.

[187] Midrash Meshiv Nefesh on Ruth 1:20.

[188] *Me'am Loez* on Ruth 1:23.

[189] Rabbi Meir Soloveichik, quoting Rav Yaakov Meidan of Yeshivat Har Etzion, Israel, in a class on the topic of the agricultural underpinnings of counting down the *omer* period. New York City, April 12, 2010, class attended by the author.

[190] *Ibn Ezra* on Ruth 2:1.

[191] *Megillat* Esther 2:5.

[192] I Sam. 17:4.

[193] Midrash Meshiv Nefesh on Ruth 2:1.

[194] *Bava Batra* 91a.

[195] *Mossad HaRav Kook* on Ruth 2:1.

[196] Midrash Meshiv Nefesh on Ruth 2:1.

[197] Judges 12:8.-10.

[198] *Bava Batra* 91a.

[199] This same Manoach would in the future become the father of Samson. Judges 13.

[200] *Me'am Loez* on Ruth 2:1.

[201] Kitzur Alschich on Ruth 2:1.

[202] Kitzur Alschich on Ruth 2:1.

[203] Kitzur Alschich on Ruth 2:1.

[204] *Me'am Loez* on Ruth 2:2.

[205] Lev. 19:9–10; also 23:22: "And when you reap the harvest of your land, you shall not. . . gather the gleanings of your harvest; you shall **leave them for the poor and the stranger:** I am the Lord your God."

[206] *Malbim* on Ruth 2:2.

[207] *Chullin* 131b; Keter Yonatan on Lev. 23:22.

[208] *Me'am Loez* on Ruth 2:2.

209 *Me'am Loez* on Ruth 2:2.

210 *Me'am Loez* on Ruth 2:2.

211 *Ruth Rabbah* 4:4.

212 Midrash Lekach Tov on Ruth 2:3.

213 *Me'am Loez* on Ruth 2:4.

214 *Shabbat* 113b.

215 *Ruth Rabbah* 4:4.

216 *Ibn Ezra* on Ruth 2:6.

217 *Shabbat* 113b.

218 *Ruth Rabbah* 4:6.

219 *Me'am Loez* on Ruth 2:3.

220 *Ruth Rabbah* 4:6.

221 *Bava Metzia* 21b; Rashi on Lev. 19:9.

222 *Chullin* 131b; *Ruth Rabbah* 4:6.

223 *Torah Temimah* 1:16.

224 *Ibn Ezra* on Ruth 2:5.

225 Kitzur Alschich on Ruth 2:7.

226 Midrash Meshiv Nefesh on Ruth 2:5.

227 Midrash Meshiv Nefesh on Ruth 2:6.

228 Kitzur Alschich on Ruth 2:6.

229 *Me'am Loez* on Ruth 2:6.

230 *Mossad HaRav Kook* on Ruth 2:7.

231 If Ruth was the marriageable age of eighteen or even twenty years old when she married Machlon, and they were married for a period of ten years when he died (1:4–5), then Ruth is about thirty years of age when she meets Boaz in his field.

232 *Ruth Rabbah* 4:4.

233 Deut. 24:19–21.

234 *Chullin* 131b.

235 *Mossad HaRav Kook* on Ruth 2:1.

236 Malcolm Gladwell, in his book *Blink* (New York: Little Brown, 2005), discusses how even just a few moments of observation can be enough to allow an accustomed decision-maker to make the correct choice. He calls it "the power of thinking without thinking." No doubt this is what Boaz does while observing Ruth; he makes up his mind in a flash.

237 *Mossad HaRav Kook* on Ruth 2:8.

238 The *midrash* teaches that within Boaz's vast cultivated acreage one side was assigned to male gleaners, and one side to female gleaners. This was enforced so as to keep the women safe from prying eyes and lewd behavior as they bent to their serious task of gleaning after the harvesters. Igeret Shmuel on Ruth 2:8.

239 *Ruth Rabbah* 4:7.

240 *Mossad HaRav Kook* on Ruth 2:9.

241 Midrash Meshiv Nefesh on Ruth 2:8.

242 *Mossad HaRav Kook* on Ruth 2:10.

243 *Me'am Loez* on Ruth 2:10.

244 *Mossad HaRav Kook* on Ruth 2:10.

245 *Mossad HaRav Kook* on Ruth 2:10; also Avivah Gottlieb Zornberg in a lecture attended by the author in New York City entitled "And I Am A Stranger: Becoming Ruth," on May 21, 2009.

246 Edward L. Greenstein, "Reading Strategies and the Story of Ruth," in *Women in the Hebrew Bible* (ed. Alice Bach; New York: Routledge, 1999), p. 215.

247 Ibn Yichyeh on Ruth 2:8.

248 Midrash Meshiv Nefesh on Ruth 2:10.

249 *Me'am Loez* on Ruth 2:10.

250 Midrash Meshiv Nefesh on Ruth 2:10.

251 Gr"ah on Ruth 2:10; also see Midrash Meshiv Nefesh on Ruth 2:10.

252 *Me'am Loez* on Ruth 2:10.

253 *Yevamot* 48b.

254 *Me'am Loez* on Ruth 2:11.

255 *Me'am Loez* on Ruth 2:12.

256 Midrash Meshiv Nefesh on Ruth 2:13.

257 *Torah Temima* on Ruth 2:12.

258 *Torah Temima* on Ruth 2:12.

259 Igeret Shmuel on Ruth 2:13.

260 Midrash Meshiv Nefesh on Ruth 2:13.

261 *Ruth Rabbah* 5:5.

262 Igeret Shmuel on Ruth 2:14.

263 *Shabbat* 113b; Kitzur Alschich on Ruth 2:14.

264 *Me'am Loez* on Ruth 2:14.

265 Midrash Meshiv Nefesh on Ruth 2:14.

266 Igeret Shmuel on Ruth 2:14.

267 *Ruth Rabbah* on Ruth 2:14.

268 Igeret Shmuel on 2:14.

269 Kitzur Alschich on Ruth 2:14.

270 Midrash Meshiv Nefesh on Ruth 2:15.

271 Kitzur Alschich on Ruth 2:16.

272 Midrash Meshiv Nefesh on Ruth 2:15.

273 Kitzur Alschich on Ruth 2:16.

274 *Me'am Loez* on Ruth 2:17.

275 Midrash Meshiv Nefesh on Ruth 2:17.

276 *Mossad HaRav Kook* on Ruth 2:18.

277 Kitzur Alschich on Ruth 2:18.

278 *Mossad HaRav Kook* on Ruth 2:18.

279 Midrash Meshiv Nefesh on Ruth 2:16.

280 Kitzur Alschich on Ruth 2:18.

281 *Malbim* and *Mossad HaRav Kook* on Ruth 2:19.

282 Igeret Shmuel on Ruth 2:18.

283 *Mossad HaRav Kook* on Ruth 2:20.

284 Midrash Meshiv Nefesh on Ruth 2:19.

285 The reader will recall our extensive discussion of the definition and requirements of the levirate law in Part Three's story of Judah and Tamar.

286 Ruth 2:1.

287 See Ruth 2:8, 9, 15, 16, and 21.

288 Ruth 2:21.

289 Ruth 2:22.

290 *Mossad HaRav Kook* on Ruth 2:22.

291 Igeret Shmuel on Ruth 2:22.

292 Judges 17:6.

293 See Judges chapter 19 where the grisly story is recounted. It is a tale of unbelievable sadistic cruelty, apathy, abuse and murder of women by Israelite men. The *midrash* wants the reader of Ruth to appreciate that Boaz's offer of protection to her is necessary and valuable, and is not mere politesse.

294 Igeret Shmuel on Ruth 2:22.

295 *Me'am Loez* on Ruth 2:23.

296 *Mossad HaRav Kook* on Ruth ch. 3.

[297] *Malbim* and *Me'am Loez* on Ruth 3:1. In Ruth's case, this assumes either that her husband Machlon had died right before she left for Judah, or that the 90 days began from the time of her roadside conversion.

[298] Deut. 25:5–6.

[299] Deut. 25:9–10.

[300] It is the *woman* — not the man — who initiates the *chalitza* ritual. Dvora E. Weissberg, *Levirate Marriage and the Family in Ancient Judaism* (Lebanon, N.H.: Brandeis University Press, 2009), p. 137.

[301] Calum M. Carmichael, "A Ceremonial Crux: Removing a Man's Sandal as a Female Gesture of Contempt," *Journal of Biblical Literature* 96, no. 3 (Sept. 1997), pp. 324, 331–336.

[302] Jacob Neusner, *How the Rabbis Liberated Women* (Atlanta, Ga.: Scholars Press, 1998), p. vii, emphasis added.

[303] Ibid., p. vii.

[304] *Malbim* on Ruth 3:4.

[305] Carmichael, "A Ceremonial Crux," p. 323, emphasis added.

[306] Rabbi Meir Soloveichik in a class on *yibum* and redemption at Congregation Kehilath Jeshurun on April 26, 2010 in New York City. Class attended by the author. See also Greenstein, "Reading Strategies and the Story of Ruth," p. 214, where he calls the *chalitza* ceremony in the Book of Ruth "quasi-levirate."

[307] The reader will recall our discussion of the levirate law in Part Three. There, when Judah denied Shelah — the true levir or *yavam* — to Tamar, her ruse and seduction of her father-in-law was sanctioned, because *he* was the *nearest male kinsman* after Shelah. Judah thus became a *de facto* "extended *yavam*." See also, Kitzur Alschich on Ruth 3:2.

[308] Boaz's use of the root-word *dbk*, or "cleave," in his conversations with Ruth in chapter 2 (verses 8 and 21) is **a hint of his intent to marry her**. This is because the root *dbk* is typically used in the Bible to connote conjugal union. See Gen. 2:24: *Hence a man leaves his father and mother and **shall cleave** unto his wife, so that they become one flesh.* See also *Shabbat* 113b, and the explanation of the Maharsha.

[309] Kitzur Alschich on Ruth 3:1.

[310] Kitzur Alschich on Ruth 3:2.

[311] Kitzur Alschich on Ruth 3:1.

[312] *Mossad HaRav Kook* on Ruth 3:1.

[313] Torat Chesed cited in *Me'am Loez* on Ruth 3:1.

[314] *Mossad HaRav Kook* on Ruth 3:2.

[315] Igeret Shmuel on Ruth 3:2.

[316] Igeret Shmuel on Ruth 3:2.

[317] Igeret Shmuel and *Me'am Loez* on Ruth 3:1.

[318] *Ruth Rabbah* 6:2.

[319] Rashi on Ruth 3:2.

[320] Rashi on *Shabbat* 113b.

[321] Kitzur Alschich on Ruth 3:2.

[322] Rashi on Ruth 3:3.

[323] *Ibn Ezra* on Ruth 3:2.

[324] *Shabbat* 113b; *Ruth Rabbah* 5:12. See also Rashi, Siftei Chachamim, and *Ibn Ezra* on Ruth 3:2.

[325] *Mossad HaRav Kook* on Ruth 3:3.

[326] Rashi and Siftei Chachamim on Ruth 3:2–3.

[327] When *Megillat* Ruth is chanted aloud, these three words are chanted in the *second*-person. The *midrashic* correction is understood and is made by the Torah reader. It is not Naomi who will *don her dress, go down,* and *lie down* at Boaz's feet; it is Ruth who does so, at Naomi's instruction.

[328] Rashi on Ruth 3:2.

[329] Zornberg, *The Murmuring Deep*, p. 368.

[330] Ibid.

[331] Siftei Chachamim on Ruth 3:2.

[332] *Berachot* 43b. Ruth is mindful of the injunction against going out alone at night, as this might raise a suspicion that she herself is promiscuous.

[333] Zornberg, *The Murmuring Deep*, p. 368.

[334] *Sanhedrin* 21a, b. This prohibition is destined to be enacted into law in years to come by the court of King David after the incident of the rape of princess Tamar by Amnon, her half-brother. See Part Five for a full discussion. An exception to this ban is a mother and her son, who are permitted to be alone together.

[335] Kitzur Alschich on Ruth 3:2.

336 Midrash Meshiv Nefesh on Ruth 3:2.

337 *Megillat* Esther 4:14.

338 Igeret Shmuel on Ruth 3:3.

339 See Midrash Meshiv Nefesh on Ruth 3:4.

340 Frymer-Kensky, *Women of the Bible*, p. 247.

341 Igeret Shmuel on Ruth 3:3.

342 Igeret Shmuel on Ruth 3:3.

343 Igeret Shmuel on Ruth 3:3.

344 *Ruth Rabbah* 5:13; *Mossad HaRav Kook* on Ruth 3:3.

345 *Shabbat* 113b.

346 Igeret Shmuel on Ruth 3:5.

347 *Me'am Loez* on Ruth 3:3.

348 Midrash Meshiv Nefesh on Ruth 3:3.

349 Likutei Anshei Shem on Ruth 3:7 describes the details of the threshing festival.

350 *Ruth Rabbah* 5:15.

351 *Me'am Loez* on Ruth 3:7.

352 *Me'am Loez* on Ruth 3:7.

353 *Ruth Rabbah* 5:15.

354 Readers will recall that in Part Three of this book, Judah's participation in the sheep-shearing festival similarly marked the end of his mourning period for his wife and sons. This is another textual and contextual connection between Boaz and his forebear.

355 Likutei Anshei Shem on Ruth 3:7.

356 The Hebrew word for "softly" is *balat*. We cannot help but notice that the word *balat* is spelled exactly as the name *Lot*; a subtle reference to Ruth's origins. *Me'am Loez* on Ruth 3:7.

357 Radak on Ruth 3:7.

358 Trible, *God and the Rhetoric of Sexuality*, p. 198, n. 23; Frymer-Kensky, *Women of the Bible*, pp. 247–248.

359 Bal, *Lethal Love*, p. 2.

360 *Mishbatzot Zahav* on Ruth 3:7.

361 *Mossad HaRav Kook* on Ruth 3:8.

362 *Ruth Rabbah* 6:1.

363 Rashi on Ruth 3:8.

364 *Ruth Rabbah* 6:1.

365 *Ruth Rabbah* 6:1.

366 Midrash Meshiv Nefesh on Ruth 3:8.

367 *Ruth Rabbah* 6:2.

368 Midrash Meshiv Nefesh on Ruth 3:8.

369 *Mossad HaRav Kook* on Ruth 3:9.

370 *Mossad HaRav Kook* on Ruth 3:9.

371 Midrash Meshiv Nefesh on Ruth 3:9.

372 Midrash Meshiv Nefesh on Ruth 3:9.

373 *Mossad HaRav Kook* on Ruth 3:9.

374 *Mossad HaRav Kook* on Ruth 3:9.

375 See Part Three of this book for the story of Judah and Tamar.

376 *Malbim* on Ruth 3:9.

377 *Malbim* on Ruth 3:9.

378 Midrash Meshiv Nefesh on Ruth 3:10.

379 Rashi on *Sanhedrin* 19b.

380 *Sanhedrin* 19b.

381 Midrash Meshiv Nefesh and Igeret Shmuel on Ruth 3:8.

382 Midrash Meshiv Nefesh on Ruth 3:8.

383 *Mishbatzot Zahav* on Ruth 3:4.

384 Igeret Shmuel on Ruth 3:8 citing the *Zohar* for the proposition that at stake was nothing less than Boaz's eternal soul. Had he sinned with Ruth he would have lost the potential reward promised to the righteous in the world-to-come.

385 *Avot* 4:1.

386 *Ruth Rabbah* 6:4.

387 *Mishbatzot Zahav* on Ruth 3:8.

388 Rashi on Ruth 3:10.

389 Targum Yonatan on Ruth 3:10.

390 Midrash Meshiv Nefesh on Ruth 3:10.

391 See Part One of this book for a complete discussion of the seduction in the cave.

392 Trible, *God and the Rhetoric of Sexuality*, p. 185.

393 *Malbim* on Ruth 3:11.

394 Kitzur Alschich on Ruth 3:12.

395 *Malbim* on Ruth 3:11.

396 Benjamin Rapoport in a conversation with the author in March, 2010.

397 *Ruth Rabbah* 6:3 and Rashi on Ruth 3:12.

398 *Bava Batra* 91a; *Ruth Rabbah* 6:3; Rashi on Ruth 3:12.

399 Ruth 3:13; see also *Ruth Rabbah* 6:3.

400 *Yevamot* 117a.

401 *Mossad HaRav Kook* on Ruth 3:12.

402 Maimonides, *Guide of the Perplexed*, Section 3, ch. 53.

403 *Yevamot* 117a.

404 See Part One, "Lot & His Daughters," where we discuss in depth the seduction in the cave.

405 Yair Zakovitch, "The Threshing-Floor Scene in Ruth [in Hebrew]" *Shenaton/Annual for Biblical and Ancient Near Eastern Studies* 3 (1978–1979), pp. 29–33.

406 *Malbim* on Ruth 3:13.

407 Kitzur Alschich on Ruth 3:13.

408 Rashi on Ruth 3:13.

409 *Mossad HaRav Kook* on Ruth 3:13.

410 *Ruth Rabbah* 6:4.

411 Rashi on Ruth 3:13.

412 Midrash Meshiv Nefesh on Ruth 3:14.

413 The reader will recall our extensive discussion on this point in Part Three, "Judah & Tamar."

414 Midrash Meshiv Nefesh on Ruth 3:15.

415 *Ruth Rabbah* 7:1.

416 *Malbim* on Ruth 3:14.

417 *Mossad HaRav Kook* on Ruth 3:14.

418 *Mossad HaRav Kook* on Ruth 3:14, fn. 16.

419 Midrash Meshiv Nefesh on Ruth 3:14.

420 Midrash Meshiv Nefesh on Ruth 3:14.

421 Midrash Meshiv Nefesh and Igeret Shmuel on Ruth 3:15–16.

422 *Malbim* on Ruth 3:15.

423 *Ruth Rabbah* 7:2.

424 *Sanhedrin* 93a.

425 Rashi on Ruth 3:15. *Me'am Loez* on Ruth 3:15 suggests that the six points of the Magen David — the Shield of David — represent these six virtues.

426 *Me'am Loez* on Ruth 3:15 and 17. The six are David, Chizkiyahu, Yishayahu, Chanania, Mishael, Azariya and Daniel (these last three are counted together as one) and the Messiah. Alternatively, the six can be David, Chanania, Mishael, Azariya, Daniel and the Messiah.

[427] Igeret Shmuel on Ruth 3:15.

[428] Igeret Shmuel on Ruth 3:16.

[429] Kitzur Alschich on Ruth 3:16.

[430] *Me'am Loez* on Ruth 3:16.

[431] Kitzur Alschich on Ruth 3:17.

[432] Kitzur Alschich on Ruth 3:18.

[433] *Yevamot* 17b.

[434] Igeret Shmuel on Ruth 4:1.

[435] Igeret Shmuel on Ruth 4:1.

[436] Kitzur Alschich on 4:1.

[437] In the rabbinic tradition, the passing-by of the nearest kinsman is far from coincidental. Instead, Boaz's words to Ruth on the threshing-floor — *Stay the night and it will come to pass **in the morning** that if Tov will redeem you . . .* —actually **cause** Ploni Almoni to pass by the next morning! The *midrash* reasons that the Almighty will step in to help matters along once the actors have set themselves firmly on the course they will take. Shoresh Yishai on Ruth 4:1.

[438] There is Boaz's ambiguous reference to Tov in Ruth 3:13. Also, numerous commentaries name Elimelech's third brother Tov (*Midrash Tanchuma, Malbim, Alschich, inter alia.*), though the *Ibn Ezra* disagrees, interpreting Boaz's words to mean "if the closer kinsman redeems, you, this is **tov** (*i.e.*, this is **good**)."

[439] Rashi on Ruth 4:1.

[440] See Part One of this book, "Lot & His Daughters."

[441] *Ibn Ezra* on Ruth 4:3.

[442] Some read verse 4:3 as saying that Naomi *has already sold* Elimelech's fields. This would still call the levirate law into play, because Elimelech's nearest kinsman is obligated to buy back or redeem the fields so as to keep Elimelech's landed portion in the family.

[443] Kitzur Alschich on Ruth 4:4.

[444] *Mossad HaRav Kook* on Ruth 4:4.

[445] *Malbim* on Ruth 4:4.

[446] *Mossad HaRav Kook* on Ruth 4:5.

[447] Carmichael, "A Ceremonial Crux," p. 335.

[448] See *Ramban*'s discussion of the law of redemption on Lev. 25:32–22.

449 Naomi explains this to Orpah and Ruth in 1:11–13.

450 *Mossad HaRav Kook* on Ruth 4:5.

451 Kitzur Alschich on Ruth 4:5.

452 *Ibn Ezra* and Kitzur Alschich on Ruth 4:6.

453 Rashi on Ruth 4:6.

454 Targum Yonatan and *Mossad HaRav Kook* on Ruth 4:6.

455 Kitzur Alschich on Ruth 4:6.

456 Targum Yonatan on Ruth 4:6.

457 *Mossad HaRav Kook* on Ruth 4:6.

458 *Ruth Rabbah* 7:10.

459 Igeret Shmuel on Ruth 4:6.

460 Kitzur Alschich on Ruth 4:6.

461 Igeret Shmuel on Ruth 4:7 describes the origin of the shoe ceremony in commercial matters.

462 This is known as *kinyan sudar*, in which one party to the transaction gives a garment to the other, sealing or binding the deal. Ruth 4:7 describes the classic case of *kinyan sudar*. *Bava Metzia* 47a.

463 *Bava Metzia* 47a.

464 Ralbag on Ruth 4:7.

465 At this point in the tale the field is Ruth's, though it is referred to in the text as Naomi's.

466 Rashi on Ruth 4:7.

467 *Bava Metzia* 47a; also *Ibn Ezra* and Kitzur Alschich on Ruth 4:8.

468 *Ibn Ezra* on Ruth 4:8.

469 Igeret Shmuel on Ruth 4:8.

470 *Mossad HaRav Kook* on Ruth 4:7–8.

471 Carmichael, "A Ceremonial Crux," p. 336.

472 Though according to *Me'am Loez* (on Ruth 4:9) Naomi was present for the sale of her (and Ruth's) land.

473 Carmichael, "A Ceremonial Crux," p. 335.

474 Midrash Meshiv Nefesh on Ruth 4:5.

475 *Ruth Rabbah* 7:12; Midrash Meshiv Nefesh, Igeret Shmuel on Ruth 4:8.

476 Or, according to the *Malbim* (on Exod. 3:5), it was Ploni Almoni who took off *his* shoe, symbolically giving it to Boaz, the second-in-line kinsman who will be redeeming the fields and

the widow of the dead Machlon. This is measure-for-measure payback; by refusing to redeem Machlon's widow, Ploni Almoni has not "stood up" for his "brother," so he must go shoeless — or barefoot — in full view of the *beit din* and his countrymen.

477 Midrash Meshiv Nefesh on Ruth 4:7.

478 *Malbim* on Ruth 4:8.

479 Igeret Shmuel on Ruth 4:9.

480 *Mossad HaRav Kook* on Ruth 4:5.

481 Targum Yonatan on Ruth 4:4.

482 Shoresh Yishai on Ruth 4:9.

483 *Me'am Loez* on Ruth 4:9.

484 According to the Talmud in *Bava Batra* 113b a legal proceeding must commence **during the daytime**. The scene at the Beit Lechem city gates on the morning after the threshing festival was nothing if not a bona fide open court. Boaz strategically convened the *beit din* in order that it give its official imprimatur to three pressing legal matters: the transfer of redemption rights from the nearest kinsman to himself; the purchase of Naomi's (and Ruth's) fields; and the propriety of (levirate) marriage to a Moabitess.

485 Midrash Meshiv Nefesh on Ruth 4:9.

486 Kitzur Alschich on Ruth 4:11.

487 Kitzur Alschich on Ruth 4:11.

488 She said, "Let us lie with him that we may perpetuate our father's **seed**." Gen. 19:32.

489 *Me'am Loez* on Ruth 4:11, emphasis added.

490 In a fascinating aside, *Mishbatzot Zahav* (on Ruth 4:12) connects Peretz and Zerach, Tamar and Judah's twin sons, to Machlon and Chilyon, saying that kabbalistically the latter are reincarnations of the former. In effect, the *midrash* is drawing a straight line from Tamar's seduction of Judah to Ruth's seduction of Boaz.

491 *Yevamot* 76b.

492 *Me'am Loez* on Ruth 4:12.

493 There is some *midrashic* opinion that Machlon died before Chilyon and that Chilyon took Ruth in levirate marriage. If this is so, then Ruth's story even more closely parallels Tamar's. *Me'am Loez* on Ruth 4:12.

494 Tzror Hamor on Ruth 4:13.

495 *Mishbatzot Zahav* on Ruth 4:13.

496 See *Mishbatzot Zahav* on Ruth 4:13 for explication of the Gr"ah's philosophy.

497 *Mishbatzot Zahav* on Ruth 4:9–10.

498 *Midrash Zuta* on Ruth 4.

499 See *Ramban* on Gen. 38:5, where Judah's wife, Bat-Shuah, names their son "Shelah" while she is in Cheziv; Judah does not appear to have been present.

500 Gen. 16:15 and 35:18, respectively.

501 Igeret Shmuel on Ruth 4:17.

502 *Mossad HaRav Kook* on Ruth 4:17.

503 *Mossad HaRav Kook* on Ruth 4:17.

504 Because of the pure intentions of Boaz and Ruth, their son was perceived, in a kabbalistic sense, to be a reincarnation of Machlon's soul. *Zohar* Vol. II, 103b.

505 *Mishbatzot Zahav* on Ruth 4:17.

506 Shoresh Yishai and *Mishbatzot Zahav* on Ruth 4:17.

507 *Mishbatzot Zahav* on Ruth 4:14.

508 *Me'am Loez* on Ruth 4:14.

509 *Niddah* 38b.

510 Choter Yishai on Ruth 4:15, as cited in Yalkut *Me'am Loez*.

511 Shoresh Yishai on Ruth 4:15.

512 Kitzur Alschich on Ruth 4:16.

513 *Me'am Loez* on Ruth 4:15.

514 Ruth 4:18–21.

515 Midrash Tzuf Devash as cited in Yalkut *Me'am Loez* on Ruth 4:16.

516 We find this in Rashi on I Kings 2:19, where the text describes Solomon sitting on his throne, having placed a chair on his right "for the mother of the king." According to Rashi, "the mother of kingship is Ruth." Literally and figuratively the commentator places Ruth in a place of honor in the court of King Solomon, her great, great-grandson. Radak (on I Kings 2:19) goes further, explicitly stating "Ruth was still alive" at the time of Solomon's court. For the same proposition see also Tzuf Devash as cited in Yalkut *Me'am Loez* on Ruth 4:16.

517 Frymer-Kensky, *Women of the Bible*, p. 253.

[518] Similarly, Tamar also "disappears" from Genesis but *midrashically* reappears holding her baby sons, Peretz and Zerach, as they migrate into to Egypt with Jacob (Gen. 46:12). That, too (Gen. 46:8–27), is essentially a male role-call (with the exception of Dinah and Serach, fruit of Jacob's loins, who are the only named females). The understanding is that of course Tamar and Ruth have not died; they are not enumerated in male genealogies because *their sons have taken their place* in the lineup. These two pivotal women have had their star turns and played them beautifully; their continued roles are present but behind-the-scenes, doing what Rachel and Leah — and all mothers through the ages — do daily: ongoing, mostly unheralded sustenance of their families.

[519] *Torah Temima* on Ruth 4:17.

[520] Obed is technically considered an orphan because his father is deceased, even though his mother is still alive (Igeret Shmuel on Ruth 4:17). But certainly the Talmud's broad principle of surrogate parenting applies regardless of technicalities.

[521] *Sanhedrin* 19b.

[522] The Bible has not shied from the notion of "additional" parenting, wherein a co-wife, mother, grandfather or uncle steps in to love and raise a child birthed by another. In Gen. 16:2 the barren Sarah gives her maid, Hagar to Abraham with the intention that she, Sarah, "will have a son through her." In Gen. 30:3 Rachel tells Jacob that she will raise "on her own knees" the son that her maid Bilhah will bear; in Gen.50:23 we are told that Joseph's grandchildren — children of Menashe's son, Mechir — are "born between his own knees." In Exod. 2:1–10 Batya, daughter of the Pharaoh, pulls the infant Moses from the Nile and raises him in the palace as her own after the baby is weaned from his natural mother's breast (Maharsha on *Sanhedrin* 19b).

To be sure, such dual parenting among the Bible's characters has varying outcomes, but it is precisely what Naomi steps in to do in Ruth 4:17, and the reader has every reason to think that it will be successful. This is because at its core is the solid relationship between Ruth and Naomi. It is a measure of Ruth's love for and trust in her mother-in-law that Naomi is given the free rein with Obed that is usually reserved for the *maternal* grandmother. The reader is not surprised; we have seen Naomi refer to Ruth in the text as "my daughter."

523 *Bava Batra* 91b.

524 Sifrei Zuta 14:29.

525 This is yet another thematic connection of Ruth to the heroes of Genesis. Genesis taught us that "chosenness" is not a mere matter of fate; rather, that a person's qualities trumped birth order when it came to inheriting the covenantal blessing. *Viz.*, Isaac over Yishmael, Jacob over Esav.

526 *Mossad HaRav Kook* on Ruth 4:17.

527 Igeret Shmuel on Ruth 4:18.

528 Frymer-Kensky, *Women of the Bible*, p. 253.

529 Ibid.

530 Ironically, the *first* word of Ruth's story, *Vayehi*, can be said to portend a pendulum-swing to family strife within the house of *David*, her story's *last* word. We have discussed this future breakdown of the royal family and its repercussions in Parts 4 and 5 of this volume. But at the time of her story, Ruth mends tears in the fabric of the house of Judah.

531 Trible, *God and the Rhetoric of Sexuality*, p. 184, emphasis added.

532 Ibid.

533 Ruth 1:16–17.

534 *Zohar* on *Vayeshev*, Vol. II, 188 a-b.

BIBLIOGRAPHY

Alter, Robert. *The Art of Biblical Narrative*. New York: Basic Books, 1981.

——————. *The David Story: A Translation with Commentary of 1 and 2 Samuel*. New York: W. W. Norton & Company, 1999.

Bach, Alice. *Women, Seduction, and Betrayal in Biblical Narrative*. Cambridge: Cambridge University Press, 1997.

——————, ed. *Women in the Hebrew Bible*. New York: Routledge, 1999.

Bader, Mary Anna. *Tracing the Evidence: Dinah in Post-Hebrew Bible Literature*. Studies in Biblical Literature 102. New York: Peter Lang, 2008.

Bal, Mieke. *Lethal Love: Feminist Literary Readings of Biblical Love Stories*. Bloomington, Ind.: Indiana University Press, 1987.

Bejerot, Nils. "The Six-Day War in Stockholm." *New Scientist* 64, no. 886 (1974): 486–487.

Ben-Barak, Zafrira. "The Status and Right of the *Gebira*." Pages 170–185 in *A Feminist Companion to Samuel and Kings*. Edited by Athalya Brenner. Feminist Companion to the Bible. First Series. Sheffield: Sheffield Academic Press, 1994.

Bialik, Hayim Nachman, and Yehoshua Hana Ravnitzky, eds. *The Book of Legends/Sefer Ha-Aggadah: Legends from the Talmud and Midrash*. New York: Schocken Books, 1992.

Bledstein, Adrien Janis. "Tamar and the Coat of Many Colors." Pages 65–85 in *A Feminist Companion to Samuel and Kings*. Edited by Athalya Brenner. Feminist Companion to the Bible. Second Series. Sheffield: Sheffield Academic Press, 2000.

Boyarin, Daniel. *Carnal Israel: Reading Sex in Talmudic Culture*. Berkeley: University of California Press, 1993.

——————. *Intertextuality and the Reading of Midrash*. Indiana Studies in Biblical Literature. Bloomington, Ind.: Indiana University Press, 1994.

Brenner, Athalya. *The Israelite Woman: Social Role and Literary Type in Biblical Narrative*. The Biblical Seminar. Sheffield: JSOT, 1985.

——————, ed. *A Feminist Companion to Samuel and Kings*. Feminist Companion to the Bible. First Series. Sheffield: Sheffield Academic Press, 1994.

——————, ed. *A Feminist Companion to Samuel and Kings*. Feminist Companion to the Bible. Second Series. Sheffield: Sheffield Academic Press, 2000.

Bronner, Leila Leah. *From Eve to Esther: Rabbinic Reconstructions of Biblical Women*. Louisville, Ky.: Westminster/John Knox Press, 1994.

Broyde, Michael J. *Marriage, Sex, and Family in Judaism*. Lanham, Md.: Rowman & Littlefield, 2005.

Bruzelius, Margaret. *Romancing the Novel: Adventure from Scott to Sebald*. Lewisburg, Pa.: Bucknell University Press, 2007.

Carmichael, Calum. "A Ceremonial Crux: Removing a Man's Sandal as a Female Gesture of Contempt." *Journal of Biblical Literature* 96, no. 3 (1997): 321–336.

Cassuto, Umberto. "The Story of Judah and Tamar." Pages 29-40 in *Biblical and Oriental Studies I*. Jerusalem: Magnes Press, 1973.

Diamond, Mia. "A Roof with a View: Differing Perspectives on the Story of David and Batsheva," B.A. thesis, Harvard University, 1992.

Ekman, Paul. *Telling Lies*. New York: W. W. Norton & Company, 2009.

Encyclopedia Judaica. Edited by Cecil Roth, et al. 17 vols. Jerusalem: Keter Publishing House Ltd., 1966–1981.

Fokkelman, Jan P. *King David (II Sam. 9-20 and I Kings 1-2)*. Vol. 1 of *Narrative Art and Poetry in the Books of Samuel*. Studia Semitica Neerlandica. Assen, the Netherlands: Van Gorcum, 1981.

Fontaine, Carole R. "The Bearing of Wisdom on the Shape of 2 Samuel 11–12 and I Kings 3." Pages 143–160 in *A Feminist Companion to Samuel and Kings*. Edited by Athalya Brenner. Feminist Companion to the Bible. First Series. Sheffield: Sheffield Academic Press, 1994.

Frymer-Kensky, Tikva. *Reading the Women of the Bible: A New Interpretation of their Stories*. New York: Schocken Books, 2002.

Ginzberg, Louis. *The Legends of the Jews*. 7 vols. Philadelphia: The Jewish Publication Society, 1968.

Greenstein, Edward L. "Reading Strategies and the Story of Ruth." Pages 211–232 in *Women in the Hebrew Bible*. Edited by Alice Bach. New York: Routledge, 1999.

Gunn, David M. *The Story of King David: Genre and Interpretation*. JSOT Supplement Series. Sheffield: University of Sheffield, 1978.

Hertz, J. H. *The Pentateuch and Haftorahs*. 2d ed. London: Soncino Press, 1994.

Herzfeld, Shmuel. "David and Batsheva: Echoes of Saul and the Gift of Forgiveness, II Samuel 11-12." Pages 227–254 in *Tanakh Companion: The Book of Samuel*. Edited by Nathaniel Helfgot. Teaneck, N.J.: Ben Yehuda Press, 2006.

Instone-Brewer, David. *Divorce and Remarriage in the Bible: The Social and Literary Context*. Grand Rapids: Wm. B. Eerdmans, 2002.

Jeansonne, Sharon Pace. *The Women of Genesis: From Sarah to Potiphar's Wife*. Minneapolis: Fortress Press, 1990.

Kaplan, Aryeh. *The Living Torah*. Brooklyn: Moznaim Publishing Corporation, 1981.

Kass, Leon R. "Regarding Daughters and Sisters: The Rape of Dinah." *Commentary* (1992): 29–38.

──────. *The Beginning of Wisdom: Reading Genesis*. 2d ed. Chicago: University of Chicago Press, 2006.

Kirsch, Jonathan. *The Harlot by the Side of the Road*. New York: Ballentine Books, 1997.

──────. *The Woman Who Laughed at God*. New York: Penguin Compass, 2001.

Klein, Lillian. "Bathsheba Revealed." Pages 47–64 in *A Feminist Companion to Samuel and Kings*. Edited by Athalya Brenner. Feminist Companion to the Bible. Second Series. Sheffield: Sheffield Academic Press, 2000.

Nehama Leibowitz, *Studies in Bereishit/Genesis* (Jerusalem: World Zionist Organization, 1972)

Levenson, Jon D., and Baruch Halpern. "The Political Import of David's Marriages." *Journal of Biblical Literature* 99, no. 4 (1980): 507–518.

Levy, Bryna Jocheved. *Waiting For Rain: Reflections at the Turning of the Year*. Philadelphia: The Jewish Publication Society, 2008.

Neusner, Jacob. *How the Rabbis Liberated Women*. Atlanta, Ga.: Scholars Press, 1998.

──────. *Tractate Yebamot*. Vol. 1 of *The Babylonian Talmud: A Translation and Commentary*. Peabody, Mass.: Hendrikson, 2005.

Niditch, Susan. "The Wronged Woman Righted: An Analysis of Genesis 38." *Harvard Theological Review* 72, nos. 1/2 (Jan./Apr. 1979): 143-149.

The Living Nach: The Sacred Writings. Translated by Yaakov Elman. Brooklyn: Moznaim Publishing Corporation, 1998.

Ogden Bellis, Alice. *Helpmates, Harlots and Heroes: Women's Stories in the Hebrew Bible*. 2d ed. Louisville, Ky.: Westminster/John Knox Press, 2007.

Pinsky, Robert. *The Life of David*. New York: Schocken Books, 2005.

Rashi. *Commentary on the Torah, Vol. 1*. Artscroll Series; Sapirstein Edition. Brooklyn: Mesorah Publications, 1995.

Rosenblatt, Naomi H. and Joshua Horowitz. *Wrestling with Angels: What Genesis Teaches Us About Our Spiritual Identity, Sexuality, and Personal Relationships*. New York: Delta, 1996.

Schwartz, Regina M. "Adultery in the House of David: The Metanarrative of Biblical Scholarship and the Narratives of the Bible." Page 335–350 in *Women in the Hebrew Bible*. Edited by Alice Bach. New York: Routledge, 1999.

Shulman, Eliezer. *The Sequence of Events in the Old Testament*. New York: Lambda Publishers, Inc., 1987.

Speiser, E. A. *Genesis*. Anchor Bible 1. Garden City, N.Y.: Doubleday, 1986.

Steinmetz, Devora. *From Father to Son: Kinship, Conflict and Continuity in Genesis*. Louisville, Ky.: Westminster/John Knox Press, 1991.

—————. *Punishment & Freedom: The Rabbinic Construction of Criminal Law*. Philadelphia: University of Pennsylvania Press, 2008.

Steinsaltz, Adin. *Biblical Images*. New York: Basic Books, 1984.

Sternberg, Meir. *The Poetics of Biblical Narrative*. Indiana Studies in Biblical Literature. Bloomington, Ind.: Indiana University Press, 1987.

Trible, Phyllis. *God and the Rhetoric of Sexuality*. Philadelphia: Fortress Press, 1978.

—————. *Texts of Terror: Literary-Feminist Readings of Biblical Narratives*. Philadelphia: Fortress Press, 1984.

Tuchman, Shera Aranoff, and Sandra E. Rapoport. *The Passions of the Matriarchs*. Jersey City, N.J.: KTAV Publishing House, Inc., 2004.

—————. *Moses' Women*. Jersey City, N.J.: KTAV Publishing House, Inc., 2008.

Weissberg, Dvora E. *Levirate Marriage and the Family in Ancient Judaism*. Lebanon, N.H.: Brandeis University Press, 2009.

Zakovitch, Yair. "The Threshing-Floor Scene in Ruth [in Hebrew]." Pages 29–33 in *Shenaton/Annual for Biblical and Ancient Near Eastern Studies* 3, 1978–1979.

Zornberg, Avivah Gottlieb. *Genesis: The Beginning of Desire*. New York: The Jewish Publication Society, 1995.

—————. *The Murmuring Deep: Reflections on the Biblical Unconscious*. New York: Schocken Books, 2009.

INDEX OF SOURCES

�֍�֍✦✦✦✦✦✦

D. M. Gunn, 349, 370, 575n45, 576nn74, 89, 579n146

Gur Aryeh (Maharal), 528n11, 529nn31–32, 49, 530nn62, 75, 531nn84, 91, 532n107, 534nn155, 157, 535n174, 538nn66, 72, 539n113, 542n182, 548n17, 556n210

Baruch Halpern, 570n188

Hemdat Yamim, 555n176

J. H. Hertz, 572n247

Shmuel Herzfeld, 255, 564n62, 570n175

Samson Raphael Hirsch, 46, 75, 228, 303, 527n6, 529n50, 530nn66, 68, 532n101, 534n158, 535nn162–63, 171, 537n48, 539n98, 540n120, 542nn175–77, 186–87, 544nn210, 218–19, 546nn236, 239, 242, 547n10, 558n242, 571n200

Ibn Ezra, 199, 386, 469, 528n9, 530n61, 533n133, 534nn142, 144, 147, 546n233, 548nn32–33, 551n87, 554nn154, 159, 168, 556nn196, 208, 559n294, 560n307, 561n329, 581n198, 582n8, 587n151, 589nn183, 190, 590nn216, 224, 594nn323–24, 598nn438, 441, 599nn452, 467–68

Ibn Yichyeh, 591n247

Igeret Shmuel, 583n21, 585nn67–68, 84, 591nn238, 259, 262, 592nn266, 268, 282, 291, 294, 594nn315–17, 595nn338, 341–43, 346, 596nn381, 384, 597n421, 598nn427–28, 434–35, 599nn459, 461, 469, 475, 600n479, 601n501, 602n520, 603n527

David Instone-Brewer, 565n69

Sharon Pace Jeansonne, 175, 532n117, 540n140, 547n8, 552n110, 555n185, 557n219

Aryeh Kaplan, 573n2

Leon R. Kass, 75, 84, 173, 537nn50, 54, 538n70, 542n181, 552nn100, 112

Keter Yonatan, 589n207

Jonathan Kirsch, 531nn85, 89, 532n100, 533n131

Kitzur Alschich, 582nn9–10, 583nn25, 27–28, 34, 584n45, 585n76, 587n136, 589nn180, 201–3, 590nn225, 228, 591n263, 592nn269, 271, 273, 277, 280, 593nn307, 309, 594nn310–11, 321, 335, 596n394, 597n407, 598nn429, 431–32, 436, 443, 599nn451–52, 455, 460, 467, 600nn486–87, 601n512

Lillian R. Klein, 265–66, 271–72, 566nn87, 93, 95, 567nn105, 114

Nehama Leibowitz, 8, 12, 22, 528n19, 529n36, 530n74

Jon D. Levenson, 570n188

Levush HaOrah, 529nn34, 51, 534n157, 538n66, 539n112, 556n191, 557n216

Likutei Anshei Shem, 582n12, 583nn20, 34, 588n159, 595nn349, 355

Haskel Lookstein, 528n21

Mahar"i, 306, 566n104, 568n125, 569n160, 571n209, 580n187

Mahara"m, 535n171, 549n39, 556n202

Maharsha, 559n289, 565n68, 593n308, 602n522

Maharsha"l, 535n171

Malbim, 75, 95, 100, 249, 294, 537n49, 539n108, 540n123, 544n223, 553n141, 554nn144,

GENERAL INDEX

✠ ✠ ✠ ✠ ✠ ✠ ✠

ABOUT THE AUTHOR

In addition to writing *Biblical Seductions*, **Sandra E. Rapoport** has coauthored two other books that tell the stories of the Bible's women. As a practicing attorney Sandra specialized in litigating sexual harassment cases. She wrote numerous articles and ran workshops on preventing sexual harassment in the workplace, and was quoted as an authority on the subject in *The Wall Street Journal*. She also has written for law reviews and *Commentary* on the issues of international law and terrorism, and consults to an auction house specializing in rare Hebrew books and manuscripts. Sandra spent the fall, 2010, semester as a Resident Scholar at Harvard University. While at Harvard, she finished writing *Biblical Seductions* and lectured and taught classes in her specialty—bringing the women and men of the Bible to vivid life by blending text and Midrash. Sandra, a popular lecturer and teacher of Bible, lives with her husband, Sam, in Manhattan, where they raised their children.